Journeys

The Teaching of Writing in Elementary Classrooms

Carolyn L. Piazza

Florida State University

Merrill
Prentice Hall

Upper Saddle River, New Jersey
Columbus, Ohio

Library of Congress Cataloging-in-Publication Data

Piazza, Carolyn L.
  Journeys : the teaching of writing in elementary classrooms / Carolyn L. Piazza.
    p. cm.
  Includes bibliographical references and index.
  ISBN 0-13-022144-9 (pbk.)
    1. English language—Composition and exercises—Study and teaching (Elementary) 2.
Language arts (Elementary) I. Title.

LB1576 .P5767 2003
372.62´3—dc21   2002069309

Vice President and Publisher: Jeffery W. Johnston
Editor: Linda Ashe Montgomery
Production Editor: Mary M. Irvin
Design Coordinator: Diane C. Lorenzo
Text Design and Production Coordination: Carlisle Publishers Services
Cover Designer: Ali Mohrman
Cover Art: Eyewire
Production Manager: Pamela D. Bennett
Director of Marketing: Ann Castel Davis
Marketing Manager: Krista Groshong
Marketing Coordinator: Tyra Cooper

This book was set in Palatino by Carlisle Communications, Ltd., and was printed and bound by Courier Kendallville, Inc. The cover was printed by Phoenix Color Corp.

Text Credits: From *Each Peach Pear Plum* by Janet and Allan Ahlberg, copyright Janet and Allan Ahlberg, 1978. Used by permission of Viking Penguin, an imprint of Penguin Putnam Books for Young Readers, a division of Penguin Putnam Inc. All rights reserved, p. 172; Reprinted by permission of Farrar, Straus and Giroux, LLC: Excerpt from *Tuck Everlasting* by Natalie Babbitt. Copyright ©1975 by Natalie Babbitt, p. 191; From *The House that Jack Built* by Emily Bolam, copyright ©1992 by Emily Bolam. Used by permission of Dutton Children's Books, an imprint of Penguin Putnam Books for Young Readers, a division of Penguin Putnam Inc. All rights reserved, p. 173; Excerpt from *The Ballad of Lucy Whipple* by Karen Cushman. Copyright ©1996 by Karen Cushman. Reprinted by permission of Clarion Books/Houghton Mifflin Company. All rights reserved, p. 115; From *Writing Without Teachers* by Peter Elbow, copyright ©1973, 1998 by Peter Elbow. Used by permission of Oxford University Press, p. 30; From *The Country Mail Is Coming: Poems From Down Under* by Max Fatchen. Copyright ©1987 by Max Fatchen (Text), copyright ©1990 by Catharine O'Neill (Illustrations). By permission of Little, Brown and Company, Inc., p. 234; From *Little Red Riding Hood*, by P. Galdone. Copyright ©1974 by McGraw-Hill. Reprinted with permission of J. Galdone and McGraw-Hill, p. 229; Reprinted with permission by Heian International, p. 113; Reprinted with the permission of Iris Hiskey, p. 212; Reprinted with the permission of Holiday House, p. 113; From *Forest Fire* by Christopher Lampton, Copyright ©1991 by The Millbrook Press. Reprinted with permission of The Millbrook Press. All rights reserved, p. 317; Text copyright ©1980 by Charlotte Pomerantz. Used by permission of HarperCollins Publishers, p. 252; Poem text copyright ©1996 by Jack Prelutsky. Used by permission of HarperCollins Publishers, pp. 231–232; Excerpted from *Little Red Riding Hood*, retold in verse by Beatrice Schenk de Regniers. All rights renewed and reserved. Used by permission of Marian Reiner, p. 229; Jacket Copy, from *Beware of Kissing Lizard Lips* by Phyllis Shalant, copyright ©1995 by Dutton Children's Books, jacket copy. Used by permission of Dutton Children's Books, an imprint of Penguin Putnam Books for Young Readers, a division of Penguin Putnam Inc. All rights reserved, p. 397; Smith, William Jay. *The World Below the Window: Poems 1937–1997* p. 100. Copyright © The Johns Hopkins University Press. Reprinted by permission of the Johns Hopkins University Press, p. 227; Reproduced by permission of the Tallahassee Democrat, p. 179; Reprinted with permission of Weldon Owen Publishing, p. 115.

Pearson Education Ltd.
Pearson Education Australia Pty. Limited.
Pearson Education Singapore Pte. Ltd.
Pearson Education North Asia Ltd.
Pearson Education Canada, Ltd.
Pearson Educación de Mexico, S.A. de C.V.
Pearson Education—Japan, *Tokyo*
Pearson Education Malaysia Pte. Ltd.
Pearson Education, *Upper Saddle River, New Jersey*

Merrill
Prentice Hall

1 0 9 8 7 6 5 4 3 2
ISBN 0-13-022144-9

To my family: Fred, Louise, Sally, Janice, Artemisia, and Taylor
With love and gratitude

Preface

"I should see the garden far better," said Alice to herself, "if I could get to the top of that hill: and here's a path that leads straight to it—at least, no it doesn't do that." After going a few yards along the path, and turning several sharp corners—"but I suppose it will at last. But how curious it twists! It's more like a corkscrew than a path!"

Through the Looking Glass (Carroll, 1872)

Teaching writing is filled with twists and turns; it is more like a corkscrew than a straight path. Seldom does it move from point A to point B without a hitch. New demands are always popping up unexpectedly, while familiar paths are often riddled with unmarked passages. Nothing about teaching writing is tension free or foolproof. It is a lifelong journey that takes persistence, commitment, and a desire to improve.

Teachers who embark on this journey will find that, although teaching writing is a lofty goal, never before in our history has so much been written about it. Countless studies building on the pioneering research of the 1970s—and now only a keystroke away—offer plenty of advice to guide instructional practice. The challenge, however, is making sense of this voluminous body of research and presenting it in a way that is conceptually sound and practical. *Journeys: The Teaching of Writing in Elementary Classrooms* provides such a conceptual framework for planning, implementing, and evaluating instruction and for presenting the strategies and skills necessary for achieving various kinds of writing. This framework is intended not only to create essential links between research and practice but also to place all writing advice and instruction within a meaningful context that considers student needs and development, types of writing tasks, curricular goals, and ongoing assessment. Accordingly, you will not find separate chapters on grammar or assessment, prewriting or reading, spelling or the writing process. Instead, strategies and skills of the craft are integrated in ways that reflect natural connections, grounded in context, and presented when most needed or appropriate.

In addition to the book's conceptual framework and set of practices, the examples and details of its application should inspire a love and passion for writing and what it can do. The journey metaphor drives this point home. The fact that writing is not simply about the destination but about the quality of the journey is something every teacher understands. Teachers want their students to enjoy writing, to see it as an adventure filled with fascination and endless discoveries. In times of accountability and widespread testing, it is all too easy to lose sight of this. As a gentle reminder about the playfulness of language and the joys and rewards of writing, quotes from *Through the Looking Glass* (1872) open each chapter. Lewis Carroll, its creator, is a genius at showing how curiosity and imagination can provide splendid adventures for children.

Another important message of the journey is its emphasis on growth and change. Like the journey motifs in children's literature, where the main character goes off on an adventure and returns changed in some way, students are transported beyond the written word to new understandings of self and the world. They perceive and look at things with increased sensitivity and sensibilities; confront writing problems and gain new confidence; and learn patience, commitment, and discipline. These destinations are important to life work and should not be overlooked on this journey.

KEY TEXT FEATURES

This text is designed for novice as well as veteran teachers responsible for teaching writing in varied contexts and content areas in language arts, across the curriculum, and in cyberspace. It is appropriate for an undergraduate or graduate class and can be used as a stand-alone text or as one of a collection. Key text features guide readers through the book's discussions and practical applications. These include the following:

- *Assessment tools*   To consider for student self-assessment and for teacher observation, evaluation, and instruction
- *Classroom vignettes*   To demonstrate classroom application of the writer's workshop across various types of writing and settings
- *Instructional methods*   To guide minilessons and offer multiple approaches to writing instruction
- *Student work samples*   To offer glimpses of children's development and responses to tasks
- *Children's literature*   To accentuate the reading–writing connection and provide suggested books to accompany writing lessons
- *Multiple forms of literacy*   To infuse drama, movement, music, and the visual arts into writing instruction
- *Journey reflections*   To summarize and highlight major points covered in the chapter

A ROAD MAP FOR READERS

The chapters comprising this book are straightforward. Each chapter presents a particular form of writing with classroom examples to illustrate its implementation, and journey reflections that summarize both. An outline precedes each chapter and an end-of-book glossary serves as a prereading and summary resource for learning from the text.

Chapter 1 provides an overview of the book. It introduces the writer's workshop, a conceptual framework that includes five interrelated components—minilessons, reading, composing, sharing, and continuous assessment—and describes three classrooms in which the workshop is implemented.

Chapters 2 through 7 are each divided into two parts. The first part includes a discussion of the five workshop components:

- *Minilessons*   Identifies two to four lesson topics that capture the striking features of the particular kind of writing under discussion.
- *Reading*   Highlights the importance of reading from a writer's perspective: as a print and language model, a content source, and a vehicle for writing activity.
- *Composing*   Includes strategies for the writing process: prewriting drafting, revising, and editing.
- *Sharing*   Provides advice for setting up literacy forums to celebrate writing and offer feedback; considers publication of a final product and its presentation.

- *Continuous Assessment*   Offers assessment, tools, such as rubrics, checklists, surveys, portfolios, and inventories, as they relate to the writer, the process, the text, and the context.

These five components anchor each chapter but address content in different ways. While the workshop components remain the same, the content, strategies, resources, teaching methods, and assessments shift and change according to the function of writing and students' needs and interests. Although these components are presented separately, in actuality, they are interrelated and should be taught as such. Moreover, the information presented in each component should be considered suggestive, not comprehensive or prescriptive.

In the second part of each chapter, vignettes are presented of three elementary classrooms in which the writer's workshop components are effectively applied in various genres of writing. For example, in the story chapter, students write animal fantasy, pourquoi tales, and science fiction. In the personal writing chapter, they compose autobiographies, letters, and personal narratives. Sample lessons and student work products grounded in the writing process are illustrative of various kinds of writing. Appearing in the table below are class rosters of students whose work will appear throughout the text. You may wish to refer to this table as you read the classroom lessons. Although each lesson is presented by grade level, most are adaptable to almost any age. Try to think *outside the box* and imagine how you might modify and use the lessons in your classroom.

Class Roster

First Grade	Third Grade	Fifth Grade
Girls	*Girls*	*Girls*
Jana	Bailey	Brittany
Keely	Brianna	Cory
Lindsey	Hannah	DiJana
Marhonda	Heather	Erin
Melissa	Jessica	Jenny
Michele	Kimberly	Jessica
Savannah	Mira	Kristal
Shelby	Nicole	LeAnne
Su Hyen	Sarah	Paige
Tina	Sonya	Rebecca
Yoshiko	Tiara	
Yumarilis	Tirzah	
Boys	*Boys*	*Boys*
Alexander (Alex)	Aaron	Andy
Alton	Branden	Bryant
John	Brian	Cameron
Jonathan	Chris	Carlos
Joshua	Daniel	Chaney
Julio	Jamey	Dario
Justin	Jeffrey	Jason
Logan	Mike	Kenny
Matt	Reggie	Nathan
Nicky	Seth	Kevin
Taylor		Lee Wung
TJ		Thomas

Discover the Companion Website Accompanying This Book

THE PRENTICE HALL COMPANION WEBSITE: A VIRTUAL LEARNING ENVIRONMENT

Technology is a constantly growing and changing aspect of our field that is creating a need for content and resources. To address this emerging need, Prentice Hall has developed an online learning environment for students and professors alike—Companion Websites—to support our textbooks.

In creating a Companion Website, our goal is to build on and enhance what the textbook already offers. For this reason, the content for each user-friendly website is organized by topic and provides the professor and student with a variety of meaningful resources. Common features of a Companion Website include:

FOR THE PROFESSOR—

Every Companion Website integrates **Syllabus Manager**™, an online syllabus creation and management utility.

- **Syllabus Manager**™ provides you, the instructor, with an easy, step-by-step process to create and revise syllabi, with direct links into Companion Website and other online content without having to learn HTML.
- Students may logon to your syllabus during any study session. All they need to know is the web address for the Companion Website and the password you've assigned to your syllabus.
- After you have created a syllabus using **Syllabus Manager**™, students may enter the syllabus for their course section from any point in the Companion Website.
- Clicking on a date, the student is shown the list of activities for the assignment. The activities for each assignment are linked directly to actual content, saving time for students.

CHAPTER 4

Story Writing   163

CHAPTER 5

Poetry Writing   227

CHAPTER 6

Expository Writing   293

CHAPTER 7

Persuasive Writing   351

CHAPTER 1

Of course the thing to do was to make a grand survey of the country she was going to travel through. "It's something like learning geography," thought Alice as she stood on tiptoe in hopes of being able to see a little farther.

The Writer's Workshop

When you embark with students on a journey, you need to know where you are headed and what you wish to accomplish. Guided by a vision—the quality and destination of the journey—you plan, implement, and assess instruction to ensure effective and meaningful learning experiences for students. Achieving this goal is no easy feat, and you may find yourself juggling many different demands not only in the writing class but in subjects across the curriculum. To assist and give direction to your instruction, the writer's workshop is proposed as a **conceptual framework** for organizing **literacy** experiences around five components—minilessons, reading, composing, sharing, and assessing.

Framing writing instruction in terms of these components is useful for several reasons. First, the components are a constant reminder of what to include in a **writing event** and how to balance instructional plans. Second, when selecting specific lessons, you can "adopt discrete activities and actions based on a set of principles rather than a potpourri of practices from a variety of sources without a guiding framework" (Jalongo, 2000, p. 263). Third, if these components are considered in writing events, it will become apparent that learners need large chunks of uninterrupted time to practice the craft. This means you will have to find ways of stretching time allotments or find places in the curriculum for integrating writing with other subjects. And fourth, because the workshop components anchor the writing events, they establish a kind of routine and predictability where learners always know what to expect and what is required of them.

In this book, the first part of every chapter addresses a particular form of writing studied from the perspective of the five components while the second part presents classroom vignettes in grades 1, 3, and 5 to illustrate the workshop in action. This introductory chapter overviews the writer's workshop and describes the three classrooms that are followed throughout the text.

WRITER'S WORKSHOP

The writer's workshop provides a road map for what can be accomplished in teaching writing during the language arts period each day. Nancie Atwell, a strong advocate of writing workshops, sums it up this way: "The workshop isn't an add-on; it is the English course—here, everything that can be described as language arts is taught as sensibly as it can be taught, in the context of whole pieces of students' writing and whole literary works" (1998, p. 97).

To understand the place of the writer's workshop in a long and well-established tradition, it is necessary to turn back the pages of time in composition history to the 1960s when writing instruction consisted primarily of giving students an assignment and correcting the written **products** for English conventions. Little was known about writers and their writing **strategies** because the focus was on examining **teaching methods** and analyzing the work of "expert" writers. Then, in 1963, three prominent scholars, Richard Braddock, Richard Lloyd-Jones, and Lowell Schoer, published a report calling for researchers to shift the focus of their work from looking primarily at products to studying the writing process. It wasn't until several years later that case studies of student writing behaviors became a significant part of the composition agenda. (For more information about past and current contributions read *Landmark Essays on Writing Process,* 1994, compiled by Sandra Perl, and *Children's Writing: Perspectives From Research,* 1998, edited by Karen Dahl and Nancy Farnan.) Two seminal works, one by Janet Emig (1971) and the other by Donald Graves (1975), contributed immensely to the popularization of what became known as process writing which is a way of thinking and working as a writer (including strategies, habits, behaviors, knowledge, and attitudes). Emphasis on process writing gave teachers a way to intervene and support learners as they moved from the assignment to the final product.

A group of 25 dedicated teachers who wanted to see the writing process flourish in schools participated in a cooperative school–university program known as the Bay Area Writing Project (Gray & Myers, 1978). During a 5-week seminar, they exchanged ideas, debated issues, and engaged in some writing of their own. When the sessions ended, they returned to their districts as consultants to share their experiences with others. Within a decade, spin-offs of the writing project sprung up in practically every state around the country, and process writing found its way into elementary classrooms.

Yet despite the enthusiastic acceptance and widespread success of process writing, there was still a need for placing it within a broader instructional framework. By the mid-1980s, the term *writer's workshop* was adopted by researchers and teachers to draw attention to the interrelationships between writing research and the study of teaching, learning, assessment, and all of the language arts (reading, oral language, drama) (Atwell, 1986; Calkins, 1983, 1986; Graves, 1975, 1983).

Although the idea of the writer's workshop is now almost 20 years old, its basic tenets continue to be just as relevant today as in the past. Some of these include the following:

- Writing is connected to all the language arts and content areas.
- Writing is both a process and product.
- Literary experiences and a variety of print resources are used.
- Various types of writing are done for **authentic** purposes in real-world contexts.
- Choice, ownership, and responsibility are encouraged.
- Writing topics are selected by teachers and students.
- Writing communities foster environments where social **interaction** is valued and experiences are shared.
- Group discussions and conferences facilitate explicit instruction for analyzing and responding to texts.
- Multiple methods of instruction are used, including modeling; explicit instruction; and guided, shared, and interactive writing.
- Adequate chunks of time are allowed for children to implement the writing process.
- Predictable routines structure and support writing.
- Writer **response** and self-assessment are the learner's responsibilities.
- Records of student behavior and conversations are part of continuous assessment.

Like all approaches, the writer's workshop continues to grow and expand to accommodate new audiences and updated research (Atwell, 1998; Calkins, 1991, 1994; Graves, 1994). In this book, we use the writer's workshop as a conceptual template for structuring instruction and learning. The writer's workshop offers five interlocking components for doing so: minilessons (instructional methods and practices), reading (literacy resources for writing), composing (the writing process), sharing (response styles and instructional formats such as the author's chair, writing circles, and conferences), and continuous assessment (observations and reflections of the writer, process, text, and context). The components are illustrated in Figure 1–1. The following sections define each of these components, beginning with minilessons.

FIGURE 1-1 Writer's
Workshop Components

Minilessons

Teachers faced with the formidable task of balancing state curricular mandates and accommodating the interests and development of students often turn to minilessons as a literacy bridge for linking the two. Minilessons are focused, interactive lessons of usually 5 to 15 minutes in length on numerous topics implemented in a variety of ways. The topics and categories as well as instructional methods are considered here.

Topics and Categories

On the writing journey, minilessons make it possible to present a variety of topics dealing with the writer's craft. There are countless minilessons from which to choose; some of the typical ones are listed in Table 1–1 to help you identify what can be accomplished with students. These topics are analyzed in three categories: content and structure (meaning–form links), writing strategies and **skills** (specific techniques in the process), and writing procedures and routines (steps or methods to follow).

Included in the content and structure category are lessons for constructing and conveying meanings. The content of writing is limitless. Students express ideas and feelings about everything from personal experiences, to nature and objects, to society and the world at large. You will have no trouble finding supplementary resources available on the market, including college textbooks of children's literature, to support the subject and content emphasis of a student's writing. On the other hand, shaping and giving form to ideas are found in the **text elements** of a particular type of writing such as story writing's plot, characters, or settings; poetry's rhythm, rhyme, or verse; or letter writing's salutations, ideas, and closings. You will become familiar with these prototypical elements because they are a significant part of your knowledge base and represent the information you will impart to students.

Overlapping and interconnecting with content and structure are strategies and skills, which are tools that writers use to practice the writer's craft. In composing, experienced writers tend to do some things automatically without much conscious thought (skills) and other things with a definite and deliberate plan (strategies). For instance, when writers draft a piece, they usually do not think about their typing or stop to sound out words for spelling. They do not worry about whether to capitalize a word at the beginning of a sentence or agonize over what punctuation mark to place at the end of it.

TABLE 1-1   Possible Minilesson Topics for Content and Structure, Strategies and Skills, and Procedures and Routines

Content and Structure
- Crafting narrative elements (openings and endings, plot structure, dialogue, strong verbs, story transitions, personification, hyperbole)
- Using poetic devices (rhythm and rhyme, onomatopoeia, alliteration, sensory details, refrains, repetition, imagery, metaphors, similes)
- Developing expository structures (compare/contrast, classification, cause/effect, general to specific, chronology, description, sequence, problem/solution, summary); expository transitions and cue words
- Producing research notes (K-W-L charts, summaries, graphs, time lines)
- Using journalistic elements (leads, facts vs. opinions, political satire, interviews)
- Addressing a letter (state abbreviations, formats, addresses)

Strategies and Skills
- Choosing a topic
- Prewriting, planning, and organizing thoughts (brainstorming, freewriting, drawing, talking, reading, role-playing, interviewing, observing, outlining, recalling experiences)
- Developing audience awareness (classmates, teacher, parents, pen pals, grandparents, neighbors, friends)
- Identifying purposes for writing (to describe, to express feelings, to entertain, to persuade, to inform, to give directions)
- Creating a rough draft
- Rereading and asking questions
- Revising using procedural techniques (sloppy copy, cut and paste, Post-it® notes)
- Revising for content, organization, word choice, voice, point of view
- Proofreading and editing (spelling, capitalization, punctuation, format, grammar and usage)
- Practicing questioning techniques
- Responding to texts
- Borrowing from literary sources
- Making a book
- Illustrating and designing
- Reflecting on work
- Self-evaluating

Procedures and Routines
- Meeting deadlines and using time effectively
- Organizing paper and everyday writing supplies
- Locating and using available print resources in the classroom (books, encyclopedias, pictionaries, dictionaries, the Internet, photo essays, telephone books, other reference tools)
- Keeping a journal or scrapbook
- Saving quotes and interesting works
- Organizing portfolios

Instead, they rely on skills they have already acquired and can apply effortlessly. Skills involve automatic behaviors during the actual writing that can be easily recognized and corrected afterward (such as handwriting, spelling, capitalization, and punctuation).

Unlike skills, strategies are deliberately selected and flexibly used throughout the process. Writers may purposely reread their work to alter content or make transitions that connect various parts of the text. They might add definitions to clarify meaning or embellish an idea with rich description. Commonly referred to with "key verbs," strategies represent critical actions and their outcomes:

analyze	define	list	relate
annotate	describe	name	rephrase
apply	evaluate	omit	reread
arrange	expand	outline	respond
classify	explain	plan	select
combine	formulate	prioritize	show
compare	illustrate	propose	sort
compile	imagine	qualify	speculate
conclude	infer	question	state
construct	interpret	quote	tell
create	label	recognize	translate

In many traditional writing handbooks, these strategies are grouped into collective categories called modes—narration, description, exposition, and argumentation—as a means of achieving a particular aim. Modes, however, describe only written products whereas the wider set of key verb strategies are applicable to both the product *and* process. Of course, strategies are always embedded and defined in the kind of writing being accomplished. For example, to *describe* in a story may mean to create a scene; in poetry, to awaken the five senses; and in expository writing, to relate facts or portray them visually on a graph. In other words, you will need to enact strategies in specific ways as they operate in various **genres** and disciplines.

Although strategies and skills are directly related to the craft, effective writers also demonstrate **literacy habits** that enable them to establish routines for productive work. Because we can't assume that children have mastered seemingly simple tasks, such as organizing a writing portfolio, using a textbook, or filling out a form, they must be modeled often and practiced regularly. Lessons on how to handle materials, where to go for help, how to work with others, and when to self-assess can often make the difference between a good writer and an outstanding one.

Clearly, for all intents and purposes, minilessons are interdependent and overlap. For instance, keeping a journal is as much a matter of meaning-making and strategic practice as it is a routine for developing positive writing habits. In addition to *what* is taught in minilessons, teachers choose instructional methods that are appropriate for the content and purpose of the lesson. Let's examine some of them.

Instructional Methods

The writer's workshop gives direction to instruction but it does not imply a single, unitary instructional approach. Instead, there are many paths for achieving similar ends, depending on the learner, the problem to be solved, the level of support needed, prior knowledge of the content, and goals to achieve. Although process writing places emphasis on students constructing their own knowledge, teachers may find themselves intervening and giving direct advice to tap into this knowledge. Many educators see value in "placing greater emphasis on the expertise, experience, and wisdom of the adult learner" (Jorgensen, 2001, p. 3) without compromising student-centered learning (Atwell, 1998; Delpit, 1987; Jorgensen, 2001; Rogoff, 1990). Workshop teachers are constantly defining problems, evaluating situations, gathering data, and contemplating alternatives. They struggle with whether to supply rules directly or allow writers to discover them on their own; to hold open-ended discussions or structure them so that major issues are raised; to let children solve their own problems or provide guidance and possible solutions. Teachers must draw on many practices and methods to ensure optimal learning in different situations. Several methods of instruction (modeled writing; direct instruction; shared writing, including language experience; interactive writing; and guided writing) fit nicely into the overall workshop framework. These methods offer varying levels of writer support and foster a balance between direct and indirect instruction. In actual practice, they are frequently combined.

Modeling Writing

"Modeling is not the best way to teach. It is the only way to teach," according to Albert Schweitzer. This insight isn't surprising to those of us who learned behaviors and skills by watching an expert. Many of us learned to cook by lending a hand in the kitchen or figured out how to fix a tire after someone showed us. Teachers model writing in much the same way: to demonstrate effective strategies and behaviors that students can imitate (Bandura, 1986). Modeling is especially appropriate when a teacher introduces something new or when she wants to take the mystery out of hidden thoughts, as in a **think aloud**, which is a running commentary of what is going on in a writer's mind. Figure 1–2 illustrates a think aloud of a teacher sharing her goals for improving an in-progress draft.

By verbalizing what she is thinking about, the teacher focuses student attention on aspects of the writing product and shows them how to approach a problem and logically solve it. Her running narrative also provides a lesson in **metalanguage**, the ability to talk about talk as though it were an object. The concept of metalanguage is explored not only in think alouds but also in children's play with sounds and words, in talk that refers to language (as when teachers use the words *nouns* and *verbs, vowels* and *consonants*), or in editing for language corrections (*this section requires a new paragraph*). When the teacher discusses her draft in Figure 1–2, she uses language concepts such as *flow, action,* and *description.*

After the teacher models decisions and strategies in the draft, she conducts a **debriefing** session to assess what students have gained from the experience. She asks, "What were some of the reasons for my using dialogue? How did I show that my character was content? How did I organize my ideas to revise? How did I add information?" During this review, students reflect on a metalanguage associated with the changes in the text.

Although modeling implies demonstration, it doesn't always have to be explicit or stated directly. When teachers hold writing circles and conferences, compose with children, share something interesting in the newspaper, or recommend a good book, they are modeling literacy habits. High-quality books and print, even graphic organizers, are models that guide students in approaching a writing **task**.

Direct Instruction

Teachers who use direct or explicit methods select and define content, introduce concepts and skills through sequenced and structured materials, and make provisions for practice and reinforcement (Eggen & Kauchak, 2001; Hunter, 1982). Some educators bristle at the mere mention of direct instruction because it conjures up images of students as passive learners under teacher control. But this is not necessarily so if instruction is based on student needs and interests, and if it encourages active participation and joint construction of knowledge. The following steps ensure this kind of involvement (Hunter, 1982):

- *An anticipatory set* at the beginning of the lesson to motivate students about what they are to learn. It is usually a verbal introduction to get students' attention and orient them to the task.
- *Teacher input* to introduce a writing strategy or skill; to provide information in oral, written, or visual form; or to explain or demonstrate.
- *Guided student practice* of what has been demonstrated or introduced. The teacher circulates and assists students by providing guidance and feedback.
- *Debriefing,* or closure, in which the teacher reviews what has been presented and the children express in their own words what they have learned.
- *Independent practice* where children apply what they have learned to future writing assignments.

FIGURE 1-2 Teacher's Draft and Metalanguage

First Draft

Emma drove to the small coast village of Seaside. A rainbow followed her and hovered over the Victorian homes of pastel pinks, blues, and violets. Emma got out of the car and walked along the brick and cobblestone roads, peering into the homes, hoping to catch a glimpse of real people walking up the spiral staircases or preparing dinner in their immense kitchens. When she reached the familiar walkway of her friend's house, she looked up and noticed Marva sitting in a rocking chair on the veranda, keeping tempo with the ocean.

Emma and her friend entered a little market. Lining the walls were floor-to-ceiling shelves with cereals, pastas, cleansers, and foodstuffs. In the center of the store was a display of meats and fishes with a large bin of nuts and grains. They purchased the groceries and headed back to the house to prepare the meal.

For dinner, they had a hearty white bean soup and hot bread. While they ate, Emma inquired about Marva's family. Marva seemed to feel comfortable talking about them. Dinner over, they walked outside to the center of a wide-open field where live music murmured through the air.

Metalanguage

> I am writing a short story and I brought it in to share with you. I was hoping you could give me some help. I will read the first part:

Emma drove to the small coastal village of Seaside. A rainbow followed her and hovered over the Victorian homes of pastel pinks, blues, and violets. Emma got out of the car and walked along the brick and cobblestone roads, peering into the homes, hoping to catch a glimpse of real people walking up the spiral staircases or preparing dinner in their immense kitchens.

> I am not happy with my opening. Does anyone have an idea?

When she reached the familiar walkway of her friend's house, she looked up and noticed Marva sitting in a rocking chair on the veranda, keeping tempo with the ocean. Emma and her friend entered a little market. Lining the walls were floor-to-ceiling shelves with cereals, pastas, cleansers, and foodstuffs. In the center of the store was a display of meats and fishes with a large bin of nuts and grains. They purchased the groceries and headed back to the house to prepare the meal.

> I don't like the way this flows (pointing to the place between the first and second sentence). Something is missing. Does anyone have a suggestion?

For dinner, they had a hearty white bean soup and hot bread. While they ate, Emma inquired about Marva's family. Marva seemed to feel comfortable talking about them. Dinner over, they walked outside to the center of a wide-open field where live music murmured through the air.

> I wanted this part (points to second sentence) to be more interesting. It seems like I have too much description and not enough action. I mentioned that the two friends talked, but I didn't tell the reader what they talked about. Do you think I need to add dialogue here? What should I say?

These suggested steps are appropriate under certain conditions and for specific purposes. Consider, more specifically, the beneficial effect of using direct instruction to zero in on concepts and skills or rules and their application. In teaching a skill, such as possessives, an *anticipatory set* occurs when the teacher calls attention to real-life uses of this punctuation mark as it appears in the titles of books, for example, *The Black Stallion's Shadow*

(Farley, 1996) or *Aunt Flossie's Hats (and Crab Cakes Later)* (Howard, 1991) or in magazine advertisements, such as Victoria's Catalog Market or The Winner's Circle. With *teacher input,* students label personal items of classmates, such as Michele's backpack or Taylor's pencils, and discover, or are told, the rule for singular possessives. During this step, the teacher may stretch the rule by examining variations (plural possessives) or nonexamples (contractions). Next, in *guided practice,* children complete a worksheet on singular possessives or engage in a hands-on activity. They review what they've learned in the *debriefing,* and apply the rule in their own work during *independent practice.*

Tompkins (2000) suggests another set of steps to follow for direct instruction. Although the guidelines summarized in Figure 1–3 pertain to story elements, they can be applied to any strategy or text element across genres.

Direct instruction is indispensable to those who require explicit guidance and manageable tasks. If not overused, it provides a worthwhile option to include in any writing program.

Shared Writing

When teachers and students write a message together they are participating in shared writing (McKenzie, 1985). The teacher typically records and **scaffolds** ideas while the children dictate. As the writing goes down, the class observes drafting and concepts of print including message construction, **structure**, letter formation, and right-to-left progression. More specific features are introduced depending on particular types of writing. For example, consider the shared story in Table 1–2. The teacher reads *The Three Little Pigs* (Marshall, 1989), leaving off the ending. She then scaffolds the conclusion by posing questions at the end of each volunteered sentence. Because she is trying to develop a sense of story, her questions call for dialogue ("What did the wolf say?"), action

FIGURE 1-3   Step-By-Step Direct Instruction
Source: Teaching writing: Balancing process and product, 3/e, by Gail E. Tompkins. © Reprinted by permission of Pearson Education, Inc., Upper Saddle River, NJ.

1. **Introduce the element.** Teachers introduce the element of story structure and develop charts to define the element or list its characteristics.

2. **Analyze the element in stories.** Children read or listen to one or more stories that illustrate the element. After reading, children analyze how the author used the element in each story. Students should tie their analyses to the definition and the characteristics of the element presented in the first step.

3. **Participate in exploration activities.** Children participate in exploration activities in which they investigate how authors use the element in particular stories. Possible activities include retelling stories orally, with drawings, and in writing; dramatizing stories with puppets and with informal drama; and drawing clusters to graphically display the structure of stories.

4. **Review the element.** Teachers review the characteristics of the element being studied using the charts introduced earlier, and they ask children to restate the definition and characteristics of the element in their own words, using one book they have read to illustrate the characteristics.

5. **Write a class collaboration story.** Children apply what they have learned about the element of story structure by writing a class (or group) collaboration story.

6. **Write individual stories.** Using the process approach, children write individual stories incorporating the element being studied and other elements of story structure that they have already learned.

TaBLE 1-2 Spoken and Written Transcript of a Shared Writing Lesson Between Students and the Teacher Involved in Writing a New Ending to the Three Little Pigs.			
Spoken		**Written**
Teacher	**Student**	
1.		The wolf huffed and he puffed but he couldn't blow down the brick house.
2. So what do you think the wolf did?		
3.	He knocked at the door.	
4.		So he knocked at the door.
5. And who answered the door?		
6.	A cow!	
7. I'm going to add some words that you find in stories before I write "a cow."		
8.		To the wolf's surprise, a cow opened the door.
9. What did the cow look like?		
10.	He had purple and pink spots.	
11.		He had purple and pink spots.
12. What did the wolf say?		
13.	Holy cow!	
14.		The wolf said, "Holy cow!"
15. What happened next?		
16.	He went inside to eat.	
17.		Then he went inside to eat.
18. What did it look like in the house?		
19.	There was a kitchen with a table.	
20.		He walked into the kitchen where there was a table.
21. What did the cow do?		
22.	Asked him if he wanted stew.	
23.		The cow asked if he wanted stew.
24. Then what happened?		
25.	The wolf ate the stew and not the cow.	
26.		So the wolf ate the stew and not the cow.

Written Text
The wolf huffed and he puffed but he couldn't blow down the brick house. So he knocked at the door. To the wolf's surprise, a cow opened the door. He had purple and pink spots. The wolf said, "Holy cow!" Then he went inside to eat. He walked into the kitchen where there was a table. The cow asked if he wanted stew. So the wolf ate the stew and not the cow.

(What happened next?), setting (What did it look like inside the house?), and description (What did the cow look like?). Now and again, to keep the action going, she repeats the question "What happened next?" or tosses in a comment of her own, such as a story transition ("to the wolf's surprise!"). Shared writing is suitable for learners of all ages, especially those who need to apprentice with an adult before writing on their own.

Another form of shared writing is the language experience approach (LEA), designed for K–2 students and carried out with individuals, small groups, or the entire class (Allen, 1976; Ashton-Warner, 1963; Hall, 1978; Veatch, 1976). The premise behind this time-honored approach goes something like this:

> What I think, I can say.
> What I say, I can write.
> What I write, I can read.

The process begins with a topic chosen from something that flows naturally from a shared experience—a familiar story, field trip, or classroom observation. Using a large sheet of paper mounted on an easel, the teacher writes the children's words verbatim, without much structuring, as they dictate an idea, sentence, or phrase.

Sometimes she asks framing questions, such as: "Who has a beginning for our story?" "Who has another idea?" "What might we title our story?" Once the children's ideas are written, the group story serves as a reading lesson to build sight and meaning vocabulary, extend experiences, or ask comprehension questions. Often the teacher masks the predictable words with flaps and children fill them in as they read. She adopts a metalanguage that labels letters and words, sentence beginnings and endings, directionality (left-to-right progression and top to bottom on a page), spacing, punctuation, and capitalization. LEA is a well-researched approach boasting positive outcomes for reading and writing. To learn more about LEA, read *Practical Classroom Applications of Language Experience* (1999) by Olga Nelson and Wayne Linek.

Interactive Writing

The children's participation in constructing text is also accomplished in interactive writing, "instruction in phonics and other linguistic patterns within the context of meaningful text" (Button, Johnson, & Furgerson, 1996, p. 453). In this unique K–2 instructional method, children and teachers discover the meaning of the text and its structure by taking turns writing letters and words to complete sentences and paragraphs. The beauty of "sharing the pen" is that it places ownership squarely in the hands of the children, without diminishing the support of the teacher. Alongside an easel or chart, a first-grade teacher calls on the children to contribute a message, encode words, and determine conventions for an episode of *The Little Red Hen* (Galdone, 1985). One of the students (S1) volunteers the opening line: "Once upon a time, Little Red Hen was walking down the road . . . ."

Teacher:	How do we write *once?*
S1:	o-n-s-e
Teacher:	That *s* sounds like another letter that sometimes makes the /s/ sound. Does anyone know what it is?
S1:	It's a *c.*
Teacher:	Yes, we need a *c* for the word *once.* Let's place some correction tape over the *s* and replace it with a *c.* Now, we need to place a space after the word. What word do we want next?
S2:	*upon*
Teacher:	Who can stretch out the sounds and write the word?

Some children make contributions, and others remain seated and copy the story on individual white boards.

The key to success in this kind of writing is having predictable content for scaffolding the overall meaning or message (such as writing an alternative plot for the ever-popular story *Alexander and the Terrible, Horrible, No Good, Very Bad Day*, Viorst, 1972). When the children already know the story, they can work letter by letter and word by word within a text and still know the direction they are heading. The retelling of *The Little Red Hen* frames the content for children and allows them to concentrate on simple changes such as substituting character names, borrowing repetitive phrases, or extending a plot.

The same thing can be done with nonfiction by identifying common experiences, such as class observations of a pet, making grocery lists, or writing directions for recipes; it can also be done with poetry by imitating well-known poems such as William Carlos Williams's "This Is Just to Say" (Williams, 1938, p. 372).

Although it is true that practicing skills in the context of meaningful texts is certainly superior to studying them in isolation, interactive writing puts a great deal of emphasis on spelling, handwriting, formatting, and punctuating sentences. In accomplished writing, seldom do these skills occupy the writer's full attention until the end of a piece, even though some in-progress editing naturally occurs along the way. However, for emergent writers, struggling writers, or non-native speakers, who often depend on spelling and letter formation to begin putting words on paper, these skills may assume top priority. Although this may be the case for some children, it is worth remembering that only a few consonants are needed (about seven) to invent spelling and create meaning independently (Calkins, 1994; Graves, 1983). Whether to use interactive writing, how often, and with whom is discussed in more detail in McCarrier, Pinnell, and Fountas's book called *Interactive Writing: How Language and Literacy Come Together, K–2* (1999).

Guided Writing

Guided writing or "scaffolding" (Cazden, 1983, 1988; Vygotsky, 1978) is even more student-centered than shared and interactive writing and involves supporting learners as they work independently. Scaffolding a task is like providing a child with a set of training wheels. The teacher slowly reduces support as confidence and ability grow. Many guided writing lessons occur at "teachable moments," those serendipitous occasions when children experience sudden breakthroughs in their work or spontaneously utter a provocative question. Teachers must have strategies and suggestions at their fingertips to answer questions and solve problems on the spot. For instance, fifth-grade teacher, Ed, moves around the room, stops at Jessica's desk, and asks, "How's it going?" She answers, "fine," and he moves on. He comes to Erin, who is erasing and crossing out information. "I can't figure out how to tell about all these things that happened on my vacation without writing for pages and pages," she utters in frustration. Ed sees that she's trying to cover too much ground and suggests elaborating the most important events and skipping over the rest. A few time transitions are offered—*meanwhile, soon after,* or *eventually*—to help Erin abbreviate parts. Next Ed moves on to work with Lee Wung, an English-as-a-second-language (ESL) student who is writing about a newly purchased computer game that turns out to be defective. Struggling to get this idea across in English, Lee Wung consults with a friend who suggests the words *ripped off*. Lee Wung doesn't understand this expression (idiom) and there are no concrete referents, authentic objects, or manipulatives to illustrate. Ed shares an incident about one of his own purchases and how cheated he felt when he discovered it was damaged. Now, Lee Wung has a concept to map onto this colloquial term, *ripped off*.

Guided writing is truly individualized and quite demanding because the teacher must know a great deal about the writers and the writing process to respond appropriately. Unfortunately, because it does not fit the traditional image of instructors standing in front of the class teaching the same lesson to all learners, it often appears to the uninitiated, as though no teaching were taking place at all. But nothing could be further from the truth. In fact, there is probably no method more effective than guided writing because students lead the way in determining how, when, and what teachers teach.

Until now we have discussed minilessons primarily from the perspective of the teacher, but child-led minilessons are also common and among the most effective. When children present ideas to their peers—Taylor telling how he selects a topic, Kristal discussing the process she goes through in creating her draft, Daniel recommending resources on snakes, and Julio speculating about what he will write next—everyone listens more attentively and with greater interest. Having an open forum to share one's knowledge empowers students and establishes a heightened level of expertise—the ability to reflect and talk about what they know and can do.

② Reading

As Donald Murray, a writer and educator, reminds us, "readers don't have to be writers, but writers have to be readers" (1998, p. 44). Two functions of reading, essential from a writer's perspective, are emphasized in the sections on reading for text conventions and reading for content and inspiration. Each is discussed in turn.

Reading for Text Conventions

Texts serve as print models, representational examples that students examine for graphic and linguistic features. As catalysts for initiating or reworking a draft, texts help to define aspects of the craft and offer examples. Scanning several books, students ask the following questions: "How do authors start a story?" "What does the author do to make me laugh?" "What information does an author report about her subject?" When children explicitly analyze and study texts, they learn how authors construct books, what decisions they must make, which topics they care about, what strategies they use, and what questions they ask (Hansen, 2001).

Coupled with an explicit search for strategic moves in discourse are reading activities that naturally immerse students in organizational structures and language in an intuitive way. In the primary grades, teachers read from oversized big books (see Figure 1–4) so the class sees and hears how discourse is chunked in phrases and sentences for fluency and expression.

With older students, frequent read-aloud experiences are equally important and bring about improved writing, specifically the producing of longer and more complex sentences (Dressel, 1990; Eckhoff, 1983) and the imitating of literacy structures and word patterns enjoyed in the literature (Winsor & Pearson, 1992). In shared readings (based on the work of Holdaway, 1979), children internalize and adopt the language and rhythms of the texts, including rhymes and predictable words and phrases. They observe spatial and directionality principles; sentence length and order; and accurate spellings, punctuation, and formatting possibilities. Having many experiences with texts enables children to internalize the structures and sounds of print (Trelease, 1995).

Reading for Content and Inspiration

Although books expose children to models of print and literary language, they also offer a rich repository of information for taking notes, arousing imagination, and inspiring top-

FIGURE 1-4   Reading From a Big Book
Source: Scott Cunningham/Merrill

ics relevant to students' lives. Teachers often group books by themes, creating text sets associated with a topic the class is studying such as friendships or families. Along with thematic titles, they make available a random set of books for browsing and pursuing independent interests. For instance, in Vivian's first grade, Jana pulls a book off the shelf on horses; she is planning to write about horse-back riding and wants to know more about it. Jonathan is exploring books about snakes for a research project; Taylor is busy copying favorite poems; and Tina and Yoshiko are adding information to their co-authored animal alphabet book. Acquainting children with books that satisfy individual interests and furnish the content they need for drafting or revising a piece brings reading and writing together in authentic and motivating ways. To illustrate this relationship even further, Vivian often plans activities with books that serve both reading and writing functions. For instance, Marhonda finds a book to inspire journal entries, whereas Nicky copies his favorite jokes to share with friends. A group of girls are writing a play based on *Rumpelstiltskin* (Zelinsky, 1986) and refer to the book for dialogue and puppet making. Planning and performing text provides rehearsal for writing and activates **schemas** or mental structures that are later called on for developing the script (Bidwell, 1990).

So far, reading has been discussed in reference to books. But children read more than books. They read a wide range of newspapers, magazines, pamphlets, and junk mail, as well as environmental print—words and texts that appear in the child's surroundings or are part of the decorative fabric of the classroom. For instance, poems and words are placed on charts and bulletin boards hanging around the room, and a word wall—a designated spot for focusing children's attention on words (see Figure 1–5)—serves as an invitation to print and a prop for instruction.

Other forms of print found on children's clothing, or labels and insignias attached to their belongings, show how writing functions in school and society and how meanings are always embedded in a context.

Although the emphasis of the reading section in this book is on children's text experiences, the sections on composing and sharing explain the role of the reading process

FIGURE 1–5 First-Grade Word Wall
Source: Cynthia Cassidy/Merrill

in writing and its effects on the quality of the written product. Reading generates ideas for drafting or clarifies them for revising. It is the focus of every sharing and response session in which students read papers to peers or the teacher. Even during editing, the act of proofreading represents a special kind of reading that leads writers to self-correct. Frankly, it is hard to find a place in the writing process where reading is not found. Yet when the reading process is used for purposes of writing, it is often invisible or simply ignored. Teachers must make a deliberate effort to teach reading not only in the literature class, but during the act of writing itself.

Composing

Composing is the core component of the writer's workshop and includes everything writers do when they write, from prewriting and drafting, to revising, editing, and publishing their work (see Table 1–3).

A writing process orientation emphasizes the *how* of writing (the process) rather than the *what* (the product) and, therefore, locates the student at the center of attention. The very idea of "process" implies adopting a particular method of doing something. In the case of writing, this includes prewriting (getting ready to write), drafting (putting ideas down on paper), revising (rethinking ideas), and editing (correcting conventions), all of which are specifically defined in terms of the writer's age, experience, individual differences, and genre requirements guided by purpose and audience (Lindemann, 1982). In a process approach, the teacher's role is to intervene during the production of the composition and guide its outcome so that it truly recognizes and showcases the writer's competence. To accomplish this, children need ample time to cycle repeatedly through the stages of writing, weaving in and out of several processes many times and in various orders. Prewriting might occur while they are talking among friends or while they are drafting. When drafting begins, it can proceed as a continuous and spontaneous flow of ideas or as a series of interruptions in which writers stop periodically to engage in more reading or revising. Revising can prompt more prewriting and discussion or suggest a complete rewrite. Clearly, the process does not involve a straight path toward the final product. The writing process is better characterized as dynamic and recursive. Writers shift skills and strategies based on the purpose and audience of the writing and its **function** (e.g., to entertain, to inform, to evaluate, or to play with language). For instance, deep revision may be necessary for fiction but irrelevant for journals, or inventing the truth may be acceptable in a fable but inappropriate for an informative report. Being prepared for the shifts and changes across diverse subjects, purposes, and audiences facilitates the process and the numerous demands competing for the writer's attention. Third-grade teacher Kate reviews the terminology and meanings associated with the process of composing during the first week of school. Kate does not necessarily cover the composing process all at one time, but gradually introduces aspects of it when children are ready. By employing a metalanguage to describe and monitor actions, she reinforces the role that language plays in gaining control over thinking processes and establishing shared knowledge with others.

Prewriting

Kate: When I find something I want to write about, something that truly interests me, I spend a great deal of time thinking about it and taking notes. We call this prewriting, which is a word that means everything you do before writing. [Kate prints the word *prewriting* on the board.] People do all kinds of things to prepare for writing, for example, brainstorming, taking notes, talking with friends, keeping a journal, or simply thinking.

TABLE 1-3   The Writing Process

Stages of the Writing Process	Activities, Strategies, and Procedures
Prewriting Everything that takes place before writing Gathering and generating ideas for writing Organizing and planning for writing	• Think about the purpose for writing • Know the audience • Take time to think and talk about ideas • Brainstorm or plan topics • Build on firsthand experiences • Practice informal writing (freewriting, quickwrites) • View films and videos • Engage in dramatic activities • Listen to and read books • Interview outside experts and classroom guests • Draw your thoughts • Look through magazines, artwork, and other print materials for ideas • Refer to journals or learning logs • Visit the library • Use graphic organizers (diagrams, outlines, charts)
Drafting Getting ideas from head to paper Putting thoughts into words in a steady, ongoing flow	• Use a word processor to get ideas down quickly • Reread work to inspire new thoughts • Leave spaces for words you can't spell • Avoid worring about correctness • Write a catchy opening (anecdote, question, dialogue) • Decide what is enough information; achieve closure • Give direction and focus to a topic • Skip every other line • Write on one side of a sheet of paper • Pause to think and contemplate • Monitor the writing • Label the work "rough draft"
Revising Rethinking and reseeing ideas in written work Making the content clearer and stronger	• Rework ideas; look at favorite books for models • Do more prewriting • Add, substitute, delete, or reorganize • Reread and discuss work • Read drafts to an audience in conferences or writing circles • Set aside writing for a while before rewriting • Cut and paste ideas, use arrows, cross out, or white out to make changes
Editing Proofreading and correcting papers for proper conventions	• Use an editing checklist to correct errors • Check for spelling, grammar, and other mechanics • Consult a dictionary or thesaurus • Experiment with the computer's spell and grammar check • Combine, clarify, and expand sentences
Publishing Celebrating and sharing work Presenting work publicly	• Place work in the library • Hang writing on a bulletin board • Have a dramatic performance • Share writing at the author's chair • Contribute stories to a class anthology • Submit a piece to a literary magazine • Enter work in a writing contest • Share work with family members and friends

FIGURE 1-6   Prewriting Activities

Making charts (K-W-L)
Using computer software programs
Creating diagrams
Doodling and drawing
Participating in drama (puppetry,
   improvisation, role-playing)
Collecting dreams
Taking field trips
Watching films and videos
Engaging in freewriting
Developing graphic organizers
Participating in hands-on experiences
Keeping journals or logs
Interviewing
Compiling lists
Listening
Following literary models
Drawing mind maps

Viewing movies
Listening to music
Taking notes
Observing
Developing outlines
Questioning outside speakers
Studying photographs
Listening to radio programs
Reading
Simulating experiences
Using study guides
Talking
Thinking
Watching TV
Viewing artwork
Making scrapbooks
Joining in movement activities (role-play,
   dance, sign language)

Here are some questions I ask myself. [She goes to a chart and reads the following.]

What is my topic and what do I know about it?

Who is my audience and what do they need to know to enjoy my work?

What am I being asked to do?

What information do I need and how will I gather it?

Indeed, all competent writers engage in some kind of rehearsal for writing. Prewriting is everything they do to get ready to write, including all preparatory efforts from the point of intention to planning and organizing thoughts. More than 70% of their time is spent framing and generating ideas (Murray, 1982). Figure 1–6 offers a list of prewriting activities for activating knowledge prior to, during, or after writing (revising).

Effective writers choose from this array of strategies, which taps into experiences, probes topics, examines relationships, discovers feelings toward a subject, and finds order in the information they are gathering. They plan and gather information not only in prewriting but also throughout the process.

Drafting

Kate: When I believe I have something to say, I try to get my ideas down quickly so I won't forget what I am thinking. I don't worry about how it goes down; I just keep writing. We call this process drafting [Kate goes to the board and prints the word *drafting*.] When I draft I usually write on every other line in case I think of something to add later. I also write on only one side of the paper so that if I decide to change the order I can cut the sentences and rearrange them. Here are some questions I ask myself. [Goes to the chart and reads the following.]

How will I start?

What am I trying to say?

How long should I continue this?
Do I need to collect more ideas?
What order would be best for my audience?
How do I want to sound?

Drafting is getting ideas down on paper before they get lost. It is making a start, finding a tone, and monitoring intentions. Often as the writing goes down, words tumble over themselves, and a free flow of associations leads to unexpected places and pleasant surprises. Unfortunately, for many children drafting remains a mystery. For this reason, Kate's think aloud and metalanguage illustrate how to recall information, reread for more ideas, and ask questions to decide what to write next. Being explicit about the strategies she follows makes the drafting process visible. Kate suggests that students write as if chatting to friends or jump right into the middle if they can't think of a beginning. As thoughts are released from head to paper, writers begin to connect and shape ideas. They pause to scan the text, make changes, or plan ahead. They don't worry about mistakes. There will be plenty of time to revisit the piece later.

Revising

Kate: Once my words are down on paper, I look at them and make changes. I might add ideas because my paper is too short or something has been left out. Sometimes I take out ideas because they don't fit what I am saying or I've changed my mind about what I've written. I often move ideas around because they need a better order or sequence. So that I don't have to copy it over, I make all the changes on my draft. This is my sloppy copy and I write "Rough Draft" on the top so others will know I'm not finished. I make my writing clearer by crossing out or inserting new information between the lines, and reorganizing paragraphs using arrows or symbols. [Kate goes to the transparency and shows the children a writer's marked draft, see Figure 1–7A, and then proceeds to share her reasoning for the revisions in a running commentary, see Figure 1–7 B.]

The E.T. draft is like a puzzle. You have to follow the symbols to read the piece. Let's read this together [Kate reads a sentence or two and points out the symbols such as carets for adding information, line cuts through words for deletions, and arrows for rearranging]. This is what we call revision [Kate goes to the board and prints the word *revision*]. At this stage, you rethink your ideas and make them better and clearer for a reader. Here are questions I ask myself. [She goes to the chart and reads the following.]

What parts do I like?
Have I included all the necessary details?
Have I made myself clear?
What would I like to change?
Are my ideas related to my topic?
Does my title reflect the content?

Revising is rethinking and reviewing written work. As Murray (1968) reminds us "writing is rewriting" (p. 11). Rewriting is not recopying, fixing spelling and grammatical errors, or redoing work considered 'wrong' the first time. It is engaging in reflective thinking and problem solving to resolve conflict between what we intend to say and

FIGURE 1-7A Visual Display of Revision: Marked Draft

Source: From Literature and Language Transparency Pack, Red Level. Copyright © 1994 by McDougal Littell Inc. All rights reserved. Reprinted by permission of McDougal Littell Inc.

large, paddle-shaped feet who waddles like a penguin. His long arms, which hang almost to the ground, end in fingers that look like prongs.

(1) E.T., the little alien, first appeared on the movie

short, stumpy

screen in 1982. (2) He is a creature with ~~long arms and~~

He has   *soft, curious*   *grotesque*   *His*

~~fingers,~~ huge eyes in a big head, ~~and a~~ stalk of a neck,

large, tightly wound   *winds and unwinds.*   *soft, chattering*

like a telephone cord. (3) E.T. makes unusual sounds

when he is with his human friend, Elliott.

(4) E.T. is highly intelligent. (5) Without knowing any

Earth language, he communicates to Elliott that he is

from a distant universe. (6) Then, quickly, he learns

including E.T., phone, and home.

some English by repeating some words. (7) Elliott

learns an important lesson from E.T.—that all creatures,

whether they are people, animals or extraterrestrials,

must be treated kindly. *As a result, when Elliott's biology class is about to dissect frogs, Elliot leads a revolt to free the frogs and return them to their natural home.*

FIGURE 1-7B Visual Display of Revision: Metalanguage

Sentences

(1) I like this first sentence. I want the reader to know, right from the start, what my paper is about. I'm going to leave it just as it is.

(2) I'm not satisfied with my second sentence. I want to create a picture of E.T. for someone who has not seen the movie. Maybe I'll slip in the words *short* and *stumpy* in the white space before the word *creature,* and I'll use a mark like this (^) to show that I've added something. I will also draw a line through *long arms and fingers* to show I'm removing it. I'll combine these words with more adjectives and maybe a comparison that will help my reader make a connection. I will need some space to write a longer sentence. I can place it up here in the margin and draw an arrow to where it belongs. Here's what I'll add: *large, paddle-shaped feet who waddles like a penguin. His long arms, which hang almost to the ground, end in fingers that look like prongs.*

(continued)

FIGURE 1-7B   (continued)

> Now I must create a new sentence out of what's left in sentence 2. I will say: *He has soft, curious eyes in a big grotesque head.* See how I added the adjectives *soft, curious, and grotesque* to my new sentence? I'm going to need a comma between them. Here's the editing mark that shows I'm inserting a comma (∧). Now if I add one more sentence to this part, I think I'll have given the reader a fairly good picture of E.T.
>
> I will begin my next sentence with a capital letter and then add more adjectives at various places in the sentence. *His* stalk of a neck *(comma)* like a *large (comma) tightly wound* telephone cord (comma) *winds and unwinds (period)*. I will draw circles around all my new periods so I'll know I have added them. Now, let me reread. Yes, that's better!
>
> (3) This sentence is okay, but I think I'll add *soft* and *chattering* before the word *sounds* so the reader will almost be able to hear E.T. Whoops! I can't forget the comma.
>
> (4) This sentence is fine. It says something important about E.T.
>
> (5) So is this one because it links to sentence 4.
>
> (6) This sentence also ties to the other two but I think I need some examples of words that E.T. is learning. I will add these at the end of the sentence after I put in a comma: *including E.T., phone, and home (period).*
>
> (7) This next sentence is fine but it needs an example to make it come alive for the reader. Maybe something that creates a moving picture. I will add a scene from Elliot's biology class: *As a result, when Elliot's biology class is about to dissect frogs, Elliot leads a revolt to free the frogs and return them to their natural home (period).*

what the text actually says. During this stage writers examine content and refine it for an audience. Kate introduces the words that begin with the prefix "re" (meaning "again") and relates them to revision:

revise	rework	redo
reread	refine	replace
rethink	revisit	reconsider

Before revising and sharing with peers, writers place drafts in a folder for a few days so that they get a little distance from the work. Letting the work rest for a while allows them to spot gaps in meaning and rework sections that need it. If they can type the draft before placing it in the folder, all the better. It's amazing how quickly writers pick up on what needs to be changed when the handwritten copy is presented in a typed form. Reading work aloud also helps the writer discover where to add, delete, change, or substitute sentences and paragraphs. When students listen to their own words they often catch accidental errors (omissions, repetitions, and so on), and discover awkward sentences that interfere with meaning or fluency. More importantly, they gain on intuitive understanding of rhythm and sense-making (recognizing sentences that are too short or too long, or ideas that go astray).

Kate often demonstrates revision by reading part of her work and saying something like the following:

- I wanted this part to sound as though I were talking with a friend. Does anyone know how I can say this differently? Can I substitute some formal words with informal ones? How can I do this?
- I don't like the way this flows. Do you have any suggestions?

- I'm not sure if this is true. Where can I find out?
- I need a catchy opening. Does anyone have an idea?

Reading aloud and questioning drafts clearly makes the point that revision is reflection; making changes and resubmitting her work to the class shows that revision is the unmistakable secret to improving writing. Over the course of a writing event, Kate attends to the physical process of revising by showing how to cut and paste paragraphs to organize them in a more effective manner. Using a sample report on medieval castles, she cuts and pastes excerpts while students follow along with copies of their own. To scaffold the exercise, the nonfiction piece is blocked into paragraphs and separated by dotted lines. Students cut on the lines and reorder the paragraphs so that the first one is the main idea and the subsequent paragraphs represent details supporting it. When the sentences are rearranged to their liking, they use a glue stick to paste them on a blank sheet of paper. The following sample is numbered out of order to show that the sentences need to be rearranged.

> **2.** Medieval castles were built higher than the surrounding land so that they would be less likely to be hit by arrows and stones. They provided a high outlook to watch for enemies. Often a whole town was built around the castle by a wall.
> --- cut line ---
> **3.** Although early castles were used largely for defense, by the late Middle Ages warfare and technology made medieval styles less effective. Many of them were preserved as private homes.
> --- cut line ---
> **1.** Castles were impressive fortresses built out of wood or stone to protect the people from their enemies.

In a second demonstration, Kate shows how to elaborate on sections of a piece without recopying. After cutting the original text into blocks, one of the paragraphs is attached to a plain sheet of paper. Under it is a large open space for additional writing. Once new information is included, the next paragraph is placed on the paper. It looks something like this.

> Castles were impressive fortresses built out of wood or stone to protect the people from their enemies. Medieval castles were built higher than the surrounding land so that they would be less likely to be hit by arrows and stones. They provided a high outlook to watch for enemies. Often a whole town was built around the castle by a wall.
>
> [Space for new information]
>
> Although early castles were used largely for defense, by the late Middle Ages warfare and technology made medieval styles less effective. Many of them were preserved as private homes.

To fill in the white space, the writer might go back to reading for the names of famous medieval castles and their locations. Maybe they will study the pictures in *Castle* (Macaulay, 1977) for details about how these buildings were constructed. By supplying missing ideas, explanations, or thoughts to the original draft, students recognize that text is neither permanent nor immovable, but always able to be improved on.

It is fun for students to participate in hands-on activities for revision. They not only learn to manipulate text for meaning but also discover a technique for making changes without having to copy a paper over.

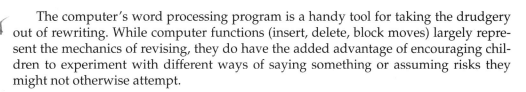

The computer's word processing program is a handy tool for taking the drudgery out of rewriting. While computer functions (insert, delete, block moves) largely represent the mechanics of revising, they do have the added advantage of encouraging children to experiment with different ways of saying something or assuming risks they might not otherwise attempt.

Editing

Kate: At the end I always go back and fix spelling, punctuation, and grammar. When I do this, I am editing. [Kate goes to the board and prints the word *editing*.] Here are questions I ask myself. [She goes to the chart and reads the following.]

Does my writing flow?
Do I have complete sentences?
Is my handwriting legible?
Is it readable?
Is my work error-free?
Is my writing the best it can be?

In this stage of the process, writers proofread and add the finishing touches to make the piece readable for an audience. Kate finds it beneficial to have students work in pairs to proofread because one may catch errors that the other misses. She provides a worksheet similar to the one in Table 1–4, to guide them as they check for mechanical errors.

Proofreading is reading for the purpose of locating and fixing errors. Sometimes students scan the text in the opposite direction of usual reading, from bottom to top and right to left, so they are less likely to focus on meaning and miss blatant errors. During proofreading, learners are naturally led to dictionaries, thesauruses, and grammar handbooks.

TABLE 1-4 Proofreading Marks

Advice	Mark	Example
Capitalize	≡	maine is our state.
Lowercase	/	Most of the Mayors agreed.
Delete word(s) or letter(s)	ℓ	He was the the group leader.
Insert word(s) or letter(s)	∧	The budding flower was opening.
Spelling	sp	She bougt a gift.
Change word or letter order	∾	The beavers dug tunnels often.
Space	#	There are a number of new students.
Insert comma	∧	Quiet she said.
Insert period	⊙	I wish to go
Insert apostrophe	∨	My mothers coat.

When they first consult these references, Kate holds minilessons to explain and demonstrate their uses.

Some teachers emphasize editing more than other parts of the process. When this happens, writers come to believe that correct grammar, punctuation, spelling, and so on is more important than their ideas. Beginning writers are naturally preoccupied with writing correctly, but paying too much attention to this, especially when they are learning about the communicative purposes for writing, undermines the goal of constructing meaning. Kate provides a time other than the writing hour to discuss the mechanics of editing. This way she maintains the emphasis on meaning and fluency without dismissing student concerns for writing correctly.

Where possible, editing for specific conventions should be taught in the context of real writing and addressed in light of the genre and function. With personal writing, children might learn personal words to spell or study contractions and possessives (because these are likely to appear in this type of writing). With journal writing, students may invent spelling and not worry about editing at all. Eventually, writers bring many skills to bear at once on a writing problem. Correcting spelling words is a good example. Researchers (Wilde, 1992; Zutell, 1978) tell us that effective spellers, such as those in championship spelling bees, have many strategies at their disposal and never rely solely on sounding out words (phoneme/grapheme relationships). Good spellers recall high-frequency and sight words (*the/is*); rely on visual factors (letter configurations, shapes, positions) to determine if a word "looks" right; use analogies to find common patterns; and are curious about word origins, pronunciations, and ways of locating words in a dictionary (Wilde, 1992). Although these strategies are inseparable when writers face spelling an unknown word, beginning writers should not be bombarded with an entire spelling program all at once. Strategies and skills are discovered or taught along the way, in small doses, as the occasion arises. Certain word lists and activities are also highlighted at appropriate times so that writers can practice, apply, or track their spelling words.

Sharing

Sharing is a regular feature of the writer's workshop and serves at least two broad purposes. The first is sharing for publication and presentation, the second is sharing to prepare for revision.

Sharing for Publication and Presentation

Sharing is the act of giving back, and students offer this gift when they write for publication. Publishing celebrates writing and provides recognition of students' efforts. It is a natural conclusion to writing but not necessarily a requirement for all pieces. As long as writers have occasions to share their work and get feedback on a regular basis, writing has reached a fulfilling end. It is hard to justify an inordinate amount of time binding books and creating or finding artwork unless the writing is being prepared for a special purpose (for example, to submit to the library, to send home as a gift, or to enter a contest). But there are many different forms of publishing books that do not take a lot of time as shown in Figure 1–8. Other informal possibilities for making work public to a wider audience involve the following:

- Display work on the bulletin board
- Contribute writing to a class anthology
- Show work to family members
- Publish writing in a magazine
- Enter work in a writing contest

This list represents a narrow definition of publishing in which language is rendered primarily in print. However, sharing can take many public forms. Within this broader view, presentations are another way to deliver a written message and build oral communication skills. The author's chair, a special chair where writers sit to read compositions

FIGURE 1-8 Simple Books for Publishing

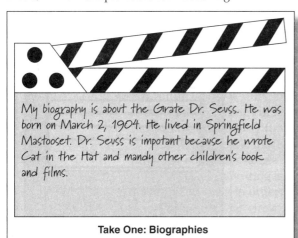

My biography is about the Grate Dr. Seuss. He was born on March 2, 1904. He lived in Springfield Mastooset. Dr. Seuss is impotant because he wrote Cat in the Hat and mandy other children's book and films.

Take One: Biographies

I have a dream . . .

That there was no wars, no fights, no bad words, no robbing, no bieng bad, and treat others as thay want to be treated, and take good care of people, be the best you can be, listen to others, share with each other.

My Winning Essay

My Winning Essay

The Missing Tooth

Once upon a time there was a boy named Daniel. He was intelligent. He was naughty. One day he was playing outside. He lost his tooth. At night he put it under his pillow. The next day when he looked under his pillow he could not find anything. His tooth was lost. When he went to school he looked on the playground. He looked in the bathroom. He found a tooth. He found it under a desk. But it was a lot bigger than his tooth. That tooth looked like Big Billy a kid in his classroom's tooth. Billy is big. Billy is mean. When Daniel gave him his tooth he was happy. At night Daniel found his tooth under his blanket. The end.

Clowning Around

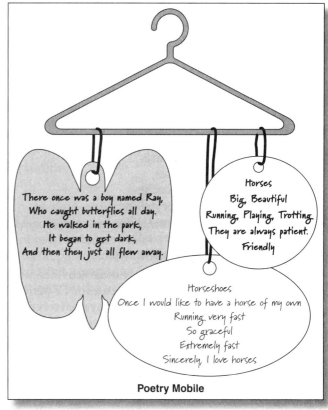

There once was a boy named Ray, Who caught butterflies all day. He walked in the park, It began to get dark, And then they just all flew away.

Horses
Big, Beautiful
Running, Playing, Trotting
They are always patient.
Friendly

Horseshoes
Once I would like to have a horse of my own
Running very fast
So graceful
Extremely fast
Sincerely, I love horses

Poetry Mobile

The raccoon is brown with a dash of white neatly ringed around a black mask.

The tail fluffs up with strips of black and broun.

They stay in a forked branch all day, when nigh comes they go out in gouroges looking for old scraps of food.

I think there veary neat sence they always wash It's food.

He carries it's pray veary carfuly, so no one else can get it.

it takes care of it's babies wile the father looks for food.

The mother also teaches her babies to hunt for food.

This is some of there food; fish apples bearrie candy scraps left overs to.

The have sharp claws so they have a wepend.

there a pretty good pet.

Slide Show

(continued)

Kenny:	I don't like how the ending sounds.
Ed:	Go ahead and read the ending for us, Kenny.
Kenny:	Have fun you'll love it.
Ed:	How had you wanted it to end?
Kenny:	I don't know. Maybe give more information?
LeAnne:	Maybe you could tell why you like collecting cards.
Bryant:	What if you would, . . . no, forget it.
Ed:	No, what? Tell us.
Bryant:	What if you would move the ending to the beginning and tell how you got started collecting? But I don't know what you would do for an ending.
Ed:	What was your purpose for writing this piece, Kenny?
Kenny:	To tell you that collecting cards was fun.
Ed:	I see. If you want to convince some of us that collecting cards is an exciting hobby, what might you say? What would we have to know to get started? Let's ask what the group thinks might convince them.

This exchange and the comments that follow lead Kenny to clarify the intent of his writing and identify details that will strengthen it. By the time the group disperses, Kenny has concrete suggestions to prepare for revision.

HOW DO PEERS RESPOND TO A WRITER'S WORK?   When writers share what they have to say through texts, their words often elicit a wide variety of interrelated responses. Responses are the postures that readers take toward an author's work. Figure 1–9 provides descriptive literary categories that represent some of the responses. They are based on Rosenblatt's (1978, 1984) two types of reading responses—esthetic and efferent—and Squire's (1964) categories of literary response.

According to Rosenblatt, an esthetic response is one in which a reader "lives through" a text and draws on private feelings, attitudes, and personal associations to discuss it. This kind of response is most likely to occur after reading stories or poetry. An efferent response, however, is one in which the reader shares new knowledge and takes away information to remember. It is more often identified with nonfiction. Although Figure 1–9 shows many and varied ways for listeners and readers to respond to an author's work, generally speaking, a particular type of text will prompt a certain kind of response. In report writing, with an emphasis on accuracy and facts, children respond efferently and analytically, whereas in personal writing, with its real-life circumstances and events, children give personal or associative responses. For instance, a fifth grader responds to a peer's written story about a white-water rafting trip.

> I really liked what you said. It made me think of the time when I was in a canoe, and the water was so rough we got soaked!

In this comment, the student offers an appreciative response—telling how she feels about the story—and makes a personal and associative connection, comparing the rafting trip to her own experience in the canoe.

The responses that emerge in a discussion may be linked not only to the genre of writing but also to the status of the draft. If the writer's work is almost ready for publication, peers might respond evaluatively; if it is a first draft, they may be more inclined to offer affective or personal responses. Teachers will want to model ways to respond to papers so that students can eventually work independently in groups and give one another appropriate feedback.

Sometimes teachers complain that young writers have difficulty articulating advice in a useful way (for example, "I don't know what I mean" or "You know" or "Something

Affective Response
Reacting to emotions evoked during the reading of the work; the actual effect provided by the reading; connotative responses and personal feelings.
>*That was so sad.*
>*When they found the puppy, I wanted to clap and cheer.*

Analytic Response
Taking apart and examining elements of the writing: meanings, structures, purposes, audience, and surface features.
>*I think the writer's reason for writing this was. . . .*
>*The writer uses emotional appeal very effectively here.*

Appreciative Response
Deriving enjoyment and pleasure from the text; valuing the work for its achievements.
>*I got lost in this adventure.*
>*This was a page turner.*

Associative Response
Making connections and analogies to one's own life or to other texts.
>*This reminds me of. . . .*
>*This book brought back memories of. . . .*

Creative Response
Constructing novel ideas and meanings that enhance the writing.
>*This could be. . . .*
>*If I were . . . I would. . . .*

Critical Response
Employing skillful inquiry, posing hypotheses, and looking for evidence to support data or literary judgments.
>*I'd like to know more about. . . .*
>*I'd like to know where the writer found this information.*

Efferent Response
Reading for information; reading to report details; for factual retellings; or to get definitions and meanings of words, phrases, or images.
>*Something I learned from this was. . . .*
>*According to the author,. . . .*

Esthetic Response
Commenting on the artistic and literary qualities of the work, such as form, style, and language, as opposed to content; perceived through intuition, images, and the senses.
>*The style of this writing is effective.*
>*The writer uses some powerful words to. . . .*

Evaluative Response
Making a prescriptive judgment based on set criteria or standards.
>*The writing achieves its purpose.*
>*I think the writing needs more examples for. . . .*

Personal Response
Identifying with the work and becoming self-involved through similar experiences, feelings, and values.
>*This reminds me of when I. . . .*
>*I began to think of. . . .*

is wrong, but I'm not sure what it is"). Suggestions from Peter Elbow's book *Writing Without Teachers* (1973) can guide writers on how to communicate their perceptions about another's work.

Pointing: They point to the words and phrases that most successfully "got through," ideas remembered. They point to any words or phrases that seem particularly weak or empty.

Summarizing: They summarize the writing by first telling the main points, then summarizing the main points into a single sentence. Then they choose one word from the writing that best summarizes it, and, finally, they choose a word that isn't in the writing to summarize it.

Telling: They tell the writer everything that happened as they tried to read the words carefully. They tell it in the form of a story: First this happened, then this happened, then this happened, and so on.

Showing: They show perceptions and reactions using metaphorical exercises such as the following:

- Talk about the writing as though describing voices, for example, shouting, whining, whispering, lecturing sternly, droning, speaking abstractly, and so forth. Try to apply such words not only to the whole but also to different parts.
- Talk about the writing as though talking about weather, for example, foggy, sunny, gusty, drizzling, cold, clear, crisp, muggy, and so forth.
- Talk about the writing as though talking about motion (marching or tiptoeing), terrain (hilly or soft and grassy), colors (golden or subdued), shapes (squared or hierarchical), animals (fierce tiger or gentle lamb), and other objects, sounds, or movements.

Learning to talk about papers involves learning a metalanguage shared by members of the writing circle and adopted by individuals as a tool for problem solving.

Writing Conferences

The conference, another writing event for sharing and receiving work, involves individualized instruction at its best and is one of the most effective ways to teach revision. It can assume many flexible shapes and arrangements (see Figure 1–10).

During a 45-minute block, Ed works with a student for 5 to 7 minutes according to a posted schedule. He and the writer sit side by side at a conference table, the writer holding the piece while Ed looks on. After the student reads her work and explains where help is needed, Ed offers expert advice or leads the writer to solve the problem. So helpful is the conference that, the writer knows exactly what the next steps are for revising the piece.

Because conference topics typically follow student concerns at various points in the writing process, Ed keeps in mind some of the following parameters:

- The writer's status with the paper
- The intentions of the writer
- The writer's request for help
- The security and confidence of the writer
- The length of time the writer has devoted to the piece
- Whether it is time to move the writer to another level
- Whether the writer is capable of implementing the suggestions provided

He shows his observance of these points in the different kinds of conferences he conducts. Brief explanations of these conferences are provided in the following sections.

TOPIC CONFERENCES.   A topic conference airs ideas and explores interests, events, and concerns. Sometimes writers talk with a teacher about the options they are considering;

FIGURE 1-10   Writing Conference Variations

Teacher–Student Conferences

The writer and teacher engage in one-on-one exchanges focused on what the writer wishes to learn. They meet at a designated place by appointment or request. Usually one or two suggestions are given so as not to overwhelm the writer. As a follow-up, the teacher might identify resources (books, media, peers) for the student. It is a matter of routine for teachers to circulate and assist students during class time. In these brief encounters, the student might request immediate help or participate in a spontaneous lesson, such as brainstorming.

Peer Conferences

The writer works with a partner who listens and offers compliments and suggestions, orally or in writing. If written feedback is provided, the responder does not write on the paper but places Post-it notes where appropriate, showing that the comments are tentative suggestions only. To guide the discussion, the partners might use a revision or editing check sheet.

Self-Response

The writer reviews the written work in anticipation of audience questions. The writer needs to gain some distance from the writing before critiquing it. Writers may want to tape readings of the paper, listen to the tape, and ask questions. If using a word processor, the writer can print the work from time to time to read and rethink the ideas.

Taped Readings at a Listening Center

Each writer records the work on tape and other students listen to the reading and write responses. The response sheets include a place for a compliment and one or two suggestions. When the responses are written, students put them in an envelope with the writer's name on the outside and place it in a box. The writer can collect these responses and read them during free time.

Written Responses

The teacher or student writes a response to the paper in summary form. Usually, the comments are a general impression that include a personal reaction, the positive aspects of the paper, and some questions about what the reader may still want to know. One or two suggestions may be made.

Parent and Caregiver Responses

Parents, older siblings, grandparents, relatives, neighbors, or other caretakers read the writer's work and give a response. To guide responses, teachers send a letter providing instructions to: (a) allow the writer to read the work aloud while you listen without interruption, (b) give the writer one or more compliments about the content and ideas in the work, (c) help the writer with one aspect of the paper (only on request), and (d) initial the manuscript. This response format provides students with another audience, identifies what is important to the parents (by considering the compliments they give), and teaches the parents about writing and the writing process.

other times they describe how to broaden or narrow a subject. Occasionally, writers need help locating a topic in something already written such as a draft or journal.

Before Ed meets with Brittany, he reads her draft and prepares for their discussion. However, when he asks about the draft, she resolutely announces that she no longer wants to continue on her personal narrative but would prefer to start a new piece. Ed finds out why she has decided to abandon her original idea, then shifts gears to support her decision.

Brittany:	I want to write something new today.
Ed:	What would you like to write about?
Brittany:	I don't know.
Ed:	Where are some places you can look?
Brittany:	I have some topics in my writing folder.
Ed:	Yes. That's a good place to start. Have you also considered rereading your journal entries? You might discover some topics there.
Brittany:	Yeah. I can do that.

Ed's comments remind Brittany of the resources at her fingertips. She reviews her journal, and when she finds an entry that catches her eye, she talks about it with a friend.

In a topic conference, the teacher and student brainstorm and exchange ideas, take notes, or pose questions. The teacher's job is to explore the student's knowledge about a subject or listen for the excitement in her voice when something really important is revealed. Some questions a teacher might ask are as follows:

- What topics have you written about in your journal?
- What topics of conversation have you had with friends?
- What ideas appeal to you that you've added to your lists?
- When you page through books, magazines, or newspapers, what catches your attention?

Ideas are everywhere. When prompted, writers begin to notice and think about ordinary things more deeply. In topic conferences, Ed taps into these ideas and elicits interests, concerns, or experiences about which students might want to write.

CONTENT CONFERENCES.   A content conference involves a discussion about meanings being constructed in a written piece. In a content conference with Ed, Carlos explains that he isn't sure whether to write about his grandmother's visit or the family celebration honoring it. Ed follows a line of questioning that eventually leads to the paper's focus.

Ed:	Tell me about your piece.
Carlos:	It's about the day my uncles and cousins were at our house and my grandma was visiting.
Ed:	It sounds as though this was a special time together.
Carlos:	Yeah. The men usually drink beer and play poker, and the women sit around the table and talk.
Ed:	What do the children do?
Carlos:	Sometimes they play on the computer or watch movies. I was showing my grandma the computer. She said she didn't have these things when she was a little girl. She used to make paper cutouts and braid bracelets.
Ed:	You mentioned that this was a special occasion.
Carlos:	Oh, we had pork roast and bean soup and other stuff. I think we had some kind of cake with peaches and cinnamon. There was music and stuff.
Ed:	You have so much to tell. Try to get some of this down and then we will talk again.

Although it is too early to determine the writer's direction, many new ideas have been generated. When more details are added and the writing unfolds, the sheer number of words devoted to one topic over the other will reveal the main idea.

A content conference is not only to discover a main idea but also to strengthen the message of the paper, guide its direction, check the accuracy of facts, consider the audience, or refine the purpose of the piece. Following are a few questions that address these matters.

- Could you tell me what your paper is about?
- What are your beliefs about this subject?
- What alternatives did you consider?
- What do you want the reader to know more about?
- What did you mean by that? Could you explain it further?
- Where did you find this information? Get your ideas?
- Were you puzzled by any information in this piece?
- What support can you provide? What does this suggest about. . . ?

Content conferences are valuable because they prompt further brainstorming and questioning to clarify or amplify the piece. It is likely that writers will revisit different aspects of the content in more than one conference.

PROCESS CONFERENCES.   In a process conference students describe the behaviors or actions performed during the writing process (prewriting, drafting, revising, or editing). Kristal's meeting with Ed is to share progress and explain the process she followed in writing her piece. Before their conference, she completes a process form (see Figure 1–11). She refers to this form from time to time to describe her work.

Kristal: Do you want me to tell you what I did so far?

Ed: Yes. Take me back to the very beginning and explain how you got started on this piece.

FIGURE 1-11 Kristal's Writing Process Description (Fifth Grader)

Concept	Student's Comments	Observer Comments
TOPIC: • Picks enjoyable topic • Sticks to topic	I have trouble finding a topic but I like the topic about the mansion	Through the prewriting activities we chose a topic based on the book we read
PREWRITING: • Show evidence of Brainstorming • Uses prewriting in first draft writing • Develops a setting • Develops a plot • Details	I like to use an outline form, but the webbing we did together made things easier. I used all the info from my brainstorming. My setting & plot could have been longer. I know I need to use more details in my first draft	She needs more help writing and developing a first draft. She needs more practice with this style of writing. We should have started by developing a character first, then creating the plot line
REVISING: • Adds or deletes info • Reorganizes ideas • Word choice	During revising I fixed punctuation and moved one sentence. The revisions we did together were very helpful & made my story better.	She is used to minor revisions but learned the proper way when we did it together.
EDITING & PUBLISHING • Proofreads for mistakes • Presentation	I proofread my story. I thought putting it in a house would be neat.	Her house idea was very cute. I think she was happy with her final story. It was a good story for her.

Student's Name Kristal

Kristal:	I made a web and wrote what I would put inside the mansion, furniture and things like that. Oh, wait. First I read *The Westing Game*. One of the characters, Turtle, made a bet that she would spend the night in the Westing House. It was a scary place, and the character chickened out until Theo and Otis went with her. I got the idea from this.
Ed:	A book is a good place to get ideas for writing. Then, you made a web?
Kristal:	Uh huh.
Ed:	What was the next step?
Kristal:	I made an outline. Like, what I would put in the first paragraph, then the second, then the third, and then the conclusion. Then I made a sloppy copy. When I finished the draft, I fixed the spelling and punctuation and here it is.

Clearly, Kristal engages in several prewriting activities to get started: reading, brainstorming, and outlining. She labels her first draft a sloppy copy and identifies what she plans to work on. Kristal's comment on the process form, *I know I need to use more details in my first draft*, is the starting place for revision.

In process conferences, learners articulate actions leading to the final product. To encourage this, teachers prompt with questions such as the following:

- How did you decide on your topic?
- What preplanning did you do for this topic?
- How did you write this introduction?
- What is the status of your draft?
- Where did you want to start?
- How did you get your information down quickly?
- How did you know when to stop?
- How can you learn more about your subject?
- How can you make changes; add, delete, or substitute information?
- What steps must be taken to complete this?

A teacher can learn a great deal about her students through the process conference: One child may chat with others to get ideas whereas another may worry about spelling and **mechanics**, or one may like to work alone whereas another enjoys performing the work for others. Ed collects observations of student literacy habits and, when he has a sufficient number, sorts them by similarities and differences to share the diversity that exists in the writing community.

EDITING CONFERENCES.   Editing conferences teach strategies and skills associated with word choice; sentence construction; or the mechanics of language, such as spelling, capitalization, punctuation, and page formatting. In the conference between Ed and Cory the topic of discussion is sentence variety. Cory has written about her gameboy and 5 of the 11 sentences begin with *My gameboy, A gameboy*, or *Gameboy*.

Ed:	Could you tell me a bit more about this game?
Cory:	You can stick it in your pocket and play it at home or in the car.
Ed:	Tell me more about the Pokemon red version.
Cory:	The first game I got with my gameboy is called Pokemon red version game. There is a little screen you can catch Pokemon on and train them.
Ed:	This is very interesting. Maybe you should add it to your piece. Let's look at the sentences you have written so far. Do you notice how most of them begin?
Cory:	With gameboy.
Ed:	Yes. I think once you add the information we discussed, you will develop more variety in your sentences. Meanwhile, can you find a place where two of your sentences might be combined to make one? This way you will only have to use the word *gameboy* once instead of twice.

Cory [pointing to the sentences]:   My gameboy color is a little handheld game. Gameboy is a square-shaped toy. [Combining] My gameboy color is a square-shaped, handheld toy.

Ed attempts to create sentence variety by expanding on the content in hopes that further elaboration will result in more complex sentences, moving beyond factual statements, which seem to be causing the monotony. Ed also wants to show Cory that short, choppy sentences with the same subject can be combined. If her next draft lacks variety, Ed will introduce sentences with conditionals (*when, if, because*) or prepositional phrases (*with the AA batteries, the gameboy; or by all means, you should get a gameboy*).

In editing conferences teachers avoid the temptation to correct everything; instead, they listen to the writer's priorities based on the text being discussed, the frequency of the error, and the need for accuracy. One or two suggestions per composition is a good rule of thumb. A few questions that reveal students' hypotheses about English conventions include the following:

- What do you do when you can't spell a word?
- How can you change your sentence beginnings to create more variety?
- How do you know where one sentence ends and another begins?
- When do you capitalize?
- Which sentences might you combine?
- Are your paragraphs in order?
- Are there transitions between paragraphs?

Students can work together to proofread work and flag problems before meeting with the teacher.

ASSESSMENT CONFERENCES. An assessment conference helps writers become more aware of strengths and weaknesses in a written product and develop their own criteria for what counts as quality writing. Ed discusses the mystery story LeAnne has been working on for several weeks. She has just finished editing her composition and is ready to share the final version. Before she reads the piece, Ed asks her to talk about its strengths.

Ed: How do you feel about this piece?

LeAnne: It's my best work.

Ed: What are the strengths of this piece?

LeAnne: The mystery and the dialogue.

Ed: I agree—the storyline keeps me on the edge of my seat. And the dialogue creates lots of suspense. How would you compare this draft to the earlier ones?

LeAnne: People told me to add more description of the jewelry store and the woods. I revised and put in more clues.

Ed: Do you think the story is stronger now?

LeAnne: Yeah. It's more interesting because I explain things better.

Although this conference centers primarily on the finished product, it is also an assessment of the writing process. LeAnne reveals that a collection of Nancy Drew books inspired her mystery story. She also tells how she drafted her work over several days and talked with peers about the plot. As LeAnne talks, Ed gets a better sense of her competence and overall efforts.

Writers such as LeAnne may use the assessment conference to reflect on previous drafts and make judgments about the quality of the final version. Some self-evaluation questions include the following:

- How's it going?
- What are you writing about?

- What do you like best about your work?
- What is your favorite part of the paper? Why?
- Which part of your paper do you want to spend more time on?
- What do you think you need help with?
- What do you plan to do next?
- How is this piece like or unlike others you have written?

As students finish one piece and begin another, the assessment conference becomes a good place to consider new goals.

PUBLISHING CONFERENCES.   A publishing conference provides an occasion to decide if a work is complete or if it needs to go through additional editing steps. Nathan has just finished a piece on football, and Ed speaks with him about his publication plans.

Ed:	What would you like to do with this piece now that it is finished?
Nathan:	Take it home.
Ed:	Is there anything you should do if you are going to take it home?
Nathan:	Spell words better.
Ed:	Yes. Go ahead and circle the words you think are misspelled and I will help you later.

Nathan decides to take his paper home, but he might have placed it in a portfolio and returned at a later time to polish it. Or he could have shared his work, put it on display, or turned it into a book. If there are plans for publication, here are a few questions the student can ask:

- Am I ready to publish my work? If not, what else must I do?
- What audience will view my work?
- What will I do with this piece now that it's done?
- What must I do to get this piece ready for publication/presentation?
- Which of my works do I want to publish? Why?
- Where and how will I publish my work?
- Are there possibilities for extending this text?
- Can this piece be changed into another form for presentation?

Publication is a gratifying and challenging accomplishment for writers who lack a sense of audience or who see no purpose for writing. At least one out of every five written compositions should be published in some form. Publication gives students pride in their work and rewards them for their achievements.

Continuous Assessment

Continuous assessment merges instruction and learning. Put another way, it asks two key questions: "What do students already know about writing?" and "What do they need to learn next?" Teachers informally monitor student progress to answer these questions (Hill, Ruptic, Norwick, 1998; Rhodes & Shanklin, 1993). This takes place during observations and in natural, ongoing interactions with students during the writing process, in writing conferences, or in minilessons. An integral part of assessment involves collecting and examining children's writing products to find value in them, strengths that guide decisions about lessons to teach, materials to gather, conversations to hold, and conventions to highlight (Hansen, 1996). Products are seen not as an end to the writing process but as the start of a dialogue or an opportunity to teach.

In any assessment, there are not only options for gathering information but also decisions about who should do the assessing. In some cases, teachers are the most appropriate choice (e.g., teachers can design and implement anecdotal records). But more often they share responsibility with students. Students should monitor and reflect on their behaviors, exploring how they've grown or how their ideas have changed. With the teacher's help, they develop checklists and rubrics for self-assessment and goal setting. As students begin to internalize the norms of good writing, self-assessments become increasingly comparable with the teacher's judgment.

Teachers are faced with many assessment choices. A few of them are presented here along with a brief description of two viable management systems. In the chapters that follow, practical teacher assessment tools are provided in the writer's workshop sections and student self-assessment tools in the classroom vignettes.

Observations

During the writer's workshop, teachers spend a lot of time *kidwatching* (Goodman, 1985), or observing children as they write. Sometimes they stand at the far edges of the room, scanning and monitoring the learning environment for interactional patterns and procedural routines. They watch how children locate and handle materials, use resources and environmental print, manage allocated time, and follow established rules and standards for appropriate social behavior.

In close-range observations of small groups, social dynamics are captured—roles children assume, questions asked, levels of assistance, and forms of sharing. A one-on-one observation involves more intense listening and waiting for pauses as writers think, erase, start over, or sound out a word. Asking a writer about what she is thinking while writing or listening to subvocalizations can reveal what cannot be readily observed.

Teachers record what they see and hear in brief and informal narratives called anecdotal records (see Table 1–5). These notes, whether written on sticky papers, a class chart, in a plan book, or on a computer screen, help them recall what they have observed. In the anecdotal example in Table 1–5, teachers can see the names of all their students. Using Post-it notes, sized to fit into the squares, teachers jot down observations and stack them sequentially under each child's name. After sufficient data is layered for each individual, the Post-it notes are lifted back in the order collected and displayed for analysis. In this way, teachers can track individual achievement over time, while surveying the whole class on any single observation. Although anecdotal records are time consuming and subject to interpretation, they are useful for developing minilessons or tracking progress to share with a parent or child in conferences.

Conferences and Interviews

To supplement observational data, teachers confer with students about in-progress drafts and finished products. In the section on sharing earlier in the chapter, various types of conferences and the potential information each could produce were discussed. A teacher can keep records of these conferences to document student behaviors and attitudes toward writing. Verbal exchanges of this sort are also ideal as interviews.

Interviews are communicative events in their own right and are sometimes prepared in advance. Seidman's (1998) interviewing guidelines for researchers are just as useful to classroom teachers. Several of these are listed below:

- listen more, talk less
- ask questions when you do not understand
- ask to hear more about a subject
- explore don't probe
- ask real questions (those you don't know the answers to)
- avoid leading questions (you like writing don't you?)
- ask open-ended questions (tell me about. . .)
- follow up don't interrupt
- ask participants to tell a story
- ask for concrete details
- share your own experiences on occasion

TABLE 1-5 Anecdotal Records for an Entire Class and for a Small Group

First-Grade Class

Taylor 11/3	Keely 11/3	Julio 11/4	Joshua 11/4
<u>Chopper</u> Check previous titles; detailed drawing; needs to add text; shares at author's chair	<u>My Sister</u> High-frequency words are spelled correctly; schedule conference for brainstorming	<u>Swimming</u> Draws pictures; invents spelling; talks with tablemates	<u>No title</u> About Nintendo; places periods after words; uses syllables to spell; shares at author's chair
Su Hyen 11/3	Alton 11/4	Logan 11/4	Lindsey 11/5
Marhonda 11/5	Savannah 11/4	Michele 11/5	Nicky 11/4

Small Group

ANECDOTAL RECORDS

Name <u>K</u>   Date <u>11/7</u>   Time <u>10:07–10:37</u>

Activity <u>At the writing table</u>

10:07–10:08	K talks with TJ about his picture. "Pretty good, pretty nice try," she comments. She says he is drawing an apple tree with worms. He points to the worm and says, "Look at my worm." TJ responds with, "I like spaghetti," and N says he does too but "his mom don't cook."
10:15–10:24	N asks K how to spell *the*. She spells it for him.
	K writes but is doing so as she talks to TJ and spells words for N.
	When K goes to write *apple* (spelled, *apl*), she says to TJ, "Is that apple? I'm trying to spell *apple* out." She is interrupted by N who continues to ask for spellings. TJ finally spells *apple* correctly for K. K announces that she doesn't need help anymore because she's "doing grass." (drawing)
10:24–10:37	Now she turns her paper over and writes the word *red* using a red crayon. She follows with the word *blue* using a blue crayon. N leaves the table. TJ asks why she is writing "red, red, red," and K says because she wants to. She says she will do two rows of red then blue. She looks at the crayon wrapper to spell *blue*. TJ says to K, "You're looking on here" (points to the wrapper). "I'm not looking on here," she says. N returns.

K = Keely
N = Nicky
TJ = TJ

- explore laughter
- tolerate silence
- role-play (if I were your mother, what would you say)
- avoid positive or negative feedback (that's good) [pp. 63–77]

For a full explanation of these and other topics, see Seidman's book *Interviewing as Qualitative Research* (1998).

Certainly, it bears repeating that the key to conducting an effective interview is to talk less than the writers do and to refrain from asking leading questions or putting words in their mouths. When unsure about students' answers, explore further. It is also important to be specific and concrete about what you request. For instance, rather than asking a child to *tell about the writing,* specify what you mean by reformulating the question as "What do you like to write about when given a choice?" Jot down ahead of time the goal or motivation for engaging in the interview and the social situation in which it occurs (including the time and place) because these factors may affect the data you collect. Student commentaries about writing can have implications for teaching, as shown in Table 1–6. Self-reports confirm or extend teacher understanding of a child. An analysis of the written product coupled with student comments provide more information and a more well-rounded assessment than either could alone. As in any type of self-report, however, there is always a chance that children will tell you what they think you want to hear. That is why it is important to supplement these interactions with other assessment tools.

Writing Sample Analyses

An equally significant part of assessment involves describing the students' products and using this description as a basis for asking questions and reporting student accomplishments in writing conferences and circles. The analysis sheet in Table 1–7 offers ways to characterize and talk about a work. As the sample questions show, the **indicators** change and are redefined in light of the writing genre.

Consider the descriptions of two writing samples: the first by 6-year-old Joshua and the second by 10-year-old Dario. Joshua's composition represents his two favorite cartoon characters, Silvester and Tweedy Bird (see Figure 1–12, p. 42). By examining this product, the teacher notes that his spellings consist of visually remembered words, such as *cartoon,* and several invented spellings that are phonemically based. Joshua chooses the middle of the page to display his drawing and uses arrows to direct readers' eyes to the print. In the lower right corner is the open cage from which Tweedy has escaped. The analysis of this single composition is part of a bigger puzzle that helps unravel the mysteries of Joshua's writing.

Dario's composition about his trip to Venezuela in Figure 1–13, pp. 42–43 shows a wider range of the descriptive categories. The content is well ordered and each paragraph focuses on a single idea. Descriptions in the opening, *soaring over the blue Atlantic Ocean toward the Caribbean Sea,* and details about his overseas classroom invite the reader to imagine the setting and get involved. Similes, such as *I was going to sizzle like bacon,* and expletives, such as *Yuk* and *HOT!,* bring voice and energy to the piece. The cultural customs and foods add interest. Although the three-paragraph theme is driving the text with words such as *first, next,* and *last,* rich ideas and colorful language show a narrative style emerging. As English conventions go, it appears that Dario has overgeneralized some phonics rules, such as *deskes* for *desks* or *activetys* for *activities,* and might profit from a minilesson on verb tense.

Although these two examples are easily described, given the lack of process data, the analysis is basically a set of hypotheses to be tested and verified with writers in conference. To increase the reliability of hunches, the teacher may want to examine multiple pieces of writing in the same genre and look for patterns.

Assessment Tools

Teachers select different tools for gathering multiple indices of writing growth, informing instruction, identifying learning goals for the writer, and tracking progress. Some of these assessment tools are listed in Table 1–8, p. 43.

TABLE 1-6   What Teachers Can Learn From Writers

What Writers Tell Us About How They Write	Teaching Implications

Children have different views about what writing is.
  I can't spell.
  First I get a piece of paper, then I sharpen my pencil. . . .
	Writing is meaning-making, not simply proper conventions or routines. For those who believe writing is spelling correctly or fixing punctuation, try to minimize correctness and concentrate on meanings and communication. For those who believe the act of writing is a mechanical process, try to involve them in meaningful experiences with writing, such as writing circles and publication.

All writers experience the writing process but express it in a range of ways.
  I make a web before I write.
  I just write until I'm finished.
  I like to draw pictures first.
	During the course of the year, show children how they can make choices based on different tasks, topics, content, purposes, genres, and writing conditions. For example, share a variety of prewriting strategies. For children who rely solely on one strategy, try to broaden their repertoire.

Children have different learning styles and preferred strategies.
  I talk better than I write.
  I don't like to copy from the board.
	Variability of strategies is a function of the individual's learning experiences and preferred modalities. Try to use a variety of communicative channels: visual, kinesthetic, auditory, and linguistic. Be sure to observe children's writing processes during particular tasks. Are they using strategies that are effective for the task? Are they aware of the general strategies inherent in a particular kind of writing?

Children require different conditions for writing.
  I like to write in front of the TV.
  When I write, it must be quiet.
  I write in the car sometimes.
	Conditions for writing are ultimately reflected in the quality of the products that children create. Teachers should constantly experiment with different writing conditions to see what works for particular children. Ask questions: Did you expect children to write within a particular time period? Alone or in a group? With or without help? What was the noise level? Did the children write the assignment at home or at school?

Children often do not distinguish between revising and editing.
  When I revise, I fix my letters and punctuation.
  When I revise, I make sure my writing is neat.
	Most children believe revision is correcting capitalization, punctuation, spelling, and other conventions. Help them understand that revision involves the content and meaning of the piece, and editing involves the mechanics. Set up situations to motivate revision. Have children read their work to others. By reading to an audience of peers, children will want to make their meanings clear. Make revision a routine in the classroom. Share revisions made by professional writers and explain how important it is to communicate meanings and intentions.

Some children find writing difficult.
  Writing is not too easy for me.
  I can't make some of the letters.
	Many children experience barriers to getting ideas down on paper because of handwriting or spelling. For example, young children are often concerned about spelling. Encourage them to use invented spellings so as not to slow down the process of getting meaning on paper. Tell them that they can fix spelling later. Have them find ways to get words down quickly during drafting: asking a friend, using pictionaries, leaving a space for the word, or dictating information on audiotape. Teach children to use word processors.

Some children do not like writing and are reluctant to write.
  I hate writing.
  I can't write.
	Often children have had negative experiences with writing and do not see themselves as writers. Try to create a positive environment to help children enjoy writing. Build a community of writers so every child sees him or herself as an author.

Children like to write about what interests them.
  I like to write about spaceships.
  I like to put my feelings in writing.
	When children write on topics they care about, they are more committed to their writing and have a greater sense of ownership. Children's purposes for writing vary, and teachers need to find out what they are.

TABLE 1-7   Analyzing a Writing Sample

Elements to Identify	Sample Questions to Consider
Purpose	What is the intent of the piece? To entertain? To inform? To express feelings? To get things done?
Audience	Who will read this? Peers? Implied audience? Teacher? Parents?
Topics	What is the subject of the writing? Objects? Family? Personal experience? Self? Abstract virtues? An issue?
Content/focus/message	What is the single, overall message or main idea? If it is a story, what is the theme? If it is an opinion paper, what is the writer's position? What ideas are presented in the paper? What is the subject matter? What details has the writer chosen to include and omit?
Organization/structure	What is the skeletal form or foundation on which all the information hangs? If it is a story, can you find the plot structure? If it is a haiku poem, can you count the syllables and lines? If it is a report, can you find definitions, cause/effect, or some other organizing text structure? How are the ideas sequenced for the reader? Are they ordered at the whole discourse level, the paragraph level, and the sentence level? How would you describe the organization?
Coherence	How does the writer keep ideas together? Do ideas flow logically throughout the piece? Are there appropriate cue words?
Linguistic devices and elements	What special uses of language create certain effects? In poetry do you find rhythm, rhyme, and imagery? Alliteration? In story do you find dialogue, action, and show don't tell? In reports do you find definitions, summaries, explanations?
Style/tone/mood	What feelings are suggested by words? Is the piece scary, humorous, or ironic? How would you describe the imprint of the writer on the page? How does the writer use words, sentence length, and other characteristic features? How can the style be characterized? Is it formal, informal, imaginative, arrogant, warm, energetic, or friendly?
Sentence complexity, variety, and cohesiveness	How would you describe the syntax? Does the writer use a variety of sentence types and patterns? Does the writer use phrases and clauses? Do the sentences string together logically and meaningfully?
Grammar/usage	Do the subject and verb agree? Is there consistency in verb tense? Are there clear pronoun referents? Is there modification?
Vocabulary/word choice	Can you describe the writer's use of word choice for the writing genre or topic (e.g., baseball words for sports writing)? Is dialect used? What functions do the words serve? Do they represent age, maturity, gender, persuasion, euphemisms, propaganda, sarcasm, or melody? Is there language play?
Spelling, mechanics, and conventions	Can you describe the spelling and patterns of errors; and use of commas, capitalization, and punctuation?
Page format	How is the writing visually displayed on the page? If it is a poem, are there white spaces or designs? If it is a news article, are there columns and lines? Are there margins set for a letter?
Length	How long is the paper? How many words? How many sentences?

The same tool in the hands of different teachers may function in different ways. For one teacher, a checklist might be a resource that frames and makes sense of anecdotal records, whereas for another, it might serve as a means of ensuring that the same behaviors are observed for each writer. Its use, even for a single teacher, may carry the dual function of informing instruction and reporting grades.

Beyond matters of function, the designs of assessment tools also vary. Some include numerical or developmental scales, others are open ended, and still others take the form

TABLE 1–9   Writer, Process, Text, and Context Factors That Influence Writing Assessment

Writer	Process	Text	Context

• Background experience
  —as a writer
  —as a reader
• Home/literacy habits
  —frequency of writing
  —kinds of writing done
• Self-efficacy
  —feelings as writer
  —attitudes toward writing
• Writing habits
  —interests
  —risk-taking behaviors
• Knowledge of writing
  —how writing is used
  —what writing does
• Development as a writer
  —novice, apprentice, proficient, independent
• Learning styles
  —multiple intelligences
	• Writing process behaviors
	  —strategies used
	  —resources used
	  —reading
	  —sharing
	  —rewriting
	  —drawing
	  —performing
	• Metalinguistic awareness
	  —self-monitoring behavior
	  —ability to self-evaluate
	  —self-regulatory behavior
		• Content
		• Task
		• Topic
		• Purpose
		• Function
		• Audience
		• Genre
		• Level of discourse (word, sentence, paragraph, whole)
		• Stylistic devices
		• Formats
		• Number of revisions
		• Voice/mood
		• Mechanics
			• Lesson objectives
			• Teacher and student expectations
			• Instruction/requirements
			• Type of literacy event
			  —dictation, copying
			  —peer tutoring
			  —shared writing
			  —conferences
			  —collaborative writing
			  —interactive writing
			  —guided writing
			• Setting
			  —in class, at home
			  —whole class, small group, with partner, alone
			  —print environment
			• Writing conditions
			  —allocated time
			  —teacher–student interaction
			  —peer–peer interaction
			  —types of writing tools and resources (e.g., computer)
			• Outcomes (private/public)
			  —evaluation
			  —publication

Source: L. Leslie & M. Jett-Simpson, *Authentic literacy assessment: An ecological approach* copyright © 1997. Adapted by permission by Allyn & Bacon.

of letters. Responses may be indicated using pictures (such as the smiley or frowning face), checkmarks, written comments, or bubble fill-ins.

An essential decision in selecting an assessment instrument is whether its content is appropriate for the function for which it was designed. A summary of content features is outlined in Table 1–9. This summary suggests four important factors that, alone or in combination, account for the items typically represented in an assessment. Sometimes a tool emphasizes writers' attitudes and feelings about writing, their perceptions of themselves as writers, prior knowledge about writing, or home literacy habits. For instance, items represented on a parent questionnaire might tap into the opportunities students have to observe and participate in writing as part of the family system. With plenty of home writing experiences, children will be far more ready for school writing tasks than those without exposure to print or with a literacy history markedly different from that of the dominant school culture (Heath, 1983). Or suppose the tool is designed to elicit student perceptions. Items on a self-report inventory may take into account students' feelings about writing and their positive or negative influences on the work

(Bottomley, Henk, Melnick, 1998; Daly & Miller, 1975). Whether items are exclusively focused on the writer or combined with other factors, the writer represents a principal source of information.

Another substantive area included in assessment tools is writing process strategies. A tool is likely to be constructed for a particular type of writing; for a certain age group; or for a stage in the piece's development, such as the rough draft, second version, or final product. Writing process behaviors often included are shown in Figure 1–14.

Documenting process behaviors and strategies helps teachers better understand the written product and credits students for problem-solving efforts, risk taking, and dogged persistence. With very young children a checklist that directs attention to reading and its role in the writing process offers added insights into the writer's hypotheses and knowledge about print [(Sulzby, 1988, 1990) see Figure 1–15].

This particular checklist also outlines the **developmental** forms of texts that children are likely to produce. For a continuum of developmental stages for writing that begins with preconventional and emergent writing, refer to the work of Hill, Ruptic, and Norwick (1998) or McGee and Richgels (2000).

Features or **traits** of a **text** (in-progress drafts or final products) are also the subject of many assessment tools (see Figure 1–16 on page 48). Agreed-on criteria regarding the quality of interrelated traits or features of writing include ideas, organization, voice, sentence fluency, word choice, and **conventions** (Spandel, 2001).

The specifications and definitions of these traits are modified based on the particular type of writing and on the development of the writer. What might a story trait look like for a first, third, or a fifth grader? What about a poetry trait? Throughout the book are prototypical traits for each kind of writing. The poetry example in Figure 1–16 illustrates the importance of particularizing the traits in terms of the student's actual work if assessment is to be useful and informative.

Because **emergent writers** represent a special group, their work is measured against a generic list, including four traits (see Figure 1–17, pp. 49–50). Again directing comments to the child that is specific to the content of the paper is essential for effective feedback (see the poetry example in Figure 1–17). It is also best to refer to multiple indicators as resources for examining and describing a product.

Knowing the traits for a variety of writing functions and modifying and adapting them to the developmental levels of children reinforces an awareness of text features, criteria for assessment, and information that you can share with writers when planning and revising.

Finally, in addition to assessing the writer, the process, and the text, teachers attend to the writing event itself including situation and **context** variables that may affect the written product: Was the work part of shared writing or did the child write independently? Was the task assigned or self-selected? Periodically, a teacher can do a writing context scan similar to the one in Figure 1–18, p. 51.

Attention to matters such as those listed in Figure 1–18 reminds teachers that learning environments make a difference in the quality of a finished work. Assessments should periodically reflect the procedures, routines, and grouping arrangements that influence the attitudes children are developing and the literacy habits they are acquiring during the process.

Balancing the context with other factors widen the lens for viewing children's competence. Teachers document as many indicators as they can to inform instruction and to accurately describe what their students know and can do. No single assessment tool is sufficient, and most teachers combine all of these substantive factors to describe development and track progress. When constructing or using predeveloped assessment forms, the content needs to be continually modified as children write in different genres and grow into the process.

FIGURE 1-16 Generic Descriptions of Six Traits

Ideas
➢ Interesting or clear messages
➢ Main points
➢ Sound or logical information marked by insight
➢ Sufficient details; evidence
➢ Theme or thesis
➢ Thoughtful or intriguing points
➢ Unity of content; development

Organization
➢ Arrangement
➢ Beginning, middle, and end
➢ Recognizable framework or skeletal structure
➢ Sequence or order
➢ Shape
➢ Transitions that hold ideas together

Voice
➢ Connection to the reader
➢ Imprint of self
➢ Point of view or attitude
➢ The sound of writing (pace, emphasis)
➢ Tone of message
➢ Topic brought to life
➢ Writer behind the text; writer's presence
➢ Writer's style, individuality, personality

Sentence Fluency
➢ Cohesive sentences
➢ Length and variety in sentences
➢ Logic of sentences
➢ Modification
➢ Readability
➢ Rhythm and flow of words

Word Choice
➢ Appropriate number of words; economical
➢ Connotation and denotation
➢ Types of words (precise words, colorful, or striking words, familiar words, quotable or memorable words, fresh words)

Conventions
➢ Adherence to standard forms
➢ Capitalization and punctuation
➢ Grammar and usage
➢ Legibility
➢ Length and format
➢ Spacing
➢ Spelling
➢ Surface features

Tree Poem

Ideas	• The idea of what is unseen about a dormant tree—or what can only be seen if one looks closely—is the theme of the poem. • Once published, this poem will catch the reader's eye because of its shape.
Organization	• Suggests organization through the visual shape of a tree. • Makes use of repetition "the tree I see" which helps with the flow of the poem. • Title is very simple — perhaps something could be added to hint at the theme of the poem. • There is a flow there but it is more narrative than poetic in nature.
Voice	• Incorporates some sound elements "creaky" and "squeaky" but it is unclear how this relates to the tree or to the other parts of the poem. • Reads fairly smoothly as a narrative. Last sentence a bit awkward.
Sentence Fluency	• Written in narrative form. Line is not compressed or broken into stanza groupings to enhance meaning and flow. • No fragments used.
Word Choice	• Written in narrative form. Line is not compressed or broken into stanza groupings to enhance meaning and flow. • No fragments used. • Some expressive language choices: "inner eye" (she probably means outer eye), "spring draws nearer," and the tree "shares its grace." • Mostly telling in nature: "little brown blossoms that are becoming beautiful." What does she see that makes her say that?
Conventions	• Conventions are used in traditional narrative manner. No special effects added through conventions. • No format was specified for the writing other than poetry.

FIGURE 1-17 Four Traits of Generic Descriptions for Emergent Writers

Source: The role of oral language in early writing processes, by Anne Haas Dyson (1983). Copyright © 1983 by the National Council of Teachers of English. Reprinted with permission.

Text Invention

1. **Sense-Making:** Creating messages that convey meanings about experiences, events, or ideas. The strategies used to carry out this element are:
   (a) *drawing, e.g.,* Labels or describes drawing with captions; draws pictures to represent complete messages; draws pictures to expand a topic or illustrate written words; uses drawing for planning
   (b) *composing, e.g.,* Generates own message; uses two to three word phrases; relates two to three sentences; writes loose factlets or messages that are thematic; displays a random collection of words or strings of letters; compiles a meaningful inventory of letters or words
   (c) *tracing or copying a message*
   (d) *modeling writing after books, e.g.,* Includes title, author, illustrator; borrows characters, plots, or themes
   (e) *dictating a message*
   (f) *writing one's name*

Text Development

2. **Identifying Form:** The structure or arrangement of letters, words, sentences, and paragraphs. The strategies used to carry out this element are:
   (a) *displaying graphic symbols, e.g.,* Abbreviates first or last letters of names or words; invents spelling (based on articulation cues, letter names, syllables, phoneme/grapheme, or visual recall); uses letter like symbols or scribbles; creates words for language play
   (b) *handwriting, e.g.,* Forms letters correctly; writes legible letters; leaves space between letters, words and sentences; positions letters on the line; scribbles; decorates letters or creates letter like strings
   (c) *considering grammar and punctuation, e.g.,* Uses upper and lowercase; recognizes nouns, verbs, adjectives, adverbs; includes end punctuation

Print Knowledge

3. **Concepts of Print:** Growing understanding that written language follows certain conventions or rules. The strategies used to carry out this element are:
   (a) *recognizing names for print, e.g.,* Identifies alphabet letters, numbers, names of objects in the world; recognizes written names; knows some punctuation; understands that names consist of letters, symbols, syllables
   (b) *knowing that print has meaning and carries a message, e.g.,* Knows that pictures communicate messages; recognizes functions of print (to make signs, send greeting cards, give directions)
   (c) *knowing that print serves many functions, e.g.,* Is aware that adults use print for many purposes; knows there are many different kinds of print (poems, signs, directions, stories, drawings)
   (d) *demonstrating concept of word, e.g.,* Recognizes that words are made of letters; understands the differences among letters, words, and sentences; detects different letter shapes; knows that sentences are made of words; is aware that letters are ordered (ABC, in words)
   (e) *identifying directionality, e.g.,* Demonstrates left to right progression, top to bottom

*Language Functions

4. **Representational language:** Language which serves to give information about events and situations (real or imagined, past or present). The strategies used to carry out this function are:
   (a) *labeling, e.g.,* That's my middle name. (Child has written MOKLLHJK.)
   (b) *elaborating* or detailing, e.g., This is a box that goes like that and see, when somebody goes in it a skeleton will pop out and eat it. (Child has drawn several objects on her paper.)
   (c) *associating* or comparing with earlier experiences, e.g., (Child has just written the word *present*.) You know what? My Grandma has a present for me in the bathroom. I can't look at it 'cuz it's a—I wannt' be surprised.
   (d) *reporting* an action or event, e.g., (Child has drawn a picture of a girl standing beside a house.) She's locked out.
   (e) *narrating* a series of actions or events, e.g., (Child is talking as she draws.) She [the girl in the picture] was swinging on the branch. She was swinging on the branch and her Mama told her not to swing on the branch and she did and her Mama said she'll knock down her playhouse and she knocked down the house and the house just got small. . . .
   (f) *dramatizing* or acting out a series of actions, e.g., (Child is talking as she draws.) "Sister, open up the door."
   (Child knocks twice on table.) "You dummy. Sister, you better come and open this door or else I'm gonna throw this pumpkin shell on your head."
   (g) *reasoning, e.g.,* (Child is speaking to an adult who has been unable to read child's writing.) You can't read it 'cuz all these letters are so teeny-weeny. Right? That's how they put it in the newspaper. Real tiny, don't they?

5. **Directive Language:** Language which serves to direct the actions of self and/or others. The strategies used to carry out this function are:
   (a) *monitoring* (strategy through which ongoing actions appear to be controlled and directed), e.g., (Child is copying someone's name.) . . . an "r" and then . . . and then . . . and then—and then an "e".
   (b) *planning* (strategy through which future actions appear to be controlled and directed), e.g., Now I'm gonna write inside my book . . . I'm gonna write a picture in the front of it.
   (c) *encoding* (strategy through which words or phrases are transferred from the oral to the written language channel: the child pronounces sounds, letters, syllables, or the word/phrase itself), e.g.,

Child's Language	Text
H-B	HB
H-B . . . O . . .	O added
HBO, HBO Box	Vivi drew a box around *HBO:* HBO

   (*HBO Box* was Vivi's term for Home Box Office television.)

(continued)

FIGURE 1-17 (continued)

(d) *decoding* (strategy through which sounds, syllables, words, phrases or propositions are transferred from the written to the oral language channel: the child matches oral letter names, syllables, words, phrases, or propositions to either some segment of the written text or to the entire text), e.g., (Child is reading text; arrows indicate where the child points as she reads.)

Text: Rudolph the Red- Nosed Reindeer
       ↑   ↑   ↑   ↑   ↑
Child: Ru   dolph   the   Red   Nosed

(e) *accessing* (strategy used to seek or to retrieve letters or words from memory: in written language situations, this strategy involves rereading) e.g., (Child is writing the *ABC*s.)

Child Language	Text
A	A
Now, *B*	B
A-B (Rereading)	
A-B-C	C

(f) *instructing* (strategy used to convey information perceived as required or needed by someone else, language to "teach") e.g., (Child is telling another how to "make people"): Let me show you how to make 'em. Let me show you how to make people how I like 'em. See? I like 'em like this. This is how you make 'em. (Child draws.) Make it curl like that, OK? (Child waits and watches.) See?

(g) *requesting*, e.g., I need a red [marker].

6. **Heuristic Language:** Language which serves to seek information, to learn about or to explore reality. In reference to written language in particular, heuristic language may be used to seek information regarding encoding, decoding, or mechanically producing print (i.e., handwriting); the print being focused on could be letters, words, phrases, or propositions (although the child may not know what linguistic unit is being focused on).

Strategies include:
(a) *seeking confirmation*, e.g.,
    What's that, a *P*?
    My God! I've been trying to make a little *e*'s 'cuz I can't make little *e*'s good . . . and → then like that?
(b) *seeking fact*, e.g.,
    How do you spell *Christmas*?
    What does this say?
(c) *seeking demonstration*, e.g.,
    How do you make a *J*?
(d) *seeking to test*, e.g.,
    (Child has written her mother's name, a word she frequently writes.)
    What does this say?

7. **Personal Language:** Language used to express one's feelings and attitudes. Examples are:
    I'm gonna' write my last name again. I like it.
    That makes me mad.
Three strategies specifically identified which serve this function are:
(a) *evaluating others*, e.g.,
    You made it very, very pretty.
    You done it wrong again.
(b) *evaluating self*, e.g.,
    I'm gonna' write a better *2*. . . . Yuch! Can't write no *2*.
    Oh my God! I done it wrong.
(c) *playing with language*, e.g.,
    I got a puppy named Bobo . . . My puppy is Slobo . . . My puppy named Klobo.

8. **Interactional Language:** Language used to initiate, maintain, and terminate social relationships. No division into strategies was done. Examples of this function are:
    Know what I'm doing?
    This one's for my mother, and I'll give you one tomorrow. I promise.

Blue

Message	• Jana writes about her favorite color, *blue*. • She synchronizes her illustration *(a heart)* with the text *(I love blue)*. • Jana relates the color to objects *(blue is the sky)*. • Jana's poem has a title *(Blue: A Poem)*.
Form	• Jana writes a four line poem. • Each line repeats the color, *blue*. • Jana uses three-five words per line. • She uses rhyme *(sky/high)*.
Print Knowledge	• Jana understands directionality and places each sentence on a line. • She invents spelling during drafting *(blu/blue; colr/color)* using phoneme/grapheme cues. • Jana spells some words conventionally *(the; of)*. • She capitalizes the first word in each line.
Language Functions	• Jana uses nouns, verbs, and adjectives *(blue is cool)*. • Jana "sounds out" words as she writes. • She talks about the topic, *blue*, in relation to objects in her bedroom. • Jana rereads her poem. • Jana asks for verification of the spelling *sky*.

FIGURE 1-18   Writing Context Scan

Student names	/	/	/	/	/	/	/	/	/	/	/
Points to scan during writing											
Uses the print environment											
Seeks help from peers											
Knows how to seek help from teacher											
Works in small group (less than 5)											
Works in large group (more than 5)											
Works in groups of mixed gender and abilities											
Works well alone											
Experiences distractions from noise or interruptions											
Seems to always have extra time											
Does not have enough time											
Makes use of a variety of resource materials											

the personal story of a student's writing journey, a vehicle for sharing writing lives along with their progress.

Writing portfolios are legal folders, accordion folders, or three-ring binders containing students' work that are kept in a place where students can access them easily. Their contents can be as creative and varied as the children want. Some sample items are listed in Figure 1–19.

The writer usually decides what materials to place in the portfolio. (Younger children may need guidance for selections and monitoring to upkeep the folders.) Sometimes the teacher asks all the students to add a special item that will inform her instruction or provide a point of reference for comparing class responses, for example, an editing checklist or an attitude survey. Because different strategies and skills are required for each kind of writing and because one or two samples often is not enough to assess a child's ability, multiple samples of a single type or several different genres are necessary to represent the range of student work. Clearly, any number of objectives might determine what to place in the portfolio.

Although the portfolio may contain many materials, it is more than a storage bin. Its very existence invites the examination of its contents and engages children automatically in appraising and reflecting on their achievements (Farr & Tone, 1994). Simply displaying the pieces in order by date provides a means for comparing or locating changes in the writing. The student might communicate any of the following through the portfolio:

- The process followed to achieve a product (the evolution of the work)
- Preferences for writing genres and topics
- Procedures for completing a particular product
- Criteria developed for assessing work
- Comparisons of drafts-in-progress and finished work

FIGURE 1-19   Writing Portfolio Contents Sample

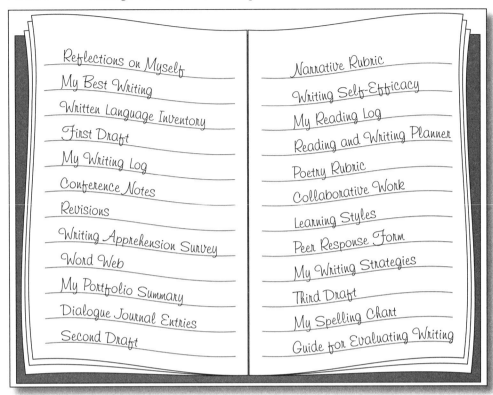

Reflections on Myself
My Best Writing
Written Language Inventory
First Draft
My Writing Log
Conference Notes
Revisions
Writing Apprehension Survey
Word Web
My Portfolio Summary
Dialogue Journal Entries
Second Draft

Narrative Rubric
Writing Self-Efficacy
My Reading Log
Reading and Writing Planner
Poetry Rubric
Collaborative Work
Learning Styles
Peer Response Form
My Writing Strategies
Third Draft
My Spelling Chart
Guide for Evaluating Writing

- Growth in specific areas over time
- Amount of information included
- Quality of individual pieces
- Variety of writing represented

In some classrooms, teachers make a distinction between working portfolios and showcase portfolios. The working portfolio is reserved for in-progress drafts, prewriting notes, revisions, assessment tools, and other artifacts. The showcase portfolio, however, includes the best work or representative pieces that sometimes follow the child to the next grade or form the basis of a presentation or public display. Because the portfolio provides samples of written products and concrete evidence of process (e.g., cut and pasted drafts), teachers are in a better position to evaluate and assign grades.

Although the discussion so far has considered only student portfolios, it is worth noting that teachers also keep portfolios to reflect on and improve their instruction. They examine class work for patterns of growth and ask, "Did I make learning expectations clear to students?" "Am I providing sufficient and varied experiences to assess children's competence?" "Do I keep sufficient levels of documentation to explain and support my assessment of children?" The teacher's portfolio can document progress toward particular benchmarks or standards; show changes and improvements in the writing program; and supply the content for conversations with other teachers, guidance counselors, or parents.

Writing Contracts

Writing contracts represent another management system for individualizing and monitoring learning (see Figure 1–20). Writing contracts are negotiated agreements between a teacher and student or between student and peers concerning workloads, deadlines for completing tasks, competency levels to be demonstrated, or literacy activities in which to engage in. They usually revolve around three questions: What do I want to study or learn? How do I plan to work on this? What will I use to document my progress?

FIGURE 1-20 Writing Contract

Name _____

Start date: _____ Finish date: _____

Reading

_____ Read a folktale

Composing

_____ Draft a folktale

_____ Include prewriting notes in my portfolio

Sharing

_____ Conference with a partner to revise work

_____ Share finished draft with a friend

Spelling

_____ Add five new spelling words to word bank

_____ Take spelling test on misspelled words in composition

_____ Edit one composition

I agree to complete these tasks by Friday.

_____   _____
Signed   Approved

Contracts are motivational because they encourage students to make decisions about their own learning. Contracts allow them to work at their own levels and to personalize tasks and activities using preferred learning styles and habits. Students who work independently to fulfill a contract may require large blocks of time. Students are responsible for self-monitoring, but they should meet with the teacher at scheduled times to discuss their progress. With this flexibility, students can tell teachers what they need and set goals for future learning.

CLASSROOM VIGNETTES

Classroom vignettes offer scenarios for implementing the writer's workshop and for detailing genre-specific practices associated with the kind of writing being discussed (for example, science fiction in story writing). From one chapter to the next, each grade level vignette builds toward a set of lessons that can help frame the writing curriculum. You'll gain an in-depth and comprehensive look at this curriculum by following the same teachers and their classes.

By way of introduction, this section examines how the teachers in three classrooms (grades 1, 3, and 5) put into place the basic building blocks that prepare students for the writing journey. Effective teachers plan long before students ever arrive at the doorstep, and this planning continues as the teachers learn more about their students each day. Any written description of a classroom, however, can never fully capture the dynamic and continuous flow of activity that takes place in real time. Nonetheless, the vignettes provide an initial set of observable indicators to think about when planning the physical environment, establishing rules and routines, and setting schedules.

FIGURE 1-21   First-Grade Floor Plan

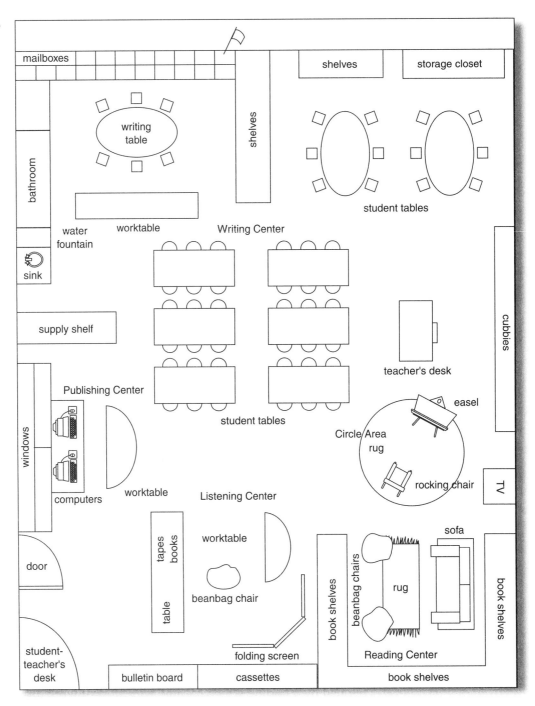

Publishing center: In front of the windowed wall are three computers on mobile carts. Computer publishing programs and electronic storybooks as well as word processing are available. Parent volunteers and aides assist the children in publishing work using computer drawing functions, font styles, and print shop software.

Vivian introduces one center per week so that by the end of the first month of the school year the children know each center's purpose and basic rules. An example of one child's version of the rules is shown in Figure 1–22. As problems arise and

FIGURE 1-22 *Play at Center,* First Draft (First Grader, Guided Writing)

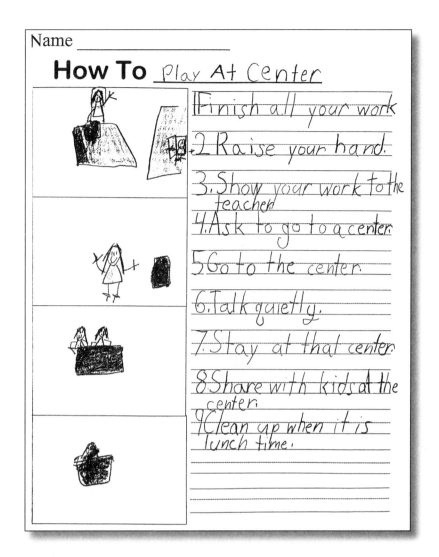

Name _____

How To Play At Center

1. Finish all your work
2. Raise your hand.
3. Show your work to the teacher
4. Ask to go to a center.
5. Go to the center.
6. Talk quietly.
7. Stay at that center.
8. Share with kids at the center.
9. Clean up when it is lunch time.

solutions are required, more specific guidelines naturally emerge. For instance, when the children discover that not everyone is cleaning up or respecting the rules of silence in the listening center, they develop a chart listing four directives: rewind tapes after listening, return books to the shelves when finished, place completed work in the folder, no talking while people are listening to a book. The chart is removed when it is no longer needed and replaced with a new one, such as a list of reminders for completing a task called "steps for taking notes on books read or heard."

Vivian allocates time for centers throughout the day: during seatwork while she is busy with a reading group, as a follow-up to a large group lesson, or during free time. Each morning, before the workday begins, the children plan the day's activities. Each child tells the teacher which two of the centers she will visit. By taking this oral inventory, Vivian can monitor the day's tasks and anticipate the literacy products she will receive. Children keep track of their schedules by filling out progress charts, as shown in Figure 1–23.

While students work at the centers during the 45-minute language arts block, Vivian might assemble large and small groups to demonstrate a concept, read a book, or teach a skill or strategy. At other times she may hold a writing conference or move around the room talking with students and availing herself of opportunities for consultation and troubleshooting.

FIGURE 1-23
Progress Chart for
Tracking Center
Activity

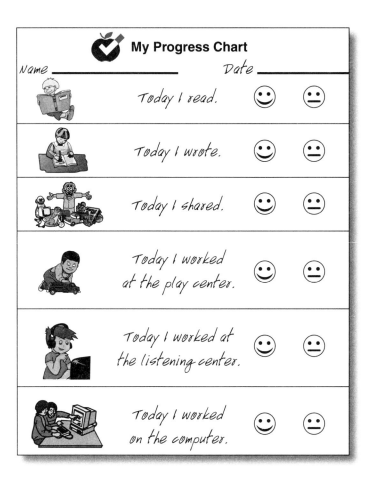

Every day she meets individually with four or five children in conference. Those who do not confer with her on a particular day share work at the author's chair or with a partner. Vivian monitors these arrangements to ensure that everyone gets feedback daily. Time to observe is also a part of each day. With clipboard in hand, she documents and reflects on center activity, grouping arrangements, and activity participation. Once routines are in place, the class begins to function on its own.

Grade 3

Kate Richardson

When entering Kate's third-grade classroom, you hear the faint sound of Mozart in the background and catch a whiff of apple cinnamon in the air. Sensory appeals such as these, coupled with a tidy learning environment, make the room an inviting and pleasant place to work.

Kate's classroom has special places and spaces that help shape the reading and writing practices and habits of her third-grade writers. As the floor plan shows (see Figure 1–24), literacy sanctuaries that offer privacy and reflection are reserved for spaces along the walls or in nooks and crannies around the room. In the center area desks are close together to encourage conversational exchanges. There is a small open space that can be used for minilessons or for class meetings.

Because storage is at a premium, Kate and the class try to keep everything in its place. Kate has devised a system that maintains order and, more importantly, ensures that she sees everyone's work on a weekly basis. On the top of the counter along the windows are three different colored crates filled with matching colored

FIGURE 1-24 Third-Grade Floor Plan

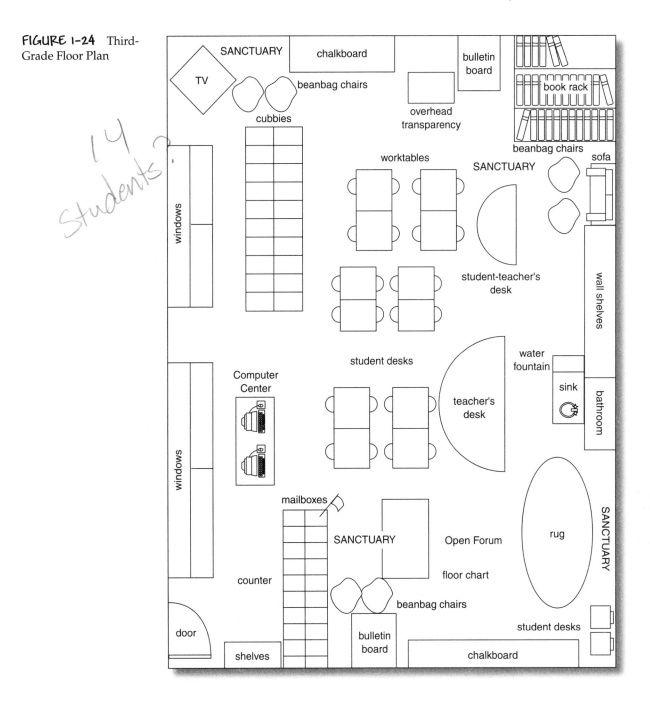

manila folders of student writing. Students with red manila folders store their work in the red crate; those with yellow folders place theirs in a yellow crate, and those with blue folders use the blue crate. Every other day, Kate reviews a set of folders, by color, to monitor progress and guide instruction. Organizing this way cuts down on the paper load and guarantees that every child's work receives special attention. A box near the crate contains reproducible forms for brainstorming, conferences, logs, and other materials required for writing. Children always know where to find what they need and how to put things away.

Beyond rules for arranging materials and space, there are rules for participating in literacy activities. If Kate is reading a book, children are to be watching and listening, not talking with one another. At the writing table, however, they are encouraged to chat with peers or leave their seats to complete one of the day's tasks. Children are taught to use time wisely and select appropriate activities to fill this time. When a rule is not working, Kate presents the issue to the entire class. "We have a problem to solve," she announces. "It is hard to find a specific book when it is not in its proper place. What can we do?" The children help solve the problem and volunteer solutions. In this instance, they decide to put round yellow self-adhesive labels on the spines of poetry books; green ones on fictional works, and red on informational books. Kate also tapes preprinted alphabet letters to the shelf and, within each color-coded genre scheme, alphabetizes the books by the author's last name.

Additional routines emerge based on Kate's decision to integrate writing and reading during a language arts block. Working back and forth between the two, she highlights connections on many different levels, including text structures, vocabulary, syntax, and sound relations (Langer, 1986; Raphael & Englert, 1990). Her planning is facilitated by combining literacies to develop lessons. For instance, she organizes books in text sets to match the writing genres and topics children are pursuing. If they are writing stories, they are reading stories and vice versa. Wherever possible, Kate includes both reading and writing in subjects across the curriculum. Students studying topics in history or geography may find that a writing lesson makes its way into social studies time.

At the beginning of class, Kate plans the day's schedule with her students. When she works with a reading group, students at their seats write about something they've read. They might choose to respond in a journal, compose a story of their own, or write a letter to a favorite author. From time to time they consult charts and bulletin boards such as the ones in Figure 1–25A (topics previously generated, workshop questions for self-reflection) and Figure 1–25B (steps to follow when offering feedback to a partner). The charts are on butcher-block paper and easily changed as new demands, tasks, rules, and reminders replace older ones. Few, if any, commercial materials are found in the room. Kate prefers print environments that provide learning tools relevant to the tasks children are doing and student work displays that instill a sense of ownership and pride.

FIGURE 1–25A Learning Charts
Source: Compliments of Ginna Plott, Second-Grade Teacher.

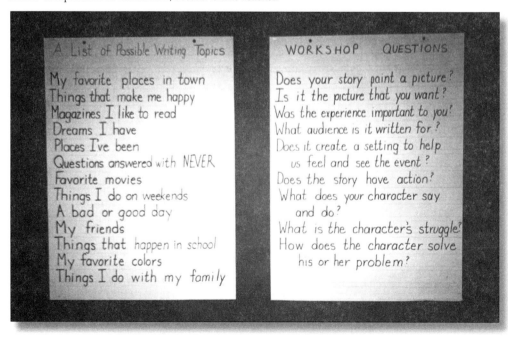

FIGURE 1-25B　Bulletin Board
Source: Compliments of Ginna Plott, Second-Grade Teacher.

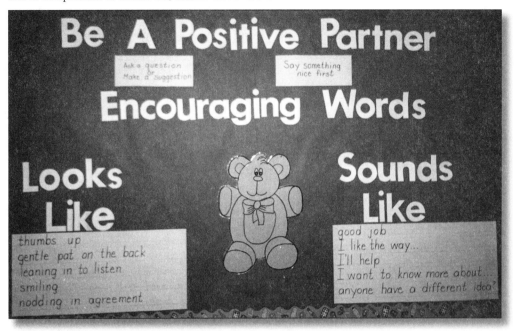

Just as writing is linked to activities in reading, so too reading is integral to writing. Kate emphasizes the fact that texts are places where authors and readers meet. Writers must always remain aware that they are constructing meaning for a reader's comprehension. When children write, they ask themselves what information the reader needs and what conventions they expect for a particular kind of writing. Two-way communication between reader and writer is reinforced at the author's chair and in writing circles. Even after the work has been published, students are urged to select and read their own compositions, bringing the writer full circle, from author to reader. In short, an interplay between reading and writing exists at all times during the language arts block—in student learning, planning, and classroom organization.

Grade 5

Ed Spinelli

In Ed's fifth grade, students are involved in collaborative projects based on a thematic unit, a curricular approach that integrates subjects, such as social studies, science, the arts, and literature. The thematic unit not only establishes connections across disciplines but can create on entire learning environment in which to work. Students in Ed's class have been known to decorate and transform the room based on a theme; for example, when they were studying the Medieval Period, they covered the walls with drawings of castles and drawbridges and filled the counters with replicas of knights in armor. Ed gathers the materials and creates the motivation for these events to happen. How he goes about this task depends on the theme and student interests. For example, the Medieval theme includes any number of possible topics and Ed helps students identify those they want to study (e.g., knights, chivalry, castles, wars, armor). He demonstrates how to interconnect subject matter (e.g., geography—hamlets, villages; music—troubadours and ballads; history—feudalism) and locate resources that offer multisensory experiences through books, videos, music, and Internet material. Finally, he suggests ways for

FIGURE 1-26 Fifth-Grade Floor Plan

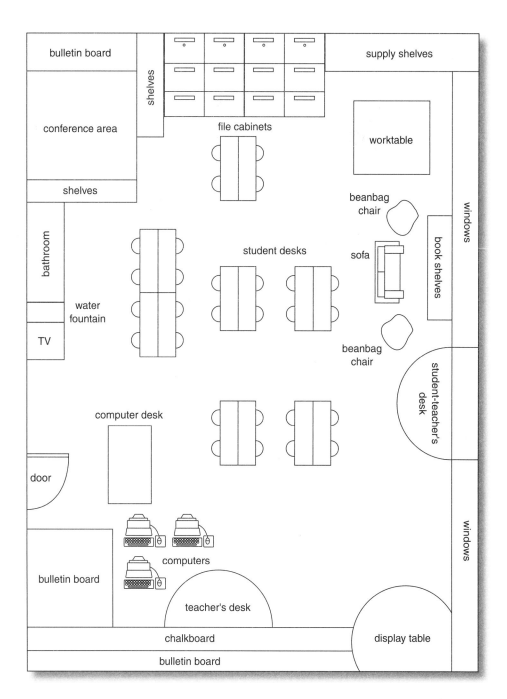

students to express their depth of understanding about a topic through writing—poems, reports, dramatic scripts, newspaper articles, short stories, reference materials (dictionaries, fact sheets)—and through multimedia projects—murals, exhibits, filmstrips, and music.

In thematic studies, students frequently collaborate on projects. For this reason, their desks are often arranged in pods to encourage social relationships and the free exchange of interaction. See Figure 1–26 for a schematic diagram of Ed's classroom.

Because students work as a team and are accountable for jointly achieving goals, they show their commitment and remind each other of the rules in a group pledge.

We pledge to
Listen to one another

Respect other team members' points of view
Share information
Treat members kindly and help one another
Complete our share of the work on time
Offer suggestions to help other groups
Put forth our best effort

During a thematic project, students meet frequently and respond to work. Small-group discussions are held throughout the process at various stages to update accomplishments and establish new group goals. Throughout the project students confer about resources, working drafts, and content. After the group divides the tasks, each member negotiates a contract with Ed. The contract empowers students to set goals and take control and responsibility for their share of the project. It also helps Ed monitor individual progress within a group.

In addition to establishing a student-centered learning environment and accountability system, the thematic unit encourages student role-playing to investigate a problem from a particular perspective. Modeled after WebQuest lessons (http://webquest.sdsu.edu/webquest.html), Ed streamlines a unit on Native Americans by asking students to select a role to play in exploring information. In each of six groups, there is an anthropologist, who examines artifacts and visits the Natural History Museum on the Web; a linguist, who studies Indian communication; a literary critic, who reads Native American legends and myths; and a historian, who investigates newspapers and historical documents. Every student has responsibilities and contributes to the group. During the investigation, Ed is available to give individual instruction. Overall contributions and concerns are shared in open forums with the entire group. Usually, the students work together to develop the rubrics, or checklists, for assessing their project. In sharing power with Ed, they determine the focus and direction of work and take responsibility for their own and others' learning.

JOURNEY REFLECTIONS

This chapter overviews the writer's workshop and the three classrooms in which the workshop is implemented. The basic components of the writer's workshop—minilessons, reading, composing, sharing, and assessment—are generically defined and illustrated with examples. Minilessons include listing and categorizing topics as well as selecting instructional methods for teaching particular students and writing tasks. Books and other print materials represent essential resources as models, and content for supporting writing activities. In composing, the writing process (prewriting, drafting, revising, and editing) is explained as a recursive one that shifts according to function and genre, student variables, and the nature of tasks. The receiving and presenting of work along with publication options underscores the need to share accomplishments and prepare for revision. The author's chair, conferences, and writing circles offer viable forums for such communicative events. Finally, strategies such as observation, interviews, conferences, and analyses of writing samples suggest how assessment can determine student growth and improve instruction. Managing this assessment through portfolios and contracts concludes the section.

The second part of Chapter 1 introduces the travelers on the journey and the environments in which they work. Regardless of whether the classroom is designed for center activity, integrated reading and writing blocks, or thematic learning, a set of predictable routines, rules, responsibilities, resources, and grouping arrangements for access to learning is guaranteed. In the chapters that follow, we consider the ever-changing and evolving nature of the workshop components and consider classroom examples of each.

We begin this journey with a type of writing that will prove invaluable across the curriculum: journal writing. All writers should carry a journal in their backpacks. No traveler should be without one.

Works Cited

Professional References

Allen, R. V. (1976). *Language experiences in communication*. Boston: Houghton Mifflin.

Ashton-Warner, S. (1963). *Teacher*. New York: Simon & Schuster.

Atwell, N. (1986). *In the middle: Writing, reading, and learning with adolescents*. Portsmouth, NH: Heinemann.

Atwell, N. (1998). *In the middle: New understandings about writing, reading, and learning* (2nd ed.). Portsmouth, NH: Boynton-Cook.

Bandura, A. (1986). *Psychological modeling: Conflicting theories*. Chicago: Aldine-Atherton.

Bidwell, S. M. (1990). Using drama to increase motivation, comprehension, and fluency. *Journal of Reading, 34*, 38–41.

Bottomley, D., Henk W. A., & Melnick, S. A. (1998). Assessing children's views about themselves as writers. *The Reading Teacher, 51*, 286–291.

Braddock, R., Lloyd-Jones, R., & Schoer, L. (1963). *Research in written composition*. Champaign, IL: National Council of Teachers of English.

Button, K., Johnson, M. J., & Furgerson, P. (1996). Interactive writing in a primary classroom. *The Reading Teacher, 49*, 446–454.

Calkins, L. (1983). *Lessons from a child*. Portsmouth, NH: Heinemann.

Calkins, L. (1986). *The art of teaching writing*. Portsmouth, NH: Heinemann.

Calkins, L. (1991). *Living between the lines*. Portsmouth, NH: Heinemann.

Calkins, L. (1994). *The art of teaching writing* (3rd ed.). Portsmouth, NH: Heinemann.

Cazden, C. (1983). Adult assistance to language development: Scaffolds, models, and direct instruction. In R. P. Parker & F. A. Davis (Eds.). *Developing literacy: Young children's use of language* (pp. 3–18). Newark, DE: International Reading Association.

Cazden, C. (1988). *Classroom discourse*. Portsmouth, NH: Heinemann.

Dahl, K., & Farnan, N. (Eds.). (1998). *Children's writing: Perspectives from research*. Newark, DE: International Reading Association.

Daly, J., & Miller, M. (1975). The empirical development of an instrument to measure writing apprehension. *Research in the Teaching of English, 9*, 242–249.

Delpit, L. (1987). The silenced dialogue: Power and pedagogy in educating other people's children. *Harvard Educational Review, 58*, 280–298.

Dressel, J. H. (1990). The effects of listening to and discussing different qualities of children's literature on the narrative writing of fifth graders. *Research in the Teaching of English, 24*, 397–414.

Dyson, A. H. (1983). The role of oral language in early writing processes. *Research in the Teaching of English, 17*, 1–23.

Eckhoff, B. (1983). How reading affects children's writing. *Language Arts, 60*, 607–616.

Eggen, P. D., & Kauchak, D. P. (2001). *Strategies for teachers* (4th ed.). Boston: Allyn & Bacon.

Elbow, P. (1973). *Writing without teachers*. New York: Oxford University Press.

Emig, J. (1971). *The composing processes of twelfth graders*. Urbana, IL: National Council of Teachers of English.

Farr, R. & Tone, B. (1994). *Portfolio and performance assessment: Helping students evaluate their progress as readers and writers*. Fort Worth, TX: Harcourt Brace.

Goodman, Y. (1985). Kidwatching: Observing children in the classroom. In A. Jaggar & M. T. Smith-Burke (Eds.). *Observing the language learner* (pp. 9–18). Urbana, IL: National Council of Teachers of English.

Graves, D. H. (1975). The writing processes of seven-year-old children. *Research in the Teaching of English, 9*, 227–241.

Graves, D. H. (1983). *Writing: Teachers and children at work*. Portsmouth, NH: Heinemann.

Graves, D. H. (1994). *A fresh look at writing*. Portsmouth, NH: Heinemann.

Graves, D., & Hansen, J. (1983). The author's chair. *Language Arts, 60*, 176–183.

Gray, J., & Myers, M. (1978). The Bay Area writing project. *Phi Delta Kappan*, 410–413.

Hall, M. (1978). *The language experience approach for teaching reading: A research perspective*. Newark, DE: International Reading Association.

Hansen, J. (1996). Evaluation: The center of writing instruction. *The Reading Teacher, 50*, 188–195.

Hansen, J. (2001). *When writers' read* (2nd ed.). Portsmouth, NH: Heinemann.

Heath, S. B. (1983). *Ways with words*. Cambridge, U.K.: Cambridge University Press.

Hill, B. C., Ruptic, C., & Norwick, L. (1998). *Classroom based assessment*. Norwood, MA: Christopher Gordon.

Holdaway, D. (1979). *The foundations of literacy*. New York: Ashton/Scholastic.

Hunter, M. (1982). *Mastery learning.* El Segundo, CA: TIP Publications.

Jalongo, M. R. (2000). *Early childhood language arts* (2nd ed.). Boston: Allyn & Bacon.

Jorgensen, K. (2001). *The whole story: Crafting fiction in the upper elementary grades.* Portsmouth, NH: Heinemann.

Langer, J. A. (1986). *Children reading and writing: Structures and strategies.* Norwood, NJ: Ablex.

Leslie, L., & Simpson, M. J. (1997). *Authentic literacy assessment: An ecological approach.* Reading, MA: Addison-Wesley (Longman).

Lindemann, E. (1982). *A rhetoric for writing teachers* (3rd ed.). New York: Oxford University Press.

McCarrier, A., Pinnell, G. S., & Fountas, I. C. (1999). *Interactive writing: How language and literacy come together, K–2.* Portsmouth, NH: Heinemann.

McGee, L. M., & Richgels, D. (2000). *Literacy's beginnings* (3rd ed.). Boston: Allyn & Bacon.

McKenzie, M. G. (1985). Shared writing: Apprenticeship in writing. *Language Matters, 1–2,* 1–5.

Moffett, J., & Wagner, B. J. (1976). *Student-centered language arts and reading K–13: A handbook for teachers* (2nd ed.). Boston: Houghton Mifflin.

Murray, D. H. (1968). *A writer teaches writing: A practical method of teaching composition.* Boston: Houghton Mifflin.

Murray, D. H. (1982). *Learning by teaching.* Montclair, NJ: Boynton-Cook.

Murray, D. H. (1998). *Write to learn* (6th ed.). Fort Worth, TX: Harcourt Brace.

Nelson, O. G., & Linek, W. M. (1999). *Practical classroom applications of language experience.* Boston: Allyn & Bacon.

Perl, S. (Ed.). (1994). *Landmark essays on writing process.* Davis, CA: Heragoras Press.

Peterson, R., & Eeds, M. (1990). *Grand conversations: Literature groups in action.* New York: Scholastic.

Raphael, T., & Englert, C. S. (1990). Writing and reading: Partners in constructing meaning. *The Reading Teacher, 43,* 388–400.

Rhodes, L., & Shanklin, N. (1993). *Windows into literacy: Assessing learning K–8.* Portsmouth, NH: Heinemann.

Rogoff, B. (1990). *Apprenticeship in thinking: Cognitive development in social context.* New York: Oxford University Press.

Rosenblatt, L. (1978). *The reader, the text, the poem.* Carbondale IL: Southern Illinois University.

Rosenblatt, L. (1984). *Literature as exploration* (3rd ed.). New York: Modern Language Association.

Seidman, I. (1998). *Interviewing as qualitative research* (2nd ed.). New York: Teachers College Press.

Spandel, V. (2001). *Creating writers* (3rd ed.). New York: Longman.

Squire, J. (1964). The responses of adolescents while reading four short stories. Research Report 2, Urbana, IL: National Council of Teachers of English.

Sulzby, E. (1988, 1990). *Emergent literacy: Kindergartners learn to read and write.* Bloomington, IN: Agency for Instructional Technology.

Tompkins, G. E. (2000). *Teaching writing: Balancing process and product* (3rd ed.). Upper Saddle River, NJ: Merrill.

Trelease, J. (1995). *The new read-aloud handbook* (Rev. ed.). New York: Penguin Books.

Veatch, J. (1976). Teaching without texts. *Journal of Clinical Reading, 2,* 32–35.

Vygotsky, L. (1978). *Mind in society.* Cambridge, MA: Harvard University Press.

Wilde, S. (1992). *You kan red this!: Spelling and punctuation for whole language classrooms, K–6.* Portsmouth, NH: Heinemann.

Williams, W. C. (1938). This is just to say. In W. Carlos Williams. *Collected earlier poems.* New York: New Directions.

Winsor, P. J., & Pearson, P. D. (1992). *Children at risk: Their phonemic awareness development in holistic instruction.* Urbana: University of Illinois at Urbana–Champaign, Center for the Study of Reading.

Zutell, J. (1978). Some psycholinguistic perspectives on children's spelling. *Language Arts, 55,* 844–850.

Children's References

Farley, S. (1996). *The black stallion's shadow.* Random House.

Galdone, P. (1985). *The little red hen.* Clarion.

Howard, E. F. (1991). *Aunt Flossie's hats (and crab cakes later).* Clarion.

Macaulay, D. (1977). *Castle.* Houghton Mifflin.

Marshall, J. (1989). *The three little pigs.* Dial.

Raskin, E. (1997). *The Westing game.* Puffin.

Snyder, Z. K. (1990). *Libby on Wednesday.* Dell.

Viorst, J. (1972). *Alexander and the terrible, horrible, no good, very bad day.* Atheneum.

Zelinsky, P. O. (1986). *Rumpelstiltskin,* Dutton.

Note-taking for bigger work.

kept, not as ends in and of themselves, but as note-taking or preparatory work for a larger effort. Henry David Thoreau's thoughts about living simply and alone became the philosophical treatise *Walden* (1971), and Carl Jung's diary (1953–1979) led to the development of his theory of psychoanalysis. It would seem that journals, endless wellsprings from which other writing flows, are a good place to start when beginning a writing assignment.

Although journals represent many things to many people, they are, above all, practical tools for capturing the ordinary: seeing something for the first time, appreciating it, and discovering its significance. Educators such as Lucy Calkins (1994) tell us that writing is about "lingering with a bit of life and layering it with meaning" (pp. 4–5). Students unwrap the significance of events and objects of everyday life to heighten experience or gain new perspectives. They write spur-of-the-moment entries about images or feelings; they write descriptions, thoughts that cannot be shaken from their minds, or advice and encouragement to themselves. They draw, sketch, and compile favorite poems, newspaper clippings, photographs, or other memorabilia. Before long just about every topic makes its way into the journals (e.g., things to do on weekends, hobbies, school happenings, books read, favorite movies, and special events).

In most writing classrooms, the goal of the journal is **invention**: discovering and exploring thoughts on a subject. However, teachers should underscore the versatile and multipurpose nature of journals by including them across the curriculum. A list of different kinds of journals is presented in Figure 2–1. The contents of these journals range from personal experiences, feelings, and events to subject matter topics and interests found throughout the world at large. In order for students to get the most benefit from journal writing, teachers should explain the purposes and procedures for each kind of journal and share examples of their own writing and those from children's literature (see the reading section later in this chapter).

For many reasons, which become obvious in this chapter, it is important to routinely set up supportive environments where children get plenty of practice writing in daily or weekly journals. A good resource for those who wish to learn more about journals in the classroom is Toby Fulwiler's edited volume, *The Journal Book* (1987).

WRITER'S WORKSHOP

Minilessons

Good luck w/ 1st graders!

Perhaps the best ways for teachers to recognize, acknowledge, and value the act of journaling is to allow time for journal writing during the school day and to write along with the students. It is hard to imagine that such simple acts can influence students so strongly, but they do. No matter how often we tell our learners that journals are instrumental in working as writers, telling is one thing, showing by example is quite another.

One of the values teachers can impress on children is the gratification that comes from "living like writers" (Calkins, 1994). Teachers do this by conducting minilessons on observing, discovering, and reflecting, which are strategies inextricably linked in one way or another to all types of journals. Although these strategies may at first seem tangential to writing, their effect changes forever how children view, respond to, and write about the world around them. Each of these is examined in the following sections.

FIGURE 2-1 Kinds of Journal Writing

Dialogue journals	Personal journals
Double-entry journals	Reading logs
Dream diaries	Simulated journals
Learning logs	Travel journals
Literary response journals	Writer's scrapbooks

Observations

Through observation, a writer becomes an eyewitness to the subject or events about which he writes. Observing is the act of consciously attending to stimuli and making a written record, an observation. In the following passage from James Michener's *Hawaii* (2002), it is easy to see how the author relies on his rich observational skills to create a scene.

> It [Molokai] lay in the blue Pacific like a huge left-handed gauntlet, the open wristlet facing westward toward the island of Oahu, the cupped fingers pointing eastward toward Maui. The southern portion of Molokai consisted of rolling meadow land, often with gray and parched grasses, for rainfall was slight, while the northern portion was indented by some of the most spectacular cliffs in the islands. (pp. 400–491)

With its visual descriptions (parched grasses) and strong metaphors (Molokai as an open wristlet), we see more than a physical map of the Hawaiian Islands, we feel the living, breathing landforms reaching out like hands into the ocean. This is the power of observation, and this is what it means to say that writing begins long before words ever are written down on paper. As Calkins put it, "Writing does not begin with deskwork but with lifework" (1994, p. 3). If we want learners to be mindful of the world, attending to ordinary things, selectively and deliberately, we must teach them to think like writers—to be inquisitive and discerning.

Planning learning experiences for students to practice observational habits is well worth the time and effort. One teacher I know takes students outdoors on an observation walk. Before they begin this walk, the teacher does a think aloud to show how an observation is made.

> When I observe, I look for something around me that I have taken for granted, something I may not have paid attention to before. For instance, this rock [holds up for all to see] that has been sitting in my garden intrigues me. I pick it up and examine it. Using my five senses [goes to chart with symbols for the five senses—eyes, ears, nose, lips, and hands], I see that the rock is brown with black streaks. It feels smooth on the surface but has rough edges that are as sharp as an arrowhead. I wonder if it may have broken off from a larger rock or boulder. The rock is solid earth in my hands. I look at the spot where I found it, to see what lives there. Did bugs or worms live under it? Why is this rock here? Could my garden have once been an empty field of rocks and stones? I think about how I can use this rock. Perhaps it might make a good paperweight.

This teacher explains how he stirs the five senses (one sense at a time) to describe his object, encouraging students to rely on vivid language through adjectives, adverbs, similes, and metaphors.

> The edges of the rock are as sharp as an arrowhead. (simile)
> The rock is solid earth in my hands. (metaphor)

He poses questions, attempting to make sense of the object, to situate it in a context, to speculate about its existence and purpose, and to relate it to personal experience or interest.

When the lesson concludes, the class goes outdoors to observe. Within a designated radius of the school grounds, each student finds a place to sit and, with notebook and pencil in hand, makes a photographic inventory of everything he sees—leaves, sticks, pinecones, stones, plants, insects, and other natural subject matter. Each student selects one item to study in detail and documents the context in which the item is found. When the students return to the classroom, they review their journal notes and develop rich descriptive paragraphs, speculate on meaning, or identify questions to be answered. The entries may later become a resource for other writing tasks.

FIGURE 2-2

Questions for Analyzing
an Artwork

1. What do you see?

2. If you see colors, what are they?

3. If you see lines, are they smooth, jagged, thick, thin, tall, short?

4. If you see shapes, what kind?

5. How many different things do you see? Name them.

6. If there is action or movement, what is happening?

7. If there are people, what do they look like? What are they doing?

8. If there are objects, how are they arranged?

Observation is a skill that should not be confined to the language arts but should be extended to subjects across the curriculum. For example, in art class, third graders study an art reproduction using questions that focus on visual details (see Figure 2–2).

Each writer takes notes on what he sees and shares his observations with others. Children are surprised to find that, although they are all looking at the same painting, some attend to the content of the piece; others, the function; and still others, the lines, shapes, angles, colors, or textures. Awareness of these possibilities assists writers in developing a unique perspective. With practice, they learn that perspective depends in large part on who is observing and how they are segmenting and organizing the world (Young, Becker, & Pike, 1970). This visual inquiry places a premium on ways of perceiving the world, attending to details, and making decisions about what to include or exclude in a written piece.

Science experiments require observation. For instance, in a second-grade classroom, students observe the metamorphosis of mealworms into grain beetles. Students place two mealworms in baby food jars covered with cheesecloth; they add a slice of raw potato to absorb moisture and oatmeal for food. Each day for 8 to 9 weeks, the students document in their journals the changes in the mealworms' colors and movements. Even if nothing happens on a particular day, they can predict what might happen or simply write, "nothing new happened today." The mealworm project gives children something to observe and write about, but it also teaches them patience.

Patience is another important function of observing. Consider sitting quietly at the beach for an hour. A patient and watchful observer might spy a seagull diving for fish, a seashell washing up on the shore, a child wading at the water's edge, or a boat sailing across the horizon. This kind of alert and wide awake patience permits the writer to appreciate observations that otherwise might escape attention.

If observing the moment and discovering the ordinary produces ideas for writers, then concentrating on an object of passion allows them to excavate deeper layers of meaning and become experts on a topic. John Audubon's sustained interest in observing and sketching birds made him one of the world's most acclaimed naturalists; his work appears in scientific books and numerous field guides. Students should not need to find a new idea every time they write. Instead, they might carve out an area of interest and explore it over weeks or months. If the topic is sufficiently rich with possibility, any number of connections will grow from it.

Observing is about acquiring knowledge and information that can be used in writing. It is a literacy habit that should be cultivated throughout the writing process and practiced until it is mastered.

Discoveries

(handwritten margin note: definition)

Observation helps writers identify and record significant events, but discovery is the meaning that grows from putting ideas on paper and finding out what is known or unknown about the subject. Discovery is important for journaling and is the impetus for the ideas behind it. How many times have well-known authors remarked that they didn't know what they wanted to say until they said it? These masters of the craft would never willingly surrender control of the word if the surprises were not part of its allure. Young children explore how journals become tools for discovering ideas, establishing voice, and enhancing personal growth.

(handwritten margin note: timed write)

Time should be set aside each day for uninterrupted, sustained journaling in which everyone writes, including the teacher. During this predetermined interval, students select a subject (perhaps one of their observations) and draft their thoughts. They keep their pens moving across the paper, without censor, without correction. Skimming their writing, they underline a phrase or sentence that seems particularly relevant or especially interesting, then they continue to write based on what they find, in a kind of repetitive chain.

Teachers can show the surprises in store for writers by drafting in front of the children, pausing to comment on the surprises.

- Remember something you may have forgotten (As I write this, I remember . . .)
- See relationships among things (This reminds me of . . .)
- Communicate something in a new way (I like the way I said this)
- Identify a new problem (I'm having difficulties showing this object to the reader)
- Find a fallacy in your thinking (I don't think what I wrote is accurate)
- Discover something you hadn't thought of before (Wow! Here's another point I hadn't thought of)

When teachers model their work, they share the false starts, hesitations, tangled sentences, and conflicting ideas that are typical of journal writing. This reassures children and they become willing to take risks and deal with ambiguity. The process of discovery is messy, and students need to be comfortable in all its messiness.

Another way to encourage discovery is to model problem-solving strategies, called heuristics. **Heuristics** help students retrieve ideas stored in the mind or draw attention to something not yet apparent (Young, Becker, & Pike, 1970). For young children, this is often accomplished using the following techniques:

- Asking the 5W questions (who, what, where, when, and why)
- Using trial and error
- Changing perspective
- Engaging in speculative playfulness
- Interrelating information
- Making analogies

Thinking flexibly in this way leads to a better understanding and explanation of events, objects, and behaviors and sets the discovery process in motion.

The process of discovery, whether arrived at systematically or spontaneously, implies that certain writing strategies are being practiced and reinforced—taking risks and experimenting, doubting, interpreting, speculating, wondering, and expressing opinions. When these strategies are activated, the potential exists for creating a lasting memory, a lucky accident, a serendipitous moment, or a profound truth.

Reflections

Reflecting on personal experiences and observations is a benefit writers get from journal writing. Students should take a few moments out of each day to attend to themselves and their work. Journals echo the writer's voice and expressive feelings to reveal personality and inner worlds. When students use journals to disclose feelings of sorrow, fear, joy or exhuberance, the writing brings them face-to-face with their most intimate thoughts and emotions. Reflections also engage writers in thinking about what they are learning or how they are learning it. Perhaps they discover a new connection with what they already know or a delightful surprise in something unanticipated. They might identify and list recurring topics, interests, or themes in their writing. In their longest or shortest entry, they discover subjects they seem to know a lot about and those that need further exploration. An intriguing sentence or question that emerges from several entries might become the start of a new entry or an entire essay or book.

Making students aware of the strategies they use in journal writing, through questioning, introduces a metalanguage that empowers them to talk *about* their process and find examples in their work.

- How did you determine which information to include in your entry?
- What guesses did you make about what you were studying?
- How did you discover this information?
- How do you feel about the information you found?
- What other possibility might you try to solve this problem?

Before long, students learn to independently probe a topic and find solutions.

Reflection not only causes writers to pause and ponder the immediate content but also serves to monitor progress over time by framing some of the following questions:

- What entries surprised you?
- Do you see any similarities in what you've written (patterns)?
- How are your early entries the same or different from later ones?
- How have your thoughts changed?
- Which entries would you like to save? Throw out?
- Is there something in your journal that you might want to write about?

Coming back to their journals after some time has elapsed helps students spot digressions (places where their minds are actively seeking meaning) and connections (places where one idea is associated with another). These reflections provide an ongoing record of language and literacy growth.

Reflection through **introspection** and self-study involves repeated reading and deliberate thinking and analysis. Too often children write journal entries and never go back to reread or revise them. Instead of continually revisiting the journal in subjects across the curriculum, students use journal writing as an exercise to fill time in the morning while the teacher collects milk money or takes attendance. The act of reflection can help change all that, especially when it is regularly used for reading as well as writing.

Reading

Children's trade books, especially full-fledged narratives stitched together by journal entries, present the teacher with rich literary print models. In many of these books, characters keep journals suggesting the pivotal role they play in expressing and resolving problems. For example, in *Jorah's Journal* (Caseley, 1997), writing becomes a safe outlet for a young child's feelings about being the new girl in school, whereas in *Strider* (Cleary, 1991), a boy named Leigh, in a series of diary entries, comes to terms with his parents' divorce. In the process of storytelling, sometimes a character, such as Catherine in *A Gathering of Days: A New England Girl's Journal* (Blos, 1979), shares more than ordinary day-to-day events and gives us a peek into the past—in this case, childhood in the 1800s. Books that take students on history excursions through journal entries woven into the fabric of fictional stories are found in Scholastic's Dear America series.

If fictional journals are inspiring to children, even more influential are journal collections written by real people who have made a significant mark in the world. *The Book of American Diaries* (Miller & Miller, 1995) is one such example. Two important books for inclusion in any text set for older students are *Diary of a Young Girl* (Frank, 1952) and

Zlata's Diary: A Child's Life in Sarajevo (Filipovic, 1994). They are stories that showcase remarkable children who used journals to express feelings and record observations of some of the darkest moments in the history of the world.

In addition to historical journals, contemporary ones suggest insights into the writing craft itself. For instance, in *My Worst Day Diary* (Altman, 1995), writers connect the theme of the journal to its contents: embarrassing moments and unfortunate mishaps at school. In Marissa Moss's American Girl series—*Ameila's Notebook* (1999b) and *Ameila Writes Again* (1999c)—the reader gets a glimpse of what to include in a journal: pages covered with words, drawings, maps, diagrams, speech bubbles, and pasted items (postcards, pennies, pictures). Reading about characters who keep journals and knowing how to begin one can be effective introductions to journal writing.

Sept. activity

Response Journals

Not all books need to be written in journal form to serve as models for writing activity. Almost any book can be linked to writing through a literary response journal. In a literary response journal, writers record personal thoughts and ideas about books. They make connections to their own lives, react to critical ideas, record quotations from book characters and famous people, or jot down powerful ideas and language expressions. The response journal offers students a wide range of options for monitoring comprehension, validating inferences and predictions, and evaluating events in a book (see types of responses in Chapter 1).

- What happened in this story?
- Will the character succeed in the goal?
- Did you ever have a similar experience?
- Does the character remind you of yourself in any way?
- Would you have acted like the character in this story?
- Do you have other knowledge or experience about this?

The entry might be written as a letter to the author or as a story retold by one of the characters. A poem might be the best way to respond. The entries, in turn, might become the basis of a book talk or a literary project, a book recommendation, or a comparison of two authors' works. There is no one way to write or use the responses in a literary journal.

In a second-grade classroom, students draw or write what comes to their minds when they think of the holiday, Memorial Day. Students design flags and patriotic emblems that depict the holiday or compose short descriptions that explain how they celebrate it. After the teacher reads *The Wall* (Bunting, 1990), a story about the Vietnam Veterans Memorial, the children go back to their drawings or writings and add or change them. Journal drawings and writing become the springboard for discussion of the book.

Although writing in a literary response journal is useful *before* and *after* reading, it is equally important *during* reading. In a think aloud, the teacher verbalizes what he is thinking *as he reads*. He finds opportune moments between sentences and paragraphs to scribble down questions that come to mind (I wonder if . . .), predictions (I think this will happen), or words he wishes to remember *(herbicides)*. Fleeting thoughts can be expanded on in a journal later.

Monitoring behaviors in reading requires keeping track of the mind's listening space, the pauses that occur when one sentence ends and another begins. An effective way to demonstrate this process is with "talking drawings" (McConnell, 1992/93, p. 3). For instance, a first-grade teacher draws as he reads *Harold and the Purple Crayon* (Johnson, 1955), a story in which the main character, Harold, takes a crayon and draws his way through a story, meandering around the pages and dropping words here and there. To help the children retell the story the teacher matches words and pictures (moon/ ☾) printed on card stock and orders them according to the plot. The steps in this talking

FIGURE 2–3
Reading Log

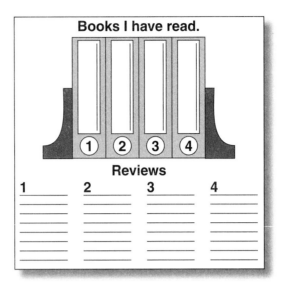

drawing are easily transferred to informational books by substituting time lines, diagrams, maps, or other graphic organizers for the drawings. Regardless of genre, the entries (drawings or graphics) in the response journal reflect what students are reading and processing along the way and underscore what they determine to be a text's high points.

Reading Logs

A type of journal that serves as both a record and reference tool is the reading log. In it the students list book titles with dates indicating what has been read (see Figure 2–3) and sometimes add one-line statements to review the book or summarize the plot, comment on elements of the author's craft, or ask questions about the content.

Logs help children take inventory of their reading (fiction, nonfiction, poetry, or magazine articles) and consider their personal preferences for certain authors, themes, genres, or characters. They may include materials read outside of class, books read for pleasure, or assigned readings. A teacher can review the log to assess student interests and attitudes about reading.

Composing

Prewriting

Because most children do not need much prompting to begin journaling, especially if they already engage in observation, discovery, and reflection, the prewriting strategies and activities introduced here simply add variety to journal writing or rekindle interest in it should enthusiasm start to wane.

Brainstorming

Brainstorming is the process of randomly tossing out ideas on a topic; making free associations and connections; and engaging in creative, nonlinear thinking. Snippets of thought are entered in the journal or visually displayed on a graphic organizer, such as a web. A brainstorming web (so called this because it looks like a spider web) has a center circle with the main topic and rays leading to other circles containing associated thoughts. A third grader named Jeffrey constructed the web shown in Figure 2–4. It presents his thoughts about camping in Tennessee. He placed the words *camping in Tennessee* in the center circle and then added everything he remembered about the trip. One word triggers another in a loosely organized fashion, expanding the main idea or subcategories that arise such as *pond* and *city*. In developing the web, the writer reflects, sorts, and links thoughts in various ways.

FIGURE 2-4 Jeffrey's Brainstorming Web for Camping in Tennessee (Third Grader, Independent Writing)

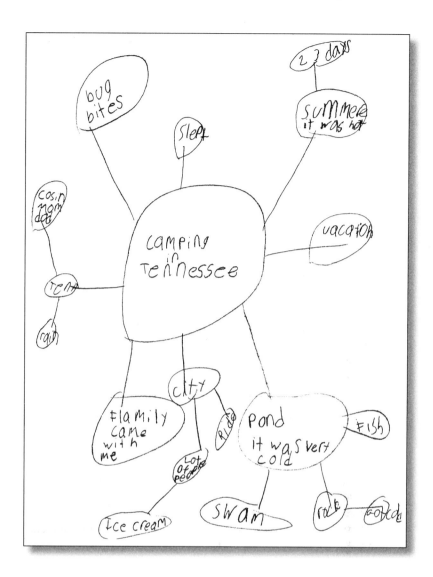

Webs are easy to do and can display various content. For example, when brainstorming informative topics, students might add facts or vocabulary words related to the subject matter. With young children, pictures may substitute for words. For a good resource on webbing, see Bromley's text *Webbing With Literature: Creating Story Maps With Children's Books* (1991). Although her examples use literature for content, the visual displays offer many excellent models that writers can borrow for their own compositions.

Another kind of graphic organizer called mapping or clustering offers conceptual and focused categories for brainstorming in order to show links between sentences and supporting details, paragraphs and key points, or text elements in story (settings, characters), poetry (onomatopoeia, rhyme), or reports (causes, comparisons). For instance, in the story map shown in Figure 2–5, fifth-grader Paige writes the focus of her entry in a center circle and fills in other circles with questions for framing parts of the narrative she will later write.

Paige's map resembles a web, but the information is sorted and arranged into a narrative sequence: first, the day she brought home her puppy from the pet store; next, a description of her puppy, followed by what was wrong with him; and finally a solution for making the puppy happy. Each ray of the map will become a paragraph when she decides to draft, so she will easily fill the blank sheet of paper. Her map will have captured the ideas and given her a way to remember them.

FIGURE 2-5 Paige's
Story Map of the New
Puppy (Fifth Grader,
Independent Writing)

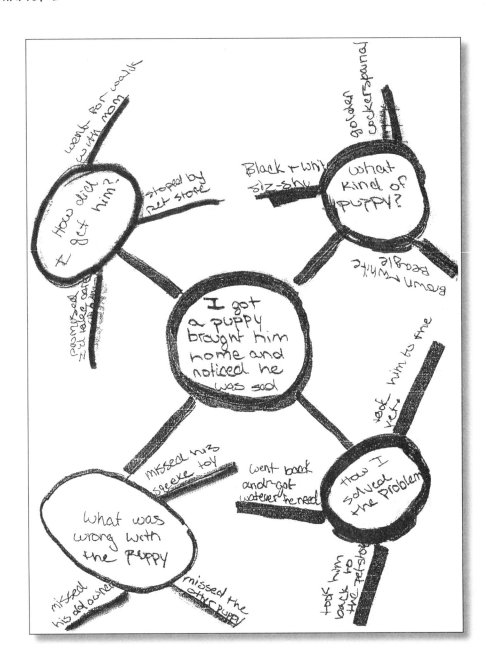

Another variation of brainstorming is listing things recalled or generated: likes and dislikes; the names of students in the classroom; the ABCs; words children know; or topic associations, such as first-grader Keely's *7 Reasons Why I Want to Be a Princess* (Figure 2–6). Although neither complete nor ordered, the list furnishes Keely with material for a future composition.

Brainstorming is a flexible strategy that cuts across nearly every type of writing and age group. Placing graphic organizers and brainstorming lists in a journal provides concrete representation of thoughts that can later be transferred to another assignment or used as a visual backdrop or prop for recalling or formulating ideas. Whether brainstorming is displayed as a graphic organizer (webbing or mapping) in journals or is part of an oral discussion leading to a writing assignment, it is both practical and invaluable. Teachers will find these entries informative because they provide insights into writers' prior knowledge and any misconceptions they might have, which can be noted and subsequently discussed with the writers in conferences or minilessons.

FIGURE 2-6   Keely's
Brainstorming List: *7
Reasons Why I Want to
Be a Princess* (First
Grader, Independent
Writing)

Doodling

Doodles, a kind of free-associating or artful scribble, are an ideal form for journal writing (see Figure 2–7). The hand, meandering and fickle, follows the subconscious mind, whereas the conscious mind concentrates on something else.

The children turn to a blank page in their journal so that they can playfully scribble all over it for 1 to 2 minutes. Adding music stimulates a sense of motion, in a sense urging the hand along. What appears on the page—circles, lines, shapes, and designs—can be shaded in to make connections with letters, numbers, faces, or familiar objects. Students examine the doodles with a partner. Are there any patterns? What do the scribbles remind them of? Much like looking for shapes and objects in the clouds, students speculate about the patterns or designs they see. Some even create secret codes to correspond to their doodling, making certain scribbles stand for letters that can be sequenced into words or messages for others to decode.

Identified objects, letters, or shapes become prompts for journal writing or are simply collected and displayed as entries in the journals. Make several of Ed Emberley's books available at the writing center—*Ed Emberley's Big Orange Drawing Book* (1980) and *Ed Emberley's Big Green Drawing Book* (1979)—along with art reproductions or postcards of expressionist painters Joan Miro, Willem DeKooning, or Jackson Pollock, the improvisational doodlers. Emberley's work outlines a combination of bold lines and circles for children to borrow for simple drawings. The abstract paintings elicit viewer response through outlines, colors, impressions, and sensations.

Music

Because music is valued in literacy learning, students listen to a wide variety of musical selections, not only for appreciation but also for developing ideas and stimulating associations for journal writing. In one lesson, a second-grade child, inspired by Cuban music *Septeto Habanero*, spontaneously wrote a journal entry to correspond with its upbeat and energetic melody (see Figure 2–8). The music activated the child's prior knowledge about Mexico and conjured up associations with its cultural traditions and symbols.

FIGURE 2-7
Directions and Samples
of Doodlings

FIGURE 2-8 Draft
Completed After
Listening to Cuban
Music, *Septeto Habanero:
75 Years Later* (Second
Grader, Independent
Writing)

According to Gardner (1993), "the aural imagination is simply the working of the composer's ear" (p. 101)—the tool for working with sound: its tones, rhythms, forms, and movement. Some educators believe that a sensitivity to sound and rhythm helps develop abstract reasoning similar to the Piagetian cognitive stages (Bamberger, 1982; Gardner, 1993). Notwithstanding music's acknowledged influence on learning, language users can build on the power of music and the euphony of words to promote journal ideas and inquiry.

Dreams

Dreams are great idea sources for journal writing since they summon thoughts and images from the unconscious mind. Authors are fascinated by dreams, which may account for the varied and numerous books on the subject including *Appelemando's Dreams* (Polacco, 1997), *The Dream Eater* (Garrison, 1986), *The Dream Stair* (James, 1990), *Ben's Dream* (Van Allsburg, 1982), *The Funny Dream* (Zemach-Bersin, 1988), and *The Morgans' Dream* (Singer, 1995). In a fourth-grade classroom, a teacher reads *Grandma's Dreamcatcher* (McCain, 1998) about a Chippewa grandmother who tells her granddaughter the Native American legend of spider, the spirit who wove a web to "catch" dreams. According to the legend, bad dreams are caught in the webbing and good dreams fly through the center and ascend to the Great Spirit. The Native American ancestors made dream catchers from twigs or pieces of jute, twisted into a circle and hung over the places where they slept. Directions for making dream catchers out of a macramé ring, lace, and leather string are printed on the last page of McCain's book. Children can make dream catchers and fill them with dreams written on strips of paper. Figure 2–9 presents some dreams recalled and written down for a dream catcher. The good dreams can be pulled out and copied into journals.

If children can't remember their dreams, they might recall feelings, moods, symbols, or objects associated with them. Daydreams can easily substitute for night dreams simply by giving students time to sit in quiet contemplation and let their imaginations run wild.

Drafting

Journal writing is, above all, exploratory. Macrorie's classic book *Telling Writing* (1985) offers at least two approaches to writing journal entries: writing freely with focus and writing without focus. Focused writings are often referred to as quickwrites; they involve writing on a subject for 10 minutes, jotting down all ideas that come to mind. A student in the second grade, inspired by the book *Squanto and the First Thanksgiving* (Donze & Kessel, 1995), wrote the quickwrite appearing in Figure 2–10, p. 81 to reflect aspects of the story that impressed her.

Quickwrites are often used with literary and social studies topics—before, during, or after reading—to direct students' attention to the learning material. Although focused writing follows a general direction guided by a subject, the mind is still free to speculate, associate, and wander within it. There are no hard and fast rules.

In "shotgun" or unfocused writing, the mind wanders and so does the writing. No topic is specified beforehand. Children scribble whatever comes into their minds—a thought, an image, a word. Even if the writer is unable to think of anything to write, simply writing "I can't think of anything to write" sustains the momentum. The goal is to cover a page with words, to write nonstop, to keep the pencil moving. Figure 2–11, p. 82 presents a sixth grader's freewrite; she moves from one topic to another—from an incident with a girlfriend, to thoughts about her father, to a little matchmaking. Without stating it directly, the child's enthusiasm about the possible relationship between two friends is implied with the bold, large, "YES!" Voice peeks through in her conversational use of words such as *kinda, anyways,* and *bunches.* One can literally hear her groan when she writes that Allison is *soooo annoying.*

FIGURE 2-9 Dreams
Recalled and Prepared
for Dream Catchers
(Fourth Graders,
Independent Writing)

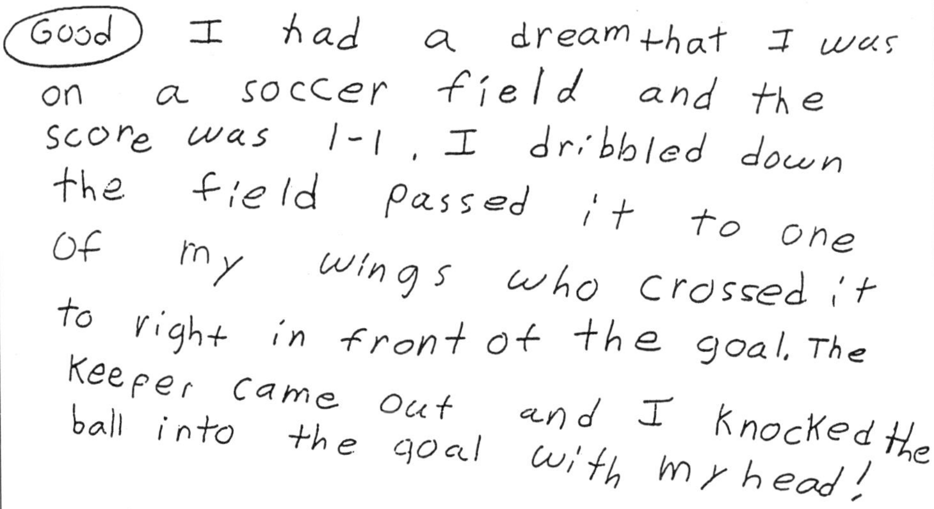

> (Good) I had a dream that I was on a soccer field and the score was 1-1. I dribbled down the field passed it to one of my wings who crossed it to right in front of the goal. The keeper came out and I knocked the ball into the goal with my head!

Good (dream)
I had a dream that I was on a soccer field and the score was 1–1. I dribbled down the field, passed it to one of my wings who crossed it to right in front of the goal. The keeper came out and I knocked the ball into the goal with my head!

Grade 4

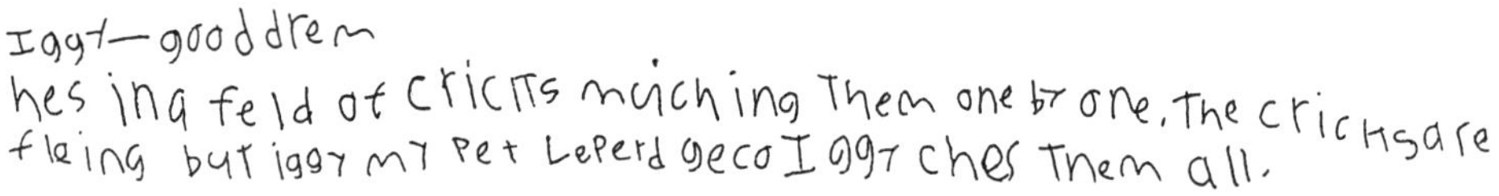

> Iggy—gooddrem
> hes in a feld of cricts muiching Them one br one. The cricks are fleing but iggy my Pet Leperd geco Iggt ches Them all.

Iggy—good dream
He's in a field of crickets munching them one by one. The crickets are fleeing but Iggy, my pet leopard gecko, Iggy chases them all.

Grade 4

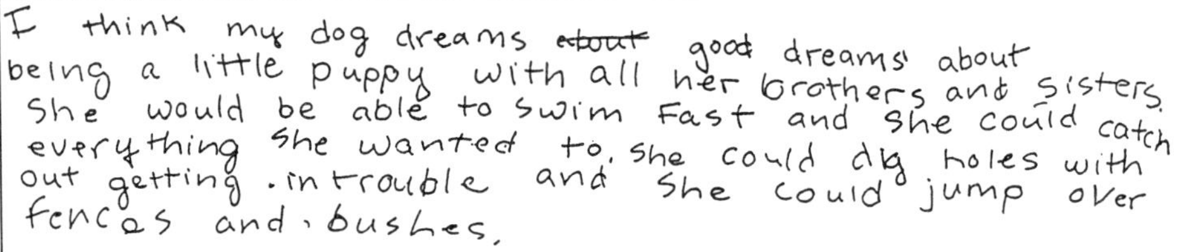

> I think my dog dreams good dreams about being a little puppy with all her brothers and sisters. She would be able to swim Fast and She could catch everything she wanted to. She could dig holes with out getting in trouble and she could jump over fences and bushes.

I think my dog dreams good dreams about being a little puppy with all her brothers and sisters. She would be able to swim fast and she could catch everything she wanted to. She could dig holes without getting in trouble and she could jump over fences and bushes.

Grade 4

New paragraphs signal new topics. This associative chaining is characteristic of unfocused freewriting and may lead writers to begin a full-fledge writing project or veer off into unpredictable and exciting new directions. Unfocused freewrites can release excess "mind baggage" for concentrating on a task at hand or allowing the mind to wander and explore.

Whether focused or unfocused, ideas flow on paper purposefully and routinely, not necessarily in correct or well-developed form (Elbow, 1973; Macrorie, 1976). Journal entries include repeated examples of children's drafting and offer a window into their levels of fluency. Fluency is the quantity of words the student produces on paper as

Fluency is the purpose, not accuracy

FIGURE 2-10
Quickwrite Based on
*Squanto and the First
Thanksgiving* by
L. Donze & J. Kessel,
1995 (Second Grader,
Independent Writing)

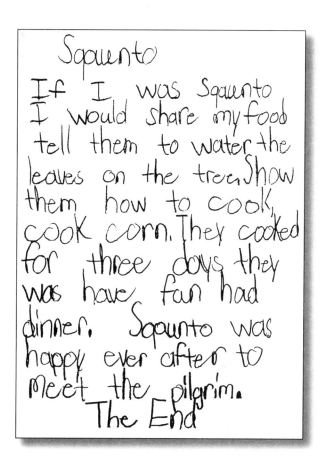

Squanto

If I was Squanto I would share my food tell them to water the leaves on the tree Show them how to cook, cook corn. They cooked for three days they was have fun had dinner. Squanto was happy ever after to meet the pilgrim. The End

opposed to the accuracy or quality of the message. The goal with freewriting is to generate as much text as possible. Most often fluency is associated with knowing a great deal about a subject. Familiarity with a subject facilitates fluency, and this, in turn, increases engagement in the piece and encourages more frequent writing.

Reviewing the length and frequency of children's entries is a natural part of day-to-day monitoring. The goal is unrestrained abundance and **automaticity**. The children should develop the ability to concentrate on meanings, ignoring skills such as spelling, capitalization, and punctuation. By dismissing the internal editor (the censor in all of us that wants to criticize what we write), students are free to concentrate on thoughts rather than correctness. When this happens, they are apt to unleash their imaginations and write more.

Revising

Because journals are directed to the self and have few, if any, audience demands, there is no need to revise journals in the traditional sense of reworking information. Instead, students are encouraged to connect and build on entries; to practice fluency; and to develop strategies of logical reasoning, specificity, sequence, and other critical thinking habits used in revision.

Students can circle main points in an entry and underline details that support them, or they can draw a box around a favorite thought and expand it into a main point. Linking focused journal entries can lead children to write stories similar to the ones they are reading in class.

Although keen observation and reflection inspire writing, they are also catalysts for refining it. As children continue to observe they develop a knack for specificity and

FIGURE 2-12 Stages of Spelling Development
Source: From Carole Cox, Teaching Language Arts: A Student- and Response-Centered Classroom. Copyright © 2002. Reprinted/adapted by permission by Allyn & Bacon.

Kindergarten Through Second Grade

Precommunicative (Preschool, 2–5 years old)
- Scribbling can be representational
- Understands speech can be written
- Lacks concept of *word,* or relationship between sounds and letters
- Makes letterlike shapes or actual letters and numbers
- May write name
    Example: MONSTER = btBpA

Semiphonetic (Kindergarten–beginning of first grade, 5–6 years old)
- Spells few words correctly but knows letters make words
- Still invents symbols for letters and words
- Makes one- to three-letter representations of words, usually consonants
- Has more control over beginnings and endings of words than middles
- Predicts words auditorially in sophisticated ways with frequently occurring patterns
    Example: MONSTER = MSR

Phonetic (First grade, 6 years old)
- Spellings include all sound features of words as heard
- Invents system of phonetic spelling that is consistent
- Understands relationship of sounds in speech to symbols in writing
- Spelling can be read by others
    Example: MONSTER = MONSR

Transitional (End of first–beginning of second grade, 6–7 years old)
- Begins to spell conventionally, and knows it is necessary so others can read the writing
- Uses knowledge of how words look as well as sound and applies this to other words
- Includes vowels in every syllable
- Uses familiar spelling patterns
- Intersperses conventional spelling and invented spelling
    Example: MONSTER = MONSTUR

Second Through Fourth Grade

Conventional (Second–fourth grade, 7–9 years old)
- Begins to spell correctly
- Has probably mastered root words, past tense, and short vowels
- Still struggles with consonant doubling, letter position (e.g., silent *e*, controlled vowels), and word affixes
- Has growing knowledge of word meanings and complicated vowel patterns
    Example: MONSTER = MONSTER

Fifth Through Eighth Grade

Morphemic and Syntactic (Fifth–eighth grade, 10–13 years old)
- Increasingly understands how meaning and grammatical structure control spelling
- Adds morphemic and syntactic to phonological knowledge
- Is better at doubling consonants, spelling alternative forms of words, and word endings
    Example: BEAR and BARE (sound alike, but spelled differently)

---

serve as diaries, they become a place where writers keep secrets and shelter thoughts they wish to protect. Free from the prying eyes of adults, these writers can pen their daydreams in private or simply enjoy the solitude that writing affords. Reading these entries may need special permission; they may be identified with a paper clip. However, a literature response journal has a wider audience; students may swap ideas on good books or interesting quotes and words. The private or public nature of the journal and the wishes of the writer determines whether sharing is advisable.

If students' journals are to be shared with the class, the teacher should model how to respond to them. Two types of response are particularly relevant to journal writing and should be reinforced across writing genres. For purposes of discussion we will consider each separately, but practically speaking they are interrelated and overlap.

Personal Responses

Since journals present an occasion for students to write about their world and experience, it seems appropriate and timely to have the teacher/reader demonstrate personal reactions to journal entries (those that are public, that is). In a personal response the teacher relates the writer's work to his own life or situation with short statements such as "I can only imagine how you felt" or "This reminds me of your last adventure." Associating personal life experience with something the child has written—"This happened to me one time, too"—conveys, by example, a reader's interest and involvement in the piece. Later, through longer autobiographical statements, teachers summarize personal experience and parallel key points to those mentioned by the writer. Young children have a tendency to digress about their lives, and require continual coaching and practice on what and how much to say about a work.

From another angle, the teacher shares ways to elaborate the piece: "My parents are divorced, too. When they first separated I remember thinking that it was all my fault. I also worried about what my friends would think. Did these things ever cross your mind?" Personal responses are a way to brainstorm common concerns and invite fresh viewpoints. To impress upon children what is being modeled and lay the groundwork for future work, the teacher periodically holds a debriefing session to discuss the language of response.

Personal responses are closely linked and often synonymous with affective responses. With affective responses, however, the teacher focuses on feelings and connotative meanings of the work.

Affective Responses

An affective response is the reader's emotional reaction to the work. In an affective response, the teacher explains how the child's words may have moved him: "Gee, this sounds like an exciting adventure" or "Your situation makes me feel sad." Affective responses oftentimes involve spontaneous nonverbal expression (facial gestures, clapping, a pat on the back) on the part of a reader who has been touched by the work. Responses should be immediate, affirming, and honest, so that the writer knows the audience is listening and is engaged. Paraphrasing or clearing up confusions should be about highlighting meaning rather than dwelling on error. A writer's work may evoke a question, an emotional attitude, or an interpretation. When readers articulate affective responses and indicate how the writing has succeeded in stirring emotions, the writer witnesses the power of the written word. Consider using the language of encouragement (Dinkmeyer & Losoncy, 1980), which includes responses that recognize student growth and contributions rather than those that suggest judgment. Phrases such as "that's great" or "wonderful" are replaced with statements such as "You are obviously learning a great deal about beetles; you've written quite an informative entry" or "Thank you for putting away your journal. It helps keep our room tidy."

Continuous Assessment

As discussed in Chapter 1, the factors of assessment include those associated with the writer, process, text, and context. Journals are particularly good at providing a window into children's inner thoughts and lives. Simply by reading some of their entries, teachers learn about student attitudes, interests, fears, background knowledge, and culture. Examining several entries, rather than only a single one, can suggest patterns that might distinguish a child's passing fancy from an enduring interest. As a record of a student's personal growth and history, journals assist teachers in making informed decisions about intervention practices, group arrangements, learning conditions, and minilesson topics. Besides using journals to learn about students, there are several other ways to obtain information. These follow.

Writer

To measure how children feel about writing and whether they perceive writing as approachable, a group self-efficacy scale can be administered, such as the one in Table 2–1. Perceived self-efficacy is a judgment about personal capability rather than self-worth (Bandura, 1997). Table 2–1 measures children's belief in themselves as writers and gauges how confident they are in performing a given task or activity in writing.

Self-efficacy is an essential attribute for high achievement, and it is believed to influence choice of activities, effort expended, persistence, and motivation (Bandura, 1997). Too many children have nagging doubts about their abilities to write. With a "can do" attitude, they will choose more challenging activities and apply what they know consistently, persistently, and skillfully (Bandura & Schunk, 1981). Instruments such as the self-efficacy scale can be used as a pre- and post-measurement scale for various modes of writing.

Self-perception scales represent yet another set of instruments that measure how learners feel about themselves as writers. Children read or listen to questions about writing performance and indicate whether they agree or disagree (young children might respond verbally or circle smiling or frowning faces). Using data results, the teacher and student set goals. If students believe they are poor writers or if they are reluctant to write, tasks might be designed to guarantee success and nurture the joy of writing. If students believe they are good writers or enjoy writing, the tasks should meet their needs and reinforce their enthusiasm. Self-perception scales can be administered at the beginning, middle, and end of the year to determine if self-perceptions have changed.

An assessment instrument that closely resembles the self-perception scale but focuses specifically on the value of writing and being a writer is an attitude survey. Attitude surveys are sets of questions such as "I like to write for fun" or "I like my friends to read what I have written" or "I think learning to write is important." Answers to these questions provide insights into the learners' feelings and values about writing and the ways of going about the work. Although there are several attitude surveys available for writing (Bottomley, Henk, & Melnick, 1997/1998; Kear, Coffman, McKenna, & Ambrosio, 2000; Knudson, 1991, 1992), administering a combination of different kinds of self-reports or supplementing them with observations will ensure that what children say they do or feel matches their behavior. If children say they like to write, do they voluntarily elect to write during free time? Do they anxiously participate in writing activity or have their own purposes for writing? How children really feel will become apparent in their actions and literacy habits.

The importance of any observation or self-report is in calling the teacher's attention to the child's perspective. Children can teach us a great deal about their writing development and their meanings and reasoning. William Corsaro (1985), an early childhood educator, reminds us that we need to modify inquiry techniques for talking with children. He suggests we subscribe to a continuous process of establishing and developing relationships with children, thus, incorporating questions into the ongoing activities of

TABLE 2-1 Writer Self-Efficacy Scale

	1 Strongly Agree	2 Agree Somewhat	3 Agree a Little	4 Don't Agree at All
I like to write	1	2	3	4
I enjoy sharing my writing with others	1	2	3	4
I have lots of ideas to share in writing	1	2	3	4
I do not mind changing my work to help others understand it better	1	2	3	4
I like my peers to tell me their impressions of my work	1	2	3	4
When writing a paper, I find it easy to make all the changes I need to make	1	2	3	4
I consider myself a good writer	1	2	3	4
When my class is asked to write a poem, mine is one of the best	1	2	3	4
When my class is asked to write a report, mine is one of the best	1	2	3	4
When my class is asked to write a story, mine is one of the best	1	2	3	4
I find it easy to help other writers	1	2	3	4
I think writing is important	1	2	3	4

Answer the following questions.

What kinds of writing do you like to do? _____

What things does a person have to LEARN to be a good writer? _____

Why do you think some people your age have trouble writing stories? _____

What things do you need to learn to be a better writer than you are right now? _____

What do you think a writer needs to be good at? _____

What good writers do you know? _____

How did you learn to write? _____

What did people do to help you learn to write? _____

How do you think you can improve your writing? _____

If you had to teach someone how to write a story, what would you do? Which of these things do you think you are good at? _____

Source: Wright Group/McGraw-Hill. (1995). Adapted from *Meadowbooks.* © Wright Group/McGraw-Hill. Reprinted with permission.

their life worlds. Special attempts are made to capture children's intentions while they are playing, presenting a special item during show and tell, casually talking at the writing table, and participating in all types of reading, writing, and language activities. Teachers can also check reading or writing logs for books they enjoy, writing topics they care about , and records of personal thoughts.

Considering the child's perspective means putting aside adult beliefs and attitudes about writing and committing to new ways of interpreting writing tasks through childhood concepts and themes, definitions and meanings, interests and beliefs, and social and emotional needs.

Process and Text

Beyond attitudes and literacy habits, teachers discover the writing strategies children have at their disposal. Observing the process of writing yields information on the following questions.

- Do the children sound out as they write or reread their work?
- Do they draw pictures?
- Do they self-correct?
- Do they verbalize while writing?
- Do they share?
- Do they take risks?
- Do they monitor the process strategies?

Jotting down brief anecdotal records of students' performance without judgmental inferences can be quite valuable. Teachers monitor student behavior before, during, and after writing, to identify positive attitudes and behaviors. For example, look for some of the following:

- General interests, energy, and passion for journal writing
- Initiation of writing
- Intellectual curiosity and risk taking
- Sense of **ownership** and commitment
- Flexibility and willingness to change directions or perspectives

In terms of the text, the six traits represent what teachers might expect to see in journals. For instance, because journals are characterized by informal **conversational styles**, there are likely to be colloquialisms, sentence fragments, slang, and contractions. Words may suggest emotion through superlatives and strong adjectives, such as *marvelous, very, terrific,* and *great.* As can be seen in Figure 2–13, the journal traits are generically defined. If the teacher introduces specific kinds of journals, some of the criteria may need to be

FIGURE 2–13   Six Trait Descriptions for Journal Writing

Ideas
- Focuses on personal reflections, insights, ideas
- Concentrates on one or more topics
- Builds on experience to shape messages
- Substitutes or embellishes ideas with drawings
- Indicates compositional risks

Organization
- Includes spontaneous short messages, words, phrases
- Presents sequenced or unconnected moments of importance

Voice
- Reveals an open, honest, and authentic personality
- Suggests self as audience
- Presents a tone that gives flavor to the message
- Portrays a unique fingerprint

Sentence Fluency
- Shows "sentence sense" or stream-of-consciousness thinking
- Emphasizes quantity and flow

Word Choice
- Focuses on personal expressive words
- Integrates accurate and appropriate words

Conventions
- Includes dated entries
- Displays regular entries
- Uses invented or creative spellings

modified. Although conventions such as spelling, punctuation, capitalization, and handwriting are never evaluated, teachers review and analyze these skills to monitor student progress. Any or all of these traits can serve as the basis for minilessons.

Context

There is one final area of assessment for teachers to monitor: the context of writing. Nowhere is this more important than in journal writing because a nonthreatening environment with unconditional acceptance makes journaling a safe haven for learning. Teachers should ask themselves the following questions:

- Do the students have privacy if they are writing in a diary? If so, where are the journals kept and who has access to them?
- Is the room set up for privacy? Is it quiet? Is enough time available to the writer?

For more public uses of journals, the teacher may consider other contextual factors such as the following:

- Are journals used outside of the writing class (e.g., responding to literature, studying subject matter, having a conversational exchange)?
- Are journals shared? Which kinds are shared?
- Are the entries written at home or in school?
- What will be done with the journals when they are completed?
- If they are written at school, are students aware of print sources available in the classroom?
- How will journals be integrated into other parts of the curriculum?

Group discussions about how children work—whether they need a quiet place to write, like to share, prefer to keep journals private, or write about sensitive topics—assist teachers in monitoring the classroom context and structuring lessons to meet individual differences and needs.

CLASSROOM VIGNETTES: JOURNAL WRITING IN ACTION

The classroom anecdotes (grades 1, 3, and 5) in this section showcase the variety of journals available to support writing and the other subjects across the curriculum. Decisions teachers make depend on instructional objectives and the developmental levels of their students. Students will often use several complementary types of journals at the same time.

Personal journals, in which the writer is the audience, are considered first, then dialogue journals, double-entry journals, learning logs, scrapbooks, and simulated journals, where the audience is extended to the teacher and peers.

Grade 1

Personal Journals

Three days a week, the first graders begin the school day by engaging in journal writing. As they enter the room, they put away their belongings and pick up their personal journals from the writing box on the counter. Their journals have blank pages for writing and are shaped like objects: a leaf for October, a pumpkin for November, and so on. They flip through the books, admiring what they have done. In the center of each table is a tin can of sharpened pencils, markers, and crayons. Walls and bulletin boards wrap the room in words and images to grab children's attention and stimulate ideas.

These reviews provide insights into children's growth and performance over time (for example, are the entries longer, more thoughtful, and more mechanically correct?). Errors are signs of progress and document the hunches children have about the language system. With continual monitoring of journals, Vivian gathers information to guide discussions with children in conferences. She might say "I've noticed you enjoy writing about your family," or "When you concentrate on spelling, your entries tend to be shorter." An account of her perceptions and observations, rather than evaluations, validates what is being learned and models her responses to journals.

As long as children do not have to write a certain amount of words every day to fill time or pages, they will discover that journals are indispensable to them. More than writing practice, and more than an occasion to write, personal journals are a welcome addition to the school day and a safe place to explore ideas for future writings.

Dialogue Journals

A dialogue journal is two-way communication between a teacher and student or a student and peers. Much like friends passing secret notes, conversational partners take turns sending and receiving messages on any topic of interest or concern. Dialogue journals provide Vivian with the opportunity to mentor a child and build a trusting relationship with him; they provide the student with a chance to communicate with the teacher and initiate topics of his own choosing.

Dialogue journals are valuable to teachers but even more so to children who write to each other. Paired with a buddy, one child initiates a topic and the other replies, asks questions, or elaborates on what is said. Sometimes Vivian assigns a specific writing task; for example, she may suggest the pair share thoughts on favorite books with one another. Written conversations about literature are effective in bridging writing and reading and often emerge naturally, as is illustrated in the exchange between Yoshiko and Vivian in Figure 2–16.

Yoshiko begins on a personal note about a skating accident and then, with Vivian's participation, ties the conversation to her experiences in America. The conversation shifts to her friend Humiko, and then on to a book review. Vivian reads Yoshiko's journal entries, asks questions, and makes comments.

Along with nurturing personal connections, Vivian models native language word order, correct spelling, inflectional endings, and conversational **discourse** (asking questions). Gradually, Yoshiko modifies her writing to reflect some of these conventions (Bode, 1989). Sentence fluency is jointly accomplished by connecting talking points: asking and answering questions, sticking to a topic, or cueing a change of topic. To read the dialogue is to hear separate voices in harmony with one another, melding into a fully developed discourse.

The dialogue journal celebrates linguistic and cultural diversity as an important resource in learning to write. The unique aspects of ESL children's experiences and personal identities, their history and culture, is shared in the content and structure of dialogue journals, which reveal unique ways of living, thinking, and behaving. In dialogue journals, teachers explore subjects never considered before and may notice that text itself manifests cultural values. For example, the Japanese culture views succinctness and ambiguity as quality features of text (Minami & McCabe, 1991), whereas in some Spanish cultures, long, flowery sentences are the ideal (Montaño-Harmon, 1991). Native American (Athabaskan) culture advocates less explicit or detailed writing because readers are believed to be co-authors of the text with the distinct responsibility of inferring what is written (Scollon & Scollon, 1981). Teachers can point out to children how culture shapes writing and how writing can be used to share culture. With an open mind, the class can explore and affirm cultural themes and subjects as well as dialects and novel uses of language. Sensitivity to these and other issues should be apparent in the responses to students' journal entries.

FIGURE 2-16   Dialogue Journal Entries Initiated by Yoshiko (First Grader, Independent Writing)

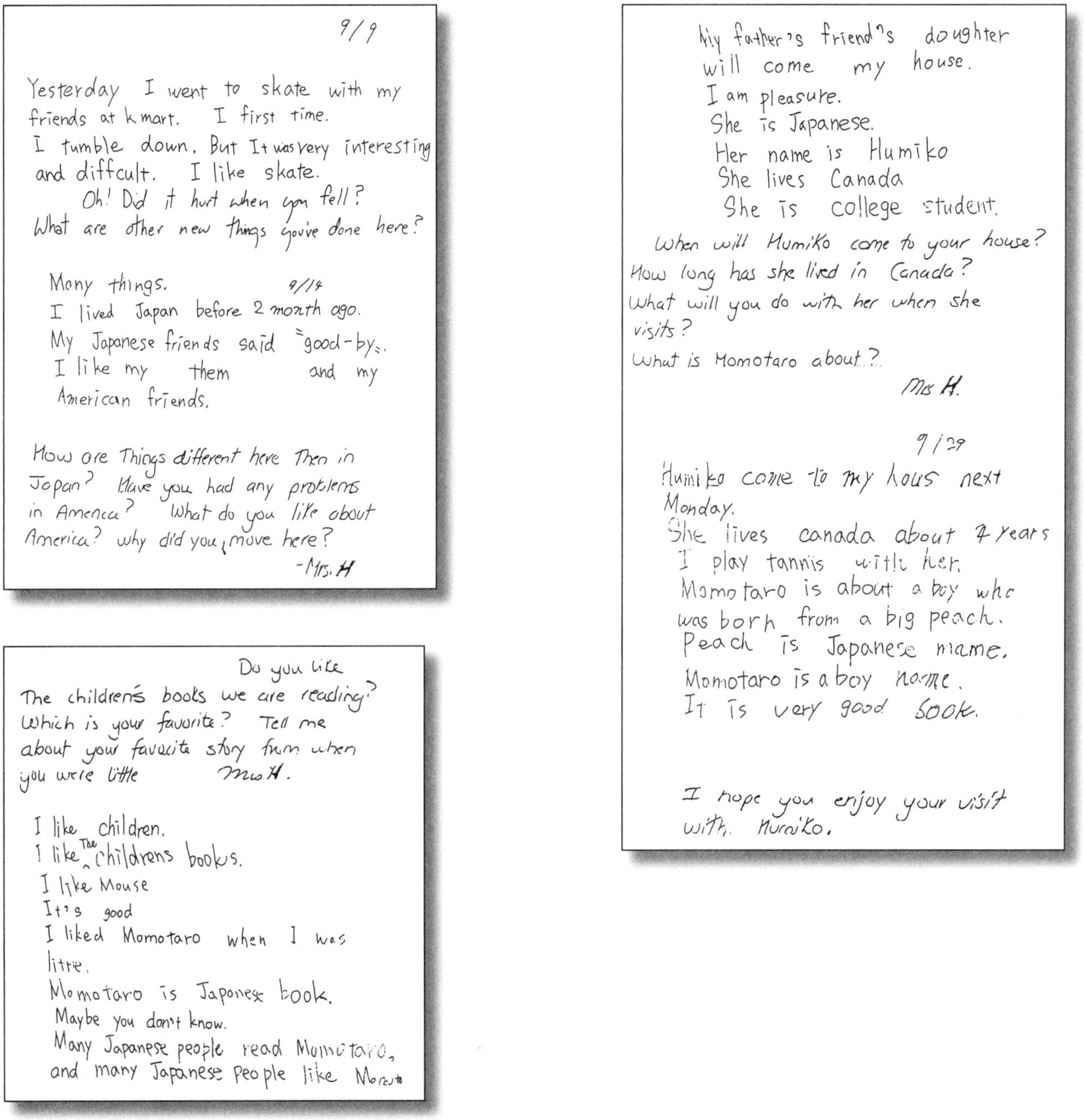

9/9

Yesterday I went to skate with my
friends at kmart.   I first time.
I tumble down. But It was very interesting
and diffcult.   I like skate.
     Oh! Did it hurt when you fell?
What are other new things you've done here?

Many things.   9/14
I lived Japan before 2 month ago.
My Japanese friends said "good-by".
I like my   them   and my
American friends.

How are Things different here Then in
Japan? Have you had any problems
in America?   What do you like about
America? why did you move here?
                              —Mrs. H

                    Do you like
The childrens books we are reading?
Which is your favorite?   Tell me
about your favorite story from when
you were little   Mrs H.

I like children.
I like The childrens books.
I like Mouse
It's good
I liked Momotaro when I was
litre.
Momotaro is Japanese book.
 Maybe you dont know.
Many Japanese people read Momotaro,
and many Japanese people like Mozzoth

My father's friend's doughter
will come my house.
I am pleasure.
She is Japanese.
Her name is Humiko
She lives Canada
She is college student.
  When will Humiko come to your house?
How long has she lived in Canada?
What will you do with her when she
visits?
What is Momotaro about.?
                    Mrs H.

                    9/29
Humiko come to my hous next
Monday.
She lives canada about 4 years
I play tannis with her.
Momotaro is about a boy who
was born from a big peach.
Peach is Japanese name.
Momotaro is a boy name.
It is very good book.

I hope you enjoy your visit
with humiko.

Reading all of the students' journals, one would be struck by how well Vivian relates to the children and how supportive her comments are. She acknowledges what the children have written, responds to their requests, replies, asks questions, and discloses personal things about herself. In turn, she requests that the child do the same. In fact, her objective is to get the children to ask most of the questions and write more than she does (Staton, 1987). Because she converses in a sincere, non-judgmental manner, students readily reveal their thoughts and feelings.

To repeat, conventions should not be a concern in dialogue journals unless they interfere with the meaning being conveyed to the receiver. If errors impede communication, Vivian models the correct form in her responses to the students. A grammarian by nature, she also makes mental notes of the kinds of sentences the students use—statements, questions, commands, or exclamations—and whether the students write in complex or simple sentences. These observations provide good examples for minilessons. Periodically, the journal becomes the basis of conference discussions in which partners review what they've learned from one another and present their feelings about writing in dialogue journals.

With access to repeated first drafts (the essence of dialogue journals), Vivian can examine entries privately and write anecdotal records about some of the following:

- Range of interests
- Fluency
- Previous experiences
- Conversational style
- Ability to sustain a topic
- Use of conventions
- Attempts at transitions or conversational ties

Dialogue journals are demanding and time consuming, but as the year progresses, neither Vivian nor the children are prepared for the remarkable writing that surfaces and the personal connections they make. Vivian may even be surprised when dialogue journals become popular with parents. Like the successful practice of book sharing, parents use dialogue writing to bond with their children and learn more about them. In a letter Vivian sends home during the first month of school, she urges parents to talk with their children on paper, producing a few words or sentences each day. She explains how to follow the child's lead and attend to his ideas and questions. Parents should not correct or evaluate the entries because that would defeat the whole purpose.

Much has been written in professional articles and books about the beneficial effects of using dialogue journals (Kreeft, 1984; Peyton & Seyorum, 1989; Staton, 1980, 1987). Some of these ideas may be discussed with parents or included in family newsletters.

Grade 3

Double-Entry Journals

The first thing you notice when walking into the third-grade classroom is the private spaces where readers can linger with a good book. Coexisting in these sanctuaries are sets of double-entry journals, notebooks with multicolumn graphic organizers (see Table 2–2). In one column, writers copy verbatim something memorable or significant from a book they are reading. In another column, they write connections or reactions to the recorded statement. A third column is available to record specific page numbers from the source book.

When the double-entry journal is first introduced, Kate models how to complete an entry using the overhead and a familiar book, for example, *Bill Peet: An Autobiography* (Peet, 1989). She reads a few passages, stopping to write when something in the book strikes her or prompts a question.

In one column, she copies the story events, and, in another column, she writes a personal response. After she finishes writing an entry in front of the students, she reads several more passages and has the class implement what they have just observed. Each day, as a new chapter is read, children independently add another double entry and share it with the class.

Kate listens for topics, feelings, points of view, and personal reactions. She also looks for reading strategies and comprehension:

- How the writer incorporates textbook features into the entry (references to pictures, cueing systems, and author studies)

TABLE 2-2	Teacher-Created Double-Entry Journal Using Bill Peet: An Autobiography	
	Story Events	**My Response**
Pages		
8	When Bill was a child he liked to draw as an indoor hobby on cold Indiana winters.	I like to draw too.
11-13	Bill wanted to catch a frog to draw.	I felt bad for the frog who died because of a snake. I would have tried to save him like Bill did.
29-31	When Bill lived with his grandparents, he would run off with his friends when his grandpa fell asleep after lunch.	Bill did things I do like swimming and playing. I used to live on a farm.
35-36	Bill wanted to be a taxidermist.	I never heard of this job. I learned a new word.
46-47	After his grandma died, Bill went back to live with his mother and dad.	Bill's mom and dad fought alot like mine.
54-55	Bill started art classes and one of his pictures got into the yearbook.	Bill was a good artist.

Source: Excerpt from *Bill Peet: An Autobiography*. Copyright © 1989 by Bill Peet. Adapted and reprinted by permission of Houghton Mifflin Company. All rights reserved.

- What the writer chooses to remember about the book
- Whether the writer makes accurate predictions
- New words and terms the writer has learned
- How the writer interacts with the ideas and language of the text
- Linkages between prior knowledge and new information
- How writers describe their reading behaviors (metalanguage)
- Evidence of the writer's reading strategies (previewing, predicting, self-questioning, self-monitoring, repeated reading, inferencing, summarizing)

There are many different ways to set up double-entry journals to make connections with print. Several excellent professional articles on double-entry journals describe their variations and uses (Barone, 1990; Macon, Bewell, & Vogt, 1991). A few of these paired prompts include the following:

Predictions/what really happened

Questions/answers

Keywords/meanings

Favorite quotes/reactions

Mira selects the *predictions* and *what really happened* prompts as she prepares to read *And Still the Turtle Watched* (MacGill-Callahan, 1991), a tale about an Indian grandfather who carves a turtle from stone for his grandson and tells him that the turtle will watch over the Delaware people and bless the land for many generations. The turtle rests on the bluff near the sea where children come to visit and honor it, until one day, many years later, a group of teenagers find the turtle and senselessly mar it with graffiti. Fortunately, a stranger also passes by, sees the rock, and recognizes it as a meaningful symbol to Manitou. He rescues the turtle and donates it to the Botanical gardens in New York City.

Predictions	What really happened
I think the turtles is going to be watch and watch all day long and the Indain is going to be watcheing the turtle for a long time and they is gets going to be looking at the turtle, they watch the turtle in the sky because he was in heaving and the boys grandpa made a turtle. they watch the teirtle and it came aluc, the turtle did not understand the people when they was talking to each other, they watch him all day long, they is not realy nice, they were not his children, they were going to spear ham. and his eye hurted he was not real, he was made by a man they put the turtle on the trunck, Nice kid watch him and love him	The turtle tired real and he they watch the turtle in the was in the sky becouse he was heaving and the boys grandpa made he and he put it on the back of the trunk and took the turtle New York city in the musum.

Mira reads the first 10 pages and studies the pictures that appear on alternating pages. At the point where the stranger appears and sees the turtle covered with graffiti, Mira closes the book to write a prediction. Her double-entry journal appears in Figure 2–17.

As can be seen from the entry, Mira has written a stream-of-consciousness summary rather than a prediction. This is not a surprise given that earlier Kate modeled a double-entry using summary prompts. Mira has simply followed the teacher's lead. The next time, Kate will encourage children to do tasks that mirror the ones she has demonstrated. Otherwise she runs the risk of introducing information that students have not yet been exposed to, such as Mira's confusion over what it means to "predict." Nonetheless, Mira has comprehended the story fully, especially given the kind of text she has selected. This particular picture book is written in a poetic style and has a tone reminiscent of a legend. It also has many indirect statements and nuances that require inferences on the part of the reader. For example, Mira infers that the turtle's eyes were sprayed with paint from the statement "he felt cool wetness on his eyes. He could no longer see." Mira also makes educated guesses based on "reading" the pictures—the faint outline of a turtle appearing in the clouds implies that he might be in heaven (although this is never stated), and the rock's placement on a ceramic-tiled floor in a large, open space suggests a museum (although the actual place is a building at the Botanical gardens). When judging writing, Kate considers text level difficulty based on style, vocabulary, illustrations, and complexity of ideas.

Although reading and writing have many commonalities, they are, nevertheless, different processes. Mira's rambling thoughts, held together with an infinite number of *ands*, take the reader in circles. Ideas are further obscured by the lack of pronoun referents. This is the kind of writing that all too frequently is dismissed by a teacher as showing "poor" thinking. It is tempting to arrive at this conclusion because of the tangled grammar, repetition, and unpunctuated text. Yet it would seem that Mira has managed to convey the essential aspects of the story. She alludes to the title of the book with the words *turtle* and *watch* and retells the story in proper sequence, beginning with an old man who made the turtle for his grandson. Her initial view that the turtle was alive is understandable given the author's personification of the rock. By repeating the words *he or they watched*, Mira captures the passing of time and the children who come through the area to see the turtle. Although the turtle is never "speared," his eye is hurt from the graffiti paint and Mira accurately states that the turtle can no longer see. Finally, she discusses the man (stranger) who sees the turtle, digs it up, and puts it on a truck. Indeed, her entry captures a remarkable amount of information about the book.

For Mira, the double-entry journal motivates interest, guides comprehension, and, in the end, serves as a springboard for clearing up misconceptions (such as the meaning of the word *prediction*). For Kate, the lessons learned from examining this entry underscore Mira's need for further writing practice.

Clearly, as the foregoing discussion suggests, the double-entry journal is relevant to reading and writing. Students can and should write all types of double-entry journals. They might be encouraged to read books by the same author and comment on writing style, topics, or memorable characters. They might also read the same book more than once, each time using a different pair of prompts. Often the entire class reads the same book and, after completing journal entries, discusses it in relation to their personal lives ("I'm sometimes afraid of these things too"), a text they've read before ("I read something like this once. It reminds me of . . ."), or anything in the world around them ("I heard about this on TV").

When children write double-entry journals, they do not have to use fictional selections only; nonfiction works just as well. The children can read different accounts or conflicting versions of historical events or famous lives, listing facts in one column and opinions in another. If they are collecting and reacting to words, they can list concepts in one column and definitions or examples in another. In Kate's class, children write double-entry journals weekly—sometimes more. Except for the double-entry format, the book titles and paired prompts offer limitless variety.

Learning Logs

A visitor to the third-grade class, on quick inspection of the room, knows what the students are learning. The visitor may see pictures of weather on a bulletin board, displays of student work celebrating Martin Luther King Jr.'s birthday, and writing activities listed on a chart. When asked to show visitors what they are studying, the children will pull out learning logs, records of their newly acquired knowledge. Based on the belief that writing is a tool for thinking and learning, these logs track students' questions, feelings, strategies, and comments. For example, in a social studies unit students might relate subject matter to their own experience or compare one subject to another. In mathematics the entry might be an explanation of operations used to solve a problem. And in language arts, it might be a collection of words for spelling.

Kate presents several alternatives for the children to respond to texts in their log:

- Tell what you have learned
- Ask questions

FIGURE 2-18D   Learning Logs (Third Graders): Sioux Name Poem and Map

self-assess, and reflect. At first, they write entries that include general "I learned" statements or summaries of what was covered. But before long, with teacher input, they respond to more complex questions:

- Am I able to formulate (historical, scientific, literary) questions?
- Have I noted information from more than one perspective?
- Did I challenge arguments?
- Did I accurately reconstruct the meaning of what I read?
- Was I able to identify problems and dilemmas?
- Did I formulate a position on an issue?

A data retrieval chart, similar to a computer spreadsheet, provides a simple means for the class to pool knowledge and log in information they have found in answer to a series of questions. Together they can outline the next steps and record these. At the end of the 6 weeks, the children discover the subjects that dominate the journal and the knowledge they have acquired about each.

Although the learning log is a self-report and will not completely reflect the full range of children's knowledge, Kate can check for the connections and meanings they are trying to make. By examining several entries she can identify patterns in topics they deem important in a lesson or words they select to describe their understandings of a subject. She also looks for signs that students are applying new information to prior knowledge. Just as learning logs document progress and content, they also contribute to the classroom routine. At the end of a language arts or social studies lesson, children bring their learning logs to the group circle and Kate assesses classwork in her record book. By questioning the students, she may offer new possibilities for log entries:

- Who read a good book today and wants to share its title?
- Who would like to recommend a book for us to consider reading next time?
- Who has a new word he learned today?
- Who reread his work today?
- Who brainstormed ideas?
- Who shared journal entries with a friend?

These questions encourage sharing, reflection, and new possibilities. During these debriefing sessions, students talk about their strategies and give examples from their learning logs.

Grade 5

Writers' Scrapbooks

Fifth graders keep writers' scrapbooks to spark memories and ideas for writing. Scrapbooks include collections of literacy memorabilia that answer the questions "Who am I?" and "Who am I as a reader and writer?" In a three-ring binder, students place newspaper clippings, letters, awards, pictures, ticket stubs, stamps, labels, or other literacy items. Print materials are glued directly into the book, whereas three-dimensional objects are slipped into pocket folders nestled in between the pages. Each page includes only one artifact or focused writing so the binder can be continuously reorganized to reflect the child's evolving understanding of himself and the world. Because the scrapbook is supplemented, reorganized, and revised on an on-going basis, it is not only a resource for writing but also a written product itself.

The essential parts of the scrapbook are the reflective writing and quickwrites, as well as the captions, labels, or special blurbs that accompany each item. Ed models how to get ideas for writing: He selects one of his objects, an Italian passport, and holds it up for students to question him about it.

- What is it?
- Why is it important?
- Who gave it to you?
- When did you get it?
- What do you do with it?

A quickwrite, projected on an overhead transparency, is read:

This stained parched passport was my great-great grandfather's. It allowed him to come to America from Italy. He was scared traveling by boat to a new country. In the early 1900s they did not have clean and safe conditions for traveling. He was alone. He had to leave his family behind because it was too dangerous.

Following his example, each class member selects an object from his scrapbook and another student interviews him about it. Ed interviews Brittany about a ruby ring. He asks, "Why is this ring important to you? Who gave it to you? Why was it your best gift ever?" When the questioning is complete, Brittany does a quickwrite (see Figure 2–19) and places the ring into the pocket folder. She will return to this entry and others during future writing topics. The scrapbooks, objects, and quickwrites ensure that writers never have to face a blank sheet of paper when they are ready to write. Students organize pages to identify themes for the items they collect. For instance, Cameron has pictures of rock stars, CD labels, concert tickets, song lyrics, and magazine articles that clearly reflect his interest in music. He asks, "How would I classify the musical collection, and what would I highlight if I were an advertiser trying to promote the music?"

FIGURE 2-19   Brittany's Ring Quickwrite (Fifth Grader, Independent Writing)

Do you know what a family ring is? Not all families have them, but my family does. A family ring is an heirloom passed down from one generation to the next within a family.

There are two rings in my family. My Dad's side, the Bridwells, have a ring. My Mother's side, the Smawleys also have a ring and this is the one that I will get. My brother will get the Bridwell ring because he is older. It's a lot like two sons in a royal family. The older one becomes king.

The Smawley ring is a gold ring. It has an impression of an armor helmet in the center. It is very pretty and finely carved. The details are so good it looks like it was printed on the ring. My mother told me that the Smawley family is from Wales and that is where the ring originated. I get it when I graduate from college.

The ring is very special to my family. It has been passed down only once, but it is special because it was passed down to a very special person—my Papa Earl. I don't remember him, but I wish I could. My mom has told me some wonderful stories about him.

Because of the popularity of scrapbooks, students continue to add to them all year long. But the scrapbook can become more than a personal keepsake and resource for ideas. In a geography lesson, Ed shares *Washington, D.C.: A Scrapbook* (Bensen, 1999), which is a story about four young tourists on a class trip to the nation's capital. The scrapbook is filled with written entries, fun facts, photographs, maps, pictures, train tickets, license plates, and other souvenirs. Using the book as a model, the students brainstorm U.S. cities they could explore. Kenny is interested in the historical significance of Boston. His family took a 3-week vacation there during the summer, and this trip fueled his interest in the city. Initially, he contacts the Boston Chamber of Commerce for brochures on the area and visits two local libraries. His brother, who works at Harvard, sends him historical fact sheets and tells him about a couple of relevant and informative Web sites. Before Kenny formulates questions to further guide his search, he reviews his collection for a report. He decides on an alphabetic tour of historic sites in Boston, where he will discuss each historical event through anecdotes and pictures (Adams Street, Bunker Hill, Commons, etc.). Throughout the project he reflects on and answers some of the following questions:

- What is my learning interest?
- How did I become interested in this?
- How did I explore my interest? What resources did I seek? Which were most helpful? Least helpful?
- What questions did I ask to facilitate my search?
- What information surprised me?
- What was my "best" find?
- What questions remain unanswered?
- What was my reason for organizing information as I did?
- What are my next strategies and tasks?
- How has my interest changed during the project?

By the time Kenny finishes his project, his scrapbook is full of information, and he has become an expert on his subject. He is ready to share his scrapbook in an assessment conference, but before doing so, he prepares a report giving a succinct account of his efforts and progress. First he summarizes the scope of the collection: the total number of objects accumulated, the number of written entries, the length of the entries, and the variety of sources represented. Then he chooses items that show evidence of quality: best works, turning points, breakthroughs, and challenges. After he discusses quantity and quality, he turns his attention to setting new goals. Committed to expanding on what he already knows, he will attempt several more compositions.

Indeed, scrapbooks are quite useful for writing and assessment, much more so than can be discussed here. *Scrapbooking for the First Time* (Carter, 1999) is a good primer for those interested in starting a scrapbook.

Simulated Journals

Around the Thanksgiving holiday, the fifth graders start a thematic unit on Native Americans. The class recently visited the Natural History Museum in town where they explored Native American artifacts, legends and myths, symbols, and language. To report on this learning event, they have a variety of writing alternatives from which to choose, and the simulated journal is one. In a simulated journal a student assumes the identity of a historical or literary figure and writes from that person's perspective. Similar to role-play, the students step into another's shoes and see the world from another's perspective. Ed conducts a minilesson to show students how to write an entry in simulated journal fashion; he begins with the article, "The Four Seasons" (Carufel, 1998). In the article, the author explains how the Indians' lifestyle and activities change in tandem with the seasons. Ed jots down two different entries to show how a writer can focus on any aspect of the text and turn it into a simulated journal entry. In the first example, he highlights the influence of the seasons on the lifestyle of the Ojibwe Indians. Ed uses many of the words from the article and changes the point of view from third person to first person.

> In winter, I easily snared the snowshoe hare because it left a trail in the deep snow. When I fished through holes in the ice, I constructed little teepees over the holes to prevent light from entering. This way, there was just enough light filtered through the ice so that I could see the fish, but they couldn't see me.

The second example shows the activities of the Ojibwe in each season, without discussing how the seasons influence their activities.

> In the winter when the food supply dwindled, I hunted the snowshoe hare and wove its fur into blankets, hats, and moccasin linings. I would fish through the holes in the ice of a frozen body of water.

Each entry stresses different aspects of the information and gives insight into how a writer interprets the piece. The personal pronoun "I" keeps the writer in the role of the Ojibwe Indian.

Ed assembles a text set that reveals the world from the perspective of characters who lived long ago. Among these are *Emma's Journal* (Moss, 1999d) and *A Journey to the New World: The Diary of Remember Patience Whipple* (Lasky, 1996), books in which the authors not only assume the role of a character to tell the story (in a simulation of sorts) but also structure the narrative in journal form. The collection also includes trade books such as *If You Lived With the Sioux Indians* (McGovern, 1992b) and *If You Lived With the Iroquois* (Levine, 1998) that familiarize students with the lifestyles of a historical period.

Jason reads the book *To Walk the Sky Path* (Naylor, 1973) and records his ideas about the Seminole Indians (see Figure 2–20), creating a personal portrait of himself as Fierce Tiger.

Each paragraph is organized by topic: what he wears, how and what he hunts, and where he lives. In assuming the role of Fierce Tiger, Jason hints at the historical

FIGURE 2-20
Jason's Simulated
Journal About the
Seminoles (Fifth Grader,
Independent Writing)

> I am Chief Schmidte. My Indian name is Fierce Tiger I am the Chief of my tribe. My people are the Seminoles. My tribe is very kind to me.
>
> I wear blue shirts, red pants, and a hat with feathers in it. I eat corn, and other crops. My people hunt buffalo. I paint with sand, animal blood, and berries. I love my tribe
>
> I live in a Chickki. I believe in the sky, earth, water, and the animals. I live with my wife, and two sons. My house is very sturdy. I love my life.
>
> I like to hunt and ride horses. I hunt with Lonesome Dove, Iron Wolt and Mighty Eagle. My Transportation is by foot and Horses. I use arrowheads, buffalo hade, deerskin, deer bones and stones to make clothes. I use spears to hunt. I love everything I have.

milieu through the topics (clothing, lifestyle, customs) and words used by the tribe (*chickee, arrowheads*). After the simulated entry is written, Jason dramatizes it for his peers and encourages them to ask questions. The questions are framed like an interview to help him maintain his particular role and develop a coherent picture of the Seminoles.

- Did you have chores that were difficult?
- How long might a hunt have taken you? What dangers did you encounter?
- What was your village like?
- How was life different back then?
- Are the historical details accurate?
- How would you have reacted to this kind of life back then?

As Jason takes on this new persona he finds himself extending journal topics into new areas. Jason wants to know about Osceola, the chief of the Seminoles, and he e-mails a local editor to find out why he named his sports newspaper *Osceola*. He notices city streets named after Native Americans (Apalachee, Apalachicola, Miccosukee), as is his favorite college sports team, the Seminoles. Before long, he is creating a scrapbook section called "Everything Seminole," adding name poems, Internet material, and items from local sports stores. The simulated journal becomes the impetus for constructing a broader understanding of the topic and for deciding to write a nonfiction text about the Seminoles complete with powerful illustrations, photographs, and other materials gathered in his scrapbook.

Simulated journals have far-reaching benefits. They allow a writer to take on the role of a fictional character to better understand a particular **point of view**. They also help prepare students for test prompts in which they must assume a role in a hypothetical situation.

Test Prompt Example

Pretend you are an animal in the Amazon Rain Forest. Describe where you are, what you see, what you hear, and what you do. Use describing words to write your narrative.

As sources of assessment, simulated journals reveal student comprehension, personal insights into reading, new vocabulary, and improved content-related spellings. Simulated journals show once again that journal writing is not exclusive to the writing class, but is a valuable resource across the curriculum.

JOURNEY REFLECTIONS

However accomplished or inexperienced the writer, journals are an indispensable resource—inspiring and gratifying. It does not matter whether students record ideas as splintered thoughts or well-formed anecdotes, there is no right or wrong way to do them. Students write as often and as extensively as they can. There are no quotas.

Journal writing is a form of **expressive writing** that need not follow the conventions and restrictions required in other types of writing (Britton, Burgess, Martin, McLeod, & Rosen, 1975). Instead, it creates its own special magic. The writing is informal and unstructured; it will not follow the writing process.

Journals serve many functions in the classroom. First and foremost, they invite students to take the time to look around, discover new things, and reflect on impressions. They also teach fluency by allowing children to take risks without fear of judgment or evaluation. Some journals, such as personal and dialogue journals, tap into valuable inner resources and invite writers to share experiences, interests, and preferences. The dialogue journal, in particular, is beneficial to ESL students because writing is shared and language is modeled. Journals also exert a powerful indirect contribution in the content areas and literature where students can activate background knowledge, broaden understanding, and react to subjects. Whether through learning logs, reading logs, double-entry journals, literary response journals, or writers' scrapbooks, journals integrate thoughts and personal experiences and provide access to subject matter across the curriculum. Because they are a part of children's day-to-day itineraries and long-term compasses for future goals, they should be portable and readily available so writers can refer to them during reading and writing assignments. The journal should to be as worn from use as any favorite book.

Writing instructors should not simply introduce the many types of journals to students; they should show their purposes by sharing books and modeling journal writing. Although journals are seldom evaluated, they should be monitored and reviewed regularly for insights into children's emerging understanding of writing, interests, and needs. This information forms the basis of minilesson topics and discussions in writing circles and conferences. Knowing and learning about children through journal writing gives direction to educational plans and guides teachers in assisting the students on their personal journeys.

Insofar as teachers are interested in children's lives and believe in the power of journal writing, the practice of expressing oneself through writing will be undeniably favorable. Other types of expressive writing that contribute comparable positive effects include personal narratives, friendly letters, memoirs, lifelines, and biographies. These types of writing, discussed in the next chapter, continue to reinforce the goal of building a writing community and, once again, underscore the belief that the journey begins with the writer.

WORKS CITED

Professional References

Bamberger, J. (1982). Growing up prodigies: The mid-life crisis. *New Directions for Child Development, 17,* 61–78.

Bandura, A. (1997). *Self-efficacy: The exercise of control* (4th ed.). New York: W. H. Freeman & Co.

Bandura, A., & Schunk, D. H. (1981). Cultivating competence, self-efficacy, and intrinsic interest through proximal self-motivation. *Journal of Personality and Social Psychology, 43,* 5–21.

Barone, D. (1990). The written responses of young children: Beyond comprehension to story understanding. *The New Advocate, 3,* 49–56.

Bode, B. (1989). Dialogue journal writing. *The Reading Teacher, 42,* 568–571.

Bottomley, D. M., Henk, W. A., & Melnick, S. A. (1997/1998). Assessing children's views about themselves as writers using the writer self-perception scale. *The Reading Teacher, 51,* 286–296.

Britton, J., Burgess, T., Martin, N., McLeod, A., & Rosen, H. (1975). *The development of writing abilities.* London: Macmillan.

Bromley, K. (1991). *Webbing with literature: Creating story maps with children's books.* Boston: Allyn & Bacon.

Calkins, L. (1994). *The art of teaching writing.* Portsmouth, NH: Heinemann.

Carter, R. (1999). *Scrapbooking for the first time.* New York: Sterling.

Corsaro, W. A. (1985). *Friendship and peer culture in the early years.* Norwood, NJ: Ablex.

Cox, C. (2002). *Teaching language arts: A student- and response-centered classroom.* Boston: Allyn & Bacon.

Dinkmeyer, D., & Losoncy, L. (1980). *The encouragement book.* Upper Saddle River, NJ: Merrill/Prentice Hall.

Elbow, P. (1973). *Writing without teachers.* New York: Oxford University Press.

Fulwiler, T. (Ed.). (1987). *The journal book.* Portsmouth, NH: Heinemann.

Gardner, H. (1993). *Frames of mind: The theory of multiple intelligences* (10th anniversary ed.). New York: Basic Books.

Jung, C. G. (1953/1979). *The collected works.* Princeton, NJ: Princeton University Press.

Kear, D. J., Coffman, G. A., McKenna, M. C., & Ambrosio, A. L. (2000). Measuring attitude toward writing: A new tool for teachers. *The Reading Teacher, 54,* 10–23.

Knudson, R. E. (1991). Development and use of a writing attitude survey in grades 4 and 8. *Psychological Reports, 68,* 807–816.

Knudson, R. E. (1992). Development and application of a writing attitude survey for grades 1 to 3. *Psychological Reports, 70,* 711–720.

Kreeft, J. (1984). Dialogue writing—Bridge from talk to essay writing. *Language Arts, 61,* 141–150.

Macon, J. M., Bewell, D., & Vogt, M. E. (1991). *Responses to literature, grades K–8.* Newark, DE: International Reading Association.

Macrorie, K. (1976). *Writing to read.* Rochelle Park, NJ: Hayden Books.

Macrorie, K. (1985). *Telling writing.* Portsmouth, NH: Boynton-Cook.

McConnell, S. (1992/93). Talking drawings: A strategy for assisting learners. *Journal of Reading, 36* (4), 260–269.

Michener, J. A. (2002). *Hawaii.* New York: Random House.

Minami, M., & McCabe, A. (1991). Haiku as a discourse regulation device: A stanza analysis of children's personal narratives. *Language in Society, 20,* 577–599.

Montaño-Harmon, M. R. (1991). Discourse features of written Mexican Spanish: Current research in contrastive rhetoric and its implications. *Hispania, 74,* 417–425.

Peyton, J. K., & Seyorum, M. (1989). The effect of teacher strategies on students' interactive writing: The case of dialogue journals. *Research in the Teaching of English, 23,* 310–334.

Scollon, R., & Scollon, S. (1981). *Narrative literacy and face in interethnic communication.* Norwood, NJ: Ablex.

Staton, J. (1980). Writing and counseling: Using a dialogue journal. *Language Arts, 57,* 514–518.

Staton, J. (1987). The power of responding in dialogue journals. In T. Fulwiler (Ed.), *The journal book* (pp. 47–63). Portsmouth, NH: Boynton-Cook.

Thoreau, H. D. (1971). Walden. In J. Lyndon Shanley (Ed.), *The Writings of Henry D. Thoreau: Walden.* Princeton, NJ: Princeton University Press.

Wilde, S. (1992). *You kan red this!: Spelling and punctuation for whole language classrooms, K–6.* Portsmouth, NH: Heinemann.

Wright Group. (1995). *Writing self-efficacy scale.* Adapted from Meadowbooks, (1994), Meadowbrook Press, Harcourt Brace & World.

Young, R. E., Becker, A. L., & Pike, K. L. (1970). *Rhetoric: Discovery and change.* New York: Harcourt Brace & World.

Children's References

Altman, S. (1995). *My worst day diary.* Bantam.

Axworthy, A. (1992). *Anni's India diary.* Whispering Coyote.

Benson, L. L. (1999). *Washington D.C.: A scrapbook.* Charlesbridge.

Blos, J. W. (1979). *A gathering of days: A New England girl's journal 1830–1832.* Aladdin.

Bunting, E. (1990). *The wall.* Clarion.

Carufel, D. (1998). The four seasons. *Cobblestone, 19,* 14–17.

Caseley, J. (1997). *Jorah's journal.* Greenfield.

Cleary, B. (1991). *Strider.* Morrow.

Donze, L., & Kessel, J. (1995). *Squanto and the first Thanksgiving.* Chronicle Books.

Emberley, E. (1979). *Ed Emberley's big green drawing book.* Little Brown.

Emberley, E. (1980). *Ed Emberley's big orange drawing book.* Little Brown.

Filipovic, Z. (1994). *Zlata's diary: A child's life in Sarajevo.* Viking.

Frank, A. (1952). *Diary of a young girl.* Modern Library.

Garrison, C. (1986). *The dream eater.* Aladdin.

James, B. (1990). *The dream stair.* Harper & Row.

Johnson, C. (1955). *Harold and the purple crayon.* Harper & Row.

Lasky, K. (1996). *A journey to the new world: The diary of Remember Patience Whipple.* Scholastic.

Levine, E. (1998). *If you lived with the Iroquois.* Scholastic.

MacGill-Callahan, S. (1991). *And still the turtle watched.* Puffin.

McCain, B. R. (1998). *Grandma's dreamcatcher.* Albert Whitmann.

McGovern, A. (1992a). *Swimming with sea lions and other adventures in the Galapagos Islands.* Scholastic.

McGovern, A. (1992b). *If you lived with the Sioux Indians.* Scholastic.

Miller, R. M., & Miller, L. P. (Eds.). (1995). *The book of American diaries.* Avon.

Moss, M. (1999a). *Ameila hits the road.* Pleasant Company.

Moss, M. (1999b). *Ameila's notebook.* Pleasant Company.

Moss, M. (1999c). *Ameila writes again.* Pleasant Company.

Moss, M. (1999d). *Emma's journal.* Harcourt Brace.

Naylor, P. R. (1973). *To walk the sky path.* Yearling.

Peet, B. (1989). *Bill Peet: An autobiography.* Houghton Mifflin.

Polacco, P. (1997). *Appelemando's dreams.* Paperstar.

Singer, M. (1995). *The Morgans' dream.* Henry Holt.

Van Allsburg, C. (1982). *Ben's dream.* Houghton Mifflin.

Zemach-Bersin, K. (1988). *The funny dream.* Greenwillow.

Media Resources

Ferrer, F., Ferro, R., Furé, M., Ibáñez, G. P., Pérez, D. M., Pérez, J. A., Sánchez, F., Teuntor, B. (1995). *Septeto Habanero: 75 Years Later.* [CD]. Corason, Mexico. Distributed by Rounder Records Corp. One Camp Street, Cambridge, Massachusetts.

CHAPTER 3

*"I shouldn't know you again if we did meet,"
Humpty Dumpty replied in a discontented tone,
giving her one of his fingers to shake. "You're so
exactly like other people."
"The face is what one goes by, generally," Alice
remarked in a thoughtful tone.
"That's just what I complain of," said Humpty
Dumpty. "Your face is the same as everybody
has—two eyes, so" (marking their places in the
air with his thumb), "nose in the middle, mouth
under. It's always the same. Now, if you had the
two eyes on the same side of the nose, for
instance—or the mouth at the top—that would
be some help."*

Personal Writing

JOURNAL WRITING

PERSONAL WRITING

STORY WRITING

POETRY WRITING

EXPOSITORY WRITING

PERSUASIVE WRITING

Humpty Dumpty makes an astute observation about being human: Individuals are, at once, both the same and different. In today's diverse classrooms, appreciating and valuing similarities and differences among individuals is an important educational goal. Teachers want students to take pride in their talents, abilities, beliefs, and experiences because, in accepting what is special about themselves, they are better able to understand and embrace uniqueness in others. When students are invited to freely express feelings, concerns, thoughts, and observations, a tapestry of diverse abilities and backgrounds emerges among the members of the class.

This interdependent relationship between the individual and social group is the driving force behind personal writing, expressive communication centered on student likes, dislikes, and experiences (Britton, Burgess, Martin, McLeod, & Rosen, 1975). Although the topics of personal writing generally focus on the self, the content is inherently **dialogical** because it reflects peer interests and communal concerns associated with relationships and nurturing human understanding (Cushner, McClelland, & Safford, 1992). When writers discover the characteristics, beliefs, and values of others, they gain a deeper knowledge of themselves in return. Personal writing is ideal for the beginning of the year because it validates what children already know (self and experience) and serves to acquaint them with class members and the teacher. Offering a broad array of choices for many situations and different individual learning styles, personal writing highlights genres that have relevancy and immediacy for children and that revolve around their intimate circle of family and friends. Some of the genres are listed in Figure 3–1. Many of the **forms** included are more public than journal writing. They require students to go beyond themselves as audience and recognize peers or other readers separated by time or distance. Because of greater audience demands, the writing is, understandably, relatively structured, and students are slowly nudged into the writing process to learn about rough drafts and revising.

Before presenting classroom vignettes on these tasks (name writing, *All About Me* books, friendly letters, personal narratives, memoirs, and biographies), the five components of the writer's workshop are considered, beginning with minilessons.

WRITER'S WORKSHOP

Minilessons

Although a full range of minilessons supporting content, strategies and skills, and procedures is available for children, two interrelated subjects of particular significance for personal writing are topic selection and voice. When students write on topics they care about, they will likely produce engaging text that others will want to read. Moreover, when they write about

FIGURE 3-1　Kinds of
Personal Writing

All About Me books	Memoirs
Anecdotes from experience	Name writing
Autobiography	Logos
Biography	Monograms
Family	Name plates
Friends	Pen pal letters
Pets	Personal journals
Dialogue journals	Personal narratives
Diaries	Photographs and captions
Greeting cards	Scrapbooks
Get well	
Sympathy	
Thank you	

TABLE 3-1　Notes on Student Interests

Name(s)	Student Interests
Reggie	Fishing, family and friends, pet dog Max, spending time with friends, church-related activity
Nicole	Family, going to the mall, cats, playing with best friend, riding her bike, fear of bugs
Hannah	Baby sister, going to Boston, pet hamster, reading for pleasure, watching Disney videos
Chris	Practicing the trumpet, playing in the school band, basketball
Jamey	Summer camp, scouting, swimming

what they know, in all probability the writing will be imbued with voice, which is the imprint of the self on writing (Graves, 1983c). Topic selection and voice are examined next.

Topic Selection

In classrooms where writing and sharing takes place on a daily basis, children seldom complain, "I don't have anything to write about." They continually identify topics in journals, share ideas with peers at the writing table, and respond to what they are reading and writing. If for any reason they can't think of a topic, the teacher may suggest one based on notes from conversations with them on the playground, in conferences, or in guided writing (see Table 3–1). If the record of a student's interests is lacking, a special attempt should be made to talk to and interact with the child.

Beyond observing and listening, the teacher models strategies for selecting a topic (following Graves, 1983c). She lists two or three potential subjects on the board and briefly describes each:

Topics and Explanations

My Favorite Doll: I have this old-fashioned doll that is very special. My mother gave it to me when I was a little girl, and her mother (my grandmother) gave it to her. The doll's tiny red lips and short, wavy hair remind me of a picture from the past. She still wears the original silk dress she came with. I don't let anyone play with her because she is very delicate and easily broken. The doll makes me think of my grandmother and the happy times I spent at her house.

Mystery Stories: I love to read mystery stories. When I was little, I read the entire Nancy Drew series. Now that I am older, I read books by P. D. James and Elizabeth Peters. In our class library, my favorites are the Encyclopedia Brown series (Sobol) and *The Westing Game* (Raskin, 1997). For me, there is nothing like a good mystery. I'd rather read than watch TV any day.

My Dogs: Many people don't realize the responsibilities of owning a pet. My two Westies are very demanding. Every day, they have to play and go for a walk. They also have to have baths and visit the vet regularly. Even so, there are many special reasons to own a pet. Maybe I will write about these.

After the teacher has revealed a little something about each topic, the children list and discuss two or three topics of their own. Sharing often inspires similar ideas in others, who may say, "Gee, that happened to me too!"

The next step is decision making. The teacher explains how she chose which topic to write about.

I've been thinking about my three possible topics. If I write about the doll, I will want to reminisce with my sister about all the things we did at Grandmother's. That would take some time. For now, I will save that topic in my folder for a future assignment.

As far as the mystery books are concerned, I'm not sure what to say. Sure, I like to read mysteries, but I wonder if there is a topic here?

When it comes to my dogs, I think I have lots to say, and, because many of my friends have pets, I might have an audience who would enjoy hearing about this topic.

As the think aloud illustrates, the teacher has decided to write about pets based on the amount of material she has and her knowledge of the audience. Other reasons for choosing one topic over another might include the following:

- Wanting to know more about a subject
- To express a happy moment
- Knowing a lot about a topic
- To tell someone about something

Children can reveal why they selected a particular topic, and the teacher can reinforce their choices. Elementary-age children typically write about some of the following subjects:

Family	Self
Friends (real and imaginary)	Traditions and customs (holidays)
	Pets (insects, birds, animals)
School	Play and magic
Relationships	Outside activities (weekends, after
Prejudices	school, hobbies, vacations, holidays)
Secrets and lies	Favorite things (subjects in
Hopes and dreams (including what I want to be)	school, sports, music, movies)
	"Firsts" (losing first tooth, first day at
Values and worldview	school, first surprise)
Likes and dislikes	Possessions (toys,
Popularity	books, video games)
Feelings	Computer games

By classroom standards, most of these subjects tend to be "safe" and reflect the status quo (Graves, 1983a; Gray-Schlegel & Gray-Schlegel, 1995–1996; Murphy & Dudley-Marling, 2001; Peterson, 2001). Considering gender, for instance, girls do not often write about armies and playing war, and boys do not often write about dolls or ballet. Personal and social concerns, such as divorce, AIDS, adoption, abuse, or gay lifestyles are also unlikely topics for students. However, if these topics surface, as they sometimes do, a good way to address them is in the context of book discussions. Rudman (1995) has gathered together a thematic collection of children's literature on some of these topics in a book, which includes a "try this" section that can be adapted for posing questions such as the following during writing.

- How does it feel to be adopted?
- How does the family change with the arrival of a new baby sister or brother?
- Where do you think elders should live?

Critical discussions that invite students to grapple with sensitive subjects that reflect the realities of their lives can pave the way for heartfelt and honest writing.

With rich experiences to draw on, children do not need "writing welfare," a term Graves (1976) associates with gimmicks and story starters used to help writers begin writing. Completing a story prompt such as, "The Martian stepped out of his spaceship and found . . . " is tantamount to completing a test prompt or fill-in-the-blank exercise. Any subject that a writer does not care about or consider worthwhile is bound to result in contrived writing. It is far better for writers to draw on personal sources for identifying topics. Locating these sources is discussed in the reading and prewriting sections.

Voice

Voice is part of a writer's identity; it is a way to speak out and be heard. Without voice, the student has little influence or authority. In personal writing, voice is revealed in the stance or attitude of a writer toward a subject ("This is what I think"). The words and sentences that writers use and the way they use them are intertwined with the events and experiences about which they care. Teachers often remark that they can identify a student's writing without ever looking at the name on the paper. Voice is the writer's presence in the text, its sound, tones, and other aural features, such as rhythm, pace, intonation, and emphasis.

To examine voice in the writing, teachers should look for features of both oral and written language because there is usually not a single voice, but multiple ones (Bakhtin, 1981).

- *Conversational voice* represents the way writers talk; it is a voice adopted for sharing with others.
- *Dramatic voice* projects the persona of a character in a particular role that a writer creates. This character may be an image of the writer or a purely invented one, as in fiction writing.
- *Audible voice* is embedded in the sounds and artistry of words that beg to be read aloud (as in poetry) or in the functional act of sounding out letters (as in spelling).

Children socially construct voice as part of development, assimilating the voices of others in their culture and developing a kind of speaking personality (Bakhtin, 1981). Observing them in spontaneous role-play reveals their intuitive understanding of voice as they adjust vocabulary, volume, and pitch to signal social roles (such as playing at being a doctor, mother, teacher, or baby) that exist in society (Corsaro, 1985).

To create voice in written language, young children label objects in pictures, add sound effects, or narrate action (Dyson, 1983, 1989). Verbal stories that report on pictures ("This is a girl") or dramatize the actions of drawings ("POW! WHAM!") frequently elaborate on or accompany the few marks that appear on paper. **Novice writers** may be overwhelmed by the task of putting words down on paper and may simply adopt a voiceless prose. Eventually, as they become more fluent, they will speak in a synthesis of voices appropriated as their own (Lakoff, 1982).

Voice seems like an elusive trait to teach; however, it is tied to the urge to express oneself and underlies the entire writing process (Graves, 1983c). An awareness of voice can be created using well-positioned questions and comments: "I like the way you put this in your own words" or "This sounds just like you" or "Show me a place in the writing that tells me you have written this?" Getting children into the habit of reading work aloud helps them appreciate and recognize the rhythms, vocabulary, and sentence structure of their own voice.

Although voice is typically discussed as something inherently natural for a writer, it can also be purposeful and selected. Writers invent new voices to add to their own, for example, the dialogue of fictional characters or the sounds and rhythms of poetry. Voice becomes "the frame of the window through which the information is seen" (Graves, 1983a, p. 228).

Because a discussion of voice is incomplete without consideration of how information is received, a fourth-grade teacher presents a small-group minilesson. "Voice and style," she states, "reflect choices writers make. It is their unique stance toward the subject and the way they reach out and connect with readers." She places several word cards on the board: *serious, objective, authoritative, conversational, formal, tense, friendly, engaging, reasoned, colorful, informal*. Students select the words they believe best describe the voice they hear in excerpts from three different books. The teacher reads the first excerpt from Dow (1990).

> This [the humpback] whale is the best known and most studied of all the large whales. Its distinctive flippers are very long—up to one-third of its body length. (Its genus name is *Megaptera*, which means "great wing.") The flippers are bumpy at the front edge. The shape of its dorsal fin is quite different from the fins of other rorquals (fin whales). (p. 20)

This text has varying effects on the students as readers. Some find the whale book *serious, authoritative,* and *reasoned;* others criticize it as boring. A few suggest that the author seems to know the subject matter because it is based on facts. The teacher reads the next passage from Patent (1989) using the same group of words to characterize voice.

> The humpback whale is a very big animal, even when it is a baby. When it's born, the young humpback, called a calf, is already 14 feet long and weighs as much as a large station wagon. By the time it's a year old, it is 30 feet long and weighs twice as much. (p. 5)

The students characterize this passage as a mixed combination of *serious, objective,* and *reasoned* writing but also *engaging* and *colorful*. One student comments on the author's objectivity in the use of numbers ("14 feet long"), whereas another remarks that the analogies or comparisons (e.g., *"weighs as much as a large station wagon"*) make the passage engaging.

Finally, the teacher reads a third excerpt from Tokuda & Hall (1986) with a contrasting style.

> Our story begins on a sunny day, far out at sea. A pod of humpback whales was traveling south together for the winter. Humpback whales are magnificent creatures that sing beautiful songs to each other underwater. (p. 1)

Students describe this voice as *friendly, informal, conversational, colorful,* and *engaging* because *story* is signaled immediately, and because images are evident in the colorful vocabulary (*sunny, magnificent*) and personification (*they sing and travel together*). This passage may be informative, but the voice is that of a storyteller, with the narrator's feelings peeking out from the facts.

Whether students succeed in sounding friendly or authoritative, colorful or serious, or a little of each, depends on their willingness to try out and refine the multiple voices at their disposal—those they've previously heard or assimilated from their culture (Bakhtin, 1981). What a paradox it must seem that although we are born with a unique voice, acquiring and mastering it in writing often take a lifetime.

Reading

Contemporary realistic fiction seems a natural companion to personal writing because its stories are consistent with the lives of real people, even though not necessarily true. A good reason for students to read realistic fiction, besides the fact that they love it, is to recognize characters who are similar to themselves or to find meaning in the unnamed feelings they share with the characters. Only in realistic fiction can students relive and resolve everyday problems without risk or reach conclusions about the consequences of certain behaviors in safe and reassuring settings (Manzo & Manzo, 1995). They consider how people react in particular circumstances; what are acceptable relationships; and how others cope with strong emotions such as anger, fear, or jealousy. In the stories they read a consistent message emerges: The making of literature is a human endeavor of self-expression and has the potential to inspire readers to reinvent experiences. This message leads readers to inspect their own lives and build bridges to writing.

Text-to-Life Interactions

During personal writing, a teacher should immerse children in realistic fiction and explicitly relate book experiences to their lives. Cochran-Smith (1984) calls this text-to-life interactions. To show how fiction imitates life, a fourth-grade teacher from Kentucky models her personal connection with a character who is called a "hillbilly" in the book *Appalachia* (Rylant, 1991).

> People sometimes make judgments about others based on where they live or form stereotypes from TV programs, such as *The Beverly Hillbillies,* or movies, such as *Ernest.* For instance, some people say I am a hillbilly because I talk with an accent and say *tahr* for *tire* or *y'all* for *you.* But my accent represents a special kind of English that others need to accept and appreciate.

By sharing her reactions to *Appalachia,* the teacher shows empathy and acceptance of people and, at the same time, demonstrates how books evoke personal meanings.

Teachers of young children use read alouds as occasions to do the same thing. For example, pausing near the end of *The Tale of Peter Rabbit* (Potter, 1902), a first-grade teacher asks children whether Peter's scolding was justified. They then discuss incidents in their own lives when they were disobedient.

Teacher: Peter Rabbit disobeyed his mother. Did you ever disobey? Do you think Peter's mother was fair in punishing him? Why or why not?

Student: I went past the stop sign on my bike when I wasn't sup'osed to.

Teacher: You did?

Student: No one saw me though.

Teacher: Your mother didn't find out?

Student: I told her.

Teacher: Did you get punished?

Student: No. She told me not to do it again. She doesn't want me to get hit by a car.

In this text-to-life interaction sequence, the student searches for personal meaning and relevance based on the book experience. As children discover glimpses of their lives in books, they are eager to share these stories through writing. Teachers will want to assemble text sets of realistic fiction for this and other purposes.

Diversity in Realistic Fiction

Making personal connections with books is essential but so is focusing on "the other," the world of diverse individuals beyond ourselves. In series books such as Beverly Cleary's Ramona or Phyllis Reynolds Naylor's Alice McKinley, readers follow the same fictional character across many incidents and situations to observe different aspects of the character's personality. Students come to understand human motivations and see that, like real people, characters often behave in predictable and governed ways.

Diversity among people with whom students come into daily contact, fill the pages of realistic fiction. They read about characters who face unique challenges such as the sixth-grade teacher who is a paraplegic in *The View From Saturday* (Konigsburg, 1996) or the two boys, one with a learning disability and the other with a birth defect, in *Freak the Mighty* (Philbrick, 1993). Characters who may appear outwardly different may share situations similar to those students themselves face. The literature on diversity presents a range of familiar predicaments but it often goes beyond what students may have experienced themselves. Putting students in touch with characters from different cultures broadens appreciation and understanding. For instance, in *Sami and the Time of the Troubles* (Heide & Gilliland, 1992), a 10-year-old Palestinian boy reveals how war is a daily fact of life in Beirut. Readers discover what normalcy means to him as he copes with missing school, retreating to the basement for safety, or cleaning up after rioters in the streets.

Life's lessons about diversity cut across many thought-provoking books that can be included in a personal writing unit: *self-image* (*ABC, I Like Me!*, Carlson, 1997; *Hatchet*, Paulsen, 1987; or *Far North*, Hobbs, 1996); *family* (*The Patchwork Quilt*, Flournoy, 1985; *Walk Two Moons*, Creech, 1994; or *Clouds for Dinner*, Perkins, 1997); *friendships* (*I Have a New Friend*, Allan-Meyer, 1995); *uniqueness* (*Brown Honey in Broomwheat Tea*, Thomas, 1993); *diversity* (*Bein' With You This Way*, Nikola-Lisa, 1994; or *Joey Pigza Loses Control*, Gantos, 2000); *social issues and popularity* (*Secret Friends*, Laird, 1999); and s*portsmanship* (*Close Call*, Strasser, 1999).

Authentic fiction mirrors real-life people and situations and shows students they are not alone. By sharing universal concerns such as moral problems, divorce, physical maturity, and special challenges, students develop personal insights that imbue their writing with the depth and sincerity that readers find gratifying and meaningful.

Realistic Fiction and Writing

If realistic fiction provides a space for students to learn about their own and others' lives, it also stimulates ideas and inspires writing. For example, a third-grade student lists all of the places she loves after reading *All the Places to Love* (MacLachlan, 1994) about a young boy who cherishes the beauty of the countryside once shared with his parents and grandparents. A second grader after losing a pet reads *The Tenth Good Thing About Barney* (Viorst, 1971) and writes 10 good things about her own pet.

Children not only write compositions inspired by books' themes but also may practice sentence structure and patterning through imitation writing, that is, substituting their own words for those of a skilled writer in rewriting a passage. For example, an excerpt from a popular children's book, *The Ballad of Lucy Whipple* (Cushman, 1996), prompts a reworking by a fifth-grade writer, Rebecca.

Cushman's Excerpt

I quickly settled into the work. From late morning to noon I'd read in the shade of a tree. At noon, I'd eat my biscuits and gravy. Early afternoon, yearning for the cool waters of spring, I'd stick my feet in the warm sticky mud of the creek and read some more. Late afternoon would find me running from bush to bush grabbing frantically at whatever berries I could reach. And at night I'd try and explain to Mama why berry picking was going so slow. (p. 80)

Rebecca's Rewrite

I quickly settled into the summer routine. From late morning to noon, I'd go to the mall with my friends. At noon, I'd stop for a cheeseburger. In the afternoon, yearning for something new, I'd try on clothes and listen to new CDs. Late afternoon would find me hanging out at the food court watching the people go by. And at night, I'd try to explain to Mama why my summer vacation was going so slow.

Part of what Rebecca is learning, as she flexibly tinkers with sentences, is the meaning of stylistic variation and narrative strategies. By rewriting and substituting words to alter a preexisting text, she is making the reading and writing connection and learning to associate her own experience with the one presented in the story, a text-to-life interaction.

Composing

Prewriting

The nature and amount of prewriting children do depends on the genre and purpose of the personal writing task. Letter writing probably requires less planning time than, say, a personal narrative. However, a biography about a family member or friend might involve far more prewriting than a personal narrative.

Children's particular learning styles also influence prewriting. Some may prefer extended prewriting time, whereas others may quickly begin drafting to discover ideas. Younger children's engaged prewriting time may fill only a fraction of the allocated time, whereas older students may require more than is available. It is a good idea to plan activities prior to drafting and revising for those who need additional preparation. Figure 3–2 lists some activities especially suited for finding and gathering ideas on a topic.

Notice that these activities represent various communicative options to accommodate children's preferred learning styles. For instance, role-playing offers a rehearsal for considering ordinary events and for developing interconnected ideas or schemas that may later be called on for composing (Bidwell, 1990). By stepping into another's shoes, children of all ages can demonstrate an idea or point of view through words, actions, and situations. Take, for example, how it might feel to be the new student in school. Here is the situation:

> You are a new student at the school. It is the first day and everyone has arrived. You hesitate. A classmate notices you are uncomfortable and tries to make you feel welcome. Show us this scene.

When children role-play a scene, they construct dialogue, actions, and interpretations that serve as springboards for drafting or revising. Short and condensed scenes scaffold the writing task, whereas visual props (pictures, cue cards, clothing) become the stimulus with which to map new words. Students can label and keep files of characters they role-play (the bully, the outsider, the jokester, the parent, the grocer, and so on) and incorporate these personalities into their narratives.

FIGURE 3-2
Prewriting Activities
for Personal Writing

Creating artwork
Collecting items
Working on hobbies
Playing sports
Taking trips
Pondering favorite things
Having hands-on experiences
Writing letters
Thinking about memories and emotions
Moving about
Listening to music
Observing
Reading books, greeting cards, or journals
Role-playing
Making scrapbooks, collecting memorabilia and photographs
Talking with a partner or friends

Ready-made scenes in powerful artwork, such as Mary Cassatt's depiction of mother–child relationships or the book cover art of *Family Pictures* (Lomas-Garza, 1990), can spur associations with writers' lives and inspire ideas for universal themes (Alexander & Day, 1991). The theme of caring, for instance, is visualized in Mary Cassatt's *Sleepy Baby* of a mother embracing her child, in Henry O. Tanner's *The Banjo Lesson* of a father teaching music to his son, in Pablo Picasso's *The Lovers* of two young adults in a romantic pose, and in Pierre-Auguste Renoir's *Woman With a Cat* of a woman caressing her pet (see Alexander & Day, 1991). Teachers can collect and discuss artworks based on the personal themes of sharing (*The Dancers* by George Segal), feelings and moods (*The Tragedy* by Pablo Picasso), or common family celebrations (*Peasant Wedding* by Pieter Brueghel).

Besides professional artworks students can create their own drawings on a storyboard, or grid, to frame a personal narrative. A third grader's drawings and sentences are shown in the **storyboard** in Figure 3–3. For the young child, the storyboard is a product in its own right; for older students it is the starting point or plan for further explorations.

Another visual prop for tapping into ideas is family photographs. These can be combined with personal items and memorabilia (baby shoes, photos, books) collected in a decorated container called a memory box. Students can work in pairs, interviewing one another about the items in the box and then write about one of the objects. At the end of the session, each student shares the written description with the class.

Along with drawings, objects, art, and drama, children benefit from a variety of informal writing situations, including brainstorming, journaling, idea mapping, and quickwrites. Posting charts of these potential sources of information and strategies reminds students of prior knowledge and helps them clarify purposes for reading or writing. The following ideas can stimulate memory and provide writing options when children get stuck.

- Reviewing journal entries
- Getting ideas from reading
- Completing an interest inventory
- Looking at old photographs and pictures
- Keeping a writer's notebook with quotes and sayings
- Listening to music
- Looking at pictures in a magazine
- Talking with others
- Interviewing a classmate
- Noting experiences of characters in books
- Drawing pictures
- Thinking quietly

Drafting

Adults know that writing down ideas is like no other form of communication. Unlike speech, which is impermanent and fleeting, or **inner speech** (talking to oneself), which tends to become repetitive and circular because of memory, written language pins thoughts down on paper and paves the way for analysis and problem solving.

Always consider having group lessons before children begin drafting independently so they have the support of others as they learn new skills and strategies. In shared writing, teachers can focus on a topic that is common to the peer group, for example, learning to ride a two-wheeler, losing a tooth, or attending slumber parties (McKenzie, 1985) (see Chapter 1). For instance, first graders dictate a story about the first day of school.

> You get up early to catch the bus and see your friends. When you get up you have to eat breakfast sometimes cause you won't be able to think cause your hungry. You have to remember your backpack and then you find your room. You see your new teacher.

FIGURE 3-3 Storyboard, *My Mother*, First Draft (Third Grader, Independent Writing)

Panel 1: Meet My Mother

Panel 2: Meet My Mother / Dedicated to Janice

Panel 3: She's as pretty as flowers. She weighs 128 lbs. and is 5ft. 8in. tall.

Panel 4: My mom's favorite food is lasagna.

Panel 5: Mom's hobby is talking.

Panel 6: I wish Mom would play games with me everyday.

Panel 7: I know Mom is really angry when she yells.

Panel 8: My mom likes to cook.

Panel 9: On Saturday, my mom sleeps

Panel 10: I think Mom looks funny when she gets up in the morning.

Panel 11: My mom's favorite outfit is her night gown.

Panel 12: My mom is happy when I don't make her mad.

Panel 13: In the good old days when Mom was little, she used to jump rope.

Panel 14: My mom is the best.

Panel 15: Thank you for being you.

Panel 16: The End

Because the teacher takes the dictation, temporarily eliminating the need for handwriting, students are free to construct meanings. Once a draft is created, students concentrate on reading and discussing it. First, they focus on meaning, then, on sentences and words.

- What is a good title for the story?
- How do you feel when you see your new friends? Can we add this?
- Look at these two sentences. How can we combine them?
- Can we substitute another word for "get up"?

Shared writing increases the amount of practice students receive in written language and promotes a safe and secure place for starting a new task. When children jointly construct texts, more ideas are generated and writing develops at a whole new level. If this collaboration continues at the writing table, where they are talking, sharing, supporting, and acting as audiences for one another, interdependence and supportive structures become part of the process. Now is a good time for teachers to observe writing process behaviors and examine the roles students play among group members.

Revising

Young writers can't wait for someone to read about their baseball game or new baby sister, and this enthusiasm conveys what writing is all about—making meaning and communication. Effective teachers listen carefully to these messages and meanings. They show children how to match intentions to words and ask questions that clear up what is vague or misunderstood. Far too often, children eagerly await the teacher's response to their writing only to hear that they have misspelled a word or need a capital letter. Placing value on correctness and dismissing the writer's message is not only hurtful to a child but also reinforces a distorted image of the meaning of writing. During revision, the teacher should provide thoughtful responses to what is written or engage in more prewriting to build text. This does not only apply to younger or inexperienced writers but to older and proficient authors as well. Their work deserves this same careful attention to content.

Young children seldom revise without teacher suggestion or guidance. At first they may see no reason to revise or believe that what they have written is unchangeable. With experience and support, they eventually accept revising as part of the process and explore its various purposes. These may include some of the following:

- Trying a new approach when an earlier one does not work
- Reorganizing the presentation of ideas
- Exploring further the feelings, ideas, or opinions in a previous draft
- Illustrating or developing main points with details
- Including information that a reader might need
- Clarifying ideas for a reader

A way to convince students about the need for revision is to involve them in writing circles where they become sensitive to an audience. Peers are quick to tell writers what they do not understand. As co-participants in constructing meaning, readers' expectations are essential to the decisions writers make about **style** and details (Flower, 1979). When students care about a reader making sense of their words, communication comes full circle. It is never too early to call attention to audience considerations by asking questions such as the following:

- What might readers want to know about this topic?
- What do readers already know about it?
- What will help readers understand this better?

In journals, diaries, and quickwrites, children write with "self as audience," but in personal writing the audience widens to include peers. When students write only for the teacher, they may simply try to please her rather than developing trusting and supportive relationships with others. With the increasing use of the Internet, electronic bulletin boards, and e-mail, today's students will likely communicate with broader and more diverse audiences than in the past.

Although the revision process unfolds differentially by age and maturity level, the children's products can be examined along several dimensions:

- Level of discourse changed (a word, a phrase, a sentence, the whole composition)
- Types of revision made (reordering, embedding, deleting, adding, substituting)
- Purposes for revising (cosmetic, mechanical, stylistic, informative, transitional)
- Rhetorical matters addressed (message, audience, purpose)

These observations anchor instruction and provide the necessary information for documenting the writer's growth in anecdotal records.

Editing

In editing, conventions are taught along with content and in response to learners' development and abilities. If personal narrative is the first type of public writing children attempt, it seems appropriate to plan short, **focus lessons** on constructing sentences. Young children observe how words combine with other words in particular orders to carry meaning. Using word builders (similar to the poetry word magnetics one can buy at a local bookstore), they put together sentences or copy favorite ones from books they are reading. With big books, children can predict words, hidden with Post-it notes, representing parts of speech (nouns, verbs, adjectives, adverbs, prepositions, conjunctions, and interjections). Several synonymous words *(run, race, dart, dash)* may be possible for making sense of the text, yet, all must fulfill the same speech function in the sentence: in this case, verbs. Older students can experiment with this procedure in their own writing, substituting different actions (verbs) and descriptors (adjectives) for an improved effect.

Teachers may spend 5 minutes before an editing session showing how categories of words can fill particular slots. *Sentence slotting*, substituting words in preset blanks, or slots, indirectly calls attention to parts of speech and word order, and more important, illustrates how words and sentences are flexible and subject to experimentation. Consider the following examples:

The _____ boy ran.   The boy _____.
silly   jumped
little   sang
clever   wrote

This process is applicable with children of all ages by substituting adjectives, verbs, and other parts of speech.

To call added attention to words, teachers introduce expressions that create informal, speechlike texts. **Idioms** fall into this category and are more habitual and customary than grammatical. For instance, a writer may use expressions such as "put up with" instead of "tolerate," or "neglect to say" instead of "ignore." Following are some common idioms.

Common Idioms

catch on	grow out of
chip in	hang on
clear up	hold up
cool off	make clear
dress up	make up
drop in	pay attention
dry up	stop off
figure out	take in
get back at	tie up
go over	work out

Humorous idioms and those that create mind pictures, such as "let the cat out of the bag" or "kick the bucket," are considered in further detail in Chapter 5 under verbal play.

Clipped words, shortened forms of preexisting morphemes, or meaning units also fit the category of speech-driven words. Consider these examples:

Clipped Form	Complete Form
Fan (sports fan)	Fanatic
Auto	Automobile
Bike	Bicycle
Phone	Telephone

Words commonly associated with everyday conversation, such as clipped forms and idioms, make good choices for displaying on the word wall.

Interpersonal expressions, such as *I think*, *it seems*, and *we should*, tend to occur in personal writing and acknowledge the writer's and reader's presence in the text (Johnson, 2001). Because these phrases are likely to appear in children's writing, it is a good idea to teach pronoun reference (ensuring that pronouns agree with their antecedents, or the words to which they are related). Young writers tend to liberally sprinkle pronouns, such as *he, she, it,* or *they,* throughout their writing, but they may neglect to identify these references for their readers. A simple question corrects this: *Who did what?*

Certain punctuation—apostrophes with possessives and contractions or exclamation marks—are likely to occur when children are writing about family, friends, or possessions. Here are some examples:

Possessives and apostrophes: Mary's jacket
Contractions and apostrophes: It's not there.
Exclamation marks: Boy, was I surprised!

A first-grade teacher may illustrate apostrophes in possessives by labeling objects around the room (first-graders' cubbies, Sally's book) or by sending the students on a scavenger hunt for contractions and possessives in stories they are reading, in newspapers, or in other forms of environmental print (billboards, yard signs, food labels). Should certain conventions arise in shared writing or in students' written work, teachers make a point of reinforcing their use and collecting them for examples in focused lessons.

Lesson objectives can start at the awareness level (labels around the room illustrating the apostrophe in possessives) and advance to more sophisticated levels such as looking for patterns in possessives using apostrophes, sorting them into two or three categories, and generating a rule governing their construction.

Rules

Use 's on singular and plural nouns not ending in s	Use s's on singular nouns that end in s	Use ' only on plural nouns that end in s

Examples

Teacher's grade book	Ross's toy	First-graders' cubbies
Children's desks	Boss's order	Students' library
Girl's bathroom	Jones's folder	Writers' portfolios

The focus of a lesson will change depending on the kind of personal writing children are doing. For instance, in letter writing, it is logical to explain the functional use of commas in addresses, salutations, and closings or to teach abbreviations such as *Mr., Mrs., St., Ave.,* or *P.O.* The conventions discussed so far may or may not appear in an individual's personal writing, but because the probability is fairly high that they might, it makes good sense to take advantage of teachable moments to present them in authentic contexts.

TABLE 3-2   High-Frequency Words

1. the	26. school	51. would	76. now
2. I	27. me	52. our	77. has
3. and	28. with	53. were	78. down
4. to	29. am	54. little	79. if
5. a	30. all	55. how	80. write
6. you	31. one	56. hers	81. after
7. we	32. so	57. do	82. play
8. in	33. your	58. about	83. came
9. it	34. got	59. from	84. put
10. of	35. there	60. her	85. two
11. is	36. went	61. them	86. house
12. was	37. not	62. as	87. us
13. have	38. at	63. his	88. because
14. my	39. like	64. mother	89. over
15. are	40. out	65. see	90. saw
16. he	41. go	66. friend	91. their
17. for	42. but	67. come	92. well
18. on	43. this	68. can	93. here
19. they	44. dear	69. day	94. by
20. that	45. some	70. good	95. just
21. had	46. then	71. what	96. make
22. she	47. going	72. said	97. back
23. very	48. up	73. him	98. an
24. will	49. time	74. home	99. could
25. when	50. get	75. did	100. or

Source: From Folger, S. The Case for a Basic Written Vocabulary, *The Elementary School Journal* 47,1 (1946).

When it comes to spelling, teachers ask what words children would like to know how to spell. The words they choose often include names of family members and friends, special events such as birthdays, or favorite objects and pets. Many years ago, Silvia Ashton-Warner (1963), author of the book *Teacher,* honored and celebrated children's requests for personal words when they dictated stories to her. She recorded the words they were especially fond of and incorporated them into reading lessons. In personal writing, highly individual, emotional, or cherished words are placed in the child's personal dictionary along with a few high-frequency words, those words that are most likely to appear repeatedly in their written work (*the, of, it, for, mom,* and others as in Table 3–2).

Several high-frequency word lists, compiled 50 or 60 years ago, still bear the names of the original researchers who cataloged them: Dolch, Fry, Horne, Rinsland, Kucer-Francis, Dale, Lyons & Carnahan. Whereas the Dolch words are popular for instant word recognition in reading, the Rinsland list, featured in an article by Folger (1946) and shown in Table 3–2, identifies keywords found in children's writing.

Memorizing or overlearning these words in combination with invented spellings develop automaticity. If children learn three or four at a time on an as-needed basis, they will eventually expand their written vocabularies. Students may place these words in personal **word banks**, pictionaries, or notebooks and refer to them repeatedly when they write. In some classrooms, words are copied on 5 × 7 flash cards for card games or for practice using the look–say method:

The student looks at the word, says it, and writes it.

Next, she looks at the word, says it, turns the card over, and spells it.

Finally a peer reads the word to her, and she writes it.

The cards are hole-punched and placed on a ring so the children can take them home to study. High-frequency words must be spelled correctly and are considered "no-excuse" words (Sitton, 1996). When it comes time to edit, writers must correct any no-excuse words before submitting their pieces. Spelling these words rapidly and easily facilitates immediate success.

Along with studying words through visual memory, students practice a technique called word sorting to examine sets of words with common characteristics. **Word sorts** can be done in many ways using many language skills. As previously discussed, sorting leads to discovering rules of punctuation or parts of speech. It also results in finding spelling patterns, such as structural elements (*repay, rework*), graphic representations of similar sounds (*bread, thread*), or words that follow predictable spelling rules (*make–making, take–taking*). Noticing patterns is one way people make sense and order of the world, and it is never too early to emphasize this pattern-seeking technique in reading and writing lessons (Jensen, 1996). Learners can create lists, add words to existing lists, inductively figure out rules, and then search in texts, magazines, and other print materials for other words that fit the pattern (Fresch & Wheaton, 1997).

Although editing should be addressed in most writing, teachers should limit the number of skills they present so that children are not overwhelmed or made to believe that the mechanics are more important than the meaning and content. Although all kinds of editing lessons are possible, the teacher must decide what to teach in depth, what to simply mention, and what to ignore. For instance, when a child runs out of space at the end of a line and has to break a word, the hyphen might be introduced, and the writer shown how to use it, but a full-fledged lesson on syllables and rules is unnecessary. With handwriting, however, legibility is important for audience participation, so several minilessons on letter formation might be a good idea. In the end, the lessons a teacher implements will depend on the child, the writing experience, previous instruction, and the goals of the curriculum.

Sharing

When children begin sharing what they think, feel, and dream, there is an intensity of spirit that must be honored. Personal topics, discussed in writing circles and the author's chair, require respect and support from others to establish a positive learning environment. Sharing is not difficult for young children. In fact, it is quite common to find them crowded around the teacher's desk or congregating on the playground vying for attention. Prepubescent children, however, sometimes find opening up to others risky. For them, revealing personal information is more an act of courage than a cause for celebration. Now is the time, if it has not already been done, to introduce the writing circle or author's chair and begin the process of community building. (Refer to Chapter 1 for a review of the basic steps in setting up procedures for the writing circle and author's chair.)

Peer Discussions

As in all sharing, the teacher is concerned with *what* children say (task talk) and *how* they say it (kinds of response). The first step in having a writing circle is to invite "grand conversations" so that the mutual concerns and interests of the peer group will emerge (see Chapter 1). Producing collective knowledge in group discussions promotes literate thinking and sets the groundwork for planning and revising. Membership and solidarity never stray far from the personal, and in writing circles, there is always a place for swapping stories in an atmosphere of affirmation and support. Children weave tales of their own lives with those of their peer group and, in the process, discover that they share a world of experience with one another. They talk about family traditions, common problems, the meaning of friendship, and many of the other topics outlined in the section on minilessons. In these conversational exchanges, students dare to question their own beliefs or established norms, to consider a new perspective, or to realize a common connection. Clearly, the intent is to offer a forum for student communication in the classroom. Meanwhile, the teacher is making moment-to-moment decisions about when to intervene and when to remain silent, how to redirect a group that gets bogged down or side-tracked, and when to allow the discussion to go on beyond the time limit because it benefits the group.

In addition to teaching students what to talk about, they need to be taught how to interact with others. Too often, "talk" is mistakenly taken for granted, believing it to be something that happens in the process of doing other things. This kind of thinking disregards the skills necessary to articulate and convey ideas to others and ignores the naturally occurring social setting in which these skills are best learned. A discussion of how to give advice to a writer begins with preserving the spirit of the writing circle and making a point of avoiding loaded words that send the wrong message about the activities that occur there. Using terms such as *constructive criticism* or *critiquing* carry negative connotations; they signal evaluation and disapproval. Writing circles are not about criticizing work, no matter how constructive it may be. They are about *receiving* a work, *supporting* a writer, *suggesting* changes, and *describing* texts. These words are not mere euphemisms; they accurately describe the purpose of the circles: to offer supportive advice and encouragement with a positive attitude that gradually seeps into the interactions. Of course, there is always the chance that when children are told to "say something nice" or preface remarks with **affirmations**, they will become conciliatory or reluctant to offer honest advice. As students learn to appreciate different viewpoints and become critical readers, they eventually strike a balance between compliments and constructive feedback. Teachers continue to set a good example and avoid the "musts" or "shoulds" that deprive the writer of ownership. Politeness formulas are often framed as follows:

- Perhaps you might try . . .
- This worked for me, maybe you want to try it.
- I get the impression that . . .
- As I understand you . . .
- Would it be reasonable to say it this way . . .
- Is the point you're making that . . .
- Are you implying that . . .
- I wonder if what you are saying could be put this way . . .
- Are you suggesting that . . .

With social matters under way, the teacher concentrates on developing reader response in the context of writing circles or the author's chair. The ultimate goal is to teach children to attend to the interests and life events of the writer, get to know her better, and create shared experiences and knowledge that will strengthen bonds and build a writing community. Because learning to listen attentively and moving beyond self-interest for the good of "the other" does not come naturally or easily, teachers continue to model various types of responses and language to assist and support writers (Freedman, 1987). In the next section, we consider a type of reader response that overlaps with personal and affective responses (introduced in Chapter 2).

Associative Responses

An associative response is one that connects writer, reader, and text. Readers may see the writer following a course of action similar to their own or they might find themselves relating to the writer's work, not because they have directly experienced the situation, but because they remember how a book character reacted. Making associations that reach across experiences and texts enables readers and writers to recognize commonalities and patterns of behavior; greater empathy and human understandings become possible. When offering an associative response, the teacher might say something like "I had an experience similar to yours" and then relate a little bit about the experience to show how it is similar or different. Another way of responding might be to say "Your situation sounds just like Ramona's predicament in the story we just read" and then explain how the situations are alike. To encourage associative responses during writing circles, the teacher asks children to think of a character or problem in a book that reminds them of the writer's story. This calls attention to the importance of bringing personal and previous text experiences to a written work.

While students are learning to respond to written work, the teacher takes notes on the kinds of responses they make. Soon, with questioning and encouragement, they develop more sophisticated reactions and gain wider repertoires of response styles.

As students attend and respond in meaningful ways, they simultaneously show courtesy and respect for others' ideas. A group can achieve no greater success than to have participants adopt a frame of mind that starts with the assumption that all comments are valuable, well intended, and supportive. When trust develops among classmates and they feel a sense of belonging to a community, they are more likely to receive and accept feedback from others.

Continuous Assessment

Teachers informally monitor student progress throughout the writing process, in writing circles and conferences, and in reviews of work portfolios. They rely primarily on observations and interactions with students, but also reflect on notes in anecdotal records or review assessment checklists or rubrics that guide their observations and reflections. No matter what form the assessment takes, the content focuses on one or more indicators within the four broad categories of writer, process, text, and context. Each category represents a piece of a bigger puzzle that unravels the mysteries of the writer and the writing. The assessment tools in this section offer teachers a way to explore an individual's uniqueness and personalize the curriculum. They provide students with a way to monitor ongoing growth and regulate their writing.

Writer

Several assessment tools are available for learning about the writers in the classroom. One especially suited for personal writing is the interest inventory. Interest inventories are instruments that tap into student interests, experiences, or habits in and out of school. Specific areas are represented through written questions for children to complete. For instance, students report *literacy interests* (favorite books, writing topics); *personal data* (a nickname, number of brothers and sisters, best friend); *school-related matters* (favorite subjects, homework, computer activities); or *general habits and lifestyles* (hobbies, TV shows, travel, pets). Data collected from this inventory allow teachers to match interests to minilesson topics, reading material, curricular themes, and learning center activities.

Interest inventories are a type of self-report and, therefore, rely exclusively on the willingness of the child to answer questions honestly and not say only what the teacher wants to hear. Knowing what children will voluntarily choose and engage in for its own sake can foster commitment and ownership in writing.

Another self-report useful in personal writing is the learning style inventory. Children respond to written questions indicating their preferences for grouping arrangements, environmental learning conditions, modes of learning (visual, auditory, linguistic or kinesthetic), and types and presentation of materials. There are many ways to discuss learning styles (Carbo, Dunn, & Dunn, 1986; Claxton & Ralston, 1978; Kagan, 1987); however, Gardner's (1993) multiple intelligences or learning habits is especially useful for examining the diversity and plurality of talents and the various communication channels that writers use to display competence and express themselves. The self-report in Figure 3–4 identifies personal learning styles: linguistic, musical, logical/mathematical, spatial, bodily/kinesthetic, interpersonal, and intrapersonal.

FIGURE 3-4 Multiple Learning Styles

Source: From *Multiple Intelligences in the Classroom* (p. 22), by T. Armstrong, 2000, Alexandria, VA: Association for Supervision and Curriculum Development. Copyright© 2000 by T. Armstrong. Adapted with permission.

Name _____ Grade_____

✓ I Like to . . .	YES	SOME-TIMES	NO
Talk with others			
Work crossword puzzles and play games like Scrabble or Password			
Draw and doodle			
Sing and listen to music			
Use my hands when I talk			
Spend free time outdoors			
Work in groups			
Work alone			
Keep a personal journal for my thoughts			
Play group sports			
Be the leader of a game			
Read books with lots of pictures			
Touch things to learn about them			
Create and read maps, graphs, and diagrams			
Play games on the computer			
Take pictures with my camera			
Work with my hands			
Explain things to others			
Watch TV and videos			
Do science experiments			
Dance and move around			
Read and write			
Learn foreign languages			
Set goals for myself			
Solve problems with numbers			

Responses can be categorized according to learner tendencies or habits: *talking with others* or *doing crossword puzzles* is linguistic, *singing* is musical, *solving number problems* is mathematical, *drawing* and *doodling* is spatial and bodily/kinesthetic, *working in groups* is interpersonal, and *working alone* is intrapersonal. Although a child may excel in one of these areas, it is likely that she will possess some degree of each. Teachers may add Gardner's eighth "intelligence": the naturalistic habit, which is sensitivity to one's environment using sensory input from nature. If teachers truly believe in the unique talents of individuals, they will construct activities that access the rich continuum of untapped resources used by creative people to perceive, interpret, and shape the world.

One of the best and most obvious ways to find out about children's literacy habits is to consider parent questionnaires or face-to-face interviews. Parents are an integral part of the assessment process, partners in the child's education, and participants in goal setting. At the beginning of the year, a first-grade teacher schedules parent–teacher conferences to find out each learner's literacy background and habits, interests, and concerns. A set of questions guides this initial interview (see Table 3–3).

During interviews, the focus of the conversation is on the child and teachers listen attentively for parental or guardian expectations. If parents are unable to attend a conference, the teacher mails a questionnaire that includes some of the interview items. If the parents or guardians do not speak English and if a questionnaire is not available in their native language, it may be necessary to translate the questionnaire into the native language or have older siblings in the family who do speak English convey the information. Parental or guardian involvement and interaction continues throughout the year. With each parent–teacher encounter, the conversation or questionnaires change to reflect the development of the child. Parental data brings another perspective to the work teachers are trying to accomplish with writers.

Talking with and listening to children on a daily basis is a primary source of data for teachers. In the natural day-to-day interactions and activity of the classroom, teachers note transactions during writing conferences and in the informal conversations at the writing table; they observe the activities children select at learning centers or the types of books they read in free time. With glimpses into the literacy behaviors and beliefs of their learners, teachers summarize the characteristics, capabilities, **dispositions,** and behaviors of class members and use these profiles to develop activities and procedures that maximize children's strengths.

Process and Text

Observing the writing process is an essential part of assessing personal writing. Each day a few minutes should be reserved for standing quietly nearby or at the writing table and observing the writing process. Because the writer's thinking or motivations are not readily visible, the teacher may bend down next to a writer and ask questions: "What had you thought to do next? Why did you change that?" With young children, teachers will want to examine self-talk, play, drawings, social interaction, or any other activity that invests the child's work with elaborate meanings not evident in print. Keep in mind that individual composing behaviors are often seen as increased time spent on the process, a broadened range of strategies, an increased control over one's thinking, or greater variability in intentions and focus at a particular moment, on a particular assignment, in a particular context (Graves, 1983c; Nystrand, 1982).

Just as teachers consider all the possible process behaviors for prewriting, drafting, revising, and editing, they also look more specifically at how children are coming to know themselves as learners and how they are regulating their learning. Noticing whether children are beginning to *self-monitor* is an integral part of observing the process. Writing is a problem-solving activity and students must recognize a problem

TABLE 3-3   Questions for Parent-Teacher Interviews

Name _____   Date _____

Sample Questions	Comments
Does your child know how to print/write at the present time?	
Does your child write at home? If so, what does s/he write (e.g., signs greeting cards, notes, letters, diary entries, homework assignments)?	
At what age did your child first show an interest in learning to write? What motivated this interest?	
If your child writes at home, how many minutes per day would you say s/he writes?	
Does your child like to read his/her writing to you or other family members?	
At home, does your child see adults write? If so, what? How often?	
Who at home helps your child with his/her writing or schoolwork?	
Does your child like to draw?	
Does your child have access to a computer?	
What kinds of reading materials are available to your child?	
Does your child enjoy being read to by family members?	
Does your child have a sibling or friend that s/he writes with?	
Is your child a member of the library? How frequently does s/he borrow books?	
What kinds of writing materials can be found in your home (e.g., a chalkboard, tablets, pencils, Magic Markers, crayons)?	
What do you think your child's greatest strength in writing is?	
What writing skills do you think need improvement?	
Does your child worry about spelling correctly?	
Does your child frequently ask for help with spelling?	
Is your child curious or interested in words?	
Is your child right handed or left handed?	
What words would you say best describe your child (e.g., persistent, curious, perfectionist, competitive, etc.)?	

before they can solve it. Can they identify what they know or need to know? Are they aware of what is difficult for them or easy? Can they recognize when learning is occurring? Do they understand that goals affect their writing? Do they know that they can seek and profit from the responses of others? Although rubrics may direct the self-monitoring process, students must also look for signals of when they are stuck or have writer's block, when and if they are taking risks, which resources they require to complete a task, or what counts as quality writing and a job well done. Knowing how to monitor this knowledge and set of behaviors is part and parcel of becoming an expert writer. Over time, children learn to examine strengths and weaknesses within the many variables at work during a writing event.

How children control and manage this learning is part of *self-regulation* or the deliberate use of strategies that afford solutions to the problems they identify. Do children know what strategies they can employ to construct meaning through written language, to correct a confusing passage, or to reorganize a message? Self-regulation is associated with having a metalanguage to talk about and adapt behaviors to different writing demands. As children become more aware of themselves as writers, they learn when, where, and how to use certain strategies to influence their writing. If a child knows that she always has difficulty organizing ideas, she might select an outline or graphic organizer to plan ahead. Or if the student knows that she writes very slowly and forgets ideas, she might use a tape recorder to help her remember ideas. Self-questioning, note taking, or getting assistance (talk with partner, ask for help) become available options in strategic learning. The act of self-regulating will develop slowly at first, but if teachers bring an awareness of this process to students, they will learn to recognize what they need to learn.

Along with observing the process and learning about the writer, teachers catalog and analyze the work products. Samples at each stage of the writing process are represented in the writing portfolio to provide a broad view of children's competence. Dated drafts, revisions, prewritings, reading and writing logs, and other informal writings are solid evidence of students' efforts in learning to write.

Certainly, the amount of work produced will be immediately evident. Some children's folders will bulge with writing, whereas others will be almost empty. What is or is not represented in the portfolio is worth noting. Do the children revise many of their works or only edit? How much prewriting and planning is done before a writing task? What form does prewriting and revising take? It is also helpful to add anecdotal records to the portfolio to explain the process. Students can write a two- or three-sentence reflection on a Post-it note and attach it to the front of the portfolio to bring their perspective to the work.

After scanning the portfolios for basic information, teachers examine and describe products against a backdrop of standards or developmental benchmarks, such as the stages of drawing and symbolic meaning (Gardner, 1980; Kellogg, 1969) or invented spelling (Gentry, 1981; Read, 1975; Wilde, 1992) (see Chapter 2). Completed *texts* can also be evaluated against the six traits for personal writing.

Keep in mind that the various types of personal writing—friendly letters, autobiographies, or memoirs, for example—will include not only features in Figure 3–5 but also unique descriptions of their own. Also remember that personal forms of writing, such as friendly letters, should not be evaluated, but rather self-checked or read by a peer editor. Any assessment tool must continually be reworked to account for the assignment, the type of writing, and, of course, the child's development.

To assess development and long-term progress, review student and teacher records at regular intervals; individual growth in writing often progresses sporadically rather than steadily. Children sometimes move forward on one assignment and then, suddenly, backward in the next. Such occurrences are frequent and to be expected. According to Graves (1983c), children's focus of attention, or "center of gravity" as he calls it, often diverts efforts from recently acquired skills to something new. Once this

FIGURE 3-5 Six Trait Descriptions for Personal Writing

Ideas
- ➤ States what is thought and felt
- ➤ Demonstrates unity of subject and purpose
- ➤ Shows the main events of an experience
- ➤ Presents sufficient information to develop a personal topic or theme
- ➤ Increases enjoyment through pictures or drawings

Organization
- ➤ Sequences events for understanding or according to a discernible plan
- ➤ Includes transitional elements that link paragraphs
- ➤ Orders ideas to build a main point

Voice
- ➤ Uses first-person point of view
- ➤ Reveals ideas through natural speech
- ➤ Considers audience

Sentence Fluency
- ➤ Develops ideas that flow from sentence to sentence
- ➤ Observes clarity of pronoun references for coherence
- ➤ Displays sentences that are concisely worded, but vary in length and pattern
- ➤ Expresses complete sentences (except where fragments provide special effects)

Word Choice
- ➤ Uses words accurately and consistently (may include informal expressions and slang)
- ➤ Conveys ideas through common idioms or conversational style
- ➤ Enhances explanations with occasional fresh figures of speech
- ➤ Employs precise nouns and verbs

Conventions
- ➤ Observes conventions of usage
- ➤ Incorporates periods, question marks, or exclamation points appropriately at the ends of sentences
- ➤ Includes apostrophes for possessives or contractions
- ➤ Uses standard and invented spellings
- ➤ Demonstrates legible handwriting

concentration becomes marginal, their strengths reemerge along with their new learning. The challenge is to capture and trace the changes in long-term development. The checklist by Sulzby in Chapter 1 is a good source for monitoring young children's efforts. It includes, among other things, the following:

- Development of concepts of print. (Do the children have a concept of directionality, basic writing conventions, print features, and spatial dimensions?)
- The role of drawing in writing.
- The functions that oral language plays in writing.
- The child's knowledge of words and spelling.

The observation guide developed by Graves (1983b) might also be useful in analyzing primary-age writing knowledge, process strategies, text development, and conventions. This guide, shown in Table 3–4, provides questions concerning changes in student writing. An accompanying discussion outlines research-based expectations in the child's natural evolution as a writer and examples of dated anecdotal entries that teachers might write.

Because progress is not fixed or predetermined, teachers must be open-minded and consider writing across diverse topics, with different purposes and audiences, under various conditions, and with varying types of instruction. Knowing the features of personal writing provides guidance.

TABLE 3-4   Developmental Observation for Composing

Questions	Discussion	Beginning of School Year	At Midyear
How does precomposing change with the young writer?	At first precomposing is visible with immediate rehearsal through drawing, building, or painting. It immediately precedes composing. Later, the child represents the message directly after writing. Next the child rehearses through experiences quite distant from the writing itself. The child merely picks up the pen and writes.	Child draws and does very little printing	Child writes longer messages; drawing continues
How does the proofreading unit change?	Children proofread at the word-unit level at first, then to the phrase. The child may proofread directly after writing or in another draft on the next day.	Child does not proofread	Child proofreads at the end of writing
How does language accompanying the writing process change?	At first children need to hear what they mean through overt expression at the time of composing. That is, you can hear what the child is going to write before he or she writes it. As the child's thinking is internalized, overt language diminishes, fades to a murmur, and disappears altogether. Under stress it may reappear.	Child sounds out words and uses many language functions to express what is written	Child uses some subvocalizing but for functions of expanding the text
How does the child's use of resources change?	At first children seem to use what is nearby. At the same time their use of resources is limited by the types of problems solved as well as their concept of the writing process itself.	Child asks tablemates for information	Child asks tablemates; uses pictionary
How do the child's rereading habits change during composing?	At first children reread constantly because their struggle is so great at the word-unit level. A struggle with spelling obliterates the actual message and the child must reread. As motor and spelling problems recede, rereading decreases.	Child cannot reread invented spelling	Child can reread work
How does the child's advance concept of ideas change?	Children who compose with unrelated ideas or action–reaction couplets have little advance understanding of what will happen next in their writing. As overt language disappears, they have a greater understanding of what will follow.	Child writes heaps or strings of information	Child has more developed sense of form for personal narratives
How does redrafting start and change in a child's writing?	Proofreading or the beginnings of redrafting come at the word-unit level. A child will be dissatisfied with a spelling; a title or a sentence may be added. Because motor demands are so great in the beginning, editing or redrafting is rare, unless taught. Redrafting is closely connected with changes in audience concept and the child's understanding of the writing process.	Child does not redraft	Child will redraft after sharing with peers

(continued)

TABLE 3-4 (continued)

Questions	Discussion	Beginning of School Year	At Midyear
How does the child's composing in several media forms change?	Many of the problems children solve in one media appear in another. For example, if ideas appear in action–reaction type couplets in drawing and drama, the same will be seen in writing. Later content develops over three to four sentences. When there is a change in the content of one media form, it can be anticipated in another.	Child uses ideas from one media to the next	No change
How does the child's concept of composing change?	A child's concept of the writing process is usually confirmed in the behaviors exhibited during the process itself. At first the child only mentions the mechanical aspects of writing, then spelling, and later organization.	Child verbalizes during writing to elaborate on limited texts	Child writes more words and longer texts
How does the child's concept of audience change?	A child's concept of audience begins with an awareness of what will happen to the paper when it is finished. This grows to include who will read the paper. Finally, the details of different persons' reactions can be recalled.	Child writes for self; no context	Child moves toward awareness of audience
How does the child's concept of a good paper change?	A child's first concept of a good paper is the drawing or the topic. Gradually affective judgments become more specific. Then the child may relate the motor components, neatness, spacing, and spelling to good writing. Later the child considers message quality for good writing.	Child believes topic is what makes good writing	Child believes topic and spelling make good writing
How does a child's use of mechanics change?	At first words and sentences may run together with little marking of meaning units. As audience sense grows, markers appear.	Child places periods after each word	Child places periods after each sentence

Source: Adapted from *A Two-Year Case Study Observing the Development of Primary Children's Composing, Spelling, and Motor Behaviors During the Writing Process.* An unpublished paper by Donald Graves. Copyright by Donald Graves. Used by permission of the author.

Context

The context influences the writer's growth and the product the child writes. Consider some of the following questions:

- Is the product a reflection of guided, shared, interactive, or independent writing?
- Was the product copied from a model or is it original?
- Did the writer have adequate time for the task?
- Did the writer receive feedback in conferences and writing circles?

When making decisions about grouping arrangements, remember that there are times during the day when individual boundaries should be observed, when writers should work alone to build self-confidence and realize their creative potential. There are also times when students need to share their work with peers, co-author a piece with a trusted friend, or work on a cooperative project. It is also a good idea to make anecdotal

TABLE 3-5   Writing Work Habits Checklist

	3/26/03	4/26/03
Is the student focused on writing about experiences?		
Does the student make meaningful contributions to others?		
Does the student show resourcefulness in solving problems?		
Does the student fill allocated time with drawing, writing, or talking?		
Does the student consult resources during writing?		
Is the student flexible and willing to change direction?		
Does the student take turns talking and listening?		
Does the student respect others' space and materials?		
Does the student clean up work areas after each project?		

notes about social behaviors that are developing during personal writing—the roles that students play during the process, including their abilities to negotiate, compromise, or motivate other group members, and the friendships and alliances they have with one another. Do not forget to consider the role of oral language in facilitating writing in the first and second grade because it is integral to getting words on paper and expanding and embellishing the message (Dyson, 1983).

Another not-to-be-forgotten aspect of context involves monitoring the work habits of students. This is especially worth noting because one of the goals of personal writing instruction should include preparing students to become responsible members of a writing community. The work habits checklist (see Table 3–5). documents students' ability to work with others, respect others' space, and take pride in their workplace. If children are always out of their seats, sharpening pencils, making noise, disrupting others, or otherwise not abiding by ordinary obligations, it is likely that engaged writing time will be compromised. Good classroom management is crucial to creating learning environments that are safe and offer a sense of emotional security for all members. Productive work habits and individual accountability go hand in hand.

CLASSROOM VIGNETTES: PERSONAL WRITING IN ACTION

As mentioned in the introduction, personal writing revolves around individuals and their families, friends, and close acquaintances. In the classroom vignettes you can explore possible tasks suited for this purpose and modified for any age—from writing one's name to writing a memoir. For instance, narratives of people's lives are found in all three classrooms but in different forms—names and All About Me books in first grade, friendly letters and personal narratives in third grade, and memoirs and biographies in fifth grade.

Grade 1

Names

One's name is the single most important word a person ever learns—it sets an individual apart, it proclaims "I am," and it symbolizes an identity (DeWitt, 1999).

Vivian initiates name writing as an entry to personal writing and reads the book *Chrysanthemum* (Henkes, 1991), which is the story of a mouse who is teased about her name but, with the support and advice of friends, learns to accept and appreciate it. Following the reading, she asks, "Who named you? Where did you get your name? Are you named after anyone? Do you have a nickname? Does your name have any special meaning? If you could pick any name you wanted, what would it be?"

Pausing for a moment to signal a shift in direction, Vivian says, "I am Vivian and I am vivacious." Then she leads the children in a game in which they describe something about themselves, using a word that begins with the first letter of their name: "I'm Tina and I like tea." When each student has had a turn, they watch Vivian write her name on the board and draw a ribbon of seashells between the letters to show a love of the beach. Then she makes the *V* look like a seagull, the *i*'s like beach umbrellas, the *a* like an octopus, and the *n* like waves. When the last letter is drawn she asks the children to brainstorm ideas about favorite objects or interests, so they can make drawings and decorations out of the letters of their names. As they finish their work, Vivian collects the papers and copies each one on plain white stationery to make personalized letterheads (Moffett & Wagner, 1992). The students' pleasure in seeing their names as letterheads on personal stationery is both thrilling and rewarding. For some examples of illustrated children's names, see Figure 3–6.

On another day, Vivian reads *Silver Seeds: A Book of Nature Poems* (Paolilli & Brewer, 2001) to share examples of acrostics, a set of vertically arranged letters that form a word. Vivian uses the letters of her name to show how it is done.

V ivacious

I nstructor

V eteran teacher

I ndependent

A rtist

N aps a lot

She says that certain letters of the alphabet, such as the *V* in her name, are difficult to find words for, so she copies some "V" words from a dictionary and circles the ones she thinks describe her best.

Vain (conceited)	Valiant (brave)	Variable (changeable, fickle)	Venturesome (bold, daring)
Versatile (many–sided)	Veracious (truthful)	Veteran (master)	Vibrant (full of energy)
Vigorous (full of physical energy)	Vigilant (alert and attentive)	Virtuoso (skilled in a fine art)	Vivacious (lively)

Vivian calls this her *bio* poem (short for autobiography), and the children follow her lead. Some work in pairs to interview each other, whereas others use the **pictionary** at each table to look up words for the letters of their name. With emergent writers, Vivian makes lists of words using letters of their names, as she did with her own, and they circle the words to copy.

Vivian interviews Alexander, writing down sentences as he talks, displaying them in front of him, and asking him to find letters in his name. Then she orders the sentences in a sequence that reveals his name (see Figure 3–7, p. 136). This acrostic illustrates the fact that letters in his name do not have to appear in initial positions but can be found in the middle or even at the end of a word.

FIGURE 3-6

Letterhead for Lindsey, Final Draft (First Grader, Guided Writing); John, Final Draft (First Grader, Guided Writing); Joshua, Final Draft (First Grader, Guided Writing); and Julio, Final Draft (First Grader, Guided Writing)

Some children, such as Melissa, write random words that begin with the letters of their names but don't necessarily describe them. (See Figure 3–8.) Vivian explains that these are also poems. The adjectives and action words become the poem's content, and its distinct shape or organization comes from writing each letter of the name vertically.

As a follow-up to the acrostics and as part of the personal writing project, Vivian introduces the *I Am* poem, in which a self-image portrait is cast in words. She writes: "I am a teacher. I enjoy racketball. I wonder about my students. I hear laughter." Before the children begin writing, Vivian reads autobiographical poetry from *A Jar of Tiny Stars: Poems by NCTE Award-Winning Poets* (Cullinan, 1996). She moves around the room during guided writing, assisting learners as they brainstorm and reflect on descriptions of themselves—physical traits, feelings and emotions, gifts and talents, special knowledge, or other personal characteristics. If they brainstorm five or six ideas

FIGURE 3-7
Alexander's *Bio* Poem,
Final Draft (First
Grader, Dictated to
Teacher)

My Name Poem

I look like **A** clown.

I **L** ook funny.

I don't lik **e** to take baths, but

I love my t-re **X** toy.

I h **a** ve money in my bedroom, but

I don't rob ba **n** ks.

My friend **D** avid jumps off the swing.

A comput **e** r is in my room.

Alexande **r** is my name.

FIGURE 3-8
Melissa's *Name* Poem,
First Draft (First
Grader, Guided
Writing)

Miss Melissa
Excellent
Lion
Intelligent
Safe
Spanish
Artist

FIGURE 3-9 Nicky's *I Am* Poem, First Draft (First Grader, Independent Writing)

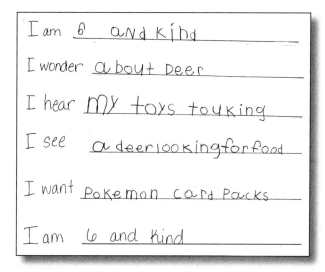

I am 6 and kind

I wonder about Deer

I hear my toys touking

I see a deer looking for food

I want Pokemon card packs

I am 6 and Kind

about themselves (this may include pictures), they will have enough to get started. With a reluctant writer named Nicky, Vivian scaffolds the *I Am* poem by writing the first part (subject and verb) of six sentences for Nicky to complete (see Figure 3–9). Interests and preferences begin to surface and Vivian scribbles some notes about Nicky in a chart of student interests similar to the one in Table 3–1. Beginning the year with personal writing yields a great deal of information about the students and their basic literacy skills. Name writing, in particular, plays a role in expressing self-identity and in creating a basis for further learning in writing (Bloodgood, 1999; Garton & Pratt, 1998).

However, name writing is not only for young children. In the upper grades, teachers can explore topics such as multicultural and ethnic names, cross-gender names (e.g., Terry), surnames, eponyms, occupational names (e.g., football teams), aliases, family names, literary names, nicknames, street names, biblical names, royal names, or pseudonyms. Besides investigating the origins and sociocultural reasons for naming, children discover that to name is one of the fundamental functions of words.

All About Me Books

All About Me books are autobiographies written by young children to express a full range of experiences and personal characteristics. Each page tells about one aspect of the child's life or one important thing about her. To introduce the lesson, Vivian gathers the children around the rocking chair for an oral retelling of *If a Bus Could Talk: The Story of Rosa Parks* (Ringgold, 1999), the story of Rosa Parks's life from her birth in Tuskegee, Alabama, to her current-day place in American history. Role-playing the talking bus and showing the bold and colorful pictures of Faith Ringgold's art, Vivian paraphrases the narrative and intersperses questions that relate aspects of the text to common feelings that all people share.

- Has anyone ever treated you as though you were different? Tell me about it.
- What do you think about white and black children having to go to different schools, swim in different pools, and eat at different restaurants?
- Why is Rosa Parks so special? What makes someone courageous?
- How did the world celebrate Rosa Parks's actions? How would you like to be remembered?

The children talk among themselves and voice opinions, sharing and learning. When they go back to their seats, Vivian distributes a me web, and everyone fills in the graphic organizer with favorite foods, songs, games, movies, hobbies, sports, and prized possessions. For an example of a me web, see Figure 3–10.

FIGURE 3-10
Michele's Me Web
(First Grader)

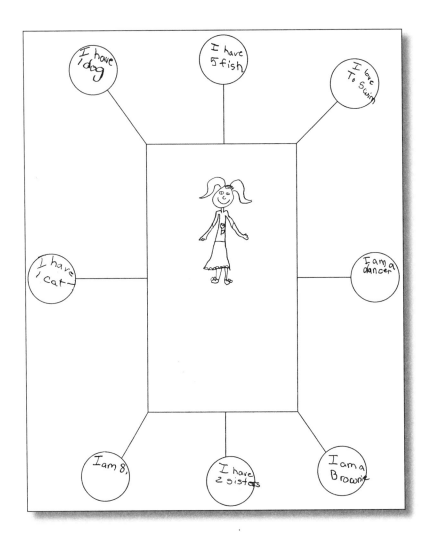

Vivian walks around the room, stopping at desks to ask questions that help generate ideas to complete the webs.

- What do you like to do on Saturday?
- Do you like to watch TV?
- Do you have a pet?
- Do you have a hobby? Collect things? If you do, what have you made or collected?
- What is your favorite sport?
- What games do you like best?
- Do you like to go to the movies? What movies are your favorites?

She may add a few questions that relate the children's lives to the story of Rosa Parks.

- Did you ever do something nice for someone? What was it?
- Did you ever do something that took courage? What was it? How did you show courage?
- Did you ever hurt someone's feelings? What did you do? How did you make up for it?

With plenty of ideas on their webs, the children are ready to write. Vivian provides sheets of 8 ½ × 11 construction paper with lined notebook pages glued to the bottom half. She models how to use each ray of the brainstorming web to complete

FIGURE 3-11 Jonathan's *All About Me* Narrative, Final Draft (First Grader, Guided Writing)

legos. I built a gigantic lego town. One thing is that I play I am an astronut in the lego town. I also play soccer very good at it. Last season I scored 15 goals.

One thing is that I play legos. I built a gigantic lego town. I am an astronaut in the lego town. I also play soccer very good at it. Last season I scored 15 goals.

different pages. Children write sentences on the notebook paper, and then, using crayons and Magic Markers, they draw pictures in the upper half. Jonathan sketches a picture of himself and shares his favorite hobby (Legos®) and sport (soccer), see Figure 3–11. Each topic on his web is used to complete the pages of the book. To expand on topics, some students stop periodically to get ideas from whomever is sharing at the author's chair. During drafting, the children check spelling against high-frequency word lists, personal spelling dictionaries, and words posted on the word wall. Invented spellings are acceptable. When finished, they organize the pages in an order that makes sense to them and get ready to decorate the front of the booklet. Vivian plans something special for the cover: a collage, or life mural. To begin, she gathers magazines, a box of scissors, glue sticks, and 8 ½ × 11-inch covers made of card stock. The writers thumb through the magazines and cut out pictures that represent things they like, dislike, wish they had, want to do, or find fascinating. Meaningful nouns and adjectives in print advertisements are superimposed on the pictures. When everything is suitably arranged they mount their items on the card stock. At the author's chair they share their collage covers and explain the significance of the words and pictures they have selected.

That same week, they work on "About the Author" pages. Each child brings in a personal or family photograph (some may include friends, relatives, or pets) and shares a little about herself (for example, who is in the picture and where and when it was taken). The photo is glued to the back inside page of the *All About Me* book and under it is written the student's name, age, number of brothers and sisters, and family name.

One last writing task completes the book. On the back will be a lifeline. Vivian models how this is done, using her own life events and making certain to include milestones that children can relate to: a birthday, meeting a special friend, the first day of school, a special book, a pet's birthday, and so on. Students follow her lead by drafting events on sentence strips and physically arranging them in chronological sequence. Then they use rulers to draw the lifelines on the back covers of their

FIGURE 3-12   Lifeline (Third Grader)

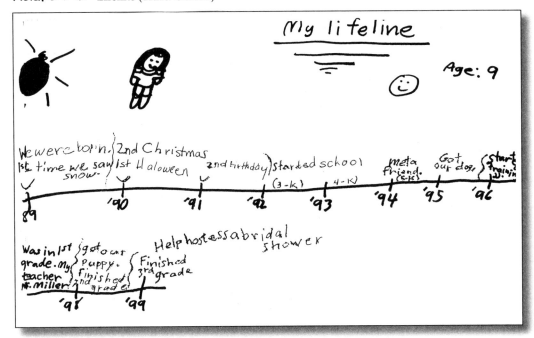

books, marking the line from left to right (using dots or carets), and copying their life events. While they are working, Vivian shares a third-grade lifeline with them so that they can see how it stretches and grows with age and experiences (see Figure 3–12). The lifeline completes the assignment, and all of the pages are bundled together to make the *All About Me* book. Vivian punches two holes on the left edges of the papers, and the children thread them with yarn. The *All About Me* book demonstrates how writing tasks are linked together to present personal information in different ways. For instance, the organization for all three tasks vary: The *All About Me* text is topical; the lifeline is sequential; and the collage is free association. From the child's perspective, the best part is becoming an author and watching the book grow in size. They take pride and pleasure when their books are placed in the classroom library.

Grade 3

Friendly Letters

Two third-grade girls approach Kate and ask if they can write a get-well note to their friend who is absent from school. They are directed to the worktable (a writing center) where there are boxes filled with paper, envelopes, a phone book, postcards, and greeting cards in a variety of sizes and shapes. The girls sit at the table chatting about the message they will convey. One child writes while the other dictates. They take turns drawing pictures before signing their names and placing the note in their friend's mailbox. The mailboxes, cubicles made from a cardboard box with dividers, line the back wall of the room. Class members correspond with one another all year, especially on holidays or special occasions. They write get-well messages to teachers and friends, invitations to birthday parties and special events, or thank-you notes for a thoughtful act of kindness. Figure 3–13 shows a letter from Tirzah thanking her classmate, Jeffrey, for an invitation to a flower show. As can be seen from Tirzah's

FIGURE 3-13
Tirzah's Friendly Note
(Third Grader)

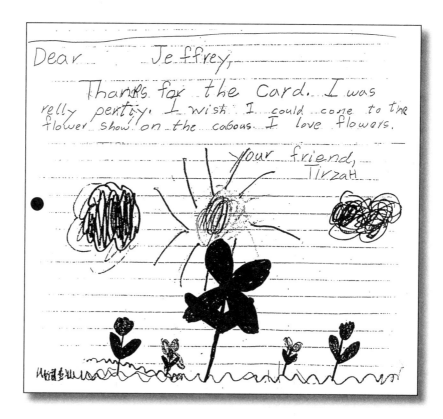

friendly note, she thanks Jeffrey for the card, which, she says, is *really pretty*, then writes a polite reply, stating her regrets about being unable to attend the flower show. She wishes she could go because she loves flowers. The decorative lower border appeals to the eye and enhances the message by bringing the text and artwork together.

Notes like this occur frequently in the classroom and reflect children's spontaneous and self-initiated purposes. Periodically, however, Kate may hold a minilesson if a letter is intended for someone who is not a member of the class. For these lessons she locates books associated with letter writing and displays them on the counter for browsing. The ever-popular *The Jolly Postman or Other People's Letters* (Ahlberg & Ahlberg, 1986) and *Dear Mr. Henshaw* (Cleary, 1983) are available along with easy-to-read titles such as *Click Clack, Moo Cows That Type* (Cronin, 2000), *I Have a New Friend* (Allan-Meyer, 1995), and *Dear Mr. Blueberry* (James, 1991).

Kate begins by sharing her own correspondence with her sister. Then she reads an episode from *Frog and Toad Are Friends* (Lobel, 1970) called *The Letter* in which Toad shares with Frog his disappointment about never receiving mail. The children then discuss how they feel about sending and receiving mail and brainstorm all the kinds of friendly letters they might write, along with purposes such as the following:

- To tell about a good book they have read
- To send news about themselves
- To tell what they are learning
- To give news of an upcoming event
- To provide information about their hobbies
- To reveal something that happened in school
- To share something from home (how they celebrated a birthday)
- To ask questions of students in other grades or schools

FIGURE 3-14
Jessica's Friendly Letter
(Third Grader)

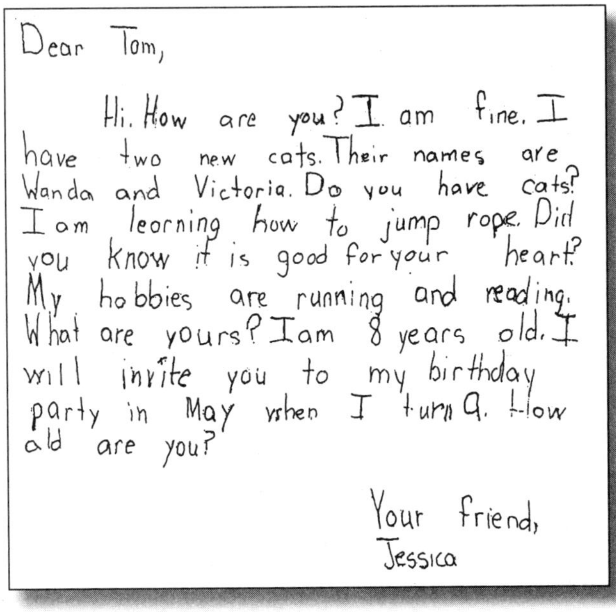

> Dear Tom,
>
> Hi. How are you? I am fine. I have two new cats. Their names are Wanda and Victoria. Do you have cats? I am learning how to jump rope. Did you know it is good for your heart? My hobbies are running and reading. What are yours? I am 8 years old. I will invite you to my birthday party in May when I turn 9. How old are you?
>
> Your friend,
> Jessica

Kate reminds the children that webbing and mapping help organize information. Those who have had lots of experience writing letters may be ready to start without prewriting. Jessica's letter to Tom is an example (see Figure 3–14). She is obviously familiar with the typical features to include in a friendly letter. She opens with a social greeting *(How are you?)*, proceeds to tell Tom about events in her life (I have two new cats and I am learning how to jump rope), and pursues the question–answer format to organize the letter and show awareness of audience. The informal style of the letter is obvious in the salutation *(Dear)*, the body, and the complimentary closing *(Your friend)*.

Not all children are ready to write immediately, and Kate provides time for students to plan their letters using the guide in Figure 3–15. Although writing personal letters may seem to require little or no planning, often writers unconsciously collect thoughts and news over time. If children are writing to relatives about what they are learning in school, they can consult reading or learning logs. If they want to tell about personal events, they can check calendars or journals.

In addition to content, Kate explains that friendly letters are personal, informal, and conversational in tone. The children explore sentence variety or word choice to make their letters more engaging or appropriate for the audience. As a group, they take a moment to list on a chart ways to address various audiences in greetings and closings:

Greetings	Closings
Hi	Bye
Dear	Sincerely
Greetings	Your pal
Ciao	Your friend
What's happening	Love

Many children include a postscript (P. S.) for adding extra thoughts they may have forgotten in the body of the letter or for stressing something they want their recipient to notice.

In the third grade, editing consists of studying the perfunctory comma in dates, addresses, and in the salutation and complimentary closing. Because as a general

FIGURE 3-15 Letter-Writing Guide

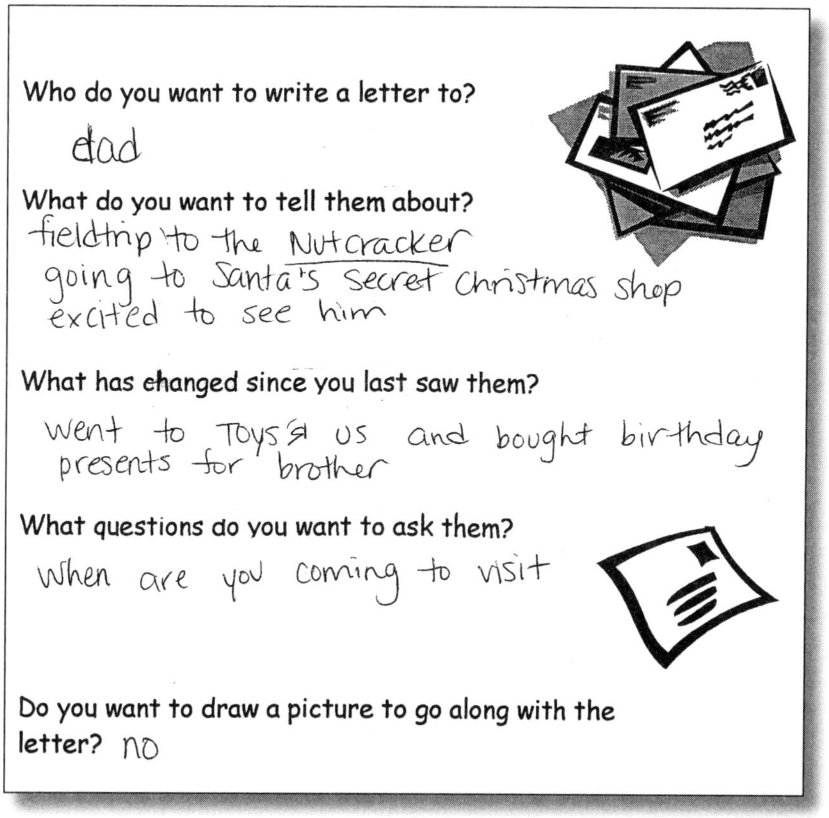

Who do you want to write a letter to?

dad

What do you want to tell them about?

fieldtrip to the Nutcracker
going to Santa's secret Christmas shop
excited to see him

What has changed since you last saw them?

went to Toys 'я us and bought birthday
presents for brother

What questions do you want to ask them?

When are you coming to visit

Do you want to draw a picture to go along with the letter? no

rule it is not unusual to ask the recipient a question or relate personal information in an emphatic manner, children should check the ends of sentences for periods, exclamation points, and question marks. Format should also be examined. Does the letter have all of the parts?

- Return address
- Greeting (or salutation)
- Body
- Complimentary closing
- Signature

Any time writing is made public, it is open for judgment. But because friendly letters are never formally evaluated, Kate and the students develop checklists, such as the one in Figure 3–16, to monitor and polish work before sending it. The checklist provides advice about the message and its form as well as details on addressing the envelope. The checklist becomes part of student's working portfolio, and the letters are sent.

Sometimes a letter-writing task becomes an extension of a book the teacher has read to the class. For example, after reading *Sarah, Plain and Tall* (MacLachlan, 1985), Kate discusses the notion of mail-order brides, and the children write letters describing an ideal friend. On other occasions, children create postcards on heavy paper or card stock for sending notes to favorite authors. On one side, they draw images related to the story. On the other side, which is divided into two parts, they write questions or summaries on the left and the author's address on the right. They find names and addresses of authors on the Internet or within the books they are reading.

Because correspondence involves more than writing postcards and letters, children exchange drawings, photos, stickers, and newspaper clippings. One of Kate's students,

FIGURE 3-16
Friendly Letter
Checklist

The Letter

_____ Message considers what the reader might like to know

_____ Message has a friendly tone

_____ Ideas are written in a logical sequence

_____ Message includes interesting details

_____ The letter includes all five parts (heading, salutation, body, closing, signature, and postscripts if desired)

_____ The salutation (*hi, dear*) and closing *(your friend, miss you)* are informal

_____ The letter is checked for correct spelling, punctuation, capitalization, and legibility

Envelope

_____ Letter is correctly folded and inserted in envelope

_____ Mailing and return address are correct

_____ Handwriting is legible

for instance, collects commemorative stamps and keeps a scrapbook with captions that describe how each stamp honors the memory of a significant person, place, or event. She sketches these stamps to send to a friend who enjoys the same hobby.

Many kinds of letters are introduced over the course of the year and in many forms. Children love novelty cards, for example, pop-up, peek, and shape cards. For the pop-up cards, they make three or four accordion folds out of thin strips of paper and tape one end to the inside of the card and the other end to the pop-up drawing or feature (a balloon, a smiley face, a greeting). Peek cards are made by cutting a small opening in the card front to reveal a design inside, and shape cards are cut in the form of objects (trees, hearts) or animals (teddy bears, frogs). Using classroom computers with desktop publishing and print shop programs students make cards or special stationery. In coordination with the art teacher, Kate helps the children create textured and interesting stationery using sponge painting, stenciling, or marbleizing.

In other chapters in this book, you will see how children write letters as part of fiction writing (see the student letter in Chapter 4, *The Flower Letters*), history writing (a simulated letter in Chapter 1), newspaper writing (letters to the editor in Chapter 6), and persuasive writing (student letter to a city official in Chapter 7).

Personal Narratives

Personal narratives express firsthand experiences and everyday occurrences. They are usually the easiest type of narrative to write because they emphasize personal ideas and experiences rather than research-based facts and details. Told from the "teller's" perspective, the personal narrative tends to adopt the first-person point of view and use the pronouns *I, me,* and *mine*. When the writer selects the third-person point of view for involving persons outside the action, pronouns *he, she,* and *they* are used.

The students in Kate's third-grade class get ideas for personal narratives from all of the visuals (charts, pictures, words) surrounding them in the classroom. For instance, on one chart several ideas are listed to activate frames of experience.

Things you like	Your best (or worst) day
Things you don't like	Something you've accomplished
Things that make you angry	Your first time at something

Things you do well	Your favorite sport or hobby
Things you don't do well	Your special talent
Things you wish for	Something you are proud of

Kate describes her inspirational sources for topic generation.

> When I am stuck on what to write about, I often read my journal entries or review topics I've placed in a manila folder. Sometimes simply leafing through magazines or favorite books sparks ideas. Whenever a thought comes to me, I write it down on a Post-it note so I won't forget.

With basic guidelines to follow, students list topics and ideas for writing while Kate moves around the room, posing impromptu questions to stimulate thinking about people and places about which the students may want to write. Sometimes the children request teacher help with spelling, but most often they get assistance from peers.

The completed narratives range in length from one paragraph to three pages. The content that emerges repeatedly in the compositions centers on ordinary events or situations, such as playing football, sleepovers, embarrassing moments, or "firsts" at learning something. In the beginning, the writing is brief; details are limited and incidents string along one after another, without reaching the heart of the event, in what Applebee (1978) refers to as "heaps." For a while students seem unable to accommodate narrative time, which is shorter than chronological time and requires the omission of extraneous details. Reggie's work (see Figure 3–17) is a good example of chronological time—a fishing excursion that lasts from morning until night. However, it is on the brink of narrative time—character action and motives that show a strong storyline emerging, waiting to be told. The middle of the piece has good ideas but they are not sufficiently detailed. Adding information and descriptions will make it more engaging and enhance its liveliness and personal flavor, which gives the writing voice.

Once the draft is finished, Kate meets in conference with Reggie to discuss what he has written. The conference proceeds as follows.

Reggie: When I'm writing the last line, and I'm just finished, I sit back for a while, think about it, then I say, this is good writing.

Kate: It certainly is good writing. Tell me about what you've written.

Reggie: Well, it's about going fishin' with my dad and Karl and Derik.

Kate: You must have felt pretty good about being the only one to catch a fish, huh?

Reggie: Yeah. My dad helped me. It was a trout.

Kate: Wow, I'll bet that tasted good when your mom cooked it.

Reggie: Yep.

Kate quotes Reggie's exact words in her comments to show that she is truly listening ("You must have felt very proud being the only one to catch a fish; I'll bet that fish tasted good when your mom cooked it"). Her next set of questions challenge Reggie to rethink the organization and add detail.

Kate: I'm curious. What do you talk about or do when you're on the boat with Derik?

Reggie: We talk and stuff like that.

Kate: Is Derik your age?

Reggie: He's about my age. I think he's 10.

Kate: What do you talk about?

Reggie: Mostly fish.

FIGURE 3-17
Reggie's Narrative *Gone Fishing*, First Draft (Third Grader, Independent Writing)

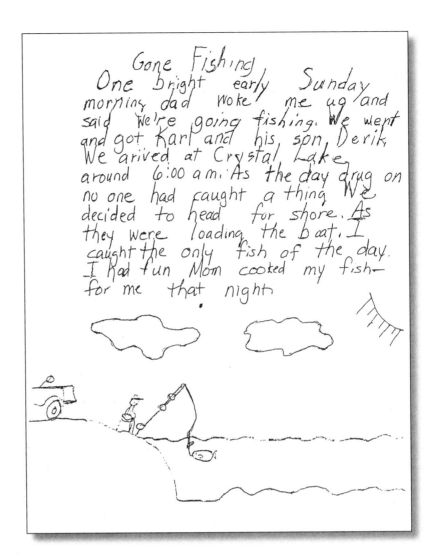

Kate: I don't know much about fishing. I would love to listen in on your conversations on the boat. You might want to add some dialogue between you and Derik or you and your father. I wonder if you could also explain a little more about what you do when you fish. Perhaps you could start by thinking about what you brought with you, then show what you did with these things. Where might you add this information?

Reggie: [Points to the space after the time "6:00 A.M." and before the words, "As the day drug on"] There?

Before Reggie returns to his seat, Kate locates her conference notes (shown in Figure 3–18) and jots down some words and phrases in front of him.

Kate: Let's see. I will write some notes about what we have discussed. [She writes as she reads.] You are going to add some information about what you did on your trip: how you hooked the bait, what you talked about while you waited for the fish to bite, how you knew when you caught the fish, and what was happening when you reeled it in.

Kate invites Reggie to borrow her notes for words and phrases *(bait, reel it in)* that are associated with the topic and already correctly spelled for him. Her written

FIGURE 3-18
Conference Notes

Name: Reggie	Date: 11/3
Title of Composition: Gone Fishing	

Teacher Notes	Student Notes
Selects a topic of interest that is well developed and has a satisfying ending; understands how to shape writing to the needs of his audience.	I need to tell about fishing.
	I can add dialogue between me and Derik.
Shares the fishing trip, adding more detail in the retelling. We talk about the people on the trip. We also discuss Reggie's feelings about catching the fish.	Tell what we talked about.
Would like him to attempt a second draft. Showed him how to cut and paste to add information about fishing: what equipment he took, what he used as bait, what happened on the boat. Reggie agrees to add dialogue between himself and his friend Derik.	
He also agrees to share his second draft with peers.	

remarks will help him recall what to do next. To make certain they have communicated, she asks Reggie to add his own conference notes. These become a part of the ongoing record of questions, observations, comments, and suggestions.

Clearly, the objectives of the conference will change depending on the status of the writer's draft. Kate and Reggie concentrate on the message in a first draft conference, but when the second draft is discussed, they consider spelling, contractions, and sentence variety. She notes the correct spelling of *arrived* and explains that quotation marks go around dialogue such as "we're going fishing." *Drug on* is substituted with the word, *dragged*. Different drafts require different comments and new points of concentration.

Grade 5

Memoirs

A memoir is a "portion of life" (Zinsser, 1998, pp. 14–15). Instead of writing about everything from birth to the present, in memoirs writers focus on a significant event or time that reveals something important about themselves.

Ed plans a lesson on memoirs and works with the school librarian to collect autobiographies and memoirs on a variety of reading levels. These books, listed in Figure 3–19, reveal autobiographical incidents or fragments of life that evoke strong impressions, turning points, or challenges leading to personal change. Many of them deal with some of the sensitive issues students experience in their own lives. Referring to a book about divorce that his student Cameron is reading, Ed gently leads him into a discussion about his own personal experience.

- How did you feel when you were first told that your parents would divorce?

FIGURE 3-19   Memoirs, Autobiographies, and Books That Evoke Memories

Ackerman, K. (1988). *Song and dance man.* Knopf.

Bridges, R. (1999). *Through my eyes.* Scholastic.

Cleary, B. (1988). *A girl from Yamhill: A memoir.* Morrow.

Cole, J. (1991). *My puppy is born.* Morrow.

Cummings, P. (1992). (Compiler/Editor). *Talking with artists.* Bradbury.

Dahl, R. (1997). *The Roald Dahl treasury.* Viking.

Dragonwagon, C. (1996). *Homeplace.* Silver Burdett.

Ehlert, L. (1996). *Under my nose.* Richard C. Owen.

Fox, M. (1993). *Wilfrid Gordon McDonald Partridge.* Trumpet Club.

Fritz, J. (1985). *Homesick: My own story.* Putnam.

Gregory, K. (1999). *The great railroad race: The diary of Libby West.* Scholastic.

Harris, M. J. (1985). *Confessions of a prime time kid.* Lothrop, Lee, & Shepard.

Hyman, T. S. (1981). *Self-portrait: Trina Schart Hyman.* Addison-Wesley.

Jiang, J. L. (1997). *Red scarf girl: A memoir of the cultural revolution.* HarperCollins.

Meltzer, M. (1991). *Starting from home: A writer's beginnings.* Puffin.

Peet, B. (1989). *Bill Peet: An autobiography.* Houghton Mifflin.

Polacco, P. (1994). *Firetalking.* Richard C. Owens.

Precek, K. W. (1992). *The keepsake chest.* Macmillan.

Rylant, C., & Good, D. (1982). *When I was young in the mountains.* Dutton.

Spinelli, J. (1998). *Knots in my yo-yo string: The autobiography of a kid.* Knopf.

Toll, N. S. (1993). *Behind the secret window: A memoir of a hidden childhood during World War Two.* Dial Books.

Yen Mah, A. (1999). *Chinese Cinderella: The true story of an unwanted daughter.* Delacorte.

Zlata, F. (1994). *Zlata's diary: A child's life in Sarajevo.* Viking.

- What are the advantages and disadvantages of having two sets of parents? One parent?
- How has your life changed because of divorce?
- Do you think kids should have a choice in deciding whether to live with their mother or father?
- Why do you think parents divorce?
- How did you cope with your parents' divorce?

After the conference, Cameron rereads the book and writes a double-entry journal, selecting certain details and writing personal reactions to it. These reactions will become part of his memoir.

Because fifth graders, such as Cameron, are becoming increasingly more responsible for their learning, they monitor daily tasks in reading and writing planners. (See Figure 3–20.) Planners are not unique to memoirs, but they are effective tools for renewing commitment to a task and reinforcing productive work habits. The planner prompts students to set goals and make realistic estimates about the time necessary for accomplishing daily activities.

In the first part of planning students reflect on their work before outlining subsequent steps. Ed reviews the plans to ensure a balance of reading and writing activities or that a realistic amount of time is allocated for each task. The 2-week projection illustrated in Figure 3–20 may be modified over time, but still requires

FIGURE 3-20   Reading and Writing Planner

NAME Brittany			TOPIC Soccer	

1. What did you learn about your writing strengths? Weaknesses?

   Strength: People like my use of words like "whamm" and "whapp"
   Weakness: Remember my reader

2. What suggestions were recommended to improve your writing?

   Tell more about how to play soccer; add a title

3. What is your literacy plan for the next 2 weeks? Please complete the calendar.

Week 1				
Monday	**Tuesday**	**Wednesday**	**Thursday**	**Friday**
Describe the people more; brainstorm	Make a picture of the soccer field and write about how to play the game	Read a book on soccer Conference with teacher	Word process my first draft; add new information	Share my work with a friend

Week 2				
Monday	**Tuesday**	**Wednesday**	**Thursday**	**Friday**
Edit my work and give it a title	Start a new writing assignment; think of ideas	Read books	Go back and read soccer piece; make changes	Conference with teacher about soccer piece

students to plan ahead. All of the children keep a writing log, in addition to a reading log, which lists composition titles, dated work entries, and self-assessments. In conference Chaney shares his planner with Ed. He has been working on his memoir and is ready to discuss it. The piece is about spending time with his family at the beach. Chaney, also a child of divorced parents, writes about a blended family reunion over Labor Day weekend (see Figure 3–21). The writing is organized, and the sentences, although not complex, tell the story. The words he uses are common to his age group, and most of them are spelled correctly.

Although Chaney has written an acceptable narrative, it falls short of "memoir status" because it fails to explain the significance of the event. Ed is aware that because Chaney's parents are divorced, this reunion at the beach represents a memorable time in his life. During the writing conference, Chaney reflects on the autobiographical importance of this event and highlights it indirectly through description, dialogue, and action.

While second drafts are being written, Ed distributes a set of questions that students can consider for self-assessment.

- Did you show or tell about something special in your life?
- Did you produce an attention-getting beginning?
- Did you maintain the personal point of view?
- Did you focus on yourself and what you thought and felt?
- Did you use the pronoun *I* (first-person point of view)?
- Did you tell what the object or event meant to you?
- Did you help the readers feel what you felt?
- Did you write a satisfying ending?

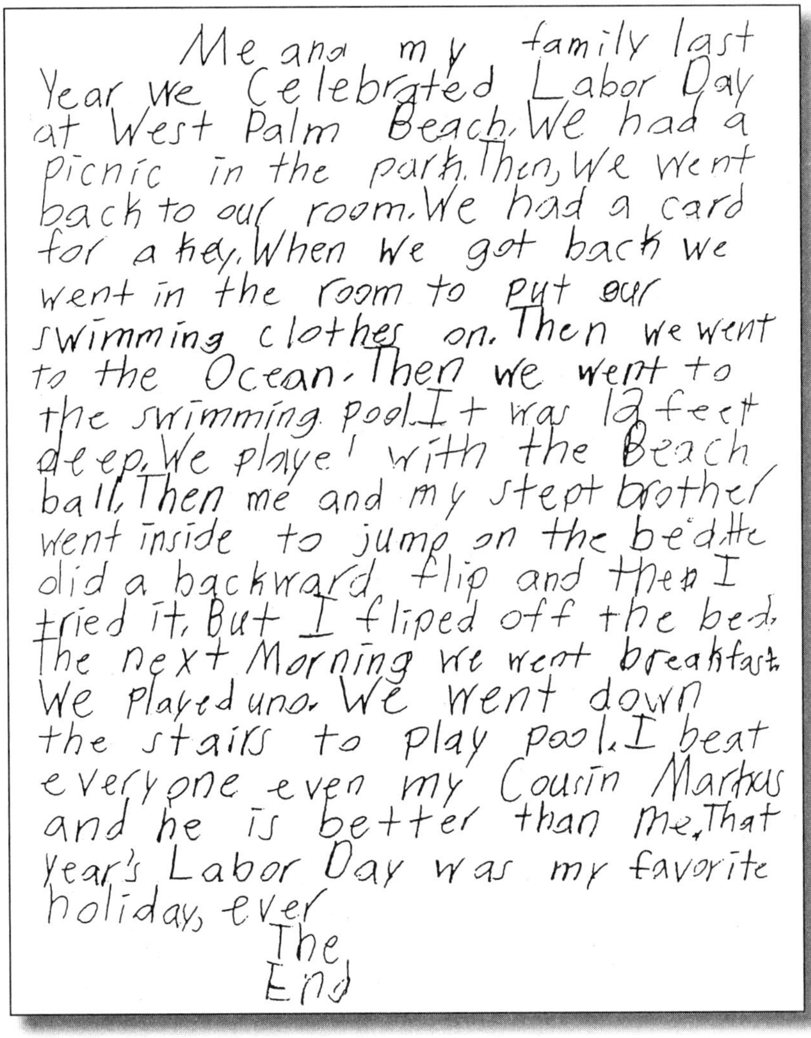

FIGURE 3-21
Chaney's Memoir,
Labor Day (Fifth
Grader, Independent
Writing)

> Me and my family last Year we Celebrated Labor Day at West Palm Beach. We had a picnic in the park. Then, We went back to our room. We had a card for a key. When we got back we went in the room to put our swimming clothes on. Then we went to the Ocean. Then we went to the swimming pool. It was 12 feet deep. We playe' with the Beach ball. Then me and my stept brother went inside to jump on the bed. He did a backward flip and then I tried it. But I fliped off the bed. The next Morning we went breakfast. We Played uno. We went down the stairs to play pool. I beat everyone even my Cousin Markus and he is better than me. That Year's Labor Day was my favorite holiday, ever
> The End

Throughout the writing project, the students share journal entries on books, quickwrites, drafts, revisions, and published works. Some of the written pieces are sent home with a letter outlining special instructions for parents to offer positive impressions and write a response of their child's work (see Figure 3–22). In this way, parents and teachers communicate with one another and collaborate on the writing effort.

At the end of the 6 weeks, the students select two to three pieces that they believe represent their best work and revise or edit once more. In preparation for a conference with Ed, the students may write notes describing their accomplishments. For instance, Dario identifies what he believes should be showcased in his portfolio (see Figure 3–23). Ed may then ask questions that require writers to reflect on their role as learners and reveal even more about themselves. Following are some examples of these questions:

- What does this piece tell about you as a writer?
- Which paper do you believe shows your greatest growth?
- What three pieces do you like best and why?
- Which one was your greatest challenge and why?

FIGURE 3-22
Sample Letter to
Families

GLENVIEW ELEMENTARY SCHOOL
1234 Child's Lane
Anywhere, USA

November 14, 2003

Dear Families,

Your child has brought home his/her portfolio for you to read and review. S/he has prepared a guide on what to read in the folder and where to focus your attention. After you have read the contents, point out what impressed you about the work and the strengths of the folder. Ask questions and listen to your child's response. On a separate sheet of paper, write your comments or reactions and sign your name.

Before you send back the portfolio on November 21, 2003, please add any samples from your child's writing at home that you think will help show his/her growth.

If you are unable to review the folder, please let me know and we will make other arrangements to discuss your child's progress. Thank you for your continued interest and support.

Sincerely yours,

Mr. Ed Spinelli

FIGURE 3-23
Dario's Note to the
Teacher

> Dear Mr. S,
>
> I read my portfolio and want to showcase these things
> my piece on snakes
> the books I read on snakes
> my piece on football
>
> Dario

- Which pieces taught you something about yourself as a writer?
- In which piece did you learn something about the subject you were writing about?

Because assessment is a dynamic process, Ed expects the students to add and re-move work throughout the year, saving only representative pieces. Eliminating older work from the portfolio helps students learn to assess past performance and plan new goals. Papers are thrown out, taken home, or transferred to a showcase portfolio with a table of contents and summary that the student creates. The following is an example:

Table of Contents

1. One of my best works
2. Reading and writing logs
3. A composition I evaluated with a rubric
4. A revision in which I added and reorganized information
5. A work I edited for spelling, punctuation, and capitalization
6. A piece in which I compared two things
7. A list of future writing topics

A portfolio summary is shown in Figure 3–24.

Biographies

In the fifth grade, students prepare to write biographies of friends, family members, or community members. They write short journal entries to identify and remember people who have been influential in their lives. Ed asks, "Who are some people you remember and why do they stand out in your mind? Is it your best friend with whom you share secrets? Is it a brother or sister who annoys you?" Students join with friends to brainstorm significant people in their lives and to interview one another about why the person is memorable.

Ed introduces the idea of interviews by sharing samples from magazine articles that students read and discuss. Ed asks, "What is the content of the questions asked?

FIGURE 3-24   Portfolio Summary

Name: _____ Date: _____

Achievements	Evidence From the Portfolio	My Goals
I wrote two personal narratives and three non-narratives	Writing samples	I want to try writing a biography
I kept a learning log of my accomplishments	There are 24 entries in the notebook	I would like to continue keeping a learning log
I read five books: three science fiction and two informational	Reading log	I would like to read more science fiction and other fiction
I was involved in weekly conferences and workshops	Conference notes	I want to participate more
I learned how to use a comma	Practice worksheet and writing samples	I would like to learn how to edit for commas

Summary _____
_____
_____
_____

Is the interviewee text section longer than the interviewer part? How would you characterize the kinds of questions asked?" The students organize the questions into those that are personal and those that are general. Then each student lists and sifts through questions of their own for the best ones. Thomas, a fifth-grade writer, diligently works on a life story about his great-grandmother. He reads and reviews interview questions to rehearse for his meeting (see Figure 3–25). Thomas tapes the interview so he won't miss anything his grandmother says. On returning to class, he shares the gathered information and determines if any follow-up questions are necessary. The questions and answers are the content for drafting the biography.

Before Thomas begins writing, he listens to the tape again to identify an interesting event that stands out. Thomas reviews the tape in the listening corner. He stops it midway and whispers, "Oh, I have one." He jots down something, returns to his desk, and writes nonstop for 10 minutes. When Thomas drafts, he balances facts with his own thoughts, and, although the overall tone is objective, he is passionate about what he is studying, and his personal imprint is evident in the piece. Figure 3–26 on page 156 depicts Thomas's art and writing. After completing the writing, he draws a picture of the incident referred to in his composition. He shares his work with peers in a writing circle, and the group applauds his efforts. The teacher's advice to review the audiotape and listen for an episode or anecdote has helped Thomas find a focus. Without this prompting, he might have simply written the interview questions and answers in chronological order. Following revisions, Thomas meets with Ed to review the biography and other pieces in his portfolio. After careful consideration, Thomas decides to evaluate the biography using a preconstructed rubric that identifies levels of performance in the six traits and various degrees of mastery, such as "exemplary," "competent," "basic," and "minimal." Thomas refers to a numerical score followed by criteria for his assessment (see Table 3–6 on page 157).

Thomas has seen this criteria before. Ed shares evaluation rubrics with the students so they know what is expected of them. Thomas and Ed sit together with the rubric in hand as Thomas rereads his work. After a few moments, he turns to Ed and says, "I think my work deserves a 'competent.'" He believes he has detailed an incident from his grandmother's life and has included other pertinent information about when she was born, how she had six children, and where she lived. Tracing his steps, Thomas explains how he completed the interview, listened twice to the tape, and selected an anecdote for writing. He also created a second draft. As the conference winds down, Thomas identifies two areas for improvement: adding more description about his grandmother and revealing more about his feelings. Thomas fills out an inventory to reflect his evaluation (see Figure 3–27 on page 158). The form has two columns: one for things he has done well and another for things that need improvement.

The inventory is a tool for assessing Thomas's progress and for setting new goals. By discussing the evaluation rating, Thomas may become more self-critical and responsible for his work. The portfolio conference directly involves Thomas in the formal assessment process so that throughout the year he can take stock of his work and answer the following questions:

- What have I learned about myself as a writer?
- What are my favorite genres to write in? In what genres have I written?
- How much did I produce during these 6 weeks?
- What strategies and skills have I mastered?
- What would I like to accomplish or continue during the next 6 weeks?

JOURNEY REFLECTIONS

Writing about personal experience and events plays a pivotal role in children's writing journey, especially in diverse classrooms where they must learn to appreciate similarities

FIGURE 3-25
Thomas's Interview
Sheet

Historical Research/Oral History

Find out about your grandmother or grandfather. Keep these questions in mind while you interview your grandparent. What kinds of things did they do when they were your age? How is that different from what you do now? What do you think has changed?

What is your grandmother's/grandfather's name?

Where and when was he/she born?

What kind of games did he/she play?

What was school like for him/her? What subjects were taught?

Did he/she have any chores? What were they?

What food did he/she eat?

What kind of clothes did he/she wear?

Did the family ever take vacations? Where to?

What is your name and age?

Where were you born?

What kinds of games do you play?

What subjects do you learn in school?

Do you have any chores? What are they?

What kinds of food do you eat?

What kind of clothes do you wear?

Does your family take vacations? Where to?

Reflect back on the differences between your answers and your grandparent's. How are they different or similar? Tell me about something that has drastically changed (clothing, for example) and why you think it changed.

FIGURE 3-26
Thomas' Drawing, and
Thomas' Biography,
First Draft (Fifth
Grader, Independent
Writing)

Once upon a time my great grandma, Mittie, who was born on November 27, 1896, had a story to tell. Her story is about my grandma, Sara, and how she had to find a place for her baby to sleep.

When great grandma Mittie had Sara she already had 5 other children and they lived in a shack that was very small. They didn't have running water like we do today. The old children would have to take turns going to get the water from the well.

Sara didn't have a place to sleep in the house so great grandma had to find a place for her. Guess where she decided to put her? She had an old chest of drawers in one of the bedrooms so she put a blanket in the top drawer. Great grandma thought this was a wonderful place since she was out of the way.

One day Sara's brother, Earl, wanted her to play with him. He was 2 years old and couldn't understand why she couldn't play. When no one was looking he went into the bedroom and pulled out the bottom drawer of the dresser just enough to stand on it.

(continued)

FIGURE 3-26
(continued)

When he looked in the top drawer to
see Sara he accidentally pulled the drawer
out onto the floor. Well, guess what
happened then? Great grandma heard Sara
crying and ran into the room and saw her
laying in the drawer on the floor. Great
grandma was so mad so she told Earl he
was going to get a whipping. After she
put Sara back in the right place she
gave Earl the whipping she promised.
Earl never touched the dresser drawer
again.

and differences, discover themselves and others, and balance the need for independence and connections. The quest for self-knowledge and acceptance brings strength and creativity. Sharing one's special gifts with a social group affirms the value and dignity of the individual and solidifies membership in a **discourse community**. Teachers begin by celebrating the uniqueness of every child. Exploring the child's world through her life story becomes the context in which all other kinds of writing are understood. When teachers have a deep understanding of their students' passions, interests, and experiences and are responsive and sensitive to their needs, they are better able to provide the positive environments in which children feel safe and thrive.

In minilessons on topic selection, teachers explore children's personal interests and experiences. Voice emerges naturally in writing based on individual backgrounds and inclinations.

During a personal writing project, children read realistic fiction about characters with concerns similar to their own. Before drafting and revising, they engage in prewriting activities that accommodate diverse learning styles. In particular, in meaningful role-play activities, students gain new perspectives and develop greater empathy for others. Interactions and feedback in conferences and writing circles encourage students to gradually build trust and shared knowledge. Children are naturally led into the writing process because personal writing is more public than journal writing, and it has greater audience demands. The process provides time for them to complete rough drafts and revise before sharing ideas with others. The teacher observes process behaviors paying particular attention to children's ability to self-monitor and self-regulate. The product itself becomes a window for reflection, a logical extension of discovery, insight, and self-awareness. Editing suggests many skills appropriate for teaching personal writing, but decisions on what to teach should be based on each child's written text.

In the three classroom vignettes, each teacher addresses different types of personal writing. Name writing, *All About Me* books, letters, personal narratives, memoirs, and biographies, although different tasks, provide opportunities to learn about the self and significant others, develop voice, and share writing publicly. In the *All About Me* book, Vivian piggybacks assignments to create task variety while focusing and sustaining the children's interest on a single project. Kate's third graders write friendly notes and letters and continue to use personal narratives for self-discovery. They complete assignments that underscore the role of peer audiences or known audiences removed in space and time.

TABLE 3-6   Six-Trait Evaluation for a Biographic Sketch

	Exemplary (4)	Competent (3)	Basic (2)	Minimal (1)
Ideas	Routinely develops a comprehensive set of questions for gathering information; presents a readily understandable message; includes relevant, accurate, and complete information about the person's life; Uses detailed and textured information to describe the informant's personality or event	Frequently develops a minimal set of questions for gathering information; presents a message that is comprehensible; includes partial information and accurate details about the person's life; Provides partial information to describe the informant's personality or event	Occasionally develops a fragmentary set of questions for gathering information; presents a somewhat comprehensible message; includes a little information about the person's life; Sketches in details about the informant's personality or event	Seldom develops adequate questions for gathering information; presents a strong message; includes information that is relevant or accurate; Provides more than a skeletal outline of the details about the informant's personality or event
Organization	Consistently relates ideas through anecdote or chronology	Frequently relates ideas through anecdote or chronology	Sometimes relates ideas through anecdote or chronology	Seldom relates ideas through anecdote or chronology
Voice	Always effectively describes the author's feelings about the person or event	Often describes the author's feelings about the person or event	Sometimes hints at the author's feelings about the person or event	Never comments on the author's feelings about the person or event
Sentence Fluency	Routinely writes meaningful and effective sentences that are appropriate in length and structure	Often writes meaningful and effective sentences that are appropriate in length and structure	Occasionally writes meaningful and effective sentences that are appropriate in length and structure	Seldom writes meaningful and effective sentences that are appropriate in length and structure
Word Choice	Consistently uses words and language that create a feeling about the person, time period, or geographic location	Often uses words and language that create a feeling about the person, time period, or geographic location	Sometimes uses words and language that create a feeling about the person, time period, or geographic location	Seldom uses words and language that create a feeling about the person, time period, or geographic location
Conventions	Always identifies and corrects spelling and punctuation errors	Usually identifies and corrects spelling and punctuation errors	Sometimes identifies and corrects spelling and punctuation errors	Seldom identifies and corrects spelling and punctuation errors

Ed's memoir and biography lessons underscore the selectivity of choosing events in one's own and others' lives. Highlighting an event and its significance is common to both tasks. During these 2-week assignments, students learn personal responsibility by setting goals and budgeting time to complete a project. In portfolio assessment conferences, they review all of their personal writing, including biographies, and rework pieces that they wish to submit for a grade. When they transfer best works to a showcase portfolio or take pieces home, the work goes through another review process. Parents become part of the review by responding to their child's work.

FIGURE 3-27 Self-Assessment Inventory

Name _____	Period of Time: __Sept.–Nov.__
Things I Can Do As a Writer	**Things I Still Need to Practice**
Writing event I can write personal narratives. I can tell about my feelings.	I need to practice writing dialogue. I need to brainstorm when I get stuck for ideas.
Writing event I keep a journal for my ideas. I write in my journal every day.	I need to remember to date my journal entries.
Writing event I can write a biographic sketch. I can conduct an interview. I can use good action words.	I should show how I feel. I need to find out more about how my informant feels.

In the next chapter, the world of personal reality is left behind for the world of enchantment and make-believe. There, writers invent characters and fictional stories that exercise imagination and extend literacy skills. Although students continue to focus on people (characters), places (settings), and events (plot), they present these elements in challenging new ways to entertain and stretch the truth. Fictional narratives extend possibilities for telling stories and diverse points of view; they equip writers with the literacy strategies and tools necessary for creating drama and literary language.

WORKS CITED

Professional References

Alexander, K., & Day, M. (Eds.). (1991). *Discipline-based art education: A curriculum sampler*. Los Angeles: The Getty Center for Education in the Arts.

Applebee, A. N. (1978). *The child's concept of story: Ages 2–17*. Chicago: University of Chicago Press.

Armstrong, T. (2000). *Multiple intelligences in the classroom* (2nd ed.). Alexandria, VA: Association for Supervision and Curriculum Development.

Ashton-Warner, S. (1963). *Teacher*. New York: Simon & Schuster.

Bakhtin, M. M. (1981). *The dialogic imagination*. M. Holquist (Ed.). C. Emerson & M. Holquist (Trans.). Austin: University of Texas Press.

Bidwell, S. M. (1990). Using drama to increase motivation, comprehension and fluency. *Journal of Reading, 34*, 38–41.

Bloodgood, J. W. (1999). What's in a name? Children's name writing and literacy acquisition. *Reading Research Quarterly, 34*, 342–367.

Britton, J., Burgess, T., Martin, N., McLeod, A., & Rosen, H. (1975). *The development of writing abilities*. London: Macmillan.

Carbo, M., Dunn, R., & Dunn, K. (1986). *Teaching students to read through individual learning styles*. Englewood Cliffs, NJ: Prentice Hall.

Claxton, C., & Ralston, Y. (1978). *Learning styles: Their impact on teaching and administration*. (Research Paper #10). Washington, DC: George Washington University.

Cochran-Smith, M. (1984). *The making of a reader*. Norwood, NJ: Ablex.

Corsaro, W. A. (1985). *Friendship and peer culture in the early years*. Norwood, NJ: Ablex.

Cushner, K., McClelland, A., & Safford, P. (1992). *Human diversity in education.* New York: McGraw-Hill.

DeWitt, K. (1999). From DeVon to La Don, invented names proclaim "I am." In A. P. Nielsen (Ed.), *Living language: Reading, thinking, and writing* (pp. 6–9). Boston: Allyn & Bacon.

Dyson, A. H. (1983). The role of oral language in writing. *Research in the Teaching of English, 17,* 1–30.

Dyson, A. H. (1989). *Multiple worlds of child writers.* New York: Teachers College Press.

Flower, L. S. (1979). Writer-based prose: A cognitive basis for problems in writing. *College English, 41,* 19–37.

Freedman, S. (1987). *Peer response groups in two ninth-grade classrooms.* (Technical Report No. 12). Berkeley, CA: Center for the Study of Writing.

Fresch, M. J., & Wheaton, A. (1997). Sort, search, and discover: Spelling in the child-centered classroom. *The Reading Teacher, 51,* 20–31.

Gardner, H. (1980). *Artful scribbles.* New York: Basic Books.

Gardner, H. (1993). *Multiple intelligences: The theory in practice.* New York: Basic Books.

Garton, A., & Pratt, C. (1998). *Learning to be literate: The development of spoken and written language* (2nd ed.). New York: Blackwell.

Gentry, J. R. (1981). Learning to spell developmentally. *The Reading Teacher, 34,* 378–381.

Graves, D. H. (1976). Let's get rid of the welfare mess in the teaching of writing. *Language Arts, 53,* 645–651.

Graves, D. H. (1983a). An examination of the writing processes of seven-year-old children. *Research in the Teaching of English, 9,* 227–241.

Graves, D. H. (1983b). *A two-year case study observing the development of primary children's composing, spelling, and motor behaviors during the writing process.* Developmental observation chart (Working paper).

Graves, D. H. (1983c). *Writing: Teachers and children at work.* Exeter, NH: Heinemann.

Gray-Schlegel, M., & Gray-Schlegel, T. (1995–1996). An investigation of gender stereotypes as revealed through children's creative writing. *Reading Research and Instruction, 35,* 160–170.

Jensen, E. (1996). *Brain-based learning.* Del Mar, CA: Turning Point Publishing.

Johnson, D. D. (2001). *Vocabulary in the elementary and middle school.* Boston: Allyn & Bacon.

Kagan, J. (1987). Cognitive style and instructional preferences: Some influences. *Education Forum, 51,* 393–403.

Kellogg, R. (1969). *Analyzing children's art.* Palo Alto, CA: National Press Books.

Lakoff, R. (1982). Some of my favorite writers are literate: The mingling of oral and literate strategies in written communication. In D. Tannen (Ed.), *Spoken and written language: Exploring orality and literacy* (pp. 239–246). Norwood, NJ: Ablex.

Manzo, A. V., & Manzo, U. C. (1995). *Teaching children to be literate: A reflective approach.* Fort Worth, TX: Harcourt Brace.

McKenzie, M. G. (1985). Shared writing: Apprenticeship in writing. *Language Matters, 1–2,* 1–5.

Moffett, J., & Wagner, B. J. (1992). *Student-centered language arts, K–12* (4th ed.). Portsmouth, NH: Heinemann.

Murphy, S., & Dudley-Marling, C. (2001). Editors' pages. *Language Arts, 78,* 412–413.

Nystrand, M. (Ed.). (1982). *What writers know: The language process and structure of written discourse.* New York: Academic Press.

Peterson, S. (2001). Gender identities and self-expression in classroom narrative writing. *Language Arts, 78,* 412–413.

Read, C. (1975). *Children's categorization of speech sounds in English.* Urbana, IL: National Council of Teachers of English.

Rudman, M. K. (1995). *Children's literature: An issues approach* (3rd ed.). New York: Longman.

Sitton, R. (1996). Achieving spelling literacy: A no-excuses approach. *California, Reader, 7.*

Wilde, S. (1992). *You kan red this! Spelling and punctuation for whole language classrooms, K–6.* Portsmouth, NH: Heinemann.

Zinsser, W. (Ed.). (1998). *Inventing the truth: The art and craft of memoir.* Boston: Houghton Mifflin.

Children's References

Ahlberg, J., & Ahlberg, A. (1986). *The jolly postman or other people's letters.* Little Brown.

Allan-Meyer, K. (1995). *I have a new friend.* Barron's Educational Series.

Carlson, N. L. (1997). *ABC I like me!* Scholastic.

Cleary, B. (1983). *Dear Mr. Henshaw.* Morrow.

Creech, S. (1994). *Walk two moons.* HarperCollins.

Cronin, D. (2000). *Click, clack, moo cows that type.* Scholastic.

Cullinan, B. E. (Ed.). (1995). *A jar of tiny stars: Poems by NCTE award-winning poets.* Boyds Mills.

Cushman, K. (1996). *The ballad of Lucy Whipple.* Clarion.

Dow, L. (1990). *Whales.* Weldon Owen.

Flournoy, V. (1985). *The patchwork quilt.* Dial/Dutton.

Gantos, J. (2000). *Joey Pigza loses control.* Scholastic.

Heide, F. P., & Gilliland, J. H. (1992). *Sami and the time of the troubles* Clarion.

Henkes, K. (1991). *Chrysanthemum.* Greenwillow.

Hobbs, W. (1996). *Far north.* Morrow.

James, S. (1991). *Dear Mr. Blueberry.* McElderry.

Konigsburg, E. L. (1996). *The view from Saturday.* Atheneum.

Laird, E. (1999). *Secret friends.* Putnam.

Lobel, A. (1970). *Frog and toad are friends.* HarperTrophy.

Lomas-Garza, C. (1990). *Family pictures (Cuadros de familia).* Children's Book Press.

MacLachlan, P. (1985). *Sarah, plain and tall.* Harper & Row.

MacLachlan, P. (1994). *All the places to love.* HarperCollins.

Nikola-Lisa, W. (1994). *Bein' with you this way.* Lee & Low.

Paolilli, P., & Brewer, D. (2001). *Silver seeds: A book of nature poems.* Viking.

Patent, D. H. (1989). *Humpback whales.* Holiday House.

Paulsen, G. (1987). *Hatchet.* Bradbury.

Perkins, L. R. (1997). *Clouds for dinner.* Greenwillow.

Philbric, R. (1993). *Freak the mighty.* Scholastic.

Potter, B. (1902). *The tale of Peter Rabbit.* Warne.

Raskin, E. (1997). *The westing game.* Puffin.

Ringgold, F. (1999). *If a bus could talk: The story of Rosa Parks.* Simon & Schuster.

Rylant, C. (1991). *Appalachia.* Harcourt Brace Jovanovich.

Strasser, T. (1999). *Close call.* Putnam.

Thomas, C. (1993). *Brown honey in broomwheat tea.* HarperCollins.

Tokuda, W., & Hall, R. (1986). *Humphrey the lost whale: A true story.* Heian.

Viorst, J. (1971). *The tenth good thing about Barney.* Atheneum.

Book Series (Selected Samples)

Cleary, B.: The Ramona Series
(1975) *Ramona the brave* (Morrow)
(1987) *Ramona forever* (Morrow)
(1989) *Ramona the pest* (Morrow)
(2001) *Ramona Quimby, age 8* (HarperTrophy)
(2001) *Ramona's world* (HarperTrophy)

Naylor, P. R.: Alice McKinley Series (Atheneum)
(1985) *Agony of Alice*
(1994) *Alice in-between*
(1994) *All but Alice*
(1995) *Alice the brave*
(1996) *Alice in lace*
(1997) *Outrageously Alice*
(1998) *Archingly Alice*

Sobol, D.: Encyclopedia Brown Series
(1963) *Encyclopedia Brown, boy detective* (T. Nelson)
(1967) *Encyclopedia Brown gets his man* (Lodestar)
(1969) *Encyclopedia Brown keeps the peace* (Lodestar)
(1975) *Encyclopedia Brown and the case of the dead eagles* (T. Nelson)
(1980) *Encyclopedia Brown carries on* (Four Winds Press)
(1982) *Encyclopedia Brown sets the pace* (Four Winds Press)

Artworks

Brueghel, P. *Peasant wedding*. Kunsthistorisches Museum, Vienna.
Cassatt, M. *Sleepy baby*. Dallas Museum of Art, Dallas.
Picasso, P. *The lovers*. The National Gallery of Art, Washington, DC.
Picasso, P. *The tragedy*. The National Gallery of Art, Washington, DC.
Renoir, P.-A. *Woman with a cat*. The National Gallery of Art, Washington, DC.
Segal, G. *The dancers*. The National Gallery of Art, Washington, DC.
Tanner, H. O. *The banjo lesson*. Hampton University Museum, Hampton, Virginia.

CHAPTER 4

"One can't believe impossible things" [said Alice]. *"I dare say you haven't had much practice," said the Queen. "When I was your age I always did it for half an hour a day. Why sometimes I've believed as many as six impossible things before breakfast."*

Story Writing

JOURNAL WRITING

PERSONAL WRITING

STORY WRITING

POETRY WRITING

EXPOSITORY WRITING

PERSUASIVE WRITING

Powerful and unbounded imaginations transport writers beyond retelling and summarizing to speculating, wondering, and pretending. Anyone who has ever watched children at play knows how easily they slip from the real world into make-believe, assuming the roles of adventure heroes, animals, sports stars, and TV personalities. They pretend about things that cannot really happen or become imaginary animals or characters who do not exist. **Fiction** allows them to forsake the well-traveled road of everyday reality for flights of fancy and "impossible things."

Stories are a natural part of growing up, and research tells us that children possess an intuitive awareness of the "concept of story" long before they come to school (Applebee, 1978; Mandler & Johnson, 1977; Pitcher & Prelinger, 1963; Stein & Glenn, 1979). Having been read to by adults or having watched TV, many children as young as 5 years old are able to put into words their notion of story (see Table 4–1).

Many older students often equate stories with the instruction they receive in story elements: character, setting, theme, plot, conflict, and point of view. Some mistakenly substitute a vivid bit of description for a strong story problem, or reveal quick cuts and nonsense for tension and genuine conflict. Only with experience do they come to realize that good fiction originates in the lives of real people with real problems and that it is not simply a matter of manufacturing pure action or contrived events that do not follow any logic (Graves, 1994). Even fantasy worlds are believable to the extent that they are grounded in actual events and make people willing to suspend disbelief. If fiction is viewed by some as pure description or action, others believe it is telling the reader what happened, when, and why, providing information and explanation, similar to personal **narratives.** They have not yet learned that fiction requires maintaining a connection to the five senses and inventing images in the reader's mind.

TABLE 4–1   Children's Definitions of Story
What Is a Story?
What you tell people so they will be happy (5-year-old)
Something you make up and it might have animals talking (7-year-old)
Little Red Riding Hood is a story. It has pages. It has words. It has a title and characters. Something happens. You can tell a story. (7-year-old)
A story is sometimes true or not true; sometimes you can write a story in books, magazines, or newspapers (8-year-old)
Telling about something and using transition words, a good opening, closing, details, and elaboration (10-year-old)

FIGURE 4-1 Kinds of
Story Writing

Animal realism
Art that tells a story
   Cave painting
   Fabric art
   Frescos
   Stained glass
Comic books
Dramatic plays and scripts
Epics
Fantasy
   Animal fantasy
   Science fiction
Fictional chronicle
Folklore
   Fables
   Fairy tales
   Folktales
   Legends
   Myths
   Pourquoi tales
   Tall tales
Historical fiction

Musical stories
   Broadway
   Fairy-tale ballets
   Opera
Narrative exposition
Narrative poems
Personal narratives
   Anecdotes
   Vignettes
Realistic fiction
   Adventure stories
   Fictional autobiography
   Fictional biography
   Fictional diaries
   Humorous stories
   Memoirs
   Mystery (scary) stories
   Sports stories
Rebuses
Screenplay
Story (prose) poems
Wordless picture books

Although fictional narratives move students beyond "telling" about experience to "showing" it through character action and dialogue, teachers often give this kind of writing short shrift. Not that they fail to include fiction writing, since it is often the most widely accepted type of prose found, but they permit students to simply report or summarize events instead of dramatizing behavior and action. In story writing, readers expect to "see" what the character sees, "feel" what the character feels, and "experience" what the character experiences. All stories use basic narrative techniques and story elements to create these happenings, even though they rely on distinctive skills and strategies from one genre to another (a list of the numerous genres of story writing is shown in Figure 4–1).

Explicit or **tacit knowledge** of the attributes, which typify genres, influences the strategies writers use for producing and manipulating texts. A "tall tale," for instance, is characterized by its colloquial phrases (likety split), **clichés** (quick as a flash), and exaggerated statements (eating billions of pancakes for breakfast or a squirrel as big as a cow); a fable, by its personification (animals talking and behaving like humans) and clever morals. Different kinds of fiction acquaint writers with the **genre-specific** conventions that distinguish one from another (see Table 4–2 for examples).

Although the conventions frequently help identify a specific genre (tall tale, science fiction) and form of writing (story, poetry, report), they are not rigid or fixed. An obvious example is the story **hybrid**, a multigenre story or mixed form of writing combined in a single text (Dean, 2000). Consider how a series of fictionalized letters comprises the plot structure for *Dear Mr. Henshaw* (Cleary, 1983) or how a set of journal entries frames the story *A Gathering of Days: A New England Girl's Journal 1830–1832* (Blos, 1979).

Proficient writers know that there is no single type of story but a continuum of mixed forms and genres that share language features, structural patterns, and overall purposes. Story hybrids, those found at the intersection of the overlapping semicircles in Figure 4–2, on p. 167, show how two familiar types of writing are combined to make a third, each borrowing features of the others. Mixed forms extend possibilities for writers to transform journal entries into stories, embed friendly letters into biographies, or rewrite stories as narrative poems or dramatic scripts. In an attempt to imitate the letter and

TABLE 4-2   Text Conventions Sampler

The World of Ordinary Experiences

Realistic Fiction

Characters
- Ordinary people (boys, girls, grandparents, dentists)
- Real animals; believable

Plotlines
- Real-life experiences with problems to solve
- Unfolding dramas with probable predicaments

Settings
- Real places (home, school, community)

Themes/motifs
- Change and challenges
- Kindness and generosity as high moral values to achieve; acceptance and loyalty
- Identity and growing up
- Adventure and survival

Literature example: *The Great Gilly Hopkins* (Paterson, 1978)

Mysteries

Characters
- Sharp-witted sleuths, private detectives, police, criminals, thieves, eyewitnesses

Plotlines
- Reviewing a problem or crime
- Series of clues to follow (footprints, tracks, secret codes)

Settings
- Dark remote places, such as haunted houses, hidden stairways, or alleys
- Mysterious places, such as graveyards, underground subways, shipwrecks, or attics

Themes/motifs
- Good versus evil; crime doesn't pay
- Simple "whodunits"; justice prevails
- Solving problems through ingenuity

Literature example: *Sparrows in the Gallery* (Brooks, 1998)

The World of Folklore and Fantasy

Fantasy

Characters
- Elves, ghosts, spirits, giants, little people, hobgobblins
- Personified animals, toys, objects

Plotlines
- Begins in reality and moves to fantasy
- Time warps; flexible time
- Invented circumstances and supernatural events

Settings
- Imaginary or future worlds, such as never-never land; unusual places, such as bath drains, cupboards, cellars, a lagoon

Themes/motifs
- Quest adventures with a broad concern for humanity
- Back-to-the-future and special insights
- Overcoming fears or threats
- Struggles between good and evil

Literature example: *Alice's Adventures in Wonderland* (Carroll, 1978)

Fables

Characters
- Cunning cat, clever fox, deceitful wolf
- Animals with human characteristics, such as greed, kindness, self-centeredness

Plotlines
- Straightforward; moral explicitly stated at end

Settings
- Nondescript backdrop for action
- Animals' natural habitats

Themes/motifs
- Moral lesson
- Universal truth

Literature example: *Aesop's Fables* (Gatti, 1992)

(continued)

TABLE 4-2 (continued)

The World of Folklore and Fantasy (cont.)

Fairy Tales

Characters
- Nobility (king, queen, prince, princess) heroes and heroines, common people (peasants), giants, dragons, dwarfs, trolls, ogres, wicked witches, cruel stepsisters, sorcerers, stepmothers, fairy godmothers, magical objects, supernatural beings
- One-dimensional: good/bad, stupid/clever, industrious/lazy, brave/cowardly, weak/strong

Settings
- Villages, castles, countryside, humble cottages, enchanted forests

Plotlines
- Often begins with "once upon a time"
- Happy endings (living happily ever after)
- Plot advanced by journey, spell, or long sleep
- Highly predictable and brief

Themes/motifs
- Rags to riches
- Magical wishes and transformations
- Abandonment
- Good and bad luck

Literature example: *Rapunzel* (Zelinsky, 1997)

Folklore

Characters
- Ethnic and racial groups
- Monster, wise or foolish beast, trickster
- Talking mirrors and other magical objects

Settings
- Usually general, settings not detailed
- Places around the world

Plotlines
- Simple and straightforward structure
- Relates events in threes (magic numbers)
- Positive and uplifting endings

Themes/motifs
- Insights into human predicaments
- Ordinary lives of "folk" people; explains beliefs, values, and customs

Literature example: *The Korean Cinderella* (Climo, 1993)

Legends and Tall Tales

Characters
- Folk heroes, such as Paul Bunyan, Pecos Bill, Johnny Appleseed, John Henry
- Real and imagined heroes
- Larger than life

Settings
- United States, mountains, the West
- Imaginary places, such as Camelot
- Wilderness, unexplored territories

Plotlines
- Describes a series of extraordinary events or quests
- Actions that reveal "what happened"

Themes/motifs
- Focus on how things came to pass
- Natural phenomena explanations
- Humor and the human imagination

Literature example: *John Henry* (Lester, 1994)

Myths

Characters
- Greek or Roman gods and goddesses, Mother Earth, sun and planets, natural phenomena, unicorns, dragons, and other mythical beasts

Settings
- Mount Olympus, imaginary kingdoms, beyond earth and sky
- Faraway and long, long ago, remote past, at the time of creation

Plotlines
- Supernatural incidents leading to explanations of nature or civilization

Themes/motifs
- The origin of the world, creation stories
- Human nature's primitive instincts and desires

Literature example: *The Woman Who Fell From the Sky: The Iroquois Story of Creation* (Bierhorst, 1993).

FIGURE 4-2 Story
Hybrids

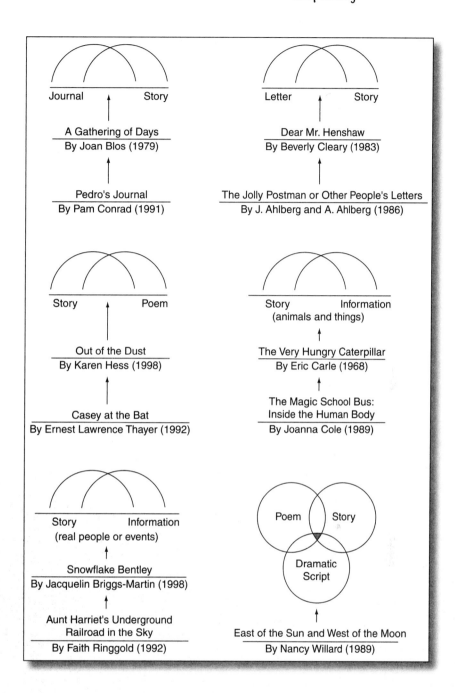

story mix, fifth-grader Jessica invites readers to eavesdrop on a conversation between two pen pals in *The Flower Letters* (see Figure 4–3).

The Flower Letters reveal Jessica's ability to move with ease between letter and story using narrative strategies learned from reading and writing. As students like Jessica broaden their understanding of text and deepen their insights into the writer's craft, they discover that lurking behind the words of their writing is often a book they have read and loved.

Writing fiction should be as much fun as reading it. If teachers project the same enthusiasm and interest for story writing that they do for reading, children will discover that the two are intimately connected. Lovers of children's literature sometimes forget that behind every good story is a writer who has created an engaging world for them to inhabit. Without J. K. Rowling, after all, there would be no Harry Potter.

FIGURE 4-3   Jessica's *The Flower Letters*, First Draft (Fifth Grader, Independent Writing)

Unedited version

Lucy McKnockwood asked her teacher, Mr. Winson, whether they would have penpals this summer or not. "Why, certainly and you will have them till the bigining of—" here he stopped. He looked at the whole class—who were anchosley waiting for him to finish, so he did "till the beginning of next year." The class groaned. "You must tell your new third-grade teacher on your progress OR write a paper." What? Lucy thought. Waist my whole summer writing to a stupid penpal? I don't think SO! "I will give you each your penpal at the end of the day." Informed Mr. W.—as they called him. So at the end of the day that was excatly what he did. Lucy made a face when she foond out who she had. His name was Michael Kennedy. Mr. W said that they would start writing right after they got their penapals on the stationary he gave out. Here's what Lucy wrote:

Dear Michael,
Hello I'm just sooo excited about being your penpal. For an entire summer! (that was a joke). I recall of other things I had to do over the summare—but this is the worst! Uh, I don't want to do this but sooo I'll tell you about my home: I live in a giant mansion, I have two million horses, and wherr I live—Needles, California. So like I said, I hate this.

                          Sincerely Bored,
                          Lucy

Dear Lucy,
    I'm sorry. I go to a all-year-round school, so it really doesn't matter to me. Since we're going to be with each other (by mail) for a while we might as well become friends. I'm 8 1/2 and I have a picture of me in school.

                                  Michael!
[picture]   P.S.
                 Bad—huh?

When Lucy got her letter she felt offended. She, a 9-year-old, writing to an 8 1/2-year-old who thinks he's hot stuff!! Lucy knew she knew more about making friends than he ever will! "I'll write him back and tell him MORE about me! Well, even though I am lying," said Lucy.

Dear Michael,
    Well I'm a 9-year-old and I'm in 3rd grade and I'm in gifted and I wear blue framed glasses, so there!

[Picture]   Offended,
                                 Lucy

WRITER'S WORKSHOP

Minilessons

Although any number of minilessons can occur during fiction writing (see Chapter 1), three interdependent topics head the list: plot, character, and narration.

FIGURE 4-4   Progressive Plotline *Source*: Based on *Charlotte's Web* by E. B. White, 1952.

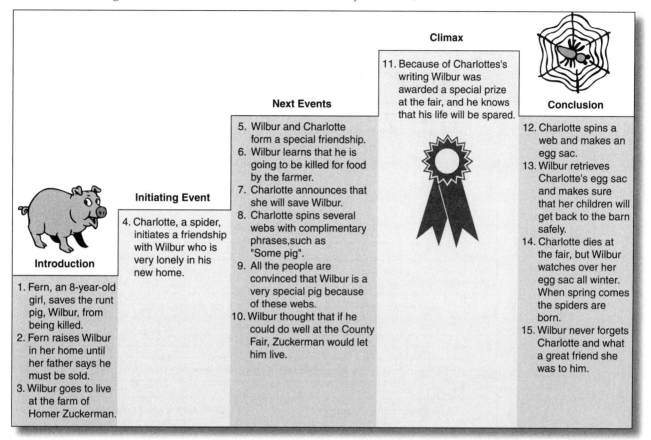

Climax

11. Because of Charlottes's writing Wilbur was awarded a special prize at the fair, and he knows that his life will be spared.

Next Events

5. Wilbur and Charlotte form a special friendship.
6. Wilbur learns that he is going to be killed for food by the farmer.
7. Charlotte announces that she will save Wilbur.
8. Charlotte spins several webs with complimentary phrases, such as "Some pig".
9. All the people are convinced that Wilbur is a very special pig because of these webs.
10. Wilbur thought that if he could do well at the County Fair, Zuckerman would let him live.

Initiating Event

4. Charlotte, a spider, initiates a friendship with Wilbur who is very lonely in his new home.

Introduction

1. Fern, an 8-year-old girl, saves the runt pig, Wilbur, from being killed.
2. Fern raises Wilbur in her home until her father says he must be sold.
3. Wilbur goes to live at the farm of Homer Zuckerman.

Conclusion

12. Charlotte spins a web and makes an egg sac.
13. Wilbur retrieves Charlotte's egg sac and makes sure that her children will get back to the barn safely.
14. Charlotte dies at the fair, but Wilbur watches over her egg sac all winter. When spring comes the spiders are born.
15. Wilbur never forgets Charlotte and what a great friend she was to him.

Plot

The plot (what happens) is the key ingredient of the story. Like a frame that holds up a building, the plot glues a set of events together. Most people think of story in the literary sense, that is, as having an initiating event, a series of consequential actions, a problem, a climax, and a resolution (Cramer, 2001; Mandler & Johnson, 1977; Stein, 1979). This type of plotline, which visually resembles a mountain and is referred to as a progressive plot, is illustrated in the graphic organizer in Figure 4–4.

By sequencing events from the well-known story *Charlotte's Web* (White, 1952), the author's development of rising and falling action becomes apparent.

Young children practice progressive plots through shared writing with wordless picture books. For instance, a group of second graders volunteers predictions and dictate the narrative plot to *A Boy, a Dog, and a Frog* (Mayer, 1978), while the teacher poses questions (What are the boy and dog doing? or Where are they now? or What might the frog be saying?). Following the group story, the students independently complete storyboards, drawings, or pictures in frames that are sequenced and labeled.

Outlining the progressive plot with a **think sheet**, similar to the one in Figure 4–5, encourages writers to consider, ahead of time, the direction in which they want to head. Many variations of Figure 4–5 exist (e.g., plot diagrams, flow charts, or storyboards), and children can select those that work best for them—with one caution: A think sheet should not direct writers to summarize story parts, as it sometimes does in reading, but should lead writers to compile specific details for producing a beginning, middle, and end. For instance, children listen for precise nouns, modifiers, and action verbs in the first part of *The Gingerbread Man* (Aylesworth, 1998) and then list words and phrases they recall.

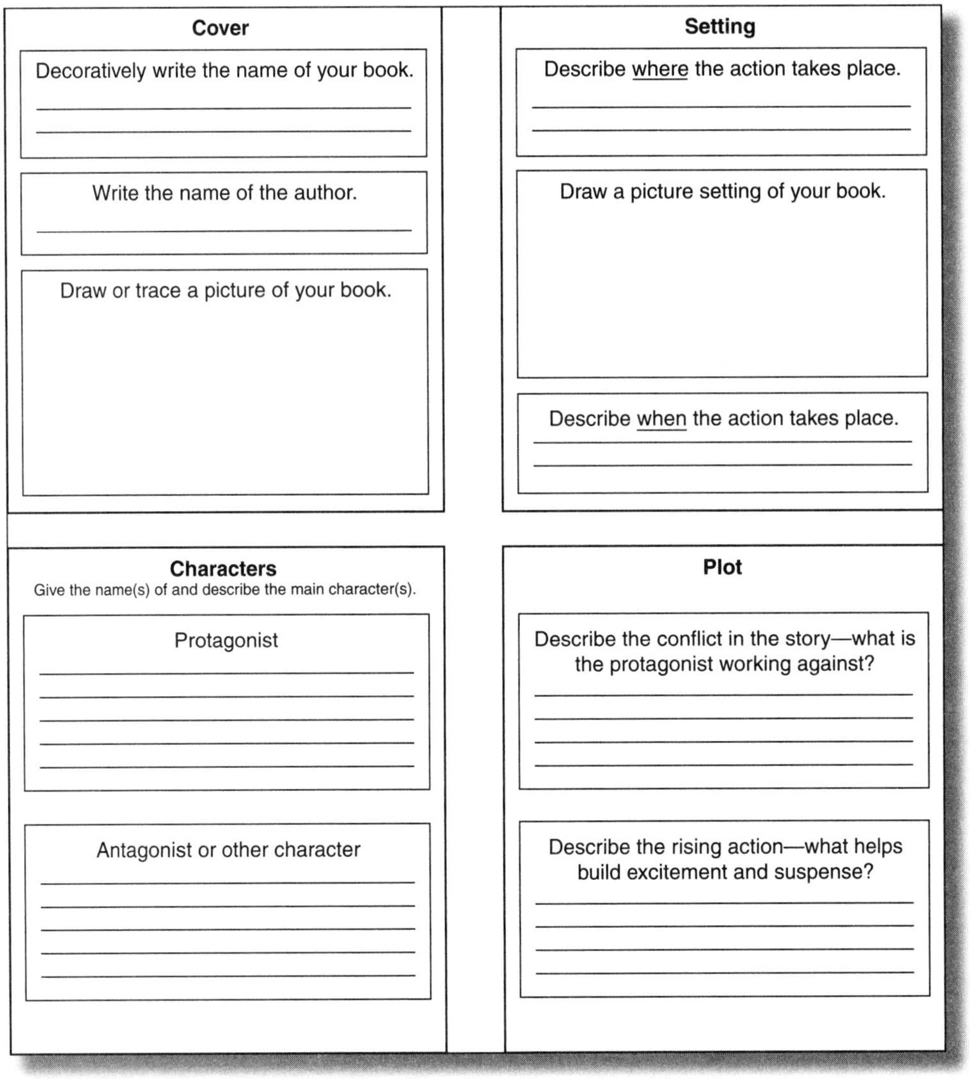

FIGURE 4-5 Think Sheet for Story Planning

Cover

Decoratively write the name of your book.
_____
_____
_____

Write the name of the author.
_____

Draw or trace a picture of your book.

Setting

Describe <u>where</u> the action takes place.
_____
_____

Draw a picture setting of your book.

Describe <u>when</u> the action takes place.
_____
_____

Characters
Give the name(s) of and describe the main character(s).

Protagonist
_____
_____
_____
_____

Antagonist or other character
_____
_____
_____
_____

Plot

Describe the conflict in the story—what is the protagonist working against?
_____
_____
_____
_____

Describe the rising action—what helps build excitement and suspense?
_____
_____
_____
_____

Little old woman	raisin eyes	sugar glaze
Little old man	batter	oven
Gingerbread man	dough	shaping arms and legs

They can use these words to write an opening scene that includes who the characters are (old man and woman), where they are (in the kitchen), what is happening (baking gingerbread cookies), and what the kitchen looks like (dough on counter, oven to one side). Drawing a picture beforehand invites description through the five senses and provides the raw material for developing the scene.

An assembly of building blocks that result in the formation of a progressive plot was shown in Chapter 1 (shared writing), where children dictated story content while the teacher asked questions to elicit dialogue, details, setting, and action. The most critical question was "What happened?" because the answer usually resulted in "an incident or action that [led] the writer towards some complication or resolution of the conflict set up in the beginning" (Egan, 1986, p. 24). At the end of the dictation, in a debriefing session, children were asked to recall the questions that the teacher used to shape the story: What happened next? Where were they? What was around them? What did they see, hear, and feel? What did the character say? In this review, implicit questioning strategies were made explicit, and tacit strategic moves, such as rereading and pausing, were revealed. Questioning strategies kept the storyline going, and rereading and pausing provided time for reflecting on words and images. In any progressive plotline it is the struggle of the main character that pushes the story forward. As part of the rising action, each attempt by the character to solve a problem must be increasingly more difficult if the reader is to remain involved in the piece. Sometimes considering the solution first "helps you [the writer] know exactly where to begin . . . and what is important for the rest of the story" (Bauer, 1992, p. 41). A solution, however, should be neither too easy (I wanted a scooter, my dad bought me one), nor unsolvable. Otherwise it is merely an incident, not a story (Bauer, 1992). When writing a progressive plotline, the writer must be able to answer the following question: Does my story have a problem that the character not only cares about, but repeatedly attempts to solve until he succeeds? With this question answered, writers are ready to proceed with the story plot.

Although the progressive plotline is the structure most commonly associated with stories, it is not the only one. Sometimes a story plot consists of repetitive structures (*We're Going on a Bear Hunt*, Rosen, 1989; *My Mom Travels a Lot*, Bauer, 1981), cumulative story sequences (*The House That Jack Built*, Bolam, 1992; Cutts, 1979; *The Cake That Mack Ate*, Robart, 1991), chained verse (*Each Peach Pear Plum*, Ahlberg & Ahlberg, 1979; *Mockingbird*, Ahlberg & Howard, 1998), question and answer dialogues (*Polar Bear, Polar Bear, What Do You Hear?* Martin, 1991), circular dream sequences (*Where the Wild Things Are*, Sendak, 1963; *The Wizard of Oz*, Baum, 1982), and other organizations (see Figure 4–6, a–e). Part of the appeal of these structures is the rhythm, harmony, and sounds that trail from the words on the page. More like games and songs than stories, they elicit singing and acting out (clapping, stamping feet, swaying bodies) as part of the children's active participation.

For instance, in *Mockingbird*, the book version of the familiar lullaby, both repetition and chaining provide a "call-and-response" structure for adding new lines. The teacher summons a story through a call or opening line: *Hush, little baby, don't say a word*, and the children answer with the response: *Mama's gonna buy you a mockingbird*. Using an *if–then* predictable pattern, teachers and children can jointly construct the story, repeatedly changing the characters and the rhyming words.

Call	**Response**
(Teacher) If that mockingbird won't sing	(child fills in something that rhymes with *sing*)

If the teacher places rhyming words with common endings (*ing, uck*) on the word wall, choices are readily available and everyone can participate.

(Call) *Sing* **(If that mocking bird won't *sing*)**	**(Call)** *Stuck* **(If that garden swing gets *stuck*)**
(Response options)	**(Response options)**
Wing	Truck
Thing	Duck
Ring	Luck

The chained structure offers another predictable pattern for adding new lines to an existing story. In *Polar Bear, Polar Bear, What Do You Hear?* the plot is stitched together in three ways: by a question/answer sequence, by a response that becomes the beginning of the next question, and by final words that rhyme at the end of sentence pairs.

> Polar bear, polar bear, what do you hear?
> I hear a lion roaring in my ear.
> Lion, lion, what do you hear?
> I hear a hippopotamus snorting in my ear.

Children brainstorm a list of animals and the sounds they make, gradually stringing together new sentences and elaborating on the piece.

Another story that gives children practice chaining and constructing rhyming couplets (a pair of sentences in which the last word of each line rhymes) is *Each Peach Pear*

FIGURE 4-6 (a) Circular Plotline, (b) Cumulative Plotline, (c) Episodic Plotline, (d) Linear Plotline, or Bed-to-Bed Narrative, and (e) Repetitive Plotline

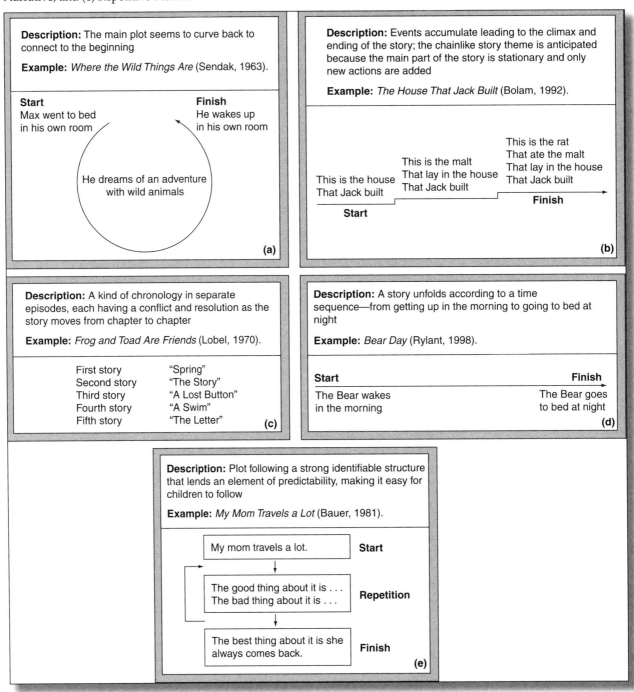

Plum. By repeating the names of nursery rhyme and folktale characters and by moving the last word of the previous sentence to the first word in the next, the story becomes a kind of musical harmony.

> Each peach pear plum
> I spy Tom Thumb
> Tom Thumb in the cupboard
> I spy Mother Hubbard

FIGURE 4-7 Graphic
Organizer for a
Cumulative Story

Children can imitate this model using the names of favorite characters (Snow White) and thinking of rhyming words that go with them *(night, right, sight/bite, kite, site)*. Sorting words according to spelling patterns can become part of this activity. Connecting story line with rhyme and repetition is just another example of how different structures and techniques work together, often in a single text, to create textured and melodious effects.

Another popular effect found in young children's books is the use of the cumulative structure, which involves adding phrases or clauses to a basic sentence, as in *The House That Jack Built, The Cake That Mack Ate*, and *A Giraffe and a Half* (Silverstein, 1964).

This is the house that Jack built.
This is the malt that lay in the house that Jack built.
This is the rat that ate the malt that lay in the house that Jack built.

With repetition, accumulation, and rhythm, these books make delightful stories out of the barest of plots. Students can emulate this model by generating topics—word pairs, a noun (thing) and a verb (action)—*bed/sleep; bench/rest; tree house/play*—selecting a pair *(bed, sleep)* and associating four or five words *(blanket, teddy bear, book)* related to it, and placing words on a pyramid like the one in Figure 4–7. Referring to the graphic organizer to remember the order of events, children may write the following sentences:

This is the bed where I sleep
This is the blanket that lays on [the bed where I sleep]
This is the teddy bear that I hug at night [that sits on the blanket, that lays on the bed where I sleep]
This is the book I read to [the teddy bear that I hug at night, that sits on the blanket, that lays on the bed where I sleep]

Children play with these sentences as if they were verbal puzzles, and the steps of the pyramid provide a visual prompt for reading them back.

A simple way to introduce cumulative stories is to have students draw a series of pictures, adding something new to each successive story frame. In a first-grader's tale about a mouse who was sad because he didn't have anyone to play with, each story frame shows an animal coming to play with the mouse (see Figure 4–8).

A familiar cumulative story can be retold with concrete props or story figures. A primary school teacher reads *The Gigantic Rutabaga* (Franco, 1993), which is a Russian folktale about a farmer who attempts to remove a giant rutabaga (turnip) from his garden. As characters are added to the story (see Figure 4–9), one at a time, in the order they come to the farmer's rescue, the children line up paper cutout figures representing the characters (farmer, farmer's wife, daughter, dog, cat, and a mouse) and join in the repetitive refrain: And they pulled, and they pulled, and they pulled, but it wouldn't come up. The oral retelling may be followed by a writing task in which the children use the paper cutouts to order their stories and add in the repetitive refrain.

FIGURE 4-8
Cumulative Story, *The Mouse*, First Draft Drawings (First Grader, Independent Writing)

FIGURE 4-9 *The Gigantic Rutabaga* by B. Franco (1993)
Source: Russia: A Literature-Based Multicultural Unit. Evan-Moor Educational Publishers. Reprinted with permission.

Children love refrains, those pleasurable interludes inspired by poems and songs. For instance, the author of *We're Going on a Bear Hunt* includes regularly recurring phrases in literary rounds, each followed by humorous alliterative words.

Refrain

We're going on a bear hunt.
We're going to catch a big one.
What a beautiful day!
We're not scared.

Children can write their own refrains or borrow them from songs and poems (e.g., the *Oompa loompa dompa de doo,* chorus in the movie *Willy Wonka and the Chocolate Factory* or the *little plumpuppets plump-up it!* passage in Christopher Morley's [1983] poem *The Plumpuppets*). Repetitive refrains make short pieces longer and, when read aloud, prompt others to join in.

Just as a repetitive or cumulative structure can drive an entire story, it can also be embedded in the middle of a complex narrative. For example, a fourth grader writes the story of Ducky following the progressive plotline: An introduction presents a problem (the animals throw a surprise party but forget to invite Ducky, the guest of honor), a middle consists of roadblocks (the animals look everywhere but can't find Ducky), and the end provides a resolution to the conflict (the animals find Ducky swimming in the pond, in the exact same place where the party is being held). A repetitive sequence of three sentences with slight variations is inserted into the middle, providing the Ducky story with suspense:

> They looked for him at Bear's house, but he was not there.
> They looked for him near the big oak tree, but he was not there.
> They looked for him down the rabbit hole, but he was not there.

By repeating the patterned sentences, the writer gives the illusion of time passing (they looked here, then there, here, then there) and brings spatial elements to the piece (at Bear's house, near the big oak tree, down the rabbit hole).

In short, writers use many different structures to add interest to the more common progressive plotline. Determining when and how to introduce these structures depends on the age and experience of the students, along with the books they are reading and emulating.

Character

If plot is the stuff that stories are made of, then the driving force behind plot is the existence of strong and memorable characters. Most readers know Harry Potter as a boy wizard, with a thin lightning-shaped scar on his forehead, who talks to snakes and rides a high-priced broom called the Nimbus Two Thousand (Rowling, 1998). The author depicts Harry in a way that makes readers care about him; she wants them to think he is real, even if he is not. Readers get to know characters by the way they are described (appearance), by what they say to themselves or others (monologue and dialogue), and by what they think and do (motivation and behavior).

The first characters children include in stories are usually peers and family members (Jorgensen, 2001). When they begin to invent characters (or animals) and give them roles, anything is possible. They assign names to characters and give them physical features, behaviors, thoughts, actions, and conversational styles to fit their personalities. They study people as they walk down the street, move through the school halls, or sit at the supper table (Bauer, 1992). Inventing these personalities, however, may mean "living" with characters awhile, to get to know them. Older students answer questions on a simple fact sheet, such as the one in Figure 4–10, to familiarize themselves with the particular attributes that make each character special. When the exercise is complete, writers set it aside to avoid copying answers sequentially into a story. They can return to the fact sheet before revising to ensure that the actions and behaviors of a character are consistent with his personality. Writers might ask, for example, would character X do this, and, if so, under what circumstances?

Short, descriptive portraits and thumbnail sketches are a good way for young children to begin practicing characterization (see Figure 4–11). For them, these pieces may be final products in their own right. Older students, however, should save character sketches as they would resumes and refer to them to "audition" characters for parts in longer, more developed stories. In complex writing, where conflict becomes the centerpiece, teachers introduce the terms *protagonist* (the good guy) and *antagonist* (the bad guy). Conflict involves a struggle between these two forces; without it, there is nothing for the main character to do.

When students start to experiment with well-rounded characters and minor ones whose actions have consequences, the story becomes richer with more texture and detail. Not surprisingly, new problems arise. For example, how will readers understand and identify the characters' personalities? Simply dropping names, without showing who's doing what, can be confusing. How do writers avoid lengthy descriptions of a character in the middle of unfolding action? If the writer doesn't weave together appearance, thoughts, words, and actions, the natural flow and rhythm of writing becomes sluggish. New strategies are needed. Asking questions about character motivations or logic, or

FIGURE 4-10   Character Fact Sheet

Directions: Please fill out these questions completely so that you can refer to them later to create a detailed character sketch.

What is your character's name? _____

What is your character's age? _____

Is your character a girl or a boy? _____

What does your character look like? _____

_____

Who is your character's best friend? _____

How is this character different from other people you know? _____

_____

Who does this character remind you of? _____

_____

What are your character's favorite hobbies? _____

What types of things does your character like to do? _____

_____

What types of things does your character dislike? _____

_____

How does your character dress? _____

What does your character like to eat? _____

What problems does your character face? _____

_____

What might your character say? _____

_____

What might your character think? _____

How might your character react to others? _____

_____

How does your character solve a problem? _____

Why is your character interesting to know? _____

_____

What makes your character likable? _____

What sort of emotions might your character feel? _____

_____

What is your character's biggest fear? _____

_____

Tell about other aspects of your character's life. _____

Examples:
Does your character have brothers or sisters?
Does your character eat breakfast?
Does your character play a musical instrument?
Does your character love animals?

FIGURE 4-11
(a) Character Sketch, *The Robot*, Final Draft (First Grader, Guided Writing); (b) Character Sketch, *The Witch*, Final Draft (First Grader, Guided Writing)

about why certain events occur (Why did your character do that? What might have happened to your character that would cause him to do that?) imbues a good story not only with tension and movement, but also with real human intrigue and struggle (Graves, 1994). Dropping one or two word clues here and there about a character (e.g., she *tossed back* her *auburn hair*) helps keep the narrative action moving and reduces overly descriptive passages that can bog down a piece. Placing a character within a simple integral setting or context enables readers to locate and follow him in the ongoing flow of events (at the kitchen table, outside the house, upstairs), just as documenting what the character does and says from moment to moment (She ran downstairs yelling, "I won!") brings him to life on the page. Characterization is at the very heart of a story—in the action, the plot, the setting, the point of view, everything. When it is done well, the character and plot are inseparable and create a unified image in readers' minds.

Narration

Narration is a basic writing strategy for presenting human action and plot (Axelrod & Cooper, 2001). According to Freeman (1995), there are two types of narrative: fictional (dramatic narrative) and nonfictional (personal narrative and informative narrative). Each tells a story but differs in purpose and style. Consider the fictional narrative *Petite Rouge: A Cajun Red Riding Hood* (Artell, 2001), which is a spin-off of the classic folktale in which the customary wolf is replaced by a "gator." The rhymed verse is full of fantasy and humor; the dialect is sheer entertainment. Now contrast this with an informative narrative such as Jean Craighead George's *The Moon of the Alligators* (1991), which is another story about an alligator but one laden with facts about the ecosystem and the Everglades. Both are narratives.

Although writers can choose from a wide range of narrative devices, certain ones are essential for fictional narrative: dialogue, description, detail, and action. Mixing and combining these four devices results in what many writing instructors refer to as *show don't tell*. All good writing is show don't tell, but many novice writers are unsure of what is involved in identifying and producing it. They may think they are spinning a dramatic or fictional narrative, when, in reality, they are merely telling and restating information. Show don't tell highlights what characters *do* or *say* in story scenes. According to Dibell (1988), "a scene is one connected and sequential action, together with its embedded description and background material. It seems to happen just as if a reader were watching and listening to it happen. It's built on talk and action. It's dramatized, shown, rather than being summarized or talked about" (p. 8). Dibell goes on to say "creating scenes means finding ways for your story to show itself, rather than ways for you to tell it" (p. 9). Although it is tempting to teach the devices of description, dialogue, detail, and action in separate exercises, these strategies are best learned together in the context of character action and plot.

Spontaneous drama, for instance, brings the four strategies of action, dialogue, detail, and description together in a meaningful context. Beginning with a set of questions, students orient themselves to a scene:

- Where would you like to be?
- Who is there?
- What is everyone doing?

With only a few ideas, they are ready to define and solve problems based on the actions of other characters and in response to cues from the teacher coaching from the side (using specific and visual action words, such as *creep* or *slither*). Props, such as hand-drawn murals for story settings (a bedroom, a storefront window, the ocean), simple costume pieces (scarves, an apron, a hat, a crown, eyeglasses), and objects (phone, umbrella, sword, candles) can enhance the drama or broaden the writer's insights for finding fresh scene material. In some schools, students collect items associated with different stories and place them in ready-made prop kits to use over and over again (e.g., a magic motif might include a top hat, feather, wand, magic cape, and four-leaf clover). This enables connections to be made between particular types of stories and their objects and words.

With props as integral parts of a scene, students express emotions and thoughts in concrete physical experiences before translating them to written words. Building on the drama, the teacher and students write a shared story, joining the dialogue and action (characterization) and the descriptions (setting and props). The details and words for the props are placed on a word wall and defined according to their use in the story events. The setting is described after viewing the mural. To recall a story action, children repeat select enactments at the teacher's request. For example, "Show me again what the boy looked like when he opened the surprise package. Yes, now let's put this into words."

Practicing dramatic invention (finger puppets, improvisation, or role-play) helps students put into action the elements of a story using behaviors, visuals, and dialogue. Acting is an important tool for writing; it transforms abstract words and summaries into show don't tell narratives and recognizes an integrated set of strategies that might be difficult to demonstrate in another way.

Another way to address show don't tell is by reading text samples that illustrate each strategy to determine whether differences can be identified. For example, the following human interest story from a local newspaper provides examples of journalistic *telling* along with *showing* sequences that engage the reader's imagination. The article from which the excerpts are taken is about a companion bird dog named Gunner who has a dangerous encounter with an alligator. Fortunately, the story has a happy ending—the owner successfully rescues the dog and takes him to a veterinarian who cleans and stitches the animal's wounds. In the first excerpt, notice how the writer uses description, dialogue, detail, and action to describe the events. The text is written as it appeared in the newspaper except for the name of the owner.

> Edwin spotted a boil of water 35 feet from the shore and figured the gator—which had snatched Gunner by his rear legs and torso—was rolling his good buddy over and over, trying to drown him. "I saw Gunner's head go by and I reached in and grabbed him with my right hand and pulled his head up," Edwin said. "The look in his eyes, I'll never forget it. It was like a glare. He was looking at me like, 'Daddy, what in the world has got me?'"

As this excerpt illustrates, the writer paints images of the lake, of the owner, and of the gator and dog thrashing around. The senses are invigorated. However, in the second excerpt, the writer switches to the telling mode to offer advice to the reader about alligators.

> Alligators are most active during warm weather when they're breeding and raising their young. Males are very territorial during breeding and females are very protective of their nests. Because dogs and small children are attractive targets for large alligators, please don't let them wade or swim in lakes and rivers inhabited by alligators.

In the reporting excerpt, the writer's purpose is to convey facts, summarize the events, and provide advice. In the showing excerpt, the writer's purpose is to capture the attention of readers. Both are effectively accomplished.

Teachers will find that most texts use a combination of show and tell strategies, to a greater or lesser degree, depending on the genre. In dramatic fiction, the proportion of showing parts far outweighs the telling parts.

Students can practice the show don't tell strategy with photographs of family and events and by asking questions that emphasize the active verbs *say, do,* and *show.*

- What do I see?
- What is the person(s) in my picture saying? How is he saying it?
- What is the person(s) in my picture doing?
- Where is the person(s) in my picture (beach, mountains, etc.)? How did he get there? What is he doing there?
- Who is the person with?
- How do the people in my picture feel about one another?
- What happened before this picture was taken? What happened after it was taken? How can I show this?

By engaging in these heuristics, the children generate content that suggests movement and affects the five senses, turning the still-life photo into an active scene.

Students can also try transforming "tell me" statements into "show me" statements using character traits, actions, setting, or other elements.

Tell Me	Show Me
He was respectful	He put all his toys in their proper place
He cried	Tears rolled down his cheek
It was a summer day	Bright blue sky, baking sun, mosquitoes swarming

Ultimately, the best place to discuss show don't tell is in conferences and writing circles. Preparing children to use this strategy strengthens their resolve to refine statements in their own work.

Reading

Adults who read to children, ask questions, dramatize what they say, or embed stories in everyday conversation are preparing youngsters for literacy (Harste, Woodward, & Burke, 1984; Heath, 1982, 1993; Taylor & Strickland, 1986). Books contain all of the marvelous literary examples writers want or need for story writing. Furthermore, when children are taught to "read like writers" (Smith, 1983) their attention is on the strategies authors use to produce specific features of text. From this perspective, literature becomes an indispensable resource for writing. First and foremost, it is a language model and an object of study for examining story elements. Second, it inspires creative drama, a literacy vehicle that positions children for the world of make-believe and role-taking. Finally, it allows for literary borrowing which paves the way for independent writing. Each of these is discussed further.

Fiction and Story Elements

Fiction is broadly defined as "imaginative narrative in any form of presentation that is designed to entertain" (Harris & Hodges, 1995, p. 83). Although there are many types of fiction (realistic fiction, historical fiction, biographies, and autobiographies), in this chapter, fiction is aligned closely with imaginary worlds and dramatic action like that found in fairy tales, folktales, and fantasy. Books representing these genres are ideal print models for studying story elements. For example, see those highlighting character and setting (Table 4–3), plot and theme (Figure 4–2), and point of view (Table 4–5, p. 190). With a teacher's repeated readings of the same book, the story elements and strategies slowly unfold before children's eyes. Initially, children might concentrate on a storyline or memorable character, and, at another time, they might focus on a captivating setting or unusual detail (Martinez & Roser, 1985; Morrow, 1988).

Reading for theme, the dominant message that unifies a story (growing up, survival, or an aesthetic appreciation of nature), may stir memories of personal events that writers can incorporate into their own works.

Basic **motifs** or motives that expand narratives (good versus evil, wishes and magic, heroes and heroines, time travel and unusual worlds) guide writers in developing episodes or scenes in their writing. For example, children recognize and intuitively understand the popular journey motif. A child (or animal) leaves the security of home because of a problem or unhappy situation and begins an adventure. The adventure, although daring and exciting, is plagued with danger and unexpected roadblocks, and, in the end, the character decides to return home (see, for example, *Where the Wild Things Are*, Sendak, 1963, or *Alice in Wonderland*, Carroll, 1978).

Characterization can be emphasized in any book. When they are reading series books, students can develop insights into favorite characters (e.g., Ramona in Beverly

TABLE 4–3   Books Representing Story Elements (Character and Setting)

Character	Setting
Belle Teal (Martin, 2001) (I)	*A Year Down Yonder* (Peck, 2000) (I)
Boston Jane: An Adventure (Holm, 2001) (I)	*Across America, I Love You*
Junie B., First Grader at Last! (Park, 2001) (P)	(Loomis, 2000) (P)
Olivia (Falconer, 2000) (P)	*Mansa Musa: The Lion of Mali*
Stowaway (Hesse, 2000) (I)	(Burns, 2001) (P)
Super, Completely and Totally the Messiest	*Nory Ryan's Song* (Giff, 2000) (I)
(Viorst, 2001) (P)	*The Breadwinner* (Ellis, 2000) (I)
When Zachary Beaver Came to Town	*The Land* (Taylor, 2001) (I)
(Holt, 1999) (I)	*The Other Side* (Woodson, 2001) (P)
	The Three Pigs (Wiesner, 2001) (P)
	Witness (Hesse, 2001) (I)

P = Primary
I = Intermediate

Cleary's books, Arthur in Marc Brown's books, or Curious George in Hans and Margret Rey's books) by observing the characters' reactions to various events, relationships they become involved in (with friends or pets), and actions or incidents that typically befall them. Citing quotations that typify a character's personality or discussing remarkable traits calls attention to the invention strategies authors use. Students also identify the book's point of view and ask themselves who will tell the story.

As students read for story elements, they begin to recognize specific writing features, such as structure and style. Mapping the plot of a book increases their understanding of story structure and deepens their knowledge of written linguistic features (Dickinson, 1987; Eckhoff, 1983; Purcell-Gates, McIntyre, & Freppon, 1995). Books that follow structural patterns, such as question/answer sequences (e.g., *Does a Kangaroo Have a Mother, Too?* Carle, 2000, and *Who Is in the Garden?* Rosenberry, 2001) or what if's (e.g., *If All the World Were Paper*, Nerlove, 1991, and *If You Hopped Like a Frog*, Schwartz, 1999), offer story frames to emulate, just as renditions of the same story (e.g., Cinderella) show the possibility of putting a new twist to something familiar (e.g., *The Rough-Face Girl*, Martin, 1992; *Cendrillon: A Caribbean Cinderella*, San Souci, 1998; or *Cinderella's Rat*, Meddaugh, 1997).

Studying the works of a single author magnifies how voice and style act as the writer's signature. For instance, *Alice in Wonderland* (Carroll, 1978) exemplifies amusing language; *Maniac Magee* (Spinelli, 1990), short, crisp, repetitive sentences; and *Roll of Thunder, Hear My Cry* (Taylor, 1976), authentic dialect. Asking children what they like about an author's works may lead to identifying and discussing style.

- What topics does the author write about? Name some.
- Does the author use long sentences, short, or a little of each? Give examples.
- How does the author use big words, special words, silly words? What are they?
- What point of view does the author bring to his work? How does this affect the story?

Style represents a writer's particular way of saying something. The presence or absence of select features and the way in which they are arranged and orchestrated often account for the story's appeal. Children can examine sentence variety (simple, complex, compound sentences), flow (one sentence leads naturally to the next; order), or precision with words (the simplest and smallest number of words needed to create meaning). Style and story elements are repeatedly discussed in the context of books to support and augment story schema. When children eavesdrop on characters' conversations, experience similar situations, or enjoy the surprise of words peeking around corners, they make personal connections to a book that they can later use in writing. The response journal discussed in Chapter 2 will aid in these associations and stimulate interests and imagination for writing.

Drama

Not only do students examine favorite books and use them as print models, but they also participate in dramatic activities based on books. Drama, as discussed earlier, introduces the children to various literary elements and enables them to journey inside an event to extend, enrich, and extrapolate basic material with ideas of their own (Fennessey, 1995; McMaster, 1998). When children improvise ideas or pose questions not answered by the text, they develop personal knowledge of plot development and story elements that prepare them for writing (Stewig, 1983). Some of the creative drama and language activities that aid in this preparation include the following:

Retelling stories: Retelling stories requires an understanding of plot and the ability to select episodes to present to someone who is unfamiliar with the story (Morrow, 1997; Pellegrini & Galda, 1982). Writers can practice retelling by examining personal incidents that are the basis of plots (sibling rivalry, risk taking, jealousy) and then enacting a story with props. In an oral retelling of a favorite book, children choose flannel board figures for settings (trees, flowers, castles), character descriptions (aprons, hats), and objects of action (swords, horses) and use these to recall events or scaffold the story. Giving children access to a utility box filled with photographs, magazines, old readers, costumes, and other hands-on materials may be just the trick for getting the creative juices flowing.

Storytelling: Storytelling is a way to rehearse ideas for writing or perform stories children have already written. Telling a story from memory encourages a strong plot for entertaining audiences and gives practice with beginnings, middles, and ends. A few suggestions guide students through the process (Piazza, 1999):

- Read and reread the story until incidents are firmly and clearly understood and remembered
- Mentally list the episodes or sequence of events
- Rely on language repetition (and he huffed and he puffed)
- Learn a few lines verbatim if they are essential to the story plot and will hold it together
- Practice

Puppet shows: Puppet shows are vehicles for trying out ideas and narrating stories. Children get to project creativity publicly while concealed behind a stage. A stage can be as simple as a cardboard box with the back cut out or the top of a desk with a makeshift curtain around the sides. When children present their stories to an audience, they bring words to life and explore events that need to be modified.

Expressive movement: Expressive movement exercises can show how readers and writers depend on words to conjure up nonverbal actions when they tell stories. For instance, after reading a book such as *Pretend You're a Cat* (Marzollo, 1990), children role-play different animal mannerisms using movement vocabulary (stretch, climb, hiss). Actions words of motion (walk, craw, leap, gallop), expression (meander, creep, bend, shake), and relations (meet, merge, shadow, congregate) are added to word walls to strengthen vocabulary.

Drama activities are too often ignored in the writing classroom, yet they provide a valuable bridge to written language. Barnes (1968) tells us that "drama is the . . . primal ocean in which the other literary forms float—monologue and dialogue, exposition, narration, description, argument, lyric, oration, epigram, apothegm" (p. 6). Through drama children are rehearsing many of the skills they will later apply to writing.

Literary Borrowing

Indeed, literature is a springboard for writing and nowhere is this more obvious than in the practice of literary borrowing, in which students appropriate story characters, plots, titles, words, or repetitive language written by their favorite authors (Lancia, 1997; Lunsford, 1997; Wolf & Heath, 1998). For example, children construct their own texts based on characters they have read about (little people, talking mirrors, greedy animals) or add compelling rhymes and refrains to their writings based on predictable patterns in books such as *Brown Bear, Brown Bear, What Do You See?* (Martin, 1992). They might adapt a memorable theme or borrow a plot structure, such as the one in *Alexander and the Terrible, Horrible, No Good, Very Bad Day* (Viorst, 1972), to write a parallel story about their own bad day.

Children can borrow any aspect of story—a theme, a plot, an episode, a transition, a sentence, a word. For instance, they might look through several articles in magazines, cut out the first sentence or paragraph of the article, place it on a note card and, on the back, write the function or strategy it exemplifies (an **anecdote,** a question, dialogue). Concrete samples of author strategies become a handy resource for writing opening scenes or story beginnings. Similarly, children can complete webs of story words, or so-called **referential words,** associated with the topic or genre (Kane, 1988). Words that signal to a reader that they are reading fiction, for instance, might include commonly used transitions (*suddenly, by and by*), and certain nouns (*ogres, princess*), verbs (*screamed, wiggled*), adjectives (*unruly, fickle*) and adverbs (*wickedly, peacefully*) on a particular topic. Since words are the building blocks for making meaning, it is good practice to call attention to them.

Literary borrowing is also valuable for developing strategies such as associating and comparing. Children might associate a new idea with something previously written or connect several kinds of conflicts to a problem they are writing about. They might compare the leads in several stories or list the likeable and unlikable characters in three different books. As children continue to write stories they bolster their understanding of the rules that govern the elements of a story and its underlying structure (Mandler & Johnson, 1977).

Story schema is further strengthened and literary borrowing further diminished as children increasingly rely on an expanding knowledge base about stories.

Borrowing is not plagiarizing. Rather, it is putting a new spin to an idea, strategy, or character personality. Any time students copy verbatim parts of another's story or alter it in only a slight way, they must cite the work or credit it with terms such as "taken from" or "based on." Children will eventually identify the difference between copying another's words and borrowing an idea that they reinvent into something original.

When borrowing is used as a temporary scaffold to structure a story, it offers a print model that writers can consult when they are stuck. The story frame is an example. To construct a story frame, the teacher chooses a passage or episode from a book the class is reading and deletes key words. Once children select and insert words into the frame, they compare their versions of the story with that of the text:

Story Frame

Once upon a time there was a _____. He/she lived _____ with his/her three _____. One day, _____ went to visit _____. He/she said _____.

Frames can focus on plots, settings, or character traits and can be designed by the teacher or students.

Choosing parts of a story to borrow is not exclusive to children's literature. Newspaper headlines can become the theme of a fable or fairytale, poetic verse may be added to a humorous story, and certainly, topics, plots, or characters can be borrowed from each other's written work.

In addition to print sources children turn to **multiple forms of literacy** for borrowing (Piazza, 1999). For example, the lyrics from folk music, country-western, Broadway songs (*The Lion King*) and musical videos (*Willie Wonka and the Chocolate Factory*) seem particularly appropriate for borrowing since they have stories to tell. Children can also turn to the Internet to view what other children have written or use storybook software that provides choices for characters, settings, graphics, and sounds. Art that tells stories, story ballets, and movies are also viable literacy forms for borrowing.

Composing

Prewriting

Thus far several prewriting activities have been discussed, including the use of wordless picture books, character sketches, storyboards, think sheets, reading, literary borrowing, and drama. These are not repeated here. The list in Figure 4–12 serves as a reminder of the possibilities that fall within the realm of prewriting.

Regardless of the activity chosen or when it is used (prior to drafting or before revising) remember that the importance of prewriting is not only to generate ideas but also to help students imagine a scene and experience their characters. The ability to get

FIGURE 4-12
FIGURE 4-12
Prewriting Activities
for Story Writing

Creating artworks	Free writing
Making story quilts	Making graphic organizers
Making mosaics	Drafting mind maps
Making stained glass	Drafting plot diagrams
Creatively visualizing	Drafting webs
Developing comic strips	Listening to music
Doodling and drawing	Viewing movies
Enacting drama	Examining photographs
Performing prop plays	and scrapbooks
Performing puppetry	Creating picture books
Performing reader's theater	Working with word
Role-playing	processing and
Writing dream diaries	software programs

into the mind and emotions of the characters and to sustain their perspectives throughout a story is essential to master. In a third-grade classroom, children practice role-taking and act out some of the characters pictured in Katherine Freeman's (1994) artwork *If Balloons Were Wishes* (see Figure 4–13). The teacher tells them to put on their magic hats and step into the painting to become one of the characters. He may say, "Tell us what is happening? What are you looking at? What are you thinking? What or who is around you? What are you feeling? What are you doing? If you are talking, what are you saying?" After initial brainstorming, volunteers start the story and others slowly join the scene.

Boy: Hello Mr. Balloon Man. How are you today?

Balloon Man: I'm fine. Would you like a balloon?

Boy: No thank you. [Dog enters]

Boy: Cute dog. [Pets dog]

Following the model, children write stories from the point of view of one of the characters in the picture. Third-grader Kimberly imagines herself in the role of the dog and details what he is doing and thinking in Figure 4–13. As this sample shows, Kimberly uses the picture to frame a story scene and suggest a point of view. Kimberly is not merely labeling items in the picture—a balloon, a man, a dog, and so on—but envisioning the scene as if it were real and being brought to life.

In the world of art all types of story elements are present in addition to point of view. Portraitures become stimuli for writing character appearances, monologues, or dialogues; landscapes, for writing descriptions of a setting; abstracts, for generating moods and feelings.

In Faith Ringgold's story quilt and accompanying book, *Tar Beach* (1991), which tell the story of a little girl's dream, visual messages are encoded into written language. Students view book illustrations or artworks to help them imagine an opening for their stories.

- Who is there?
- What are they doing?
- What is happening?

Once students have an opening scene, a moving picture, in their minds, they then refer to the 5W questions (who, what, when, where, and why) as a heuristic for amplifying the content. At the end of each sentence, they ask questions to keep the writing going: "What happened next?" They should cast these questions in such a way as not to result in facts and examples but to develop sensory descriptions, actions, dialogue, and details (of the story). It is best to focus on verbs: What are the people doing or saying. What happened?

Karen Jorgensen (2001) suggests taking students on "story trips," neighborhood walks to the park, shopping center, or playground. When children sketch places and happenings on their outings, they "hone observation skills and learn to use sense impressions" (p. 37).

It is not necessary for children to wait for the story unit to begin writing stories. In daily journal writing, they can record overheard conversations (dialogue), events in their lives (plot), problems they encounter (conflicts), and solutions to those problems (resolution). Remind students that writers are always looking for story material and that their journal entries are simply waiting for a story to unfold around them.

Drafting

The writer's primary goal during the drafting stage is to sketch the story's beginning, middle, and end. Various types of plots that comprise and shape these parts have already been discussed; however, when writers actually apply what they have learned

FIGURE 4-13
Kimberly's *The Park*, First Draft (Third Grader, Guided Writing)
Source: Based on the painting, *If Balloons Were Wishes* by K. Freeman. Courtesy Tatistcheff Gallery, New York.

To day we went to the park I started to look at the girl feeding the birds. I say to myself I'm sleepy and I wont to take a nap. Im also saying I bet the people wont a dog like me. Also they are skat boarding and buying balloons. The suddenly a man is flying with a balloon. Then I start barking. Then my owner

(continued)

FIGURE 4-13
(continued)

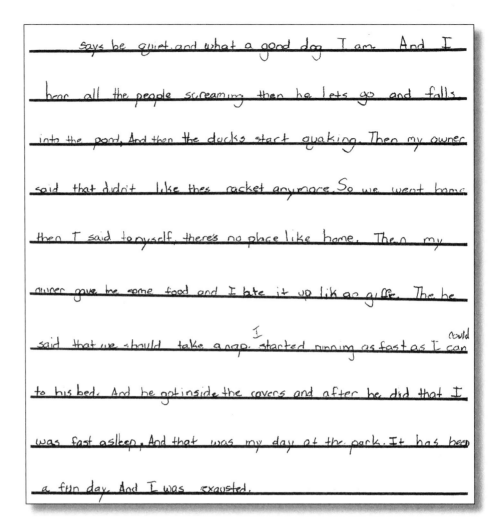

says be quiet. and what a good dog I am. And I hear all the people screaming then he lets go and falls into the pond. And then the ducks start quaking. Then my owner said that didn't like this racket anymore. So we went home then I said to myself, there's no place like home. Then my owner gave me some food and I ate it up like as giff. The he said that we should take a nap. started running as fast as I could can to his bed. And he got inside the covers and after he did that I was fast asleep. And that was my day at the park. It has been a fun day. And I was exausted.

about plot to a story, there are no specific rules for putting ideas on paper. Some start smack in the middle of the story and work from there; others begin with bits and pieces—a word, dialogue, an image.

When young children begin drafting, they often recount a series of verbatim events from their personal lives that, in their minds, are equally important. These drafts tend to be bed-to-bed narratives involving trivial or unremarkable happenings from morning to night that they string together and that typically omit sensory impressions of settings and characters. In these cases, the teacher can encourage literary license, the freedom to take risks and allow one's imagination to soar. Some students will embellish events or guess at what their characters might do and say; others may need a special technique to develop a text. A writer can find a favorite line of writing or a snippet of dialogue and repeat it throughout the story (as in the refrains of *The Gingerbread Man*), or the writer might include a question that becomes the beginning of a repetitive pattern as, for example, in the book *Are You My Mother?* (Eastman, 1988). Now is a good time to go back to drawing pictures, analyzing scenes that others have created in books, or doing observation exercises.

When drafting a beginning, middle, and end, writers depend on transitions with (cue words) to move from one part to the next. Readers rely on these words to connect what they have previously read with what they are about to read. Students can search literary texts for cue words and place them in lists for future reference (see Table 4–4). They should notice that fictional transitions are typically spatial and temporal in nature, suggesting events occurring in a particular place, in clock and calendar time.

TABLE 4-4 Story Transitional Words		
Beginning	**Middle**	**End**
At first	After a short time (or a while)	At last
At the beginning	All at once	From that day on
Far away	In next to no time	Happily ever after
Long, long ago	Instantly	Last
Once upon a time	Just when	Last of all
	Not long ago	
	Of late	
	Previously	
	Recently	
	Suddenly	

During writing events, teachers should circulate around the room asking questions as students finish sentences they are writing or asking the students to reread their work for momentum and flow. The key to drafting a story is to allow the character and plot to push the story forward. The specifics of description, transitions, and vocabulary can always be dealt with in revision.

Revising

Just as writers work diligently to draft ideas for a piece, so they must learn to match words to their intentions. Oftentimes, writers have a logical reason for what they have written or meant to write. They clearly know and see everything in their heads and find it difficult to imagine why anyone who reads their story is unable to understand it as they do. Gaps can originate from sentences that do not logically follow one another or from extra sentences that stray from the focus. Teachers can inquire about story happenings by asking clarification and extension questions.

> Where is your character now?
> What's in your drawing that is not in your story?
> What does your character say?
> How does your character react?

If teachers comment on the content and details of the piece as it unfolds in drafts, the resulting drama is likely to be more coherent and comprehensible.

The changes children make during revision will reflect the status of the draft and their ability level and experience. For a beginning writer, revising might mean adding a title, a picture, a descriptive word, or an additional page in the form of a new chapter. It may mean trying out a transitional phrase or substituting a name for a vague pronoun reference. More advanced students might rewrite an introduction, change a character's perspective, reorganize events, or put more obstacles in the character's way to achieve a stronger conflict. The choices are many, and teachers should follow their best judgments, keeping in mind where students are in the draft and what they wish to accomplish. Following are some questions to help students solve specific problems dealing with meaning/form, style, dialogue, or point of view.

Meaning/Form

- Where does this incident begin? End?
- Is this a scene? What image do you form in your mind when you think of this place?
- What action could you use there?
- How can you tell what the character feels, wants?
- What happened next?

- Where is your character now? What is in front of (behind) him?
- How did your character get to this place?

   Sending children back to literature to examine story beginnings or unusual endings provides the examples they need to produce their own. If setting is being revised, the writer might take a moment to sketch the scene and use it as a reference for adding or changing words. In revising for meaning and form, children are concentrating on fictional scenes and interrelating detail, description, action, dialogue, and story elements. They can review some of the following:

- Add a picture or drawing to extend or enhance the text
- Make certain there is a beginning, middle, and end
- Delete scenes or add new ones
- Make sure the plot is logical; avoid plot jumps or gaps in thought
- Examine problems and roadblocks to be sure they are plausible and believable
- Create an engaging beginning
- Remember to settle the conflict
- Describe a character (integrate the description rather than listing attributes)
- Emphasize what the characters do and say
- Make characters move and locate them in settings
- Connect characters with their feelings and motivation; make them convincing
- Use a plotline to structure the story

Style

Style is the manner of telling the story or how ideas are expressed. Writers can examine aspects of style in second or third drafts by asking the following questions:

- How does the story reflect real life?
- How does the writer grab your attention?
- Did the story create moving pictures in the reader's mind?
- Does the writing flow?

   When revising for style, students consider the following changes:

- Removing extraneous detail
- Including sensory words
- Providing specific, concrete nouns and adjectives
- Using transitions to show time passing or places and locations
- Determining when to summarize and when to expand
- Considering language devices, such as simile, metaphor, personification, exaggeration
- Weaving in details and descriptions throughout the piece; not placing descriptions all in one chunk
- Adding new sentences or phrases to show movement
- Attending to word choice; using words that are understandable or appropriate to the context; checking for out-of-place words

   A teacher demonstrates style using 4 to 5 paragraphs from his own writing or from a familiar book. He removes all the description and detail, leaving behind only the nouns and verbs. Students are given a list of adjectives, adverbs, and prepositional phrases to add back to the passage. Children see how various versions emerge based on their linguistic choices.

Dialogue

Dialogue is an essential feature of dramatic narratives. It makes a story seem like it is really happening while the audience listens. Writers consider the following questions:

- How would you describe your character's speech?
- What can you learn about your character from his speech?
- What does the dialogue add to the piece?

When students rewrite for dialogue, they enact some of the following:

- Add dialogue
- Omit meaningless chatter or distracting and endless conversation
- Ascertain who is talking
- Balance talk and narrative
- Make dialogue reveal aspects of character, setting, conflict, or plot
- Show *how* the character talks (add expressive tag lines)
- Create authentic speech (such as conversation)

Students can complete cartoonlike strips with dialogue bubbles to show how characters interact with one another. Pictures and photographs of people or animals offer ideal props for eliciting dialogue.

Point of View

Point of view is the perspective from which a story is told. It is the position of the author during the story's evolution. Is the writer in the story? Watching from the sidelines? What does he know or not know? Stories are usually told from a particular angle and are grammatically signaled by a pronoun that indicates the appropriate person. These points of view include the following:

First person point of view: The author tells the story through the eyes of the main character using the first person *I.*

Omniscient view: The author is outside the story, watching the action externally. He sees everything and knows what is going on in all of the characters' minds. The reader gets to see the characters as they are rather than as how the main character might see them. Second- or third-person pronouns are used *(you, he, she, it).*

Limited omniscient view: The author enters the mind of one character and explores feelings and emotions internally. Rather than the character telling the story, the author reports what the character thinks and feels. Usually, third-person pronouns, such as *he, she,* or *it,* are used.

Objective view: The author is detached, reporting events seen or heard. The writer is an eyewitness to the events. Readers do not learn about what characters think but simply observe what they are doing and saying. Third-person pronouns, such as *he, she,* or *it,* are used.

Multiple-character views: Sometimes an author uses several different character viewpoints, each bringing a new perspective to different chapters or episodes in a single book, such as in *Witness* (Hesse, 2001), the story of racism in a small Vermont town told from the perspectives of several townspeople.

Writers select a viewpoint that creates the effects they want. For instance, most children are acquainted with *The True Story of the Three Little Pigs! By A. Wolf* (Scieszka, 1989), in which the author evokes sympathy for the wolf's point of view. Children's literature provides a range of viewpoints for writers to explore (see Table 4–5). Children can use these books, rewriting stories from the perspective of various characters.

Point of view is usually discussed in prewriting; however, it must be reviewed during revision. As the writer reflects on what he has written, he poses some of the following questions:

- Who is telling the story?
- What does the author know about the character's feelings or thoughts? What does the character think or feel?
- What does the character see and do?
- How do I show the attitude of the character?

TABLE 4-5 Books for Teaching Point of View

Objective Point of View	First-Person Point of View	Omniscient Point of View	Limited Omniscient Point of View
Anno's USA (Anno, 1983) (P, I)	*Because of Winn-Dixie* (DiCamillo, 2000) (I) *Joey Pigza Loses Control* (Gantos, 2000) (I) *Osceola: Memories of a Sharecropper's Daughter* (Mays, 2000) (I) *Radio Rescue* (Barasch, 2000) (I) *The Wanderer* (Creech, 2000) (I) *Virgie Goes to School With Us Boys* (Howard, 2000) (P) *Wings* (Meyers, 2000) (P)	*The Amazing Life of Ben Franklin* (Giblin, 2000) (P, I) *The Word Eater* (Amato, 2000) (P, I)	*Crazy Horse's Vision* (Bruchac, 2000) (P) *Surviving Brick Johnson* (Meyers, 2000) (I)

P = Primary
I = Intermediate

Some aspects to consider with point of view include the following:

- Deciding who will be the main character; asking "whose story is it?"
- Changing words to maintain a consistent point of view
- Reviewing the selection of pronouns (*I, he, you*)
- Seeing places and events as the character sees them

Teaching children to revise requires plenty of modeling and frequent minilessons. Sometimes the purpose is to introduce a new strategy that facilitates the writer's growth; other times it may be necessary to review something already taught, and still on other occasions, it may be desirable to focus on a skill that several children need to develop. In the following think aloud, the teacher communicates his intentions about adding description to a piece.

> I want to describe how my character is dressed and what she looks like. Here are the details. She is wearing a T-shirt and jeans and has flippers on her feet. She is about 8 years old, with brown hair and green eyes. She pulls her hair back in a ponytail. Her name is Rosie. If I put all this in right here (points to the text), it will interrupt the story I am trying to tell. I think I will sprinkle this information along the way. Here at the beginning, I will say, "As Rosie got dressed, she slipped her T-shirt over her brown ponytail." Now, where might I squeeze in that she is 8 years old? Let me see. . . .

Even if all the students are not ready to use a particular technique, modeling the idea "plants a seed" and provides a new strategy for them to explore.

Editing

The detail and description, necessary for inventing story scenes and characters, present a wonderful opportunity to discuss sentence expansion—that is, taking a kernel sentence with a noun and verb and extending it with adjectives, adverbs, phrases, and clauses. Only 5 minutes a day are needed to guide students in a sentence expansion activity. Read aloud a simple two-word sentence—*flowers blossom*—and challenge the students to ask questions about the subject, expanding it into longer and more complex sentences.

Basic sentence: Flowers blossom.

What kind of flowers?	Daisies blossom.
What color are the daisies?	Yellow daisies blossom.

Where are the daisies?	Yellow daisies blossom on the hillside.
Why are they there?	The farmer planted yellow daisies that blossom on the hillside.
How did they get there?	The farmer cast seeds to plant the yellow daisies that blossom on the hillsides.

Of course, the object is not to pile on adjectives but to show how sentences are manipulated and simple words transformed into detailed and strong images. If sentences get lengthy and tangled, the writer always has the option of trimming them.

Along with sentence expansion, teachers can point out the importance of verbs. Verbs are the engines that fuel movement and imagery in stories, and have many characteristics and functions. Although dramatic fiction involves several types of verbs, the most common are precise, action verbs that are written in the past tense and active voice (the boy *jumped*). These verbs suggest that something has already happened, yet they give readers a sense of the "here and now." For instance, consider a description of a road in the opening scene of *Tuck Everlasting* (Babbitt, 1975):

> It *wandered* along in curves and easy angles, *swayed* off and up in a pleasant tangent to the top of a small hill, *ambled* down again between fringes of bee-hung clover, and then *cut* sidewise across a meadow. (p. 5)

Readers can almost see the road and feel themselves moving along its curves. These strong verbs create images, movement, and pace.

Students can examine age-appropriate literary passages and underline or copy vivid and precise action verbs, contrasting these with weak auxiliary verbs *(is, am, are, was, were, been)*, present tense *(jump, run, skip)*, or passive voice (the castle *was built* by the serfs). The best place to apply their knowledge, however, is in shared writing or in editing.

As regards punctuation, the convention that seems most pertinent to story writing is quotation marks because they frequently enclose the dialogue of the characters. Although quotations have many uses (quoting sources, marking concepts, or citing titles of books) and appear in various types of writing (exposition, poetry, persuasion), all children find an authentic need for them when they write dialogue in stories. Older children can examine literary passages to compare indirect quotations (that is, a restatement of the thoughts or comments of a person) and the actual words of a speaker.

Indirect Quotation	**Direct Quotation**
She said that she was going to be late.	She said, "I'm going to be late."
I thought that it would be great if only I could spend three days alone on the beach.	I thought, "If only I could spend three days alone on the beach."

In editing conferences, children will identify quotations in their own writing and learn to punctuate them with simple rules. The rules can be posted on a chart for reference. (For example, use a comma to separate a quotation from the rest of the sentence: *Jane asked, "Do you like him?"*) Usually, a quotation is accompanied by a tag statement that shows how something is being uttered and who is doing the uttering (e.g., Mary said). When writers realize that they are overusing the word *said*, they jot down a substitute on a Post-it note and add it to a chart called "Other Ways to Say 'Said'."

Other Ways to Say "Said"

cried	whined
asked	interrupted
groaned	promised
grumbled	joked
laughed	shouted

Spelling lists are compiled using referential story words. For instance, in a spelling conference with first-grader Jana, the teacher asks about words she wants to learn to spell based on a piece she wrote, *The Princess Named Flower*.

Teacher: I can read your story the way you have written it. Many of your spellings are very close to the actual spellings. Are there any words you would like to know how to spell correctly?

Jana: Yes, "happily ever after."

Teacher: Those are good choices because they end many fairy tales. I'll give you the spellings for "And they lived happily ever after."

After they discuss the spellings and use of upper- and lowercase letters, Jana outlines a section in her spelling notebook called "words for fairy tales." There the teacher jots down the phrase *happily ever after*, and adds *princess, prince,* and *castle* from Jana's writing. The pronoun *her* is placed on a card ring for Jana to study because it is one of those so-called high-frequency words that she must memorize or figure out with phonics. Children find examples of referential words in their writing, and post them on the word wall. When the children accumulate a sufficient number of words, they analyze and sort them. The teacher might ask if the students notice anything surprising about the spellings, if they can think of a way to remember a word, or if they recognize words that are similar. The children sort the words by letters (in various positions in the word), by type (fairy-tale words versus baseball words), by rhyme (*bake* and *take*), or by other means. Students enjoy contributing to the word wall and being involved in selecting spelling words.

Sharing

The primary purpose of reading and responding to work in writing circles and conferences is to support writers and celebrate the work. Grand conversations reveal remembrances of events in students' lives or stimulate connections to other stories they've read; task talk emphasizes feedback on the craft and inadvertently teaches the students and writer how to self-monitor and assess writing. Inherent in sharing is the frequent opportunity to interact and give advice. Specifically, students are given time to rehearse the broad range of interrelated responses available to them so that as they improve, they are better able to work in groups without the teacher. Since the kind of text being read will influence response, various types of response are presented in this book. However, it bears repeating that in actual practice, responses are not usually compartmentalized but tend to occur in combination. What's more, they are not exclusively verbal but emerge artistically, physically, nonverbally, and dramatically. Noticing behaviors that signal the array of ways in which children express responses can indicate their engagement with texts.

The next sections describe two types of responses especially attuned to fiction writing: esthetic and appreciative responses. Adding these responses to the mix of available options can help children avoid reliance on stock statements such as "It was good" or "I liked it."

Esthetic Responses

As noted in Chapter 1, Rosenblatt's (1978, 1984) concept of esthetic response is associated with literary engagement. Entering the world of the writer's work, students report what they are thinking about as they are reading, what feelings are evoked, or what images strike them. Esthetic response builds on satisfaction through the senses and on the feeling states of the reader. These responses are often tied to the reader's disposition and background knowledge. Some students will respond favorably to humor, action, or suspense while others might be enthralled by the appearance of the piece, its fanciful illustrations, or its readable handwriting.

Esthetic responses should also focus on the writer's flair with language or artistic skill. An esthetic response might go something like this: "Your drawing shows how sad the characters are in your story" or "Your descriptions of the setting paint images in my mind and make me feel like I am there." Since esthetic responses involve lingering with language, children attend to words and images that are stimulating and engaging, pleasurable and beautiful: "I laugh each time I read the words 'jumblies' and 'gurgle'" or "You make the forest seem so scary." If students read for the purpose of entertainment, they begin to recognize special words or favorite parts that appeal to their emotions and sensibilities.

Of course, there is always an interplay between feelings and the metalanguage associated with describing these feelings. Special "how to" storybooks introduce the metalanguage of story writing so that children can extend their knowledge of the craft and learn terminology for techniques they are already using and discussing in writing circles. *From Pictures to Words: A Book About Making a Book* (Stevens, 1995) tells about one illustrator's story process from idea generation to publication. *What Do Authors Do?* (Christelow, 1995) accomplishes a similar goal. A full-color *How a Book Is Made* poster by Betsy and Guilio Maestro (2000), published by the Children's Book Council, is a visual reminder of the steps writers go through to construct a story. With practice and heightened understanding of the story elements, students can offer esthetic responses using the metalanguage of stories—dialogue, description, action—and the vocabulary associated with multiple forms of literacy—movement, texture, images, color, and shape (Piazza, 1999). For example, a listener who can identify a detailed and vivid scene in a story is better able to convey these qualities through an esthetic response. An author who recognizes point of view can manipulate it to assume a new perspective (e.g., *The True Story of the Three Little Pigs! by A. Wolf* by Scieszka, 1989). A metalanguage makes it possible to communicate advice and control one's writing. Teachers can assume the role of guide-on-the-side for a while, modeling and assisting students as they practice esthetic response. In the meantime, students can follow some of the advice provided in Chapter 1—pointing and showing (through metaphors)—to express the indescribable. Having students draw pictures to visually interpret the writer's story or inviting them to alter their voices to repeat lines spoken by a character ("How do you think the character might say this?") are other ways of capturing the esthetic features of the writer's work.

Appreciative Responses

If esthetic responses reflect what to focus on in the text, appreciative responses overlap and extend what is valued about the literary work—the emotional and intellectual pleasure derived from it. Students who truly appreciate the work of a peer may express their response in several ways. Most obvious is a verbal statement of feelings about the work. Children may make direct remarks such as "This is the funniest story I've ever read" or ask lots of questions such as "Why did you call your character Silly Sam?" During sharing time, teachers may want to model how to show appreciation for a work. An appreciative response can highlight an author's achievements: "I loved the conclusion of your story" or "I found the plot very suspenseful." It may also recognize the process the writer went through in producing the piece: "You really worked hard on this revision."

Active involvement with a story can take many nonverbal forms as well, for example, grinning or laughing at something amusing or conveying a serious demeanor when something is sad. Facial expressions can show interest, sadness, and enjoyment just as physical responses such as clapping, standing, sighing, or sound-making can express appreciation.

During conferences and writing circles, the teacher will want to observe behaviors that indicate student appreciation. Do children willingly participate in discussions or demonstrate particular content preferences—topics on animals, magic, familiar experience, or nature? Do they tend to select certain genres for writing—adventure, fairy tales, fables, or mysteries? What character attributes most appeal to them (clever, considerate, ambitious)? The more teachers learn what pleases children, the more examples they will have for practicing appreciative responses during sharing: "I think Marhonda's animal stories are always such fun to read."

Signs of appreciation are sometimes more apparent after sharing time than during it. Do children voluntarily select to read a peer's work during recreational time? Does a peer choose to read several stories by a student author or imitate and borrow ideas from him? Do they repeat a favorite phrase from the writer's story *(pigs in wigs)* or play with the name of a character *(Silly Sam)* during casual talk at the writing table?

At the conclusion of story writing, formal acts of appreciation might occur. Do the students celebrate efforts by presenting or performing written stories (see previous discussion of storytelling, puppetry, and drama activity) or contribute student-made books to the classroom or school library (see Chapter 1 for bookmaking)? These and other gestures of appreciation, even those that often go unnoticed, augment the learning of reader response and are just as relevant as verbal response during sharing.

Continuous Assessment

The major function of assessment is to facilitate teaching and learning in an integrated writing program. Teachers of writing have many tools available for observing and collecting data on student interactions in guided writing, conferences, and writing circles. Although these tools center on writer, process, text, and context, they are always defined according to the kind of writing being studied. In this section we consider story writing. First is a summary of the four factors as they relate to story writing; then are process and product indicators for select genres of the story form.

Writer, Process, Text, and Context Factors

All of the assessment tools for story writing are associated with the writer, the process, the text, or the context. In terms of the writer, teachers can review students' self-reports of reading and writing habits or examine writing records and logs for topic preferences, books read, and compositions completed. Observational data might include some of the following:

- The kinds of stories students read and enjoy
- Previous knowledge about stories
- Attitudes toward story writing
- Preferred manner for sharing and presenting stories

The genre choices students voluntarily select (fairy tale, fable, legend) and embed in play, in show and tell, or in performances at school can also tell a great deal about writers as can the retelling of stories they've read or seen on TV.

Children are also growing in their knowledge about writing. They may no longer view the initial draft as the final one, or recognize that sharing with an audience is a necessary part of revising. They may be realizing that there are many ways to write stories and different options for implementing strategies. Parents and guardians report on the use of stories in the home, in social events, in religious affairs, or in their professional careers. Children who are told stories or who observe parents reading and writing learn how literacy functions in the lives of family and friends.

Children are also adopting a particular disposition, or stance, toward story writing. They should have an interest in writing stories and be willing to participate in activities that will widen their imaginative experiences. Since most literary stories are based on conflicts and resolutions it helps if children are curious or sensitive to problems.

Nowhere is this demonstrated more clearly than in their approaches to finding and solving problems and in their ability to produce ideas easily. Believing they can write stories and having a sense of humor are also pluses.

To add to a teacher's unfolding knowledge about writers, they design story writing checklists to frame their observations during the writing process. Some indicators might include the following:

- Does the writer use repetition, refrains, or cumulative storylines?
- Does the writer ask the question, "What happened next" to keep going?
- Does the writer choose action or description words?
- Does the writer stop or pause to plan sentences?
- Does the writer show revising by erasing or scratching out words?

Seeking information from students in face-to-face interactions may be the best way to determine what they know and what they need to learn. During conferences, for instance, students can share their hypotheses and new understandings of story elements.

Another way teachers study children's growing knowledge about writing is by observing the process of self-evaluation. Self-evaluation involves making judgments about what to value in a work and what to improve. This is an important goal of the writing process since the act of self-evaluating cultivates independence in writers and empowers them to take responsibility for their own learning. When writers can follow their own good advice, they gain greater control over their writing and a better understanding of themselves as writers. Children who are excited about assessing and observing their own growth may be motivated to pursue life long habits of writing. Process behaviors that suggest that self-evaluation is taking place include the following:

- Self-questioning (does this sound right?)
- Selecting a written piece and giving reasons why it is the best, unique, challenging, or easy
- Identifying things they are doing well and where they need improvement
- Outlining next steps and setting goals
- Revising

Self-evaluation takes many forms: as verbal analysis in conferences, reflective narratives, self-evaluative comments, or summaries of work. In doing a self-evaluation, children reflect on and analyze their work against a set of **standards** or criteria. Some of the tools in this and other chapters require students to answer questions with a simple "yes" or "no" ("Is your paper well organized?" or "Did you spell words correctly?"). Yet it is seldom the case that a complex process such as writing can be answered so easily. Open-ended questions ("What do you like best about your drawing?") or statements that call for explanations and narratives of the work ("Tell about the changes you made in this revision") are more likely to produce a thoughtful response.

The process of self-evaluation can begin with the teacher saying something like: "Circle all the words you think are spelled correctly" or "Underline the sentence you like best" or "Compare this drawing to a previous one." The class might work together to assess a sample story or develop a story rubric. At the same time, teachers are always listening carefully to the child's perspective of what counts as quality writing. Children may say that the writing is good because the words are spelled correctly or because it has a pretty drawing or shows nice handwriting. Building on these remarks, teachers direct children's attention to process and product factors they may be overlooking such as effort, range of projects, number of revisions, type of genres attempted, and aspects of story elements—strong action, plot, dialogue, and so on. Before long, children accumulate many new descriptions and criteria for judging their work.

Besides routinely gathering information about the self-evaluation process, teachers collect writing samples and analyze them using rubrics or descriptive categories (see

FIGURE 4-14 Six Trait Descriptions for Story Writing

Ideas
- Entertains the reader
- Considers audience
- Makes sense (ideas fit together, few plot jumps)
- Develops character, setting, story conflict, and resolution
- Emphasizes a central theme or idea
- Presents a title that captures the story ideas
- Shows compositional risks

Organization
- Creates a strong plot structure (beginning, middle, end)
- Locates the reader within settings (in time and space)
- Includes smooth story transitions to link ideas
- Develops an interesting and arousing introduction

Voice
- Projects a consistent point of view
- Gives voice to the character
- Engages the reader; keeps the reader in mind
- Expresses a mood
- Uses active voice
- Employs dialogue that sounds authentic

Sentence Fluency
- Follows appropriate pacing—slows down or speeds up at the right moments
- Incorporates sentence variety
- Suggests a readable text
- Infers rhythm and flow

Word Choice
- Shows what is happening
- Builds action through strong, lively verbs
- Provides sensory words for mental images

Conventions
- Uses quotation marks correctly
- Illustrates with drawings and print
- Includes conventional spelling
- Demonstrates legible handwriting

Chapter 1). The text can be assessed according to the six traits and modified by genre and student development.

The six traits (see Figure 4–14) reveal what to look for and what to record. In the classroom, these traits are modified to account for a child's developing knowledge of features that comprise story. This knowledge is frequently outlined as benchmarks or performance statements for each particular grade level. For fiction writing (grades 3–5) benchmarks might include some of the following (Sunshine State Standards, Florida 2002):

- Uses simple graphic organizers for clustering ideas
- Uses peer reader response to improve the organization of a draft
- Demonstrates a command of subject/verb agreement; has correct verb and noun forms
- Generally follows the conventions of punctuation, capitalization, and spelling

Teachers will want to review materials in children's portfolios to reflect on instruction and check that the curricular goals and benchmarks are being met. Remember, however, that the benchmarks are only guides and that the instructor is ultimately responsible for making sound decisions about what to teach and when to teach it. These judgments are always based on an understanding of the subject matter and the development of children.

Finally, during the story writing period, context factors and decisions are also considered:

- Does the story reflect the work of a group or an individual?
- Were words selected from the word wall?
- Did the writer use literature as a model or resource?
- How long (time/days) did the writer take to compose the story?

Experimenting with different grouping arrangements and conditions that promote diverse learning styles, may significantly influence the kind of product students create.

Genre-Specific Indicators

The story domain is comprised of many genres each of which has its own descriptive indicators and each of which can be modified to reflect student development. While teachers can refer to text conventions in Table 4–2 to assist them in setting up process and product indicators, here are three examples for getting started.

Tall Tales

Product

- Presents oral language features (colloquial phrases and clichés)
- Includes exaggeration and humor (eating millions of pancakes)
- Experiments with similes and metaphors (as big as a mountain)
- Shows unusual descriptions (Babe—the blue ox)

Process

- Reads tall tales
- Watches filmstrips
- Rehearses or shares through storytelling or vignettes
- Revises for features characteristic of the product

Mysteries

Product

- Sprinkles clues throughout the piece
- Solves a mystery
- Develops strong settings and characters (suspects)
- Provides a solution

Process

- Reads mysteries of the "whodunit" variety
- Brainstorms clues and how to incorporate them in the story
- Draws pictures of mysterious places
- Revises for features of the product

Historical Fiction

Product

- Represents historical facts and events accurately
- Offers authentic details of the time period (customs, behaviors, morals, clothing, homes)
- Includes fictional elements (theme, plot, characters, setting)
- Adds dialect or uses the language of the period

Process

- Brainstorms topics and time periods (new frontiers, wars, medieval times, ancient civilizations)
- Reads about famous historical figures or social traditions
- Takes notes on the customs and traditions of the historical period
- Revises for features of the product

These genre indicators are modified for rubrics by delineating the features at various developmental stages and specifying levels of quality (see Chapter 3, biography example). Rubrics are generally organized along a developmental continuum (emergent, developing, fluent, proficient, and independent writers) or along numerical levels of competence, for instance, a scale of 1 to 5, with 1 being low and 5 being high. Within each developmental category, the genre indicators are qualified by numbers (e.g., includes at least two similes) or adjectives *(most, some, few)*, hence, turning them into evaluation criteria. In other words, while the genre indicators are an essential starting point for assessment, to formalize these for evaluation or report card grades, teachers will need to consider what they know about development, what is expected in standards and benchmarks, and what constitutes generally accepted design for assessment.

CLASSROOM VIGNETTES: STORY WRITING IN ACTION

The final sections of this chapter highlight components of the writer's workshop approach across three grade levels to explore how writers shape stories by topics and genres, personal experience, and narrative strategies. As in earlier chapters, the classroom vignettes are meant to be illustrative rather than comprehensive. Teachers can build fictional units and make genre choices based on children's interests and abilities, preferences, and needs. The three genres discussed here—animal fantasy, pourquoi tales, and science fiction—illustrate the ways writers confront different kinds of texts and find solutions to the problems they face. We begin by peering into the first-grade classroom to consider a popular genre of story writing: animal fantasy.

Grade 1

Animal Fantasy

Vivian's classroom is vibrant with colorful pictures of animals, only these animals are not the kind typically found in nature magazines or seen on the Discovery Channel. They are pigs carrying purses, wolves dressed in cloaks, and hens in aprons, holding trays of cookies. On the wall hangs a big chart with the names of animal friends, such as Alexander (*Alexander and the Wind-Up Mouse*, Lionni, 1967); Flopsy, Mopsy, Cottontail, and Peter (*The Tales of Peter Rabbit*, Potter, 1902); Charlotte the spider (*Charlotte's Web*, White, 1952); and Corduroy, the bear (*Corduroy*, Freeman, 1986). The countertop is lined with animal fantasy books, their tantalizing pictures openly displayed. Vivian is at the rocking chair holding the book *Three Billy Goats Gruff* (Galdone, 1961). The children are gathered around her playing with paper plate puppets that represent the main characters in the story. Chiming in on cue to repeat refrains, a few of them are on their feet, bouncing up and down in anticipation of their parts.

When the dramatic reading ends, the children return to their seats to write their own make-believe stories. Vivian presents the book cover for *Nosey Mrs. Rat* (Allen & Marshall, 1985) and discusses how the illustrator personifies animals. "How do you know these animals aren't real?" she asks. The animals are wearing people's clothing and doing people things, they respond. Some infer that the animals are talking and propose on-the-spot scenarios of their actions.

With no shortage of story ideas, the children settle down to write. A dizzying swirl of voices begins filling the room as they talk with tablemates about the pictures they will draw and the stories they will tell. Vivian edges toward a worktable to observe a young writer named Matt who is diligently working on his piece, rehearsing aloud what he will say before writing it down. Stretching out the sounds in a word, he systematically orders the graphemes (letters) to go with them. His final written product appears in Figure 4–15. He draws a picture to reinforce the plot: one lonely bunny at the beginning and two bunny friends at the end. Matt is what Anne Dyson (1983, 1989) refers to as a "symbol weaver." He uses drawing, talking, and writing to plan his sentences and construct meaning.

The events and feelings he expresses in the piece are certainly familiar. Going to school and making new friends is a frightening experience for many first graders.

FIGURE 4-15 Matt's *The Shy Bunny*, First Draft (First Grader, Independent Writing)

The Shy Bunny
By Matt

One day he went
to school. He was shy.
But he found a friend. And that
cheered him up.
　　　　　The End

The story organization is a simple progressive plot with a character (rabbit), a problem to overcome (shyness), and a resolution (finding a friend). Matt begins with the formulaic opening *one day* and ends with an event reminiscent of *they lived happily ever after*. Although written in simple language with the sketchiest of plots, the story holds much promise. It is readable and has a sense of completeness.

During a conference, Vivian asks Matt to verbally expand on his work. Blank sheets of paper are stapled to his initial story to encourage new chapters or sequels without having to rework the original. In the sequel, he might talk more about the shy bunny's experiences at school with his friend or start a brand new episode about the bunny. According to Calkins (1994), revision in the primary grades usually involves "growing the story's meaning" (p. 18) and developing plot (beginning, middle, and end).

Children who are not yet ready to write complete sentences are told to label and arrange pictures and sentence strips. Vivian discusses the arrangement of text and pictures on the page. For example, "Should the writer place the text on the top or bottom? Should he surround the text with illustrations? Should the illustrations extend or match the storyline?" Authors grapple with these kinds of decisions all the time.

As Vivian moves around the classroom during guided writing, she asks questions to ensure sentence fluency and meaning making. For instance, in a story about a bat, Marhonda explains how Ellen the bat gets from the zoo to the cave. (See Figure 4–16.)

Vivian:	How did the bat get from the zoo to the cave?
Marhonda:	It flies.
Vivian:	Where does it fly?
Marhonda:	Over trees and mountains.
Vivian:	I see. The bat flies over trees and mountains to get to the cave.

This young writer adds missing information to strengthen plot and achieve sentence coherence and fluency.

After attending to individual writers with unique problems, Vivian leads the class on a "text walk," proceeding page by page through a storybook looking for colorful story language: sound words such as *clamor* and *screech*, descriptive words such as *blustery* and *powerful*, and strong action words such as *bellow* and *crash*. She places the words on the word wall under labels: *Noun, Verb*, and *Adjective*.

Writers edit for conventions during drafting, using punctuation marks and symbols that have their counterparts in speech—intonations, volume, rhythm, and pauses. They read aloud from their work and insert periods where they pause. Vivian gathers the class at the easel and points out end punctuation in sentences from a big book. Alternatively, she uses unpunctuated literary passages and lets the children determine where periods, question marks, and exclamation points belong. Editing by ear is effective for determining where to place these.

Children "look for" punctuation in literature and hypothesize about punctuation rules. Before publishing, students work with editing partners to fix accidental errors, such as omissions or repetition. Because most compositions are short, Vivian either accepts invented spelling or corrects referential words *(wolf, castle, queen)*.

Self-assessment, a continuous part of the writing experience, provides insights into children's perceptions of quality writing. Vivian poses simple questions such as, "What do you like best about your work?" or "If you were writing this story again, what changes would you make?" When she asks Matt to share the best part of his story, he replies, "When the bunny found a friend." This is a typical response, but so are those that focus on drawing, handwriting, or spelling. As Vivian interacts with writers in conferences, she points out features they overlook (a great ending or a strong image), gradually expanding the criteria and array of indicators they use to examine their work.

From time to time, Vivian shares observations from her anecdotal records with the class: "I noticed that Taylor took a risk and tried to spell a difficult word"; or Matt took time today to plan his writing before getting started. Maybe he would like to share what he did." Doing so inspires confidence, and before long students eagerly volunteer their successes, announcing how they worked through trouble spots or mastered a skill.

Students complete a self-assessment form during or after a writing task. In the open-ended example in Figure 4–17 (p. 202), Shelby reveals her assessment of her piece and what she would do differently: she would change the ghost's attitude.

Self-assessment tools such as these reflect children's growing understanding of quality story writing. If they complete several types of assessment over time, the teacher gains a broader picture of their competence (see Chapter 1, writer, process, text, or context factors in assessment).

Meanwhile, every 6 weeks, Vivian discusses the portfolio contents with students. At a conference with Savannah, three stories from her portfolio are laid out on the table: *Kittens and Goldfish*, her earliest work (Figure 4–18, p. 203); *Lizzie*, a work

A bat named Ellen lived at a zoo.

She lived in a bat cage.

She had big teeth and she unlocked herself.

She flew away because she didn't like the zoo, and she had to go to an emergency to the bathroom.

Until she found a cave she saw her family.

They had a great big party for her little sister, Annie.

Annie's favorite toy was a car that drives all around to America.

Because they had no food, they were starving.

Ellen search for food.

She looked under the log and it was their favorite snack, ants!

They had nets and catched them all.

They put them in a jar and ate them.

Ellen and all of her family they search for her friends.

They drove Annie's car to the zoo.

When they got to the zoo they found their friends.

Ellen's friends was a leopard, a cheetah and an anteater.

Annie was scared because she though the anteater would think she was an ant and eat her.

Until she found her friends to come with her.

She knew she wasn't scared anymore.

And then she knew her friends were good so they took them to their happy home.

She didn't drink their blood.

FIGURE 4-17
Shelby's Self-
Assessment (First
Grader)

> **Self-Assessment**
>
> Name __Shelby__   Date __2.28.00__
>
> The best thing about my story is...
>
> The Ghost has a half faces.
>
> If I could change one thing about my story it would be...
>
> Changeing the Ghostes atatat.
>
> **A Story Passage**
>
> Aney is frightened of this mean ghost. Her friend Julie got medicine. for her. Then She got better. Aney called her father in the castle and said, "John the Gost poisoned me with Flower I was sick, but now I'm better."

done midpoint during the 6 weeks (Figure 4–19, p. 204); and *The Bees and the Bear*, her most recent composition (Figure 4–20, p. 205). Turning to these pieces, Vivian poses three questions.

1. "Let's look at these three pieces. What surprises you about what you have done?"

   Savannah replies, "I didn't think I could do all of this! This one [pointing to *The Bees and the Bears*] is the longest."

2. "What is new in this writing that wasn't there before?"

   Savannah says her early piece, *Kittens and Goldfish*, didn't have a picture and so it wasn't as good as the other two.

3. "Do you see anything that is the same in all of your writings?"

   Savannah points out that all of her stories are about animals.
   Vivian adds notes to her ongoing documentation of Savannah's literacy growth:

- Less static drawings (more movement implied in bumblebee design and sequence of pictures in *The Bees and the Bears*)
- Stronger plot structure in *Lizzie* and *The Bees and the Bears*; less pure description as in *Kittens and Goldfish*

FIGURE 4-18
Savannah's *Kittens and Goldfish*, Final Draft (First Grader, Guided Writing)

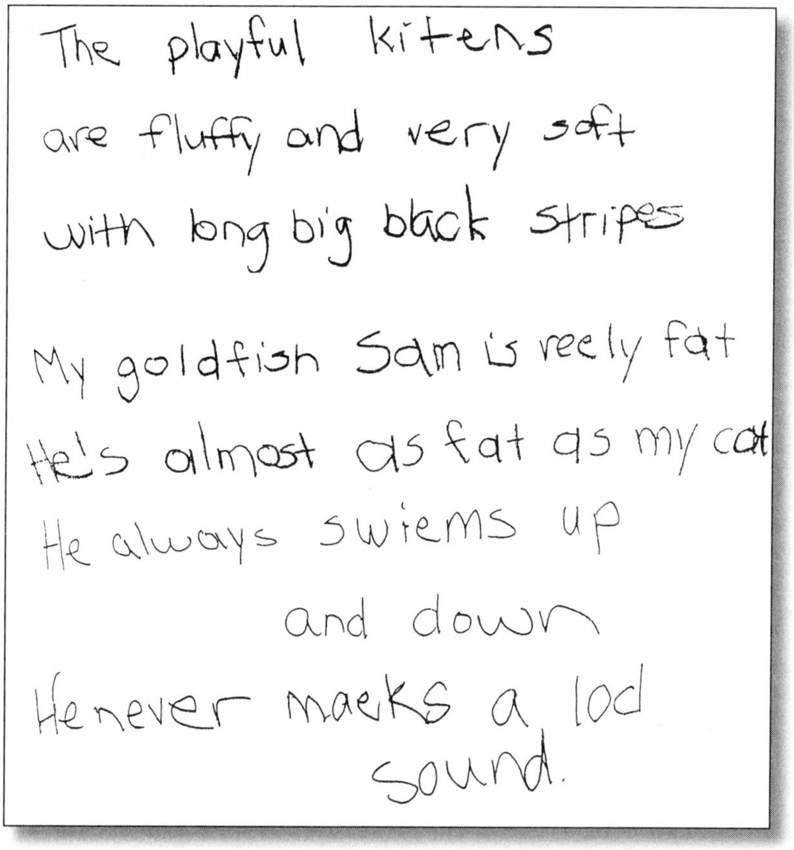

> The playful kitens
> are fluffy and very soft
> with long big black stripes
>
> My goldfish Sam is reely fat
> He's almost as fat as my cat
> He always swiems up
> and down
> He never maeks a lod
> sound.

- Increasingly more complex writing leading to experimentation with verb tense (see mix of present and past tense in *The Bees and the Bears*)
- Increasingly greater use of conventional spellings; invented spelling is phoneme-grapheme based
- Continued and effective use of language devices in all three pieces, such as rhyming and half-rhyme patterns in *Kittens and Goldfish* (fat/cat; down/sound), alliteration in *Lizzie* (Lizzie the lizard, Freddy the frog), and onomatopoeia (yummy) in *The Bees and the Bears*

Regarding Savannah's self-evaluation, Vivian may add:

- Increasingly able to judge her own work; noticed topic similarities and length; viewed illustrations as an important accompaniment to writing
- Gaining self-confidence as a writer; commented that she was surprised to see how much work she had done

Savannah is asked to select a favorite piece and tell about it. She chooses the story *Lizzie* (Figure 4–19) "because I like the drawing" and "I spelled some words good. I wrote a lot." Turning to Savannah, the following dialogue takes place:

Vivian: I really like the drawing too. I especially like the way the picture matches your words.

Savannah: Me too.

Vivian: Your story plot really kept my interest. I could see ugly Lizzie in the swamp going to look for food and getting lost. She must have been very relieved when Freddy helped her find her way home. The order is

FIGURE 4-19   Savannah's *Lizzie*, Final Drawing and Draft (First Grader, Guided Writing)

Lizzie

Lizzie the lizard lifed in the swamp. She was green and very ug[y and had a pinck pers. She was hungry and went looking for food. But she was lost for 10 hours, Lizzie fond her boyfrend Freddy the frog and asked for direxons. Lizzie went to bed when she got home.

The End!

clear, too. You introduce the character, Lizzie, place her in a setting, and then give her a problem that has to be solved.

Vivian's comments reflect the metalanguage of story (plot, organization, setting, and problem) and echo Savannah's written words, allowing her to hear what she has done.

Next, Vivian refers to the six-trait writing rubric (see Table 4–6, pp. 206–207) to guide discussion with Savannah. A possible teacher–student dialogue and Vivian's "between the lines" analysis are presented here.

Vivian [to Savannah]: Let's look at the final draft of your story about Lizzie. Your ideas for this story are creative and I really like your picture. In the beginning of the story your words help paint a vivid image of Lizzie in my mind. Was she strolling, crawling, or hopping?

Based on a general impression of *Lizzie* (see Figure 4–19), Vivian determines that Savannah is a capable writer. Savannah's ideas make a point, and her illustration adds to the message. The details of the climax and ending, however, are not as developed as the opening.

Vivian [to Savannah]: You have all the parts of the story in order, but I am curious about some details that you haven't written about. How did Lizzie feel being lost for 10 hours?

FIGURE 4-20 Savannah's *The Bees and the Bear*, Final Draft (First Grader, Guided Writing)

The bees came out of the tree. The bees stung bear in her head. She said ouch! Then when the bees left the hollow tree the bear went to get some honey for her cubs.

2

When she ate it she said was sticky. Her cubs yummy. Now the bear knows how to get honey when the bees go some place else. She can get honey for her cubs and her.

3

THE END

Bears are curious. They are almost always hungry, too. Mother bear and her cubs are looking for something to eat. Mother bear sniffs the air. Her nose tells her that bees are living in the hollow tree.

Regarding organization, Vivian acknowledges the clear skeletal outline of the story but notes the lack of texture and details necessary for a well-developed plot. A narrator's voice, telling about the fictional lizard's feelings and emotions is necessary to identify with Lizzie's dilemma. (Was she afraid when she got lost? Relieved when she saw her boyfriend, Freddy the frog?)

Vivian [to Savannah]: I simply love the vivid color words you use (green and pink). I also like the word *swamp* because it makes me imagine wet mushy land covered with grasses.

At the beginning of the story, Savannah paints a verbal picture of Lizzie to match the illustration. Although the sentences are well written and in logical order, most of them follow a noun–verb–noun (NVN) or a noun–verb (NV) pattern with little variation. Moreover, it is difficult to demonstrate sentence fluency in such a brief plot.

Vivian [to Savannah]: I can read your words and most of your spellings. You do such a good job sounding out words.

TABLE 4-6 Six-Trait Developmental Assessment for Beginning Writers

	1 Experimenting	2 Emerging	3 Developing	4 Capable	5 Experienced
Ideas	— Uses scribbles for writing — Dictates labels or a story — Shapes that look like letters — Line forms that imitate text — Writes letters randomly	— Some recognizable words present — Labels pictures — Uses drawings that show detail — Pictures are supported by some words	— Attempts a story or to make a point — Illustration supports the writing — Meaning of the general idea is recognizable/understandable — Some ideas clear but some are still fuzzy	— Writing tells a story or makes a point — Illustration (if present) enhances the writing — Idea is generally on topic — Details are present but not developed (lists)	— Presents a fresh/original idea — Topic is narrowed and focused — Develops one clear, main idea — Uses interesting, important details for support — Writer understands topic well
Organization	— Attempts to write left to right — Attempts to write top/down — No sense of beginning and end yet — Experiments with spacing	— Consistently writes left to right — Consistently uses top/down — Experiments with beginnings — Begins to group like words/pictures	— A title is present — Limited transitions present — Beginning but no ending except "The End" — Attempts at sequencing	— An appropriate title is present — Attempts transitions from sentence to sentence — Beginning works well and attempts an ending — Logical sequencing — Key ideas begin to surface	— An original title is present — Transitions connect main ideas — The opening attracts — An effective ending is tried — Easy to follow — Important ideas stand out
Voice	— Communicates feeling with color, shape, line in drawing — Work is similar to everyone else's — Ambiguous response to task — Awareness of audience not present	— Hints of voice present in words and phrases — Looks different from most others — Energy/mood is present — Treatment of topic predictable — Audience is fuzzy—could be anybody, anywhere	— Expresses some predictable feelings — Moments of individual sparkle, but then hides — Repetition of familiar ideas reduces energy — Awareness that the writing will be read by someone else — Reader has limited connection to writer	— Writing is individual and expressive — Individual perspective becomes evident — Personal treatment of a standard topic — Writes to convey a story or idea to the reader — Attempts nonstandard point of view	— Uses text to elicit a variety of emotions — Takes some risks to say more than what is expected — Point of view is evident — Writes with a clear sense of audience — Cares deeply about the topic

Sentence Fluency				
— Consistently uses sentence variety — Sentence structure is correct and creative — Variety of sentence beginnings — Natural rhythm, cadence and flow — Sentences have texture which clarifies the important idea	— Simple and compound sentences present and effective — Attempts complex sentences — Not all sentences begin the same — Sections of writing have rhythm and flow	— Uses simple sentences — Sentences tend to begin the same — Experiments with other sentence patterns — Reader may have to reread to follow the meaning — Dialogue present but needs interpretation	— Strings words together into phrases — Attempts simple sentences — Short, repetitive sentence patterns — Dialogue present but not understandable	— Mimics letters and words across the page — Words stand alone — Patterns for sentences not in evidence — Sentence sense not yet present
Word Choice				
— Everyday words used well — Precise, accurate, fresh, original words — Creates vivid images in a natural way — Avoids repetition, clichés or vague language — Attempts at figurative language	— Uses favorite words correctly — Experiments with new and different words with some success — Tries to choose words for specificity — Attempts to use descriptive words to create images	— General or ordinary words — Attempts new words but they don't always fit — Settles for the word or phrase that "will do" — Big words used only to impress reader — Relies on slang, clichés, or repetition	— Recognizable words — Environmental words used correctly — Attempts at phrases — Functional language	— Writes letters in strings — Imitates word patterns — Pictures stand for words and phrases — Copies environmental print
Conventions				
— High-frequency words are spelled correctly and very close on other words — Capitals used for obvious proper nouns as well as sentence beginnings — Basic punctuation is used correctly and/or creatively — Indents consistently to show paragraphs — Shows control over standard grammar	— Transitional spelling on less frequent words (MONSTUR, HUMUN, CLOSSED, etc.) — Spelling of high-frequency words usually correct — Capitals at the beginning of sentences and variable use on proper nouns — End punctuation is correct (.!?) and other punctuation is attempted (such as commas) — Paragraphing variable but present — Noun/pronoun agreement, verb tenses, subject/verb agreement	— Uses phonetic spelling (MOSTR, HUMN, KLOSD, etc.) on personal words — Spelling of high-frequency words still spotty — Uses capitals at the beginning of sentences — Usually uses end punctuation correctly (.!?) — Experiments with other punctuation — Long paper may be written as one paragraph — Attempts standard grammar	— Attempts semiphonetic spelling (MTR, UM, KD, etc.) — Uses mixed upper- and lowercase letters — Uses spaces between letters and words — Random punctuation — Nonstandard grammar is common	— Writes letter strings (prephonetic: dmRxzz) — Attempts to create standard letters — Writes word strings — Attempts spacing of words, letters, symbols, or pictures — Student interpretation needed to understand text/pictures

Savannah's work suggests progress in spelling. Her invented words are readable and based on an emerging understanding of phoneme-grapheme relations.

In this conference, Savannah receives feedback based on the six-trait descriptions for story writing. Eventually, the other two pieces she has written will be evaluated and added to her 6 weeks' accomplishments. Savannah's portfolio of work samples documents the array of topics selected, the types of story plots and narrative strategies implemented, the number of revisions completed, and the accuracy of proofreading accomplished.

Grade 3

Pourquoi Tales

Children's natural tendency to ask "why" is a springboard for writing pourquoi (French for *why*) tales. In these stories, the author asks about the origins of something in nature and then goes on to explain how it came to be. Animals seem to be favorite topics. Questions concerning how the zebra got its stripes or *Why Mosquitoes Buzz in People's Ears?* (Aardema, 1975) stimulate curiosity about animal characteristics and habits.

Kate introduces pourquoi tales with *Beast Feast* (Florian, 1994), which is a set of poems and paintings about animals and their unique characteristics (e.g., the anteater's long and tacky tongue or the shaggy sloth who hangs by its claws). She also reads from Rudyard Kipling's (1902) classic *Just So Stories*, which is a collection of tales that explain many aspects of nature. Following the readings, each child selects an animal sticker with a special or unique characteristic and generates a "why" question: Why does the raccoon have a mask? Why does the tiger have stripes? Why does the anteater (or echidna) have spikes? The children then head to the library to research the habits and behaviors of the animals chosen. The goal is to invent a story that explains the animal's special characteristics and, at the same time, weave in actual facts that make the story believable. Using the Internet, Brianna researches credible and intriguing information about the *echidna* (an anteater, see Table 4–7). After locating the echidna's habitat (Australia) and noting details about its behaviors and physical attributes, Brianna combines factual knowledge with imagination to answer the question, "Why does the echidna have spikes?" In Figure 4–21, Brianna writes about what she has learned.

TABLE 4-7   Brianna's Fact Chart on the Echidna (Third Grader)

What the Echidna Looks Like	Where the Echidna Lives	What the Echidna Eats	Habits of the Echidna	Other Australian Animals
Medium size Covered with spines Stocky body Long snout Like a pig Long tongue	Australia Those in cold climates have more spines Will share same hole with other animals Burrows	Ants Termites Licks early morning dew from plants	Solitary Can climb tresses and fencing Makes a cooing sound Lives 49 years Uses snout to turn over soil for ants Can move sizable rocks	Platypus Koala bear Wombat Kangaroo

How the Echidna Got its spikes

In Australia, there's a echidna that lives in a Jungle. she is surrounded by high grass, and waterfalls. She is black and she has a long tongue. She comes out at night for food

She was robbing her back on the tree but it was not a tree. It was a snake.

The snake wants to eat her, but she got away. The echidna eats ants.

The echidna stepes in the ant bed so the ants bite her.

The ants that bit her gave her bumps. She got poison from the queen ant. Every day

the echidna gets five spikes from the bumps. It take five hours to get five spikes. After a few months, she got six million spikes.

Thats the way the echidna got its spikes.

Her story has two noticeable episodes leading up to the theme. The first reveals the hazards of living in the jungle—the snake that wants to eat the echidna. The second deals with the change in the echidna's smooth skin: a formidable enemy, an army of ants, attacks the echidna, and the queen's bite injects a poison that causes the echidna to break out in bumps. The bumps multiply and turn into spikes.

When her draft is finished, Brianna confers with Kate, who praises her original storyline and descriptive passages. Brianna's piece is easy to read and the events are sequenced. She has a well-prepared plan of development with conflicts (the snake and the queen ant) and a climax (the ant bite and spikes). Brianna takes her own personal experience of getting bitten by fire ants and arrives at the plight of the echidna: red blotches on the skin. Yet much of what is written sounds like expository writing (telling style) rather than narrative (showing style). Brianna has rattled off a list of facts without transforming them into fiction. At this point Kate worries that her directive to find facts about an animal may have steered the class in the wrong direction. Without dialogue and action, Brianna's first draft does not resonate as a story. The pourquoi tale requires a deft balance between telling facts, as a journalist does, and creating scenes, as a novelist does. Transforming expository information into fictional narrative is not an easy task for young writers. So as not to overwhelm Brianna, Kate asks questions that can be easily answered.

- (For the beginning) Where does the echidna make her home in Australia? What does it look like there? What does she do each day inside her home? Outside it? Who does she meet on a daily basis?
- (For the middle) How does the echidna react to the snake? What does the echidna say? Do? How does the echidna feel when the ants bite her?
- (For the ending) Are there advantages to the echidna having spikes? What can she do now that she couldn't before?

Brianna's next step is to look in *National Geographic* for pictures that resemble the scenes in her story: a backdrop for the echidna's actions, responses, movement, and conflict. The pictures help her ascertain what she wants the animal to do and say in these settings. Kate poses a few questions about the pictures and suggests that Brianna generate lines and quotations specific to the echidna by reading passages of dialogue from other pourquoi tales.

Meanwhile, Kate organizes small-group minilessons with children who have common writing problems to solve. One of the lessons highlights story transitions of space (behind, in the corner, around the bend) and time (season change, clock time, days and years). Students collect and list transitions found in literature, place them on sentence strips, and hang them on the wall. When students are writing, they refer to these transitions, applying them to disparate parts of their stories to achieve greater coherence and sentence fluency.

Appropriate verbs and their tenses are essential for writers to bring movement to pourquoi stories. Kate holds an entire class focus lesson on a passage from *The Little Red Hen* (Zemach, 1980) that she projects onto a screen. Omitting words from the sentences allows students to select regular *(turned)* and irregular *(came)* verbs to fill in the blanks (see Figure 4–22). Students notice when simple past tense occurs and when the verb changes to the present tense (between quotation marks). In several cases, more than one word is appropriate.

After the lesson, students are told to search for verbs in their own writing samples. "See how many verbs you can find," Kate says. "Underline your verbs. Remember, there will be a verb in every sentence. Once you have found the verb, decide if you want to change it."

Children locate auxiliary verbs *(is, am, are, was, were, be)* in their papers and replace them with strong, concrete ones that can be "acted out." They brainstorm synonymous verbs with different effects and write them in notebooks. Figure 4–23 illustrates verbs that can be used instead of *talked*.

FIGURE 4-22 Fill-in-the-Blank Exercise for Verb Study

Source: Reprinted by permission of Farrar, Straus and Giroux, LLC: Excerpt from *Little Red Hen* by Margot Zemach. Copyright © 1983 by Margot Zemach.

The Little Red Hen

Once upon a time a little red hen _____ with her chicks in a small cottage.
            (live, lived)

She _____ hard to keep her family well fed. In the evenings she sang
    (work, worked)

while she _____ .
        (work, worked)

"Oh, _____ and _____ the green wheat growing!" she _____ to
    (come, came)   (see, saw)   (called, yelled, whispered)

her chicks.

All summer the wheat _____ taller and taller. It _____ from green to gold.
                  (grow, grew)   (turn, turned)

"Who will harvest this wheat?" _____ Little Red Hen.
                          (says, said)

FIGURE 4-23 Verb Web (Synonyms for *Talked*)

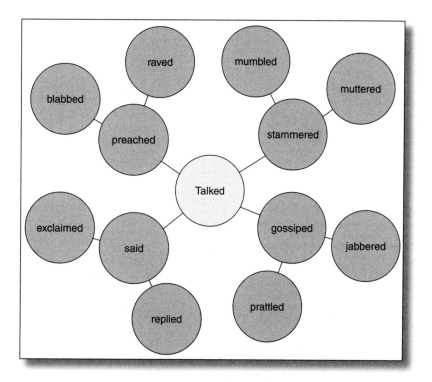

In an editing conference with Bailey, Kate introduces past tense, which is the preferred verb form for fiction. Using *Cassandra Who?* (Hiskey, 1992), she reads the following excerpt.

> One Friday morning, when Cassandra *stepped* out onto her porch to water the flowers, she *saw* the mail carrier coming down the road.
>
> "Anything for me today, Maisie?" she *called*. The mail carrier *looked* up.

"I'd like you to point to the verbs," Kate says. Bailey selects the words and Kate jots them down on paper.

Stepped

Saw

Called

Looked

Examining the final two letters of each, Bailey determines which one is different. When she correctly identifies *saw*, Kate explains that it is an irregular verb. Most past tense verbs end in *-ed*, unless they are irregular. Bailey chooses a writing sample from her portfolio and examines it for verbs. Her piece, *The Lake* (see Figure 4–24), is written in mixed tenses. In revising *The Lake*, Bailey removes forms of "to be" and, where possible, replaces them with strong action verbs. Kate lists word choices appropriate to fill in the blanks as in Figure 4–25. Simple context or synonym prompts encourage Bailey to try alternatives: What word would fit here? Is this word like any other word you know? Before publishing, Bailey should check for repeated connectives, especially *and, then,* and *so,* and substitute time transitions for these words. Kate then checks whether Bailey can correct the past tense of *teach* (taught).

As the third graders continue to work on several pourquoi tales, they incorporate many of the strategies learned in minilessons. Because only one or two key

FIGURE 4-24 Bailey's *The Lake*, First Draft (Third Grader, Independent Writing)

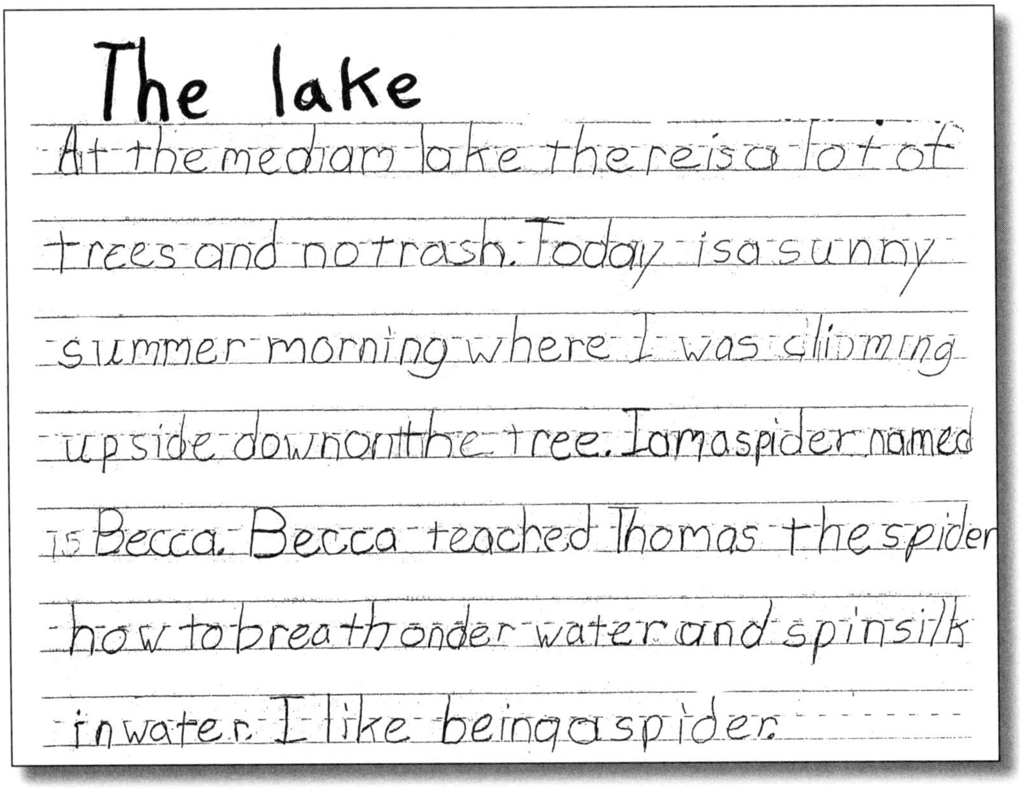
The lake

At the mediam lake there is a lot of
trees and no trash. Today is a sunny
summer morning where I was climing
upside down on the tree. I am a spider named
is Becca. Becca teached Thomas the spider
how to breath onder water and spin silk
in water. I like being a spider.

FIGURE 4-25   Sentence Slotting to Substitute Verbs for Revision

At the medium lake _____ a lot of trees and no trash. One sunny summer
        (stood, stretched, rose, swept, jutted)

morning a spider named Becca _____ upside down on a tree. Becca
        (climb, climbed, climbing)

_____ Thomas the spider how to breath under water and spin silk in water.
  (teach, taught)

She _____ being a spider.
(enjoyed, liked, delighted in)

FIGURE 4-26   Story Strategies Log

Story Strategies Log

Name _____

What I Do	Title/date The Echidna 2/04	Title/date The Penguin 2/07
Planning		
I made a storyboard or map	✓	
I drew a picture	✓	
I read stories and borrowed from books	✓	✓
I pictured images in my mind		✓
I used artwork for ideas		
Drafting		
I asked questions about the five senses	✓	✓
I read the story to myself	✓	✓
I asked, "What happened?"	✓	✓
Revising and Responding		
I read my story to others	✓	
I acted out parts of my story		
I changed my writing to show what people did or said		✓
Editing and Publishing		
I corrected quotation marks	✓	✓
I changed weak verbs into action verbs	✓	✓
I wrote my story in the past tense	✓	
I made a book cover		
I placed my story in the class library	✓	✓
I sent my story to a magazine for possible publication		

editorial skills are discussed in each piece, Kate will hold the children responsible for the ones she has taught, and before long, writers will have a body of editing skills they can call their own.

All the while, the children track progress and document various writing process behaviors in their story strategies log (see Figure 4–26). This log, along with brainstorming webs, story drafts, conference summaries, and editing checklists, is placed in a working portfolio. For assessing the final product, children attach colorful stickers to questions, and circle responses about their work and attitudes (see Figure 4–27.) A new assessment form is prepared for each writing assignment, detailing different objectives and eliciting something new from the learners. Reviewing the working portfolio from time to time helps them determine what to keep and what to discard. Kate will meet with each writer to select a writing sample that represents his best work, which is then dated and placed in a showcase portfolio.

Grade 5

Science Fiction

"What if?" questions open up all kinds of extraordinary and remarkable tales. Although many fifth graders take their everyday lives for granted, when they are faced with a "what if" question, they are quick to transform the ordinary into something amazing and dramatic. "What if there was no more food? What if the rivers all dried up? What if you lived on another planet?"

Students in Ed's fifth grade read classic "what if" stories such as *A Wrinkle in Time* (L'Engle, 1963), which is a space story of suspense and adventure, or contemporary favorites, such as *Harry Potter and the Sorcerer's Stone* (Rowling, 1998), in which wizards frolic in magic and mayhem. Although these stories are not real, the characters are believable and the plots are conceivable.

Brittany, a prolific writer, enjoys writing fantasy—especially science fiction. In her piece, *Little Purple Alien* (see Figure 4–28) written over three writing periods, she follows a progressive plotline and selects words consistent with science fiction. Although she tells the story from the point of view of the little purple alien, Nubu, new scenes introduce and follow minor characters (e.g., Shirone) in an imaginary world full of description, strong images, and clear settings. As with most types of fantasy, *Little Purple Alien* demonstrates the good versus evil motif. Nubu forges battles on earth and in space to bring goodwill to a newly created world.

Because students find it easy to invent characters, Ed highlights strategies for developing and organizing plot. The class reads favorite books and brainstorms a list of criteria that make the opening especially satisfying.

- Captures readers' attention with immediate action
- Provides fresh or original ideas
- Arouses suspense
- Sets a mood
- Establishes writing style from the start (narrative not expository)
- Poses a question to the reader
- Foreshadows what is to come
- Starts with dialogue

Students who have difficulty drafting a plot can fill in events along the progressive plotline and quickwrite a few paragraphs on each point (see Chapter 2). Writers "round out" a scene by asking, What's next? What does the character want? What is his/her goal? Because story characters are typically thwarted in their goals, students may need to rethink conflict and consider major roadblocks facing the characters. Without such tension, the story fizzles.

If writers' compositions became lengthy and unwieldy, Ed calls their attention to important threads or gems worth saving. Like most writers, the fifth graders find cutting information difficult.

FIGURE 4-27 Self-Assessment with Stickers

My Personal Self- Assessment

Title of Paper: By:_____   Circle your choice:

I lliked my paper.

Not too much   It was great!

I had fun thinking of ideas for my story.

No way   Yipee!

I did not like _writing drafing_   OOPS!

The best part of my story is _I like wat I rotc about_

If I could change one thing about my story it would be: _that he sleepsalthe time_

I would like to write more stories!   Yes!   No way

I enjoyed changing and revising my story.   _gad yes_   Yeah!   Nope!

Next time I would like to: _color draw paint_

In fantasy, detailed settings are often the main attraction, playing a significant role in developing plot and building a story's suspense. After all, what would Alice be without Wonderland or The Wizard without Oz? Readers have to believe in the imaginary place. They must see where the character is, what is in front of him, and what lurks behind. They have to know when a character leaves one place to go to the next. Forgetting to mark these locations leads to confusion. To illustrate an integral setting, Ed projects on the overhead reproduction of an underwater space odyssey by the celebrated artist, Robert McCall (see Figure 4–29, p. 218). He places a mark in the left corner of the artwork and says; "Pretend this is you. Describe what you see in front of you, to your left, to your right. Who is next to you? Now tell what is happening, detail by detail, as the undersea ship opens its door in front of you. Where are you now? Use your five senses. What do you smell? What do you feel? Turn around and look behind you. What is there? What can you touch? What happened before this picture and what will happen after it?" The students write a moving account of what is happening, and, when they finish, they see how two narrative

FIGURE 4-28
Brittany's *Little Purple Alien*, First Draft (Fifth Grader, Independent Writing)

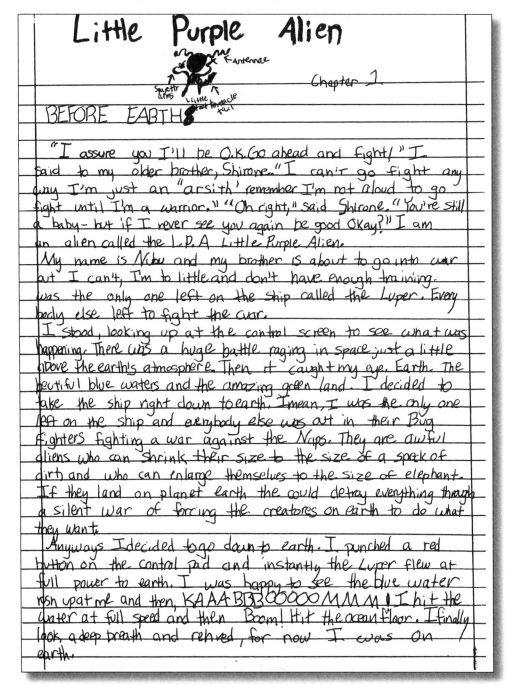

(continued)

FIGURE 4-28
(continued)

L.P.A

I knew this adventure would be fasinating, but I was worried about my appearance. I didn't think I looked like any animal on Earth. So, I swam on. Up, up, and up thragh the ocean. And when I was about halfway up, my oxygen ran out. I couldn't breathe, but I kept going. My lungs gasped for air, but it was impossible. I could feel my face turn from purple to blue.

And then, I hit the top. I flew off my spacesuit helmet and breathed fresh air. I was relieved. I looked around, and all I saw was blue ocean all around me. When I was looking around I spotted a red button on my suit. I decided to press it. And instantly my suit inflated into a blow-up boat. "Well, maybe I can paddle to shore, at least I have a boat." I said. So, I began paddling.

MEAN WHIIE?
"Load all systems and FIRE!" cried Shimone. The ship, number 411 fired its biggest blow it had at the Nap ships. But when the air had cleared, there were the Nap ships, sitting there as if this was no big deal. Then, without a moment's notice, the Nap ships fired lazers upon the unsuspecting L.P.A ships. The L.P.As quickly flew in another direction, towards the Earth's moon. But the Naps didn't let up. They followed and fired. One by one, the L.P.As abandoned they're ships in their spacesuits. The plan was simple. The L.P.As would float down to the moon and Then... well... they would figure it out.

To be, Well, you know.

strategies, description, and action work together. They then return to their work and draw scene sequences on a storyboard. With the drawings in front of them, they are ready to add words to the in-progress draft.

In a conference with Cameron, Ed discusses voice from the perspective of a character's speech. Cameron must decide whether to use the first person *I* for the main character or the third person *he* or *she* to talk *about* the main character. He must also concentrate on the functions of dialogue: Will it carry the plotline, reveal the character, or quicken the story's pace? To practice writing dialogue, Cameron spends time eavesdropping on conversations and listening to TV news

FIGURE 4-29
Undersea Exploration by
Robert McCall.
Source: Copyright by
Robert McCall. Used by
permission of the artist.

commentaries and sit-coms. These activities will help him understand that casual talk includes false starts, interruptions, inexact words, repetitions, and fillers (such as *hmm* or *uh*). Although dialogue is not raw conversation, but crafted speech, Cameron develops an ear for natural sounds, rhythms, and emotional overtones in speech.

A cursory look at the fifth-grade papers illustrates two sentence-level extremes. Some papers have elegantly written sentences that vary in length and style. Others have monotonous sentences with unclear referents, or words that are helplessly tangled. Because sentences can either fuel the plot or act as the speed bumps, varying sentence length is considered for individual papers. For the most part, minilessons on sentence fluency address advancing a story by coherently linking thoughts together and creating narrative pace. The writers decide whether to use detailed sentences to slow action and increase drama, or short sentences and phrases to quicken the pace.

Interesting transitional words and phrases also create movement and serve to unify a text. In fifth-grade writing, transitions become whole paragraphs that serve as bridges between scenes. Brittany's action episode in the second chapter of her story is an example of this application.

> Then I skuddled over to the main doors, pressed a button on one of the doors and they instantly opened. Then I pushed my way out, spun around, pressed another button on the outside of the ship and the doors shut instantly.

Her transition not only brings suspense but also chains the events of the plot.

Fifth graders have extensive vocabularies and will search for words that exhibit precision (*gasped for air, speck of dirt*) and passion (highly charged words such as *Kaaabbboooommm, Boom*, and *FIRE*). Although most students understand the importance of a direct and forceful tone, a commonly held myth by some is that "big words" mean better writing. They are quick to pull out a thesaurus and insert a million-dollar word when a simple one will do just fine. These students, like younger children, require rich language experiences so they can begin to realize the appropriate context for words. The feedback they receive in writing circles and conferences helps them improve vocabulary and other language skills.

Before publishing, Ed insists that the writers examine papers for letter and punctuation omissions and other random mistakes (e.g., repeated or extra words). In notebooks they categorize incorrect spellings into common error patterns. For example, in Brittany's notebooks are three categories: confusing homonyms, words that sound alike but are spelled differently *(aloud/allowed, to/too, they're/their)*; letter omissions caused by relying solely on visual memory *(beutiful/beautiful, fasinating/fascinating, detroy/destroy, relising/realizing)*; and erroneous word strings in which compounding is done instead of using two words and vice versa *(lifeforms/life forms, every body/everybody)*.

Because many of Ed's students are experimenting with dialogue, he refers them to an English handbook for the correct application of punctuation rules. After editing, students use word processing to produce an attractive appearance for their final works. Uniform letters, margins, and consistency of style provide readers with easy access to meaning.

Self-assessment occurs during and after writing. Before writing begins, students work in groups to determine essential features of a story—ideas, plot structure, narrative strategies, sentence fluency, word choice, and mechanics—and to create their own rubrics. Figure 4–30, shows how students draw or cut out pictures to go with simple descriptions of the criteria they develop in each of the achievement categories across the traits. These criteria help guide their work throughout the writing process and determine the quality of the written product. During the process, students explain to the class the particular strategies they are using. For example, Brittany tells how she moves characters back and forth between real and imagined environments and how she includes several battle and adventure scenes along two independent storylines. Bryant shares how transitions link his story episodes together. When written products are complete, a developmental category (novice, apprentice, proficient, or distinguished) is assigned by the authors and two others who read and assess the work.

At various times throughout the writing process, students might use additional assessment tools designed for specific purposes. For instance, in a follow-up to a minilesson on combining and expanding sentences, they refer to a sentence construction checklist (Figure 4–31) while editing their work. This checklist is used in combination with other assessments and placed in working portfolios.

JOURNEY REFLECTIONS

Story writing is an important stop along the path of learning to write. It cultivates children's aesthetic sense and imagination, allowing them to temporarily leave behind their daily lives and enter the world of make-believe. In personal narratives, students "tell" or summarize real experiences; in fictional narratives, they show human dramas and "dwell in possibility" (Huck, 1992).

Most children do not need a story prompt to jump-start their writing. They are always seeking and gathering topics, reading and talking about characters in books, and informally considering story elements so that when they are ready to write they have a rich reservoir on which to draw. In some cases, researching information for a story is integral; in other cases, elaborating on the truth is encouraged. The concept of revision often takes the form of "making sense" or "adding text." As stories become more sophisticated—with embedded episodes and new insights into protagonists' thoughts

FIGURE 4-30 Picture Story Rubric

Six Traits of Quality Writing	Novice	Apprentice	Proficient	Distinguished
Ideas	My story needs more details. 	My story is taking shape. 	My story makes sense and shows insight. 	My story is engaging and unforgettable. 
Organization	I have loose factlets that don't seem to fit.	I skip from point to point.	I have a reasonable sequence.	I have a developed structure.
Voice	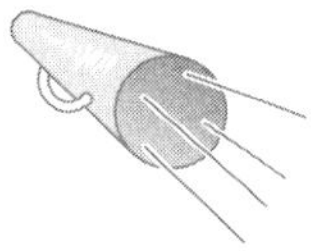 No voice can be heard.	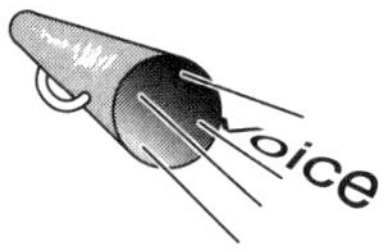 My voice is barely there.	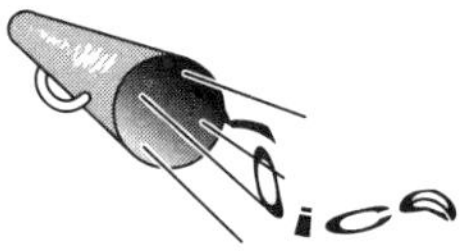 My voice comes and goes.	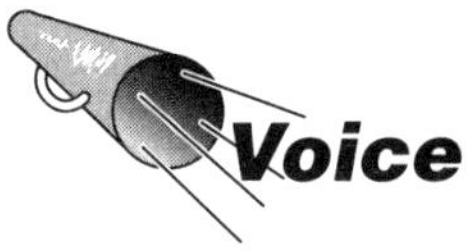 My voice explodes from the page!
Sentence Fluency	My sentences are incomplete or tangled. 	My sentences are readable and varied. 	My sentences are strong but need bridges. 	My sentences are smooth and seamless. 
Word Choice	 animal My words are too general or vague.	 dog My words are familiar but not memorable.	 beagle My words create a mental image.	 Snoopy My words are precise and colorful.
Conventions	I use  .	I use  .?!	I use  .?!""	I use  .?!"",

FIGURE 4-31   Sentence Construction Checklist

Name _____ Date _____ Genre _____

Sentence strategies (combine, expand, clarify, reduce)	Comments
Can I make my composition more interesting to my readers by making some sentences short, some medium length, and some long?	
Can I vary my sentence beginnings?	
Will my composition be more interesting if I use varied sentence patterns (NV, NVN, NLvN)?	
Can I take some short sentences and combine them into one sentence to give the same information but in fewer words?	
Will my whole composition become more readable if I take out some sentences or words?	
Can I make my writing more interesting by adding words that answer questions such as "What kind of? Which one? Whose? How much? How many?"	
Can I make my writing more interesting by placing additional modifiers in some of my sentences (e.g., adjectives, adverbs, prepositional phrases, appositives)?	
Do I need to attach anything I have written to a nearby sentence because it is not itself a sentence?	
Can I make my composition more interesting if I use matter of fact (declarative), asking (interrogative), commanding (imperative), or exciting (exclamatory) sentences where I think they will fit best?	

and feelings—students begin to use a full range of revising skills, from rewriting introductions to changing the style of sentences.

Although there are numerous story types, the writing represented in the classroom vignettes—animal fantasy, pourquoi tales, and science fiction—shows how the basic story elements can be shared among the different genres, depending on students' experiences, interests, and age. Variety and novelty allow students to develop a repertoire of skills that shift according to the nuances of the genre.

Teachers should model for students how to assess their efforts along both process and product dimensions and monitor work throughout the process to determine the writers' attitudes and behaviors toward story writing.

Traveling the road of "once upon a time" and opening the gateway to the imagination is time well spent. Story writing allows children to practice narrative strategies that not only enhance fiction writing but also reinforce an enjoyment and love of the genre. In the next chapter, fiction writing sets the stage for creating the magical features of poetry. Word play, sensory images, music, and visual aesthetics intensify the joyful celebration of literacy and inspire children to continue the adventure of learning to write.

Works Cited

Professional References

Applebee, A. N. (1978). *The child's concept of story: Ages 2–17*. Chicago: University of Chicago Press.

Axelrod, R. B., & Cooper, C. R. (2001). *The St. Martin's guide to writing* (6th ed.). New York: St. Martin's Press.

Barnes, D. (1968). *Drama in the English classroom*. Champaign, IL: National Council of Teachers of English.

Calkins, L. (1994). *The art of teaching writing*. Portsmouth, NH: Heinemann.

Cramer, R. L. (2001). *Creative power: The nature and nurture of children's writing*. New York: Longman.

Dean, D. M. (2000). Muddying boundaries: Mixing genres with five paragraphs. *English Journal, 90*, 53–56.

Dibell, A. (1988). *Plot*. Cincinnati, OH: Writer's Digest Books.

Dickinson, D. (1987). Oral language, literacy skills, and response to literature. In James R. Squire (Ed.), *Dynamics of language learning* (pp. 147–183). Urbana, IL: National Conference on Research in English.

Dyson, A. H. (1983). The role of oral language in writing. *Research in the Teaching of English, 17*, 1–30.

Dyson, A. H. (1989). *Multiple worlds of child writers*. New York: Teachers College Press.

Eckhoff, B. (1983). How reading affects children's writing. *Language Arts, 60*, 607–616.

Egan, K. (1986). *Teaching as storytelling*. Chicago: University of Chicago Press.

Fennessey, S. (1995). Living history through drama and literature. *The Reading Teacher, 49*, 16–19.

Florida State Department of Education (2002). *Sunshine State Standards*. Tallahassee, FL.

Freeman, M. (1995). *Building a writing community: A practical guide*. Gainesville, FL: Maupin House Publishing.

Graves, D. H. (1994). *A fresh look at writing*. Portsmouth, NH: Heinemann.

Harris, T. L., & Hodges, R. E. (Eds.). (1995). *The literacy dictionary: The vocabulary of reading and writing*. Newark, DE: International Reading Association.

Harste, J., Woodward, V., & Burke, C. (1984). *Language stories and literacy lessons*. Portsmouth, NH: Heinemann.

Heath, S. B. (1982). What no bedtime story means: Narrative skills at home and school. *Language in Society, 11*, 49–76.

Heath, S. B. (1993). *Ways with words*. Cambridge, U.K.: Cambridge University Press.

Huck, C. S. (1992). Literacy and literature. *Language Arts, 69*, 520–526.

Jorgensen, K. (2001). *The whole story. Crafting fiction in the upper elementary grades*. Portsmouth, NH: Heinemann.

Kane, T. S. (1988). *The new Oxford guide to writing*. Oxford, U.K.: Oxford University Press.

Lancia, P. (1997). Literary borrowing: The effects of literature on children's writing. *The Reading Teacher, 50*, 470–475.

Lunsford, S. H. (1997). "And they wrote happily ever after": Literature-based mini-lessons in writing. *Language Arts, 74*, 42–48.

Mandler, J. M., & Johnson, N. S. (1977). Remembrance of things parsed: Story structure and recall. *Cognitive Psychology, 9*, 111–115.

Martinez, M., & Roser, N. (1985). Read it again: The value of repeated readings during storytime. *The Reading Teacher, 38*, 782–786.

McMaster, J. C. (1998). "Doing" literature: Using drama to build literacy. *The Reading Teacher, 51*, 574–584.

Morrow, L. M. (1988). Young children's responses to one-to-one story readings in school settings. *Reading Research Quarterly, 23*, 89–107.

Morrow, L. M. (1997). *Literacy development in the early years* (3rd ed.). Boston: Allyn & Bacon.

Pellegrini, A., & Galda, L. (1982). The effects of thematic fantasy play training on the development of children's story comprehension. *American Educational Research Journal, 19*, 443–452.

Piazza, C. (1999). *Multiple forms of literacy: Teaching literacy and the arts*. Columbus, OH: Merrill.

Pitcher, E. G., & Prelinger, E. (1963). *Children tell stories: An analysis of fantasy*. New York: International Universities Press.

Purcell-Gates, V., McIntyre, E., & Freppon, P. A. (1995). Learning written storybook language in school: A comparison of low SES children in skills-based and whole-language classrooms. *American Educational Research Journal, 32*, 659–685.

Rosenblatt, L. (1978). *The reader, the text, the poem.* Carbondale, IL: Southern Illinois University.

Rosenblatt, L. (1984). *Literature as exploration* (3rd ed.). New York: Modern Language Association.

Smith, F. (1983). Reading like a writer. *Language Arts, 60,* 558–567.

Stein, N. L. (1979). How children understand stories. A developmental analysis. In L. Katz (Ed.), *Current topics in early childhood education,* vol. 2 (pp. 261–290). Norwood, NJ: Ablex.

Stein, N. L., & Glenn, C. G. (1979). An analysis of story comprehension in elementary school children. In R. O. Freedle (Ed.), *New directions in discourse processing* (pp. 53–120). Norwood, NJ: Ablex.

Stewig, J. W. (1983). *Exploring language arts in the elementary classroom.* New York: Holt, Rinehart & Winston.

Taylor, D., & Strickland, D. S. (1986). *Family storybook reading.* Portsmouth, NH: Heinemann.

Wolf, S. A., & Heath, S. B. (1998). Wondrous worlds: Young children's rewritings of prose and poetry. *The New Advocate, 11,* 291–309.

Children's References

Aardema, V. (1975). *Why mosquitoes buzz in people's ears.* Dial.

Ahlberg, J., & Ahlberg, A. (1979). *Each peach pear plum.* Viking Penguin.

Ahlberg, J., & Ahlberg, A. (1986). *The jolly postman and other people's letters.* Little Brown.

Ahlberg, A., & Howard, P. (1998). *Mockingbird.* Candlewick.

Allen, J., & Marshall, J. (1985). *Nosey Mrs. Rat.* Viking.

Amato, M. (2000). *The word eater.* Holiday House.

Anno, M. (1983). *Anno's USA.* Philomel.

Artell, M. (2001). *Petite Rouge: A Cajun Red Riding Hood.* Dial.

Aylesworth, J. (Retold, 1998). *The gingerbread man.* Scholastic.

Babbitt, N. (1975). *Tuck everlasting.* Farrar, Straus & Giroux.

Barasch, L. (2000). *Radio rescue.* Farrar, Straus & Giroux.

Bauer, C. F. (1981). *My mom travels a lot.* Puffin.

Bauer, M. D. (1992). *What's your story?* Clarion.

Baum, F. (1982). *The wizard of Oz.* Henry Holt.

Bierhorst, J. (1993). *The woman who fell from the sky: The Iroquois story of creation.* Morrow.

Blos, J. (1979). *A gathering of days: A New England girl's journal 1830–1832.* Aladdin.

Bolam, E. (1992). (illus.). *The house that Jack built.* Dutton.

Briggs-Martin, J. (1998). *Snowflake Bentley.* Houghton Mifflin.

Brooks, W. B. (1998). *Sparrows in the gallery.* Atheneum.

Bruchac, J. (2000). *Crazy Horse's vision.* Lee & Low.

Burns, K. (2001). *Mansa Musa: The lion of Mali.* Gulliver.

Carle, E. (1968). *The very hungry caterpillar.* World.

Carle, E. (2000). *Does a kangaroo have a mother, too?* HarperCollins.

Carroll, L. (1978). *Alice in wonderland and through the looking glass.* Grosset & Dunlap.

Christelow, E. (1995). *What do authors do?* Clarion.

Cleary, B. (1983). *Dear Mr. Henshaw.* Morrow.

Climo, S. (1993). *The Korean Cinderella.* HarperCollins.

Cole, J. (1989). *The magic school bus: Inside the human body.* Scholastic.

Conrad, P. (1991). *Pedro's journal.* Boyds Mills.

Creech, S. (2000). *The wanderer.* HarperCollins.

Cutts, D. (1979). *The house that Jack built.* Troll Associates.

DiCamillo, K. (2000). *Because of Winn-Dixie.* Candlewick.

Eastman, P. D. (1988). *Are you my mother?* Random House.

Ellis, D. (2000). *The breadwinner.* Groundwood.

Falconer, I. (2000). *Olivia.* Atheneum.

Florian, D. (1994). *Beast feast.* Trumpet.

Freeman, D. (1986). *Corduroy.* Puffin.

Galdone, P. (1961). *Three billy goats gruff.* Seabury.

Gantos, J. (2000). *Joey Pigza loses control.* Farrar, Straus & Giroux.

Gatti, A. (1992). *Aesop's fables.* Harcourt.

George, J. C. (1991). *The moon of the alligators.* HarperCollins.

Giblin, J. C. (2000). *The amazing life of Ben Franklin.* Scholastic.

Giff, P. R. (2000). *Nory Ryan's story.* Delacorte.

Hall, D. (1994). *I am the dog, I am the cat*. Dial.

Hesse, K. (1998). *Out of the dust*. Scholastic.

Hesse, K. (2000). *Stowaway*. McElderry.

Hesse, K. (2001). *Witness*. Scholastic.

Hiskey, I. (1992). *Cassandra who?* Simon & Schuster.

Holm, J. L. (2001). *Boston Jane: An adventure*. HarperCollins.

Holt, K. W. (1999). *When Zachary Beaver came to town*. Henry Holt.

Howard, E. F. (2000). *Virgie goes to school with us boys*. Simon & Schuster.

Kipling, R. (1902). *Just so stories*. Doubleday.

L'Engle, M. (1963). *A wrinkle in time*. Farrar, Straus & Giroux.

Lester, J. (1994). *John Henry*. Dial.

Lionni, L. (1967). *Alexander and the wind-up mouse*. Pantheon.

Lobel, A. (1970). *Frog and Toad are friends*. Harper.

Loomis, C. (2000). *Across America, I love you*. Hyperion.

Martin, A. M. (2001). *Belle Teal*. Scholastic.

Martin, B. (1991). *Polar bear, polar bear, what do you hear?* Henry Holt.

Martin, B. (1992). *Brown bear, brown bear, what do you see?* Henry Holt.

Martin, R. (1992). *The rough-face girl*. Putnam.

Marzollo, J. (1990). *Pretend you're a cat*. Scholastic.

Mayer, M. (1978). *A boy, a dog, and a frog*. Puffin.

Mays, O. (2000). *Osceola: Memories of a sharecropper's daughter*. Hyperion.

Meddaugh, S. (1997). *Cinderella's rat*. Houghton Mifflin.

Meyers, C. (2000). *Wings*. Scholastic.

Meyers, L. (2000). *Surviving Brick Johnson*. Clarion.

Morley, C. (1983). The plumpuppets. In J. Prelutsky & A. Lobel (Eds.). *The Random House book of poetry for children* (p. 213). Random House.

Nerlove, M. (1991). *If all the world were paper*. Albert Whitman.

Park, B. (2001). *Junie B., first grader at last!* Random House.

Paterson, K. (1978). *The great Gilly Hopkins*. Cromwell.

Peck, R. (2000). *A year down yonder*. Dial.

Potter, B. (1902). *The tales of Peter Rabbit*. Warne.

Ringgold, F. (1991). *Tar beach*. Crown.

Ringgold, F. (1992). *Aunt Harriet's underground railroad in the sky*. Crown.

Robart, R. (1991). *The cake that Mack ate*. Little Brown.

Rosen, M. (1989). *We're going on a bear hunt*. Simon & Schuster.

Rosenberry, V. (2001). *Who is in the garden?* Holiday House.

Rowling, J. K. (1998). *Harry Potter and the sorcerer's stone*. Scholastic.

Rylant, C. (1998). *Bear day*. Harcourt.

San Souci, R. D. (1998). *Cendrillon: A Caribbean Cinderella*. Simon & Schuster.

Schwartz, D. M. (1999). *If you hopped like a frog*. Scholastic.

Scieszka, J. (1989). *The true story of the three little pigs! by A. Wolf*. Viking.

Sendak, M. (1963). *Where the wild things are*. Harper.

Silverstein, S. (1964). *A giraffe and a half*. HarperCollins.

Spinelli, J. (1990). *Maniac Magee*. Little Brown.

Stevens, J. (1995). *From pictures to words: A book about making a book*. Holiday House.

Taylor, M. D. (1976). *Roll of thunder, hear my cry*. Puffin.

Taylor, M. D. (2001). *The land*. Phyllis Fogelman Books.

Thayer, E. L. (1992). *Casey at the bat*. Putnam.

Viorst, J. (1972). *Alexander and the terrible, horrible, no good, very bad day*. Aladdin.

Viorst, J. (2001). *Super, completely and totally the messiest*. Atheneum.

White, E. B. (1952). *Charlotte's web*. Harper & Row.

Wiesner, D. (2001). *The three pigs*. Clarion.

Willard, N. (1989). *East of the sun and west of the moon*. Harcourt.

Woodson, J. (2001). *The other side*. Putnam.

Zelinsky, P. O. (1997). (Reteller). *Rapunzel*. Dutton.

Zemach, M. (1980). *The little red hen*. Farrar, Straus & Giroux.

Educational Resources

Franco, B. (1993). *The Gigantic Rutabaga*. In *Russia: A Literature-Based Multicultural Unit*. Monterey, CA: Evan-Moor Educational Publishers.

Freeman, K. (1994). *If Balloons Were Wishes* [Art transparency]. In *Literature and Language Transparency Pack*. Evanston, IL: McDougal-Littell. Courtesy Tatistcheff Gallery, New York.

"Gunner's Brush With Death by Gator." (1997, August 2) *Tallahassee Democrat* (p. 9A).

How a Book Is Made [Poster]. Betsy & Guilio Maestro. The Children's Book Council 2000, P.O. Box 2640 JAF Station, New York, NY 10116.

McCall, R. *Undersea Exploration* [Art transparency]. Prentice Hall.

Taymor, J. (Director). (1997). *The lion king* [Film]. (Available from Disney Theatrical Productions, New York: Disney Enterprises and ABC Inc.

Stuart, M. (Director). (1971). *Willie Wonka and the chocolate factory* [Film]. (Available from Warner Home Video, New York: Time Warner.

CHAPTER 5

"Somehow it [a poem] seems to fill my head with ideas only I don't exactly know what they are!"

Poetry Writing

If words make us feel like clapping our hands or waving our arms, or if they bring us laughter and arouse our senses, it must be poetry. Poems speak through the language of sensations, rhythms, colors, and images. A poem is experienced by exploring and traveling through it, discovering what it has to reveal rather than what it actually says (DeHaven, 1983). Suppose one is writing about a lion. To get facts about the lion one simply goes to an encyclopedia to find out that it is a large, carnivorous, nocturnal cat found in the rocky or open areas of Africa and Southern Asia. But to experience the power of the lion, its fierce nature compared to the fragility of the other animals, or the grandeur of the lion's surroundings, a poem like this one by William Jay Smith (1998) might be considered:

Lion

The lion, ruler over all the beasts,
Triumphant moves upon the grassy plain
With sun like gold upon his tawny brow
And dew like silver on his shaggy mane.

Into himself he draws the rolling thunder,
Beneath his flinty paw great boulders quake;
He will dispatch the mouse to burrow under,
The little deer to shiver in the brake.

He sets the fierce whip of each serpent lashing,
The tall giraffe brings humbly to his knees,
Awakes the sloth and sends the wild boar crashing,
Wide-eyed monkeys chittering through the trees.

He gazes down into the quiet river,
Parting the green bulrushes to behold
A sunflower-crown of amethyst and silver,
A royal coat of brushed and beaten gold.

This poem suggests a vision of a lion strikingly different from the information found in the encyclopedia. It engages emotions, intellect, imagination, and senses. As Alice in Wonderland proclaims in the opening quote, "it seems to fill my head with ideas only I don't exactly know what they are!" The multidimensional ways poems speak to us may account for why this is so.

Although poems may intuitively be understood, they are not always easy to define. Rather than attempting to do so, it is often better to let them show themselves through words (*Inner Chimes: Poems on Poetry*, Goldstein, 1992), through art (*Imaginary Gardens: American Poetry and Art for Young People*, Sullivan, 1989), or through music (*Just the Two Of Us*, Smith, 2001). Sharing

JOURNAL WRITING

PERSONAL WRITING

STORY WRITING

POETRY WRITING

EXPOSITORY WRITING

PERSUASIVE WRITING

TABLE 5-1 Children's Definitions of Poetry	
What Is Poetry?	
Things that rhyme (6 year old)	Poems make you laugh. They are
I like poetry about birds (6 year old)	things about people (8 year old)
Poetry is fun to say. I like poetry in the morning	Some things actually happen and
(7 year old)	some are made up (8 year old)
Poetry is funny; some poetry is sad (7 year old)	Shorter than a story (9 year old)

FIGURE 5-1   Kinds of Poetry Writing

Elegy	Musical poems
Epigrams (concise, witty poems)	Chants
Dramatic poems	Odes
Free verse	Rap
Invented poems	Rounds (rondeau)
Alphabet	Songs
Chants	Spirituals
Color	Narrative poems
Concrete	Epic
Descriptive	Lyric
Dialogue	Ballad
Five senses	Nonsense
Found	Puns
I am	Syllable and count poems
I remember	Cinquain
Imitation	Diamante
List	Haiku
Name (acrostics)	Limerick
Phone number	Lune
Preposition	Pantoums
Question and answer	Senryu
Shape	Word play
Movement poems	Jokes
Multiethnic poems	Puns
	Riddles

how authors write poems (*Near the Window Tree: Poems and Notes*, Kuskin, 1975) or asking children for their meanings are other ways of defining them. You might be surprised by what children have to say (see Table 5–1). Some think poems must rhyme, others associate them with a special time or a particular subject. A few explain how poems affect them. The more children are exposed to poetry, the more they begin to understand that poems come in many forms and are about many things. In fact, there are hundreds of different poetic forms (Padgett, 1987; Williams, 1986), too many to cover in this chapter or to address in a single classroom. Some of the more popular ones taught in school are shown in Figure 5–1.

These poetic genres—rhymed verse, lists, graphic humor, song lyrics, advertising jingles, and stories—are plentiful and offer many choices for writing and reading. Moreover, they can be found everywhere—on buses and billboards, in graffiti and joke books, in greeting cards, in songs, in bedtime stories, and in lunch boxes. A poem that everyone recites at a moment's notice seems almost magical. If it is a distracting or disquieting time, clapping to "Pease porridge hot/Pease porridge cold/Pease porridge in the pot, nine days old" captures everyone's attention. On a rainy day, the class comes alive by joining in a jingle: "Rain, rain, go away/Come again another day." Even a tense or somber moment can erupt into laughter when the teacher refers affectionately to a child as "Little Miss Muffett"or "Tony Baloney" (Lee, 1983). Poems celebrate a holiday or welcome a new season, boast the ordinary or tug at deep emotions, spark laughter or bring tears.

WRITER'S WORKSHOP

Minilessons

When introducing poetry to young children, teachers should make it concrete, relevant, and immediately accessible. Although many topics are suitable for minilessons, those dealing with visual, aural, and humorous effects seem especially pertinent to the craft.

Visual Effects of Poetry

According to Spender (in Ghiselin, 1952, p. 112), "the poet should be able to think in images; he should have as great a mastery of language as a painter has over his pallet." Poetry's meanings and feelings are often expressed through line length, shapes, white space, symbols, punctuation, and formatting (Piazza, 1999). Because the poem's distinct "look" on the page makes it as much a visual experience as an auditory one, an appropriate way to introduce poetry is to compare its visual features with that of prose. Consider the two different versions of *Little Red Riding Hood*.

Poetic Verse	**Prose**
So, Red Riding Hood ran	Her grandmother lived away in the wood,
For almost a mile.	a good half hour from the village. When
Then she sat down	she got to the wood she met a wolf, but
To rest a while.	Little Red Riding Hood did not know
Along came MR. WOLF!	what a wicked animal he was, so she
	was not a bit afraid of him. . . .
But	In the meantime the wolf went straight off
The wolf ran fast–	to the grandma's cottage and knocked
Faster than fast.	on the door. "Who is there?"
He reached the grandma's	"Little Red Riding Hood, bringing you a
Door at last.	cake and some wine.
Tap-tap!	Open the door!"
[deRegniers, 1972 (pp. 6, 16)]	[Galdone, 1974 (pp. 4, 12)]

The poetic version illustrates end rhyme and short sentences, with white space defining its shape and meaning. Most children are surprised to find that well-known fairy tales can be transformed into narrative poems by replacing the long sentences of prose with the thrifty ones of poetry and keeping the story's plot and characters in tact. Following the Red Riding Hood example, the teacher reads *Cinderella* (Brown, 1954), stopping occasionally for children to retell an episode while she converts responses into verse. The first four stanzas of "The Ball" follow.

The Ball

Her clothes in rags
And her hands full of blisters
Cinderella worked hard
For her wicked stepsisters.

She swept and she scrubbed
To make the house clean
But still her three stepsisters
Were angry and mean.

Cinderella always dreamed
About attending the ball
The castle, the music,
The dancing and all.

But her stepsisters laughed
Said "Start scrubbing the floor"
And with a loud slam
They went out the door.

Although making a poem out of a story appears easy, it is a bit trickier than this example might suggest. In fact, it requires the ability to summarize a familiar story *and* write poetry. The point here is simply to model the construction of a poem and show visual distinctions and connections between prose and poetry and reading and writing.

Among the most visual of poetic forms is shape and concrete poetry (more is said about these in the classroom vignettes). Shape poems derive their meanings from words that look like the thing they represent. Oftentimes phrases and sentences replace the lines of the pictured object, as in the basketball poem constructed by a fifth grader in Figure 5–2. Concrete poetry exploits the visual plan or "look" of the poem but creates its effects through **stanza** groupings, line breaks, varying line lengths, or other typographical arrangements of words or letters on the page. In the Pokeman sample in Figure 5–3, a fifth grader groups words to lead the eye and uses font styles and graphic features (size, shape, slant, proportion, decoration) to energize content and achieve playfulness.

Graphic artists tell us that the "look of words" can imbue a work with meanings and feelings (Brier, 1992). Because English words and lines have distinct personalities (fat or thin lines, long or short, wide, curved, closed), they can be organized or decorated to express mood or give the illusion of movement.

FIGURE 5-2
Basketball Shape Poem, Final Draft (Fifth Grader, Guided Writing)

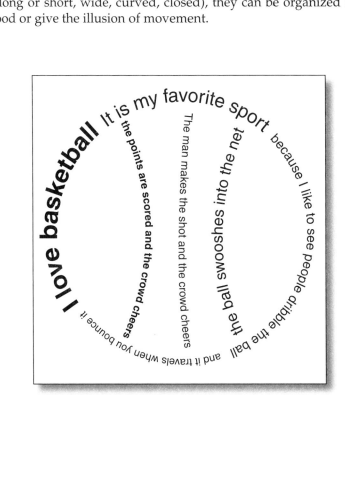

FIGURE 5-3
Pokemon Concrete
Poem, Final Draft (Fifth
Grader, Guided
Writing)

POKEMON
All kinds of
CREATURES
FIGHT OFF enemies
PIKACHU
CHARIZARD
MEWTWO
MACHAMP

Trading cards
They're **RARE**
They have different
POWERS!!!
They are different Colors
I LOVE to play the games

A river is w i d e

Jammedtogether

The building is TALL

Shadow

To capture interests and stimulate interaction, the teacher distributes a list of words *(laugh, soft, stiff, tree, wind),* along with stencils, cutout letters of different sizes and shapes, Magic Markers, and crayons, and has the children depict word meanings using typographic features. On hand are sample graphics (CD covers, magazine clippings, bumper stickers, or book jackets) and professional poems which show how deviations from norms of spelling, punctuation, or layout can also surprise the eye and add humor. A case in point is the poem "I'm All Mixed Up" (Prelutsky, 1996), which mixes upper- and lowercase letters within a word to coincide with the poem's meaning, or "I Am Your Mirror Image" (Prelutsky, 1996), a poem that must be held up to a mirror to be read.

Graphic effects are concrete and easily identified but, some visual appeals are mediated by sensory words and descriptions. Imagery and the many strategies associated with it (simile, metaphor, personification, and hyperbole) build on connotations, comparisons, and sensory descriptions to represent ideas, objects, or experiences. A good way to illustrate the power of imagery is through creative visualization, an invention technique that makes use of sensory words.

A second-grade teacher reads the descriptive poem "I'm Proud of My Preposterpus" (Prelutsky, 1996) while the children close their eyes and imagine what the Preposterpus looks like. Here are the first two stanzas of the four-stanza poem:

Stanza 1

I'm proud of my Preposterpus,
so ponderous and pale,
I love the way it whistles

Stanza 2

It has talons like an eagle,
shiny flippers like a seal,
rows of webbing at its elbows

when it swizzles ginger ale.
It's magnificent in stature,
fully twenty-four feet tall,
so it tends to draw attention
when I take it to the mall.

and a head of solid steel.
With its pickle-like proboscis
glossy antlers rosy beak,
its apparent my Preposterpus
is practically unique.
(pp. 150–151)

Following the reading, the children draw a picture of the "Preposterpus" based on the sensory words they've heard.

Another way to teach third graders the power of descriptive vocabulary for imagery is to give each child a grab bag with a secret object inside and a five-senses chart to record notes (see Figure 5–4). At first the writers do not look in the bag but only smell what's inside. Based on what they smell, they fill in the space on the chart for "I smell." Then they feel the object (still without looking) and describe its touch. Again, the appropriate box is filled in. Next they pull out the object and record what they "see." If the item is edible, they taste it and complete the chart. After the object is fully examined, the children write a description. Some may choose to add details about the object's function or make possible comparisons (similes and metaphors) with it.

Similes are tools that poets use to compare ideas, actions, feelings, or objects using the words *like* or *as (legs like a crane, quiet as a mouse)*. At first children might write from a prompt that compares *similar* items:

FIGURE 5-4   Five Senses Chart

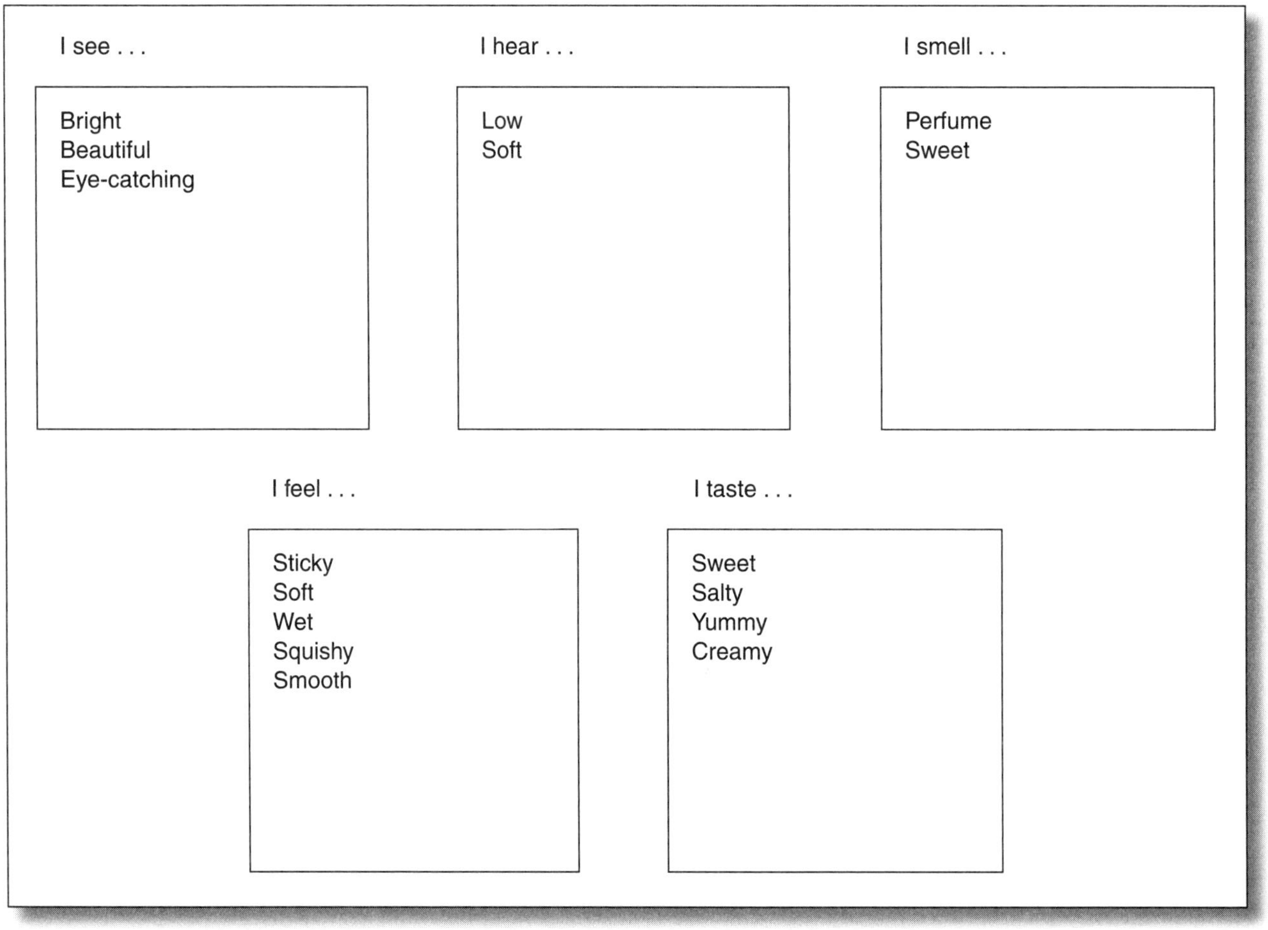

I see . . .	I hear . . .	I smell . . .
Bright Beautiful Eye-catching	Low Soft	Perfume Sweet

I feel . . .	I taste . . .
Sticky Soft Wet Squishy Smooth	Sweet Salty Yummy Creamy

As small as _____
As simple as _____
As stupid as _____

Then they practice writing comparisons between things that are essentially *dissimilar*. For instance,

A moon is like a soccer ball.
A toothpick is like my sister.

Before long, they find their own subjects and experiment with this device to structure poems.

The second-grade author of "The Statue of Liberty" (see Figure 5–5) considers the visual features of Lady Liberty (her eyes as big as a puppy's, her crowned spikes resembling pencils) and makes other comparisons to the torch and chains. She ends by underscoring the symbolic meaning of the statue: She is as free as a bird.

In another poem, "The Thing!" (see Figure 5–6), also written by a second grader, simile is sprinkled in as part of description. The thing has a tail like a spade and feet like a duck, but it is also very dangerous. In this example, expression and technique come together to form new images and ideas.

Like similes, metaphors make associations and comparisons. Apart from this, however, they are distinguished by the absence of the words *like* or *as*. For example, *the night was a visiting traveler* or *lucky is a star* imply a connection and new idea so subtle, that it is less seen than sensed. Children will discover metaphors popping up in everyday conversations—*It's a lemon* (a defective car)—or in symbols all around them—*the flag* (patriotism).

Sometimes poets construct imagery by assigning personal qualities to inanimate things or ideas. This is called *personification*. Note how the attributes of human dialogue and action are assigned to the ocean tides and a gatepost in two excerpts found in *The Country Mail Is Coming: Poems From Down Under* (Fatchen, 1987).

FIGURE 5-5 Simile Poem, "The Statue of Liberty," First Draft (Second Grader, Independent Writing)

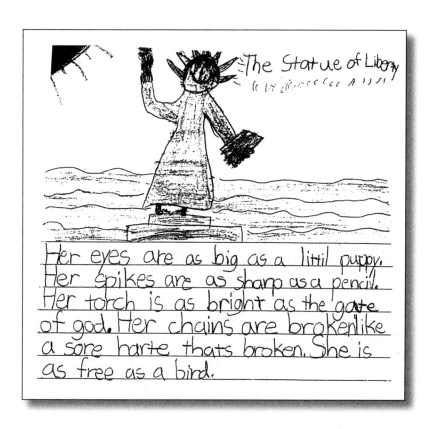

Figure 5-6 Simile Poem, "The Thing!", First Draft (Second Grader, Independent Writing)

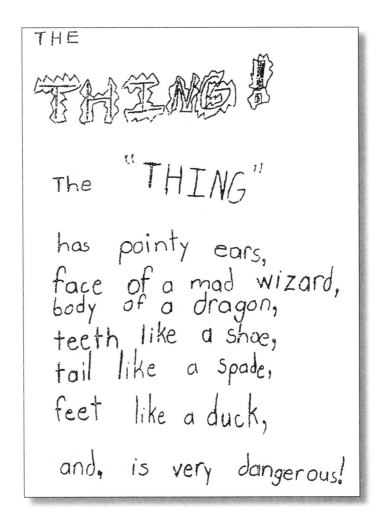

The tide, quite crossly, said: "The sea
Is always out there pushing me.
And just when I am feeling slack,
It sends me in then drags me back.
It never seems to let me go.
I rise. I fall. I'm to and fro."
(From "Tide Talk," p. 40)

The gateposts lean,
A little tired,
With fences stretching
Rusty wired.
(From "Gate Gossip," p. 20)

In these excerpts, images of people come to mind as the "tide" speaks about being pushed around by the sea, and the worn-out "gatepost" frets over years of neglect. Because personification can pictorially render an inanimate object human (dressing up a dog or cat), young children can have fun drawing pictures to go with statements such as

The star winked at me.
The moon slept behind the clouds.
The rain beat against the window pane.

TABLE 5-2   Books of Visual Poems

Color
A Song of Colors (Hindly, 1998)
Hailstones and Halibut Bones (O'Neill, 1961, 1989)
Out of the Blue: Poems About Color (Oram, 1995)

Graphic Displays
Animalia (Base, 1986)
Anno's Alphabet: An Adventure in Imagination (Anno, 1975)
Walking, Talking Words (Sherman, 1980)

Shape and Concrete
Concrete Poetry: A World View (Solt, 1980)
Eats Poems (Adoff, 1979)
Flicker Flash (Graham, 1999)
If Dragonflies Made Honey (Kherdian, 1977)

Simile
As: A Surfeit of Similes (Juster, 1989)

Collections
A Moon in Your Lunch Box (Spooner, 1993)
Knock at a Star: A Child's Introduction to Poetry (Kennedy & Kennedy, 1982)
The Country Mail Is Coming: Poems From Down Under (Fatchen, 1987)

Learning from examples such as these, they can begin to write and illustrate their own phrases.

Hyperbole, or exaggeration, is another type of imagery that uses visual pictures for humorous or fanciful effects. Usually hyperbole intentionally makes a point.

He laughed his head off.
I turned red with rage.
It rained buckets.
The airplane split the sky in two.

Statements of hyperbole stretch the truth for emphasis and say one thing but mean another. Unrestrained and impertinent, they can make a poem deliberately dramatic or wonderfully wacky. Table 5–2 is a list of books to teach imagery or visual poems.

Aural Effects of Poetry

Poetry is as much for the ear as it is for the eye. The marriage of music and poetry has a long history. In Western culture, the first poems were sung by bards and troubadours who knew that their listeners would remember information longer if they sang songs with catchy rhythms and simple plotlines. In more contemporary times, poems of great writers are commonly recreated in music (e.g., the lyrics of Ogden Nash and the music of Saint-Saen's *Carnival of Animals*) and great music frequently inspires poetry (e.g., Debussy's *Prelude to the Afternoon of a Faun* as the muse for the symbolic poetry of Mallarme).

Children intuitively understand this poetry–music connection. Perhaps this is because their earliest developmental experiences involve soundmaking in language learning (Piaget, 1952). From the discovery of speech sounds and their production (ma-ma, da-da) to the first nursery rhymes and lullabies, children delight in sounds that are pleasant to hear and say.

Musical poetry may also be well received because it mimics everyday activity—jumping, running, and singing. On the playground in jump-rope songs and jingles, hopscotch, and hide-and-seek games, children use strong action verbs, rhyme, and word sounds (Fisher & Natarella, 1982; Terry, 1974). Familiar chants and ritual repetitions, such as "Mable Mable set the table / Don't forget the mustard, ketchup, red, hot, pepper, pepper, pepper" or "Cinderella dressed in yellow / Went upstairs to kiss her fellow," are found in every culture and across many generations (see collections such as *Miss Mary Mac All Dressed in Black*, Hastings, 1990).

Just as children's physical activity spawns creativity for poetry, so do experiences with TV and the media. Educators often talk about children's ability to learn literacy from the print environment, but they are just as likely to learn it from media jingles and catchy tunes heard on TV. McDonald's "We love to see you smile," Campbell's® "Mmm mmm good®", or Bounty's "quicker picker up-per", provide repeated exposure to word order, repetition, rhyme, and verbal play.

Traditional songs such as "Twinkle Twinkle Little Star," "Eency Weency Spider," or "Ring Around the Roses" are also a part of childhood lore and peer culture (older students examine song lyrics as texts, looking for rhyme at the ends of sentences or the number of syllables per line). Teachers can take advantage of children's natural joy of melody and rhythm by purchasing or making musical instruments to accompany poetry. For example, in a first-grade class the children ring bells and the teacher asks, "What sound do you hear?" Children invent words, such as ting-a-ling, jingle-jingle, ring-ring. "What does this sound remind you of?" The children think of associations, such as sleigh bells, telephones, jingling coins, and charm bracelets. These steps continue with several instruments: triangles (wind chimes), tambourines (spice jars with rice), bells, sticks (chopsticks), and sand blocks (wood and sandpaper). A poem is born.

> Ting-a-ling go the sleigh bells
> Click clack go the horses
> Swish swish through the snow
> Ping ping drip the icicles on the roof

Older students can accompany a poem with instruments to create a rhythm or natural pulse through **meter**, cadence, or syllable stress. The limerick offers a good example. Instruments mark the beat on the accented syllable while voices substitute words with nonsense expressions such as *ta tum* or *duh dah*:

> Duh DAH duh duh DAH du duh DAH
> Duh DAH duh duh DAH duh du DAH
> Duh DAH duh duh DAH
> Duh DAH duh duh DAH
> Duh DAH duh duh DAH duh duh DAH

Finger snapping, hand clapping, or foot stomping work just as well for measuring rhythm.

> There ONCE was a BUN ny named SCRATCH
> Who RAI ded the VEG etable PATCH
> From CAR rots and LEEKS
> To LET tuce and BEETS
> He ATE every THING he could SNATCH.

In the limerick, keeping the tempo and mood (slow and soothing or quick and vigorous) paces the reading to match the poet's desired intent. Older children can learn how rhythm is formalized into meter, a pattern of regularity identified according to the number of words or syllables per line, placement of stress or **accent** in the words, the number of syllables, or both a fixed number of syllables and accents.

By repeating a word or phrase in a particular arrangement (e.g., rhythm), the poet structures ideas and sets expectations. Both rhythm and rhyme are types of repetition that scaffold the poem and emphasize key points for memorization or recitation. Depending on the repetitive length and patterning of words and sentences, lines can saunter or stop, bounce or behave.

FIGURE 5-7 The Sounds and Rhythm of Poetry

> **Alliteration:** Repeating beginning consonant sounds in words, such as *purple pansy in a pewter pot*
>
> **Assonance:** Repeating vowel sounds in words, such as *please, legal,* or *sleezy*
>
> **Consonance:** Repeating consonant sounds anywhere in the words, such as *black, dark, jacket, cat*
>
> **Onomatopoeia:** Using words that imitate the thing or action being described, such as *wham, twitter, bang*
>
> **Repetition and refrain:** Repeating a word or phrase to emphasize an idea and add rhythm and cadence, such as *Oh where have you been, silly goose, silly goose? Oh where have you been, silly goose?*
>
> **Rhyme:** Placing similar sounding words at the end or in the middle of lines, such as *hippity, hippity hop, can't get my feet to stop;* and *After he broke the seal, the wheel began to reel*
>
> **Rhythm:** Repeating stressed and unstressed syllables or sound patterns, such as *bump and bang, twist and turn, / dents and scratches, tires burn / fast and furious, swing and sway / It's a slam-dunk bumper-car day*

Above all, the sounds of words will bring a melodious dimension to poetry. Teachers can share **stylistic devices** that poets use for sound effects—rhyme, assonance, consonance, onomatopoeia, and alliteration (see Figure 5–7). These devices refine students' poetic sensibilities and turn the silent words on the page into vocal scores that beg to be read aloud. Through pronunciation and phonology, the poem invents its own music.

Rhyme is probably the stylistic device best known to children. Simply put, rhymes are similar sounding words, usually at the ends of poetic lines. They organize meaning and structure sounds for rhythm. Children enjoy rhymes in all kinds of poems and songs. More is said about teaching rhyme in the classroom vignettes.

Assonance and consonance are techniques poets use for manufacturing both sound and rhythm. Assonance is the repetition of vowel sounds, and consonance, the repetition of consonant sounds. Note the long *e* sound formed in four different ways (*ee, ea, e, ei*) in the following poem by Piazza (1999, p. 71):

> A naughty sleezy weasel
> Stole a painting from an easel
> While a measley eager beagle
> Stole it back to please an eagle
> "Not for me, this is not regal"
> Said the cunning hawk-eyed eagle
> "I cannot seize a weasel's work
> Until this deal is legal."

As this short verse illustrates, recurring vowel sounds echo one another to accomplish harmony and coherence. The same repetition might be done with consonant blends (*truck, sultry*) and digraphs (*batch, botched*), manipulating them in various positions in a word. Clearly, poetry is a phonics lesson in the making.

Onomatopoeia, the device for making words mimic what they mean, such as *buzz, hiss,* or *snap,* produces an effect of motion and sound. Several books and poems that highlight such words prepare students to hear poetry's cadence and melody. Children can also listen to audiotapes such as *Soundtracks* (1993) and verbalize the sounds they hear: frog (*ribbit*), sneeze (*aahchoo*), cat (*meow*). They add these words to a chart, pick three of their favorites from the list, and write sentences in their journals for reference in future assignments.

Another poetic device for making sound effects is alliteration, the repetitive sequencing of initial sounds. Poets are very picky about the letters they use, intuitively considering place and manner of articulation. Words that begin with a *b* or *p* seem to explode from our lips while those that use *l* and *r* seem to glide and calm. Renowned writer Eudora Welty (1984, p. 11) offers her thoughts on the melodious formation of a word.

> The word 'moon' comes into my mouth as though fed to me out of a silver spoon. Held in my mouth, the moon became a word. It had the roundness of a Concord grape grandpa took off his vine and gave me to suck out of its skin and swallow whole, in Ohio.

A poet can also link every word with the same sound and end up tangling our tongues (see the section on verbal play later in this chapter). In the alliterative sentence in Figure 5–8, a second grader chooses the letter *n* to begin her words. The picture that accompanies the work extends the sentence and gives it coherence.

Natural sounds are found everywhere—birds singing, motors humming, crickets chirping, dogs barking, and footsteps pounding on the pavement. Attending to these sounds can result in a sonorous or rhythmic poem. At a listening center, a third-grade writer is inspired to write **free verse** (see Figure 5–9) after listening to a tape on the sounds of nature. Her piece presents a list of words that express the forms and sounds of water.

A close second to listening to poetry is reading it. Just about any book that focuses on the phonemic and structural properties of language—from a simple rhyme to a carefully planned song is suitable for reading during prewriting or revising (see Table 5–3). Some of the prose and pattern books discussed in story writing also have the tonal shape and flow of poetry. Children will discover that poetry shares techniques with fiction such as the refrains in *Traveling to Tondo* (Aardema, 1991) or *The Pied Piper of Hamelin* (Browning, 1997).

Humorous Effects of Poetry: Verbal Play

Poetry is full of "just for fun" expressions and language play, where words are turned on their heads to make us laugh or presented as puzzles for our amusement. They add a light note to the normal school day and expose children to the power of language. We

FIGURE 5-8   Alliteration Poem, "Nice, Nerdy, Nephew," Final Draft (Second Grader, Guided Writing)

FIGURE 5-9 Hannah's "The Sound of Water," First Draft (Third Grader, Independent Writing)

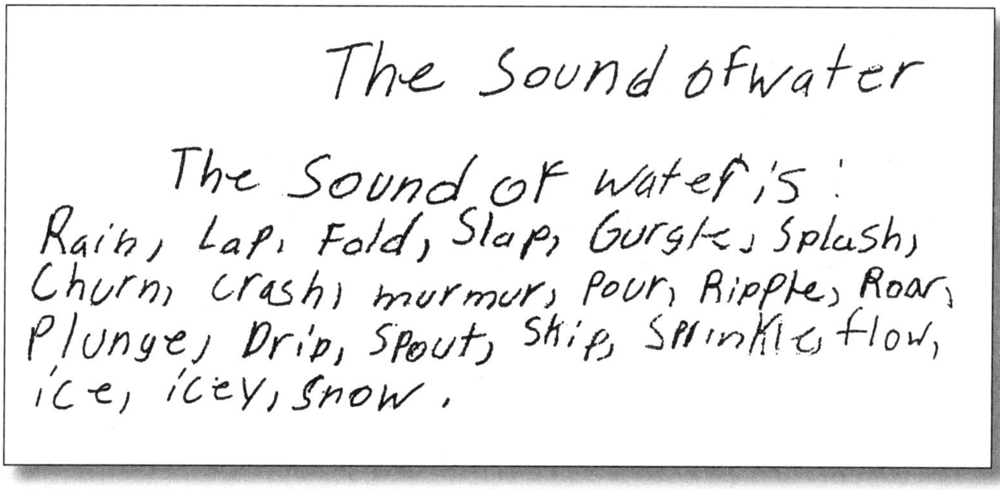

> # The Sound of water
>
> The Sound of water is:
> Rain, Lap, Fold, Slap, Gurgle, Splash,
> Churn, crash, murmur, pour, Ripple, Roar,
> Plunge, Drip, Spout, Skip, Sprinkle, flow,
> ice, icey, snow.

TABLE 5-3 Books of Musical Poems and Sound Effects

Alliteration
Clara Caterpillar (Edwards, 2001)
Hoot, Howl, Hiss (Koch, 1991)
Six Dinner Sid (Moore, 1991)
Six Sleepy Sheep (Gardon, 1991)
Some Smug Slug (Edwards, 1996)

Assonance
Feed Me (Hooks, 1992)
Frank Was a Monster Who Wanted to Dance (Graves, 1999)
Henny Penny (Wattenberg, 2000)
Touch the Poem (Adoff, 2000)

Onomatopoeia
Click, Clack Moo: Cows That Type (Cronin, 2000)
Off We Go (Yolen, 2000)
The Remarkable Farkle McBride (Lithgow, 2000)
Zin! Zin! Zin!: A Violin (Moss, 1995)

Rap
Just the Two of Us (Smith, 2001)
Lunch Money: And Other Poems About School (Shields, 1995)
Yo Hungry Wolf? A Nursery Rap (Vozar, 1985)

Rhythm and Rhyme
Cats, Cats, Cats! (Newman, 2001)
Park Beat (London, 2001)
Shells (Franco, 2000)
When Moon Fell Down (Smith, 2001)

Songs
Arroz Con Leche: Popular Songs and Rhymes From Latin America (Delacre, 1989)
Big Talk: Poems for Four Voices (Fleischman, 2000)
Don't Worry, Be Happy (McFerrin, 2001)
I Have a News: Rhymes From the Caribbean (Jekyll, 1994)
The Star-Spangled Banner (Kent, 1995)

Collections
Knock at a Star: A Child's Introduction to Poetry (Kennedy & Kennedy, 1982)
Ride a Purple Pelican (Prelutsky, 1986)
Sing a Song of Popcorn (deRegniers, Moore, White, & Carr, 1988)

have seen how poets use sound for stylistic purposes, but they also exploit it for verbal play and humor. Not only do they depend on phonology (the sound system) to accomplish this, but they borrow from the entire structure of language, including morphology (word formation and the make-up of words), syntax (the order of phrases, clauses, and sentences), and semantics (the meanings of words, phrases, and sentences). These linguistic features are embedded, combined, or freestanding in short forms or **terse verse**. In this section is an introduction to an array of verbal play techniques that bring humor to poetry and constitute rich topics for word study. It concludes with a few minilessons on short written forms—riddles and jokes—that are products in their own right.

Playing With Sounds of Language (Phonology)

The sound system of language, called phonology, may be the smallest unit of speech, but it can be a potent tool for the poet who combines and assembles sounds for different humorous effects. Here are a few.

TONGUE TWISTERS.   Tongue twisters involve a series of consonants that usually appear in the initial positions in consecutive words. What makes these consonants funny is that they deviate from the normal use of sounds found in everyday conversation. You literally trip over your tongue as you say the words; kids love to say them very fast. The first two lines of some popular tongue twisters follow.

> Sally Sells Seashells at the Seashore
> The Shells She Sells are Surely Seashells.

> Betty Botter had some Butter
> "But," she said, "this Butter's Bitter.

> Peter Piper Picked a Peck of Pickled Peppers
> A Peck of Pickled Peppers Peter Piper Picked.

> How much Wood Would a Wood Chuck Chuck
> if a Wood Chuck Could Chuck Wood?

MALAPROPISMS.   Malapropisms are words that are similar in sound but not in meaning. Intended words are replaced by those with similar sounds causing verbal blunders that have a comic effect.

> The imminent president (should be eminent meaning distinguished; not imminent meaning something is about to happen)
> He has no conscious (should be conscience meaning an inner ethical sense; not conscious meaning alive and in a state of awareness)
> The states are contagious (should be contiguous meaning next to one another; not contagious meaning infectious)

Sometimes malapropisms are found in knock-knock jokes.

> Knock knock
> Who's there?
> Dwayne
> Dwayne who?
> Dwayne the tub I'm drowning

Other examples occur in everyday experience. Just ask students to recite the pledge of allegiance (I pledge *the legions/allegiance* to the flag) or sing the national anthem (By the dawn's early *night/light*) and see for yourself.

PUNS.   Puns are whimsical plays on words that add color to stories, poetry, and even nonfiction. They make us laugh because of the incongruity of meanings. Two totally un-related ideas are brought together in a single word to produce a witty statement. Puns in newspaper headlines and TV commercials show that writers are exceptionally clever at skewing language to make a point.

> A legend is Bjorn (born) (headline following Bjorn's fifth Wimbledon victory)
> Too much whine (wine) with dinner? Leave the whine behind. (part of a TV commercial about children wanting their favorite macaroni instead of a meal prepared for them)

Children enjoy playing with puns that involve double meanings made from homonyms *(might/mite)* or syllable parts *(lettuce/let us)*.

> Read between the li-ons (lines)
> Take the Monet (money) and run

SPOONERISMS.   Spoonerisms are linguistic flip-flops in which writers transpose initial sounds, syllables, or letters in words to make readers laugh.

A well-<u>o</u>iled <u>b</u>icycle	A well-<u>b</u>oiled <u>i</u>cicle
<u>Sn</u>ow and <u>sl</u>eet	<u>Sl</u>ow and <u>sn</u>eet

These kinds of words gain our attention as "bloopers" on TV or speech boners in conversations. Although these transpositions usually happen accidentally, children can purposely switch letters in words to add wit or a sense of the ridiculous.

Playing With Word Formation and the Structure of Words (Morphology)

Morphology is concerned with the structure of words and is essential to the word for-mation process. Poets blend words from two existing forms (portmanteau words), clip words to shorten ones that already exist (*fan* for *fanatic* or *fax* for *facsimile*), or compound words by combining two known terms (fire + fighter). Let's consider a few.

PORTMANTEAU.   These words combine two or more elements to make new forms.

Chuckle and snort	Chortel
Clack and crash	Clash
Motor and hotel	Motel
Smoke and fog	Smog

Lewis Carroll, the author of *Alice in Wonderland* (1865) and *Through the Looking Glass* (1872) first coined this term to explain many of the unusual words in his stories and po-ems. Blending known words into nonsense also brings humor to children's poetry.

WORD PARTS.   Writers often manipulate elements of word structure and word bound-aries to produce humor. Tampered typography and word parts are commonly found in greeting cards. For instance, a picture of a cow is accompanied with the split meaning and words: MOOv over. Or words are divided in unusual ways to make silly names such as Dan D. Lion (dandelion).

Playing With the Structure of Phrases, Clauses, and Sentences (Syntax)

Syntax describes the grammatical aspects of language, oftentimes cast as parts of speech. Writers play with syntax by violating constraints ("The moose whacked the rose." when "whacked" requires human action), or toying with word order or usage rules ("The car got hit by the boy"). Parts of speech and order are exploited to achieve the poet's intent.

DANGLING AND MISPLACED MODIFIERS.   Dangling and misplaced modifiers are in-correct in standard English but can have a humorous effect on sentences or aspects of

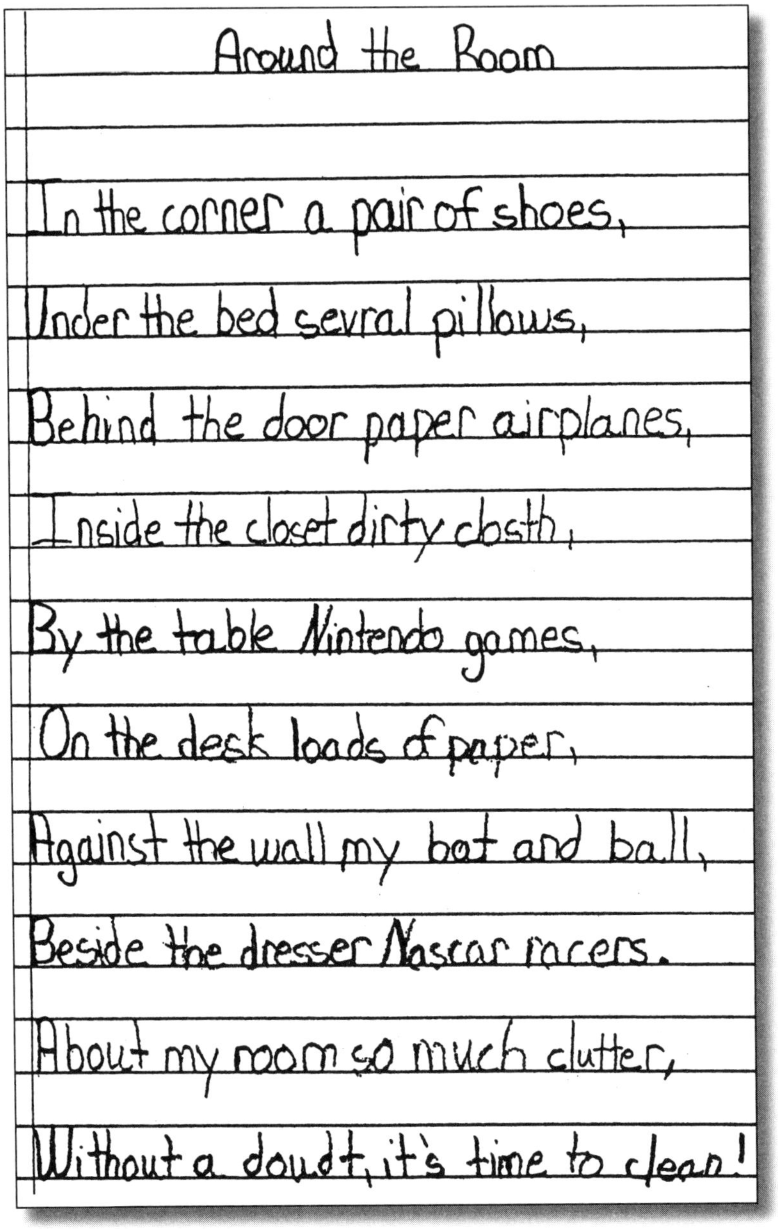

FIGURE 5-10
Preposition Poem,
"Around the Room,"
Final Draft (Third
Grader, Guided
Writing)

> ## Around the Room
>
> In the corner a pair of shoes,
> Under the bed sevral pillows,
> Behind the door paper airplanes,
> Inside the closet dirty closth,
> By the table Nintendo games,
> On the desk loads of paper,
> Against the wall my bat and ball,
> Beside the dresser Nascar racers.
> About my room so much clutter,
> Without a doudt, it's time to clean!

jokes. A dangling or misplaced modifier is a phrase that is unattached to the word or phrase that it modifies. Often the words are in the wrong order in the sentence or require additional words to make sense.

We're having your mother-in-law for dinner tonight.	I'd rather have chicken.
While reading a book, the birds on the railing caught my eye.	What book were the birds reading?

PREPOSITION POEMS.   These poems begin every line with a preposition. With so many prepositions to choose from (e.g., *around, of, by, next to, with, in, for*), children can easily get started with a list of 10 to 12 words. The example in Figure 5–10, written by a third grader and titled "Around the Room," shows a poem that is stuffed with prepositions.

Lining up prepositional phrases in this way scaffolds the writing through repetitive rhythms and draws attention to the grammatical construction. If teachers want to underscore the poem's meaning and integrity, rather than structure, they may need to accept variant openings to the sentences.

TOM SWIFTIES.   These puns got their name from the Tom Swift books popular with children in the 1940s. Humor is created by matching meanings in a sentence with a tag—a word, phrase, or clause attached to a sentence to form a question or add emphasis. The swifties are usually adverbs and adjectives, sometimes written in the sentence and other times in the tag line.

Adverbial Swifties	Adjectival Swifties
"Wouldn't you prefer a poodle?" asked her father, *doggedly*.	"I am totally *disinterested*," said the bank manager.

Children take a list of adjectives and change them into adverbs with *-ly*; then they write the statement or question following the models. Adjective swifties are constructed from nouns and adjectives that play off one another.

Playing With the Meanings of Words, Phrases, and Sentences (Semantics)

Semantics explores the relationship between the form of language and its function. Poets select words with more than one meaning or those with similar or near meanings to amuse their audiences. Here are a few categories of words and phrases that seem to accomplish this.

IDIOMS.   Idioms are complex expressions whose meanings cannot be derived from the definitions of individual words. **Figurative expressions** are used all of the time in speech, but in poetry, these short snappy statements attract a reader's interest and produce an air of familiarity.

A frog in her throat
Apple of my eye
It rained cats and dogs
Hit the nail on the head

Children can collect idiomatic expressions and illustrate them. For example, *a frog in one's throat* figuratively means that the individual's voice is hoarse. Literally it means you have a little green amphibian in your mouth. This visual picture is what causes the humor: the juxtaposing of the literal or exact meaning with the figurative one.

FRACTURED PROVERBS.   A proverb is a wise saying that embodies habits of thought, customs, and values: *Look before you leap* or *the early bird catches the worm*. This folk wisdom allows poets to poke fun and make mischief. A fractured proverb breaks the expected literal translation often with a clever twist or transformation. The writer starts with a predictable proverb and crafts an unexpected ending. For example, instead of *Don't put all your eggs in one basket*, a fractured proverb might say: *Don't put all your eggs in the microwave*.

HOMOPHONES OR HOMONYMS.   Homophones or homonyms include words that are pronounced the same but have different meanings and spellings:

Bear/bare
Blew/blue
Doe/dough
Sent/cent
Tale/tail
Vane/vein/vain

Homonyms or homophones are often used in children's riddles and jokes:

Question: What's a measuring stick for a monarch?
Answer: A ruler for a ruler. (Gwynne, 1970)
Question: Why do you take rabbits to the barber shop?
Answer: Because they need a hare cut.

Words that resemble one another in sound cause the reader to pause and process the puzzle or punch line.

HOMOGRAPHS (DOUBLE AND MULTIPLE MEANINGS).   Multiple meanings of words, when illustrated or used in a surprising or unintended way, can make poems funny. One category of words that do this is homographs, words that are spelled alike but differ in meaning or in pronunciation *(read, dove)*. Take the word *run* for instance and the variety of interpretations it has:

Run an automobile
Run for office
Tears run down a cheek
A run on free Popsicles
Hit a home run
Run a race
Run in a stocking

Older children can work with a partner to list words with double meanings *(dust, bank, fish, scale, show, loaf)*, drawing pictures to illustrate. They can locate homographs in classified ads (*The Cutting Edge Lawn Care Service*) or comic strips ("Did you see that sign? [Fine for Parking] "Yes Officer, and I heartily agree with it"). Collections can be placed in a book.

Young children will enjoy double meanings in the Amelia Bedelia stories by Peggy Parish. For instance, in response to the boss's request to "stamp the envelopes" in *Good Work, Amelia Bedelia* (1976), the author shows Amelia Bedelia in an office jumping up and down on white letter envelopes, leaving her footprints all over them. Students can dramatize double meanings through charades, a nonverbal game in which one person acts out or draws a word and others try to guess it.

Play With Short Forms or Terse Verse (Discourse)

Riddles and jokes are short forms of discourse, products in their own right that combine many of the language features already mentioned.

RIDDLES.   Riddles are verbal guessing games with question-and-answer structures. The idea is to ask a deliberately ambiguous question and come back with a clever answer.

What is the smartest kind of bee?	A spelling bee
What is black and white and red all over?	A newspaper
What is in the middle of Texas?	An *X*
What kind of rock can be shot in the air?	A rocket

To answer the first riddle, you identify the double meaning of the word *bee* and make associations. In the second riddle, you understand *red* as *read* and *all over* as *everywhere*. The riddle about Texas purposely omits information to throw you off. It leads you to think about *middle* as a geographic location rather than a letter. Finally, to solve the rocket riddle, you recognize the play with syllables in a word.

Children can copy favorite riddles from humorous greeting cards and books. After reading a variety of materials and choosing subjects to write about, they borrow some of the typical questions that begin a riddle:

What do you call a _____?
Why is _____ like ____?
What is the difference between _____ and ____?

They will especially enjoy rhyming riddles, called hink pinks, in which words that answer the riddle have rhymes of one syllable *(hink, pink)*, two syllables *(hinky, pinky)* or three syllables *(hinkity, pinkity)* (Geller, 1985). Here is a hinky pinky.

What do you call a lame turkey?   A hobbler gobbler

A flip book is a handy way to present a riddle. Children write the question on the top of a folded piece of paper and lift the flap to find the answer. Collecting riddles in books by subject categories, such as animals or objects, is a great addition to the classroom library.

JOKES.   Jokes are short one-liners or sentences that present a clash in expectations or frames of reference. Jokes engage the audience and can bring groans or laughter. As early as first grade, children tell jokes to their friends, especially those that use malapropisms or silly "sound alike" words. Fashioned after Moffett and Wagner's (1992) activity card idea, jokes and other wordplay tasks are written on 5×7-inch note cards and placed in a recipe box. Printed on the card is the task, step-by-step directions, the number of participants involved, and examples of the end product. Students performing these tasks are often led to books, Web sites, or other literacy activities. Figures 5–11 and 5–12 show both sides of the "Write a Joke" card that involves sound alike and look alike words and word

FIGURE 5-11 Joke Activity Card, Side 1

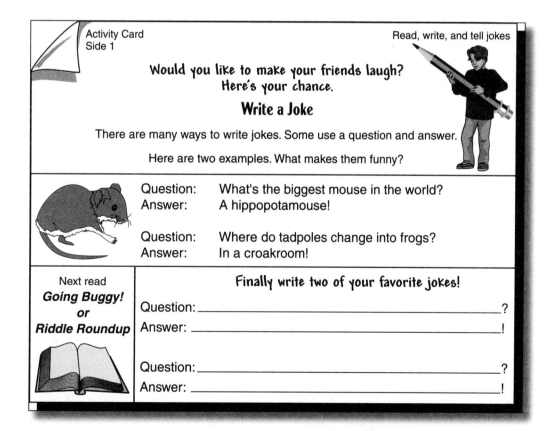

FIGURE 5-12   Joke Activity Card, Side 2

Activity Card
Side 2

Read, write, and tell jokes

Read the joke below:

Question: What's a wolf's favorite holiday?

Answer: HOWLoween!

Here are some "sound alike" and "look alike" words that you may want to use in your joke.

hiss/history purr/purple bus/buzz nap/gnat moo-er/mower sneaker/squeaker wars/arts

flies/fries chip/chimp croak/cloak litters/letters chick/check herring (a fish)/hearing

Remember to start your joke with a question. A question begins with one of these words:
Who   What   When   Where   Why   How
It ends with a question mark like this: (?)
At the end of your answer, you can use a period (.) or an exclamation mark (!).

Now write your own joke. Draw a silly picture to go with it.

Question: _____ ?
Answer: _____ !

Try out your joke on a friend.
Collect jokes from friends and family.
Make your own joke book.
Perform your jokes.

FIGURE 5-13   Nicky's Joke, "Crackers/Quackers," First Draft (First Grader, Independent Writing)

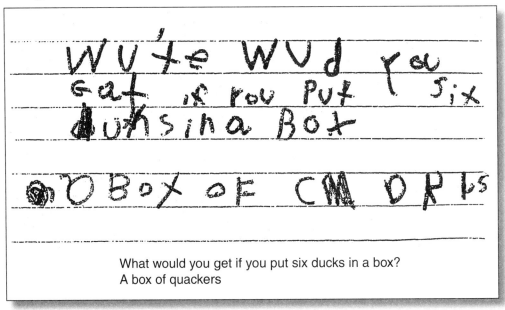

What would you get if you put six ducks in a box?
A box of quackers

parts. Nicky, a first grader, takes advantage of the similarity in word pronunciations and constructs the joke seen in Figure 5–13 using invented spelling:

Question: What do you get if you put six ducks in a box?
Answer: A box of quackers.

FIGURE 5-14   Lindsey's Jokes, "Shellfish; Kindergarten," First Draft (First Grader),
Independent Writing)

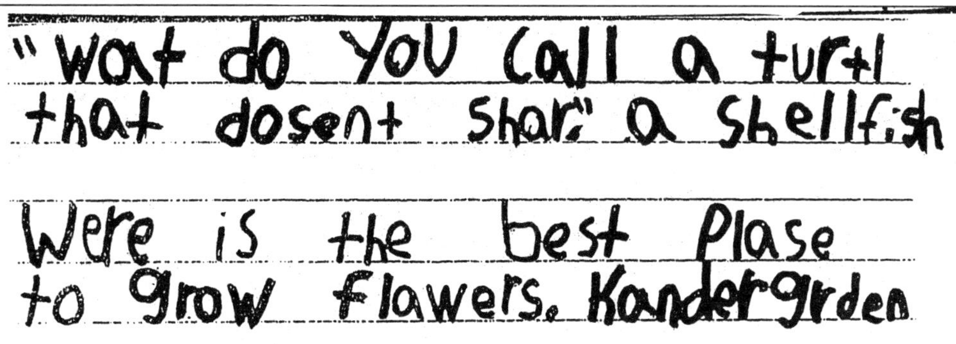

> " wat do you call a turtl
> that dosent shar" a shellfish
>
> Were is the best Plase
> to grow Flawers. Kandergrden

What do you call a turtle that doesn't share?
A shellfish

Where is the best place to grow flowers?
Kindergarten

Nicky laughs at his joke and explains why it is funny: "See crackers and quackers,
it's almost the same word." Lindsey, who is inspired by Nicky's joke, writes two of her
own. They are provided in Figure 5–14.

Question: What do you call a turtle that doesn't share?
Answer: A shellfish. (selfish)
Question: Where is the best place to grow flowers?
Answer: Kindergarten.

Jokes, riddles, and puns, which build on wordplay, are a chance to use language for
its own sake, construct meaning, and make friends laugh. Many books are available on
verbal play and can be added to the classroom library (see Table 5–4).

Reading

As teachers, we want children to fall in love with poetry, to experience its magic,
beauty, and honesty. When poetry is a welcome part of the daily routine, learners imitate favorite authors or write poems of their own. They read a broad range of contemporary and traditional poems, the best of which are told from a child's perspective, and
gain a tacit understanding of a poem's construction and technique. In the reading sections, we consider poems that inspire writers and serve as models and resources.

The Writer's Inspiration

Saucy and witty, gripping and dark, poems capture the common and insignificant (a pair
of shoelaces) or the grand and unusual (UFOs). Because class preferences may be wide and
eclectic, a variety of poetry selections should be read. For instance, young writers take special pleasure in the rollicking verse of Jack Prelutsky and Shel Silverstein, but are equally
captivated by serious and reflective poems such as "The Road Not Taken" (Frost, 1959).
Feeling a poem's amusement or melancholy, may remind students of ordinary events or
objects. They learn to mine daily experiences and make connections to their own lives.

Poems show how to look for surprises and notice unexpected relationships. As keen
observers, poets know how to sort through experience to collect an abundance of details

TABLE 5-4   Books of Verbal Play

Homonyms
Eight Ate: A Feast of Homonym Riddles (Terban, 1982)
The King Who Rained (Gwynne, 1970)
The Sixteen Hand Horse (Gwynne, 1980)

Idioms
In a Pickle and Other Funny Idioms (Terban, 1983)
It's Raining Cats and Dogs—And Other Beastly Expressions (Ammer, 1989)
Punching the Clock: Funny Action Idioms (Terban, 1990)

Prepositions
Behind the Mask: A Book About Prepositions (Heller, 1995)
Elephants Aloft (Appelt, 1993)

Riddles
Count Draculations!: Monster Riddles (Keller, 1986)
Ribbit Riddles (Hall & Eisenberg, 2001)
Super Silly Riddles (Keller, 2001)
The Little Giant Book of Riddles (Rosenbloom, 1996)
What's a Frank Frank? Tasty Homograph Riddles (Maestro, 1984)

Tongue Twisters
Busy Buzzing Bumblebees and Other Tongue Twisters (Schwarz, Miesel, & Schett, 1982)
Oh Say Can You Say? (Seuss, 1979)
Six Sick Sheep: 101 Tongue Twisters (Cole, Calmenson, & Tiegreen, 1993)

that will make a subject rich and lively. An author takes something that may seem to have little value (a paper clip or a toaster), turns it upside down, or makes it extraordinary. Just by switching point of view a poet can illuminate the same subject matter in many fascinating ways. Thematic collections such as Hopkins's (1989) *Still as a Star: A Book of Nighttime Poems* and Livingston's (1987) *Cat Poems* are good examples.

Readers of poetry can observe how traditional poems, such as nursery rhymes, are given a new lift. Since children prefer contemporary to traditional poetry (Fisher & Natarella, 1982; Terry, 1974), modern day versions of favorite nursery rhymes, with their unquestionable charm, can be rewritten to renew the genre's popularity. For example, *And the Dish Ran Away With the Spoon* (Stevens, 2001) tells the story of Dish and Spoon who run away and cause their rhyme friends to rescue them in time for the next evening's reading of their evocative tale. *Some From the Moon, Some From the Sun: Poems and Songs for Everyone* (Zemach, 2001) includes traditional poems and songs that can be reworked using trendy language or newfangled illustrations.

Children who are receptive to a poem will experience the author's appeal to the five senses. Through language, they might feel the sting of a rubber band, hear the buzz of a bee, or smell the smoke of a bonfire. They might envision clouds chasing each other across the sky or taste the sweetness of a ripe red tomato.

Although poetry is read during the language arts block, it lives not only in children's literature, but also in science and social studies. In science are poems about raindrops and tree frogs, the dew on the morning grass, or the snow in the forests. Social studies poems are about famous events (the Fourth of July), people in history (Martin Luther King, Jr.), or patriotic symbols (Statue of Liberty). Through a factual poem, children learn the subject matter but also capture the dramatic mood or attitude of an event. Pursuing curricular studies from the perspective of a poem establishes its place outside the language arts class and reinforces learning.

Children enjoy reading and hearing professional works, but they also like poems written by peers their own age such as *Kids' Poems: Teaching Children to Love Poetry* (Routman, 2000), *Wishes, Lies, and Dreams* (Koch, 1970), and *Ten-Second Rainshower Poems by Young People* (Lyne, 1996). With the introduction of the World Wide Web, students can select poems from around the world or contribute their own to Internet sites. Knowing that their peers are authors makes them want to become poets too. By reading poems on any and every topic, writers explore subjects they may not have considered before.

But poetry is more than content. It is also a valuable print model and resource for writing and rewriting. Let's consider this particular purpose in more detail.

Poetry Models

With frequent poetry reading comes an increasing awareness of the anatomy of a poem. When children find poems that suit their fancy, they read them silently or aloud and reread them more than once. Doing so helps them internalize text conventions, formulas, or stereotypical structures and meters that carry the author's meaning. If teachers read poems, it is best to recite them in their entirety without stopping to comment or explain. This preserves the mood of the poem, and, with repeated readings, children peel away the layers of meaning and uncover the poet's strategies. With time, avid readers of poetry will feel a connection with other poets' ideas and become influenced by them.

Reading poems aloud focuses children's attention on the sounds and pictures words make, the patterns they form, the stories they tell, and the meanings they express (Nodelman, 1992). Indeed, poetry can serve as a literary model for writing if students' attention is directed to linguistic features like those portrayed in special collections (see Tables 5–2, 5–3, and 5–4).

Although a tacit knowledge of poetry is valuable, the writing teacher should not be afraid to offer explicit information about the structures and strategies inherent in poems. In learning to write, it is valuable to have specific tools for writing and samples that illustrate form and technique.

Borrowing or imitating poems gives students a structure to follow while they grow in confidence as poets. For example, the refrains or repetitive patterns in *The Important Book* (Brown, 1949, 1977), involve the author starting and ending a verse with the words "The important thing about (snow, grass, apple, wind, sky) is. . . ." Children finish the sentence with something they believe is noteworthy to extend or mimic the pattern.

As valuable as inventing poems are, copying favorite ones in a journal gives practice writing words and sentences that are embedded in rhythmic phrasing and stanzas. It impresses on writers the shape of a poem, its punctuation, its length, and its format. Even improved handwriting and spelling are positive consequences.

Poems are often a response to something else and may be the structure of choice for communicating content knowledge. While studying the Civil War, for instance, a fifth-grade girl composes a five senses poem titled "Violet."

> Purple hearts seem violet
> Like the honor of a soldier.
> I *see* guns firing,
> I *hear* screaming from pain,
> I *smell* blood,
> I *touch* the wound of my friend,
> I *taste* the loss.

Her poem captures the ravages of war and the bravery and honor of a soldier decorated with the purple heart. Through poetry she breathes life into what otherwise might be difficult concepts to understand or accept.

Sifting through student likes and dislikes about the poems they are reading calls attention to the criteria and metalanguage they will encounter in their own poems. What makes poetry enjoyable to them: Is it the rhyme? The topic? The language choices? The arrangement? These questions and the ensuing discussions reflect what children are learning from the master poets and enable them to hold minilessons with peers about how they write their poems. Short minilessons in which children select books of poetry and collect rhyming words, metaphors, similes, alliteration, or other stylistic devices provide multiple examples for children to write or copy in their journals. Children can refer to these for ideas or samples when writing their own poems.

Composing

Prewriting

Children's ideas for poems come from everything about which they know and care (Heard, 1989). They live in feelings and experiences and spring naturally from interacting with others, observing the world, and asking questions. The teacher should make a special effort to show that topics are about the everyday world of people and play as well as ordinary things, such as bubble gum (Payne, 1983) or pizza (Prelutsky, 1996). Viewed through the lens of a vivid imagination, a simple happening can be transformed into an extraordinary one. Observing is a good starting point for writing poetry. Displaying a chart of "things to notice" can call attention to objects in the students' surroundings.

Notice

Sensory details	Seemingly unimportant details
What's in front of you, behind you, beside you	Striking features
Contrasts and similarities	Movements
First impressions	Colors, shapes, sizes, textures

Each day the teacher focuses on one of these items, and the children make a list of everything they noticed (e.g., seemingly unimportant details: a door knob, a scrap of paper, an empty jar, an untied shoe). When they talk together and fill the pages of their journals with impressions and fleeting images, common objects take on new possibilities.

Reading, of course, is the most obvious place to find poems, but inspiration can burst forth from many different literacy activities as shown in Figure 5–15. For instance, after studying a reprint of a famous abstract painting, small groups of children brainstorm ideas about what they see and how it makes them feel. They examine the mood of the painting by studying its color and lines (smooth, thick, thin, bold), or stretch the imagination for new ideas and vocabulary. Sometimes they make their own art and read the designs, pictures, rhythms, and patterns to start ideas flowing (following Olshansky, 1994).

Music also has the potential for stimulating ideas. Listening to music encourages free association and can serve to suggest memories of special events, places, people, and times in our lives. Children can jot down words or draw pictures that come to mind when they hear a particular song. They examine these free associations to look for something that suggests a theme or the start of a poem.

Notwithstanding poetry's musical effects (rhythm and action, repetition and line breaks, and literary beats and sounds), children benefit from engaging in movement and dance to rehearse and gather ideas through spatial channels of communication. With some easy-to-follow movement prompts, children can create and interpret thoughts.

- Create a movement (What does it look like?)
- Change it (What does the movement become?)
- Associate it (What connections between a movement and something else come to mind?)
- Combine it (What parts of two movements can be blended together? What transitional movements might connect two movements?)

Poetic collections such as *Dance With Me* (Esbensen, 1995) offer a rich array of choices for interpreting poems as well as enhancing children's sensibilities and awareness of language rhythms and movement. Whether actions and gestures influence written description (with words such as *leap, roll, flutter*) or guide displays of print on the page (as

FIGURE 5-15   Prewriting Activities for Poetry Writing

Creating artwork
   Abstracts
   Landscapes
   Portraits
Reading children's literature
   Nursery rhymes
   Poetry collections
Collecting items
   Artistic objects
   Favorite things
   Sensory words
Making creative visualizations (guided imagery)
Listening to everyday sounds
   Footsteps
   Barking dog
   Doorbell
Writing in journals
Miming
Moving about
Playing Music
   Critical listening
   Rhythm activities
Observing
Creating pictures
   Greeting cards
   Magazine prints
   Photographs
   Wordless picture books
Observing with the five senses (see, hear, taste, touch, smell)
Singing
Using wordplay
   Hink pinks
   Homonyms

in concrete poems), the aesthetic elements offer a valuable strategy for suspending poems in time and space (Piazza, 1999).

Drafting

Collaborating on group poems prior to writing individual ones is a positive initial experience for children and provides teachers with an opportunity to model strategies and structures. The group identifies a topic and decides whether it will rhyme or not. Each participant contributes a single line, helping one another with word choice and spelling, and pulling the lines together at the end to form several verses. Sometimes a poem is held together by word arrangement, the pattern of sounds and repetition, or a certain number of syllables and lines. As the instructor records the poem, she demonstrates unique ways of seeing and thinking beyond words to that of shapes, lines, rhythms, and movement.

- Could you read a line of the poem you think is particularly appealing? Why do you like this line?
- How many words should I place on this line? Where should the thought break? Why?
- Let's clap our hands to the rhythm of this poem.

- How might this poem look (sound) if I wrote it in a column? In one long sentence? In short ones?

Independent student work follows, with the teacher stepping in only to guide and facilitate. Children dabble with a word or phrase, select a line to repeat elsewhere in the poem, or return to poetry books and examine how authors construct their poems.

Several types of structures seem to emerge during drafting. Rhyme patterns, for instance, offer order and suggest a certain number of syllables and words to complete a phrasal thought. Repetitive arrangements are another. A favorite line or verse is repeated to add to the poem's rhythm and coherence. Of course, shape poems have their own unique configurations, as do many formula poems with word and syllable counts. Narrative poems embed an abbreviated story plot (initiating event, roadblocks, and climax) for structure. Writers will learn that sometimes the shape of a poem is discovered, while at other times it is purposely designed as part of a formulaic task.

Invented poems are a case in point. They are easy to draft because they provide a scaffold, yet encourage freedom of expression (see examples in Figure 5–16). These kinds of poems are readily accessible and can serve as warmups for other types of verse.

Revising

The overhead transparency is a beneficial tool for whole-class revision of poetry. Projecting a poem for all to see, the teacher calls for a precise word, sensory detail, or punctuation mark. Even minor revisions can dramatically improve the poem. For example, in one case, a student creates a whole new meaning for her poem simply by changing the white paper on which it is written. She places her butterfly shape poem on a background of pastel-colored flowers and, with this decision, invites the viewer to speculate on a solitary butterfly in an open field of flowers. A first grader writes three sentences about an apple in black ink and adds a dash of red on the last word, *Yummy*, to draw attention to it. Manipulating font styles, letter size, backgrounds, or formats are acceptable forms of revision when they accentuate meanings or alter interpretations. Some other possibilities include the following:

- Writing the same poem in another language (see *If I Had a Paka: Poems in Eleven Languages* by Pomerantz, 1982) or substituting English words with those from another language. A good example is the poem "My Mami Takes Me to the Bakery" (Pomerantz, 1980, p. 21). Here is a stanza from that poem.

> Inside the panadería,
> There's the hot sweet smell of pan
> Good day, says the plump panadero
> (The baker's a very nice man.)

- Adding color, clip art, or drawings.
- Using decorative backgrounds or borders.
- Changing font styles or line quality (continuous or broken).
- Experimenting with size and shape.
- Selecting different paper textures.

In the third-grade classroom, many of these options are posted on a chart called "Things I can do to make my poems *really cool*."

Beyond surface changes, children rethink the subject matter by writing a poem that is a response to another one, writing two different poems on the same topic, two poems in the same style, or two poems each in a different style. They explore a possible title for a poem—a question to entice the reader or a double meaning based on words already embedded in the poem. During revision, children make additions, substitutions, or changes to ideas, words, sounds, and rhythm.

FIGURE 5-16 Invented Poems

Source: By William Carlos Williams, from *Collected Poems: 1909–1939,* Volume 1, copyright © 1938 by New Directions Publishing Corp. Reprinted by permission of New Directions Publishing Corp.

1. **Alphabet Poems**: Use sequential parts of the alphabet to make a list, phrase, sentence, or verse

   Animals   Come
   Bear   Do
   Cat   Enter
   Dog

   Amy asked an aardvark to appear
      to an awkward adolescent.
   Bonnie blew bubbles to the bear
      who blew them back.
   An **m** for mum
      It seems to hum
   A **p** for pop
      Why does it flop?

2. **Chants**: Repeat the same fixed phraseology

   Yes I am
   Yes I know
   Yes I will
   Yes I can
   Yes I am
   Yes I know
   Yes I will
   Yes I can

3. **Color Poems**: Describe by focusing on a color

   Red is anger
   Red makes me happy
   It's the color of apples
   And the color of royalty
   Red

4. **Comparison Poems**: Relate two things on the basis of their similarities

   Hiccups are like speed bumps. You can't talk very fast when you've got periods after every word.
   Speed bumps are like hiccups. They have their own tempo whether you like it or not.

5. **Five Senses Poems**: Build on sight, sound, taste, smell, and touch

Sight/color:	The bird was yellow
Sound:	It sang so clearly
Taste:	The air was sweet
Smell:	It smelled like rain
Feeling/action:	The bird landed on a branch

6. **Imitation Poems**: Take well-known poems by a professional poet and use them as models for writing

* This is just to say	This is just to say
I have eaten the plums	I have fed the cat
That were in	That was sitting
The icebox	on the porch
And which	And which
You were probably	I know we can't keep
Saving for breakfast*	

(continued)

Figure 5-16   (continued)

---

7. **List Poems**: Include one word or phrase per line, written vertically and based on a theme; place a collection of words or a sentence placed in a column; create a numbered list

I	Fall
collect	leaves
and	scarlet
trade	gold
Pokemon	play
cards	rake

Five Things That Can't Happen

Dogs flying
A soda talking to the drinker
A bird doing the laundry
Cats rock 'n' rollin'
Grass growing to the sky

8. **Phone Number Poems**: Develop each line of the poem with words containing syllables that match a real or imaginary phone number (224-6632)

2   My mom
2   Likes dogs
4   She plays soccer
6   Over at the ball park
6   The dog follows her there
3   No Rover
2   Stay home!

9. **Dialogue Poems**: Show conversation or talk directed to animals, people, or inanimate objects

Oh tiger, Oh tiger	Dear pizza box
Why are you stripped?	You carry such
Do you enjoy going	Wonderful smells
After the zebra?	And yummy hot
Why do you bite?	Slices of pizza

10. **Synonym Poems**: Use two lines that rhyme; the first line is made up of synonyms and the second describes the subject or tells how one feels about the subject

Blab, gossip, chatter, talk
Chit-chat is better than taking a walk.

Dip, plunge, douse, dunk
All day in the pool, my skin has shrunk.

Ideas

Making a mediocre poem sparkle may involve rethinking the ideas in the poem. Students may want to talk to others about their views of the subject or engage in more observation or reading. During revision, children check their poems for the following:

- A metaphor or simile
- An original or unusual idea
- A new perspective on an old idea
- An ordinary idea cast in a fresh way
- A title that piques the interest of the reader

Words

The poem uses special types of words for effect—aesthetically pleasing words or strong, vigorous ones, for example. Students can categorize the types of words found in their poems based on their own interpretations and descriptive categories. While specific concrete nouns and verbs add force to the poem, adjectives and adverbs *(nice, excitedly)* can weaken it. Students can check their poems for the following:

- Sensory words
- Precise words
- Concrete words rather than abstract
- Condensation of words (removing unnecessary clutter or surplus words)

Sounds

As already mentioned, poets often choose words based on how they are formed in the mouth or reverberate in the vocal cords. For instance, pleasant sounds include fricatives *(f, v, th)*, sibilants *(s, z, sh)*, liquids *(l, r)*, and nasals *(m, n)*; harsh sounds include plosives *(p, b, tk, j)* or affricates *(ch, j)*. Children can develop auditory perception by listening to how consonants *(b, t)* and consonant clusters *(ch, bl)* feel when they produce them. Have children review their poem for the following:

- Recurring sounds
- Beginning, middle, and ending sounds
- Patterns at the ends of words *(ack, ite)* for rhyme
- Blending sounds

Rhythm

If a poem begs to be read aloud, it is often because of its sound and rhythm. Have children read to someone and listen for fluency, beat, or pace. Then have them review their poem for the following:

- Sentence length
- Words per line
- Syllables and stress
- Rhyme
- Repetition of words or phrases

Again, these are only a few points to consider. Referring to assessment checklists and rubrics for poetry can guide the revision process. Of course, returning to prewriting and drafting is always a good idea.

Editing

Because the poet often flouts conventional editing rules to achieve visual and aural effects, you may want to provide the same literary license to children. In exchange, you can explore students' reasons for breaking rules and determine whether they are accidental or purposeful. A few unusual but purposeful conventions already discussed include the following:

- Mixing upper- and lowercase letters
- Using capital letters for emphasis
- Placing periods after each word
- Writing words upside down
- Using unusual directionality

Reading widely provides even more examples.

Another possibility is to build on the prototypical features of poetry to teach conventions. Spelling is perfect for this. Poets love the word's aesthetic features, visual configurations, and sound patterns. Children can imprint visual images of words by drawing a box around the letters of a word, highlighting its graphic characteristics. English words have distinct shapes based on length, width, and form. Ascenders such as *h*, *l*, and *t* or descenders such as *g* and *p* are examples.

Letter names are examined and used in language play (E-Z Floor Care), and assonance and onomatopoeia are learned by sorting words and placing them on the word wall (see Chapter 2). Because rhyme is one of the poet's tools, the teacher explains how to produce rhyming words from patterns, drawing attention to spelling by segmenting a word into onsets and rimes. The **onset** is the part of the syllable before the vowel, and the **rime** is the rest of the unit. In the word *stand*, "*st*" is the onset; "*and*" is the rime (36 rimes are found in over 500 words). Children volunteer a list that rhymes with *sn -ake*.

awake	cake	Jake	rake
bake	drake	make	snake
blake	flake	quake	wake

When rhyming, children learn words that end in the same way. They get additional practice rhyming verse and playing with graphophonic cues and sound blending (*bl, dr, fl, sn*). Clever handheld devices are used for word building.

The baseball example in Figure 5–17A reveals a ball with a rime written on it and an open square (window). A strip of paper, much like a filmstrip, slips into the window and exposes a letter to complete a word. The children use the strips of tag board to move the letters up and down matching different onsets with the rime.

In constructing the flipbook (see Figure 5–17B), the teacher cuts out a rectangular piece of card stock approximately 4 inches long and 2 inches high. She writes a rime *(ake)* on the right side leaving room on the left for the onsets. Onsets are written on separate card stock rectangles that are about 1 inch long and 2 inches high. All the cards are lined

FIGURE 5-17A   Word Building Tools: Baseball

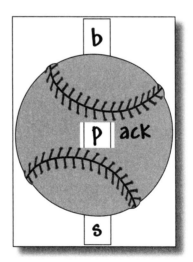

FIGURE 5-17B   Word Building Tools: Flipbook

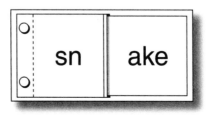

FIGURE 5-17C Word Building Tools: Wheels

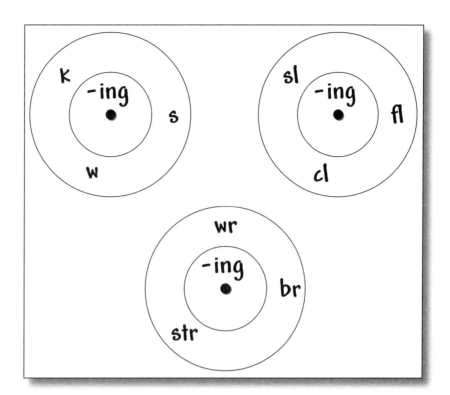

up, hole punched, and attached with a brad or yarn. Children flip the onsets in front of the rime and line them up to make new words.

Finally, the teacher can choose to make wheels from two concentric circles held together with a brad (see Figure 5–17C). A small center circle holds the rime and a larger, outer one holds the consonants or consonant clusters. With the brad placed in the center, the outer circle turns like a dial to form a variety of words.

In addition to manipulative tools, students build new words from known ones using analogy. For instance, if a child knows how to spell *play* and wants to write *slay*, she can guess at the correct spelling based on similarities. When children recognize the number of words they can create by using analogy, they gain a sense of control over their learning and develop another strategy for figuring out how to spell a word.

The study of words is also addressed in terms of grammatical parts of speech (nouns, pronouns, verbs, adjectives, adverbs, prepositions, conjunctions, and interjections). Ruth Heller, a children's author and illustrator, has an entertaining and informative book series on parts of speech. These include the following:

> *Up, Up and Away: A Book About Adverbs* (1991).
> *Behind the Mask: A Book About Prepositions* (1995).
> *A Cache of Jewels and Other Collective Nouns* (1998).
> *Fantastic! Wow! and Unreal! A Book About Interjections and Conjunctions* (1998).
> *Kites Sail High: A Book About Verbs* (1998).
> *Many Luscious Lollipops: A Book About Adjectives* (1998).
> *Mine, All Mine: A Book About Pronouns* (1999).

The parts of speech represented by Heller's series create an awareness of language forms and functions, rendering these books valuable reference tools. Students should know, for instance, that concrete nouns paint better poetic images than general or abstract ones (for instance, *yellow* instead of *color*, *Japanese Maple* instead of *tree*, or *Blue Jay* instead of *bird*).

Parts of speech can be practiced in **formula poems** that specify set rules and meta-language (for instance, the preposition poem shown in Figure 5–10 or the diamante or diamond-shaped poem presented here).

Lines 1 and 7 state subjects (nouns) that are opposites. Line 2 contains two adjectives describing the subject of line 1. Line 3 contains three action words (-*ing* words) specific to the subject of line 1. Line 4 contains four nouns, the first two related to the first subject and the second two related to the second subject in line 7. Line 5 contains three action words (-*ing* words) specific to the subject of line 7. Line 6 contains two adjectives describing the subject of line 7. Line 7 states the noun opposite the one in line 1. A completed diamante follows:

Cold

Chilly   Frosty

Skiing   Skating   Sledding

Winter   Snow   Blossoms   Summer

Swinging   Swimming   Sweating

Sticky   Humid

Hot

Learning parts of speech offers another way to share knowledge about the craft and discover a metalanguage to use as an analytic tool for examining sentences during editing (for example, recognizing a sentence from a fragment by the presence of a noun and a verb, or using Tom Swifties to identify adjectives and adverbs).

Finally, handwriting may be a requirement of the curriculum but except for legibility, it seems of little importance here because the poet may want to distort, exaggerate, or tinker with letters for poetic impact. Even so, experimentation with graphic effects can only heighten children's attention to letter formation, alignment, slant, proportion, and size.

Sharing

All things considered, conferences and writing circles are the best places to celebrate students' risk taking and their efforts at becoming poets. In writing circles, students wishing to get feedback or reactions to their work can frame the following questions:

Do you like my word choice?
What words appeal to you?
Should I use alliteration or onomatopoeia?
What rhythm does this remind you of?
Do you like the look of my poem?
How should I display this poem?
What images do you see as you read this poem?
Should I add a drawing?

Writers explain where help is needed and peers are prepared to give appropriate advice. During interactions, students demonstrate the types of responses introduced earlier, especially those associated with literary writing. They comment on the esthetic features of poetry, its imagery, sounds, or verbal play ("I like the words you use, for example, *pop* and *bam*"). Feelings evoked from the poem are expressed appreciatively ("Your poem was fun"). In addition to these responses, the teacher emphasizes creative response because originality and surprise are important features of the poetic form. The creative response is discussed further.

Creative Responses

A creative response is a vehicle for gradually molding a draft into an imaginative poem. It places demands on the writer's intuition and spurs the novice poet into considering unique ideas or descriptions. Peers ask writers to think about their words in terms of analogies or associations such as similes and metaphors ("What are hands like?"). They pose unusual or unexpected question prompts to foster original thinking ("Which is heavier a mountain or an ocean?") or "what if" questions to suggest scenarios the writer may not have entertained ("What if the wolf was shy instead of ferocious?").

The creative response is not an "anything goes" remark but follows conventions of **divergent thinking**. It is aimed at concocting something new ("What if you made the animals in your poem speak like people?"), inventing words for humor ("What would happen if you changed the word *pretty* to *razzle dazzle?*"), or inspiring memorable word-play ("Maybe you can use the letters *E* and *Z* as a substitute for the word *easy*"). Creative responses also emerge when students connect disparate ideas or think in word opposites called oxymorons *(bitter sweet; jumbo shrimp)*. Children who provide creative responses are flexible and speculative thinkers. Does a spoon always have to be used to eat? Can it be a musical instrument or a tool for prying open a window? Writers must be willing to challenge the mundane or common. For a while, teachers may need to model how to reframe actions and ideas so that new possibilities present themselves.

A creative response activates the drama or surprise in a poem. It unleashes writers' imaginations and encourages possibilities. Since children are always growing and changing, a creative response is always appropriate for eliciting thoughts and feelings about the happenings in their lives.

Presenting Poems

Poetry is meant to be read aloud. Only when children recite their poems can they fully appreciate the richness of their words and the rhythms of their sentences. If children want to present poems through choral reading, they can type and distribute them to all class members. When the poems are read in harmony, students pay attention to punctuation marks, white space, and graphics that signal meaning, emphasis, and fluency. Depending on the type of written poem, children might participate in musical rounds (two or more voices entering at different times), call-and-response (a question or request followed by a statement or answer), or echoic chorus (a line is read and then repeated by the audience). As children experience the many presentational arrangements, they discover new structures for use in future poems.

The poetry performance, in which a narrator reads the words and the children enact movements, can heighten the poem's meaning with new interpretations. Performing in unison, children can follow directive actions (swaying heads, clapping hands), facial expressions (smiles, frowns, or wrinkled nose), body language (arms folded, hands on hips, gestures), or movement (walking, galloping, skipping) in a choreographed presentation of the poem. Another recommended means for expressing the interpretation of ideas and feelings in poems is to explore mime, a kind of body speech with gestures rather than words.

The student's work typically finds its way into anthologies to be placed in the library or exhibited in local businesses around the community. Some writers choose to enter contests or submit their poems to magazines (see *The Young Writer's Guide to Getting Published* by Henderson, 2001), whereas others copy their poetry on greeting cards to give as gifts. Poems are framed like family photographs or dangle on mobiles hung from the ceiling. Shape and concrete poems are often displayed in art exhibits.

Just as students publicly share their work, so should teachers and other poets. Through the poet-in-the-schools program, for example, published authors can read their work or teach poetry either as visiting consultants or poets-in-residence. Teachers can contact their local arts council for further information about these programs.

Continuous Assessment

Ongoing assessment of writer, process, text, and context (see Chapter 1) occurs in mini-lessons, in conferences, in sharing, and in daily interactions. Like the other kinds of writing discussed thus far, poetry has its own unique lens with which to view the four assessment factors.

Writer, Process, Text, and Context Factors

With a checklist and clipboard in hand, teachers observe and write anecdotal reports about student attitudes, perceptions, and feelings about poetry. Children's attitude toward poetry can make the difference between a child who writes and the one who does not. Because poetry is to be shared and enjoyed, teachers will want to examine their own attitudes as well. Catching the poetry delight from teachers who love and savor language is a key ingredient to writer motivation.

To learn more about students' attitudes toward poetry, the teacher asks herself some of the following questions:

- How do students feel when asked to write poetry?
- Have their feelings changed from the beginning of the poetry unit to the end? Are they more confident?
- Do students initiate poetry writing and make a place for it in their lives?
- What do they already know about poetry?
- What do writers believe they do well in poetry?
- What is their favorite (least favorite) poem?

A few of these questions are designed to tap into children's personal dispositions toward poetry. Are students curious? A curiosity will drive the need to investigate "why" questions and challenge the common or familiar. Are they intuitive? Intuition nurtures the spirit within and develops trust in one's ideas. Are they playful? A playful attitude will inject the work with experimentation, variety, and laughter.

To determine if students exhibit some of these qualities teachers may want to observe preferred learning styles. A poet, with a gift for music, might enjoy choosing sound words or creating rhythmic patterns whereas the introspective poet might use her intrapersonal strengths to tap into deep feelings about a subject. Certainly, linguistic aptitude will be demonstrated in a poet's use of wordplay or highly descriptive language. It's worth examining the multiple intelligences as they relate to the children's strategic propensities toward poetry.

Any checklist that addresses process strategies should direct attention to behaviors that are specific to poetry, such as making associations, engaging in relational thinking, or viewing situations in a different light. Perhaps the writer compares and contrasts two seemingly unrelated ideas or rearranges words to make a new statement. Four particularly creative behaviors, associated with early work done by Torrance (1963), and especially suited to poetry writing should be noted.

- Fluency – Can children generate a large number of ideas?
- Flexibility – Can children create ideas in different categories and explore them in versatile ways? Can they think "out of the box"?
- Originality – Do children generate unique or unusual ideas?
- Elaboration – Are children able to extend an idea or expand on its details?

These four elements challenge students and fuel creative input. Teachers can add these elements to the typical process questions they might ask:

- How do they prepare for writing?
- Are they willing to share their poetry aloud?
- Do they draw pictures to go with their poems?
- What strategies do they use to figure out words?
- Is there an "aha" moment when children discover or arrive at a new idea?
- Does the poem have an unusual layout?

In regard to the text, although the six traits (see Figure 5–18) seem more attuned to prose than poetry, they are just as relevant.

FIGURE 5-18 Six Trait Descriptions for Poetry Writing

Ideas
➢ Includes original and fresh ideas that evoke feelings, moods, or emotions in the reader or listener
➢ Catches reader's attention

Organization
➢ Expresses visual shape, repetition, syllable or word counts, or other rhythmic patterns or rhyme schemes
➢ Displays a title that augments the poem
➢ Presents a natural flow

Voice
➢ Invites listener appeal (may include sound, movement, or rhythm)
➢ Suggests that words be read aloud

Sentence Fluency
➢ Provides line breaks, stanza groupings, or compressed length for meaning and flow
➢ Uses fragments to add style and flair

Word Choice
➢ Eliminates excess words
➢ Emphasizes precise words
➢ Produces word pictures, visual images, colorful expressions
➢ Includes words that appeal to the ear (onomatopoeia, assonance, rhyme, consonance)
➢ Creates wordplay and action (synonyms, homonyms)

Conventions
➢ Uses conventions purposely for desired effects (mixing upper- and lowercase letters in same word, using repetitive exclamation marks, placing periods after every word, capitalizing for emphasis)
➢ Follows the required format

All of the descriptors can be accounted for through interviews, self-reports, observation checklists, rubrics, or combinations thereof. Teachers can add to, remove, or re-word them to suit particular circumstances.

When teachers are examining the context in which poetry is being studied and written, they ought to check children's literacy habits. Are they keeping a journal for their observations, idea flashes, jokes, analogies, metaphors, and similes? Are they reviewing their ideas periodically? Are they reading poetry? Routines should be adjusted from time to time so that diversity and spontaneity are part of the poetry event. Collaborative partnerships, for example, inspire a free flow of ideas that motivate and expand writing.

The context also provides a window into whether or not the poetry process is being nurtured or hindered. A teacher can revisit the context set up for poetry by considering some of the following:

- Are students immersed in enough poetry writing experiences?
- Have I displayed all kinds of visual images and words for writing?
- What aspects of poetry are modeled for the child?
- Do students work in small groups before writing independently?
- Have I created a community of poets?
- Is there a balance between teacher and student selected poetry?

Finally, how might the sensory environment contribute to poetry writing? Should the classroom be highly charged to enhance alertness and stir the senses or should it be filled with soothing aromatic scents, and background music that helps students relax? In what kinds of places do children feel inspired? Invigorated? Teachers can experiment with different aesthetic effects to match environments to student needs.

Genre-Specific Indicators

Poetry has hundreds of different forms and teachers will want to fully investigate those they are teaching in order to convey expectations to the students. Throughout this chapter are descriptions of poetry from which to extrapolate indicators for process and product. Here are examples for three music-based poems, discussed in further detail in Piazza (1999).

Ballads

Product
- Tells a story (typical topics of love, adventure, intrigue, outlaws)
- Focuses on a single important episode
- Uses incremental repetition (refrains) and quatrains (4 lines per verse)
- Employs words consistent with the historical era *(lass, yonder, fortnight)*

Process
- Collects ballads
- Sings or listens to ballads on CDs
- Reads aloud or performs one's own ballad
- Revises for features characteristic of the product

Rap

Product
- Tells a story (a social commentary)
- Uses language that is short, curt, sharp-witted (slang, exaggeration)
- Stylizes speech with short, choppy phrases (speechifying)
- Has a strong beat (rhythm and meter)

Process
- Engages in verbal art performance (hand clapping, voice effects)
- Sings along with recordings of raps, delivering them at a very fast speed and using gestures and movements
- Lists possible refrains or repetitive sequences
- Revises for features characteristic of the product

Ode

Product
- Involves one central theme (commemorates public events, state ceremonies, dedications)
- Presents a tone that is sentimental, intense, emotional, exalted
- Pays homage or tribute to an object
- Has a rhythm and beat (lyrical poem)

Process
- Brainstorms ordinary objects (pizza box, ice cream, birdcage)
- Reads and studies odes
- Lists possible reasons for tribute
- Revises for features characteristic of the product

Teachers and students can analyze and outline descriptive indicators for any number of poetic genres. If students join teachers in developing evaluation criteria, they learn more about the genre qualities at their specific developmental level and expand their knowledge of what makes good writing.

Classroom Vignettes: Poetry Writing in Action

The remaining sections focus on the creation of poetry collections within the framework of the writer's workshop. In the three grade levels, you will see the many kinds of poetry that children write. As was true for the other writing functions, the genre collections are neither comprehensive nor exclusive to a particular grade level. They are simply representative works completed in a poetry unit. When modified to meet student experiences, interests, and abilities, writers of any age can enjoy them.

Grade 1

Vivian's classroom is filled with eye-catching bulletin boards, writing samples, and poems from favorite authors. The room itself vibrates with the energy of 6-year-olds who maneuver their shared space with a sense of ownership and pride. At the reading center Vivian has assembled text sets (collections of books) of all kinds of poetry books, a few of which are propped open on their spines for display. Paper of all sizes is easily accessible and jars with pencils and crayons sit in the middle of the tables.

Vivian especially loves to teach poetry because of the creative power it releases in her students. When the school year begins, she introduces free verse and invented poems because they are short, fun, and free of rules. Although these poems may appear deceivingly simple, children curl interpretations around them that are full of insight and imagination. Because most first graders love rhyme and wordplay, nonsense and rhyming verse are included in the unit.

Free Verse

Free verse is a place to break with tradition and assume complete freedom to follow natural thought patterns, pauses of speech, or desired effects. Because it is fluid, with emphasis on meanings and feelings over form, it never constrains writers. Unbound by rules, students can concentrate on what they have to say, leaving the length, placement of words, and poetic devices to emerge from their purposes.

Vivian schedules a minilesson to model where poems come from. She relays a personal incident that happened to her.

> I was working in the garden one morning, weeding through some of the flowerbeds, when a snake slithered into my path. I could have jumped 10 feet high when I saw it. I thought it was a rattlesnake or some other poisonous one, so I grabbed my shovel to strike it. Before I could hit it, the snake disappeared. Later when I described the incident to my friend, she said that I was probably frightened over a harmless garter snake.

After sharing the story about the snake, she shows how the narrative can be turned into verse.

> Snake in my flowerbed
> Slithers in my path
> I grab for my shovel
> It is gone!

She lists persons, places, and things gleaned from her story and circles one of these for the subject *(snake)*. Then she asks, "What happened?" and writes words, phrases, and condensed sentences to form the answer. The children watch what she

FIGURE 5-19 Yumarilis's Free Verse, "Ladybugs," First Draft (First Grader, Independent Writing)

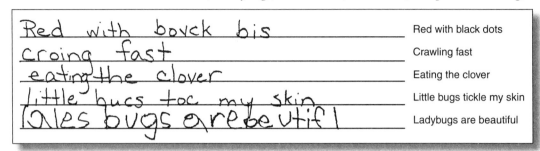

Red with black dots
Crawling fast
Eating the clover
Little bugs tickle my skin
Ladybugs are beautiful

does and prepare to follow her lead. They recall events in their lives—an observation, a person, an experience, a feeling—and share their stories with friends, brainstorming keywords. For those who can't think of something to write about there is always the option of reading more poetry or returning to journal entries to underline words or phrases that spark ideas or pleasing images. Vivian is available at the worktables to assist writers and remind them about adding sensory details—what they see, touch, hear, taste, and smell.

Yumarilis writes a poem, direct and simple, with no wasted words. (See Figure 5–19.) What is striking about the work is its reliance on keen observation, apparent in her description of the ladybug and its tactile impact on her skin. She seems to have a special knack for expressing ideas in a fresh way and finding words and phrases that appeal to the senses. Precise nouns, such as *clover* rather than *grass*; color adjectives, such as *red* and *black dots*; and verbs, such as *crawling, eating,* and *tickle,* provide vivid images and give voice to her work. A recognizable organization that centers on the ladybug and its activity fits the meaning and feelings she wants to convey.

Contrast this with Taylor's three-line poem in Figure 5–20 in which repetition and word placement build structure and fluency. The picture of colored leaves that he draws to accompany his thematic content produces coherence. Vivian confers with writers after they have a draft, not to ask them to change what they've done but to comment on skills they have mastered (I can read many of the words you have tried to spell), or interpretations of their work (Your poem reminds me of *X*). She also questions them about their process (How did you come up with this topic?) and sensory descriptions (How does *X* sound? Feel?).

In a writing conference Yumarilis talks about her ideas, and Vivian responds.

> Your poem made me think that I should look more closely at ladybugs. What details! You even captured the movements of ladybugs and how they feel when they walk across your skin.

She points out what Yumarilis is doing well and makes her aware of a metalanguage to describe her strategies (that is, use of detail).

Sharing poems is a major event in the first grade. Children read their poems at the author's chair while Vivian emphasizes special techniques found in the work. Even the intonation, pauses, and speed with which a poem is read conveys its subtle moods. The class poems are as diverse as the writers. Some of the poems are long and others are short. Some rhyme; others do not. Some are written in stanzas; others are not.

Rhyming Poems

When children are learning about rhyme in the reading class, it usually finds its way into writing. Michele composes a simple four-line stanza called "Sam." (See

FIGURE 5-20
Taylor's Free Verse, "Leaves," First Draft (First Grader, Independent Writing)

Down down
down Leaves
fall down

FIGURE 5-21
Michele's Rhyming Poem, "Sam," Final Draft (First Grader, Independent Writing)

> **Sam**
>
> My goldfish Sam is really fat,
> He's almost as fat as my cat.
> He always swims up and down,
> He never makes a loud sound.

Figure 5–21.) The ideas for her poem grow out of personal experience—she owns a goldfish and a cat. The poem is written in exact *(fat/cat)* and half *(down/sound)* rhyme with an irregular rhythm. Because several children, including Michele, show an interest in rhyme, Vivian reads nursery verses, such as "Jack be nimble/ Jack be quick/ Jack jump over the candlestick," or storybooks, such as Dr. Seuss's *The Cat in the Hat* (1952). Prior to writing their own poems, they are reminded to first put down thoughts and add rhyme later. Any subject is suitable for a rhyming poem, but generally they are light and humorous. Vivian holds a group minilesson to be certain everyone understands the concept of rhyme. Together they brainstorm rhyming pairs—*bug–hug, boy–toy, beat–heat, log–hog*—and then Vivian writes a sentence on the board and underlines the final word.

I saw a black and white <u>dog</u>

In a second sentence, she omits the end rhyme and the children insert a word to complete the couplet, creating successive lines of verse.

He snored and slept near a _____
[hog, bog, frog, log, jog, cog, fog]

In the subsequent examples, Vivian slowly gives the students more responsibility for creating sentences. Some rhyming couplets are better than others because they have similar syllable and word counts for even rhythm. When children hear this constraint, Vivian shows them how to add or subtract words for flow.

Children frequently start with couplets and then extend these to triplets. Triplets consist of three rhymed or unrhymed lines arranged in what are commonly referred to as rhyme schemes. The most popular scheme of *a, a, a* involves rhyme in the last words of all three lines.

Rain, rain go away	*a*
Come again another day	*a*
Little Tommy wants to play	*a*

A rhyme scheme of *a, b, a* presents another popular structure where the final words in the first and last lines rhyme.

Jingle bells, jingle bells, jingle all the way,	*a*
Oh what fun it is to ride	*b*
In a one horse open sleigh!	*a*

As the children become more comfortable with rhyme, some write quatrains, four-line verse patterns, with many different rhyme schemes. Three examples follow:

A rhyme scheme of *a, a, b, b* where the final word of lines 1 and 2 rhyme and 3 and 4 rhyme, as in the following verse from *Jack and the Beanstalk*:

a Fee, fi, fo fum
a I smell the blood of an Englishman,
b Be he alive, or be he dead
b I'll grind his bones to make my bread

A rhyme scheme of *a, b, c, b* where the final word of lines 2 and 4 rhyme; lines 1 and 3 do not rhyme:

a Take a simple purple pansy
b In a perfect pewter pot
c Sit it on a painted porch
b Where the sun pours down a lot

A rhyme scheme of *a, a, b, a* where the final word of lines 1, 2, and 4 rhyme:

a Mary Maple went to France
a "Time" she said, "to take a chance"
b I'll open up a brand new school
a And teach young children how to dance

Older children often revise poems for better rhyming pairs or accents that fit a stronger rhythmic pattern. Attention might be given to the number of words and syllables that make rhyme work. Vivian's first graders use rhyme primarily for its sound and structure. It invites them to read poems out loud. Often the words from their writings are added to the word wall. During spelling they will use them for sorting or placing in flipbooks to study onsets and rimes.

Nonsense and Humorous Poems

Humorous poems, such as "Sir Smasham Uppe" (Rieu, 1983), or sheer nonsense, such as "Slithergadee" (Silverstein, 1964), are popular because they convey comical or amusing events, or nothing at all (Norton, 1999).

Children follow along as Vivian reads the poem "Jabberwocky" (Carroll, 1978), posted on oversized paper in the front of the room. The first two verses are reproduced in Figure 5–22. After completing the second reading, she poses some questions:

FIGURE 5-22 First
Two Verses of
"Jabberwocky," by
Lewis Carroll (1978)

Jabberwocky

'Twas brillig, and the slithy toves
Did gyre and gimble in the wabe:
All mimsy were the borogoves,
And the mome raths outgrabe.

"Beware the Jabberwock, my son!
The jaws that bite, the claws that catch!
Beware the Jubjub bird, and shun
The frumious Bandersnatch!"

Lewis Carroll

Vivian:	What did the slithy toves do?
Class [laughter]:	Gyre and gimble.
Vivian:	Where did they gyre and gimble?
Class:	In the wabe.
Vivian:	Who should the Jubjub bird shun?
Class:	The frumious Bandersnatch!

In the same way that Alice in Wonderland understood the gist of the poem but didn't know what it meant, the children easily respond to the questions but aren't quite sure what they have answered. Although the words and sentences are nonsense, the expected rules of morphology, grammar, and syntax are in tact. A few of the words are blended to form distinctly new ones (portmanteau words such as *chortle*—*chuckle* plus *snort*—and *galump*—*gallop* and *triumph*), and initial consonants or consonant clusters at the beginning of common words make for predictable and readable nonsense (*gimble* or *frumious*).

The children decide to write humorous or nonsense poems, but before they begin, Vivian reads *Superdupers: Really Funny Read Words* (Terban, 1989) and lists on the board some invented words that add color to the language.

Big wig	Hokey pokey
Doodad	Jibber jabber
Fiddle faddle	Topsy turvy
Hocus-pocus	Wishy washy

She also implements some of the minilessons discussed previously in the section on poetry's humorous effects.

The class completes a poem together before writing independently. They begin by volunteering a list of nonsense words that rhyme with *snake*.

bibblebake	nake
crake	slake
fiddlewake	splake
frake	twake

Vivian models a poem using these words. She writes:

> I saw a big *snake*
> He looked like a *crake*
> He ate a hot *splake*
> And fell on his *twake*

Children enjoy this lighthearted verse and respond with clever refrains:

And fell on his twake, his twake, his twake!

When the lesson concludes, children work in groups at the writing table crafting their own nonsense verse. They think of an animal or object, describe it with unusual characteristics, and make up nonsense words for its actions. Some pencil in silly drawings and use these as the springboard for writing.

During the process, Vivian reinforces children's efforts at trying untested words or experimenting with new ideas and rhymes. Often she recommends they review poetry books to examine how authors create humor. After experimenting with titles and sharing their poems, students place their work in the writing folders with other in-progress drafts and list the titles in their writing logs.

Formula Poems

Children frequently "borrow" poems from their favorite poets, taking the basic structure and making it their own. For example, a first grader imitates the popular "This Is Just to Say" by Williams Carlos Williams (1938) and writes a mirror image of it substituting a personal experience—playing drums at church (see Figure 5–23). The child's imitation is true to the poet's original verse, mimicking division of lines, opening words, tone, and structure. To continue children's interest along these lines,

FIGURE 5-23   This Is Just to Say Poem, "Drums at Church," Final Draft (First Grader, Guided Writing)

Vivian consults Kenneth Koch's book, *Wishes, Lies, and Dreams* (1970), a collection of poems written and compiled by children. She lists on the chalkboard poetry prompts for learners to complete.

I used to _____ but now I _____
I used to think that _____ but now I see _____
I seem to be _____ but really I am _____
I remember _____
I wish _____

Before they work independently, Vivian invites the class to contribute lines to one of the prompts. Children watch her chain several responses together to make a collaborative poem.

Michele selects the *I remember* opening to reflect on things she recalls (see Figure 5–24). Ideas for Michele's poem are drawn from her experience and offer insights into her memories and desires. The imitated poem has a built-in unity and an organization with internal regularity created through repetition. Her voice comes through in the words and phrases that complete this predetermined framework and in the way she adorns or formats the poem.

When the students have a collection of three or four poems, they bind them together in a simple book (as shown in Figure 5–25) made from five sheets of 8½ × 11-inch paper, spread horizontally, hole punched on top, and threaded with yarn. The books are shared with peers and later given as gifts to parents.

FIGURE 5-24 I Remember Poem, "Losing a Tooth," Final Draft (First Grader, Guided Writing)

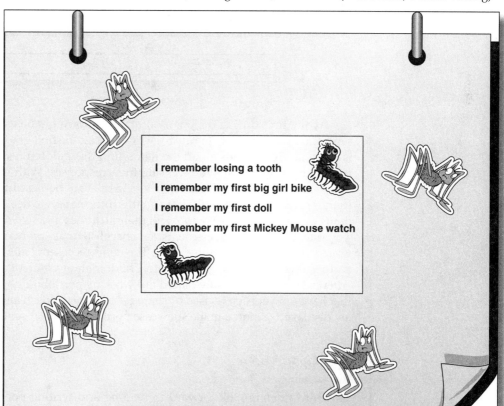

FIGURE 5-25 Easy-
to-Make Poem Book

At any time during the poetry unit, students might be asked to complete a self-report such as the one in Figure 5–26 given to all the first graders after the first poem is written. Vivian reads aloud the items, and the children respond by placing colorful stickers appropriately to indicate their responses. With information from these self-reports, she is able to guide writers to relevant books, authors, genres, or topics. In the ensuing tasks she will draw on this information to design minilessons. As students grow and change so, too, will their attitudes and feelings about the work.

Many of the self-assessments are checklists that summarize the various poems writers have done (see Figure 5–27). The items represent criteria for the specific poem and are developmentally appropriate. Children stamp smiley faces next to the achieved criteria. These checklists are placed in a working portfolio along with sample products that have not yet been revised or shared. As learners polish and complete pieces, they are displayed or stored in the showcase portfolio and later sent home.

Grade 3

The third graders look forward to reading and writing poetry during the 6-week unit on visual and invented poems. They start out with found poems, an invented form for demonstrating the visual and aural distinctions between prose and poetry.

FIGURE 5-26 Self-
Report About the
Poetry Experience

SELF-REPORT
(Place sticker on line)

1. I enjoyed working on my poetry.

Yes _____   No _____

2. How do I feel about my poems?

Happy _____   Neutral _____   Sad _____

3. Did I like making my poetry book?

Yes _____   No _____

4. Did I like revising my poetry?

Yes _____   No _____

5. Would I like to write more poetry?

Yes _____   No _____

FIGURE 5-27 Poetry Checklist for Free Verse Poem, Rhyming Poem, Nonsense or Humorous
Poem, and Formula Poem

Poetry Checklist

Free Verse Poem:
☺ I select words and phrases that are descriptive
☺ I write 2–4 sentences that relate to one another
__ I draw a picture to go with my poem

Rhyming Poem:
☺ I use rhyming words
__ I follow a consistent rhythm throughout the poem
☺ I write 2–4 sentences that paint an image
__ I read my poem to a friend

Nonsense or Humorous Poem:
☺ I make up words with interesting sounds
☺ I write 2–4 "funny" sentences
__ I share my poem with the class

Formula Poem:
☺ I repeat 2 or 3 words from a favorite poem
__ I make my poem sound like another's but use my own words and topic
__ I draw a picture to go with my poem

Then they tackle descriptive and cinquain poems. The collection is complete with an artistic shape or concrete poem.

Found Poems

The found poem is exactly what the name implies—a poem that is found in the texts of others (Dunning & Stafford, 1992). Poems can be found in any type of text, for example, children's literature, magazines, or even travel brochures. The following three essential steps were adapted from Dunning and Stafford:

1. You find 50 to 100 words you like from something you've heard or from printed material, such as newspapers, books, magazines, junk mail, or letters. Just about anything will do as long as it is not already "artistically arranged," such as song lyrics or other poems.
2. You "cut everything that's dull, unnecessary or sounds bad" (p. 4). You must trim back by half. If you have 50 words, cut back to 25; 100 words are cut to 50. There are only three rules in creating found poems: You can add no more than two of your own words, you can change punctuation, and you can change tense.
3. Finally you arrange your poem, determining where to break lines and how to lay words on the page. Be sure to cite the text from which the poem was crafted.

Kate distributes local and student newspapers (e.g., *Tallahassee Democrat, Weekly Reader*) to the third graders who select an article and underline the phrases and words they think will make a good poem. Brian goes directly to the sports section, looking for a piece on hockey. When he finds an article about the Tiger Sharks, he underlines information and records it in the order it appears in the article (see Figure 5–28A). Although the article provides a ready-made organization, Brian makes decisions about word choice, number of words per line, and number of lines. Kate hands him two different-colored markers so that he can highlight different word and phrase combinations if he doesn't like his first choice. This review and scanning of the material constitutes part of the revision phase of the lesson.

To add a unique fingerprint (voice) to his work, Brian chooses certain words and omits others (see Figure 5–28B). He also structures lines and stanzas (sentence fluency) to give the poem its shape. By altering script style (handwriting or word processed) and punctuation marks, he purposefully applies conventions to his poem. As shown in Figures 5–29A and 5–29B, some children go back to stories or reports they have written to "find" poems.

While the children are writing, Kate walks around the classroom reminding learners of the rules of the poem or talking with them about their interesting reading material. She comments on surprising word combinations and line breaks. When the poems are complete, they are shared and displayed in the classroom next to the original article or text from which the poem was extracted. Class members can read both the prose and poetic versions. By reading potential poems in a variety of texts, they recognize that poetry exists everywhere.

Descriptive Poems

The descriptive poem is an invented form that assembles details to conjure up a picture in the reader's mind. When Kate teaches these poems, she reads examples and identifies a handful of words that illustrate description (colors, shapes, textures, and feelings).

Before writing, class members complete a five senses chart (see Figure 5–4) based on their topics. In Jeffrey's "Pokemon" piece (see Figure 5–30, p. 276), strong adjectives and action verbs coupled with a simile produce a clear picture of the lizard. Although color words are commonly used by this age group, adjectives, such as *chubby* and *hot glowing*, are unique. The drawing and the placement of the poem

FIGURE 5–28A *"T-Sharks in a Deadline Flurry," Cited in the* Tallahassee Democrat, *February 29, 2000, First Draft*
Source: "T-Sharks Deal Oates in Deadline Flurry" by Jack Corcoran reproduced by permission of the Tallahassee Democrat, p. 1c.

T-Sharks Deal Oates in Deadline Flurry

by Jack Corcoran

The captain has disembarked.

Matt Oates wanted nothing more than to lead the Tallahassee Tiger Sharks out of the ruins and into the playoffs. But Oates, who had a team-high 28 goals and 49 points, **will not get the chance.** He was dealt to Dayton at the ECHL trading deadline Monday as the Tiger Sharks made major changes in the middle of the playoff race while keeping an eye on next season.

The Tiger Sharks, who got defenseman Jim Baxter, cash and two players to be named at the end of the season for Oates, were able to deal their No. 1 center because they signed speedy veteran center Jeff McLean on Monday.

McLean was awesome down the stretch last season with the Tiger Sharks, collecting 16 goals in 21 games. But he **hasn't done much since.** McLean played two games with Quebec of the AHL in October and then decided to **return home to South Carolina.**

Tallahassee also traded defenseman Jason Kelly at the deadline, sending him back to Greenville for forward Jay Panzer and a player to be named at the end of the season. Veteran forward Kimbi Daniels, who has been playing with Quebec since Dec. 14, is also expected to return to town before the Tiger Sharks begin a five-game homestand against Jackson on Friday.

Tiger Sharks general manager Larry Kish said the moves were made partially with next season in mind, although he said the changes should not be seen as the team giving up on making the playoffs.

"It's done in the best interest of the present, but it's also done for our organization in the future," said Kish, whose team trails Baton Rouge and Mississippi by five points for the final two playoff spots in the Southern Conference. "When we started this year, we didn't have too much. But now we have a lot to build off for next year. I have been **holding my breath** for such a long time. Yeah, we have been winning some, but we've been losing some. This is the **final injection into the team** to get us over the hump. It's a gamble. If we make the playoffs, we look great. If we don't make it, we don't look so great. But what do we have to lose?"

Baxter and Panzer are both first-year pros.

Baxter, who played his junior career with Oshawa of the Ontario Hockey League, had 10 goals and 26 assists in 58 games with Dayton. Panzer, who played four years at the University of North Dakota, had 11 goals and 23 assists in 45 games with Greenville.

Kish said Kelly, who helped turn the season around after being acquired from Greenville via Johnstown in January, never wanted to play for the Tiger Sharks. He wasn't expected to return next season. Kish said he also feared Oates might look elsewhere in the summer, leaving the Tiger Sharks with nothing in return for their assets.

But will the remaining Tiger Sharks feel sold out?

"I don't think so," said Tiger Sharks coach Terry Christensen, whose team plays 11 of its final 16 games at home. "The bottom line is nobody should think we're cashing in the chips. Not when you add a guy that had 16 goals in 21 games last year. I am hoping McLean can give the same production he gave the hockey club last year."

Oates said he was upset at the news.

"For what I've done for the team, it's kind of a striking blow," said Oates, the team's most consistent scorer and top faceoff man. "After dealing with the problems and trying to keep this thing together, it hurts. I liked it here. It's been a trying year. I thought I was one of the pieces of the puzzle and part of the glue that helped keep this thing afloat when times were bad."

Kish said veteran defenseman Andy Silverman, who has a disc problem in his back, will not return this season. That means the Tiger Sharks will not have a problem with the league's veteran rule with the addition of McLean and Daniels.

add to its appeal; the words seem to emerge from the mouth of the lizard like a speech bubble. The reader sees the lizard and feels the impact of his actions. In "Pokemon," the details and meanings as well as the point of view give it voice.

Although Jeffrey's poem is descriptive, some of the others are not. Vivian conducts an on-the-spot minilesson to show how descriptions are formed from definitions and personification as follows.

FIGURE 5-28B Brian's Found Poem, "T-Sharks in a Deadline Flurry," First Draft (Third Grader, Guided Writing)

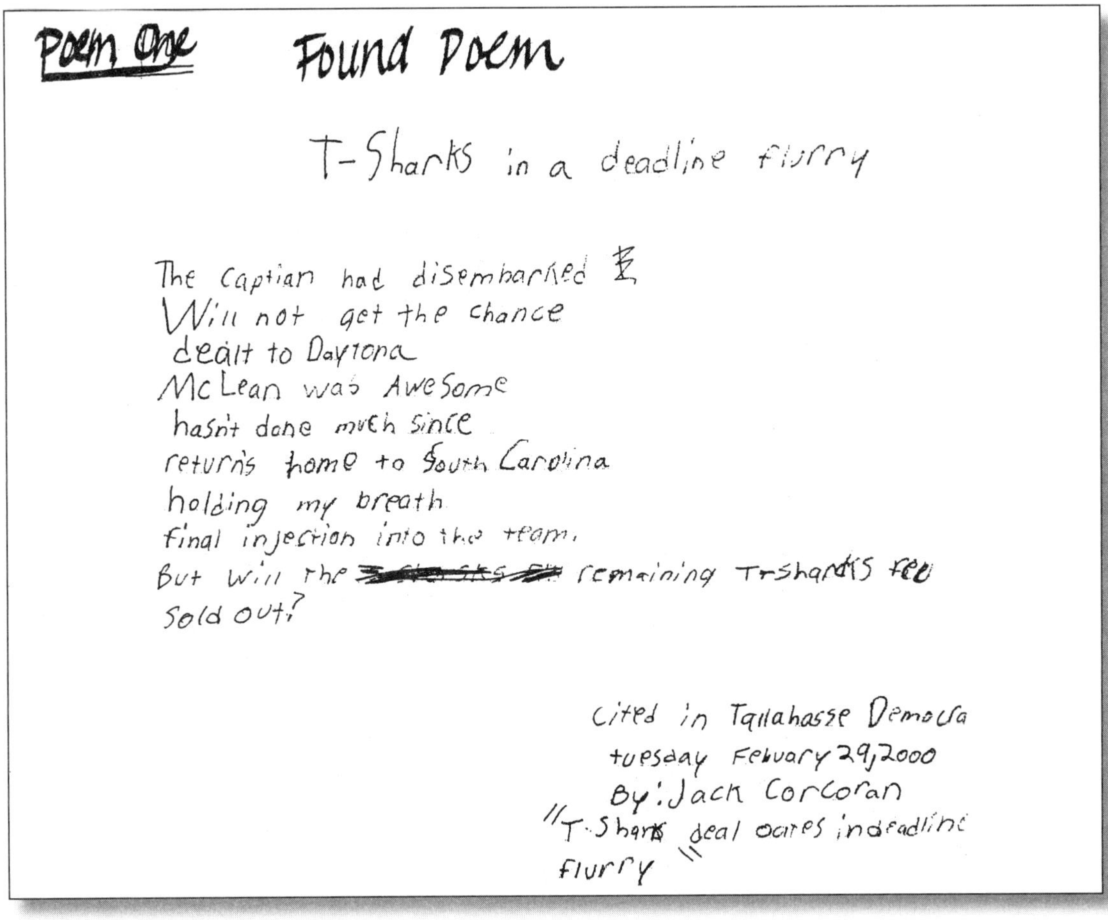
Poem One Found Poem

T-Sharks in a deadline flurry

The Captian had disembarked
Will not get the chance
dealt to Daytona
McLean was Awesome
hasn't done much since
returns home to South Carolina
holding my breath
final injection into the team.
But will the ~~[illegible]~~ remaining T-sharks fee
Sold out?

cited in Tallahasse Democra
tuesday Febuary 29, 2000
By: Jack Corcoran
"T-Sharks deal ocres in deadline
flurry"

Definition

Red is a cardinal hiding behind a black mask
Red is the tip of my nose on a cold day
Red is love

Personification

My garden rake uses its teeth
To gobble up the leaves

She holds up a seashell and asks children to formulate questions about it. What does it look like, smell like, feel like? What can it do? What shape does it have? In publishing conferences, students discuss how to enhance meaning through colors, decorative borders, and textured papers. Some decide to make "shape" books for compiling theme-related poems. For instance, a book shaped as a flower holds several descriptive poems about flowers. Sharing poems with an audience of peers celebrates the work and acknowledges the author.

Cinquain Poems

A cinquain is a five-line poem of 22 syllables in a 2–4–6–8–2 syllable pattern. But rather than adhering to syllable counts, Kate has students follow a different formula. Writers start with a one-word topic or the name of an object (e.g., apple). Then they find two words that describe it (e.g., sweet, juicy). Next they make up something

FIGURE 5-29A
Third grade Story Text
for Creating a Found
Poem)

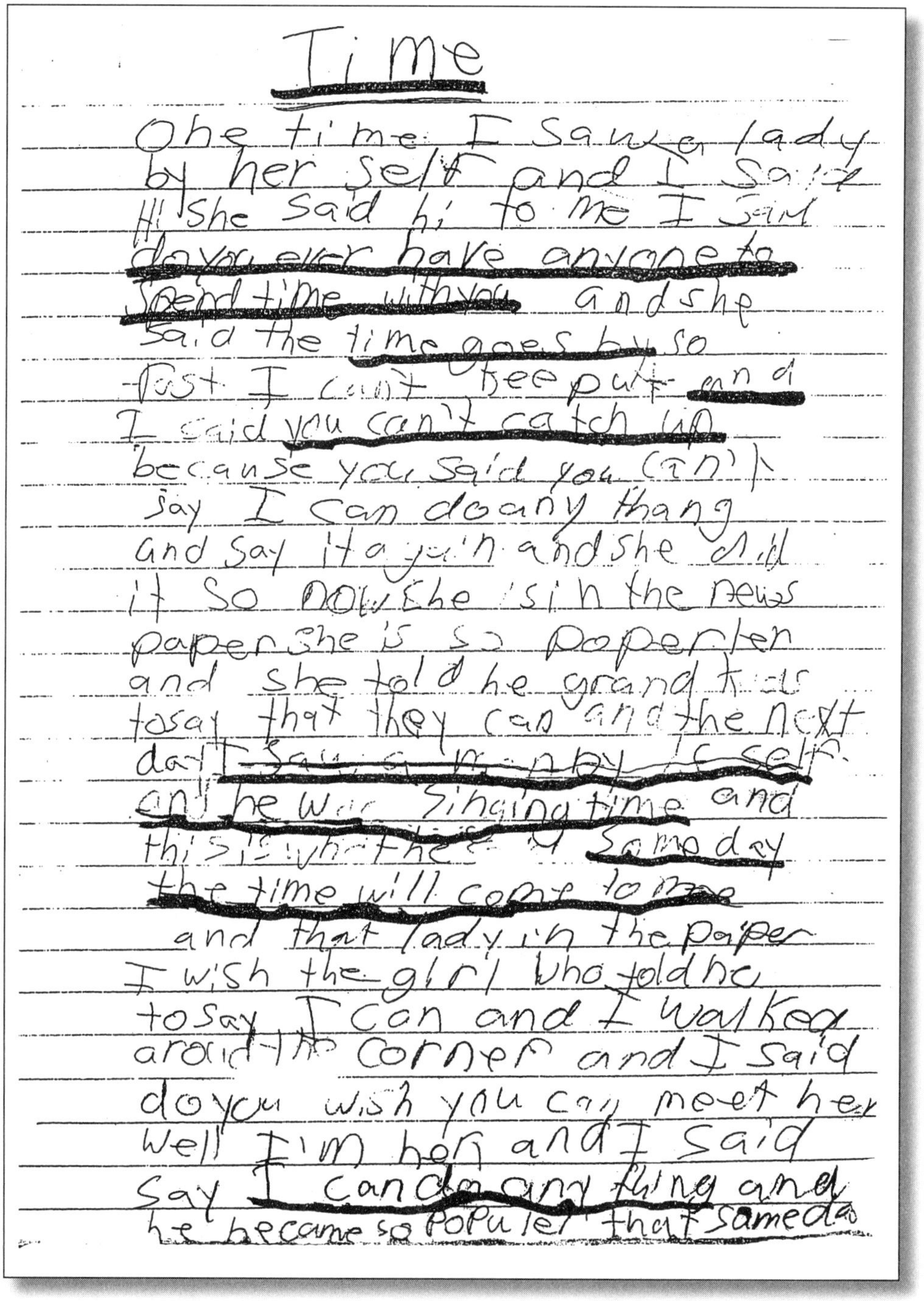

that the topic can do (an action) using three words (e.g., *growing, nourishing, feeding*). Based on feelings or observations about the topic, they think of four words to make a phrase (e.g., *nutritious, full of water*). Finally, they decide on another word for the topic (e.g., *fruit*).

Line 1, one word: title

Line 2, two words: describe title

Line 3, three words: show action

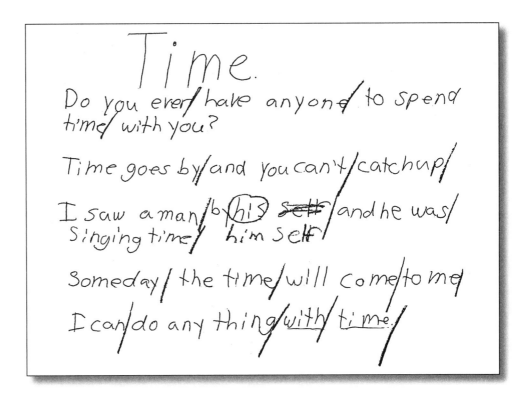

FIGURE 5-30 Jeffrey's Descriptive Poem, "Pokemon," Final Draft (Third Grader, Guided
Writing)

Line 4, four words: show feelings

Line 5, one word: another word for title

Kate demonstrates the cinquain to streamline the process and provide a point of reference for decision making. She explains that to find a subject for the cinquain, she is attentive, observing and noticing details about people, places, or things around her. If she needs a memory jogger she might consult her journal or talk with others. Oftentimes, she sits quietly and visualizes an image. Once an idea (*books*) pops into her mind, she thumbs through magazines, mail, Internet material, and newspapers to make a collage of words that are associated with her subject. Finally, she is ready to write the poem and talk aloud the decisions made to create it.

> Books
> Treasured friendship
> Mysteries to explore
> Chapters laughing and echoing
> Sanctuary

I love books and I think they'd make a good topic. In the opening, I place the word *books* as the title. I use the word *treasured* instead of *prized* because I like the way it sounds, and when I think about a treasure, I think of jewels and gold. Friendship is like gold. I add *mysteries to explore* because there is always something to discover in books. I also think it heightens interest in my subject. Because I think of books as friends, I use the words *chapters laughing and echoing* to make the books seem like people and let the reader know that books can make you laugh. The word *echoing* lets them know that the messages of the book remain with us long after we finish reading. I end the poem with a word that reminds me of the comfort I derive from a book. A book can provide a quiet place for me in my busy life. I want the reader to know that books can do the same thing for them.

Talking through the poem in this way Kate shows children her prewriting steps and walks them through decisions made during drafting and revising. She leaves them with a few other techniques that they can use to start their own poems. For example, they can make a list of synonyms or antonyms for their first and last words. Synonyms will reinforce the title and antonyms will emphasize a contrast. They might also ask themselves a few questions:

- How does the subject make you feel?
- What does it remind you of?
- What can you compare it to?
- How can you describe the subject?

The cinquain is just one of many syllable and count poems that third graders write (see Figure 5–31). All syllable and count poems have an organization that is strictly defined, which some students find welcoming and others, constricting. Sometimes the formula is purposely specified in grammatical terminology so children will learn to distinguish a noun from an adjective, from a verb.

Cinquain Poem

Noun (one word, title)
Adjectives to describe nouns (two words that describe the title)
Verbs or action phrases (three words that show action)
Adjectives (four words that show feelings)
Noun (another word for title)

Because cinquains follow "given" rules, Kate discusses the formula in small-group focus lessons and makes certain that students can identify descriptive words (adjectives) and action words (verbs). These are added to the word wall.

FIGURE 5-31 Syllable and Count Poems

Cinquain: Five-line verse that follows this pattern:
    Line 1: One word (title)
    Line 2: Two words (describing the title)
    Line 3: Three words (an action)
    Line 4: Four words (a feeling)
    Line 5: One word (referring to the title)

Diamante: Seven-line diamond-shaped poem that follows this pattern:
    Line 1: Subject noun (one word)
    Line 2: Adjective (two words)
    Line 3: Participles (three words)
    Line 4: Nouns (four words)
    Line 5: Participles (three words)
    Line 6: Adjectives (two words)
    Line 7: Noun—opposite of the subject (one word)

Haiku: Nonrhyming poem about nature; few articles or pronouns are used; consists of three lines patterned as follows:
    Line 1: Five syllables
    Line 2: Seven syllables
    Line 3: Five syllables

Lanterne: Five-line poem with a 1–2–3–4–1 syllable pattern. When completed, it should look like a Japanese lantern.

Limerick: Humorous five-line poem with lines 1, 2, and 5 rhyming (each providing three beats) and lines 3 and 4 rhyming (with two beats each).

Lune: Variation of the haiku in which words are counted instead of syllables; the pattern consists of 3–5–3 words.

Renga: Form comprising a series of tankas written by several people; combines the images and topics of haiku and the humor of senryu; alternating three lines and two lines of as many stanzas as desired (36 stanzas are a popular length).

Senryu: Humorous poem of three lines; a poem that follows the haiku form but is not about nature (any topic is acceptable).

Sestina: Unrhymed six-stanza poem of six lines per stanza. The words at the ends of the stanzas give a sense of motion. It ends with a three-line stanza, or tercet, usually of six end words. The pattern is as follows:

Stanza 1	A		Stanza 4	E
	B			C
	C			B
	D			F
	E			A
	F			D
Stanza 2	F		Stanza 5	D
	A			E
	E			A
	B			C
	D			F
	C			B
Stanza 3	C		Stanza 6	B
	F			D
	D			F
	A			E
	B			C
	E			A
		Tercet: AB		
		CD		
		EF		

Sijo: Nonrhyming form written in six short lines, each line containing seven to eight syllables for a total of 48 syllables; uses contrasts, such as sun and rain, earth and sky.

Tanka: Haiku with two extra lines of seven syllables each added at the end.

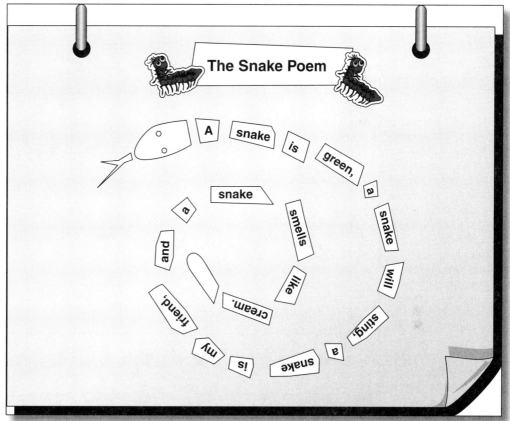

FIGURE 5-32 Seth's Shape Poem, "The Snake Poem," Final Draft (Third Grader, Independent Writing)

Shape and Concrete Poems

The shape poem is a picture sketched with words, phrases, or sentences to resemble the thing it represents. Its meaning comes from the arrangement of letters and words that outline the shape of an object. The visual form is integral and essential to its content and interpretation. Figure 5–32 shows a shape poem that places word labels in specific locations on the page to combine art and writing. The snake's body is composed of tiny paper word cutouts, and the head and tail are drawn. The cutouts are from a set of word builders, manipulatives that can be assembled in many ways to adjust or revise the shape of the poem. Unraveling the snake poem and placing the words in a stanza suggests it is a quatrain with an *a, a, b, a* rhyme scheme.

Kate takes coloring books, pictures from calendars or magazines, and visuals with strong lines to provide templates for those who feel they can't draw. With an image from a coloring book, the students place a transparent sheet of paper over the dark outline and write words or sentence around it. When they remove the top sheet of thin white paper, a picture shaped out of words appears (see Piazza, 1999, p. 35).

Ideas for shape poem designs are found not only in language arts books but also in content-related areas of the curriculum. In geography class, the children select map outlines of countries and continents and write facts around their contours. In science, Kate shows pages from the book *Splish Splash* (Graham, 1994) in which all the shapes that water can take are in the form of concrete and shape poems—icicles, ice cubes, Popsicles, waves, and waterfalls. In math class, Aaron draws a geometrical figure and describes its properties (see Figure 5–33).

One way to talk about organization as regards shape poems is to examine the visual positioning of words on the page and its implications for meaning. Drawing

FIGURE 5-33   Aaron's Shape Poem, "Disfigured," Final Draft (Third Grader, Guided Writing)

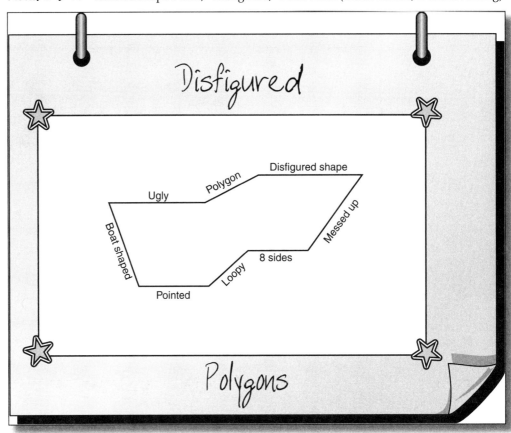

and using predrawn shapes, in essence, offer their own unique word orders. Children write words on a curve and then outline, shadow, or stagger them for special organizational effects. Any level of text is suitable for a shape poem: words, sentences, or whole stanzas. Writers often mix these in varying combinations.

When concrete poems are introduced, the learners take special note of how poets use *white space*, the empty areas around words that create the visual and aural pause in poetry. Depending on where white space appears—at the end of a line, between words, or between stanzas—the potential exists for creating unity, variety, and balance in the work (Piazza, 1999).

The unusual conventions of concrete poems—represented by punctuation, alignment, and visual symbols—produce emphasis, suspense, surprise, or satire. A dash might emphasize motion or action and words written down the page might suggest dribbling or falling. In Sonya's concrete poem (see Figure 5–34), linguistic and visual clues offer several meanings and interpretations: someone nagging, reflecting on oneself, or questioning life. The seemingly endless stream of repetitive words "you have to keep asking . . . on and on and on and on" wrapped around concentric circles creates a kind of dizzying effect that makes us feel as though we were being hurled into infinity. As this poem illustrates, concrete verse can have subtle interpretations based on what you see as well as what is said.

Concrete poems and other poems being written in Kate's class are continually shared and assessed as children go through the process.

For example, third graders select assessment tools such as the "How Did I Do?" checklist in Figure 5–35 to monitor process strategies and reflect on the written product. Before asking students to try this, Kate demonstrates and interprets criteria with

FIGURE 5-34

Sonya's Concrete Poem, "Just When You Think," Final Draft (Third Grader, Guided Writing)

FIGURE 5-35 "How Did I Do?" Checklist for Process Assessment

How Did I Do?	Yes!	Kind of	I Need to work on this
1. I used brainstorming or visualization to help myself get started.	X		
2. I used similes or metaphors to add impact or details to my poem(s).	X		
3. I used language that *shows* rather than tells (lots of descriptive words/details).	X		
4. I reread my poem(s) to myself and other people.		X	
5. I changed the appearance of my poem(s) to make it more exciting or fun to look at.	X		
6. I gave my poem(s) a title.		X	
7. I am happy with my poem(s)!	X		

examples from her own work. A line of questioning during conferences may also help students to self-assess.

- What makes your poem special?
- How do you know what to write first, next, and so on?
- What do you like about the way your poem looks? Are there decorative features that set your poem apart from others?
- What do you like about the words you selected? Can you find surprising or interesting word combinations?

When students have a collection of poems, they might complete a summary checklist such as the one in Figure 5–36. Over time, children develop on increased awareness and understanding of each poem's traits and are better able to develop and revise their work in light of them.

In addition to assessing the writing of the poem, children are asked to examine their reading or recitation of it. Students are given the choice of memorizing the poem or reading it from the paper. Over several days, they practice with a partner using a checklist that identifies speaking criteria. When it is time to share, Kate captures the reading or recitation on tape and the poets later listen and rate their performances using this criteria:

- Did you pause during the poem? At what places? Why?
- Did you read with emotion and expression? What parts?
- How fast or slow did you read? Was there a reason for this?
- Did you speak loudly enough? Did you change your volume for certain reasons?
- Did you pronounce words clearly?

There are no right or wrong answers to the questions. Kate wants children to think about these features as part of the performance of a poem and use their voices to convey interpretations.

FIGURE 5-36 Poetry Checklist for Found Poem, Descriptive Poem, Cinquain Poem, and Shape Poem

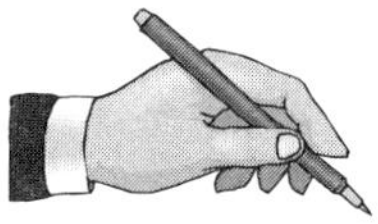 Poetry Checklist For _____	Found Poem	Descriptive Poem	Cinquain Poem	Shape Poem
Original or creative	☐	☐	☐	☐
A recognizable shape or organization	☐	☐	☐	☐
Colorful or imaginative words	☐	☐	☐	☐
Interesting sentences or phrases	☐	☐	☐	☐
Special visual effects	☐	☐	☐	☐

Grade 5

Fifth graders experience poetry, not only in language arts class but also across the curriculum. In the examples presented in this section, haiku and narrative poems are incorporated into the science and social studies lessons. The haiku and limerick represent types of syllable and count poems, and the narrative poem similar to the one introduced earlier in the minilesson of *Cinderella* is a blend of poetry and story.

Haiku Poems

Haiku is a 17-syllable unrhymed poem arranged in three lines of 5–7–5. It expresses the poet's feelings about something in nature and creates a scene for the reader, using the sparest of language. Because the translation from Japanese to English makes the strict syllable count irrelevant, some teachers may prefer to concentrate on capturing the essence of the haiku rather than worrying about its syllable count. Cory's haiku in Figure 5–37 is written as part of a science unit on the rain forest. Her word pictures reflect the Japanese love of nature, and the personification she includes (the earth is thirsty and the flowers drink) brings imagery and insight to the poem. The three sentences are grouped to tell a little story that depicts nature.

Cory and the other students get ideas by reading science textbooks and taking stock of unusual words, colorful aspects of nature, and animal habitats. They view footage from *Rain Forest Voices* (Godfry, 1990), a beautiful videotape of lush forests, colorful birds, insects, and waterfalls with recordings of natural sounds (no words), and jot down words or phrases that come to mind. Later they place these words in three lines according to syllables. Because the poems are short, they write several

FIGURE 5–37 Cory's Haiku Poem, "Rain," Final Draft (Fifth Grader, Independent Writing)

The Earth is thirsty
The clouds in the sky rain down
Flowers drink the rain

haikus on rain forests and string them together. Ed shares Richard Lewis's book *In a Spring Garden* (1965) and Patrick Lewis's book *Black Swan White Crow* (1995) as examples of how a collection of haikus can dramatically represent a theme.

During a minilesson, Ed models how to arrange sentences or phrases for effect. He displays a picture representing a seasonal scene and lists what he sees. Next he brainstorms what is happening, the hour of day, time of year, or words describing the scene (in the winter, at nightfall). The *what, where,* and *when* are written out in phrases.

What: the moon is shining

Where: over the mountain

When: at nightfall

Finally, he organizes and reorganizes the lines for different effects. Only at the end does he adjust the poem to fit the haiku syllable pattern:

The moon is shining (5 syllables)
At the top of the mountain (7 syllables)
In the winter night (5 syllables)

Before Ed's learners revise words or phrases, they talk about the original intent behind the haiku. In Japanese society, members frown on verbosity. Words in haikus are succinct and reflect what the Japanese refer to as "wa" or "harmony," a value highly treasured in the culture. The fifth graders read several Japanese haikus to examine these cultural effects before reworking their piece.

Although surveys of children's poetry preferences rank haikus low in popularity, students in Ed's class like them because they are brief and challenging. For them, haikus are more fun to write than to read.

Limerick Poems

The limerick is a funny five-line story with a clever, unanticipated punch line. It follows the *a, a, b, b, a* rhyme scheme in which the last words in the first, second, and last lines rhyme, and the last words in the third and fourth rhyme. Lines 3 and 4 are usually shorter than the other three and have the same number of syllables or beats. Lines 1, 2, and 5 also have the same number of beats. This syllable count constitutes not only the "rules" for writing limericks but also the organization it follows. In Figure 5–38 Paige's limerick illustrates the appropriate rhyming patterns and rhythmic scheme. Her inspiration comes from a nursery rhyme, "Little Bo Peep," and the humor is derived from a play on its original words and meaning. A poetic limerick spans a broad range of subject matter and ideas, and *what, where,* and *when* questions form the meaning. Students work in groups to write limericks. For those who need special assistance, a "how to" sheet is provided.

1. Write your first line (e.g., There once was a . . .)
2. List words that rhyme with the last word in your first line.

FIGURE 5-38
Paige's Limerick, "Bo Peep and the Lamb," Final Draft (Fifth Grader, Guided Writing)

Bo Peep and the Lamb

There once was a shepherd named Bo.
She was fat and very slow.
But one little lamb
Did not eat any ham,
So she gave it to a boy named Mo.

3. Make your next line rhyme with the first.
4. Write two short lines that rhyme and tell about your topic.
5. Create a final line that rhymes with your first line.
6. Complete the limerick on the lines below.

Another guide available to assist students is the limerick "frame."

There once was a _____ from _____	There was a small boy from _____
Who _____	Who couldn't remember his _____
_____	His friends thought him _____
_____	And a little too _____
That silly _____ from _____	But he was the best of his _____

Ed borrows several books from the library so that students can enjoy reading poems by Edward Lear (1990) or contemporary authors (e.g., *Pigericks: A Book of Pig Limericks,* Lobel, 1983). During minilessons on word choice, students practice word-play, double meaning, tongue twisters, or variant spellings as strategies for inventing ridiculous situations or incongruities that take people by surprise. At another time, they discuss sound devices such as alliteration or rhyme to create internal rhythm and smooth seams within sentences. A limerick is said to have come from the chorus of an old song in which the city of Limerick, Ireland, is mentioned. To introduce the rhythm behind this culturally specific poem and the link between the syllables, their stress, and the meter, students listen to music from *James Galaway and the Chieftains,* dialectal songs that embed limericks as part of the lyrics. For sentence flow, they draw on their intuitive understanding of the singsong pattern (meter) that comprises the musical beat of the limerick (see the musical effects of poetry section earlier in the chapter). Ed introduces terminology for the two poetic measures in the limerick: one iamb (u/) and two anapests (uu/) in lines 1, 2, and 5; one iamb (u/) and one anapest (uu/) in lines 3 and 4 (where u = the unstressed beat and / = the stressed beat). These terms are units of rhythm each of which is called a **foot**. The iambic and anapestic feet dominate the limerick. Attention to syllables and their accents in words (MEANwhile or RABbit) contributes to the proper beat and word choice. During discussions in writing circles and conferences, students consider limerick features and use checklists to rework poems. The criteria on the checklist is later applied to assessing poems.

Narrative Poems

Narrative poems tell stories with elements such as plot, characters, and dialogue. *The Night Before Christmas* (Moore, 1980), *Paul Revere's Ride* (Longfellow, 1990), and *Casey at Bat: A Ballad of the Republic Sung in the Year 1888* (Thayer, 2000) are among the most well known. LeAnne writes the following narrative poem about van Gogh.

Born in the Netherlands in 1853
A child is born
Whose name is Vincent.

From a family of peasants
Three sisters and two brothers
Vincent's brother Theo is his favorite.

A master of four languages
And a passion for painting
He leaves home at 16.

From the Hague to London
From London to Paris
He is a preacher, a student, a book clerk.

> But van Gogh wants to paint
> And teaches himself
> To draw like the masters.

LeAnne's poem is written as part of a biography unit that integrates language arts and social studies. Each day in social studies, she reads a chapter from the biography *Vincent van Gogh: Portrait of an Artist* (Greenberg & Jordan, 2001), and selects main ideas for quickwrites in a journal. During language arts, she uses keywords from her entry to transform the narrative into verse. By the time she finishes reading the biography, she has written a narrative poem of 6 to 10 stanzas. Working with a partner, she gets advice on content and style. This may lead to reordering stanzas for flow, adding or changing details for accuracy, or going back to the biography to get ideas for a stronger storyline. It may also mean substituting words for purposes of rhythm or rhyme: lengthening or shortening a line based on syllable count or replacing a word based on accented syllables.

Organization typically follows the biography's sequence, but students make decisions about the words and ideas. Even if two students read the same biography, each poem will have its unique voice and style. Writers build coherence and sentence fluency through meaning, repetitions, or sound patterns, or through rhythms that carry a poem's logical flow from one idea to the next. Discussions of narrative poems in writing circles are similar to those in story writing because they share story elements and use many of the same narrative techniques.

The van Gogh poem requires historical accuracy, but not all narrative poems do. Children can write from their imagination, drafting a prose passage to get started and using show don't tell techniques and story elements to make narrative come alive. If they have a story, report, letter, or essay that previously has been written and revised, they can review it and underline phrases and words to use in verse. They proceed just as the third graders did in the found poems, but with freedom to add or change words to emphasize visual and aural features. One time it might be a dash of suspense or surprise; the next time it might be a fresh metaphor or simile.

Ed recommends that students let their poems "rest " for a while before going back to them to revise. This way, they are more likely to know what to omit, what to add, or what to substitute.

In revision conferences and at the end of units, students explore various self-assessment checklists that elicit process and product information. The open-ended self-reports are examples (see sample assessment tools in Figures 5–39 and 5–40). As the samples indicate, some items address general features of poetry writing and others are specific to the genre being written. Some reflect process *and* product criteria, whereas others feature one or the other. The goal is to have children construct their own self-assessment sheets.

Quite often, Ed projects a student poem on the overhead for the class to see while he discusses it, without overanalyzing, commenting on what the writer has accomplished. He might say something like the following:

- Look how she changes the tone with the word *fragile*.
- Notice where she places the periods.
- Look at the writer's skillful use of transitions.
- Isn't this topic a clever one!

This running commentary teaches the class how to find value in a piece and highlights the strategies writers use to develop poems.

Writers also keep track of the number of minutes per day spent writing poetry, the types of poems written, their length, varieties of activities used to develop the poems (music, movement, drama), and whether the writing occurred at home or in school.

FIGURE 5-39 Open-Ended Self-Assessment: My Poetry Writing

My Poetry Writing

1) My favorite poem is

   about Rusty

   Because

   She is my dog

2) My least favorite poem is

   about Manites

   Because *I've never seen one*

3) Something new I learned about poetry writing is *I learned that Mantes are endangered. I never knew that there were so meny kinds of poems that don't ryme.*

FIGURE 5-40 Open-Ended Student's Assessment, for a Shape Poem, an Acrostic, and a Ballad

Student's Assessment

Type of Poem	Why did they choose this selection?
Shape Poem	I think they are neat.
Acrostic	The letters in my name are hard to find good words
Ballad	I like sound of rhyming poems.

Did you make revisions?
Yes I revised all three poems. I tried to add more description so that my poems could create visualizations for the read

Were your poems "pleasing to the ear"?
I thought so. I also read my revisions to my family and they agreed with me.

Did you publish them neatly?
I tried to do something different for each one. I wanted to make my final products colorful.

Were you happy with your work?
Yes, I was very proud of my work and I felt that it represented my ability well.

287

Journey Reflections

Journeying down the path of poetry is a rich experience for children. Along the way they bring fresh meaning to everyday facts of life and exercise creativity and wordplay. As with all poetry, ideas come from the imagination and from being in a state of mindfulness. Poetry teaches children to wait, watch, and listen for "the place words are looking for" (Cedering, 1990, p. 42). Yet, because it is not one of the forms assessed on standardized tests, poetry is often woefully neglected. This is unfortunate given poetry's power to refine aesthetic sensibilities and improve immeasurably the quality of life. Poetry's visual, aural, and humorous effects highlight the beauty and playfulness inherent in the child's world and help them weather life's changes. More than entertainment and more than a catharsis, poetry offers unique meanings, skills, and strategies not found in other kinds of writing. A balanced writing program should support children as they choose a variety of poetic forms for many purposes. Those that are discussed in the three classroom vignettes provide a good start. Free verse and invented poems offer immediate success because there are no strict rules. Children select virtually any topic and create a composition of sounds and meanings. More strict and disciplined are syllable and count poems which provide formulas to follow for measured verse. At all grade levels, narrative and found poems provide a way to transform prose into poetry while using story plot as support.

In the next chapter of the journey, expository writing advances children's curiousities and quests for meaning. This time, however, the purpose is to get things done, inform, explain, and report. In doing so, writers harness their passions and dig deep into new and familiar subjects. They will follow proven strategies for assisting in this endeavor. Now, more than ever, in a media-driven and technological world, it is imperative that children learn to manage and shape large amounts of information for presentation to others.

Works Cited

Professional References

Brier, D. (1992). *Great type and lettering designs*. Cincinnati, OH: North Light Books.

Cedering, S. (1990). Suppose. In P. B. Janeczko (Ed.), *The place my words are looking for* (p. 42). New York: Bradbury Press.

DeHaven, E. (1983). *Teaching and learning the language arts* (2nd ed.). Boston: Little, Brown.

Dunning, S., & Stafford, W. (1992). *Getting the knack*. Urbana, IL: National Council of Teachers of English.

Fisher, C., & Natarella, M. (1982). Young children's preferences in poetry: A national survey of first, second, and third graders. *Research in the Teaching of English, 16*, 339–354.

Frost, R. (1959). *You come too: Favorite poems for young readers*. New York: Henry Holt.

Geller, L. G. (1985). *Word play and language learning for children*. Urbana, IL: National Council of Teachers of English.

Ghiselin, B. (1952). *The creative process*. New York: Mentor Books.

Heard, G. (1989). *For the good of the earth and sun*. Portsmouth, NH: Heinemann.

Henderson, K. (2001). *The young writer's guide to getting published*. Cincinnati, OH: Writer's Digest Books.

Koch, K. (1970). *Wishes, lies, and dreams*. New York: HarperPerennial.

Moffett, J., & Wagner, B. J. (1992). *Student-centered language arts, K–12* (4th ed.). Portsmouth, NH: Heinemann.

Nodelman, P. (1992). *The pleasure of children's literature*. New York: Longman.

Norton, D. (1999). *Through the eyes of a child* (5th ed.). Upper Saddle River, NJ: Merrill/Prentice Hall.

Olshansky, B. (1994). Making writing a work of art: Image-making within the writing process. *Language Arts, 71*, 350–356.

Padgett, R. (Ed.). (1987). *The teachers and writers handbook of poetic forms*. New York: Teachers and Writers Collaborative.

Piaget, J. (1952). *The origins of intelligence in children*. (M. Cook, Trans.). New York: International Universities Press.

Piazza, C. (1999). *Multiple forms of literacy: Teaching literacy and the arts*. Upper Saddle River, NJ: Merrill/Prentice Hall.

Routman, R. (2000). *Kids' poems: Teaching children to love poetry*. New York: Scholastic.

Terry, A. (1974). *Children's poetry preferences: A national survey of the upper elementary grades*. Urbana, IL: National Council of Teachers of English.

Torrance, E. P. (1963). *Creativity*. Washington, DC: National Education Association.

Welty, E. (1984). *One writer's beginnings*. Cambridge, MA: Harvard University Press.

Williams, M. (1986). *Patterns of poetry: An encyclopedia of forms*. Baton Rouge: Louisiana State University Press.

Children's References

Aardema, V. (1991). *Traveling to Tondo: A tale of the Nkundo of Zaire*. Knopf.

Adoff, A. (1979). *Eats poems*. Lothrop, Lee, & Shepard.

Adoff, A. (2000). *Touch the poem*. Scholastic.

Ammer, C. (1989). *It's raining cats and dogs—And other beastly expressions*. Dell.

Anno, M. (1975). *Anno's alphabet: An adventure in imagination*. Thomas Y. Crowell.

Appelt, K. (1993). *Elephants aloft*. Harcourt Brace & Company.

Base, G. (1986). *Animalia*. Abrams.

Brown, M. (Trans.). (1954). *Cinderella*. Atheneum.

Brown, M. W. (1949, 1977). *The important book*. HarperCollins.

Browning, R. (1997). *The pied piper of Hamelin*. Dover.

Carroll, L. (1978). "Jabberwocky." In L. Carroll, *Alice in wonderland and through the looking glass* (pp. 164–166). Grosset & Dunlap.

Cole, J., Calmenson, S., & Tiegreen, A. (Compilers). (1993). *Six sick sheep: 101 tongue twisters*. Morrow.

Cronin, D. (2000). *Click, clack moo: Cows that type*. Simon & Schuster.

Delacre, L. (1989). *Arroz con leche: Popular songs and rhymes from Latin America*. Scholastic.

deRegniers, B. S. (1972). *Red Riding Hood: Retold in verse by Beatrice Schenk deRegniers*. Atheneum.

deRegniers, B. S., Moore, E., White, M. M., & Carr, J. (1988). *Sing a song of popcorn*. Scholastic.

Edwards, P. D. (1996). *Some smug slug*. HarperCollins.

Edwards, P. D. (2001). *Clara caterpillar*. HarperCollins.

Esbensen, A. J. (1995). *Dance with me*. HarperCollins.

Fatchen, M. (1987). *The country mail is coming: Poems from down under*. Little, Brown.

Fleischman, P. (2000). *Big talk: Poems for four voices*. Candlewick.

Franco, B. (2000). *Shells*. Children's Press.

Galdone, P. (1974). *Little Red Riding Hood*. McGraw-Hill.

Gardon, J. R. (1991). *Six sleepy sheep*. Boyds Mills.

Goldstein, B. S. (1992). *Inner chimes: Poems on poetry*. Boyds Mills.

Graham, J. B. (1994). *Splish splash*. Ticknor & Fields.

Graham, J. B. (1999). *Flicker flash*. Houghton Mifflin.

Graves, K. (1999). *Frank was a monster who wanted to dance*. Chronicle.

Greenberg, J., & Jordan, S. (2001). *Vincent van Gogh: Portrait of an artist*. Delacorte.

Gwynne, F. (1970). *The king who rained*. Windmill-Wanderer.

Gwynne, F. (1980). *The sixteen hand horse*. Windmill-Wanderer.

Hall, K., & Eisenberg, L. (2001). *Ribbit riddles*. Dial.

Hastings, S. (Ed.). (1990). *Miss Mary Mac all dressed in black: Tongue twisters, jump-rope rhymes, and other children's lore from New England*. August House.

Heller, R. (1991). *Up, up and away: A book about adverbs*. Scholastic.

Heller, R. (1995). *Behind the mask: A book about prepositions*. Grosset & Dunlap.

Heller, R. (1998). *A cache of jewels and other collective nouns*. Putnam & Grosset.

Heller, R. (1998). *Fantastic! wow! and unreal! A book about interjections and conjunctions*. Grosset & Dunlap.

Heller, R. (1998). *Kites sail high: A book about verbs*. Putnam & Grosset.

Heller, R. (1998). *Many luscious lollipops: A book about adjectives*. Putnam & Grosset.

Heller, R. (1999). *Mine, all mine: A book about pronouns*. Puffin.

Hindly, J. (1998). *A song of colors*. Candlewick.

Hooks, W. H. (1992). *Feed me*. Bantam.

Hopkins, L. B. (1989). *Still as a star: A book of nighttime poems*. Little, Brown.

Jekyll, W. (Compiler). (1994). *I have a news: Rhymes from the Caribbean*. Lothrop, Lee, & Shepard.

Juster, N. (1989). *As: A surfeit of similes*. Morrow.

Keller, C. (Compiler). (1986). *Count Draculations!: Monster riddles*. Prentice Hall.

Keller, C. (2001). *Super silly riddles*. Sterling.

Kennedy, X. J., & Kennedy, D. (Compilers). (1982). *Knock at a star: A child's introduction to poetry*. Little, Brown.

Kent, D. (1995). *The star-spangled banner*. Children's Press.

Kherdian, D. (1977). *If dragonflies made honey*. Greenwillow.

Koch, M. (1991). *Hoot, howl, hiss*. Greenwillow.

Kuskin, K. (1975). *Near the window tree: Poems and notes*. Harper & Row.

Lear, E. (1990). *Of pelicans and pussycats: Poems and limericks*. Dial.

Lee, D. (1983). Tony Baloney. In J. Prelutsky (Ed.), *The Random House book of poetry for children* (p. 109). Random House.

Lewis, P. (1995). *Black swan white crow*. Simon & Schuster.

Lewis, R. (1965). *In a spring garden*. Dial.

Lithgow, J. (2000). *The remarkable Farkle McBride*. Simon & Schuster.

Livingston, M. C. (1987). *Cat poems*. Holiday House.

Lobel, A. (1983). *Pigericks: A book of pig limericks*. Harper & Row.

London, J. (2001). *Park beat*. HarperCollins.

Longfellow, H. W. (1990). *Paul Revere's ride*. Dutton.

Lyne, S. (1996). *Ten-second rainshower poems by young people*. Simon & Schuster.

Maestro, G. (1984). *What's a frank Frank? Tasty homograph riddles*. Clarion.

McFerrin, B. (2001). *Don't worry, be happy*. Welcome Books.

Moore, C. (1980). *The night before Christmas*. Holiday House.

Moore, I. (1991). *Six dinner Sid*. Simon & Schuster.

Moss, L. (1995). *Zin! zin! zin!: A violin*. Simon & Schuster.

Newman, L. (2001). *Cats, cats, cats!* Simon & Schuster.

O'Neill, M. (1961, 1989). *Hailstones and halibut bones*. Doubleday.

Oram, H. (1993). *Out of the blue: Poems about color*. Hyperion.

Parish, P. (1976). *Good work, Amelia Bedelia*. Greenwillow.

Payne, N. (1983). "Bubble gum." In J. Prelutsky (Ed.), *The Random House book of poetry for children* (p. 106). Random House.

Pomerantz, C. (1980). "My mami takes me to the bakery." In C. Pomerantz, *The tamarindo puppy* (p. 21). Greenwillow.

Pomerantz, C. (1982). *If I had a paka: Poems in eleven languages*. Greenwillow.

Prelutsky, J. (Ed.). (1983). *The Random House book of poetry for children*. Random House.

Prelutsky, J. (1986). *Ride a purple pelican*. Greenwillow.

Prelutsky, J. (1996). "I'm proud of my preposterus." In *A pizza the size of the sun*, pp. 150–151. Scholastic.

Rieu, E. V. (1983). "Sir Smasham Uppe." In J. Prelutsky (Ed.), *The Random House book of poetry*. (p. 167). Random House.

Rosenbloom, J. (1996). *The little giant book of riddles*. Sterling.

Schwarz, A., Miesel, P., & Schett, S. (1982). *Busy buzzing bumblebees and other tongue twisters*. Harper & Row.

Seuss, T. G. (1952). *The cat in the hat*. Houghton Mifflin.

Seuss, T. G. (1979). *Oh say can you say?* Beginner Books.

Sherman, I. (1980). *Walking, talking words*. Harcourt Brace Jovanovich.

Shields, C. D. (1995). *Lunch money: And other poems about school*. Dutton.

Silverstein, S. (1964). "Slithergadee." In S. Silverstein, *Don't bump the glump*. Simon & Schuster.

Smith, L. (2001). *When moon fell down*. HarperCollins.

Smith, W. (2001). *Just the two of us*. Scholastic.

Smith, W. J. (1998). "Lion." *The world below the window: Poems 1937–1997*. Baltimore, MD: Johns Hopkins University Press.

Solt, M. E. (1980). *Concrete poetry: A world view*. Indiana University Press.

Spooner, M. (1993). *A moon in your lunch box*. Henry Holt.

Stevens, J. (2001). *And the dish ran away with the spoon*. Harcourt.

Sullivan, C. (Ed.). (1989). *Imaginary gardens: American poetry and art for young people*. Abrams.

Terban, M. (1982). *Eight ate: A feast of homonym riddles*. Houghton Mifflin.

Terban, M. (1983). *In a pickle and other funny idioms*. Houghton Mifflin.

Terban, M. (1989). *Superdupers: Really funny real words*. Clarion.

Terban, M. (1990). *Punching the clock: Funny action idioms*. Houghton Mifflin.

Thayer, E. L. (2000). *Casey at bat: A ballad of the republic sung in the year 1988*. Handprint.

Vozar, D. (1995). *Yo hungry wolf? A nursery rap*. Doubleday.

Wattenberg, J. (2000). *Henny Penny*. Scholastic Press.

Williams, W. C. (1938). "This is just to say." In W. C. Williams, *Collected earlier poems* (p. 372). New Directions.

Yolen, J. (2000). *Off we go*. Little, Brown.

Zemach, M. (2001). *Some from the moon, some from the sun: Poems and songs for everyone*. Farrar, Straus & Giroux.

Media Resources

James Galaway and the Chieftains [CD]. New York: BMG Music.

Rain Forest Voices. (1990) [VHS]. Michael Godfrey (Director). Natural Science Network, 108 High Street, Carroboro, NC 27510.

Soundtracks. (1993). Living and Learning. Cambridge, England: Abbeygate House.

CHAPTER 6

Here the Red Queen began again, "Can you answer useful questions?"

Expository Writing

C hildren are full of the whys and wonders of the world. A 7-year-old runs over to the teacher and inquires about a ladybug in the palm of her hand. A 9-year-old watches a spider build a web and wants to know what the web is made of and how insects get trapped there. Through the eyes of a child, ordinary curiosities and inquisitive ponderings illuminate, in a fresh way, what most adults take for granted. "Useful" questions reveal their natural inclination to explore the world and unveil its complex mysteries. Whatever teachers do to foster these questions only deepens student understandings and meanings. Such a resolve is at the heart of instruction in expository writing, a large, sprawling domain that offers various forms and strategies for knowing a subject and presenting it to others. In its broadest sense, expository writing includes all texts in which facts and information dominate be they pop-up books, alphabet books, "how to" manuals, newspaper articles, biographies, poems, stories, or TV scripts.

Although many of the genres in Figure 6–1 are familiar by their common labels, such as business letter or research report, or by belonging to a literary category, such as **nonfiction**, there are no sharp dividing lines between narration, description, exposition, and persuasion. For example, *narrative exposition* simultaneously tells a story *and* teaches facts, as in the picture book *The Very Hungry Caterpillar* (Carle, 1971) or the historical biographies *And Then What Happened, Paul Revere?* (Fritz, 1973) or *Beethoven Lives Upstairs* (Nichol, 1994).

Conversely, *informative exposition* concentrates on facts but doesn't ignore the reader's need to be entertained. Good examples are the *Poke and Look Learning* books, in which die-cut holes allow you to peek through to pictures to discover content, and *Robert Crowther's Deep Down Underground: Pop-Up Book of Amazing Facts and Feats* (1998), in which pulling tabs and lifting flaps dispatch readers to tunnels, caves, and mines.

Because informative exposition dominates popular **trade books**, textbooks, reports, and reference materials, this chapter focuses on this form, referring to it simply as expository writing and identifying it by some of the following features:

- Purpose is to inform, to report, or to explain
- Explanations are precise and accurate
- Examples are given to clarify concepts
- Unfamiliar concepts and vocabulary are defined
- Facts and opinions are clearly distinguished and well documented
- Purpose of questions is clear
- Important points are emphasized
- Information is technically sound
- Legitimate differences are explained and supported
- Recommendations are offered

JOURNAL WRITING

PERSONAL WRITING

STORY WRITING

POETRY WRITING

EXPOSITORY WRITING

PERSUASIVE WRITING

FIGURE 6-1 Kinds of
Expository Writing

Applications	Solutions to problems
Biographical sketches	Story problems
Captions	Memos
Case studies	Newspaper writings
Historical problems	Nonfiction trade books
Local issues	Phone books
National concerns	Photo essays
School problems	Poster displays
Scientific issues	Process journals ("how to")
Collages, montages	Puzzles and word searches
Commentaries	Radio scripts
Concept books	Recipes
Demonstrations	Reference books
Dictionaries	Almanacs
ABC books	Encyclopedias
Visual dictionaries	Thesauruses
Directions	Requests
"How to" manuals	Responses and rebuttals
School or neighborhood maps	Résumés and summaries
Survival manuals	Reviews
Fact books and fact sheets	Books (including texts)
Graffiti	Documentaries
Histories	Films
Political cartoons	Music and dance
TV documentaries	Television programs
Interviews	Science notes
Journals	Lab reports
Labels	Observations
Letters	Reading reports
Informative writings	Science notebooks
To businesses	Surveys
To public officials	Technical writings
Literacy prints	Telegrams
Logos	Text books
Math	Travel guides
Notes, observations	
Record books	

Although these features can be assembled and combined to craft many different genres, the one most commonly found in schools, largely because of the emphasis on testing, is the five-paragraph theme, or, in the case of younger children, the three-paragraph theme. Recognized by its familiar format—an introduction; three to five facts sequenced in a list and connected by the words *first, second, next*; and a conclusion—it is not difficult to find numerous compositions constructed this way, regardless of the topic (see Figure 6–2). Wholesale adoption of this genre by teachers and students makes it the preferred, and sometimes the *only*, model of expository writing. The texts in Figure 6–2 show how two third graders respond to the same expository writing prompt, "Why I like going to the beach." Although sample A is longer than sample B, they are practically carbon copies of one another. Both have topic sentences that tell the reader what the paper is about, three facts that comprise the body of the paper, and a conclusion that restates the main points and topic sentence. They are logical and easy to follow but their formats are so rigidly structured that the reader literally trips over them looking for the

FIGURE 6-2 Sample A: Three-Paragraph Theme, *Why I Like Going to the Beach*, First Draft (Third Grader, Independent Writing) Sample B: Three-Paragraph Theme, *Why I Like Going to the Beach*, First Draft (Third Grader, Independent Writing)

Sample A

Expository Writing

There are three reasons why I like going to the beach. First, I like to collect shells. Next, I love going boating. Last, I like fishing with my dad.

First, I like to collect shells. I like collecting shells because I sometimes find shells. Also, I find very pertty shells on the ground. Last, I very often find a bunch of sanddollars in the water.

Next, I love going boating. Really it's because I get to wach some pretty fish go by. The next thing is because once I saw a dolphin go by the boat, and I almost touched it. Oh and when my dad and me were on the boat we saw a big starfish.

Last, I like going fishing. This is why I like fishing. I like it because once my dad and me and other friends where on the boat, I cought the most fish. Last time we went fishing and I saw a lot of dolphins going by. Afterwords I got a lot, I got ten fish and I gave one to a dolphin.

In conclusion, those are my three reasons why I like going to the beach. When I go again I know what I am going to do. I just can't wait until I go fishing whith my dad, and mabe my big sister can come to. If my mom lets her.

Sample B

Expository Writing

There are three reasons why I like going to the beach. First, I like swimming. Next, I like collecting shells. Last, I like building sandcastles.

First, I like swimming becauses I get to toch the sand with my nose.

Next, I like collecting shells becase some of them are big and pertty or some of them are small and pertty too.

Last, I like building sand castles becase when you put the sandcastles by the water they will fall and get wet and you will have to make anather one.

In conclusion, thats why I like going to the beach.

meaning. Clearly the writers are displaying knowledge for the teacher-as-examiner who is looking for the "correct" form.

Although we ought to retain some of the commendable qualities of the three-paragraph theme (focus, order, explanations, and summaries), limiting student expression to a fixed and inflexible structure that refuses to recede into the background inhibits literacy growth and reinforces writing that lacks spirit and energy. Such texts may be easy to teach and grade, but they do not inspire ownership of ideas or engagement in a process of **inquiry** and critical thinking synonymous with the writing process.

The classic research report is another case in point. Approached by most students with great angst, it often conjures up images of countless hours sitting in the library, plowing through information, and taking copious notes. No wonder it is met with such trepidation, when it ought to be fun, no matter what a child's ability, no matter what the age. Practically speaking, we are all researchers whether shopping for a new computer or weighing the pros and cons of getting a new pet. Researchers are people who are curious and love to learn. In following a passion, they are never bored.

WRITER'S WORKSHOP

Minilessons

As discussed in Chapter 1, teachers conduct countless minilessons even though certain ones seem to be essential to a particular craft. Because expository writing is driven by the quest for information, teachers plan lessons on two major topics: inquiry strategies for producing knowledge and expository structures for shaping it. Together these topics provide alternatives to opening an encyclopedia and paraphrasing other people's ideas.

The Inquiry Cycle

Inquiry, a systematic way of thinking, provides the strategies for constructing one's own knowledge. Although it is often defined in terms of the scientific method—asking questions, formulating hypotheses, collecting, analyzing, and evaluating data—as you will discover in this chapter, these are the same strategies embedded in the expository writing process, especially during the preparatory stage of writing. Similar to the writing process, the inquiry cycle invites writers to complete a project by circling around a topic several times rather than committing to a lockstep linear path.

Asking a Question/Finding a Topic

Questions put the inquiry process into motion and drive the search for information. Yet, regrettably, in some classrooms students spend far too much of their time answering questions instead of asking them (Cazden, 1988; Rosenblatt, 1978, 1984). If students are to follow a passion and develop an area of expertise to proudly share with others, they need to pose their own questions. As suggested in the opening of the chapter, questions come naturally to children. The teacher's job is to show the many ways authors formulate questions to get the creative juices flowing.

> *Wonder questions:* Big questions that they are curious about, such as "Why is the sky blue?"
> *Rhetorical questions:* Self-questioning, such as "Do I really want to own a pet?"
> *"What if" questions:* Prediction questions that pose the world of possibility, such as "What if I were the leader?" or "How would you like to visit Sea World?"
> *Detail questions:* Who, what, when, where, why questions, such as "Who lived there?"
> *Critical questions:* Questions that reexamine the value of rules, norms, or taken-for-granted practices, such as "Why do we have to eat vegetables?"
> *Doubting questions:* Questions that explore an incongruity, dissatisfaction, or contradiction that is perceived as a problem in need of solving, such as "Why do Americans say they are peaceful when they start wars?" (Banks & McGee-Banks, 1999)

Reading and sharing question and answer (Q&A) books also illustrates the questions authors pose. See, for example, the Usborne Starting Point Science series in which answers are provided to questions such as "How does a bird fly?", "Why is night dark?", and "Where does rubbish go?" or the Scholastic series of history titles, including *If You Lived in Colonial Times* (McGovern, 1992), *If You Traveled West in a Covered Wagon* (Levine, 1992), or *If You Sailed on the Mayflower in 1620* (McGovern, 1991), and science titles, such as *How Do Flies Walk Upside Down? Questions and Answers About Insects* (Berger & Berger, 1999b) or *Can It Rain Cats and Dogs? Questions and Answers About Weather* (Berger & Berger, 1999a). Although answers accompany questions in these books, children's unanswered questions will spur similar searches and discoveries. Questions emerge naturally as a result of observation, brainstorming, literary response, or firsthand experiences. Lucy Calkins, a noted writing educator says, "Living like a nonfiction writer means watching for surprise and perplexity and mystery. It means knowing that even the subjects we know very well can be endlessly new to us" (1995, p. 438). Familiar topics, understood only at the surface level, become opportunities for deeper explorations. Conversely, topics students know little about, but that originate out of sheer curiosity, capture the imagination and intensify new interests. A set of questions to expand these interests can be placed on a chart for easy reference (Murray, 1980, p. 69):

- What do I know?
- What don't I know about what I know?
- What do readers need to know about what I know?
- What do I need to know?
- What would I like to know?
- What would I like to do?
- What problems need solving?
- Who might have solutions to those problems?

Requiring children to ask and answer their own questions, not for purposes of testing but for authentic reasons, will place them squarely in the middle of the inquiry process.

Another way to promote inquiry or keep momentum going is to follow heuristic procedures. The questions in Table 6–1 can be used before and during writing and serve the dual function of encouraging discovery and problem solving. Students identify their audience and figure out the information they will need. Students also reflect on their research and alter questions for the particular purpose intended. Typically, this leads to the formation of new ideas or unconventional approaches to old problems.

Hypothesizing

Hypotheses are statements of prediction and are often hunches about the question or problem identified. We are always making rational guesses about happenings in our lives. Suppose you are listening to music on the radio and the sound begins to fade. You guess that it could be poor reception, trouble at the radio station, or a weak battery. You try the radio several days later. When the sound doesn't improve, you decide it must be the battery. You change it, and the volume is restored. You have just

TABLE 6–1 Heuristic Questions for Planning Exposition

What am I being asked to do?	What else can I try?
How can I explore this?	How can I get around that?
What do I want?	What have I got?
What does the reader want?	Do I want to do any more?
What does the reader need to know?	Have I made myself clear?
What isn't working?	

supported your hypothesis. In expository writing, students make hypotheses about the subjects they are studying, for example, what killed the dinosaurs? The children volunteer hypotheses:

- It was the climate
- There was not enough to eat
- Bigger animals ate them

Jotting down as many hypotheses as possible and testing new speculations against an ever-expanding range of collected data, students achieve control over the direction and slant of their research and extend the avenues they might follow to support or reject their claims.

Collecting Data

Although students have a tendency to go directly to books for information, whenever possible they should be encouraged to seek out primary sources, data prepared by authors and communicated directly to readers/viewers through literacy forms (speeches, letters, diaries) and artifacts (human objects, works of art, or photographs). Students might also get involved in firsthand experiences, such as charting plant-growth experiments or weather conditions, measuring heights of peers, or conducting surveys. These types of inquiry tasks remind young writers that they are their first and best resource. Students interview family members and friends or invite local authors, newspaper writers, or university professors to their schools to share expertise on specific subjects. (In advance, the teacher and students can brainstorm questions to ask and the teacher can review the guidelines in Chapter 1 or read professional works such as "The Lively Art of the Interview" (Graves, 1989) or *History Workshop* (Jorgensen, 1993). To encourage self-reliance and communal support, lists of peer names and areas of expertise appear on a chart with a pocket underneath each name for class members to swap book references, Internet sites, or other valuable messages.

Secondary sources, those based on primary evidence but written and reshaped by others, represent the lion's share of information. Books, newspapers, and magazines are the most common (more is said about print resources in the section on *reading*). Some nonfiction books are especially well suited for inquiry because they use primary data as an integral part of their presentation rather than relying solely on author interpretations. Two examples are *The Black Americans: A History in Their Own Words 1619–1983* (Meltzer, 1984) and *Lincoln: A Photobiography* (Freedman, 1988).

Because a large amount of data comes from books and print materials, students must evaluate these sources for currency, objectivity, and accuracy. For instance, they discuss "publication dates" on science books and magazines because facts change rapidly and become outdated by the time they get to print. They also ask questions such as the following:

- Is the author qualified to write about the subject?
- Are there alternative views?
- Is the text biased?
- Is there evidence for what the writer says?

Making notes of the book's title, author's name, date and place of publication, and page numbers is invaluable if students decide to write a bibliography.

The Internet represents another major resource for gathering data. Using scaffolded tasks from an Internet guidebook published by *Class Connect*, third graders take electronic field trips to visit the home of Betsy Ross (http://libertynet.org/iha/betsy/house/room1.html), then compare life in the 1700s to today. They set out on a virtual tour of Philadelphia to explore major landmarks and historical symbols (http://libertynet.org/iha/postcards/hd2.html). Each tour is accompanied by prompts that focus students' attention on key information.

Enlarging on this experience, students access simulated government documents (http://www.earlyamerica.com/earlyamerica/milestones/commonsense/index.html)

and historical newspapers (http://www.earlyamerica.com/earlyamerica/past/index.html), to learn about printing presses, preservation, and archaic language.

Internet sites that encourage interaction with photographs and pictures are particularly useful because they involve more than simply reading; they require visual literacy and viewing skills. For instance, consider how the photos of the Old West and gold rush (http://gopher.nara.gov:70/Oh/inform/dc/audvis/still/amwest.html) acquaint students with data about the gold miners and their living conditions:

- What is the most important thing you see in the photo? Tell two things about the photo that surprise you.
- Find and list two things in the photo that might not be seen if the photo were taken today.
- Give the photo a title that describes it accurately.

Whether the class participates in simulated experiences or explores primary and secondary sources, some advance planning, on the part of the teacher, is necessary to pull together resources for children to review. Table 6–2 provides a list of authentic materials used by researchers. Data exists in many places and students are directed to libraries, archives, museum exhibits, and even attics. Based on what they discover, more refined questions are formulated and topics further explored.

Analyzing and Displaying Data

Once students complete the fact-finding stage, they sort through materials to associate and establish logical relationships. Now the writer must read for information to include in the work. The writing educator Donald Murray (1984) explains what it takes to read as a writer:

> This means that the writer has to be able to sift through random words, phrases, sentences that half work, scribbled outlines, telegraphic notes, incomplete paragraphs, false starts, the way an archeologist has to sift through the excavated refuse of an ancient civilization. The archeologist has to be able to read these fragments to recreate what was; the writer has to read the fragments to recreate what may be. (p. 202)

Teachers model this process with their own notes, showing what to save and what to discard, how to make connections between bits and pieces, how to write and transform the fragments into sensible prose. This constructed knowledge is supplemented with visual displays of information such as charts and think sheets.

An attribute chart or semantic features analysis (Johnson & Pearson, 1984), as shown in Figure 6–3, helps separate and organize data into manageable units that can be examined for patterns. Writers list traits or characteristics of subjects they are studying and then indicate the presence or absence of these features on a chart using checkmarks, symbols, or other means. Let's consider the details about snakes displayed in Figure 6–3.

On the top and bottom 5×5 grids, the rows identify facts about snakes and the columns list kinds of snakes. In the first grid, X's indicate the presence of the feature, whereas in the second grid words do, instead. For example, some snakes are 2 to 4 inches long, and others are 6 to 18 inches long; some snakes' young are born alive, whereas others are hatched from eggs. Displaying data as graphs, tables, time lines, matrices, or inverted triangles (large general topics narrowed down to specific ones) provides a visual interpretation of relevant questions and shows where more information is needed. Classifications of data may serve to later organize paragraphs in a text and guide decisions about the best way to display and communicate findings.

Evaluating Findings

Based on the analysis, students accept or reject their initial hunches. They detect faulty thinking or elaborate on previous understanding, asking themselves what they now believe, what they can conclude, or what they will accept based on available evidence. They may return to gather more data, correct predictions, or ask new questions. At some

TABLE 6-2 Authentic Research Sources for Reading and Writing

Books

Anthropology	History	Nonfiction
Autobiography	Legends	Physical science
Biography	Myths	Poetry
Fiction	Natural science	Political science
Geography		

Experiences

Demonstrations	Family vacations	Laboratory
Experiments	Field trips	Observation museums

Media

Films	Radio	Television
Filmstrips	Slides	Videodiscs
Microfilms	Tape recorder	Videos

Newspapers and Magazines

Book, movie, play reviews	Narratives in magazines
Cartoons	Political news—local, state, national, international
Editorials	Stock market reports
Feature articles	Want ads
Financial sections	Weather reports

Primary Sources

Architecture	Family documents	Paintings
Artifacts	Government documents	Photographs
Buildings	Historical markers	Plaques
Business ledgers	Interviews	Record books
Cemetery records	Journals	Relics
Church records	Letters	Ruins
Clothing	Logs	Samples
Coins	Memoirs	Speeches
Cornerstones	Military records	Surveys
Court documents	Monuments	Telephone conversations
Diaries	Organizational records	Tools

Reference Materials

Almanacs	Biographies	Histories
Atlases	Encyclopedias	Textbooks
Bibliographies		

Symbolic Sources

Blueprints	Globes	Photographs
Calendars	Graphs	Scales
Cartoons	Illustrations	Thermometers
Census records	Maps	Topographical sketches
Diagrams	Models	Works of art
Formulas	Music	

Technology

CD-ROM	Hypertext	World Wide Web
Computer programs		

Source: Reprinted by permission from *The Theme Immersion Compendium for Social Studies Teaching* by Maryann Manning, Gary Manning, and Roberta Long. Copyright © 1997 by Maryann Manning, Gary Manning, and Roberta Long. Published by Heinemann, a division of Reed Elsevier Inc., Portsmouth, NH.

FIGURE 6-3
Semantic Features
Analysis

Snakes	Poisonous	7 inches or longer in length	Young born alive	Recognizable design and color on skin
Boa constrictor		X	X	X
Garter snake			X	X
Mud snake				X
Rattlesnake	X	X	X	X

Snakes	Poisonous	Length	Young born	Design and color
Boa constrictor	no	6–18″	alive	striped
Garter snake	no	2–4″	alive	striped
Mud snake	no	4–6″	from eggs	red diamonds
Rattle snake	yes	3–8″	alive	V-shaped bands and rattler tail

point, however, when the learner is satisfied that his questions have been answered, he is ready to write the report.

Expository Text Structures

All along the inquiry process, as facts are being gathered, organized, and analyzed, students are drafting and taking written notes to shape the material and construct knowledge. At some point, when they decide to culminate the research, they must figure out the best structure for presenting their findings to an audience. Just as a building's framework connects rooms together and gives it form, "a text's structure binds several segments together, and keeps it from being a random ordering of sentences" (Moore, 1995, p. 599). Expository text structures are the backbone of nonfiction and, when effectively implemented, allow the writer to present large amounts of information to others. Some of the text structures writers typically use in exposition are description (lists or attributes) and conceptual organization (classified and categorized descriptions), sequence (chronology), compare/contrast (alike or different), cause/effect (one thing affects another), and problem/solution. For instance, if writers are exploring similarities and differences between frogs and toads, reptiles and amphibians, or Floridians and Californians, it makes sense to follow a compare and contrast organization. However, if they are listing characteristics, features, and details about an animate object or animal, a descriptive structure may be more appropriate. Researchers suggest that children who are aware of text structures typically found in nonfiction material will be better prepared to write texts of their own (Armbruster, Anderson, & Ostertag, 1989; Englert & Hiebert, 1984; Englert, Raphael, & Anderson, 1992; McGee, 1982; McGee & Richgels, 1986). In minilessons, the teacher will want to acquaint children with text structures and model strategies that signal when these structures are being used. Several are considered next.

Description

Description in nonfiction involves listing characteristics and presenting facts about a person, place, event, or thing. The kinds of questions that exemplify description include the following:

- What is X?
- How would you define X?
- What are X's features?

Most writers rely on observation through the five senses to describe the thing they are studying. In nonfiction, where accuracy dominates, description might take the form of numbers, sizes, dimensions, dates, and other exact or precise facts rather than relying on emotive, aesthetic, or imaginary details. For example, compare the following two descriptions.

1. Florida's coastline stretches 1,350 miles along the Atlantic Ocean and the Gulf of Mexico.
2. Florida's warm sunshine touched my skin and brightened my spirits.

In the first example, likely to appear in a textbook, the writer sticks to the facts to provide information. The second description, likely to appear in fiction or poetry, paints sensory images to evoke a mood or feeling through personification *(sunshine touches)* and aesthetic vocabulary *(warm, spirits)*. Although there are no hard and fast rules about the presence or absence of variant modes of description in nonfiction, the context in which certain details appear and fulfill reader expectations can serve as a litmus test for their use.

Descriptive sentences carry factual messages and further the overall expository aim of the text. When multiple paragraphs arise, writers often use cue words to tell the reader that the text is being organized in a certain way, in this case, description.

A number of
As an example
Characteristics are
Features are
For example, for instance
Several
Small sized, medium sized, large sized
Tallest, shortest

These and many other words facilitate the reader's navigation of the text and help him remember and comprehend information. From the standpoint of writers, however, these words bring coherence to the work (transitions within and across sentences) and offer readers a glimpse into the author's thinking patterns.

When students are deciding whether to use description to organize a text, sometimes they wait to see what details emerge from the compiled data (form follows function). In other cases, they determine from the outset that this is the structure they will follow. Certain open-ended prompts can indicate ahead of time the direction in which the topic and content might go.

- All about _____ (dinosaurs, frogs, etc.)
- My favorite _____
- Interesting _____
- Types of _____

Any number of topics can fill the slots of these open-ended prompts, giving children choices while steering them into the descriptive mode used in exposition.

Children as early as first grade can begin to write expository description by labeling and creating entries for visual dictionaries, such as the one in Figure 6–4. Bound books of children's labeled pictures can share the bookshelf with concept selections such as *Tool*

FIGURE 6-4   A Visual Dictionary Entry on Dogs

Book (Gibbons, 1982), which is an assortment of tools classified by name, or *Spiders* (Gibbons, 1993), which shows illustrations of spider body parts and types of webs with words to accompany and distinguish one from the other. Children of all ages find labeling an important aspect of description. Graphic aids and labels are plentiful in complex nonfiction whether the author illustrates the anatomy of a flower, drawing a picture and listing parts such as *leaves, roots, stamen,* and *petal* or writes an entire architectural description of a castle with labels such as *drawbridge, moat, tower,* and *dungeon* to accompany the narrative explanation (McCauley, 1977).

In addition to using description for captions and illustrations, teachers will find multiple descriptions pulled together around a central controlling theme such as how animals snag their prey (*Catching a Meal,* Bennett, 1994), what animals eat (*When Hunger Calls,* Kitchen, 1994), varieties of bears (polar, grizzly, black; *Bears,* Barrett, 1988), or types of fish (angel fish, minnows, *A Swim Through the Sea,* Pratt, 1994). The author may create a conceptual or thematic structure that answers the following questions:

- What makes X an X?
- What are the kinds of X?
- How are the X's the same?
- What does X do, or how does X act?

For example, in *The Big Bug Book* (Facklam, 1994), details of which appear on the graphic organizer shown in Figure 6–5, each of several insects has its own encyclopedic entry yet all are included in a single book. A graphic organizer such as this associates details or categories around a thematic idea that structures a written piece.

Description is a big part of trade books, textbooks, dictionaries, almanacs, fact books, and encyclopedias. In many ABC books, such as *Ashanti to Zulu: African Traditions*

FIGURE 6-5
Description
Organization

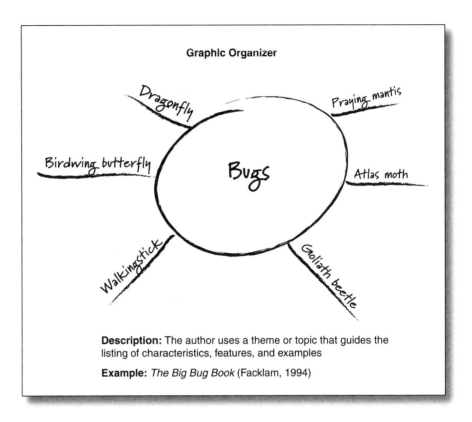

Graphic Organizer

Bugs

Dragonfly

Praying mantis

Birdwing butterfly

Atlas moth

Walkingstick

Goliath beetle

Description: The author uses a theme or topic that guides the listing of characteristics, features, and examples

Example: *The Big Bug Book* (Facklam, 1994)

(Musgrove, 1976), *Animalia* (Base, 1987), and *The Path of the Quiet Elk: A Native American Alphabet Book* (Stroud, 1996), each letter of the alphabet becomes the device for organizing and presenting descriptions.

Sequence/Chronology

The sequence structure lists items; events; processes and happenings by calendar days; clock time; numerical order; time lines; and concepts such as today, yesterday, or tomorrow (similar to present, past, and future tenses). A writing genre that is entirely built around the sequence structure is the "how to" report. In a "how to" report the writer describes a process or common event (following a recipe, preparing for a camping trip, riding a bike, or training a dog) in step-by-step, or time order, fashion. Some questions that are associated with this structure include the following:

- Does X come before Y?
- What follows X?
- Where is X in the arrangement?
- When did X happen?
- Did X happen before Y?
- Did X happen after Y?

Several children's books are available for presenting an entire text in the sequence/chronology structure. For example, *A Beekeeper's Year* (Johnson, 1994) shows how the chores and duties of a beekeeper are arranged over time. In Aliki's (1989) *The King's Day: Louis XIV of France*, the reader is privy to the activities that fill a king's day from morning until night. Print materials, such as a health pamphlet that details the steps to take in the case of choking, or a set of directions that specify how to play and follow the rules of a board game, offer authentic examples of the sequence structure.

The sequence structure can be visually displayed as an outline or a series of linear steps as shown in Figure 6–6.

FIGURE 6-6
Sequence Organization

> **Event Organizer**
>
> 1. A beekeeper and his bees
> 2. A beekeeper's tools
> 3. Looking for brood
> 4. A "queenright hive"
> 5. Other spring jobs
> 6. Bees at work
> 7. The nectar flow
> 8. Preventing swarms
> 9. Supering up
> 10. Taking honey
> 11. In the honey house
> 12. Chores in autumn
> 13. The long, cold winter
>
> **Description**: The author lists items or events in numerical or chronological order
>
> **Example**: *A Beekeeper's Year* (Johnson, 1994)

Although sequence can order an entire expository text, it may also embed itself in other genre structures such as a biography, historical fiction, or scientific report (lab experiment). Certain cue words signal the reader that the writing is organized by logical sequence or time. Here are a few of them.

After, after a few days, after a short time, at last
Finally
First, second, third …
In conclusion, in closing, last of all
In the past
Next, then, finally
Starting with
To sum up, to review

Sequence is a structure that pervades activities in the classroom from following a daily schedule to checking for comprehension in texts: What happened first, next, and last? For a writer it is one of the many ways to present information.

Compare/Contrast

Comparison and contrast is a structure that signals the examination of two or more items to establish how they are alike or different. Writers compare new things to what is already known, make connections between items, or ensure that certain points stand out.

- Are X and Y associated?
- Are X and Y different?
- What group of things does X belong to?
- How is X related to Y? What is X similar to? Different from?

Authors develop whole books around the compare/contrast structure, such as *Animals in the Wild: Crocodile and Alligator* (Serventy, 1984) or *I Am the Dog, I Am the Cat* (Hall, 1994). If students want to write a compare and contrast essay, they can compare two books on the same topic, two books by the same author, or two books with similar conflicts or settings. Farris and Cooper (1997) suggest using a collection of texts to compare regions across the country in a unit they call "around the world with exciting books."

Northeast: Winter Barn (Parnell, 1986) takes place in New England
Southeast: On Granddaddy's Farm (Allen, 1989) takes place in Tennessee
Midwest: Plowie: A Story From the Prairie (Kirkpatrick, 1994) takes place in Iowa
Southwest: The Best Town in the World (Baylor, 1983) takes place in Texas
Far West: Long Ago in Oregon (Lewis, 1987) takes place in Oregon

When it comes to comparing things, the possibilities are endless: favorite movies, tracks or footprints of animals, toys in different cultures, colors of caterpillars, or characters in literature.

Children can frame topics ahead of time to guide the way they explore and present information. Open-ended prompts start them thinking in terms of compare/contrast.

- Best and worst _____
- A comparison of _____ and _____
- Do's and don'ts of _____
- Strengths and weaknesses of _____
- _____ versus _____

These prompts don't tell children what to write about but position them for researching and organizing a topic. During the inquiry process children use graphic organizers, such as the Venn diagram, to consider similarities and differences (see Figure 6–7). A Venn diagram is two overlapping circles that show relationships, characteristics, or attributes. The intersecting portion represents common features, whereas the nonintersecting parts show differences. To compare and contrast, the writer must be able to identify the critical attributes of objects, ideas, and other entities (e.g., two different reptiles' eating habits, behaviors, habitats, or physical characteristics). Children use these similarities and differences to organize paragraphs in texts.

FIGURE 6-7
Compare/Contrast
Organization

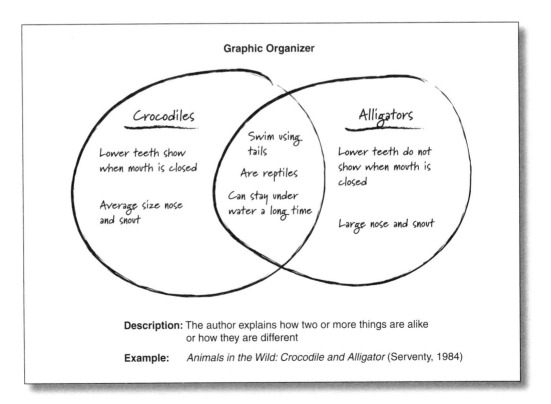

Graphic Organizer

Crocodiles
- Lower teeth show when mouth is closed
- Average size nose and snout

(intersection)
- Swim using tails
- Are reptiles
- Can stay under water a long time

Alligators
- Lower teeth do not show when mouth is closed
- Large nose and snout

Description: The author explains how two or more things are alike or how they are different

Example: *Animals in the Wild: Crocodile and Alligator* (Serventy, 1984)

As with the other expository structures, the compare/contrast structure involves cue words, a few of which are provided here:

Alike, different from
Although
And yet
Even though
In much the same way, instead
Looks like, same as
On the other hand, on the contrary
Unlike, whereas

In addition to these cue words, students may want to review the inflectional endings *-er* and *-est (faster, slower, tallest, biggest)* or invent similes and metaphors *(my cat is like a lion)* to compare or show relationships. These strategies remind the writer that compare/contrast represents not only a structure for an entire text but also a thinking pattern that reveals itself in words, sentences, and paragraphs.

Cause / Effect

Cause/effect is a relationship in which one thing may have a resulting impact on another. Many firsthand experiences prepare children for writing cause and effect. In science, for instance, students hypothesize about the effects objects will have in the presence of a magnet (will the objects attract or repel?) or they consider how certain objects react in water (do they float or sink?). Cause and effect is also demonstrated in art class when students combine paints and discover that yellow and violet make gray, or blue and yellow make green. Mathematics activities likewise reinforce cause and effect when children place items of differing weights on a teeter totter made from a ruler and observe what happens. In many ways, these experiences are like expanded versions of the open-ended prompts in that they position children for writing cause and effect simply by the way they are set up. Following are some of the questions frequently used for probing cause and effect:

- What causes X?
- What conditions make X possible?
- If X then Y?
- Does X relate to Y?
- What can you conclude from X?

An example of an entire book structured as cause/effect is *The Amazon Rain Forest and Its People* (Morrison, 1993). The first part of the book details how people are destroying the vegetation and wildlife, and the second part proposes how they can save the rain forest. A graphic organizer that displays this structure is found in Figure 6–8.

Because cause/effect examples are oftentimes indistinguishable from problem/solution, it is best to think about expository structures as falling along a continuum, where they overlap or intersect with one another. The cue words to use in cause and effect include some of the following:

Accordingly
Because, because of
For this reason
Gradually
If/then
Little by little
On account of
Since/therefore

These words show that causal relationships exist between events. Linking sentences and paragraphs, a writer can explain how several causes produce one effect or how one

FIGURE 6-8   Cause/Effect Organization

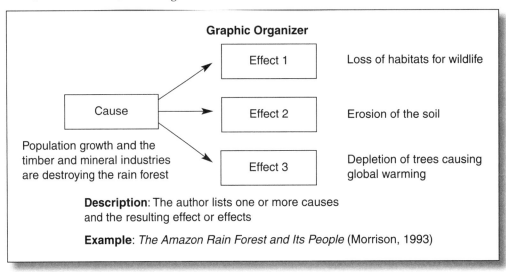

cause creates multiple effects. By focusing attention on consequences and outcomes, a reader may be moved to find remedies or take corrective action.

Problem/Solution

Problem/solution involves analyzing and resolving a perplexing or difficult situation. It answers some of the following questions:

- Why is X a problem?
- What can be done to solve X?
- What are some concerns associated with X?
- How can X be solved?

Sizing up a problem and seeing it in its broadest possible context enables children to select information relevant to it. Whether problems are personal (curfews), school related (vandalism), or global (saving endangered species), students debate them with classmates and write journal entries describing possible solutions. It is worth reminding children that they first became acquainted with problem/solution through stories. Questions dealing with conflict and resolution include the following:

- Is this a problem for the character? Would this be a problem for you?
- Why was it a problem?
- How did the character solve the problem?

Social and community events in the newspaper are another source for identifying and discussing problems and what might be done to solve them.

Throughout these experiences, students learn that problems are relative, depending on point of view or comparative magnitude. Knowing how to identify and formulate a problem initiates the inquiry process. Certain prompts can move problem/solution writing along:

- Six ways to stop _____
- Deciding on _____
- Finding solutions for _____
- Ways of handling _____

The teacher introduces the children to nonfiction titles that capture the problem/solution format such as *On the Brink of Extinction: The California Condor* (Arnold, 1993).

FIGURE 6-9   Problem/Solution Organization

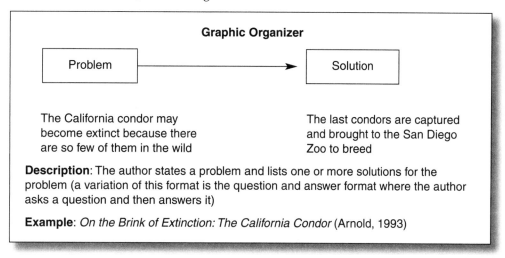

Figure 6–9 illustrates the problem/solution strategy, and cue words that suggest the presence of this structure include some of the following:

A case in point
Although it is true
As a result
As a result of
For one thing
In effect
On account of
To reexamine

At this point, it is important to emphasize that, although we have discussed common structures in their purest forms, it is more likely that all five structures will be combined within a single piece, as shown in Table 6–3. Not only are these structures represented as whole texts but they are also found across paragraphs or within a single sentence. Consider, for example, the following sentences:

Descriptive sentence: A hurricane is a severe storm whose winds have reached or exceed 74 miles per hour.
Sequence sentence: You know a hurricane is coming, first, by a change in the waves, then dark and gloomy clouds, and finally the rain.
Compare/contrast sentence: Winds that average more than 75 miles per hour are no longer tropical storms but hurricanes.
Cause/effect sentence: Hurricanes cause severe winds that destroy homes and threaten human lives.
Problem/solution sentence: If people live in an area that is at risk from hurricanes, it is important to pay extra attention to weather advisories during this time.

As these examples suggest, writers draw on multiple strategies to build text. Although the structures provide good organizers for writing, they are not, by far, the only ones available and they are not exclusive to expository text.

Reading

Noted literature educator Donna Norton (1999) sums up the wide range of nonfiction genres in a single phrase: "from who's-who to how-to" (p. 670). The next two sections explain how to use expository genres as print models for writing and study strategies.

TABLE 6-3 Combining Expository Structures in a Single Text	
Description (What is a hurricane?)	Hurricanes are natural phenomena that occur every year at about the same time. They are powerful, whirling storms whose winds reach or exceed 74 miles per hour.
Sequence (What is the order of events that indicate a hurricane is coming?)	The first sign of a hurricane is a change in the waves. Where once they broke gently against the beach, they are now larger and more violent. The second sign is in the sky. Dark and gloomy, the clouds start gathering thickly over the ocean. Then they roll inland, blackening the sky. At last it begins to rain, not just a gentle spring rain but a powerful torrent.
Cause/Effect (How do hurricanes develop and what effects result?)	Hurricanes develop from easterly winds. These long, narrow regions of low pressure occur in ocean winds called trade winds. Easterly winds may grow into a tropical depression. When the tropical depression begins to sustain winds with an average speed of at least 39 miles per hour, it is no longer a tropical depression. It becomes a tropical storm.
Compare/Contrast (What is the difference between a tropical storm and a hurricane?)	Many tropical storms simply die out, never to be heard from again. But others grow strong. The winds blow faster and faster as more and more air containing hot water vapor is sucked up into the clouds. When the winds in the tropical storm average more than 75 miles per hour, the storm becomes a hurricane.
Problem/Solution (What dangers are posed by hurricanes and how can people prepare for them?)	The greatest single destructive force in a hurricane is a storm surge, an increase in the water levels brought about by strong winds causing the sea level to rise. Of every ten people who die in a hurricane, nine are killed by the storm surge. When people hear that a hurricane watch is in effect, they should check that the family car has gas in it, in case it becomes necessary to evacuate unexpectedly. Stock up on emergency supplies, such as medicines and first-aid kits. Put fresh batteries in flashlights, in case the lights go out, and in portable radios, to listen to emergency broadcasts in the absence of power. Tape windows or close shutters to avoid broken glass.

Nonfiction Print Models

Although nonfiction has many writing applications, one of its chief functions is to provide print models that not only introduce content but also illustrate how exposition is structured to communicate information effectively. With first graders, the teacher checks whether students can distinguish fiction from nonfiction. He reads three different books about bears on three consecutive days: On the first day, he reads an informational text, *Bears* (Barrett, 1998); on the second, poetic fiction, *Brown Bear, Brown Bear* (Martin, 1967); and on the third, a fictional story, *The Berenstein Bears and Too Much TV* (Berenstein & Berenstein, 1989). After the children hear all three, the following questions are asked:

- Which one is probably true?
- Which one was most likely written by a scientist? A storyteller?
- Which one uses language to have fun?
- Which one is make-believe?
- Which one would you choose if you wanted to learn about bears?
- Which one is the least believable?

Through questioning, the children become aware of authors' purposes for writing and of differences between real and imaginary.

Another worthwhile minilesson is to share books that inspire questions or put the inquiry process in motion. A nonfiction book that entices the reader with a question in the title, *Why Did the Dinosaurs Disappear? The Great Dinosaur Mystery* (Berger & Berger, 1995), builds an entire text on this query. The fictional story, *Homeplace* (Dragonwagon, 1996), presents an interesting anomaly that leads to asking questions and putting pieces of a puzzle together. A family is taking a stroll on a Sunday afternoon, and they come upon a stone foundation and some daffodils growing in an otherwise barren place. As the story unfolds and artifacts are uncovered, questions and conjectures emerge to explain the identity and whereabouts of the previous occupants.

A trip to the library to browse book titles will generate ideas. Trade books, once in limited supply, are now written on nearly every subject imaginable. Contemporary trade books abound with compelling content and visually attractive illustrations in forms suitable for all readers, including concept books (*26 Letters and 99 Cents*, Hoban, 1985), ABC explanation books (*Ashanti to Zulu: African Traditions*, Musgrove, 1976), fact books (*Guinness Book of World Records*, McFarlan, 2001), and praiseworthy series (*Eyewitness* books, Dorling Kindersley, or *The Magic School Bus*, Scholastic). Equally engaging are newspapers (*The Weekly Reader*, Scholastic), magazines (*Cobblestone*, Cobblestone Publishing), and reference books (dictionaries, almanacs, encyclopedias). Topics and research questions come from everywhere. In fact, if teachers take time to read aloud excerpts from magazine or newspaper articles on a regular basis as adults do when they want to share something of interest with a friend or family member, they are likely to stimulate curiosities and develop the student's "ear" for informative writing. Keeping literary response journals or learning logs handy will help children capture interpretations and document what they have heard.

Many of the students begin their research by reading authors with similar interests to their own.

Read these authors	If you are interested in
Rhoda Blumberg	U.S. history
Kathryn Lasky	Archaeology and ancient civilizations
Patricia Lauber	Science
Rick Reilly	Sports
Seymour Simon	Earth science
Diane Stanley	Arts and humanities

Reading multiple books by the same author shows children what it is like to have a sustained passion that is explored at deeper and deeper levels on many topics related to a subject. It also provides them with documentation of an author's ongoing development as a writer and scientist/historian/artist. If students follow their own passions, they too will become experts with a traceable lineage.

Lastly, nonfiction opens a window for viewing all the expository structures discussed previously. Children consider the decisions authors make about the structures for their writing and identify how these structures work in sentences and paragraphs. For instance, they ask "What is it about this information that is best revealed through compare/contrast? Sequence? What strategies did the author use to achieve this structure?"

Study Strategies

Children who read nonfiction assume what is called an efferent stance (Rosenblatt, 1978, 1984). This means they read for purposes of acquiring information and increasing their body of knowledge. Since reading nonfiction and other secondary sources is an essential part of inquiry *and* the writing process, teachers share study strategies for gathering information and note taking. Study strategies are "all those things one can do to apply literacy to one's best advantage in a school setting" (Manzo & Manzo, 1995, p. 413). For the writer this may mean learning to ask questions before reading, using chapter overviews or headings in a book, identifying technical terms, deciphering graphs and charts, or reading end-of-chapter summaries. A common study strategy practiced in reading is to transform chapter subtitles into questions to predict and guide a search. An example from *Extinction Is Forever* (Silver, 1995) illustrates this:

Chapter Subtitles	Changed to Questions
Digging Up the Past	What has been found by digging up the past?
Extinction Is a Part of Nature	In what way is extinction a part of nature?
Extinction Is Forever	Why is extinction forever?

As children read books written by novelists, historians, geographers, and anthropologists, they also ask questions that go behind the text.

- What questions did the writer ask?
- What does the author think is important? How do you know?
- How did the author deal with conflicting accounts of the same thing?
- How did the writer discover information and form opinions?

These focus writers' attention on ways to approach their own investigations and decision making.

In the fifth grade, students use a **mnemonic** to remember information that they read. It is called SCAN: *S* stands for surveying headings, *C* for capturing the captions and visuals, *A* for attacking boldface words, and *N* for noting and reading chapter questions. Having a routine procedure to follow increases student awareness of expository structure and guides comprehension.

Another way to prepare students to read content-area and informational texts across disciplines is to introduce anticipation guides (Head & Readence, 1986). The teacher develops a set of statements about a book's subject to discuss before reading. The statements are usually those that students "think" they know the answers to but may need to verify. An example is provided in Figure 6–10.

FIGURE 6-10
Anticipation Guide

Before Reading	After Reading	
_____	_____	Cockroaches have been on Earth since the dinosaurs.
_____	_____	Bugs and insects are the same thing.
_____	_____	Most large bugs live in the tropical rain forest.
_____	_____	There are thousands of kinds of bugs.
_____	_____	A bug can be as big as a mouse.

Students decide beforehand which statements they believe are true. After reading and discussing the text, they defend correct responses or note misconceptions. Anticipation guides stimulate interest in reading and foreshadow the main ideas. Before reading, students predict information, tap into their background knowledge, and set purposes. After reading, they compare responses and discuss content. A variety of preview guides for dealing with content can be found in the informative and comprehensive text *Teaching Children to Be Literate* by Manzo and Manzo (1995).

Showing children how to glean key ideas from a typical textbook will help them organize and shape their writing into an expository style. Students of all ages can go on a "text walk" through a book to survey its overall landscape including table of contents, units, sections, subheadings, italicized words, glossaries, index, graphs, and tables. A magazine feature presents short narratives using illustrations and captions; a newspaper article highlights its leads, bylines, and 5W's. Many pamphlets and reference materials are highly visual with only a modicum of print (consulting the study skills section of any reading textbook yields numerous methods for previewing and **scanning** many types of materials).

Composing

Prewriting

When teachers involve children in the inquiry process, they are preparing them for writing. Children identify topics (some of which are listed in Table 6–4) in their personal and school lives by looking for interests in everything they do and say: their class presentations, the books they read, and the subjects they talk about. If students select topics that teachers know little about, the teacher becomes the learner and the student becomes the expert. Empowered by the switching of roles, students teach what they

TABLE 6-4 Subject Matter Topics			
Social Studies	**Science**	**Math and Technology**	**Literature and Art**
Famous Americans	Plants	Spending money	Well-known painters
Rivers and streams, mountains and oceans	Earthquakes, hurricanes, and natural disasters	Explaining word problems	Favorite music
Buildings and statues in the community	Planets, galaxies, and space	Having an allowance	Navajo ceremonial clothes
Hieroglyphics	Animals	Using the Internet	Mythical figures (vampires, monsters)
Antarctica	Insects	Playing computer games	Favorite characters
Seeing eye dogs	Endangered species	Measuring objects	Caldecott books
Olympic events	Inventions (computer, paper)	Finding shapes in nature	Author study, illustrator study
People around the world	Foods around the world	Using surveys and graphs	Famous detectives
Genealogy	Eating well	Employing probability and making guesses	Reading/writing habits

FIGURE 6-11 Thematic Web

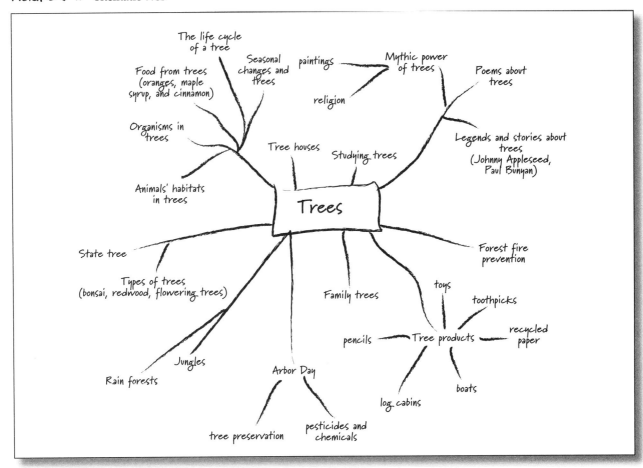

have learned to others. Meanwhile, teachers share their own passions with students and lead by example. Being passionate about something is always catching!

Writing in social studies and science offers yet another chance for students to learn subject matter and discover new topics. These topics are particularly effective when they are part of a theme because the broad spectrum of subtopics accommodates a variety of personal interests and student choice. For instance, the subject of trees can be expanded to reveal any number of subtopics that might be of interest to a writer (see Figure 6–11).

Having settled on a topic, students practice strategies for the informal writing that occurs during the inquiry process. Note taking allows writers to remember information from print materials or monitor visual presentations or lectures. A fourth-grade teacher shows students how to take notes using information downloaded from the Internet. Instead of copying or paraphrasing sentences, students employ shortcuts:

- Underline outstanding details and definitions
- Annotate with comments in the margins
- Place vertical bars at the sides of paragraphs
- Circle words or "star" certain sentences
- Underscore in different colors

They codify important ideas with shorthand symbols such as initials, asterisks, abbreviations, or invented spellings (e.g., *cmctn* for *communication; w* for *with*). Placing the

FIGURE 6–12   K–W–L Chart

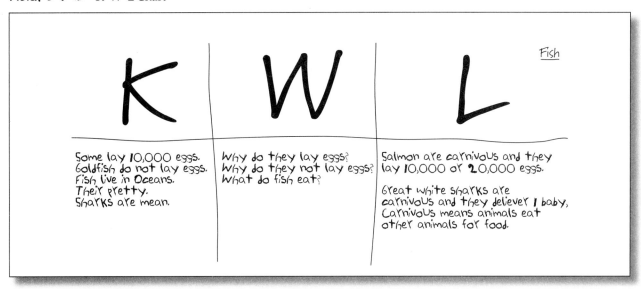

marked note sheets in a three-ring binder with subdividers makes it easy for them to be located and examined later. Although Internet materials can be marked up, school books cannot. If students cannot write directly in a book, they can place sticky notes on the pages or use colored, transparent, highlighting tape that is made for easy removal.

Because there is no one way of taking notes, the teacher introduces a combination of methods and students select the ones that work best for them. However, as part of all note-taking lessons the teacher provides specific direction on how to write summaries. He projects a text on a transparency and shows the children how to skim for main ideas and supporting details. (As a rule, key points are usually found in the author's organizational plan, the first and last sentences, or the subheadings.) Removing the text from view, the teacher writes what he remembers, choosing his own words to avoid plagiarism and pointing out how he captures major ideas or interesting details without repeating. The summary is then compared with the original to check that major points have been retained. Students practice summarizing from the texts and graphic organizers they develop. Summarizing is a valuable strategy in its own right because it often concludes a report. It takes skill to recognize material that is worth condensing in one's own words. Teaching children to separate relevant from irrelevant details based on purpose will help writers stay focused. Remember, however, that what is considered "relevant" or "important" will vary as students come from diverse backgrounds and cultures.

Because taking notes longhand can be a time-consuming and arduous process for young writers, there are other forms of note taking that teachers can share, including graphic organizers such as webs and maps (see Chapter 1) or the Venn diagram shown in Figure 6–7.

A strategy, popular across all grade levels, is the knowledge or K–W–L chart (an acronym that stands for *Know, Want* to know, *Learn*). The K–W–L chart (Ogle, 1986) gives students ownership of their learning and provides insights into their abilities to draw on background knowledge for prediction. Based on facts compiled while completing this chart, the teacher prepares resources appropriate to student needs and interests. Usually, a K–W–L chart is presented in three separate columns to guide inquiry (see Figure 6–12). Prior to reading, children draw on previous experiences or interests

FIGURE 6-13
Prewriting Activities
for Expository Writing

Conducting interviews
Creating artwork
Developing graphic organizers/charts
    5W (who, what, where, when, why) questions
    K–W–L charts
    Time lines
    Venn diagrams
    Webs and clusters
Doing quickwrites
Finding resources
Inviting guest speakers
Making learning scrapbooks
Making outlines
Posing *I search* questions
Reading
    Skimming/scanning
Reading/keeping journals
Taking field trips
Taking notes
Using media
    Computers
    Film
    TV
Using the Internet

FIGURE 6-13
Prewriting Activities for Expository Writing

and list in the first column what they already know about the topic. In the second column, thoughtful questions suggesting purposes for reading propel the quest for information and offer a means for sifting through materials more efficiently. After reading, students complete the third column (information learned) with answers to the specific questions posed.

When a single reference is insufficient for finding answers to the questions, or if students want to confirm the accuracy of prior knowledge, they research the topic further and consult multiple sources. From time to time, teachers review the quality of responses on the K–W–L charts and make note of this in anecdotal records. K–W–L charts are a great way to provide a structure for learning and develop research skills as well.

Beyond note taking and K–W–L charts, there are numerous other activities for accessing information (see Figure 6–13). For instance, when students go on a field trip, they directly witness facts and details that they can refer to for writing. At a museum, they might examine an artifact and write notes about it. On a tour of the local newspaper building, they might observe the process of publishing the daily newspaper.

Listening to musical lyrics increases vocabulary and reveals information about its period. For example, in *Multiple Forms of Literacy* (Piazza, 1999), a third-grade class studies the U.S. cowhand by singing selections from *Songs of the Wild West* (Axelrod, 1991) and piecing together a portrait of the cowgirl and cowboy in the mood and spirit of the Old West. After all four verses of "Home on the Range" are sung, the teacher asks the following questions:

- What is a range?
- What words in the song describe the range?

- What words in the song are new for you (e.g., zephyr was a god of the west wind and refers to a breeze from the west; balm means soothing)?
- Why do you think this song was written?

Information from the songs are enhanced by watching TV and film clips of westerns on DVDs or videos to provoke some of the following questions:

- Was the information accurate? How can you find out?
- Whose point of view is projected in this film? Are there others we should know about?
- What does the film assume the viewer already knows?
- What other information is needed?
- Does the filmmaker manipulate facts and evidence to create a good story?
- How accurate are the details of the period (clothing, setting, dialogue)?
- How are all histories selective in terms of what is presented and how?

Selecting resources other than books (music, media) accommodates various learning styles. If the class is studying a certain part of the world, there is nothing like a National Geographic film or documentary for finding a topic or beginning research.

Drafting

When students draft, they usually have to juggle many things all at once. That's why it is a good idea to keep resources handy—notes, graphic organizers, or other raw material—to support memory and help writers get started. Reading these resources, however, requires strategies that most adult writers take for granted. Donald Murray (1984) illuminates some of these strategies:

> It's easy to read a text after it has been drafted, but the writer has to develop the skill to read a text when there is no text. The writer has to see which words are code words, words that have special meaning for the writer when they appear in the notebook. The writer has to pick the phrase that gives the hint of a special meaning or an effective voice. The writer has to see how a fragment can be developed and to spot the meaningful connections that may be made between specific details. (p. 202)

It is up to the teacher to demonstrate how to carefully select language for the text being created. They might begin by having students respond to prompts such as "Underline a word from your notes that you think should be defined in your writing" or "Choose a sentence that you think would make the best lead for your writing." Learning to read for writing requires special training and children need instruction and practice on how it is done.

Rereading professional words during drafting is also encouraged. Some writers return to reading nonfiction to determine how authors create strong leads and conclusions. For instance, in the book *Forest Fire* (Lampton, 1991) the author uses description to set the scene:

> It was a long, hot summer. It hadn't rained in weeks, and the forest was parched with thirst. The debris that lay between the trees and shrubs were bone dry, like old paper. Even the leaves on the trees were becoming brittle. All that was needed to start a fire was a single spark. (p. 27)

Such an introduction captures the essence of the book and invites the reader to enter the story to learn about forest fires. The book concludes as follows:

> Fires have been around much longer than human beings have been, and they are part of the life of the forest. By learning about fires and allowing beneficial fires to burn instead of stopping them, we can help maintain the balance that nature created long before we arrived on this planet. (p. 57)

This conclusion ends on an upbeat note by reassuring the reader that some forest fires are natural occurrences. Beginnings and endings are framed differently in various books. Children can make lists of ways in which nonfiction authors begin books:

> *Setting:* A yellow dandelion appears in the middle of a smooth green lawn. A wildflower pushes its way up through a crack in a city sidewalk. (Bix, 1982)
> *Personification:* A warm and gentle wind is blowing today. My leaves are rustling in the breeze. It's a great day to be a tree. (Kallen, 1993)
> *Fantasy:* Imagine traveling back in time 65 million years. Your mission is to find out what really happened to the dinosaurs. You are there: What evidence are you looking for? (Berger & Berger, 1995)
> *Facts:* This book is about . . .

Most endings are like good beginnings and end with a quote or a question, an anecdote or a directive. Some typical endings in books include:

- Reminders
- Solutions
- Summaries
- Calls to action
- Reassurances
- Positive/upbeat conclusions

In the middle of texts, students find substantive content to inform others. Like the plot structures introduced in story writing (Chapter 4), expository writing has its own preferred methods for developing and presenting ideas. Students return to their graphic organizers, such as the Venn diagrams (for compare/contrast), graphs and tables (for listing attributes), or webs and clusters (for free association and categorizing), to guide them as they present the body of the paper.

Revising

Of the many genres and forms available to writers, none is more suited for recognizing the power of "writing as problem solving" than exposition. During revision, children describe, classify, and categorize data, separate facts from opinions, sort relevant from irrelevant information, and ask questions. Any aspect of the inquiry process or strategy for structuring exposition is worth revisiting. Above all, the writer makes certain that the message is clearly communicated to the reader. Content and credibility are essential. Authors decide what to include and what to omit. They establish authority on the subject. The ultimate goal is to entice the reader to want to know more. During revisions students cross-check references, look for not only cold facts but also personal observations, and reassure readers that the facts are accurate. Within the content, three strategies are discussed in more depth: defining, giving examples, and classifying.

Defining

Authors define words they believe their audience will not know. For instance, consider the following sentences.

1. These rocks, called asteroids and meteoroids, sometimes crash into Earth.
2. A flu outbreak is called an epidemic. An epidemic is the rapid spread of a disease—many people having it at the same time.

In the first example, an appositive (a phrase set off by commas) defines the rocks in context. In the second example, the words *is called* and *is* signal the definition of *epidemic*.

Deciding what to define depends on children's growing understanding of audience. For instance, if a veterinarian were addressing fellow veterinarians, he would not find it necessary to explain "whelping" because his readers would probably already be familiar with the term. However, a veterinarian writing to the general public might have to define it and give examples. In expository writing, meanings must be made explicit or put into words, rather than assuming shared knowledge. Teachers are often heard saying: "Pretend your audience doesn't know anything about _____," so that children will fill in missing details. Because the experiences, interests, and concerns of a peer audience shape what writers choose to select and present, writers must attend to their audiences' needs.

Writing that draws on social studies and science content may make special use of foreign words and expressions. In the following sentence, a Native American term is defined using English words so that readers can understand.

> The Native Americans drove their cows across at the narrow bend, so they gave it the name Wacca Pilatka. Those Native American words mean "cows crossing."

Sometimes words that are new to readers and difficult to pronounce are placed in parentheses and spelled the way they sound.

> The chameleon (kuh-MEEL'-yun) flicks out a long tongue that sticks to an insect like flypaper. (Moses, 1999, p. 10)

These and many other examples from text and trade books are used to teach revision and awareness of audience demands.

Giving Examples

Examples make a concept or idea more comprehensible. When giving examples, many authors use similes so that readers can picture what they are saying:

> A chameleon's tongue shoots out like a spring. (Moses, 1999, p. 10)

At other times, the author tries to associate new information to an analogous personal situation to build on what is already known.

> Mom tells you to wash your hands before dinner but you don't need to remind the raccoon about cleanliness and good manners. In fact he has a habit of washing his food in water!

Illustrations and visual aids, such as pictures, graphs, or maps, are other ways to offer readers examples. To direct readers to the illustrations, writers use direction words such as *right, below, above left, above right, opposite,* or they number the illustrations and write captions to go with them. The teacher will want to explore details of layout, such as headings and subheadings, or make sure photographs complement the printed text and are informative rather than decorative. They can look for some of these features in the students' final products.

Classifying

Organizing information into categories is a prominent feature of expository writing. Children classify objects in school all the time, whether they are sorting buttons, blocks, or library books. During revising, however, they are sorting facts (i.e., language) rather than objects. Facts are observed, compared, and clustered according to common attributes.

- Statements that represent facts vs. opinions
- Statements that describe size, shape, color, physical characteristics
- Statements that can be prioritized (general to specific)
- Statements that represent a theme

In text they are represented by key words, bullets and lists, subtopics, graphs or illustrations. Some examples follow:

Key Words	Examples
Types of, kinds of, numbers of an entity (Six characteristics of), members of a class	• There are three kinds of small trees: flowering dogwoods, Japanese maples, and crape myrtles. • Blue jays are part of the crow family; pine siskins and grosbeaks are members of the finch family.
Lists	*Examples*
Use of bullets, prioritized information	*Tips for Having a Party* • Select a theme • Send invitations • Decorate the house • Plan activities • Serve refreshments • Have prizes and favors
Subtopics	*Examples*

Categories that belong to a major topic and help to expand it	Dinosaurs
	When They Lived
	What They Ate
	    Meat-Eaters
	    Vegetarians
	How They Disappeared

Graphs or Illustrations	*Examples*

Use of diagrams, labels, or other visuals	*A tree diagram:*
	                    Animals
	        Cold-blooded Warm-blooded
	Amphibians Reptiles Mammals
	        Lizards Snakes
	                    Poisonous Nonpoisonous
	
	An illustration:
	Labeling the parts of a flower: *petal, stamen, root*

Forms of representation such as these give writers a way to emphasize, clarify, or simplify data for readers. Classifying also allows the writer to organize the paper and establish specific relationships for meaning.

Editing

It is usually best to teach selected editing skills when children need them or when they naturally appear in a specific genre of writing. Because the inquiry process leads children to primary and secondary sources, many of which include reading materials with polysyllabic words and complex vocabulary (technical words, specialized content of a discipline), the teacher may want to revisit word building strategies and encoding skills that benefit students in the long run, even if they never again encounter the same complex words they are reading.

Introducing **derivations** is a good choice. Most derivations are formed by affixes, a letter or sound, or groups of letters or sounds, added to words to change their meanings. Two common affixes are prefixes, units attached to the beginning of a word as in *unhappy* where /*un*/ is a prefix, and suffixes, attached to the end of the word as in *happiness* where /*ness*/ is a suffix. Children of all ages can form new words by taking a root word, the basic part that usually stands alone, and adding prefixes and suffixes to it. Or they can select a particular prefix or suffix and construct new words from the parts. To make this activity developmentally appropriate, the selection of words and affixes should come from children's own writing or the materials they are currently reading and comprehending.

friend (root)	bi (prefix meaning two)	ish (suffix meaning like, belonging to, somewhat)
*friend*ship	*bi*annual	
un*friend*ly	*bi*polar	sty*lish*
*friend*liness	*bi*focal	child*ish*
	*bi*cuspid	pigg*ish*
		snobb*ish*

Based on what children already know and understand, they are able to generate new possibilities that widen their reading and writing vocabulary.

Derivations, however, are not just associated with affixes but are often discussed in historical linguistics as the origins of a word's meaning or form (etymology). Learning about the history of words creates semantic awareness and serves as a memory device for spelling. For instance, do students know that many English words have been borrowed (loan words) from different parts of the world (*tortilla* from Mexico, *goulash* from Hungary, *entreé* from France)? Or do they know that surnames were once indicative of a person's occupation (*Taylor*: a clothes maker, *Brewster*: a female brewer), description (*Brown*: dark hair), or place of residence (*Hatfield*: wooden field)? And why might it be useful for students to know that the modern words *knight, know,* and *knee* were once pronounced with the /*k*/ sound in Old English? Studying word origins is, in itself, a curiosity and can be explored as a topic for expository writing as well as a spelling strategy. The book *Mother Tongue: English and How It Got That Way* (Bryson, 1990) offers a valuable reference for teachers who wish to share tidbits about the history and eccentricities of the English language.

In addition to derivations and borrowed terms, authors frequently provide definitions and pronunciations of words to unlock meaning in context. It makes sense to introduce dictionary work if it has not been already. When dictionaries are first distributed, children browse through them like they would any other book and find favorite words, strange words, or other distinct words. Then, depending on their age, they are shown what the book has to offer: alphabetic order, guidewords, pronunciation keys, syllables, definitions, and variant meanings. If a writer can't spell a particular word, he may have to imagine how it looks, writing it out on paper and spelling it as best as he can before looking it up. Alphabetical order and guidewords, the first and last entry found at the top of the page, are reinforced and practiced in other reference materials with similar organizations, such as pages from the phone book.

Because the expository writing process highlights semantic features analysis and graphing of data, these strategies can be extended to spelling. Using self-correction techniques and spelling logs (Figure 6–14), a group of fifth graders follows a four-step problem-solving routine to discover rules and patterns.

Step 1: Each author reads another's work, line by line, and puts a checkmark in the margins of the paper near each spelling error.

Step 2: After the paper is fully examined for spelling errors, it is returned to the writer who uses the checkmarks to locate errors.

Step 3: The writer places the incorrect and correct version of the word, side by side, and hypothesizes about the cause of the error.

Step 4: The writer reviews all the errors for patterns and generates a rule or solution for correcting the error. (See Figure 6–15.)

FIGURE 6-14   Spelling Log

My Spelling Log			
Correct Spelling	My Misspelling	Why the Word Confuses Me	Ways to Remember the Correct Spelling
happy	hapy	I use one p instead of two	hap-py
I'm	i'm	I don't capitalize I	I is a proper noun and always capitalized
could	culd	I spell it how I think it sounds	o before u
placid	plasid	It sounds like an s instead of c	remember to listen before I write
Mississippi	Misisippi	I didn't think it had many letters	I can sound it out more better
whether	weather	the weather I keep thinking about	I can think more brilliantly
Kentucky	Centucky	It sounds like a C	I can remember about the word
pints	pintes	It sound like a long E	I can learn more

The analysis is recorded in the log and the words are used for weekly spelling tests, which students administer to one another. To practice the words on their list, the students create crossword puzzles, card games such as Go Fish or Old Maid, and board games such as Scrabble and Concentration (see Figure 6–16). Constructing a game becomes another type of expository writing assignment in which children are engaged in writing definitions, developing visual formats, writing directions, and arranging and playing with words.

Along with spelling practice, upper-elementary students reinforce copyediting skills by eliminating all the punctuation from a short paragraph in a trade book and exchanging the unpunctuated excerpt with a partner whose job it is to replace the punctuation. After the paragraphs are returned to the scribe, the partners check their paragraphs against the original text, gaining practice in punctuation and proofreading.

Students will notice specific functions of punctuation marks found in expository writing, such as commas that set off illustrator transitions: *for example, on the other hand,* or *in addition to.* Because expository transition words and phrases can appear at the beginning of sentences, at the end, or in the middle, the teacher illustrates each.

> For example, the dolphin is an intelligent animal.
> The dolphin is an intelligent animal, for instance.
> The dolphin, on the other hand, is an intelligent animal.

Another function of the comma in expository text is in appositional phrases. The inserted information, grammatically known as "appositives," serves as nouns or noun equivalents functioning as adjectives to rename or categorize and are easily recognized ways to define or clarify meanings. Because renaming, definitions, and categorizations are essential elements of exposition, the teacher may want to introduce the appositive construction. The appositive clue is usually a parenthetical expression, set off by commas, such as the following:

> Ballads, lyrical poetry, were sung by troubadours. (renaming)
> An apple, a juicy fruit grown on trees, is red, green, or yellow. (definition)
> Italy, a country in Europe, is east of Spain. (categorizing)

FIGURE 6-15   Spelling Analysis Chart for Self-Correction

Name_____

My Running List of Spelling Corrections

Week of _____		Week of _____	
Incorrect	*Correct*	*Incorrect*	*Correct*
summerize	summarize	changeing	changing
infation	inflation	tomatos	tomatoes
		rideing	riding
		recieve	receive
		oun	own

Week of _____		Week of _____	
Incorrect	*Correct*	*Incorrect*	*Correct*
basikly	basically	alchol	alcohol
gooy	gooey	satelite	satellite
heros	heroes		
extremly	extremely		

The use of parenthetical information for definitions and descriptions draws attention to sentence variety and construction. Students continue to work on sentence-level strategies through sentence combining. In sentence combining, children join short choppy sentences to form complex ones (Mellon, 1969; O'Hare, 1973; Strong, 1993).

Mary is a friend.
Mary is trustworthy.
Mary is honest.
Mary is a trustworthy and honest friend.

FIGURE 6-16
Spelling Game
Formats

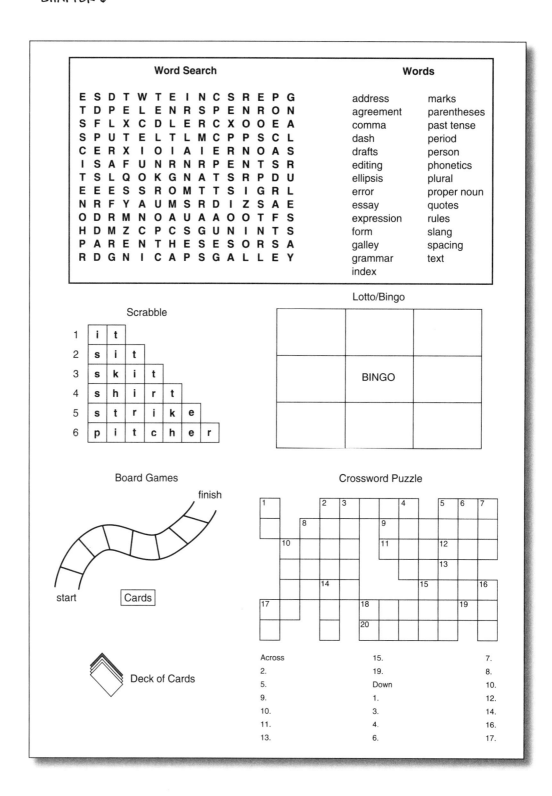

They select sentences from their writing and explain which ones they think might be combined to enhance meaning. Sentence combining exercises are useful for all kinds of writing and require only 5 to 10 minutes each day. Organized around different parts of speech and grammatical structures, they encourage variety (simple, complex, and compound sentences) and flow.

Compound Subject

a. Kittens are good pets.
b. Puppies are good pets.
c. Kittens and puppies are good pets.

Compound Object

a. I like games.
b. I like parties.
c. I like games and parties.

Subject and Object Modifier

a. The girl had a toy.
b. The girl was little.
c. The toy was new.
d. The little girl had a new toy.

Parallel Structure to Coordinate

a. The teacher walked out the door.
b. The teacher walked down the street.
c. The teacher walked to the school.
d. The teacher walked out the door, down the street, and to the school.

Compound Sentence

a. The sun is shining.
b. The sky is blue.
c. The sun is shining and the sky is blue.

Adjectival Clause (using *who* or *that*)

a. Mary found the book.
b. The book was new.
c. Mary found the book that was new.

Complex Sentence (using *or, because*)

a. I got a present.
b. It was my birthday.
c. I got a present because it was my birthday.

Relative Adverb (using *when* or *where*)

a. This is our school.
b. We learn.
c. This is our school where we learn.

Tinkering with sentences for various effects and meanings gives children flexibility for constructing complex ideas.

Depending on the genre of expository writing, sentence conventions will vary. In a recipe or "how to" paper, for instance, sentences are short and direct; phrases or single words may be common. In a report, sentences follow a combination of orders and lengths, oftentimes, with embedded phrases and words.

Although it may be tempting to introduce several sentence conventions as well as editing and formatting skills during an expository writing project, only those found in students' writing or necessary for a particular genre (report, newspaper) are selected. An example would be modeling the proper form of a bibliography (how to list titles, authors, year of publication, publisher, and place of publication) or paragraphing to group ideas for a report. Other conventions are addressed in minilessons when they are most needed or where they make the most sense.

Sharing

Sharing expository writing is the author's time to shine. Young children read from the author's chair, display their work on the bulletin board, or add their self-made books to the classroom library. A popular activity for older students is to present their written work as a speech. In a speech, the writer highlights main points and relevant details; cross-checks organization; makes certain there are transitions between main points; reworks the introduction and conclusion for audience appeal (using quotes or anecdotes); and creates visually interesting props, overhead transparencies, posters, charts, graphs, or other artifacts. In transforming the written version into a public speech, writers may actually construct a more engaging text by connecting to the audience.

The most common type of sharing is discussion, debating, and talking informally. By reading a draft in the writing circle, writers expose peers to a wide range of interesting topics and perspectives. In return, the peer audience responds to the draft-in-progress, encouraging the writer to reflect on his information for revision. The writer asks himself some of the following heuristic questions:

- Is my information accurate?
- Is my information in order?
- Do I adequately explain and give examples?
- How current is my information?
- How reliable are my sources?

Through collaboration, the children actively construct knowledge and acquire new facts. The author who is an expert on his subject might coach others or lead minilessons. Reversing roles empowers him to share expertise. From time to time, the writing circle is videotaped so that students can examine group interactional patterns.

Meanwhile, the teacher listens for all types of peer responses (including those mentioned previously such as personal, affective, and esthetic). In particular, he considers two types of responses that are essential for logically examining ideas. First is an efferent response in which peers explain what they learned from reading the author's work. Second is an analytic response in which readers break down the text into component parts that can be examined for details and strategies. Let's consider each of these two types of responses further.

Efferent Responses

Like other responses, efferent responses encourage interaction and openness of opinions. Peers retell the facts as they find them in the text or make inferences based on these facts. Reacting to the writing as readers, they attempt to comprehend and follow the logic or chain of events that the writer has communicated. Reversing this process for purposes of giving the writer feedback, peers formulate comprehension questions, such as "What is the main idea (focus)? What is the problem the writer is trying to solve? What details or examples support the main idea? Is the information accurate?"

Readers attempt to find meaning by generalizing information or drawing reasonable inferences from multiparagraph texts. They ask writers to validate concepts and definitions, research sources, or conclusions by framing questions for clarification ("Can you tell me about the leopard?") or for making predictions ("What is the result of polluting the air?"). Throughout all of this, students are becoming better readers and writers.

Efferent responses also seem to tap into prior knowledge by sharing individual observations and experiences on the subject or questioning the writer about information that might not be included in the writing. The children ask "Does the work leave questions unanswered? Has the writer verbally expressed information that is not included in the paper?"

Basically, an efferent response will mirror the concerns necessary for revising: definitions, summaries, examples, and other relevant strategies that explain and clarify. These constructive suggestions will prepare the writer for the revision he must do.

Analytic Responses

An analytic response is one in which students reduce writing to its constituent parts in order to fill in information gaps or strengthen the presentation. Peer audiences look for thought patterns that hold the content together and **frame** questions and comments about comparisons ("What is the difference between a porpoise and dolphin?" or "This seems to be a fact and this is your opinion") and categories ("If this dodo is a bird why doesn't it fly?" or "You might reorganize the information with subtitles"). Through discussion, students are likely to determine what it is about the topic the writer really cares about. Without evidence of this, it will be difficult to direct meaningful comments to the writer.

Peers are not the only ones, however, who ask questions. Writers may ask the group which details are relevant and which are not ("Which of my data support this problem?"), where more elaboration is needed ("Do I need to say more here?"), or which strategy is best to implement in a particular situation ("Should I organize this as compare/contrast?)". Naturally, depending on the form of exposition (e.g., the "how to" essay, newspaper article, or report), questions will be slightly altered.

An analytic response is cloaked in metalanguage and goes hand-in-hand with critical reading. In other words, if students can identify stated assumptions, relevant data, evidence, conclusions, and other significant aspects of the report, they will be better able to offer analytic responses.

Analytic responses often lead to introducing or borrowing new strategies. Suppose peers are discussing a word's definition. With guidance, students recall examples from their own work or from texts they have previously read. For instance, maybe a definition is directly stated: *An astronaut is a person who travels in a spacecraft into outer space.* Other possibilities, however, might include the following:

- Defining by examples: Boa constrictors, pythons, and rattlesnakes are all reptiles.
- Defining with synonyms: A kitten is playful. (*kitten* is used instead of *young cat*).
- Defining by description: An Oreo is a round, chocolate cookie with a cream filling in the center.
- Defining by comparison: Astronomy is the science of the stars; astrology is a prediction about the stars' influence on human affairs.

As these examples show, an analysis of discourse uncovers strategies for experimentation and cultivates practices for thinking through problems more clearly.

Continuous Assessment

The assessment component of the writer's workshop, as has been discussed throughout the chapters, considers key elements of each of four factors: writer, process, text, and context. Here we revisit these factors, but from the perspective of expository writing. Like the other forms of writing, constrained by specific characteristics of meaning and form, expository writing itself is an important consideration for mapping the terrain of assessment.

Writer, Process, Text, and Context Factors

Teachers use observation along with self-reports to glean information about the writer. They are looking for positive attitudes and student commitment to expository writing. Students acquire a positive disposition toward writing by catching the delight of teachers who love to learn. When children care about what they are studying, they will spend time and effort developing their interest in depth and breadth.

Since discovering and developing information takes persistence and commitment to a task, students should write daily in a journal or learning log, read widely, and display some of the following behaviors:

- Initiates problem solving
- Exhibits a sense of self-efficacy and confidence
- Cares about how well people understand the work
- Encourages others to share expertise
- Carries on conversations with peers, seeking answers to explanations for ideas through questioning and answering

These actions shed light on students' willingness to assume responsibility and ownership of writing and speak volumes about the level of tenacity necessary for completing a project.

Students must also be honest about their writing, examining the text with a critical eye. Are they willing to admit that what was intended or hoped for in the writing is nonexistent on the page? Do they feel comfortable wrestling with problems or handling ambiguity or contradictory information? Are they ready to subject their ideas to scrutiny or shift perspectives and reverse thinking if new information warrants it?

Another angle for learning about writers is to explore their prior knowledge and background on subjects through use of expository writing tools: K–W–L charts and anticipation guides, and journal entries and logs. Information from these tools trace the process of inquiry and provide answers to questions that tap into students' knowledge about exposition, such as, Do they know the difference between expository and other types of writing? Can they recognize a fact from an opinion? Are they aware of techniques for classifying and analyzing data? Do they understand that facts can and should be verified?

Learning styles including linguistic, logical, and interpersonal are also visible in expository writing. With audience demands for precise language and verbal skills, exposition benefits those writers with strong linguistic styles. Moreover, because expository prose uses methodical thought structures and language strategies, it offers an added advantage to those who take a logical approach to problems. Finally, children with sophisticated interpersonal skills, who respond well to others in writing circles, contribute significantly to discourse communities that engender honest feedback without jeopardizing rapport and friendships.

To extend an assessment beyond writer dispositions, teachers look for certain strategic behaviors and actions exhibited during the inquiry and writing process, for example, the ability to formulate problems or questions, make hunches, identify appropriate resources, analyze and rethink predictions, and develop new questions. Informal writings—journals, observation charts, graphs, or half-completed drafts—are part of this continuous cycle of exploration.

Working with the teacher, students can create checklists that take into account some of the process factors:

- Raising a pertinent question or one that is practical and feasible to explore
- Following an inquiry plan to guide the search (e.g., K–W–L, notes, journals)
- Using at least three appropriate resources (that immediately bear on the topic)
- Knowing how to navigate the pages of a reference book, textbook, or other resource to find information
- Graphing and analyzing information
- Writing drafts to explore ideas with others
- Engaging in a continuous cycle of inquiry

Inviting children to assist in defining behaviors, in their own words, provides a balance of power between the teacher and students and centers activity on the construction of text. Students, however, can always use practice in self-monitoring and self-regulation. For a while the teacher might need to apply a prompt that will assist students with this ("Do you think you might find this definition in a dictionary or encyclopedia?" or "Had you considered testing your idea on several readers to find out what information they already know about this topic?"). The process of being a researcher also requires self-evaluation and self-correction. Writers need to know what they do well, what they enjoy, how they solve problems, and what is most difficult for them.

In addition to process factors for constructing meaning and producing knowledge, the written product is examined for content, reasonableness, and intellectual integrity. The six traits are a good start because they are built on purpose and audience, the rhetorical basis for content, organization, and style.

Of course, rubrics for these traits must be modified to meet instructional goals, particular genres within expository writing and developmental levels. For instance, descriptive structures in a report will look very different from those in a travel guide just as defining at the first-grade level might look very different from defining at the fifth-grade level as seen in first graders' visual dictionaries versus fifth graders labeling to embellish an explanatory narrative. In any case, the generic indicators of expository writing for the six traits suggest what educators value in this kind of writing and serve

FIGURE 6-17 Six Trait Descriptions for Expository Writing

Ideas
- ➢ Presents content that is informative or explains
- ➢ Includes accurate facts or evidence to support thesis
- ➢ Develops a clear main idea
- ➢ Reports interesting, supporting details
- ➢ Gives examples and nonexamples to support facts
- ➢ Limits or narrows the topic

Organization
- ➢ Demonstrates an identifiable organization structure and expository strategies for shaping ideas (description, sequence, compare/contrast, cause/effect, problem/solution)
- ➢ Exhibits paragraphs that are unified
- ➢ Incorporates transitional devices and cue words to connect main ideas and show text structure *(first, next, as a result)*
- ➢ Follows a logical sequence of events (an effective lead, informative middle, summary or conclusion)
- ➢ Employs subheadings to aid understanding

Voice
- ➢ Sounds objective
- ➢ Presents authoritative tone, full of conviction
- ➢ Reveals a unique perspective
- ➢ Conveys a clear sense of audience
- ➢ Discloses a passion for the topic

Sentence Fluency
- ➢ Combines sentences
- ➢ Expresses sentences that are concise and varied

Word Choice
- ➢ Uses specific informative words with appropriate connotations
- ➢ Provides vocabulary that accurately specifies the subject or facts
- ➢ Defines unfamiliar concepts or terms

Conventions
- ➢ Identifies citations, footnotes, quoted information
- ➢ Includes bibliography
- ➢ Delineates page numbers
- ➢ Establishes correct margins
- ➢ Indents paragraphs
- ➢ Displays accurate spelling

as a starting point for defining quality exposition (see Figure 6–17). If children know the goals for a particular type of writing beforehand, they are more likely to account for these traits during revising and editing. It is good practice to have them join in and develop rubrics for evaluating their work. By examining sample papers and discussing features of high, average, and low quality products, students gain a better idea of what readers expect in an exemplary work.

Analysis of text also occurs in the collections of drafts and final products stored in portfolios. Children chronicle progress by comparing multiple drafts or examining a single draft for features of quality writing. Some typical comments include:

- It is long; or short
- The spelling is correct
- It includes lots of details and examples

- It has paragraphs
- I stuck to the topic
- I know what I'm talking about

Finally, the teacher takes an inventory of the classroom context to examine its influence on the writer and his product. Is the environment rich with possibilities so that ideas find their way into classroom life (e.g., having a pet in the classroom to motivate observation or posting a National Geographic photo to instigate questions)? Are new alliances and shared expertise fostered by arranging the class into interest groups? Do writing circles provide a free exchange of ideas in contexts beyond language arts (math, science, the arts, history, geography, and political science) where children cooperate with one another as authorities on their topics? Teachers will also want to determine if expository writing is being enhanced by contexts beyond the school. How often do students take a field trip to an archaeological site, biology lab, or cultural center? Do they ever visit local libraries or museums? Fieldwork outside the classroom is part of assessing children's overall opportunity to learn.

Genre-Specific Indicators

Expository writing involves a large domain of genres, many of which might be included in a child's elementary experience. The teacher determines which genres are most appropriate for particular developmental levels and which fit into the requirements of the curriculum. Once the genres are selected, teachers spend time analyzing and studying the form to outline its features. The resulting descriptions serve as the starting point with which to consider whether writing goals have been adequately met. If evaluative criteria is added (the writer includes three facts; or the student distinguishes between fact and opinion 95% of the time), the results are a set of benchmarks for students to accomplish.

Here are three genres, not previously addressed in the chapter, with process and product indicators for each. These represent the teacher's first step in developing assessment criteria, that is, the analysis and study of the genre's characteristics.

Book Reviews

Product

- Includes the title and author of the book
- Summarizes the plot
- Presents an evaluation with convincing reasons
- Begins with an interest catcher (a quote from the book, an anecdote, a question)

Process

- Selects a graphic organizer or outline for main idea and details
- Reads online book reviews of popular titles
- Discusses parts of the story to critique
- Revises for features characteristic of the product

Bumper Stickers

Product

- Includes slogan appropriate to the topic
- Displays designs and print features that are eye-catching
- Has audience readability; may include language play
- Conveys a message

Process

- Collects and reads bumper stickers
- Considers art elements of color, size, textures, designs, and shapes
- Brainstorms places to attach bumper stickers
- Revises for features characteristic of the product

Fact Sheets

Product
- Shows a well-designed format; single page; clear headings
- Limits data for interpretations
- Provides important facts about a topic
- Uses words or visuals to specify the facts

Process
- Practices reading charts and maps
- Discusses facts vs. opinions
- Establishes key ideas
- Revises for features characteristic of the product

All of these descriptions can be added to the six traits and assessed along with process behaviors such as critical thinking, hypothesis building, analyzing, and other related measures. Any combination can be put together with evaluation criteria (levels of proficiency required) to report development and achievement.

CLASSROOM VIGNETTES: EXPOSITORY WRITING IN ACTION

In the final sections, we consider the inquiry process and the many forms it takes as students in three grade levels explore various kinds of expository writing. All writing is thinking, but nonfiction deals specifically with facts, concepts, and generalizations and includes purposes that allow the writer to record, instruct, explain, summarize, inform, and/or report. As readers will see, informative writing for all three classrooms is found not only in the language arts block but also across the curriculum: in social studies, science, the arts, mathematics, and literature.

Grade 1

Observations

In Vivian's classroom, off to the side of the room, is a cage occupied by two gerbils. When the room is quiet, you can hear them digging through wood chips and scurrying up and down a ladder, chasing each other in play. The class has assumed responsibility for the care of these pets, making sure that each day they are fed and have clean drinking water. During a science lesson on animals, the children decide to study their classroom pets. Vivian divides a single observation chart into categories and, over the next several days, information is added: when and how much the gerbils eat; how they play; and how they are cared for.

When the learners have compiled plenty of ideas, Vivian says, "Let's write about what we have observed." The students volunteer responses from the chart, and Vivian takes dictation on butcher-block paper. Throughout the process, students are referred to the chart of observable data so that they remember the reason for prewriting in the first place.

> Our gerbils' names are Mable and Sable. They are little animals. Mable is gray and black and Sable is black. They have brown eyes and black noses. They are little with long tails. We keep our gerbils in a cage. You have to be careful what you feed the gerbils. If you put a toilet paper roll in the cage the gerbils will run through it. They get exercise by climbing the ladder. We give them a handful of food. They eat carrots and lettuce, parsley, apples, and grapes and sunflower seeds, but you can't give them some things cause they will get sick. You have to be careful they don't get out. We have to wash our hands before we hold them, and after too. If you are not careful you can squeeze them to death. You have to feed them every day just a little bit of food. We help clean the cage.

While recording information verbatim, Vivian models where to place conventions and how to write simple and complex sentences, rereading each sentence before calling for the next response. When the last sentence is written and the students have reread the passage, she prepares them for rewriting by underlining sentences with colored markers based on categories of information: red for what the gerbils look like, blue for how to care for them, yellow for what they eat, and green for what they do. She explains that, in a rewrite, all of the sentences underlined in red will be placed together, all the blue, and so forth. The next day she uses the revised version for a reading lesson and asks the students the following questions:

- Who can find the word *gerbil?* (A child comes forth using the pointer and touches the word *gerbil*).
- Who can put their hands around a whole sentence with the words *lettuce* and *carrots* in it?
- How does this sentence begin and what is at the end of a sentence?
- Who can read the words I point to (she points to individual words)?
- Does anyone see something similar in the words *squeeze, feed, keep*, and *seeds?* (The long /e/ sound made by the double e's.)

Children spell out a few keywords that are semantically associated such as *gerbil* and *cage* and place high-frequency words such as *they* and *have* on the word wall. In this way, they are acquiring vocabulary in the context of direct experience.

In math class, while children are working on measurement activities, Vivian brings in a food scale to weigh the gerbils. Mable is 4-1/2 ounces and Sable is 4 ounces. The children note the number of times the gerbils are fed (once a day) and how often they clean out the cage (every three months). When revisiting their class report during language arts, they substitute precise measurements and terms for more general words. They change *little animals* to *4 inches high*, substitute *1 tablespoon of grains* for *a little bit of food*, and decide whether to change *a handful of food* to *a half cup*. Vivian makes it clear that not every word and phrase must be turned into numbers. The facts make it credible, but their opinions give it voice. As the learners revise ideas in the original draft and continue to watch gerbil activity, they ask more questions. Answers not directly observable must be explored elsewhere. Vivian assembles a text set about gerbils so that they can search the collection for more information. To prepare for reading, children use anticipation guides that reflect key ideas about gerbils. They read five statements with a partner and decide whether they agree or disagree with the content. Then they circle the word *fact* or *opinion* to characterize each statement.

Gerbils are strange-looking animals	Fact	Opinion
Gerbils live 3 to 4 years	Fact	Opinion
Gerbils are the best pets	Fact	Opinion
Gerbils are about 4 inches high	Fact	Opinion
Gerbils need our care and protection	Fact	Opinion

The next step is to read the text to validate responses. If they wish to search beyond a single text, they might consult an encyclopedia, a dictionary, or another trade book. They might also consider people resources such as a pet store owner or a vet.

This lesson is rich with opportunities for honing observation skills and for writing informative exposition. Firsthand experiences offer a vehicle for students to construct their own knowledge and gain insights into questions that will sustain them over several assignments. For example, how are hamsters like gerbils? Or what do mice have in common with gerbils? Children will pursue new topics on their own, or work in study groups with individuals who have similar interests.

"How To's"

In daily routines, teachers expect students to follow directions. They utter directives frequently and unconsciously, assuming listeners know exactly what to do:

- Go to the writing box and pull out your folders.
- Circle the picture that begins with a *B*; underline the correct word.
- Get the book from the desk in front of the bookcase.

Giving and following directions are part of classroom life, and all children, especially students for whom English is a second language (ESL), must learn to successfully navigate the tasks they are assigned. Vivian builds on these valuable oracy skills and helps students choose precise language and chronological sequence for a "how to" report. A "how to" piece explains a process or enumerates the steps necessary to follow it. Some examples include:

How to . . .
- Care for an animal
- Play soccer
- Blow bubbles
- Study for a test
- Make a peanut butter sandwich
- Build a birdhouse
- Prepare for a camping trip
- Ride a bike
- Make a model airplane
- Train a dog
- Read a book
- Take a photograph

Vivian engages the first graders in a shared writing experience on how to make ice cream. On a large rectangular table, she sets out milk, vanilla extract, sugar, salt, ziplock bags, plastic teaspoons, plastic cups, and ice. Behind the table, taped to the chalkboard is a "sample" recipe that displays a typical layout: first a list of materials and ingredients written in two columns, then a few paragraphs with step-by-step directions for mixing the ingredients. (See Figure 6–18.) Turning to the task at hand, Vivian holds up each ingredient and writes its name on the board. After the children complete each step in the ice cream making process, Vivian records the actions (e.g.,

FIGURE 6-18 Recipe for Ice Cream

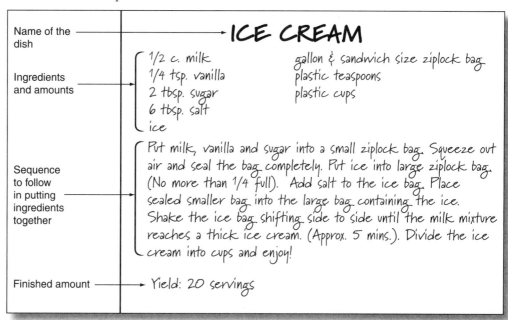

add 6 tablespoons of salt to the ice bag), pointing out transition words and phrases, such as *then, next, while the milk freezes*, to emphasize the order.

Reducing the number of words in sentences, such as "put ice into a large ziplock bag" or "divide the ice cream into cups," keeps directions easy for readers to follow and remember. During dictation, the children watch Vivian translate actions into simplified, but grammatical sentences. Because most of the sentences begin with a command word, children intuitively observe the imperative mood of verbs. The structure of sentences contributes to the matter-of-fact and impersonal voice, even though the actions hint at a "doer" and a knowledgeable person giving directions. Vivian mentions a few of these characteristics even though they are not objectives of the lesson.

Once the recipe is drafted and the children have enjoyed their treat, Vivian goes to the chart, covers her hand over a step, and asks the question: "What would happen if we left out this part?" An audible groan by the class tells her that steps cannot be omitted. Now she covers the line that says "6 tablespoons of salt" and substitutes "a little." "What would happen if we wrote 'a little' salt? Would we know whether to add a pinch, a teaspoon, a tablespoon, or a cup?" Children quickly figure out that choice of words can make a difference in whether the directions are accurately applied. Finally, Vivian reverses the sequence of steps in the recipe and the children's voices pile up over one another to let her know that the organization can't be changed.

One of the benefits of writing "how to's" is that students see the immediate effects of properly following directions (e.g., sampling the ice cream). From a writer's standpoint, now is a good time to create an awareness of the "other," the reader. Children are taught to notice where readers get stuck and why.

- Do you need to add explanations?
- Did you leave out anything?
- Do you need to reorder information?
- Do you need to define words in parentheses?

If the directions raise questions instead of answering them, the writers must go back to the trouble spots and revise. This may mean substituting an abstract word *(some)* for more explicit ones *(3 tablespoons)* or elaborating procedures with additional sentences or words. Children usually assume their readers already know what to do. However, the best kind of "how to's" tell the reader, up front, what results will occur if they follow the directions.

Conventions often take the form of editing for accuracy and clarity. As with all writing, conventions are discussed only when students are satisfied with the content. A "how to" is never complete until a reader tries it out. Writers can ask their peers or someone from another class to follow their directions and see if they work.

Although many "how to" topics are concrete and immediately verifiable, some are not. In cases where they are not, students may need to simulate the activity, consult a book, or interview someone who has experience in the area in order to test the directions. Lindsey found a practical way. She drew pictures to illustrate the steps and dictated a few sentences to go with each. A few of the steps are shown in Figure 6–19.

Collecting the "how to" compositions in a book and placing it with professional "how to" manuals for future reference shows that writing has a utilitarian purpose as well as an academic one.

Grade 3

All About Animals

In Kate's third-grade class, students are excited about authoring a book on animals. They read non–narrative genres to immerse themselves in content and a variety of styles, and then they compile a general list of animals (loosely defined as anything

FIGURE 6-19 Lindsey's *How to Climb With Concentration*, Final Draft (First Grader, Guided Writing)

from mammals, birds, and fish, to insects and reptiles). Then they select an animal, brainstorm what they know about it, and talk about their ideas with peers (Graves, 1989). On the board are questions they ask each other:

- How did you get interested in this?
- What have you read about this?
- What about this topic fascinates you?
- What do you already know about this topic?
- What would you like to know?

The learner's topic choice must be relevant to him, and the text he is writing must spring from his own authentic questions rather than a verbatim report of data from a secondary source. To that end, Kate has students complete a K–W–L chart for locating at least three independent sources of information. She meets with the students in the library, and surrounded by books and muffled silence, they go to work. Kate is available to modify the task and formulate questions for those who need additional assistance. For example, Sonya is given a think sheet on dogs (see Figure 6–20). Together she and Kate develop the questions that will be used to research the answers. As the ideas are being collected, another third grader, Tiara, classifies and displays data about Pomeranians as shown in Figure 6–21. Referring to the chart, she drafts a report that includes paragraphs on the history, grooming, and feeding of these dogs. Then, with draft in hand, she meets in a writing circle with peers to discuss her work. As soon as she finishes reading, the classmates promptly ask:

Sarah: What is your dog's name? How old is your dog? How long have you had him?

Mike: What does he look like? Do you have a picture?

FIGURE 6-20
Questions for Research
on Dogs and Responses
by a Third Grader

What do dogs look like? (What sorts of things do they have that make them look different from other animals?)	dogs have wet noses. dogs have a tail. dogs are furry.
What is this animal like when it is a baby?	puppies are small. puppies are blind when they are small.
Name three different types of dogs. Talk about how you can tell them apart from other dogs.	1. Australian Kelpie, they herd sheep. 2. Maltese, its skeleton is like a wolf. 3. airedale terrier it has a long tail.
Do dogs do sports? What sorts of things do they do?	hunting racing, sled racing,
How do you care for dogs?	water food brushing exrsising, chocolate is bad.

FIGURE 6-21 Tiara's Graphic Organizer for Categorizing the Study of Pomeranians

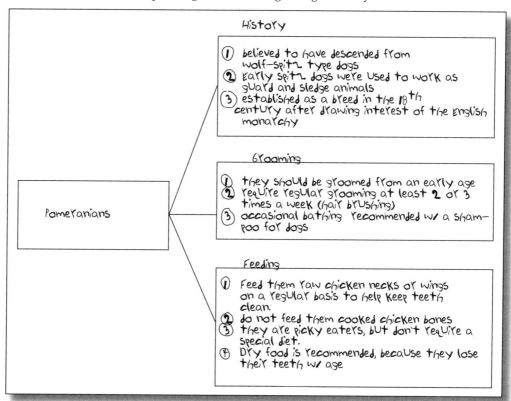

History
① believed to have descended from wolf-spitz type dogs
② Early spitz dogs were used to work as guard and sledge animals
③ established as a breed in the 18th century after drawing interest of the English monarchy

Grooming
① they should be groomed from an early age
② require regular grooming at least 2 or 3 times a week (hair brushing)
③ occasional bathing recommended w/ a shampoo for dogs

Feeding
① Feed them raw chicken necks or wings on a regular basis to help keep teeth clean.
② do not feed them cooked chicken bones
③ they are picky eaters, but don't require a special diet.
④ Dry food is recommended, because they lose their teeth w/ age

Pomeranians

Tiara realizes she will have to personalize the piece in addition to providing facts. The readers need to be able to envision her dog in their minds. Could she add a photograph or describe the dog in her writing? The dialogue continues, and with new questions emerging, Tiara is able to begin a more refined search and add personal experiences, anecdotes, and analogies. As can be seen in Figure 6–22, Tiara's final draft injects voice and breathes life into the piece without compromising the facts. What starts out as densely compressed prose with pure facts ends up as a more engaging piece that resonates with readers.

Although students may, at first, be tempted to copy information found in books, they soon learn to see facts through the lenses of their own backgrounds and experiences. Filling in drafts with personal observations and experiences loosens up texts that sound like encyclopedia entries and infuses them with features that exude passion and interest. Having students explore primary sources will assist in this objective.

In writing circles, after content is discussed, students turn to task talk and examine specific topics of the writing craft, for example, word choice. Although technically it is the writer who controls the selection of words, the fact is that, in fluid, communicative relationships, readers and writers negotiate meaning. That is why children need audiences: to learn how their words are being received by others. They might discuss whether a word is precise or vague, accurate or misleading, narrow or general. They might brainstorm new words for richer descriptions. As a follow-up to the circle, the writer takes a corpus of referential words (e.g., *breed, groom, stray, coat*) and adds at least three new entries to his word bank. Each word is written on a separate index card and includes information about where the word was found, what it means, and a sentence using the word. When the writer needs vocabulary for drafting and revising, he refers to the word bank.

FIGURE 6-22 Tiara's Report, *Pomeranian Dogs*, Final Draft (Third Grader, Independent Writing)

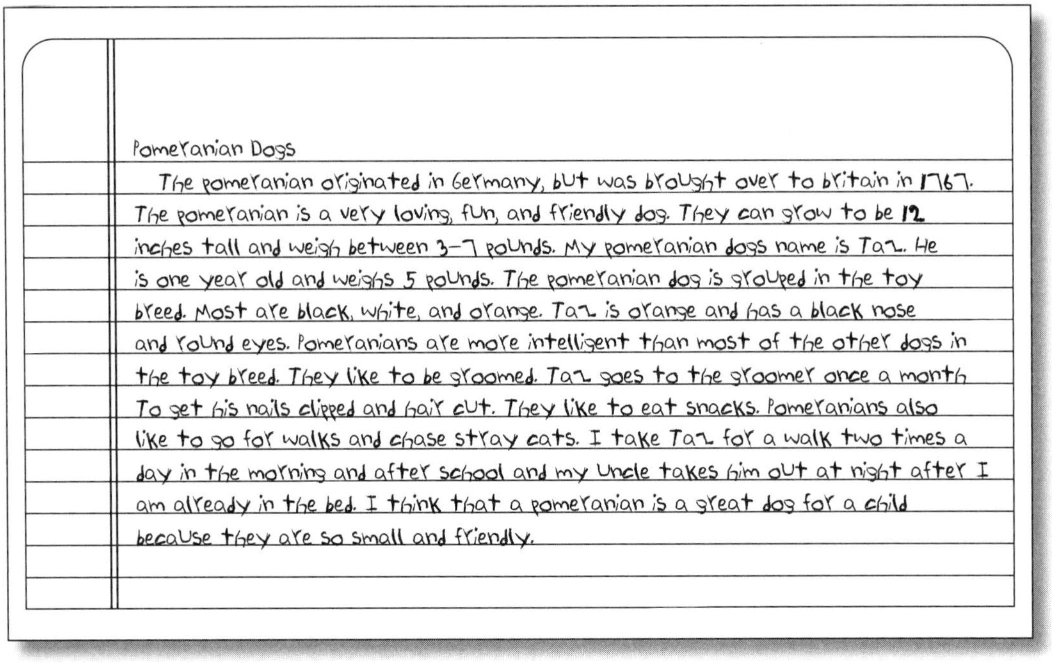

Pomeranian Dogs

The pomeranian originated in Germany, but was brought over to britain in 1767. The pomeranian is a very loving, fun, and friendly dog. They can grow to be 12 inches tall and weigh between 3-7 pounds. My pomeranian dogs name is Taz. He is one year old and weighs 5 pounds. The pomeranian dog is grouped in the toy breed. Most are black, white, and orange. Taz is orange and has a black nose and round eyes. Pomeranians are more intelligent than most of the other dogs in the toy breed. They like to be groomed. Taz goes to the groomer once a month To get his nails clipped and hair cut. They like to eat snacks. Pomeranians also like to go for walks and chase stray cats. I take Taz for a walk two times a day in the morning and after school and my Uncle takes him out at night after I am already in the bed. I think that a pomeranian is a great dog for a child because they are so small and friendly.

Before publishing, the children examine products against an editing checklist to be sure conventions are in place:

- Did I cite my references?
- Did I spell words correctly?
- Did I illustrate something about my animal?
- Did I capitalize the title of my book?

This is the perfect time for Kate to introduce simple rules of punctuation for bibliographic citations, such as underlining or capitalizing words in a title. She also models how commas set off descriptive details and definitions of animals and places (appositives). These rules are discussed in the spirit of "here is something you might need or want to include in the kind of writing you are doing."

The dog's ears, short and clipped, can detect the slightest sound.
The Amazon, one of Africa's largest rivers, is the home of the alligator.

When the reports are complete, they are bundled in packets of five or six and the writers collaborate to prepare a cover for each packet. Before starting, they volunteer design criteria to consider.

- Make it relate to the content and details of the book
- Make it colorful and eye-catching; use your imagination
- Write a title and your name
- Decorate it

Everyone adds something to the front cover, and the students all sign their names on the back. The reports bound together with the cover page are placed in the class library. Kate creates an "experts" board and lists the children's names next to their topics. "Who are our experts on sharks?" Kate asks, and the child who has written about sharks raises his hand with pride.

Survey Research Reports

In another expository writing task, Kate integrates the inquiry process with basic graphing skills and concepts in mathematics. The third graders set out on a scientific writing project using a survey tool for gathering data. In this research report, they must trace the steps they follow to conduct a survey and report the findings. The class begins with basic questions.

- What do scientists want to know?
- What makes a science writer?
- How do science writers ask questions?

Next they brainstorm topics of interest suitable for surveying: birthdays; accelerated reading points; favorite drawing materials (crayons, paints, markers, colored pencils); kinds of shoes they wear (sneakers, slide-ons, boots, dress shoes, sandals); how they get to school (bus, car, walk); and preferred sports (soccer, baseball, football), animals (giraffe, elephant, bird), or colors (red, blue, green). Kate reads *How Many Snails?* (Giganti, 1988), a book that shows numerous items, suitable for graphing, and *17 Kings and 42 Elephants* (Mahy, 1987), in which the reader journeys through the jungle searching for different animals to count along the way. These and other number and measurement books (*Anno's Counting Book*, Anno, 1975; *Poems to Count On*, Liatsos, 1995; or *So Many Cats*, deRegniers, 1985) reveal topics that are appropriate for picture graphing.

Once students have a topic, they formulate the question they will ask. Kate models a few examples from topics they have generated.

- Do you come to school by bus, by car, or do you walk?
- What is your most enjoyable sport? Soccer, baseball, or football?
- What is your favorite animal? (List several.)

She shows them how to formulate questions that give respondents discrete choices (Do you come to school by bus, by car, or walk?) and contrasts these with open-ended questions (How many accelerated reading points do you have?) that, although easily tallied, don't make good picture graphs. She circulates around the classroom listening to children try out survey questions and assisting those having trouble.

Once students have a question and some potential responses, Kate reviews how to gather and tally information. She uses *birthdays* as an example. The months of the year are written on poster cards and placed on the floor with masking tape. Children stand behind the appropriate birth month and the number of people in front of each is tallied (see Figure 6–23 for partial list). Because a spread of 12 months is not large, each tally mark equals one person. On an overhead transparency, Kate shows a picture graph, in which she places smiley faces to correspond to the marks on her tally

FIGURE 6-23 Tally Table for Birth Months

Third-Grade Birth Months	
January	I
February	IIII
March	II
April	I
Each tally mark equals one person	

FIGURE 6-24
Picture Graph for Birth
Months

Third-Grade Birth Months	
January	☺
February	☺☺☺☺
March	☺☺
April	☺
☺ = 1 person	

table (see Figure 6–24 for partial list). Kate distributes several visual representations of picture graphs and directs students to newspapers and magazines to collect graphs of their own.

Now it's the children's turn to construct graphs. They are given rulers to make the lines on the graph and stickers for the responses. Each morning for a week, selected students administer surveys to classmates. After the entire class has had a chance to complete their graphs, they are ready to write. Kate engages in a think aloud to show children how she reports the process and data from her investigation of birthdays. She writes her thoughts as she speaks.

> I began my study because I was curious about the birthdays of my students. I wanted to know when they were born so I could plan a celebration for them. However, rather than having a separate party for each person, I decided to hold one celebration every two or three months and include several people. I needed to find out the months of my students' birthdays so I conducted a survey. I asked students to line up behind the months of the year. Then I created a table to show what I found. As you can see, it appears that there are no birthdays in September, three in October, two in November, none in December, one in January, four in February, two in March, one in April, two in May, two in June, five in July, and none in August.

> The most frequent number of birthdays per month seems to be two and the month with the most birthdays (July) has five. On the basis of my findings, I decided to group the celebrations into three time periods. The fall birthdays would be celebrated in November and they would include all the birthdays that took place from September to December. The winter birthdays would be held in February and would include birthdays between January and April, and the spring/summer birthdays would be held in May and this would include all the birthdays from May to August. My study helps me plan birthday celebrations for the year!

In the think aloud, students listen to the tone of the report and consider how Kate carries out her purposes and research process. Kate methodically reviews the essence of her draft to provide students directions on what to include in their reports. She explains how she selected a particular topic to investigate (the predictions or curiosities she had), the questions she asked, the steps she followed, and the discoveries she made, pointing out how surveys often produce surprises (two birthdays a month is the most frequent number) or the need for further observations, experiments, or follow-up interviews. She wants the children to understand that a report can grow into something more than simply the mere massing of facts. Finally, she points out where she will leave space in the writing to insert her graph. Once student reports are drafted, they are examined by others for accuracy, originality, and exploration. Completed reports are compiled as research publications for future reference.

Grade 5

Neighborhood News

In the twenty-first century information is growing exponentially. By working in teams, students can bring various experiences and knowledge to the group to define a common goal that is rewarding to all members. Each year, Ed's fifth graders cooperate on a class newspaper, writing editorials (opinions of citizens), feature articles (interest stories), or classified ads (marketing jobs and objects). This year, the class focuses on neighborhood news. As always, Ed begins the project by reading *Deadline! From News to Newspaper* (Gibbons, 1987) so that students have an idea of the overall project they are about to undertake. Planned minilessons also include a broad spectrum of writing issues aimed at the craft of newspaper writing (see Table 6–5).

The project begins with students examining articles from the community sections of the local newspaper and noticing the various topics and issues covered. Then students and their partners answer a set of questions.

- What does my neighborhood look like?
- Where is my neighborhood located?
- What events take place in my neighborhood?
- What is special about my neighborhood?
- Who are my neighbors?
- What is my favorite place in the neighborhood?
- What after-school activities occur in my neighborhood?
- What rules must I observe in my neighborhood?

TABLE 6–5 Suggested Minilessons for Newspaper Writing

What is newsworthy?
How to make decisions about which stories should be printed. Find an athlete, entertainer, or politician featured in the news. Why is this person in the news? Find an event in the news. How did this event make an impact on peoples' lives?

Writing a lead.
How to write the first paragraph or first few sentences to hook the reader. It may contain a summary of the article or an introduction to why the story is important. Students read leads and categorize them by type. They will discover many purposes of leads: to raise questions, set a tone, inform, or surprise.

Answering the 5W and H (who, what, when, where, why, and how) questions.
The answers to the 5W and H questions constitute the content and body of the writing. Oftentimes they are all included in the lead and the rest of the article expands the details. Students learn to capture the essence of the article and choose a chronology that best tells the story.

Distinguishing fact from opinion.
Front-page headlines consist primarily of facts. Using colored markers, students circle words or phrases in the paper that are facts with one color and those that are opinions with a different color. Then discuss.

Writing a headline.
The headline summarizes the main idea of the article and promotes interest. Students are taught to write a short and simple statement, leaving out unnecessary words. These sentences are written without punctuation and in the present tense. The size and style shows the degree of importance.

After discussing the questions, they meet as a class to brainstorm general neighborhood concerns and topics:

Lost pets	Garage sales	New babies
Neighborhood parties	Parks	Picnics
Biking	Animals on leashes	Litter
Street hockey	Wildlife	Speeding cars
New neighbors	Traffic	Street signs and names
Trespassing	Vandalism	Statues in parks

They organize the topics into three broad categories and form cooperative groups to work on each of the areas. Here is the gist of the three groups' tasks.

Neighborhood Description

The first group will contribute the photos, maps, and other illustrations for the newspaper. Each member takes a neighborhood walk, snapping pictures and making drawings that detail the physical layout of the neighborhood, including storefronts, stop signs, parks, roads, and other interesting details. One member of the group proposes they study the origins of street names. In one area, the streets are named after horses that won the Kentucky Derby. Others are named for flowers and famous people.

Neighborhood Events

Another group considers social events in the neighborhood, brainstorming several research tasks for individual members. One student will examine the entertainment section of the newspaper for dates of upcoming events such as picnics and festivals. Another will consult the chamber of commerce to locate fun and interesting places for people to visit in town (museums, libraries, or theaters).

Still another student takes responsibility for conducting a survey on the relative popularity of certain outdoor activities in the community (bike riding, street hockey). With predesigned forms for note taking, students take a virtual tour, on the Internet through several community neighborhoods. Before they write, the group will consider several different kinds of products that they can contribute to the class newspaper including articles, social announcements, and social calendars.

Human Interest Stories

A third group writes human interest stories, interviewing families and neighbors in the community where they live: a sports athlete at the school, a family who has lost a pet, and a community member who has turned 100 years old. Many interviews are personality profiles of unsung heroes. The group generates a list of questions to include in their interviews and makes arrangements with people they will interview. The writing products emerging from this group will be feature articles that are single or co-authored.

The success of the final task depends on individual and group efforts. Once the group knows what tasks need to be accomplished, the individual members generate a contract listing the specifics for which they are responsible.

A quick minilesson on print layout provides the groups with a template to use for judging space available for each section of the newspaper. This is one time where word count matters.

The groups consult with each other to plan the layouts. The photographers prepare captions and size pictures and maps to fit the space. Feature writers limit reports to answering the 5W questions, and social coordinators reduce descriptions to include with their social calendars.

Throughout this cooperative project, the students meet in writing circles to respond to working drafts and ideas. Sometimes they are authors (or scribes) writing the pieces; other times they are the readers or editors for a classmate's work. Ed scaffolds these tasks beforehand. For instance, in writing circles, the editors review the work with a set of questions that encourage several types of responses.

Efferent questions

- Did the writer develop content (and visuals) in such a way that it is easy to read?
- Can a reader scan the article (map, picture) and pick up important information?

Critical questions

- Did the writer get the facts (details) straight or interpret them reasonably?
- Are there parts that are confusing?

Analytic questions

- Did the writer say too much or too little about the subject? Is the visual too complicated?
- Did the writer select terms associated with this topic? Can the reader follow the visual?

The responses to these questions guide the writers on what to revise. This may mean recording more information from observations, sticking to facts, or verifying and referencing sources so that readers get the impression of fair and balanced coverage.

A spin-off of the writing circle is the "staff" planning meeting, in which students work with other members of the newspaper board to make decisions about the presentation of their individual articles or contributions. Occasionally, when disagreements arise at these meetings, Ed intervenes, talks with the students about how to handle discrepancies, and offers constructive feedback.

- Paraphrase or summarize the speaker's points
- Ask the speaker for more information or clarification
- Acknowledge ideas and messages
- Identify common themes or make insightful observations
- Ask questions that express interest

During a second revision, the students meet in pairs to analyze language use in their respective texts. For example, in a feature article about football they might discuss referential word choices such as *defensive end, goal, score,* and *Super Bowl.* For an interview, students check to be sure they captured verbatim informant quotes or anecdotes. A map or photograph is examined for accuracy of labels or captions.

Children return to the local newspaper as a model for examining sentence fluency. When they discover that, for the most part, sentences are short and to the point, Ed offers a few explanations. Sentences must be comprehensible and readable because readership will vary widely in terms of literacy abilities. Because people are busy, and sometimes scan an article quickly, short sentences, consecutively arranged, allow for a rapid reading.

Newspapers are public documents and assume an educated readership, therefore, capitalizing headlines and proper names, and correcting spelling and punctuation are in order. Once editing is complete, students self-evaluate by reviewing their individual contracts and completing a group assessment form similar to the one in Table 6–6. The group assessment captures the social behaviors and communal tasks that the individual contract may not pick up. At the conclusion of the project, the finishing touches of design and publication are achieved with desktop publishing, and the newspaper is delivered to the rest of the school population.

TABLE 6-6   Assessment Form for Evaluating Behavior in Cooperative Groups

Purpose

a. Effectively worked to achieve team goals and aspirations.
b. Contributed to the shared vision of the group.
c. Shared experiences to enhance team learning.

Empowerment

a. Respected other team members' diverse points of view.
b. Enabled other team members to do their best work.
c. Listened to and validated the work of fellow team members.

Productivity

a. Contributed to the quality of the team's thought and dialogue.
b. Encouraged team's success through personal effort and performance.
c. Met team performance schedules in a timely manner.

Recognition

a. Celebrated team accomplishments.
b. Commended team members for their individual contributions to goals and objectives.

Morale

a. Encouraged and validated feelings and opinions of other team members.
b. Engaged in a spirited sense of fun while accomplishing the team goals and objectives.

Participant: Evaluator:

Personal Histories

Writing history should begin with one's own life and times. Over several days, Ed assigns students to the library to read materials he's placed on reserve. Students look at both current newspapers and those from the year that they were born. Everyone takes with him a worksheet, "What Happened on the Day I Was Born," that lists sections of the newspaper to explore and questions for note taking. A copy is shown in Figure 6–25. After the ideas for writing have been gathered, students are ready to draft. As Ed moves around the room offering advice, he notices that many students are transferring information verbatim from the worksheet, without any concern for organization. He decides to conduct an on-the-spot minilesson on comparison and contrast.

He draws a Venn diagram on the board to distinguish similarities and differences between current events and those that occurred on the days the students were born. Borrowing responses from one of the students, Ed completes the diagram and assembles information differently from the way it appears on the worksheet. Other expository structures are reviewed as well, and, when the minilesson concludes, the students select one of the organizers to develop the second draft.

Ed glances over the students' shoulders to check on their progress. They are organizing notes, asking questions, and discussing gaps in their research. Ed feels certain that their second drafts will be more refined than their first.

On another day, Ed conducts a writing circle with a small group. Kevin, who is an average writer, reads his paper aloud and then opens the floor for the students to re-

FIGURE 6-25   Research Data Gathering Form for "What Happened on the Day You Were Born?"

Name **Kevin**

What Happened On the Day You Were Born?   Date __7/7__

Do you ever wonder what happened on the day you were born? What were the top news stories? Who were the sports heros of the day? What fashions were in style? How have things changed in the years since you were born?

Instructions:
Read today's paper and then take a trip to the library and find a newspaper (will be on microfiche) from the date you were born, and compare the following things.

Headlines	Television shows
Local news	Want ads
Sports stories	Apartment rentals
Advertisements	Homes for sale
Fashions	Comics
Movies	Automobile ads

Headlines _A striking Shift Is Seen in Haiti In AIDS Victims, Recent Gorbachev Note Hints at_
a Solution on Missiles in Europe and in Asia.

Local News _George Tapper dies of cancer - 69 year old GCCC Board chairman._
School Board to award contstruction contact

Sports Stories _Drugs tied to 2d Athlete's Death Ruthe Boris Beeker and Martina Navratilova_
high score sizzle at Wimbledon.

Advertisements _Winn Dixie 1/2 gallon ice milk 99¢ (1986) (1999) Winn Dixie 1/2 gallon ice_
cream 98¢

Fashions _____

Movies (include who stars in them) _"Ruthless People" Danny Devito Bette Midler (1986)_
(1999) "Austin Powers The Spy who shagged me." Mik Myers

Television Shows (prime time) _"Murder she wrote" (1986) 3rd rock from the sun" (1999)_

Want Ads (notice the types of jobs advertised) _(1985) House keeper-$4 per hour   (1999) House_
keeper-$40 per day

Apartment Rentals (how much did it cost to rent a 2 bedroom apartment then? How much does it cost now?)
2 bed apt. #300 per month (1985)   (1999) 2 bed apt $475 per month

Homes for Sale (how much did a 3 bedroom 2 bath house sell for then? Try to find homes for sale in the same neighborhood and compare what they sell for now) _Grand Lagoon - $80,000 (1985)_
(1999) Grand Lagoon $120,000

Comics (are the subjects similar to today's comics?) _____

Automobile Ads (find a model of car that is still made today, such as a Chevrolet 1/2 ton pickup, what did they sell for then, and what are they sold for today?) _Chevy 1986 1/2 ton pickup-$9,454_
_(1999) $15,500_

spond. (See Figure 6–26.) A few of the boys tease Kevin about his fashion statements, laughing at words such as *big hair, sweaters,* and *make-up.* Others note his serious tone in reporting the country's problem with drug use among athletes and other role models. Ed pushes the group to specify how Kevin presents these topics to achieve a personal style. One student cites Kevin's example of inflation. "He wrote it in a logical, mathematic way." Another comments that he has structured his written piece into three paragraphs with a summary.

With this newfound awareness of style and development, the students are encouraged to give more opinions and feelings about their topic so readers can really hear their voices coming through. "Leave your fingerprints on the work," Ed proclaims.

FIGURE 6-26   Kevin's Report, *What Happened on the Day I Was Born*, First Draft (Fifth Grader, Independent Writing)

> Kevin
>
> Since I began this project, I learned much about how things were around the time I was born and how much they've changed. From reading some newspapers from then and comparing them to whats going on today, I found out how much and how little has changed.
>
> Topics of news stories haven't changed much since 1986. For example, in June of that year there were articles about the use of drugs by professional athletes. 13 years later we're still having problems with the drug-use of the role-model athletes of today.
>
> One thing that has definitely changed over the years is fashion. Back then, big hair, sweaters, and lots of makeup was the trend. Fashion has come a long ways and now pretty much about what individuals want to wear.
>
> Infation? I found that in 1986, a 1 ton Chevy 1/2 pickup cost about $9,500. Today, for a 1999 model of the same truck would cost $15,500. Another example of infation is that 13 years ago, a 3 bedroom 2 bath home in Grand Lagoon shores would cost about $80,000. Now for the same home in the same neighborhood it would cost $120,000. Although, some products like newspapers, clothing, and some foods have neither increased or decreased in price. And, some natural resources such as gasoline, oil, and gold have even reduced in value as they became more abundant.
>
> In conclusion, I summerize everything I've learned in saying that alot has happened since the summer of 1985; most things have changed, some haven't.

JOURNEY REFLECTIONS

The domain of expository writing includes a range of purposes and audiences that often go unrecognized by the teacher. Although there is no magic rule that separates one genre from another, the overriding purpose of this kind of writing is the presentation of facts and information. With that in mind, minilessons address the inquiry cycle for developing critical habits of mind and research, and draw on expository structures as the blueprints for constructing and presenting information. During inquiry students ask questions, formulate hunches, and collect data. They consult primary sources, consider firsthand experiences and available materials, and discover themselves and their peers as experts. Secondary sources, represented in magazines, newspapers, videos, the Internet, and the arts, complement and extend primary sources. When children are involved in inquiry, they discover ways of analyzing data using charts and other schemes, but they also examine ideas on paper by drafting and revising. Reflecting on what they have written, they often go back to the data to define their subjects, give better examples, or gather more material. Occasions for expressing analytic and efferent responses help writers shape ideas for revision. During editing, students center on accuracy of meanings, correct spelling of specialized vocabulary, inclusion of citations, and appropriate punctuation and capitalization. Older students view editing as problem solving and chart spelling errors to look for patterns and rules.

A closer look at a writer's work habits during assessment will reveal his engagement in the inquiry process and the concomitant products that result. It is important to keep in mind that each genre of exposition, with its own purpose and audience, will require its own rubric.

The classroom examples, which reveal the robust nature of the informative domain, stand in stark contrast to the shortsighted practice of requiring only the research paper or a five-paragraph theme. On any journey, teachers will want students to have many opportunities to write for many purposes and in so doing learn to shift their skills across the wide expanse.

In the final chapter on persuasion, students apply and extend their skills in exposition by writing to influence, convince, or defend opinions. Although the writers are still concerned about providing facts and accurate information on a topic, they go beyond descriptions, comparisons, and explanations to argue a point of view, opinion, or perspective to an audience. Children who learn to write persuasively inherit writing's power and social influence not only in school but also in many journeys throughout life.

WORKS CITED

Professional References

Armbruster, B. B., Anderson, T. H., & Ostertag, J. (1989). Teaching text structure to improve reading and writing. *The Reading Teacher, 43,* 130–137.

Banks, J. A., & McGee-Banks, C. A. (1999). *Teaching strategies for the social studies.* New York: Longman.

Bryson, B. (1990). *Mother tongue: English and how it got that way.* New York: Avon Books.

Calkins, L. (1995). *The art of teaching writing* (2nd ed.). Portsmouth, NH: Heinemann.

Cazden, C. (1988). *Classroom discourse.* Portsmouth, NH: Heinemann.

Englert, C. S., & Hiebert, C. (1984). Children's developing awareness of text structure in expository material. *Journal of Educational Psychology, 76,* 65–74.

Englert, C. S., Raphael, T. E., & Anderson, L. M. (1992). Socially mediated instruction: Improving students' knowledge and talk about writing. *The Elementary School Journal, 92,* 411–449.

Farris, P. J., & Cooper, S. M. (1997). *Elementary and middle school social studies: A whole language approach* (2nd ed.). Madison, WI: Brown & Benchmark.

Graves, D. H. (1989). *Investigate nonfiction.* Portsmouth, NH: Heinemann.

Head, M. H., & Readence, J. E. (1986). Anticipation guides: Meaning through prediction. In E. K. Dishner, T. W. Bean, J. E. Readence, & D. W. Moore (Eds.), *Reading in the Content Areas* (2nd ed.) (pp. 229–234). Dubuque, IA: Kendall Hunt.

Johnson, D. D., & Pearson, P. D. (1984). *Teaching reading vocabulary* (2nd ed.). New York: Holt, Rinehart & Winston.

Jorgensen, K. L. (1993). *History workshop: Reconstructing the past with elementary students.* Portsmouth, NH: Heinemann.

Manning, M., Manning, G., & Long, R. (1997). *The theme immersion compendium for social studies teaching.* Portsmouth, NH: Heinemann.

Manzo, A. V., & Manzo, U. C. (1995). *Teaching children to be literate: A reflective approach.* Fort Worth, TX: Harcourt Brace.

McGee, L. M. (1982). Awareness of text structure: Effects on children's recall of expository text. *Reading Research Quarterly, 22,* 581–590.

McGee, L. M., & Richgels, D. J. (1986). Attending to text structure: A comprehension strategy. In E. K. Dishner, T. W. Bean, J. E. Readence, & D. W. Moore (Eds.), *Reading in the Content Areas* (2nd ed.) (pp. 234–245). Dubuque, IA: Kendall Hunt.

Mellon, J. (1969). *Transformational sentence combining* (Research Report No. 10). Urbana, IL: National Council of Teachers of English.

Moore, S. R. (1995). Focus on research questions for research into reading–writing relationships and text structure knowledge. *Language Arts, 72,* 598–606.

Murray, D. (1980). The handout page. *English Journal, 69,* 79.

Murray, D. (1984). *Write to learn.* New York: Holt, Rinehart and Winston.

Norton, D. (1999). *Through the eyes of a child: An introduction to children's literature*. Upper Saddle River, NJ: Merrill/Prentice Hall.

Ogle, D. (1986). K–W–L: A teaching model that develops active reading of expository text. *The Reading Teacher, 39*, 564–570.

O'Hare, F. (1973). *Sentence combining: Improving student writing without formal grammar instruction* (Research Report No. 15). Urbana, IL: National Council of Teachers of English.

Piazza, C. L. (1999). *Multiple forms of literacy*. Upper Saddle River, NJ: Merrill/Prentice Hall.

Rosenblatt, L. (1978). *The reader, the text, the poem*. Carbondale, IL: Southern Illinois University.

Rosenblatt, L. (1984). *Literature as exploration* (3rd ed.). New York: Modern Language Association.

Strong, W. (1993). *Sentence combining: A composing book* (3rd ed.). New York: McGraw-Hill.

Children's References

Aliki. (1989). *The king's day: Louis XIV of France*. Crowell.

Allen, T. B. (1989). *On granddaddy's farm*. Knopf.

Anno, M. (1975). *Anno's counting book*. HarperCollins.

Arnold, C. (1993). *On the brink of extinction: The California condor*. Harcourt Brace Jovanovich.

Axelrod, A. (1991). *Songs of the wild west* (arrang. D. Fox). Simon & Schuster.

Barrett, N. S. (1988). *Bears*. Franklin Watts.

Base, G. (1987). *Animalia*. Abrams.

Baylor, B. (1983). *The best town in the world*. Scribner.

Bennett, P. (1994). *Catching a meal*. Thomson Learning.

Berenstein, S., & Berenstein, J. (1989). *The Berenstein bears and too much TV*. Random House.

Berger, M., & Berger, G. (1995). *Why did the dinosaurs disappear? The great dinosaur mystery*. Ideals Children's Books.

Berger, M., & Berger, G. (1999a). *Can it rain cats and dogs? Questions and answers about weather*. Scholastic.

Berger, M., & Berger, G. (1999b). *How do flies walk upside down? Questions and answers about insects*. Scholastic.

Bix, C. O. (1982). *How seeds travel*. Lerner.

Carle, E. (1971). *The very hungry caterpillar*. Crowell.

Crowther, R. (1998). *Robert Crowther's deep down underground: Pop-up book of amazing facts and feats*. Candlewick.

deRegniers, B. S. (1985). *So many cats*. Clarion.

Dragonwagon, C. (1996). *Homeplace*. Silver Burdett Ginn.

Facklam, M. (1994). *The big bug book*. Little, Brown.

Freedman, R. (1988). *Lincoln: A photobiography*. Clarion.

Fritz, J. (1973). *And then what happened, Paul Revere?* Coward/McCann.

Gibbons, G. (1982). *Tool book*. Holiday House.

Gibbons, G. (1987). *Deadline! From news to newspaper*. Crowell.

Gibbons, G. (1993). *Spiders*. Holiday House.

Giganti, P. (1988). *How many snails?* Greenwillow.

Hall, D. (1994). *I am the dog, I am the cat*. Dial.

Hoban, T. (1985). *26 letters and 99 cents*. Greenwillow.

Johnson, S. (1994). *A beekeeper's year*. Little, Brown.

Kallen, S.A. (1993). *If the trees could talk*. Abdo & Daughters.

Kirkpatrick, P. (1994). *Plowie: A story from the prairie*. Harcourt Brace.

Kitchen, B. (1994). *When hunger calls*. Candlewick.

Lampton, C. (1991). *Forest fire*. Millbrook.

Levine, E. (1992). *If you traveled west in a covered wagon*. Scholastic.

Lewis, C. (1987). *Long ago in Oregon*. Harper & Row.

Liatsos, S. (1995). *Poems to count on*. Scholastic.

Mahy, M. (1987). *17 kings and 42 elephants*. Puffin.

Martin, B., Jr. (1967). *Brown bear, brown bear, what do you see?* Henry Holt.

McCauley, D. (1977). *Castle*. Houghton Mifflin.

McFarlan, D. (Ed.). (2001). *Guinness book of world records*. Sterling.

McGovern, A. (1991). *If you sailed on the Mayflower in 1620*. Scholastic.

McGovern, A. (1992). *If you lived in colonial times*. Scholastic.

Meltzer, M. (1984). *The Black Americans: A history in their own words 1619–1983*. Crowell.

Morrison, M. (1993). *The Amazon rain forest and its people*. Thomson Learning.

Moses, B. (1999). *Munching, crunching, sniffing, and snooping*. DK Publishers.

Musgrove, M. (1976). *Ashanti to Zulu: African traditions*. Dial.

Nichol, B. (1994). *Beethoven lives upstairs*. Orchard.

Parnell, P. (1986). *Winter barn*. Macmillan.

Pratt, K. J. (1994). *A swim through the sea*. Dawn Publications.

Serventy, V. (1984). *Animals in the wild: Crocodile and alligator*. Scholastic.

Silver, D. (1995). *Extinction is forever*. Silver Burdett.

Stroud, V. A. (1996). *The path of the quiet elk: A Native American alphabet book*. Dial.

Book Series, Magazines, and Internet Guides

Cobblestone: The History Magazine for Young People. Cobblestone Publishing, 7 School Road, Peterborough, NH 03458.

Eyewitness books. Dorling Kindersley Publishing Inc., 375 Hudson St., New York, NY 10014.

The Magic School Bus. New York: Scholastic.

Poke and Look Learning books. New York: Grosset & Dunlap.

Teaching American History With the Internet. Classroom Connect, 1866 Colonial Village Lane, Lancaster, PA 17601–0488 (800-638-1639). http://www.classroom.net.

The Weekly Reader. Scholastic, 555 Broadway, New York, NY 10012.

Usborne Publishing Ltd. Educational Development Corporation (U.S. distributor), 10302 E. 55th Place, Tulsa, Oklahoma 74146.

CHAPTER 7

"When I use a word," Humpty Dumpty said in rather a scornful tone, "it means just what I choose it to mean—neither more nor less."
"The question is," said Alice, "whether you can make words mean so many different things."
"The question is," said Humpty Dumpty, "which is to be master—that's all."

Persuasive Writing

As Humpty Dumpty reminds us, individuals make choices about words to persuade others of their meanings and interpretations. No one knows better than young children the power of words in getting needs and self-interests met. They are always trying to persuade adults about one thing or another: why they should be permitted to stay up late or buy a new toy, have a slumber party or adopt a new pet. Although they may not always choose the best means for persuading an adult to their side (cajoling or whining), they are aware of the function that words and actions serve. They grow up learning that words "do" things, such as provide information, bind friendships, control others' behaviors, or satisfy personal needs (Halliday, 1975). Older students also come to understand that words and power go hand-in-hand and that language is a battle over meaning—over whose beliefs, values, and views of reality will dominate (Gee, 1996). To become accomplished writers of persuasion, they must convince others that their opinion or perspective is the one that counts! "The question is," as Humpty Dumpty puts it "which is to be master—that's all."

The art of persuasion, referred to as **rhetoric** by early Greek philosophers, involves the presentation of facts and ideas in clear, convincing, and attractive language (Thrall, Hibbard, & Holman, 1960). When writing persuasively, the aim is to influence others to think or behave in a certain way. Much like lawyers who argue a case before a jury, writers attempt to convince a reading audience that their contentions about an issue are right. First, they identify the issue and consider their personal beliefs and positions toward it. Then they find pertinent literature to support their point of view and critically examine the evidence they find. After writing their argument, citing as many examples or reasons as necessary, they submit the work to an audience in hopes of reinforcing agreement or changing attitude or behavior.

To some degree, all writing is persuasive because writers are always trying to win acceptance of their ideas, whether to entertain or inform. However, the genres listed in Figure 7–1 promote persuasion as the primary aim and are particularly applicable for classroom writing instruction. This extensive list suggests that there is something for children of all ages and developmental levels. It also highlights relevant and functional forms that pervade all of society, not only education.

Persuasive writing is a valuable tool for empowering students. It provides for practice in logical reasoning and argumentation and encourages new roles: as concerned citizens, as social activists, and as leaders. Yet as important as persuasive writing is, students are seldom exposed to it or taught its strategies (Applebee, Langer, Mullis, Latham, & Gentile, 1994; Kinneavy, 1980). When it is taught, the essays are often reduced to rigid structures consisting of a statement and three reasons. Until students reach beyond the

JOURNAL WRITING

PERSONAL WRITING

STORY WRITING

POETRY WRITING

EXPOSITORY WRITING

PERSUASIVE WRITING

FIGURE 7-1 Kinds of
Persuasive Writing

Advertisements
Billboards
Book jackets
Book reviews
Classified ads
Editorials
Entertainment reviews
   Dance
   Movies
   Theater
   TV
Persuasive essays
   Family problems
   Moral questions
   School issues
   State or national affairs
Political cartoons
Posters and signs
Proposals
Requests
Résumés and summaries
Speeches
Travel brochures

simple formulas required for passing state tests, and engage in the process of forming opinions and supporting them, the true benefits of persuasion—acquiring power and voice—will be lost. For reasons discussed in this chapter, persuasive writing needs to be included in the language arts and in subjects across the curriculum. This chapter shows how to get started.

WRITER'S WORKSHOP

Minilessons

This section on minilessons covers several topics essential to the craft of writing persuasion. In particular students learn that to give power to ideas they must know their purpose and audience, build and structure arguments, and select words with the clear intent of influencing others. Each topic is discussed in turn.

Purpose

As in all genres of writing, purpose or aim is everything (Kinneavy, 1980). A surefire method for identifying the overall purpose of a persuasive piece is to ask children what they want the writing "to do." This may be the first time they think in terms of writing "doing" something, but words have the power to move people, incite them to anger, or induce action: Do you want your words to encourage people to vote or buy Girl Scout cookies? Are your words intended to convince the family to take a trip to the Bahamas or spend money to buy you a new pair of sneakers? Asking the questions, What is the job of my writing? and What will be the result of my argument? requires writers to determine exactly what purpose they have in mind and to what end their writing will be used.

A significant part of carrying out the purpose involves writing a statement or proposition, that is, *proposing* or *posing* an idea that allows the reader to discern the thoughts or assertions that are being put forward for consideration (Wallat & Piazza, in preparation). Young children state propositions all the time: I'm better on this scooter than you are; or My baseball card collection is better than yours. They can turn these statements into questions to support the propositions they make: How would I convince my friends that I am good at riding a scooter? How might I persuade peers that my card collection is better than theirs?

Older children won't have any trouble finding propositions because they appear everywhere—in editorials, campaign speeches, newsletters, and political debates. The difficulty is sorting through them, identifying those they feel strongly about, evaluating alternative perspectives, and forming an opinion. Once they know their positions, writers are ready to summarize them in a proposition. They substitute the word *proposition* for *topic sentence* because they are no longer simply explaining or reporting information but are stating something that must be defended or proved, using clear and convincing evidence that readers are willing to embrace or at least consider. There are two types of propositions for persuading: propositions of fact and propositions of action. Propositions of fact are generalizations that can be checked by facts for truth or falsity. Children are always exaggerating statements as if they were propositions of fact: Did you know that the moon is a million miles from here? or Did you know bumble bees could kill you? Now they must defend these statements and ideas with appropriate evidence to satisfy their audience. Students need practice writing propositions of fact. Some examples include the following:

- Riding a scooter takes practice.
- Dogs are more loyal than cats.
- Children should get an allowance.
- People should not be mean to others during playtime.
- Teachers are supposed to assist students with their lessons.

When they are well written, propositions encourage a person to verify the information.

Propositions of action are attempts to arouse readers' interests and show them the wisdom of acting in accordance with the writer's aims (take a trip, read a book, go see a movie). Action propositions are often found in advertisements, travel brochures, junk mail, book or movie reviews, or in consumer-related print materials. Children can practice writing them as well.

- Everyone should read *Bud, Not Buddy* (Curtis, 1999).
- Citizens should not litter.
- Children should do their homework.
- Families should go to Disney World for a vacation.
- People should be friends with everyone.
- Adults should not smoke.

Both propositions of fact and propositions of action begin with a generalization that reflects the writer's convictions and can be defended by evidence. It is a good idea to jot down propositions on note cards and hang them were they can be continually referred to throughout the project.

Audience Appeals

For whom am I writing this paper? What might my reader want to know about my subject? Why should my audience care about this subject? These are questions that writers must ask themselves if they want to influence their readers' beliefs or elicit action. They also find out everything they can about the audience—their education, gender, lifestyle, interests, experiences, and preferences—so that the argument is tailored accordingly (Ede, 1984; Ong, 1977; Park, 1982). Advertisers are masters at this. They literally "argue to the people" or tell them what they want to hear.

TABLE 7-1 Audiences to Address and What to Know About Them	
Audiences	**What to Know About Them**
Classmates	Where they live
Students in the school or other schools	How old they are
Students across the world (e-mail)	What they like to eat
School personnel (secretaries, nurses, coaches, crossing guards, bus drivers, cafeteria workers)	What they typically wear
Teachers, student teachers, librarians, principals, school board members	What hobbies they enjoy
Family, relatives, friends	Whether they own an animal
People in the community (gardeners, grocers, dentists)	What consumer products they buy
Government officials (city, state, national)	How they spend free time
TV and sports personalities	What TV or radio programs they regularly listen to
Businesses (travel bureaus, restaurants, chambers of commerce)	Whether they like movies, sports, or other forms of entertainment
	Whether they collect anything
	Whether they read, and if so, what (magazines, newspapers, books)

Identifying an appropriate audience is always an essential first step. However, in schools it is far too often the case that "teacher as audience" is selected. This is a problem for two reasons. First, students cannot write from a position of power if the teacher is already the expert on the subject being argued, and second, students don't learn to struggle with the decisions about what evidence to present to whom if they know what the teacher already expects. The best thing a teacher can do is broaden the available audiences for children and give them the tools for finding out as much as they can about them. Some examples are listed in Table 7–1. Writing to a familiar audience is a lot easier than writing to an unknown one in which students have to guess at the background information necessary for orienting the reader to an issue. Suppose a group of fourth graders wants to persuade the principal that they should be allowed to go on a field trip. They start with what they already know about their principal and these concerns are written on a graphic organizer similar to the one in Figure 7–2. Then students discuss each point strategically plotting solutions.

To arrive at solutions, the teacher frames problem-solving questions or heuristics that go beyond audience characteristics and habits to discovering a need for persuasive strategies.

- How can I change my audience's thinking about . . . ?
- What will motivate my audience?
- How can I make my audience feel sympathetic toward my cause?
- What actions do I want my audience to take?
- How can I convince my audience that my issue is important?

Answering these questions, in turn, paves the way for introducing persuasive appeals, or hooks, to reel in an audience. Most students can relate to a discussion of appeals because, whether they know it or not, they use them all the time: simple pleas, testimonials, friendship solidarity, put-downs, rejections, or threats. Starting with what they already know, students are led to discover successful strategies that writers favor.

FIGURE 7-2

Graphic Organizer for Arguments and Counterarguments (Convincing the Principal)

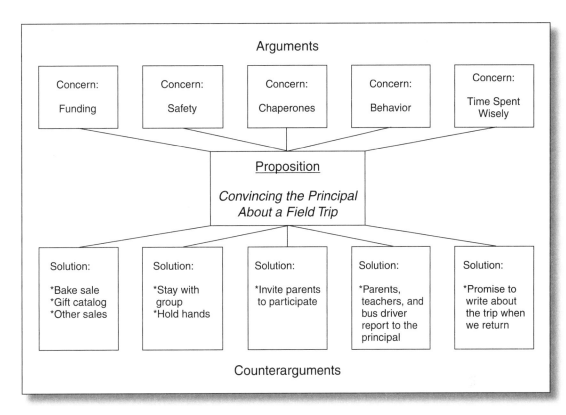

The first strategy is the *logical appeal* (appeal to reason), in which the writer asks the question, "Does it make sense and can I prove it?" Strategies that stimulate and reinforce a reader's logic include the following:

- State facts
- Sprinkle in statistics and explain what they show
- Make the argument seem like common sense; make it part of the status quo
- Give credibility to authoritative sources
- Present a similar situation or idea
- Include counterarguments
- Offer examples
- Explain reasons/causes

Say, for instance, a class wants to persuade someone that they have increased their book reading over the past 6 months. If they survey and tally the number of books the class has read each month and place the results on a graph, allowing the numbers to speak for themselves, they can convince the audience of the report's credibility (see the pictograph in Chapter 6).

A second way to appeal to an audience is to tap into emotions. When writers are attempting to make an *emotional appeal*, they ask the question, "Does my argument arouse certain feelings in the audience?" Strategies that tap into emotions include the following:

- Offer an enticement or reward
- Challenge the audience to action
- Associate the idea or product with a celebrity
- Make the reader feel something (regret or concern, sympathy, gratefulness, patriotism)
- Accentuate the personal; allow the reader to feel special
- Make the reader feel connected to an idea
- Place doubts in what the reader normally thinks; create conflict

Students implement these appeals by mentioning something that the audience can relate to personally: stating a name, referring to a birthday, or endorsing a sense of entitlement. If the audience members are competitive, the writer can challenge their desire to compete. If they are thrifty, the writer can make them feel financially secure.

Finally, *ethical appeals* (appeals to someone's character and credibility) beg the question: "Is it the right thing to do?" A set of strategies that draw on a reader's ethical sense include the following:

- Draw on the audience's sense of responsibility
- Make a reader feel she must follow the rules
- Tell the reader it is the right thing to do
- Make yourself appear trustworthy
- Talk about the fairness of the idea
- Suggest the reader needs to intervene in something
- Appeal to the reader's values
- Give the reader a sense of commitment

Writers can implement ethical appeals in very concrete ways, such as showing pictures of endangered animals and asking for support, presenting a cause that calls for doing the right thing, or simply issuing commands to take actions that are sympathetic to their argument (vote, buy, sponsor).

Knowing an audience's tendencies and characteristics and then finding ways to appeal to them goes a long way toward mastering the art of persuasion. The next two sections consider how writing to a real or hypothetical audience connects persuasion to decisions about content and style.

Arguments

When students are arguing with peers for something they want, they seldom mince words. They may threaten, "If you don't do this, I won't play with you"; resort to one-upmanship, "I'm allowed to do this because I am older", or announce that everybody else is doing it and so should they. Whether they barter with friends, defend their actions, or simply cajole, developing written arguments requires new alternatives.

Unfortunately, persuasive models for structuring such arguments suffer the same difficulties that expository ones do. Like the three-paragraph theme, the three-reasons **argument** has become firmly inflexible and lockstep, often representing the only structure students are exposed to, and reinforcing the mistaken belief that all persuasion is written this way. Although this structure may be a good starting place, if used exclusively, it limits possibilities for building rich arguments and convincing audiences.

In a little book called *A Rulebook for Arguments* (Weston, 1987), several kinds of arguments are outlined and worth considering for instruction: arguing reasons, multiple perspectives, two sides, analogies, and authority. Many of exposition's strategies—compare/contrast, cause/effect, and problem/solution—are embedded in these arguments or provide structures of their own. Each type of argument is considered separately.

Arguing by Reasons

The three-reasons argument is the template many instructors follow to teach persuasion. Its development and structure is illustrated in the graphic organizer in Figure 7–3. A young writer's enactment of this structure might appear as simple and straightforward as the following:

You should go see this movie because
   1. It has lots of action
   2. It is fun
   3. It has a rabbit in it

FIGURE 7-3 Arguing
Reasons

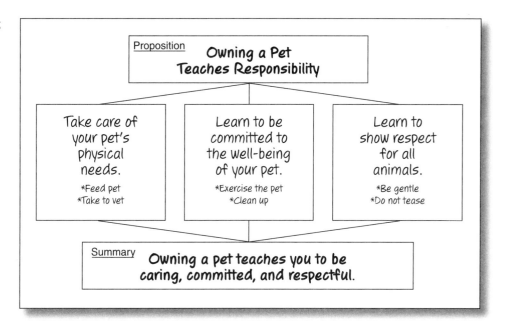

This short argument is a good beginning but can be revised and improved by including one or two examples as evidence of a statement (e.g., it is fun because the rabbit is flying in an airplane). Although beginning writers display a somewhat skeletal form of argument, older students can expand on the reasons not only with more textured details and examples but also with illustrative scenarios and anecdotes.

Anecdotes, or short narratives, bring a personal voice to the argument that lends credibility to it. Readers are often more convinced if they can see a real person behind the argument. For instance, if the argument is against drugs, writers include testimonials of average people or public figures who may have been involved in substance abuse and are now on the road to recovery. Creating a hypothetical scenario of what happens to a person on drugs is another way to make the argument concrete and real for the audience (see the DARE essay at the end of this section). Imagined events or projected courses of action force them to step into the shoes of another and attempt to personally identify with the issue. A hypothetical situation can also make difficult ideas more meaningful to the reader. Scenarios and anecdotes prove that the three-reasons argument does not have to be formulaic and uncompromising but it can be rich with narrative creativity.

Arguing Multiple Perspectives

A second way to make a point is to argue from multiple perspectives, or from several points of view. Some audiences are more convinced when the issue is presented from many sides and they can make their own decisions and educated guesses about a position. Involving older children in a WebQuest (see Chapter 1) is a good way to offer practice in exploring different views. For instance, in Figure 7–4 fifth-grade students argue multiple perspectives on saving the rain forest. They view a single problem from the perspective of a geographer, a historian, or an artist and develop arguments and viewpoints from that vantage point. During the process the writer contrasts her position with those of others to enhance thinking about a particular problem. When each individual finishes her part, the group pulls the essay together from all angles. The paper becomes a well-rounded argument of the rain forest's impact on people, nature, and animals.

Arguing Both Sides

Another way to build an argument is to consider both sides of an issue, the good and the bad, the for and against, or the arguments and counterarguments (see Figure 7–5). In these kinds of arguments, if writers dialogue with those holding opposing views, a broad

FIGURE 7-4 Arguing
Multiple Perspectives

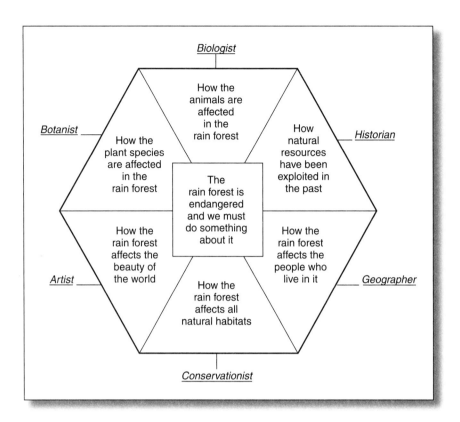

FIGURE 7-5 Arguing Both Sides

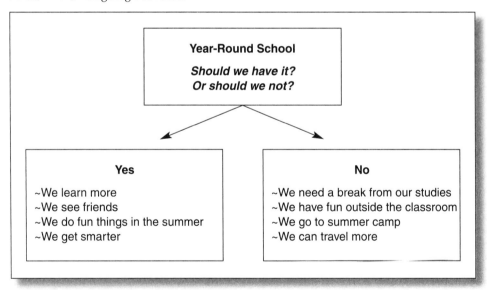

range of potential issues are available to contemplate and refute. Some open-ended prompts that frame this structure include the following:

- Should parents set a curfew?
- Is watching too much TV bad for you?
- Should there be year-round school?

A good way to begin is to consider arguments for and against, list pros and cons, or detail arguments and counterarguments, depending on the issue. Showing both sides will strengthen the writer's position and create a sense of integrity around the argument, making an audience believe the writer is fair-minded.

Debates provide good rehearsal for this kind of argument. The best topics are those that present an enduring interest, genuine opposing opinions, and a slight tension among values. It goes without saying that topics should be developmentally appropriate and related to the students' lives. Children split into teams to debate the two sides, divide the tasks among themselves, and find materials and resources representing both sides of the controversy.

Each team takes about 10 minutes to present. The team begins with an opening statement (1 minute) that clearly reveals the side of the issue they support. The group then proceeds to offer supporting arguments (5 minutes). In the next segment of the debate, the opposing team asks the first team questions (3 minutes), and then the first team makes a closing statement (1 minute) that summarizes their position. Not only do debates provide rehearsal for writing but they also demonstrate the work involved and discipline necessary for arguing a case.

A drama activity that is especially effective in rehearsing a two-sided argument is role-playing. For instance, older students might role-play the parent–child struggle and sibling rivalry in the book *The Pain and the Great One* (Blume, 1984). By enacting more than one role, they hear arguments from perspectives other than their own.

The two-sided argument is especially suitable for co-authorship. Students can work in pairs on the same question, one persuading the audience in the affirmative, the other in the negative.

Should There Be Year-Round School?

Yes

I think that year-round school sounds like a great idea for three reasons. First, you get a bunch of breaks during the school year instead of only one long break. Second, there would be no summer school! And last, my mom wouldn't have to worry about finding someone to watch me all summer long—only for a few weeks at a time. These are all good reasons to have year-round school.

By Brittany

No

I don't think year-round school is a good idea for three important reasons. First of all, I read that if we went to school year-round, we would be in school for 40 more days than we are now! We are in school enough as it is. Second, we wouldn't have the same long summer vacation. What about summer camp and staying out late with friends to play games? Finally, my family always goes on vacation during summer break. When would we be able to go if we were in school during that time? I think these are three good reasons to stick to the 9-month school year.

By Andy

Each writer presents facts and opinions on one side of the controversial issue and shares them in a point/counterpoint session. The audience determines which claims they believe are relevant and fully developed.

Arguing by Analogy

A fourth way to argue is by analogy, a comparison that suggests that because *A* gives certain results, *B*, which is like *A* in vital respects, will also accomplish the same results (Thrall, Hibbard, & Holman, 1960, p. 17). For instance, consider the analogy *school cooperation is like team sports* represented in Figure 7–6. Writers develop an analogical argument by asking the reader to take an imaginative leap: in this case, relating cooperative teams in school activities to those in sports. Documenting the advantages and disadvantages of each, arguing points in tandem, and using the attributes of one to support

FIGURE 7-6
Arguing by Analogy

Cooperation = Team Sport

- There is one clear, consensual goal.
- All players must work together.
- Motivation is interpersonal and interdependent.
- Teammates are seen as resources.
- Individuals' combined skills and efforts are valued.
- Accomplishments are shared and celebrated.

and reinforce the other, in essence, creates a parallel argument. Certainly, the premise that school cooperation is like team sports is easy enough to support if the analogy resonates with a reader who is either a supporter of school cooperation or involved in team sports. But this may not be the situation, and the writer may be forced to take a more moderate stand rather than continuing to stretch the analogy. It is rare for an analogy to consistently cover all points of comparison, but it can provide the vehicle for relating something unfamiliar to something familiar. In order to write a multiparagraph analogy, students select an idea that is familiar to the audience (sports) and use this as a means for explaining a more abstract concept (cooperation). They brainstorm the parts of the analogy in detail to view the ways in which one idea is related to the other. Naturally some characteristics of the familiar topic will not be applicable to the less familiar one.

By looking for pieces that fit together, students begin to recognize how experiences in life are related. A good place to find analogies for argumentation is in metaphors and similes. These figurative expressions are the "architects of our conceptual system; they build scaffolds of ideas" (Wujec, 1995, p. 133). In *Metaphors We Live By* (Lakoff & Johnson, 1980), the authors pose numerous comparisons that people make to structure their thinking and experiences (time is a commodity, the mind is a machine, the mind is a brittle object, love is madness, ideas are products, theories are buildings, and so on). Some metaphors are quite creative and alter an individual's outlook: Imagine a culture where an argument is viewed as dance instead of war (p. 5). Children can find their own analogies (reaching a goal is like climbing a tree; doing homework is like having a job) and then brainstorm facets of the argument to defend or refute.

Arguing by Authority

Arguing by authority is another common way to develop ideas. If you are a nurse practitioner and you argue that healthy people eat well, exercise daily, manage stress, and refrain from smoking, readers will accept the argument because nurses are supposed to know such things. But what if you are not a nurse? How could you show you were qualified to report on this issue or any other one for that matter? Writers use several different strategies to establish authority.

Winning over an audience may need to begin with legitimating one's own credentials. Writers can report firsthand experiences or verify those of someone they know. Any time anecdotes, testimonies, or eyewitness accounts are part of an argument, it assumes greater validity and authority. After all, persuading someone about the joys of being a musician is more convincing if the writer is a musician herself or knows a lot about musicians (that is, she has a sister or brother who is a musician, she is a groupie, or she is a talent scout).

A close second to relevant experience is proving one's determination and commitment. Writers appear more trustworthy when they show numerous and sustained efforts to get at the truth no matter how long it takes, no matter what the circumstances. For example, did they verify and double check records, take time to talk with informants, continue to write letters to their legislator?

Of course, there is no substitute for establishing faith in the work. This comes from meticulously demonstrating a thoughtful approach to a problem and proposing a relevant and feasible solution. To develop authority, writers show their line of reasoning in two ways. They make a general claim and systematically take the reader through specific statements as proof (deductive reasoning) or they begin with specific instances of an issue and move to a general proposition (inductive reasoning). More is said about these approaches in drafting.

Offering substantial and sufficient supporting information (what are some examples?) is another way to establish authority. The writer shows she has done a thorough investigation of the subject by presenting facts and examples that are verifiable and tested for currency (is the data too old to use?), relevancy (is it directly related to the topic at issue?), and reliability (can we trust that there is no self-interest in the statistics we read?).

Finally, facing a dubious audience, the writer can always cite outside authorities on the topic, using quotes by known experts whose highly respected status makes the argument credible. Since the author's claim and possible bias is always in question, it is essential that she guard against any flaws in the argument and test for the points suggested.

Combining Lines of Argument

Developing a persuasive text is usually best accomplished by borrowing from several lines of argument. This is illustrated in the persuasive essay in Figure 7–7 written by a fifth-grade boy after a presentation on the drug abuse resistance education program (DARE). He begins with the proposition that the DARE program will help younger children make the right choices and goes on to blend two types of arguments: the list of reasons argument coupled with the argument/counterargument. According to the writer, there are at least four reasons to support DARE: It helps peers avoid the temptation to do wrong things; it tells about the true effects of smoking and drinking; it may prevent vandalism; and it discourages children from getting involved in gangs. To explain these claims and guard against refutation, the writer adds counterarguments. He includes hypothetical statements typically heard by peers in defense of drugs and appeals to the peer group's need for friendship and respect, fear of getting in trouble, or the likelihood of death. At one point, however, the writer weakens the argument by feeling obliged to qualify his opponent's view of "gangs." In doing so, he detracts from his main argument of a violence- and drug-free school and begins discussing good versus bad gangs, another topic. As mentioned previously, writers must be unwavering and headstrong once they take a stand. Although there may be two sides to every argument, this is not the time to shift to the other side or contradict oneself. The DARE essay is a good example of a first draft, a piece full of potential and ready for discussion and revision.

Language Devices and Tactics

The art of persuasion through careful word choice can result in a positive effect on an audience (Woodson, 1979). Many of the persuasive devices in the following sections build on knowledge associated with spoken language and social discourse.

FIGURE 7-7 Persuasive Essay on Drugs, First Draft (Fifth Grader, Independent Writing)

> ⋮
> # TAKING
> # A STAND
> ⋮
>
> This is the time for you to think about all the things you have learned in DARE. Take a few minutes to look through your notebook to see all the information contained in the DARE program. Think of the things your officer has taught you. You've learned a lot!
>
> Now, you will be writing your commitment to stay drug-free and avoid violence. Be sure to express:
>
> - How you feel about the DARE program
> - What you have learned in DARE that can help you stay drug-free and avoid violence.
> - Why you think it is important to be drug-free and avoid violence.
>
> The D.A.R.E program did, can, and will help younger children make the right choices. They might be tempted into doing wrong things. The D.A.R.E. program helps these kids learn the flaws of those wrong things.
> There are many kids that do not know the true effects of smoking and drinking. Sure, they say one puff won't hurt and one drink is all it takes for relaxations. The truth is one puff and drink is all it'll take for trouble or worse, death, to find you. It's no good for your body no matter what anyone says. 
> Vandilism can have a horrible effect on your personality and your respect. People won't want you as a friend. They know better than to be as stupid as someone that vandilizes. They won't give you the respect you think you deserve. If you vandilize, you don't deserve anyones respect. 
> If your in a gang more likely than not, your going to do all of the above of what I stated. They may want you to do bad things for initiation. Then again it may be a good gang. For instance neighborhood gatherings.
> Everything about D.A.R.E. is to keep kids away from drugs and alchole. They keep so many kids out of gangs and off of drugs. I feel the D.A.R.E. program will be running long after I graduate. Thanks Officer Skundberg.

Word Choice

Words shape attitudes. No where is this more true than in persuasive writing where learners are always making conscious decisions about lexical (word) choices for emphasis, manipulation, or enlightenment. They purposely select terms to communicate or conceal messages to an audience. Here are some of these persuasive choices.

EUPHEMISMS: CONCEALING WITH WORDS. One of the ways individuals persuade others that unpleasant events are not as bad as they may seem is to use euphemisms, words that sugarcoat or distort, oftentimes with good reason. Following are some examples of euphemistic language.

Laundry (dirty clothes)	Downsized (fired from a job)
Senior citizen (old person)	Intelligence gathering (spying)
Custodian (janitor)	Dentures (false teeth)
Casket (coffin)	Memorial park (cemetery)

Euphemisms may be used to give a more impressive sounding title to a job (working for waste management instead of being a garbage collector), to spare someone's feelings on a delicate and possibly painful subject (death is referred to as a time of grief, hour of sadness, bereavement, or passing), or to avoid taboo words (*darn it* for *damn*). As you can see, not all euphemisms are evasions of the truth; some provide socially acceptable words to express what would otherwise be tactless or uncomfortable. In today's society, euphemisms oftentimes become issues of political correctness. The term *deaf* for instance was initially changed to *hearing impaired* and later to *aurally challenged.*

However, as harmless as most euphemisms are, a few of them may be questionable if their intent is to "cover up" a reality, such as collateral damage (killing enemy civilians in war) or low-income housing (slums). Avoiding the truth can inadvertently foreclose debate or prevent possible solutions from being realized.

DOUBLESPEAK: AVOIDING THE TRUTH WITHOUT LYING.   Doublespeak is a blended word comprised of the words *newspeak* and *double think*, two terms that originated in George Orwell's *1984: A Novel* (Crystal, 1995). They are words that pretend to communicate but don't. In many ways they are similar to euphemisms; however, rather than being a part of everyday discourse, they are more frequently associated with the language of power.

Doublespeak	Plain Speak	Origins
Agricultural structures	Pig pens and chicken coops	Agricultural Industry
Media courier	Newspaper delivery person	Journalism
Encore performances	Reruns	Movie Industry

Lutz (1999), a grammarian and wordsmith, says "it is language which makes the bad seem good, the negative seem positive, the unpleasant appear attractive or at least tolerable" (p. 298). One might dazzle a reader with doublespeak, not saying much of anything or saying nothing but in the required way (Lanham, 1992).

Political speech writers and advertisers sometimes use doublespeak to confuse or circumvent the truth. During the 1970s, the National Council of Teachers of English (NCTE) began hosting the Doublespeak Award, given to the most outrageously deceptive, evasive, or confusing language spoken by politicians, journalists, academics, or advertisers. These awards were published in newspapers throughout the United States.

As it turns out, newspapers are a rich source of doublespeak. Students can find examples of these words and include them in writing campaign speeches or school mottos.

CONNOTATIONS: SUGGESTING THROUGH SHADES OF MEANING.   Connotations are implied meanings or a word's overtones. For example, *color words* can elicit emotions and imply or suggest feelings that represent meanings not found in the dictionary. Here are a few generated by a group of fifth graders:

Pink: feminine, love
Green: jealousy, carefree
Black: scary, empty
Blue: cold, vast
Orange: goofy, fruity
Brown: earthy, dirty
Gray: stormy, neutral
Purple: royal, different
Red: hot, angry

Teachers can illustrate this same idea by dictating 10 words for students to list down the left side of the paper (see Table 7–2) and asking students to draw a checkmark in the right column to indicate their first impression of the word (favorable, neutral, or unfavorable) (see Lass & Davis, 1996). On completion, they share responses. Some associate the word *daydreamer* with being constructive and creative; others view it as goofing off

TABLE 7-2   Connotations Exercise

How Do Words Make You Feel?

Test your reactions to the connotations of these ordinary words. Place a checkmark in the column that best describes your feelings about the word. What makes you feel this way? How do your answers compare to others?

Words	Favorable	Neutral	Unfavorable
Daydreamer			
Black			
Popular			
Tough			
Skinny			
Shy			
School			
Talkative			
Critique			
Old			

Source: Adapted from *Elementary Reading: Strategies That Work,* by B. Lass and B. G. Davis, 1996, Boston: Allyn & Bacon.

or avoiding what needs to be done. The word *popular* arouses thoughts of "being liked" but also conjures up memories of snobs, cliques, or exclusive groups. The class discusses how each of the words might be received in ways that writers had not intended. Depending on how words are used, they can be good servants or bones of contention.

JARGON: TALKING LIKE AN INSIDER.   Jargon has been described as the idiom of a group, a roundabout way of expression or pretentious use of language (Crystal, 1995). Just as certain terms often mark a group as part of a distinct community, the same terms can also confuse and bewilder outsiders, locking them out. For persuasion's sake, writers acquire the specialized language of a disciplinary field in order to write with insider knowledge and establish credibility and membership. For instance, educators use jargon such as *developmental, invented spelling*, and *authentic assessment*, and business employees recognize words such as *outsource, bottom line*, or *cost effective*. In the computer industry, individuals refer to *spam* (to flood someone with e-mail), *flame* (an angry response), or *surfing the net* (visiting different sites on the Internet). As a rule, most editors advise writers to avoid jargon and simplify language, but in writing persuasion directed to a particular audience, the technical terms and concepts may be more economical, stating in a single word what would otherwise take several sentences and paragraphs to convey.

LOADED WORDS: CREATING HIGHLY CHARGED MEANING.   Loaded words are those that carry opinions or have associations and meanings that cause something to be prejudged, for example, *welfare, untrained*, or *improved*. Although these words often express the opinion and attitude of the writer toward a subject, the persuasive purpose of loaded words is to sway emotions and grab people's attention. Even so, loaded words have different effects on audiences. Highly charged or inflammatory words can turn off readers to an argument or rally and make staunch supporters of them. Skimming the editorial page of any newspaper will result in finding plenty of charged terms: *reckless* drivers, sports *fanatics, harassed* students, *disgraceful* behavior. What effects do these words have on the overall tone or slant of the piece?

WHOOPEE WORDS: MAKING US FEEL GOOD.   Whoopee words make things look better than they are, even though they are basically meaningless. *Wonderful, great*, or *perfect* are good examples. To provide an increased awareness of these words, students collect menus from a local deli or restaurant and write descriptions that pile on whoopee words to make the menu more inviting *(perfectly seasoned roast beef, deliciously cooled Boston cream pie)*. They use whoopee words to change a drab meal into a delectable cuisine.

WEASEL WORDS: AVOIDING MEANING.   Weasel words are those that whitewash or deliberately evade to conceal facts. Advertisers or lawyers play with these words to avoid saying something directly. In this way, there is room to maneuver meaning and interpretation to suit many situations. Take, for example, terms that are found in advertising.

Affordably low price	Incredibly low price	A price you will appreciate
Finely crafted	Professional quality	Lasting beauty
Reasonably priced	Preferred customer	Exclusive and revolutionary
At a discount	Advanced design	A top seller
High quality	Feature packed	Innovative

Students read a variety of ads and copy down words that manipulate or confuse, persuade or sell. They use this same list to create their own advertisements.

SYNONYMS: SLANTING MEANINGS IN SUBTLE WAYS.   Synonyms are words that are similar to each other. Yet it is hardly the case that every word does the same work as another. In fact, if you have ever learned a second language and found yourself groping for a word, you recognize immediately that dictionary definitions are of little help in showing which synonyms belong in which contexts. In persuasion, writers use shades of meanings to their best advantage. For instance, they think carefully about whether to call someone *skinny* or *trim* or to refer to a place as *enjoyable* or *gratifying*. These words are synonyms, but one will be more appropriate than the other in a particular situation.

Younger students can act out shades of meaning for words such as walk *(saunter, stroll)* or eat *(nibble, gobble, munch)*. Older students can check dictionaries and thesauruses to define and locate expressions for pairs of nouns *(manager or boss)*, verbs *(flaunt or reveal)*, adjectives *(bighearted or openhanded)*, and adverbs *(slowly or leisurely)* as in these examples:

Word	**Definition**	**Expression**
Flaunt	Shameless, boastful	Flaunting his wealth
Reveal	Open up, expose to view something hidden	Revealing a secret

Children learn that although the thesaurus offers viable options, decisions about words are based on their purpose and position in a particular text.

Propaganda

A writer makes deliberate use of certain language strategies and word choice to soften or hide certain facts, suggest values, exaggerate the truth, or establish believability. A term that describes the spread of ideas through such practices is *propaganda*. Students might wonder if there really is a difference between persuasion and propaganda. Persuasion is often associated with positive motives for convincing others whereas *propaganda* is typically used to discredit an adversary's ideas or deceive through point of view. Because we tend to link propaganda and politics, it is usually the one area most individuals view with suspicion and are quick to cast in a negative light. According to William Safire (1978), a well-known language expert, "despite occasional efforts to insist the word is neutral, that there is 'good' propaganda, current usage is definitely pejorative" (p. 573). He goes on to say, however, that there is a shift in this view because of "increased public recognition and acceptance of the use of powerful channels of communication by special interest groups" (pp. 573–574). In other words, students should

TABLE 7-3 Propaganda Techniques

Propaganda Device	Definition	Example
Bandwagon	Claim that everyone is doing it or that it is common knowledge	"99 out of 100 physicians recommend this product"
Card stacking	Presenting only part of the facts, half-truths, information that is out of context; failing to present essential information	"The president was always away from his desk"
Emotional appeal	Using emotionally laden pictures and words to sway opinions; use of sentimentality to influence	"Hallmark has the way to say you care"
Glittering generalities	Promises made in ambiguous or vague terms	"If elected, the candidate vows to be tough on crime."
Name calling	Using labels to refer to someone instead of providing the necessary information for allowing individuals to make their own decision	"He's a snob"
Slanted words and phrases	Trying to make people believe that something is tried and true	"Laboratory tested"
Snob appeal	Appealing to people's interest in status, admiration, or recognition	"Only Domino's™ supreme deluxe is good enough for my guests"
Testimonial	Getting prominent people to endorse an idea	"Michael Jordan uses Sprint®"

be reminded that it is sometimes acceptable to include propaganda devices in certain types of writing (see Table 7–3).

For instance, no political campaign would be complete without a few glittering generalities, and no advertisement gains popularity if it doesn't occasionally use card stacking (bringing to light the favorable characteristics without mentioning any undesirable ones). Even solicitations from charities depend on an appeal to compassion and pity in order to get donations of time or money.

From the perspective of the reader, however, these techniques might seem disingenuous or suspect. Readers understand that if they can't recognize misinformation or manipulation, they will certainly be susceptible to its influence. By identifying propaganda in reading and print materials, readers become critical consumers and more informed citizens.

Perhaps rather than arguing whether propaganda is good or bad, it is better to discuss its purpose and motivation based on different perspectives. For instance, if you are the creator of an advertising campaign, the propaganda techniques may be effective in getting the consumers' attention and selling the product. Conversely, if you are the buyer of the product and believe the claims are filled with half-truths or faulty thinking, then you are more likely to label it as propaganda. For the advertisers, propaganda techniques are favorable; for the consumer they are not.

Complicating this a bit further is the role that individual differences play in determining what is manipulation and what is persuasion. For instance, telling people they should do something because *people have always done it that way* may seem like a persuasive argument to one person but a manipulative strategy to another, in much the same way that a political campaign speech may be received favorably by supporters and unfavorably by opponents. Exposing discrepancies such as these should be a welcome part of persuasive writing and discussed openly in writing circles and sharing exercises. Because propaganda is used and received differentially, teachers should not negatively label the term but teach children how to make sound decisions about when and how to use it, for what purposes, and by whom.

Reading

Barr (1987) and Golden (1987) tell us that certain kinds of texts stimulate and influence specific responses from readers. Nowhere is this more true than in contemporary books and materials with controversial messages. In this section you will consider using controversial print with students for two purposes: identifying social problems to write about, and analyzing the strategies authors select to make a work persuasive.

Controversial Print

One of the first things a teacher might do when starting a persuasive writing unit is to locate materials that elicit strong convictions. Newspapers seem a perfect place to look because they are filled with geopolitical, social, and legal dilemmas. Reading headlines on covers of current magazines and discussing startling facts or opinions arouse curiosity or stimulate thoughts. Students can compare how different newspapers handle or address a controversy. Are some conservative and others sensational?

Social studies textbooks are equally powerful for evoking questions, identifying propositions, and establishing background documentation for persuasive writing. Students read them with an eye toward identifying problems that need attention, such as the consequences of certain policies or legal actions or the call for individual and social justice. These problems are not only valuable topics for persuasive writing but they also promote activities in which students exercise the rights and privileges of good citizenry. Parlaying reading into social action strengthens beliefs and attitudes on an issue and prepares students to write. If, for instance, writers argue that the elderly in their community deserve more attention, they might volunteer to spend one day a month writing letters to the residents at a nursing home. Or if they discover that littering is a problem in the neighborhood, they can take steps to argue for a clean-up campaign. The term *critical literacy* is being used to discuss students' ability to recognize their role in society, find solutions to its problems, or question the status quo (Fairclough, 1989; Freire, 1970). Persuasive writing gives voice to young people's commitment to social change.

Children's literature is another source for stirring controversy or locating pressing social or political issues. After reading *The Bracelet* (Uchida, 1993), older students take a stand on their feelings about internment camps and government actions. Discussions focus on questions such as: How would you feel if your country moved you from your home and sent you to a camp because they did not trust you? Do you think this is justified?

For students wishing to enter the debate about civil and political rights, there is *Freedom's Children: Young Civil Rights Activists Tell Their Own Stories* (Levine, 1994) or *American Women: Their Lives in Their Words* (Rappaport, 1990). Concerns related to **censorship** and access to information excite discussion in *Who's to Know? Information, the Media, and Public Awareness* (Weiss, 1990). Based on books such as these, students form their own opinions about the issues that have shaped (and are still shaping) people's lives.

Throughout history, changes in social consciousness and attitudes have often stirred controversy over entire books. Take, for example, the heated discussions of racism in *The Adventures of Huckleberry Finn* (Twain, 2000) or the implication of witchcraft in the Harry Potter series (Rowling, 2001). In some cases, books have been revised to reflect contemporary views, such as *The Story of Little Black Sambo* (Bannerman, 1995) written as a more acceptable modern version, *The Story of Little Babajii* (Bannerman, 1996). It would seem that censorship and book revisions are persuasive subjects in their own right.

Serious political and social concerns, however, are not the only topics that invite persuasive writing. Traditional literature, including fables and folktales, often includes worldly philosophy and moral lessons that students can defend through persuasion. In the third grade, students write a two-sided argument for a mock trial of the three little pigs. The class begins by drawing on their previous knowledge about trials (for example, those seen on court TV). After they brainstorm and assign roles for the principal and minor players, they write dramatic scripts using *The Three Pigs* (Wiesner, 2001) story to argue the perspective of the pigs, and *The True Story of the Three Little Pigs by A. Wolf* (Scieszka, 1989) to argue the perspective of the wolf. Working in groups, each student writes her own lines, whether they are short statements for the witnesses or longer ones for the attorneys. When the writing is complete, the dramatic enactment begins.

A court official opens the trial and a judge (a student dressed in a black robe) enters, taking her place at the teacher's desk. A selected jury (12 members of the class) seated to the left of the judge hears the case and takes notes. On trial is the wolf who is accused of destroying the houses of the little pigs. In an opening statement, the prosecuting attorney explains to the jury the wolf's disastrous deeds. Meanwhile, the defending attorney explains the wolf's side of the story, rebutting the pigs' accusations. During the trial, the three little pigs and other storybook characters are called as witnesses. They are examined by the prosecutor and cross-examined by the defense. When all the witnesses have testified, the prosecuting and defense attorneys each give a closing statement; the prosecutor argues that the wolf should be punished; the defending attorney makes a plea for his acquittal. The jury deliberates, votes, and reports a verdict. Writing comes alive in this dramatic activity as the children learn the skills of oral and written persuasion in an authentic situation.

Inspecting beliefs and arguing the merits of classic or contemporary proverbs in fables or folk wisdom from countries around the world is another way to make connections between reading and writing.

> He that lies down with dogs, shall rise up with fleas. (United States)
> A bird in the hand is worth a hundred flying. (Mexico)
> You will gain three moons if you wake up early in the morning. (Japan)
> To begin is to be half done. (Korea)

Students who collect proverbs from parents and grandparents gain valuable insights into family traditions and produce interesting topics for persuasive arguments. Children also relate proverbs to something in their own experience, something read, or something viewed on TV: haste makes waste is translated into a proposition of fact—students who hurry carelessly through their work get poor grades; a penny earned is a penny saved becomes the proposition of action—saving your allowance teaches responsibility. If proverbs are used, they should be commensurate with the students' ages and developmental levels.

Author Strategies

Books not only inspire persuasive writing topics and activities but also represent print models for examining the strategies authors use to position readers to take sides on a controversial topic. When children read a broad range of persuasive texts on a particular issue, they discover how various authors feel about a subject. Some are for an issue, others against it, and still others remain neutral. In studying these varied accounts, students explore reasons for differences of opinion and discover arguments that might alter their own thinking. They can gain an awareness of these possible arguments by asking questions that map the text.

- What does the author believe about _____?
- Does the author tell readers why this was written?
- What are the arguments?
- How does this argument fit with what the writer believes?
- What is the author's purpose?

After answering these general questions, students select several passages that they believe are convincing and discuss how the author argues her proposition. The way in which the author shows her interests, opinions, knowledge, intended audience, or purpose can be found in the words, sentences, or structure of the argument. For example, an author's advocacy for democracy over socialism might be evident in word choice. Perhaps she associates the word *freedom* with democracy and *oppression* with socialism. Similarly, if an author is arguing that comic books have no place in the curriculum, her bias might be reflected in the adjectives she selects (a *worthless* book).

There are many other points for students to address in regard to the author's strategies. To begin, students read about the same topic across several texts and compare information that is included or omitted. Sometimes an author will select only those arguments that support her case, ignoring obvious counterclaims. At other times, an author might purposely clutter or pad the argument with irrelevant information simply to distract the reader from the real issue at hand.

When students read work representing many sides of the issue they obtain a more balanced account in which to form their own opinions. They are also better able to determine discrepancies in evidence from one piece to the next, making it easier to separate reasonable differences from misrepresentations and inaccuracies. Additionally, when students read several works by the same author, they have an opportunity to explore the writer's patterns of thinking. For example, are the author's ideas always radical or mainstream? Has the writer shifted her views on the subject from one point in time to another?

Over and above determining whether the argument is reliable and sound, there is also the question of integrity. Children should be shown how to skim a work to discuss conflict of interest or motives in writing from a particular perspective.

Affiliation: The writer is a member of a particular organization or agency. Members of the national humane society are apt to be opposed to animal testing.

Credentials and Expertise: The writer has been studying something for many years. The dietician is an expert in arguing what are good foods for healthy bodies because she has an academic degree and has been working in a clinic for 20 years.

Special Interests: The writer has a vested interest in selling a product or promoting an idea. An employee of playground equipment is being paid to convince the consumer of the safety of a jungle gym.

Citations: The writer lists as references only those with opinions similar to her own rather than including authorities who represent diverse points of view.

Readers must always remain alert to the author's reasons for arguing a particular position since integrity is an essential property of persuasion.

Although students may scrutinize books and articles for arguments, a **text analysis** can go beyond extended prose to short forms, such as pamphlets, bumper stickers, junk mail, and business cards as well as consumer products and labels. These written "sound bites" are oftentimes persuasive for reasons other than logical argument and rely on illustrations, graphic displays, clever language, or format and length. Students will find that the Internet is a goldmine for exploring these short forms. Lessons learned from the advertising pop ups on search engines and websites can expand the few strategies that have already been mentioned. Of course, to explore the full range of writer strategies, the class might use texts that go beyond books to those associated with films, videos, music, or art, or gather data from eyewitness testimony, interviews, or other verbal sources.

Composing

Prewriting

Persuasive writing puts the inquiry process into motion beginning with the identification of a controversial issue or problem. If a topic is assigned it should be broad enough

TABLE 7-4　Persuasive Writing Topics

Opinions	Refute or Defend
Most entertaining movie Best food (book, hobby) My idea of a good teacher My biggest gripe The best mom (dad, brother, sister) in the world	Spanking School dress codes Helmets for bike riding Year-round school Book censorship Eliminating tests

Questions	Pros and Cons
What factors contribute to school violence? What rights should children have? Should animals be kept in zoos? Are snack foods good for you?	Having a job Getting an allowance Joining scouts Homework

Convincing Someone	Arguing Values
Going to a slumber party Buying a new toy Extending recess	Saving endangered animals Adopting an animal Stopping pollution

FIGURE 7-8
Persuasive Essay, *What Makes a Good Friend?*, First Draft (Second Grader, Independent Writing)

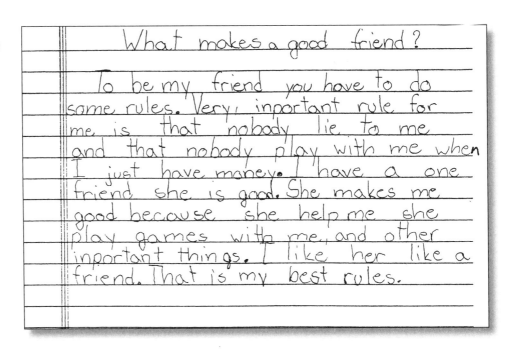

for several different aspects to be individually explored. In the report on drugs, for instance, a student might choose to argue physical harms, social implications, government policy directions, or medical perspectives. Self-selected topics can be gleaned from day-to-day events in students' lives. The class brainstorms some of these (see Table 7–4).

Young children write about permission to go to the park, to walk home from school with a friend, or to prepare their own lunches. "Pet peeves" galvanize thoughts for solving problems and enacting change. The second-grade essay in Figure 7–8 written by an ESL student is an attempt to persuade others of the values of friend-ship. This was written in response to her annoyance with the behavior of several peers. The writer argues that to be a friend, one must follow certain rules: You can-not lie or be someone's friend simply because that person has money. Her argument ends by contrasting this statement with the meaning of true friendship, showing that persuasion leads to innovative solutions of unfavorable events or existing social obligations.

Asking questions that disrupt well-established ideas representing the status quo can offer another way to approach a problem. For instance, if students are discussing computers and everyone is arguing their benefits, a writer might take the nonconven-tional position by discussing their limitations or drawbacks. Or the writer might agree that the computer is a marvelous invention but claim that it needs to perform better. In this case the task is to convince others that the suggested solution can be new and improved—going beyond what is known or taken for granted and entertaining even better ways of doing something.

Some children rethink the significance of their problems by engaging in more prewriting before revision. They test their propositions and draw on problem-solving heuristics to generate ideas or think through arguments. Questions such as the follow-ing are considered:

- What have people been saying about my problem?
- Are solutions easy to implement?
- What have I read about my problem?
- Who can I talk to about my problem?
- What will I have to do or say to make my reader believe my proposition?
- What does this problem mean to me? How does it affect others?
- What kinds of evidence help prove my problem?
- What counterarguments must I provide to my critics?

Many of the answers will be based on a continued search for facts and information that help defend what writers have to say.

Once the topic of persuasion has been identified, students complete an audience analysis so that they will know how to choose the "right" kind of evidence and argu-ment to achieve the desired outcome (see the previous discussion on audience). When this is accomplished, they begin gathering facts, time lines, examples, quotes, and expert testimony. They search archives or special data banks for statistics, government and law documents, scholarly research, directories, consumer sourcebooks, invoices, obituaries, marriage announcements, telephone records, or other special or unusual print sources. As was true for reading, the writer must evaluate the credibility of all sources before choosing them as evidence.

Drafting

How the writer chooses to arrange the argument determines what constitutes the be-ginning, middle, and end of a piece. Whatever arrangement is constructed, it is likely that expository writing structures will be embedded somewhere within it (problem/ solution, definition, cause/effect, compare/contrast). A sample serves to illustrate this. In the second-grade draft in Figure 7–9 about lending a hand at home, the writer devel-ops a list of arguments with a problem/solution component. The student begins with the problem/proposition—I think that I should always help my mom when she is clean-ing up by herself—and uses the middle as the solution (clean room, take out trash, etc.). She ends with the question that naturally evolves from the solution (Now do you see how important it is to help your mom?).

FIGURE 7-9

Persuasive Essay,
Helping Mom Clean,
First Draft (Second
Grader, Independent
Writing)

> I think that I should always hep
> my mom when she is cleaning up by herself
> Because that is what a child should do if it
> seems like your'e mother is just doing all the
> work, and you are not helping. Because that is what
> you call being down right stubborn right there.
> And these are the things that I would do to help
> my mom out I would clean up my room. Take
> out the trash. Wash the dishes so that she wouldn't
> have to do it. And of course clean out from under
> my bed and clean out my closet. Now do you
> see how impotant it is to help your mom when
> you perpusly see her strugeling cleaning up
> the house.

In another organization (see Figure 7–10), a fourth-grade writer starts with the proposition, "In life, there are many reasons that you need to be able to cooperate with others," and then makes three points, expanding on each in the paragraphs that follow. This organization mimics the expository three-paragraph theme and includes a predictable cause/effect structure (if you couldn't cooperate, you would have trouble finding a job).

Although the "cooperation" and "helping mother" essays follow typical list-of-reasons arguments, some writers achieve a persuasive end by changing the entire form of writing as in the fourth-grader's acrostic poem shown in Figure 7–11. Randy's acrostic shows how writing often achieves dual aims (to persuade and to play with language) and how messages are sometimes shaped to fit more than one written form.

During minilessons children discuss various ways of arranging an argument for greatest impact. Rather than listing all of the reasons of an argument as equally important, as in the earlier essays, the writer can follow a deductive line of reasoning. When the teacher introduces deductive reasoning, she illustrates it using an inverted pyramid as shown in Figure 7–12. In a deductive approach, the writer begins with a general proposition of fact or action and then proceeds to prove it with specific details. The writer should end with a statement that leaves the reader wondering about the issue or thinking about it more deeply—a question, a surprising twist, a striking event, or a call to action—something that won't be quickly forgotten.

In an inductive approach, the writer begins with the specific details of an argument and builds toward a general proposition. A pyramid structure (see Figure 7–13) can show how specific statements are expanded, qualified, or refuted to move the reader's attention to the generalization. This approach takes specific, detailed reasons and organizes them from the known to the unknown, the least to the most important, the concrete to the abstract. By following this arrangement, writers conclude the essay with a generalization that will stick in the reader's mind.

Along either line of reasoning, opening words should introduce the topic, grab the attention of the reader, and establish credibility. Writers pose a question and then answer it (Did you ever hand glide? It's the best sport in the world). Or they begin with a surprising statistic, a memorable quote, or a rhetorical question. In the book *Extinction Is Forever* (Silver, 1995), the author catches the audience's attention immediately when he tells a lively anecdote about how a snake manages to get into an airplane headed for an island where a rare bird's only predator is this uninvited passenger. The story heightens the reader's interest and lays the foundation for the argument to follow.

In life, there are many reasons that you need to be able to cooperate with others. Just three of these reasons are that if you couldn't cooperate with other people you would have trouble finding a job you would get into numerous fights, and you would have to do everything on your own. Luckly, most people can cooperate with their peers!

Getting a job would be pretty hard if you couldn't cooperate with the outside world! Just one of the multiple jobs that requires cooperation is football, in which not cooperating with your team would mean that you would run the wrong way, purposely fumble and other things that aren't terribly great. Another job that requires loads of cooperate is being a lawer where not cooperating would mean not listening to the judge and disagreeing with the person you are trying to defend! Think about it... every job requires cooperation because if you don't cooperate with your boss, you will most likely get fired!

If you couldn't cooperate with anybody, you would get into many fights. You would never agree, which would trigger lots of people's tempers. Other people could also forget the idea of you ever listening and taking in any of their ideas! Even worse, it would be quite hard to get along in life!

The last reason that it is important to be able to cooperate with others is because if you couldn't, you would have to do everything on your own. Make your own food, money, house, and, basically, your own everything else! Life would be no fun either you would end up sitting around the house all day with nothing to do. Also if your A/C ever broke down, you wouldn't be able to cooperate with the repairman! Jeez!

In conclusion, cooperation is a pretty important thing to learn! I'm glad I learned cooperation!

FIGURE 7-11
Persuasive Poem:
Acrostic on Staying
Drug Free, Final Draft
(Fourth Grader,
Independent Writing)

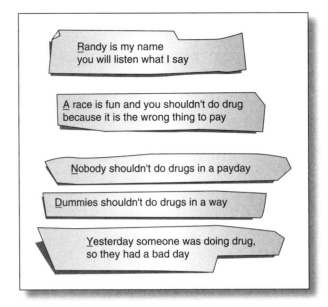

FIGURE 7-12
Deductive Reasoning:
The Inverted Pyramid,
Arranging an
Argument From
General to Specific

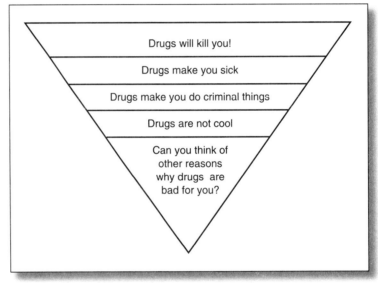

FIGURE 7-13
Inductive Reasoning:
The Pyramid,
Arranging an
Argument From
Specific to General

Making a controversial statement can excite interest by attracting readers that are either pleased supporters or antagonized opponents. The supporters will read to reinforce and validate their beliefs while the opponents will read to find flaws in the argument or counterargument. If writers want to show that they have considered both sides before launching into a defense of their position, it may be useful to start with a qualifying statement that shows this (e.g., although the Japanese system has shown the benefits of year-round school, this type of system also has negative aspects). Because writing often takes off after the first couple of sentences, sometimes finding a compelling opening is as simple as checking the sentences in the middle paragraphs. There the writer might discover something that would make a good lead such as a strong conviction or relevant anecdote. Depending on the structure of the argument, the middle of the piece should delineate the evidence in support of the writer's proposition and refute or cite **fallacies** in the opponent's view. The content is presented without clouding the major points with uninteresting or irrelevant information. If writers are asking someone to follow a course of action, they must make sure the details reveal why the reader should take a side or do what they ask: What are the arguments for or against each side? What alternative courses of action are there? What would be the consequences for each alternative?

Connecting the examples and tightening the information requires transitions that intensify, show evidence, and cue the reader to the order (see Figure 7–14). These transitions serve not only to group or tie ideas together but also to orient the audience to the argument, signaling a logical connection using the if–then construction. To concede to an opposing view, the writer might begin with *certainly* or *it is true* and then resume the argument with *nevertheless*. Interweaving the transitions with the argument, the appeals, the structure, and the language tactics is much too big a feat to be handled in drafting alone. It is addressed again in revising.

FIGURE 7–14
Persuasive Transitional
Words

Add a point
    Again
    Also
    Although
    As well as
    But . . . then
    Equally important
    Repeatedly
    Yet
Emphasize or intensify
    Above all
    Absolutely
    Certainly
    Even more important
    Especially
    More important
    Obviously
    Primarily
    Surely
    Without fail
Provide an example
    For example
    In this case
    In this instance
    To clarify
    To demonstrate

The ending to the persuasive essay is just as important as the beginning because it is what the audience remembers and takes away with them. If a proposition of fact is being defended, the writer may want to repeat key points, summarize, or tie the ending back to the beginning to remind readers of the argument and give it final emphasis. If the details have been leading up to the proposition, then, in effect, a kind of climax has been created in which the conclusion summarizes everything that has been said. For propositions of action, the writer may want to end with a call to action:

- Call your representative.
- Sign your name to the petition being circulated.
- Cast your vote for me.

Statements such as these reduce the number of words and make action-oriented commands more explicit than general vague statements, such as "we need to be kinder to one another" or "we should be patriotic." Detailed directives that are easy to follow motivate others to act.

Endings that inspire a plan of action or restate the advantages of the persuasive point of view are common. Writers must also be prepared to tell what will happen if they get their way or what will happen if they don't. In a persuasive letter, for instance, a statement conveying willingness to accept a decision, however it turns out, adds persuasive power by showing that the author is broad-minded and willing to see more than one side of an issue.

Revising

The focus of revising should be to develop and strengthen an argument. No one is convinced by a flimsy thread of facts or a rambling set of disconnected statements. The writer may need to cross-check sources or find quotes for credibility, add more examples or explore another side of the issue.

When all the information is gathered and written, the argument is crafted and shaped for maximum effect. Students reread their papers from the perspective of an outsider or potential reader and consider what is questionable, misunderstood, or unclear. As readers of their own work, writers are now interested in structuring their positions to vigorously defend their ideas.

- What is my strongest argument? Why?
- What is my weakest argument? Why?
- Have I ordered my information to have the greatest impact?
- Have I argued points about which my audience will care?
- Are there alternatives to my point of view? Did I cover all counterarguments?

The writer may want to display the major points of the argument on a graphic organizer. Perhaps shuffling the information around will marshal the material to convince or predispose an audience to believe in and support the claim. Examining the draft for effective transitions or bridges serves to hold the argument together and cue the reader when the writer is shifting focus.

Of course, even after the structure is in place and the parts of the argument seem solid, writers must consider the inferences and chain of reasoning that connect their proposition (claim) to the data (Toulmin, Rieke, & Janik, 1984). Revision is a good time to teach **critical thinking** skills to guard writers against fallacies, faulty reasoning, or misleading statements, which may contribute to erroneous facts or conclusions.

Overgeneralization: Making an all or nothing statement (e.g., *She never does her work*). The writer can look for and eliminate terms such as *always, all, never, everybody,* and *only,* making certain that they are not overgeneralizing.

Hasty generalization: Drawing a conclusion based on too little evidence, too few examples, or unrepresentative samples (e.g., *My scooter cost $40.00. All toys for kids are expensive*). Without more information on the kind of toys being compared or the definition of "expensive," the counterexamples and arguments will prove this statement incorrect.

Mistaking the cause: Assuming that because one thing follows the other that it happened because of it (e.g., *I had a bad week. I lost my book*). There are other reasons to account for a bad week in school. A lost book is probably not the cause. Children can look for faulty cause/effect statements.

Rationalization: Making excuses for something (e.g., *People can't do homework because they need help*). Writers need to underline those statements that others find objectionable because they can't be supported.

Ignoring the issue: Arguing issues that are irrelevant to the proposition. The paper may be about recommending a particular movie to an audience but the writer argues that the theater is beautiful or that the popcorn is tasty. Neither is relevant in evaluating the film's quality.

Ad hominem: Attacking a person rather than the merits of the argument (e.g., *He is a phony*). The argument loses credibility because it detracts from the matter at hand.

Teachers can expose these fallacies with skillfully placed questions appropriate to the genre being constructed. For instance, overgeneralizing weakens a research report (*None* of my friends say it is true) but strengthens an advertisement (*Everyone's* doing it). Or loaded language may embellish a humorous story but sound like an exaggeration in a letter of complaint to the principal (Homework is *torture*). Common pitfalls often stem from assuming knowledge without proving it (Brushing with Colgate will whiten your teeth) or linking two unlikely things as if they were a cause/effect relationship (Nikes are the best shoes because Michael Jordan wears them). Other issues that must be questioned and explored in persuasive writing include the use of stereotypes, categorizing a group based on some presupposed characteristic, or prejudices, making judgments about people whose ideas differ from one's own. Showing children examples that shatter the myths of stereotyping or prejudice will not only improve their writing but also make them better citizens.

Editing

In editing lessons, students discuss the persuasive thrust of paragraphs, sentences, and words. Although young children are introduced to paragraphs as a way to give the reader's eye a little rest, older students are shown how blocks of text can accentuate ideas in an argument. If writers want to draw emphasis to sets of ideas, they place each set in its own paragraph, or if they want to show a connection between related ideas, they use transitions. Refining the piece even further involves examining sentences for power or flair. They hunt for various sentences in prose and collect examples of different lengths, decorative features, and style. When they record their examples, they indicate the function a particular strategy will serve (see page 378).

When writers move sentence parts around for emphasis or repeat sentences for force, include parenthetical asides, or interject a conversational expression, they make connections with the reader and intensify their arguments

Along with sentence structure, it is worth discussing at least one part of speech: the pronoun. In persuasive writing, certain pronouns are directly connected to audience involvement. The pronoun *we* as a strategy of persuasion can have a bandwagon effect. Who does "we" refer to? Everybody and nobody? The "we" might allow the writer to be deliberately obscure and avoid claiming responsibility. Directly addressing readers *(you)* can call them to action or make them feel personally involved in the argument. A

Make something emphatic (repetition)
Energy, tenacity, curiosity—these are the signs of genius.
Americans are always giving *of time, of money, and of effort.*

Voice a command (imperatives)
Witness the major rush to department stores when there is a sale. (*You* is understood.)

Change common sentence order (surprise or emphasis)
Only in the world of Harry Potter could a broom be suspended in air. [A broom can be suspended in air in the world of Harry Potter.]

Suggest conditions or effects (paired conjunctions)
Just as individuals benefit the group, *so* the group benefits the individual.

Mimic speech (fragment)
She is not cynical. *Quite the opposite.*

Address the reader (direct address)
If *you* buy these sneakers, *you* will certainly win the marathon.

Use exclamations (highly expressive statements)
The supermarket cart was filled to the brim. *How plentiful is America!*

Highlight with quotes (for idioms or slang)
A burglar can spot a *"target"* a mile away.

metalanguage that consists of learning grammatical labels to discuss these issues can assist the writer in orchestrating the changes.

As far as word study is concerned, any of the topics discussed under language tactics are worth reviewing. Along with these, derivations of Latin or Greek origins seem especially suitable for persuasion because they are prominent in political and legal circles and are a significant part of public and private documents, contracts, and other administrative publications.

Latin

audire (to hear): audience, audio, auditorium, audible
dicere (to speak): dictate, dictator, dictionary, diction

Greek

ology (study of): anthropology, sociology, biology
graph (drawing, writing): phonograph, autograph, biography
Root words that are part of an entire set are also introduced. For instance *ast* (star): aster, asterisk, astrology, astronaut, astronomy

By examining derivations and suffixes of many types, writers discover new meanings and spell any number of words that have similar endings. Moreover, it is no surprise that accurate spellings lend authority to the argument. Because persuasive writing is audience based, it is important for the reader to conclude that the author is an effective thinker and communicator. Right or wrong, if the persuasive piece is filled with spelling errors, readers will form negative opinions and attitudes about the writer's abilities and expertise and, perhaps, give less consideration to the argument.

Students can do their own analyses of any misspellings using a spelling chart similar to the one shown in Figure 7–15. In the first column they identify the misspelled word, then find the correct spelling and place it in the second column. In the third column is a hypothesis about the nature of the misspelling and finally, in the fourth column, a reasoned explanation of how to fix it. Independence in learning to spell is essential for older writers, and analysis and self-correction will facilitate their abilities to find patterns and make hypotheses (see also the spelling log in Chapter 6).

FIGURE 7-15 Spelling Chart: An Analysis of Spelling Words

My Spelling Chart

Name_____ Date_____

Source of my words (journal, story, poem, writing log, other_____)

My spelling of the word	The correct spelling of the word	Source of the misspelling	A solution to the problem
becaus	because	omits silent letter *e*	memorize high-frequency words
opend	opened	omits silent letter *e*	study inflectional ending *ed*
though	thought	notorious confusable	attend to detail; use meanings; find a mnemonic
realy	really	omission of *l*	review suffix, *ly*
I	It	accidental error	proofread
spoung	sponge	*ou* for *o*, omit silent letter *e*	study phonics; vowels
tride	tried	drop *y* and add *ed*	apply rule or word sort patterns
Caliconnia	California	proper name	add to personal spelling words
who ever	whoever	two words versus one	practice compound words
pin	pen	short vowel	study phonics; vowels
adress	address	double consonant	break word into syllables
nedil	needle	invented spelling	sort words according to ending *le* and double vowels *ee*
hade	had	overgeneralized phonics rule	consider analogy (*bad, mad, dad*)
maby	maybe	invented spelling	practice compound words
supish	suspicious	omitted letters	break words into syllables; study phonics
to	too	homonyms	memorize meanings

Number of words in my text_____ Number of misspellings_____

Emerging patterns to note

_____
_____
_____

Contracts are another useful tool for spelling instruction (see Figure 7–16). They are particularly suitable for persuasive writing because, in many ways, contracts are a way for students to convince the instructor that they are committed to goal setting and finding solutions. In the contract, students list spelling words they need in their compositions along with words they are studying in minilessons (in this case, Latin and Greek affixes).

FIGURE 7-16 Spelling Contract

My Spelling Contract

Name_____

Beginning date _____   Completion date_____

I agree to learn the following spelling words:

1.	6.
2.	7.
3.	8.
4.	9.
5.	10.

And complete at least five of the following tasks:

Spelling Practice Activities	(✓)	Date
I will read three documents or texts and locate 10 words with suffixes.	✓	
I will post 10 words on the word wall that end with *ology*.		
I will play two games that will help me • Classify related words *(local, locate, location, locality, dislocate)* • Generate names of the sciences *(zoology, archaeology, biology)* • Build word parts *(self, selfish, selfishness, unselfishness)* (Games and activities: spill and spell, letter builders, anagrams, cards, crossword puzzles, bingo, spelling bee, spelling relay race)	✓	
I will work with a partner. First I will select 8 to 10 words from my personal writing and my partner will give me a pretest. Misspelled words will be corrected and practiced with my partner. After practice, my partner will give me a posttest to see if I learned the words.		
I will add to my spelling chart, list misspelled words, correct them, and make guesses about why the errors occurred.		
I will proofread two of my writings and circle any words I think I may have misspelled. Then I will look up these words to see how they are spelled. I will add the correct spellings to my notebook.		

Signed,   Approved by,

_____   _____

They outline a plan for practicing spellings and sign an agreement that the words on their list will be mastered. In addition to spelling, the appearance of writing is now an important matter. Length must be discussed in terms of the target audience. How much does a reader need to know? How much is too much? What does the audience need? Will they read this if it's too long? In the age of technology, where writing is becoming more and more visual, tables and graphs may be an efficient way of presenting information.

Visual appeal and its link to authority emerges as a topic of editing. In persuasive writing, students will want a professional-looking product. For instance, handwriting neatness and legibility make the first impressions. Nothing frustrates a reader, or diminishes an argument more than writing that has to be deciphered. Students should examine handwriting for legibility and readability.

- Are the spaces between my letters even? (spacing)
- Are the letters proportionate to one another: Are some too large and others too small? (size)
- Do all the letters touch the line? (alignment)
- Do all the letters lean the same way? (slant)
- Are round letters round *(m, u, w)*, tall letters straight *(b, f, k)*, closed letters closed *(a, d, o)*? (letter formation)
- In cursive writing, are the letters in words joined properly? (connections)

Besides handwriting, graphs, colors, artwork, and design in advertising and promotional material can position readers to approach an argument with a positive attitude. In persuasion, writers are presenting themselves and their authority in many different and subtle ways.

Sharing

Students who interact with their fellow classmates take intellectual risks by posing their own problems, clarifying and defending conclusions, exploring possibilities, and using results to make informed decisions. Asking a simple question, such as "Where did you learn that?," can reveal sources of evidence and set the groundwork for future discussions.

Older students participate in writing circles to test arguments with an audience and determine whether their reasons are convincing. Because the aim of persuasive writing is to influence others, it helps if writers have an immediate audience who can offer feedback. As students discuss their papers, the teacher listens for the kinds of responses they make. Two responses particularly related to persuasive writing are emphasized: critical responses and evaluative responses.

Critical Responses

Critical responses employ reasoning and healthy skepticism in determining hidden values and meanings in a written piece. Peers who share work in writing circles approach evidence cautiously and reject the presence of faulty thinking and logical fallacies. Some of the questions they ask include the following:

- How did you learn about this?
- When did you learn about this?
- What resources did you use (and when were they dated)?
- What is suggested in this statement?

When students make a critical response they are actively using knowledge and reasoning to weigh opposing points of view or deduce relationships among ideas in the text. They might go beyond what is explicitly stated, reading "between the lines" to get at what the author is really saying. As they refine critical responses, they become more reflective, growing in their ability to offer effective advice and work with others in problem-solving situations.

If students have difficulty verbalizing a response, they can participate in a spontaneous oral debate. Another possibility is to pose scenarios relevant to the issue, thus, offering a range of options to consider. For example, if they are arguing for or against the subject of weekly allowances they might entertain scenarios representing multiple vantage points: those who receive allowances for doing nothing, those who work for allowances, those who use allowances to learn about money, those who spend an allowance foolishly, those who save allowances, those who receive allowances solely because of age, or those who receive privileges in lieu of money. In this way, students consider the topic from many angles and viewpoints.

Another way to practice critical responses is to ask rhetorical questions. A rhetorical question doesn't need an answer. The readers play devil's advocates by bombarding the writer with strings of questions, one after the other, in order to impress upon her the tenets of the argument. For example, in the situation mentioned earlier about persuading the principal to go on a field trip, the rhetorical questions might be:

- Who will pay for it?
- What special arrangements need to be made?
- Who will be chaperons?
- How will students get where they need to go?
- What are the objections?

An approach that borrows liberally from Peter Elbow's (1973) believing and doubting game is useful for critical response. In the believing game you try to find the truths in what the writer has asserted and "get inside the head of someone who saw things this way" (p. 149). In the doubting game you question what is common sense or self-evident and, instead, look for logic and evidence. The first game emphasizes involvement and experience and the second game, doubting, nurtures rigor and healthy skepticism. These approaches are interdependent and offer a balanced way of responding to a persuasive argument.

Evaluative Responses

Evaluative responses position the reader to examine the information as it relates to the expectations and criteria of persuasive writing. At this point, students use external criteria or standards to appraise a work and make judgments about its merits. Maybe they use the six traits or a specialized rubric to guide their responses. Peers talk about whether or not the information is relevant, if there are enough examples, if the writer has interpreted the evidence correctly, or if other inferences or conclusions are possible. Of course, in applying criteria to a text, there should be leeway regarding interpretations since students come from diverse backgrounds and cultures. Over time, students develop shared meanings of the criteria and learn to question assumptions behind debatable points or call for proof to justify claims. Some questions for peers to ask writers include the following:

- What is most convincing about your argument?
- What will move your audience to take action?
- What makes you think that this is true?
- Have you checked for fallacies or flawed ideas?

Sharing gives students an opportunity to assess the power of their ideas with an audience. Without this, the work suffers. All writers need feedback from others if they are to amend or defend their work. Although they should defer judgments during the production of ideas, they do just the opposite during sharing. Now is the time to examine misconceptions, illusions, or ideas not based on logic, consistency, or probability. Are ideas reasonable?

When peers volunteer evaluative responses to a writer's work, they can choose either an oral or written form. If they select to write comments, they might participate in an exercise adapted from *A Writing Project* by Daniels and Zemelman (1985). The teacher generates a list of possible roles for children to play: editor, friend, parent, or critic. In role, the children evaluate an anonymous writing sample and compare responses. Here is what might be contained in several types of written comments from different perspectives.

Comments from an editor: May suggest errors to correct such as fixing spelling, use of apostrophes, and capitalization.

Comments from a friend: May want to know why the writer has taken a particular position on a controversial topic.

Comments from a parent: May be interested in the position the child has taken on a controversial topic as it relates to family values and upbringing.

Comments from a literary critic: May show opposing arguments that the writer has not considered.

Writing comments from many points of view show that evaluation is influenced by a person's experience and concerns. It also makes writers aware of the many possible aspects of writing that can be evaluated.

Another way peers might appraise a work and offer evaluative responses is by requesting that the author direct them on what to discuss. For instance, the writer might ask the group "Do I have all the necessary information?" or "Do you think I have overgeneralized here?" Regardless of the kind of evaluative response that is projected, it should be done in the spirit of improving the paper, not correcting it for a grade.

Continuous Assessment

Assessment is always a work in progress and always a balancing of multiple factors—the writer, process, text, and context. What makes these factors unique to persuasion are the specific purposes, audiences, strategies and stylistic features related to this kind of writing. Therefore, the four factors in this section are addressed from the perspective of persuasive writing. Teachers can use the information outlined for each factor in self-made checklists, rubrics, inventories, questionnaires, and other assessment tools.

Writer, Process, Text, and Context Factors

Through persuasive writing, teachers learn about writers: what issues or topics move them to action, where they stand on the issues, what values they hold dear, and what misconceptions they may have. Simply noting the verbal appeals students use in the classroom (how they persuade the teacher to go outdoors for recess, have a test cancelled, or be excused from a homework assignment) provides insights into their understanding of persuasion. Not only are teachers interested in how students make persuasive appeals to others, but they also want to find out what strategies are effective in convincing the students themselves. How do TV and print advertisements influence them as consumers? What tactics might a peer use to influence an other's behavior, whether it's seeing a movie or suggesting the type of clothes to wear? The power of persuasion, as it affects students at a particular age level, will sensitize teachers to peer pressure and social influences.

As children debate and write arguments, teachers mediate and model behavior to show that argument is not quarreling or verbal contention but reasoned discourse. Ruggiero (1988) offers critical thinking guidelines that teachers can use to assess whether writers have a healthy attitude toward argumentation. These include some of the following indicators:

* Admits being wrong; won't rationalize
* Reflects and is candid about ideas or argument
* Refuses to settle for the easy answers
* Examines beliefs in light of new evidence
* Entertains opposing views without reacting defensively
* Listens to new ideas and is open-minded
* Remains unbiased; judgment is not affected
* Gives ideas fair and impartial hearings; defers judgements

Teachers keep anecdotal records of these observed characteristics and the contexts in which they emerge. For instance, interviewing as described in Chapter 1 and applicable across all writing, may elicit individuals' attitudes and meanings. It is necessary to remember, however, that because 65% of the young children's communication is nonverbal (Birdwhistell, 1970), teachers will have to remain alert to behavior (gestures, facial expressions, actions) in addition to words.

Just as it is necessary to know how children feel about persuasive writing, it is also important to have an idea about their working knowledge of persuasion: Are they able to anticipate questions an audience might ask or are they able to enter into the role of a specific reader? Understanding a reader/audience of a different age, sex, or opinion requires writers to assume new roles and move outside themselves to anticipate a reader's position. Along with demonstrating a sense of audience, students should also exhibit information literacy, that is, the ability to know when there is a need for information, how to find, organize, and evaluate it, and how to use it effectively to address a problem (American Library Association, 1989). These strategies require they go beyond merely collecting information and show that they can use it effectively.

Ascertaining students' learning styles may also be of immense value to teachers. Having interpersonal skills and understanding an audience's motives, needs, and goals allows writers to get into others' minds and select appeals that will most likely influence them. Similarly, a child who has a strong verbal preference will be sensitive to the nuances of words or the presence of effectual phrases in proof building and argumentation. We all know the power of language in moving an audience to action. Knowing what to say and how to say it is, by far, the most important ingredient in learning to write persuasively. Of course, there are exceptions. In some types of persuasion, particularly advertising, the teacher will want to assess the students' sensitivities to rhythms and word play or their visual-spatial tendencies. After all, writing a catchy jingle and designing an unforgettable image can be just as convincing, if not better than words. Finally, a logical style in which the writer differentiates the parts of an argument and assembles it in a manner that shows deductive or inductive reasoning is a significant plus in getting a point across to others.

During the writing process, the teacher will want to observe whether students take advantage of all available resources for shaping an argument. The students develop a checklist similar to the one in Table 7–5 based on process indicators.

The process begins with deciding on a persuasive topic and learning as much as possible about the issues surrounding it. The writer then takes a position on the topic, writes a proposition, identifies the audience, gathers the "right" evidence, drafts and revises an argument, and edits for accuracy. At this point writing circles are an important forum for instructors to determine how learners are testing their work on an audience and using the feedback to strengthen the work.

Product indicators focus on the writer's ability to hook the audience and draw them into the piece. Most of the questions are cast in terms of how the writing affects the reader: Is the writing clear to a reader? Do readers like it? Does it compel the reader to want to read more? How does it affect the reader? Can the reader follow it? Does the reader have to reread a sentence to make sense of it? As outlined in the six traits (see Figure 7–17), an assessor looks for controversial topics; a sound argument; credible and plausible explanations; rival perspectives, and implicit or explicit appeals to logic, authority, emotions, or ethics.

TABLE 7-5　Process Checklist for Persuasion

	Student	Teacher
I researched my proposition and took notes	___	___
I discussed my proposition with someone who had a different opinion or preference	___	___
I explored the characteristics (preferences and habits) of my audience	___	___
I used a graphic organizer to lay out my argument	___	___
I experimented with visual techniques for presenting my ideas (color, size, paper texture)	___	___
I reviewed language and persuasion/propaganda techniques	___	___

FIGURE 7-17   Six Trait Descriptions for Persuasive Writing

Ideas
➢ Specifies a definite purpose and well-defined problem
➢ Builds a convincing or significant argument
➢ States a position on the topic
➢ Provides assertions or points about the position taken
➢ Develops the main points with details and examples that strengthen the argument
➢ Supports the position with three or four thoughtful reasons
➢ Offers promising or feasible solutions; valid deductions

Organization
➢ Connects ideas with transitions that emphasize sequence, explanation, cause/effect
➢ Orders arguments or counterarguments effectively
➢ Makes connections that avoid logical fallacies (sweeping generalizations, inaccurate causes and consequences)
➢ Creates a beginning that captures reader's attention

Voice
➢ Anticipates reader's questions
➢ Persuades through reader appeals and personal tone (conviction, passion, authority)
➢ Uses quotations accurately
➢ Projects a reasoned tone; shows respect for reader
➢ Suggests a provocative or compelling text
➢ Shows a consistent voice throughout

Sentence Fluency
➢ Expands or shortens sentences for effect
➢ Varies sentence structure; length

Word Choice
➢ Employs forceful adjectives and adverbs
➢ Includes words to persuade the reader

Conventions
➢ Demonstrates appropriate punctuation
➢ Presents accurate spelling

The list of traits along with process indicators are typically consulted when students present portfolios for a grade. Students write a letter to the teacher indicating why they deserve a particular grade and use their informal writings and work products in the portfolios as evidence. The argument should consist of proofs, such as the amount of writing done (drafts, revisions), the quality of work (strength of arguments, types of revisions, length, range of topics), the nature of the inquiry and research process (sources consulted, note taking, webs), and the appropriateness of goals set for the future. All of this can be written in the persuasive letter.

In regard to context, once again, teachers will want to consider whether ample space and time is provided for students to interact or work alone and whether a variety of materials is available for conducting research. Teachers also continue to reflect on whether they are reinforcing student choice, collaboration, and meaningful activity.

Besides the classroom environment, contexts outside the school can take assessment to new heights. In the role of social activists, students implement an action plan for making change or serving others whether it be for reasons of public health and welfare (better care in nursing homes), public safety (the need for stop lights, appropriate behavior on the bus), or global awareness (encouraging people to recycle). Bridging classroom environments with the community at large and engaging students in service roles ought to be an important part of the student's overall social competence.

Genre-Specific Indicators

It can be argued that just about all writing is persuasive. However, despite the widespread applicability of the six persuasive traits, as was true in other forms of writing, genres within a particular domain often have their own unique features. The examples that follow represent some of these genres and offer a starting point for determining evaluative criteria for modifying traits along developmental lines.

Movie Review
Product
- Identifies the title of the movie
- Summarizes the content and gives reasons for evaluation
- Mentions technical production (lighting, camera, music, animation)
- Describes the acting

Process
- Develops standards/criteria for judging movies
- Reads computer online movie reviews and views trailers
- Discusses and rates movies
- Revises for features characteristic of the product

Proposals
Product
- Defines the problem and solution
- Evaluates the alternatives
- Avoids logical fallacies
- Engages the reader; considers readability

Process
- Lists problems and analyzes them for solutions
- Interviews potential informants
- Reads and discusses proposals
- Revises for features characteristic of the product

Classified Ads
Product
- Identifies the object for sale
- Presents persuasive descriptions of the object
- Includes short, clear sentences with details
- Provides appropriate details (costs, phone numbers, location for pick-up)

Process
- Uses a graphic organizer for details
- Reads classified ads from newspaper
- Discusses details to include and exclude
- Revises for features characteristic of the product

With a basic set of descriptors for each genre, the teacher will be able to pick and choose from the six traits or add to them. As in any genre associated with a particular type of writing, criteria is guided by developmentally appropriate expectations. Identifying indicators is only the first step in conveying expectations to the writer and holding them accountable.

CLASSROOM VIGNETTES: PERSUASIVE WRITING IN ACTION

In the final sections, students in grades 1, 3, and 5 convince someone about something through persuasive writing, sometimes transferring oral language appeals and strategies to the written text. Children construct persuasive arguments for advertisements and posters, travel brochures and book jackets, and editorials and persuasive letters. These texts are approached according to their overall aims: to convince, advise, arouse action, influence, defend, and appeal.

Grade 1

Advertisements

Literacy is more than reading books. It is learning to read the world. Growing up in a media- and consumer-oriented society, children are immersed in persuasive writing from restaurant billboards and vehicle bumper stickers to TV commercials and print ads. Never mind that many of these print literacies are learned outside of school, Vivian brings them into her classroom and builds on students' implicit understanding of these symbols as they relate to advertising. To get started she reads two books: the first, *Harriet Reads Signs and More Signs: A Word Concept Book* (Maestro & Maestro, 1986), shows all of the environmental signs Harriet sees on a walk to her grandma's; the second, *Truck* (Crews, 1980), is filled with images of environmental print on trucks, billboards, and road signs. Following a discussion of these books, children collect and bring to class examples of print advertisements and objects: classified ads from the yellow pages of the telephone book, bumper stickers, junk mail, campaign buttons, and newspaper and magazine clippings. As the items trickle in, Vivian arranges them on the counter near the windows. Children huddle over them talking with friends, revealing what they already know about popular culture and consumerism.

At the beginning of the first minilesson, Vivian calls the children to the rug to ask a series of questions: "Has anyone ever had a lemonade stand? Who has a T-shirt bearing the name of a designer or rock star? Who can recite a jingle to a favorite TV commercial?" They discuss what people might do to create interest in products and how they get others to remember these products. Vivian suggests they create advertisements of their own.

At each writing table is a collection of magazines, catalogs, and Toys "Я" Us inserts from the newspaper. The children rummage through them to find pictures that are pleasing or interesting, while Vivian asks what it is about the advertisements that catches their attention. Without knowing it, children's responses tap into the persuasive techniques of advertisers. Some point to a particular toy that all their friends own (they are referring to bandwagon), others comment on specific details that strike them, such as the crown on Imperial® margarine (they have identified a symbol or mnemonic device that helps consumers remember the product). One child focuses attention on the Pillsbury dough boy (she recognizes a personality invented by the advertiser), another on a particular celebrity featured in an ad (she has identified an endorsement by an expert). Some enjoy reciting words, Fingerlickin Good (they are identifying a technique that involves mimicking conversational style) or Leggo My Eggo® (they are witnessing how advertisers use rhyme and verbal play to remember a product) (see Chapter 5).

Vivian jots down their responses and adds them to a list of "things they can do" to create stimulating and interesting advertisements that capture the attention of a reader. This list becomes the guide for planning a rubric to be used in self-assessing.

- Draws a colorful picture
- Makes the picture funny

FIGURE 7-18

Logan's Print
Advertisement,
Calvin Klein T-shirt
(First Grader,
Guided Writing)

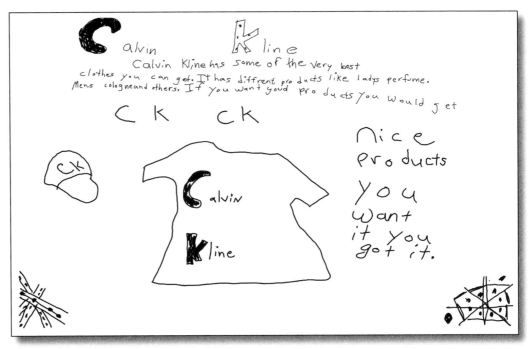

- Introduces a known person or character
- Uses a familiar object or symbol
- Sells only one product at a time
- Tells consumers why they should buy the product
- Writes words to go with the picture

Children begin the writing process by brainstorming products for advertising—pizza boxes, fast foods, toys, and wearable art—and drawing pictures or finding them in magazines.

They carefully work on one-line captions to go with their pictures. Some use the wordplay they have learned in poetry; others include jingles; and still others use a sales pitch with an imperative or persuasive technique. Logan's advertisement for a Calvin Klein® T-shirt (see Figure 7–18) shows the advertiser's power to construct desire for social status through symbols. His drawing includes a shirt with the CK monogram and next to it is a short caption: *You want it you got it!* It appears that these words are a mix of his own creation and an automobile commercial. With the words "Calvin Kline" at the top of the poster and a few sentences about the product under it, Logan's ad is complete and ready to be discussed with others. During sharing, Vivian comments on the persuasive language features of all the children's products, such as Logan's T-shirt ad (what an unforgettable phrase, "You want it you got it") or the sensory descriptions in Marhonda's cookie ad ("My mouth puckers when I hear the words lemony taste"), or the humor in Savannah's McDonald's hamburger ad ("Your advertisement caught my eye because the picture was so silly"). By making these comments she outlines the criteria that constitutes an effective advertisement (catchy slogans, sensory descriptions, or humor). Before long, children imitate her metalanguage, commenting not only on the content but also on the use of language and images. The completed ads are hung around the room.

At the writing center, tasks outlined on activity cards continue the advertising theme. One of the cards directs children to make a cereal box cover. Boxes and white paper are available along with stickers, crayons, Magic Markers, glue sticks, and

FIGURE 7-19
Graphic Layout.
Source: Piazza, C. L. 1999.
Multiple Forms of Literacy.
Reprinted with Permission. Merrill/Prentice Hall,
p. 28.

scissors. A few "snack pack" cereal boxes are displayed as models. The writers wrap the boxes in white paper, draw their pictures, give the cereal a name, and add words or phrases to sell the product. Another activity card guides experimentation with graphic features. Words have certain looks to them. The children use stencils as they did in the poetry lessons (see Chapter 5) and create graphic meanings out of words. Attracting attention with bold, catchy letters and colors is creative and fun for the children, as is experimenting with graphic layouts (see Figure 7–19). They arrange words (written on a separate strip of paper) with a picture in a variety of spatial positions learning concepts such as top, bottom, right, and left. As they become more familiar with criteria for judging an ad, they develop their own checklists. The one in Figure 7–20 includes items that can be adapted for the developmental level of students. They practice using this checklist to evaluate magazine advertisements or other mass media before assessing their own.

Posters and Charts

The first graders extend the advertising campaign and continue their study of persuasion by making health posters. The idea grows out of recent visits from a police officer and nurse who talk to the children on consecutive days about health and safety. The question and answer sessions with the nurse and officer become the prewriting discussion for topics on cleanliness, school safety, eating well, and exercise. Because the children seem excited about these topics, Vivian asks if they would like to work in groups to make health and safety posters. There is a resounding *yes*.

Walking over to the storage closet, Vivian pulls out three large posters—one of a recent movie, another for military service recruitment, and the third for travel abroad programs. She tacks them up on the board so that the children can get an idea of the size and layout of posters, their styles (color, size, and nature of print), and messages (advice, action, summaries). But before discussing how these posters were

FIGURE 7-20   Advertising Checklist for Self-Assessment

I targeted an audience	☺☹☺
I had a gimmick or appeal for the ad	☺☹☺
I used pictures or symbols that related to the words	☺☹☺
I grabbed the audience's attention and showed them where to look first	☺☹☺
I caused my audience to act or think in some new way	☺☹☺
I used words to create a lasting image (special typeface, connotations)	☺☹☺
I let the audience know why they needed this product or experience	☺☹☺
I arranged the parts of my ad for the best possible effect	☺☹☺

made, she underscores their social significance by sharing where they were found, who viewed them, and what they were intended to accomplish.

With this social context established, Vivian trumpets the start of the writing lesson by calling the children to the large rug in the open forum where she is seated in a rocking chair with a hanging chart next to her. She asks children to volunteer possible topics for health and safety and she writes them down:

Not littering	Bicycle safety
Dressing for safety	Brushing your teeth
Not talking to strangers	Picking up toys
Emptying the garbage	Doing homework
Not smoking	Caring for belongings
Washing your hands	Taking a bath
Watching both ways when you cross the street	Obeying patrol helpers

Some of the children grumble that they can't see and squeeze their way up to the inner circle. So as not to break the momentum, Vivian continues writing responses adding a few suggestions of her own. Once several ideas are brainstormed, the children return to their seats and table helpers distribute scratch paper to them. Before they are allowed to use the large poster paper, they must draft their sentences on a separate sheet of paper and sketch a picture that can be cut out and attached to the poster board. Vivian explains that they will draft something short (a few sentences), making it simple enough to read quickly. The message should be forceful or clever so that readers will not only notice it but also remember the advice. The children are grouped in threes to talk about experiences they may have had with bike safety, littering, or community rules. After they agree on an idea to pursue, they share their advice with Vivian, who lists some "advice" words on the board: *don't, do, should, remember*. Time is provided for exploring and drafting. One child completes a simple draft about brushing your teeth, shown in Figure 7–21. In this draft, she cautions class members to brush their teeth, providing three reasons for doing so: your teeth will get yellow, you get cavities, you have to go to the dentist.

As Vivian moves around the room with her clipboard, she reads children's work and scribbles down snippets of conversations overheard at the tables. She is not only examining the writing but also getting a better glimpse into peer culture and the overall dynamics of the class. While she is monitoring, she notices that although most of the children write their advice for peers, a few write to adults, as in the example in Figure 7–22. In this draft, the student offers several reasons for not smoking, personalizing it with the pronouns *I* and *you* (I don't want you to smoke) and appealing to the audience's emotions with strong declarative language (you can die) and (it makes your lungs black and it can make you have cancer).

This draft becomes a springboard for an on-the-spot minilesson about audience. Vivian asks the group, "Who do you want to see your poster and take your advice?"

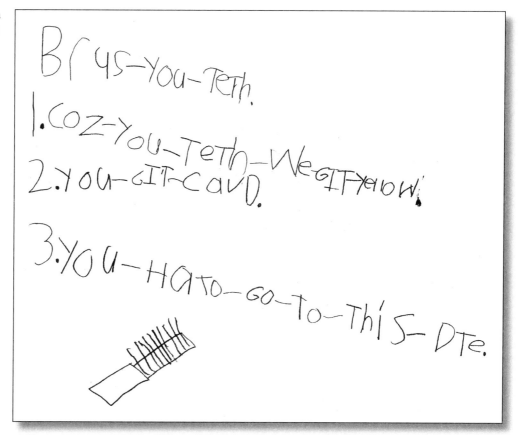

FIGURE 7-21 Health and Safety Poster, First Draft (First Grader, Guided Writing)

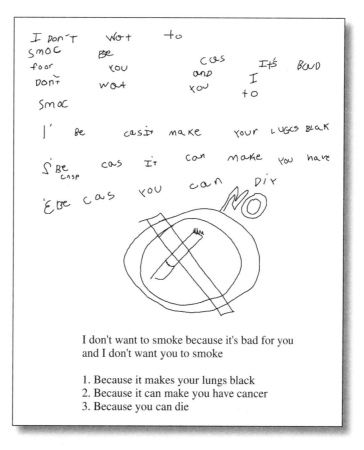

FIGURE 7-22 Health and Safety Poster, First Draft (First Grader, Guided Writing)

I don't want to smoke because it's bad for you and I don't want you to smoke

1. Because it makes your lungs black
2. Because it can make you have cancer
3. Because you can die

The children discuss public audiences for their work and what is appropriate to say. But not everyone completely understands this concept. For example, one student offers the following personal warning about the dangers of drinking: Don't drink beer! It makes you cuss. And it makes you fall down. It makes you throw up!

As students complete drafts, Vivian works with groups on editing sentences for accuracy. Because their posters will be public, students must spell all of the words correctly. This will make the work appear valuable and the author knowledgeable. Others will be more inclined to take the advice seriously. With the editing finished, the children copy their sentences to the poster board and add their pictures.

They are now ready to add the final touches and consider visual elements that enrich the poster. To make their posters attractive, colorful, perhaps even bold, they use markers for dark lines around the pictures or stencils to make words large enough to read from a distance. Now Vivian loops back to the first minilesson to stress the importance of placing the posters in a social context where the intended readers will see them. Some children decide that their advice is for peers, so they will hang them in the school hallways and cafeteria. Others are more specific about where the work should appear. Posters for washing hands are placed on the door of the bathroom or above the sink; those for bicycle safety are located on the outside walls or doors of the school building; and those on littering are attached to the flag pole or near the swings on the playground. Before the posters are displayed around the school, the children judge them by putting a blue ribbon next to the ones they believe have the best visual appeal, yellow ribbons near those that have catchy messages, and red ribbons near those that show important advice. The teacher makes sure that all the posters get ribbons for one feature or another as children practice assessing and extending criteria for this kind of writing.

In a follow-up task that introduces students to a two-sided argument, Vivian writes the labels *dos and don'ts* under the topic, *Washing Your Hands* and the children volunteer responses.

Do's	Don'ts
Do keep healthy	Don't spread germs
Do wash hands before meals	Don't shake hands with someone
Do wash hands after going to	whose hands are dirty
the bathroom	Don't have dirty fingernails
Do use soap	Don't touch garbage

The children work with partners to create their own *do and don't* charts. One child fills in the affirmative statements, and the other fills in the negative ones. The topics range from using the bathroom to lining up at the door for a fire drill. When the charts are finished, they are hung on the doors, near the sink, and next to the TV.

Grade 3

Travel Brochures

Writing a travel brochure is an attractive alternative to the old standby "what I did on my summer vacation." In Kate's third-grade class, students share experiences they have had preparing for or going on trips with family and friends. They volunteer places where they have been (the city, neighborhood parks, swimming areas) or would like to visit (vacation spots, places and settings they have read about in literature). Because the ideal vacation will vary by audience—some enjoy sightseeing, the beach, leisure, mountain climbing, and so on—each brochure will be unique. As enthusiasm mounts, Kate distributes sample travel brochures and magazines from local travel agencies and takes the class on a text walk to look for pictures, captions, maps, colors, words, and sentences. Who has a map in their brochure? What colors are used? What do you notice about the size and style of print? Are there pictures? Where are the pictures or photographs in relation to the words? How long are the sentences? Are there words and labels? The children enjoy hunting for these features and sharing what they find.

When the students have a sense of what makes a brochure, Kate calls their attention to style. She reads an encyclopedia entry and a travel brochure about the same place. "Which is more exciting?" she asks. Several hands go up in the air. It's not that the brochure lacks information but that it is more interesting than the encyclopedia entry. Kate wants them to know why. She plans to call their attention to the language tactics during revision.

For now, the children consider a place of their choosing (a beach, an amusement park, a mountain range) and cluster ideas to answer questions such as, What is your place like? (tropical, cold, scenic, swampy), What activities can you do there? (biking, snorkeling, hiking, amusement rides), Where might you stay? (hotel, campsite, beach house, chalet), and How might you travel? (bus, car, plane, train).

The world map is displayed on the bulletin board for them to take turns locating their travel destinations using colored pushpins to mark the spots. Imaginary trips sparked by science fiction or fantasy literature are drawn on a blank outline that serves as a map.

Over the next few days, Kate encourages the children to bring in photographs taken during their trips or to browse through travel magazines, postcards, photos, catalogs, and the Internet for vivid pictures and decorative print to add to their brochures. On a brochure template, divided into panels and used as a "dummy" copy, they draft words and position pictures without gluing them in place. Although the organization is prescribed through "blocked" spaces and front and back folds, the students are free to design their versions of attractive covers and to slot three or four enticing reasons for visiting a site. Because the children will travel to different places, they make their own personal word walls on a manila folder and prop it up on the desk. If, for example, they plan to go deep sea diving at the beach, they may need words such as *snorkel, swim fins,* or *underwater;* if they are going camping, they might have words such *insect repellent, flashlight,* or *sleeping bag.*

Before students finalize the brochures, Kate holds a minilesson on descriptive words using adjectives and adverbs. She reads from travel sections in the newspaper and projects sample texts on the overhead. The children underline phrases that authors use to make the writing come alive, such as *clear blue waters* and *brilliant colored fish.* Here are some other examples:

Warm summer breezes

Tropical paradise

Sun-drenched playground

Opulent surroundings

Wind-swept beaches

Crystal clear waters

Overblown adjectives, such as *wind-swept* to describe beaches and *sun-drenched* to depict the location, appeal to the reader's five senses. The children brainstorm more words from the professional brochures and from their own mock-up copies. They paint pictures with words by piling on sensory adjectives (e.g., *warm, restful, beautiful, fun*). Exaggeration (a once in a lifetime event), and "catch phrases" (don't just stay—explore; swim with the dolphins) entice the audience with the promise of excitement and action.

After they add "marketable" information and move parts around on the "dummy" copy, they are ready to complete the final brochure, rewriting words and sentences, tacking down photos and pictures, and drawing in borders and special effects, as shown in Figure 7–23.

FIGURE 7-23 Travel Brochure, Final Draft (Third Grader, Guided Writing)

Children are inventive; they explore type styles and boldface, underlining, size, directionality, color, and other intrinsically exciting features that will entice the readers. If they do not grab the readers' attention, they have little chance of selling their dream vacations. The travel brochures are displayed on a table designated as "The Travel Agency." Children take turns discussing and promoting their special places with classmates.

Book Jackets

The third graders are getting ready to publicize a favorite book by designing a book (dust) jacket. Kate brings in several dust jackets and, while the class examines them, she identifies the parts. An effective front cover makes a good first impression. It reveals the title and author's name, along with a sneak preview of the content, which is communicated through a combination of words, graphics, colors, print size and style, pictures, and other decorative touches. The back cover, which may include quotes from the book or endorsements from other writers, also carries a bar code and special ISBN (international standard book number) for cataloging the book. On the inside front flap is usually a summary of the book, and on the back flap an author profile. The spine (the part of the book that is visible when it is shelved) repeats the title and may use symbols or decorations. Although each cover differs slightly, these major parts are typical.

In Figure 7–24, third-grader Sarah designs a dust jacket for the Harry Potter book series (Rowling, 2001). She has completed the front and back covers and is arranging clip art for the flaps. These, however, will not be glued into place until the promotional narrative is written. The front cover depicts a colorful image of

FIGURE 7-24 Book Jacket, *Harry Potter*, Final Draft (Third Grader, Guided Writing)

Hogwarts, the school Harry attends, along with the name of Harry Potter written on the spine in uppercase letters. Not shown in Figure 7–6 but also included on the back, in the center of the cover, are the words *school of witchcraft and wizardry* to describe Hogwarts. Above the words is the school's crest; below, a picture of the four student houses. The right and left flaps display pictures of characters, spells, and potions.

The children have no trouble selecting a favorite book as the inspiration for their dust jackets and Kate reviews some of the artistic features for decorating the jackets by asking pointed questions.

- What first catches your attention?
- What feelings are evoked by the script style and words?
- How do the images represent the book?
- How does the artwork convince the audience to read the book?
- What techniques did the writer use to make you remember the book?

The students cut a piece of construction paper large enough to cover a book from top to bottom and long enough to fold the edges around the inside and front, adding about a half inch for the spine. They work for a few days creating drawings and labels for the front, back, and flaps of the jackets. Many design elements emerge through colors (e.g., black for mysterious), print styles (regal, bold), and photographs or symbols. When the dust jacket designs are finished, the children write the material that will appear on the inside flaps. The writing blends features of exposition (a summary of the book, without revealing the end of course) with a promotional sales pitch (the persuasive ad); the children read the narratives on sample covers to see how they are done. As they review several of these, they discover different approaches, such as a character sketch, an anecdote, a mood, or a plot summary.

Type of Expository Synopsis	Gathering Information	Book Examples
Plot summary	Summarize the major events of the plot	*Hugh Can Do* (Armstrong, 1992); *The Star Maiden: An Ojibaway Tale* (Esbensen, 1988); *The Gorilla Signs Love* (Brenner, 1986)
Anecdotal	Find a favorite passage, quote, or excerpt from the book; make sure it represents the theme	*Everywhere* (Brooks, 1990); *Deerskin* (McKinley, 1993); *Who Was That Masked Man Anyway?* (Avi, 2001)
Mood/setting	Draw an image or scene from the book and capture it in words	*Meet the Witches* (McHargue, 1984); *July* (Stevenson, 1990)
Character sketch	Describe the main character's actions, values, dialogue, or physical traits	*Beware of Kissing Lizard Lips* (Shalant, 1995); *Sounder* (Armstrong, 2001)

The children read a plot summary example and take notes. Kate shows them how to organize the information to produce a cliffhanger, the place where the writer stops short of giving away the ending. This leaves the reader "hanging" and wanting to know more. Following the cliffhanger is the promotional sentence or paragraph. This part critiques the book in a favorable way and applies persuasive terms to convince new and loyal audiences of its merit.

This story sparkles with a humorous sympathy for what it takes to weather the ups and downs of friendship and social life in the sixth grade.

Beware of Kissing Lizard Lips (Shalant, 1995)

Rhythm, invention, humor, and a catch-your-breath twist are completed by animated, richly colored illustrations. Plucky, energetic Hugh is an unforgettable character . . . a sparkling and spirited original folk tale.

Hugh Can Do (Armstrong, 1992)

Deerskin is an unforgettable journey of discovery, where the secrets of a hidden world meet the dark forces of our own. . . . *Deerskin* is Robin McKinley at her finest.

Deerskin (McKinley, 1993)

The children discuss the concept of audience. For example, in *Beware of Kissing Lizard Lips*, the readers are elementary students who are at an age when peer approval and socializing are significant in their lives. The "we are in this together" strategy is an effective draw with this audience.

Word choice is extremely important in marketing the book. The students return to the sample dust jackets to find colorful or inflated language, such as *unforgettable, animated*, and *spirited*. When the children are writing promotional sentences, their voices must resound with the passion of an advertiser. Sentences are varied and follow many of the techniques of both exposition and narrative. When the draft is edited, they copy the information onto the dust jacket, wrap it around their marketable book, and place it on a special table for others to view.

Grade 5

Editorials

Students have been working on the school newspaper for more than a week and are preparing to write the editorial section. Ed begins by reading letters to the editor from the newspaper and pointing out how **tone** can affect audience perceptions. Consider his definition of a courteous tone and its contrast to a quarrelsome one.

- Courteous tone: The writer is perceived as serious, reasonable, and helpful. She recognizes the best interest of the reader and tries to create a win–win situation. Her goal is to offer viable solutions to a problem and positive words to express concern. Questions imply a willingness to entertain another perspective, if there is one. The writer intends to establish a rapport with the reader.
- Quarrelsome tone: The writer is demanding and leaves no room for negotiation. No solutions are offered, and the writer blames the reader for what she has failed to do. Negative words abound. The writer is accusatory, abrupt, rude, or critical.

He then highlights how words are carriers of tones and personalities. Words such as *failed to, problem*, or *lacks* signal the writer's negative or accusatory position just as qualifying words, such as *sometimes* or *might*, seem neutral and negotiable.

Following the examples provided in the newspaper, the fifth graders decide to write letters to the editor on the pros and cons of homework. All of the students are gathering facts to write an affirmative or negative position on homework. Ed provides them with a newspaper template so that they will know the expected lengths for their arguments. Some articles will be short, others will be long. The children can sign up and reserve the block of space they would like for their work. Before filling the space, however, they will draft a full-fledged essay.

Students spend the first day polling classmates and individuals outside the classroom on their opinions about homework. Are they *for* or *against* homework (see surveying in Chapter 6)? Others conduct interviews and work with Ed to discuss a few key questions.

- Do you have homework?
- Do you think kids should have homework? Why?
- What would change your mind about homework?

The third question provides insights into how the students can convince others. Brittany asks Ed if she can take a middle-of-the-road-perspective, that is, homework can be either good *or* bad. This idea prompts a discussion concerning the nature of many controversies: Issues often fall along a continuum. People may neither strongly agree nor disagree. Instead they may be neutral or express levels of agreement or disagreement. Ed suggests that if she wants to argue this position, she might consider a few additional questions.

- Describe a homework assignment that was a waste of time.
- Describe a homework assignment that was helpful.
- Tell how much time you spend doing homework? Do you think it is too much, too little, or just right?

In some cases, the interviews and survey results cause the children to change their minds and reverse their position. In other cases, the firsthand research confirms what they originally believed and gives them additional evidence for their arguments.

Once students form opinions and brainstorm more ideas, they draft their papers. Then they meet in writing circles to present them. While the audience poses questions, the writer takes notes of points raised. Peers might question the reliability of the evidence or ask the writer to distinguish between relevant and irrelevant material. They may also discuss omissions and determine whether the writer reaches a fair conclusion. A sample of DiJana's draft essay is shown in Figure 7–25. The opening sentence immediately draws readers into the debate with the pronouns *you* and *us*. Following the typical three-reasons argument she fulfills the intended purpose to convince readers that they should do homework. Although there is nothing in the paper to counter possible rebuttals, the pillars of the argument are present. She will combine the last two points by using them as examples then a third point will be added. Meanwhile, she works on adjusting the length of the essay for the newspaper copy. Based on space allotment, she must decide which parts of the argument to include. The first paragraph and first point are selected. The essay appears on the same page with two other articles, shortened to fit length requirements and reproduced in Figure 7–26.

Those who have very short columns, such as Chaney, opt for one important point to emphasize. He decides to stress homework's relationship to the Florida Comprehensive Assessment Test (FCAT). DiJana and Carlos include their opening paragraphs and one or two points from their list of reasons. Ed suggests that for the final drafts, they remove the cue words so that the arguments appear complete.

Before the final publication is assembled, each writer corrects usage, punctuation, spelling, and other mechanics using a checklist similar to the one shown in Figure 7–27, p. 401. Once the writer looks over the article a final time, the template is retyped and ready for publication. When the newspapers are finished, students hurriedly grab copies to take home to read.

Letters to Public Officials

Ed thinks it is important that students choose issues of personal interest to write about, issues about which they have strong views. Critical awareness and conscious

FIGURE 7-25

DiJana's Persuasive Essay, *Why I Should Do Homework*, Final Draft (Fifth Grader, Independent Writing)

> For most of us who attend school, homework is a part of school. You always need to do your homework, it is very important. If you do your homework it could help you on your test alot. I am going to give you examples of why you should do your homework.
>
> The first is, you should do your your homework because you can earn alot of credits. Those credits can also bring up your grade alot. You also can get points and earn parties. Thats what I like to do.
>
> The next thing is, it can help you out on your test. If you have a big test like the FCAT you should always turn it in. The test could be really hard. You might want to turn in you homework to show you practiced
>
> Last but not least is, It can bring up your grade, up to an A. If you have a F or D it can really help you. I bring a B up to an A. You should always bring up your grade.
>
> All these examples should have tought you a lesson. It is very and important to do your homework, also turning it in. I think homework its to very important. You should too!

engagement in persuasive writing prepares children to become social activists in their schools and communities. Many will write letters to the editor or opinion articles based on school subjects or local news. Others will speak out in letters to their legislators or public officials for or against personal rights or social or political concerns that impact their community. Because the students have previously learned

FIGURE 7-26 Letters to the Editor in the School Newspaper. "Should Kids Have To Do Homework?" First Drafts (Fifth Graders, Independent Writing)

Your Comment Page

Editorial Board

Brittany   Cory   Kevin

by DiJana

For most of us who attend school, homework is a part of school. You always need to do your homework because it is very important. If you do your homework it could help you on your test a lot. I am going to give you examples of why you should do your homework.

The first is, you should do your homework because you can earn a lot of credits. Those credits can also bring up your grade a lot. You also can get points and earn parties. That's what I like to do!

by Chaney

Doing homework regularly can help us on our tests. If we have a big test like the FCAT then doing homework and turning it in shows that we have practiced working on the subjects.

Should Kids Have To Do Homework?

by Carlos

Lots of people don't like to do homework and wonder why they have to do it, but it can be useful. Homework can be useful for practice. It can also be fun, like special projects. You can also finish classwork as homework.

First of all it can be used for practice. For example, if you have trouble on some math or spelling you can work on some extra practice for your homework.

Second of all, it can be used for fun. Some of the worksheets I do for homework are really fun. Also, some of the problems are like puzzles. They're really, really fun.

about persuasion, they apply many of the same principles to this project. The first step is to identify and clearly define a problem that needs to be resolved and a solution that will benefit others.

Ed sets up experiences in which the students become aware of problems that require action. They read the community newspaper, interview family and friends, observe events in neighborhoods, or simply spend time on the school grounds looking for potential problems (vandalism, unsafe playground equipment, dangerous intersections, noise pollution, littering). Chatting with friends about these problems

FIGURE 7–27

Checklist for Mechanics

Name_____ Date_____ Type of Writing_____

Checking Mechanics

Punctuation	Checked(✓)
End punctuation (period, question mark, exclamation mark)	
Comma use (in quotations, introductory elements, appositives)	
Apostrophes in contractions, possessives	
Quotation marks	
Other punctuation (dash, slash, hyphen, colon, semicolon)	

Other	
Capital letters (names, places, beginning of sentences)	
Abbreviations	
Spelling	
Legible handwriting (formation, slant, alignment, spacing)	

enables them to sort and clarify ideas. Ed provides a list of questions to guide the discussions:

- What is the problem and who sees it as a problem?
- How serious is the problem?
- What is the cause of the problem?
- Are there similar problems you know of?
- Is the problem solvable and if so what are some possible solutions?
- Who needs to know about this problem or who can do something about the problem?
- Why should this person care about solving the problem?

The questions that Ed poses lead to an empirical problem, one that can be tested by research (interviews, surveys, experiments, questionnaires). A fifth grader named Andy is prompted to write a letter to the transportation department urging officials to erect a stop sign at a busy intersection near his family's vacation home. Before he ever puts pen to paper, he researches traffic patterns at various hours during the day, draws a map of the site (see Figure 7–28), and counts the number of pedestrians and cars passing through the intersection. The data is graphed on a chart as shown in Figure 7–29.

The graph and map illustrate a real community problem and Andy has plenty of data to convince others of the problem's significance. Andy decides to send this information in a letter to the public official in charge of city transportation and safety. But first he must complete an audience analysis. He lists reasons that will persuade his reader of the problem and, using three of the best reasons, drafts his letter

FIGURE 7-28
Andy's Map (Fifth
Grader)

FIGURE 7-29 Andy's
Graph (Fifth Grader)

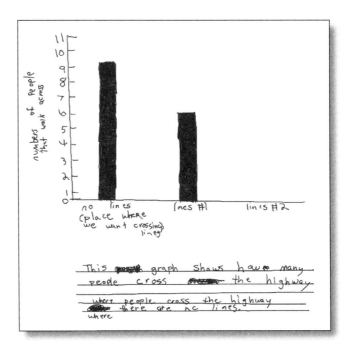

(see Figure 7–30). In the opening Andy explains that he's been conducting research on a location that he believes needs a pedestrian walkway. He then goes on to present data to convince the public official that the matter has been thoroughly investigated. At the end, Andy states briefly why the official should care about the issue—his data speak for themselves, and many neighbors think his suggestion is a good one. The final sentences bring the letter to a courteous conclusion and infer that the official will take action.

However, before Andy sends the letter, Ed holds several minilessons to encourage revision. In the first lesson, he asks several questions that direct students to audience concerns.

- To whom are you writing?
- What does your audience already know?

FIGURE 7-30 Andy's Letter of Concern, First Draft (Fifth Grader, Independent Writing)

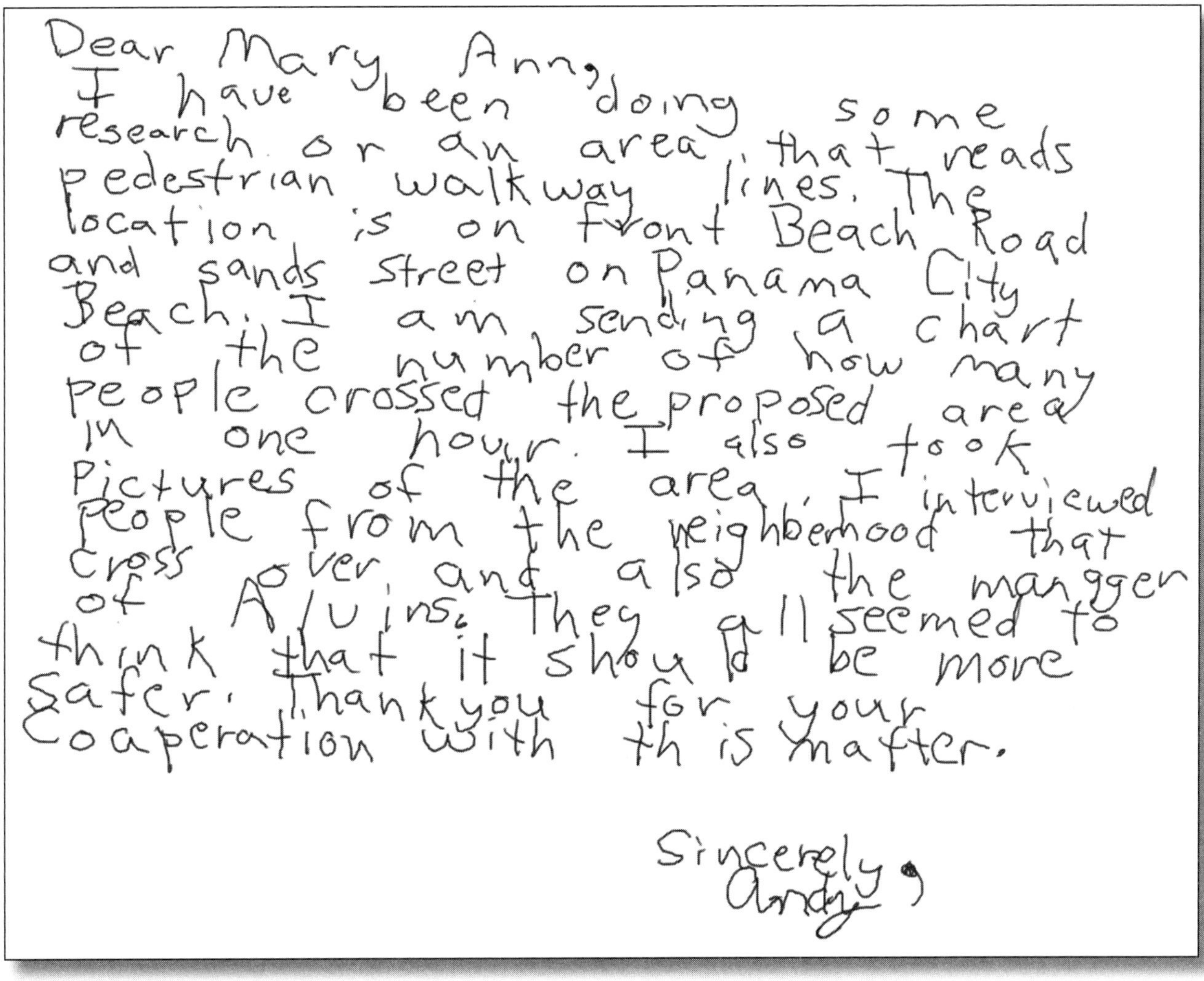

> Dear Mary Ann,
> I have been doing some research or an area that reads pedestrian walkway lines. The location is on front Beach Road and sands street on Panama City Beach. I am sending a chart of the number of how many people crossed the proposed area in one hour. I also took pictures of the area. I interviewed people from the neighberhood that cross over and also the manggen of Aluins. They all seemed to think that it should be more safer. Thank you for your cooperation with this matter.
>
> Sincerely
> Andy

- What does the audience need to know?
- What are the reasons for the letter and what exactly do you want your audience to know?
- Why should the audience care about the issue?

Ed explains to Andy and the others that they need to be certain that the letter fully incorporates the following points:

- Makes a clear and concise expression of concern; tells why you are writing
- States the problem, request, demand, or appeal
- Provides background and context so the reader knows what action is needed
- Tells why it is important and how the reader benefits
- Offers solutions or helpful suggestions about the action someone can take

Clearly, before Andy documents the problem and provides proof, he needs to state the purpose of his letter, explaining why the problem is of public concern. This will alert the reader immediately to the seriousness of his letter. The context is fairly well outlined in his research and Andy infers that he has spoken to several neighbors for validation. Although the logical appeals (the data) and the bandwagon tactic (neighbors think this is a problem) are quite convincing, the ending is a bit abrupt and Andy has not given a suggestion. Because the solution (a walkway) appears to be feasible, he might analyze the consequences of his advice by thinking about cost effectiveness, convenience, or the impact of a pedestrian walkway on traffic, business, and residents. In this way, he shows the public official that he has given considerable thought to his solution and has provided a tentative plan of action that might be followed. The recipient of the letter may feel more inclined to respond to Andy's request if she believes he has given this matter detailed attention. The added information will also balance and structure the message—the first part discussing the problem and the final part offering the solution. Another possibility is to offer more than one solution and allow the public official to decide the best course of action.

Finally, Ed wants Andy and the students to proofread their letters. He holds a minilesson to show what they are to look for. They examine format and select the proper salutation and closing to the letter:

Formal Openings	Formal Closings
Dear Sir/Madam; Mrs. and Mr.	Sincerely
Honorable Legislator	Respectfully yours
Dear Chief Justice/Mr./Madam Vice President	Best regards
Ladies and Gentlemen	Cordially
Dear Senator/General	Yours truly

They also discuss commas in clearly defined places such as dates, salutations, and closings, and check for accuracy and neatness because these are natural requirements for establishing credibility with a real audience or professional readership. Ed explains that the students must proofread carefully and leave a good impression of themselves on the writing.

Spelling correctly is a required skill of persuasion because all writers want to appear competent, conscientious, and precise. Errors detract from even the best thinking, so spelling (including typographical errors), punctuation, and grammar is checked. The writers review their work using an editing checklist.

- Avoid slang ("rip off" or "far out")
- Correct spelling
- Make certain references are correct
- Eliminate unnecessary words

After Andy types his final draft and sends it to the public official, he waits patiently for a response. He receives a letter back several weeks later thanking him for bringing the problem to the department's attention and complimenting him on his thorough investigation. The public official promises Andy that she will consider the matter. Andy is quite proud of what he has accomplished, and rightly so!

JOURNEY REFLECTIONS

Persuasive writing is indispensable for empowering students. By taking a stand or arguing a point, elementary students come to view themselves as "doers" who can exercise power to effect change in the world. Writers begin with a problem, a statement, or a proposition that they feel strongly about and then champion their cause. They learn about their target audience so that just the right evidence is collected. To strengthen the argument they use logical, emotional, or ethical appeals, greasing the wheels, so to speak. In the process, they determine not only what to say but also how to say it. They may adopt certain language tactics to conceal, impress, appease, or rally the audience.

Persuasion takes many forms, as seen in the three classrooms. Young children build on their exposure to environmental print and accomplish persuasion through advertising and health posters. The third graders discover how print and art come together to promote travel and influence readers to buy books. In the fifth grade, students initiate public service projects: letters to the editor and letters to public and government officials. These and many other lessons suggest that students can and will write persuasively if offered the opportunity. Given the time and freedom to develop an interest in several presentational forms, through labels, slogans, letters, book jackets, and essays, students discover the joys and rewards of persuasive writing, surprising even themselves with how powerful a tool writing can be. Nothing could be more valuable than to discover writing as a way to engage with the world (Britton, 1970; Halliday, 1975).

Indeed, as all the chapters in this book show, there are numerous rewards associated with writing, whether expressing self, developing the imagination, playing with language, or reporting and arguing information. As teachers expose children to a variety of writing along the journey they travel many of the old roads and discover new ones. At the end of the year, just as they reach the final stretch, the work begins again. If it is true that the journey of teaching writing has no clear beginning, then it is even more true that it has no magical end. A quote by T. S. Eliot best captures the nature of the journey described throughout the book:

> The end of all our travels
> Will be there again
> At the beginning of our journey

So it is for teachers and their writers. They come full circle. Each time they approach writing, they bring with them a storehouse of accumulated knowledge, memories, and acquired skills to start the process again. Each time they start the process again, they experience the surprises and limitless dreams that make it possible for them to discover writing anew.

WORKS CITED

Professional References

American Library Association. (1989). *The American library association presidential committee on information literacy: Final report*. Chicago: American Library Association.

Applebee, A. N., Langer, J. A., Mullis, L. V., Latham, A. S., & Gentile, C. A. (1994). *NAEP 1992 writing report card*. Washington, DC: Office of Educational Research and Improvement. U.S. Department of Education.

Barr, R. (1987). Classroom interaction and curricular content. In D. Bloome (Ed.), *Literacy and schooling* (pp. 150–167). Norwood, NJ: Ablex.

Birdwhistell, R. (1970). *Kinesics and context: Essays in body motion communication*. Philadelphia: University of Pennsylvania Press.

Britton, J. (1970). *Language and learning*. Hammondsworth, Middlesex, England: Penguin.

Crystal, D. (1995). *The Cambridge encyclopedia of the English language*. New York: Cambridge University Press.

Daniels, H., & Zemelman, S. (1985). *A writing project: Training teachers of composition from kindergarten to college*. Portsmouth, NH: Heinemann.

Ede, L. (1984). Audience: An introduction to research. *College Composition and Communication, 35*, 140–154.

Elbow, P. (1973). *Writing without teachers*. New York: Oxford University Press.

Fairclough, N. (1989). *Language and power*. New York: Longman.

Freire, P. (1970). *Pedagogy of the oppressed*. New York: Seabury Press.

Gee, J. (1996). *Social linguistics and literacies: Ideology in discourses* (2nd ed.). New York: Falmer Press.

Golden, J. (1987). An exploration of reader–text interaction in a small group discussion. In D. Bloome (Ed.), *Literacy and schooling* (pp. 169–192). Norwood, NJ: Ablex.

Halliday, M. A. K. (1975). *Learning how to mean: Exploration in the development of language*. London: Edward Arnold.

Kinneavy, J. (1980). *A theory of discourse*. Upper Saddle River, NJ: Merrill/Prentice Hall.

Lakoff, G., & Johnson, M. (1980). *Metaphors we live by*. Chicago: University of Chicago Press.

Lanham, P. A. (1992). *Revising prose* (3rd ed.). New York: Macmillan.

Lass, B., & Davis, B. G. (1996). *Elementary reading: Strategies that work*. Needham Heights, MA: Allyn & Bacon.

Lutz, W. (1999). From the world of doublespeak! In A. P. Nielsen (Ed.), *Living language: Reading, thinking, and writing* (pp. 298–302). Boston: Allyn & Bacon.

Ong, W. (1977). *The interface of the word: Studies in the evolution of consciousness*. Ithaca, NY: Cornell University Press.

Park, D. (1982). The meanings of audience. *College English*, 44, 247–257.

Piazza, C. L. (1999). *Multiple forms of literacy*. Upper Saddle River, NJ: Merrill/Prentice Hall.

Ruggiero, V. R. (1988). *Teaching thinking across the curriculum*. New York: Harper & Row.

Safire, W. (1978). *Safire's political dictionary*. New York: Ballantine.

Thrall, W. F., Hibbard, A., & Holman, C. H. (1960). *A handbook to literature*. New York: Odyssey Press.

Toulmin, S., Rieke, R., & Janik, A. (1984). *An introduction to reasoning* (2nd ed.). New York: Macmillan.

Wallat, C., & Piazza, C. (in preparation). *College students' explorations of power in discourse through analysis of hypertext documents*.

Weston, A. (1987). *A rulebook for arguments*. Indianapolis, IN: Hackett.

Woodson, L. (1979). *A handbook of modern rhetorical terms*. Urbana, IL: National Council of Teachers of English.

Wujec, T. (1995). *Five star mind*. New York: Doubleday.

Children's References

Armstrong, J. (1992). *Hugh can do*. Crown.

Armstrong, W. H. (2001). *Sounder*. HarperPerennial.

Avi. (2001). *Who was that masked man anyway?* HarperTrophy.

Bannerman, H. (1995). *The story of little black Sambo*. Applewood.

Bannerman, H. (1996). *The story of little Babajii*. HarperCollins.

Blume, J. (1984). *The pain and the great one*. Bradbury.

Brenner, B. (1986). *The gorilla signs love*. Ballantine.

Brooks, B. (1990). *Everywhere*. HarperCollins.

Crews, D. (1980). *Truck*. Greenwillow.

Curtis, C. P. (1999). *Bud, not Buddy*. Dell.

Esbensen, B. J. (1988). *The star maiden: An Ojibaway tale*. Little, Brown.

Levine, E. (Ed.). (1994). *Freedom's children: Young civil rights activists tell their own stories*. Avon.

Maestro, B., & Maestro, G. (1986). *Harriet reads signs and more signs: A word concept book*. Crown.

McHargue, G. (1984). *Meet the witches*. Lippincott.

McKinley, R. (1993). *Deerskin*. ACE Book.

Orwell, G. (1981). *1984: A novel*. Signet Classic.

Rappaport, D. (1990). *American women: Their lives in their words*. HarperCollins.

Rowling, J. K. (2001). *Harry Potter boxed set: Harry Potter and the sorcerer's stone; Harry Potter and the chamber of secrets; Harry Potter and the prisoner of Azkaban; Harry Potter and the goblet of fire*. Scholastic.

Scieszka, J. (1989). *The true story of the three little pigs by A. Wolf*. Viking.

Shalant, P. (1995). *Beware of kissing lizard lips*. Dutton.

Silver, D. (1995). *Extinction is forever*. Silver Burdett.

Stevenson, J. (1990). *July*. Greenwillow.

Twain, M. (2000). *The adventures of Huckleberry Finn*. Prentice Hall.

Uchida, Y. (1993). *The bracelet*. Philomel.

Wiesner, D. (2001). *The three pigs*. Clarion.

Weiss, A. E. (1990). *Who's to know? Information, the media, and public awareness*. Houghton Mifflin.

About the Author

Carolyn L. Piazza is an associate professor of reading and language arts and elementary education at Florida State University, where she teaches graduate and undergraduate courses in language arts, written composition, and applied linguistics. She also spends each semester supervising student teachers and working with classroom teachers in the public schools. Dr. Piazza is the author of several professional works on language and composition and, for a time, wrote a weekly literacy column, Ask Carolyn, in the local newspaper. Her most recent book, *Multiple Forms of Literacy: Teaching Literacy and the Arts,* brings together her passion for language with the visual and performing arts. She enjoys gardening, studying Italian, and, above all, her two Yorkies.

Glossary

Accent   An emphasis on certain syllables or words; vocal stress that calls attention to a particular syllable.

Affirmations   Strong positive statements to oneself or others during the writing process.

Anecdote   A short written narrative of an amusing or interesting incident.

Argument   A line of reasoning aimed at employing proofs to achieve the truth or falsity of an idea.

Authentic   Real-life and genuine tasks, materials, or contexts; authenticity is important in creating assignments, developing prompts in assessment, or selecting materials.

Automaticity   The process of overlearning a skill to the point where it becomes second nature; exerting little mental effort or attention.

Censorship   The act of limiting, suppressing, or deleting ideas because they are objectionable to certain persons or groups; frequently related to books or artwork.

Clichés   Trite or commonplace expressions or ideas that writers often try to avoid; may be used for humor.

Conceptual framework   A set of ideas, concepts, or organizers that guide thinking about teaching or writing; a basic structure of ideas.

Context   A constructed activity, a situation, or a phenomena in which messages, created and received are better understood; the set of interrelated conditions in which something occurs.

Conventions   Commonly agreed on ways of doing things, such as following acceptable practices for creating a story or spelling a word correctly; established through habitual use.

Conversational styles   Oral exchanges represented in everyday talk and casual communication; the unique way people convey intentions through tone of voice, volume, pace, and other verbal and nonverbal skills.

Critical thinking   Higher level thinking skills and logical thought processes typically associated with the scientific method; involves skills such as analysis, synthesis, and evaluation.

Debriefing   A recap or review; discussing a process previously demonstrated.

Derivations   Linguistic term referring to the process of word formation (use of affixes, such as prefixes and suffixes); the origins and variants of words.

Developmental   Changes in behavior and growth over the course of the life span; gradual and successive changes in writing ability.

Dialogical   An interaction consisting of several voices; participating in a dialogue; a relational-responsive kind of exchange.

Discourse   Text longer than a sentence; oral or written communication beyond a sentence.

Discourse community   A social group who shares knowledge through a common language, set of experiences, or rules of conduct.

Dispositions   Writers' temperaments during writing including values and attitudes associated with the work, the degree of commitment and ownership, and the stance taken toward another's writing; tendencies to act in a particular manner consistent with a writer's role in enacting literate behaviors.

Divergent thinking   Mental activity manifested in acts of elaborating and associating thoughts from many perspectives and directions; the aim is to go beyond the status quo and spin out countless ideas and original interpretations; synonymous with creative thinking.

Emergent writers   Children who demonstrate a growing understanding of print and the behaviors that accompany it.

Expressive writing   Forms of writing that represent self and tend to bring forth the writer's emotional state; considers self as the audience.

Fallacies   Invalid inferences or errors in reasoning rather than facts; pitfalls to avoid in making an argument.

Fiction   Narrative that is imaginative and entertaining rather than telling or explaining.

Figurative expressions   Departures from the normal meaning or structure of language; simile, metaphor, and imagery are examples; purposeful distortions of language for making an impact.

Fluency   The ability to write smoothly and effortlessly to produce a generous amount of text; emphasis on quantity and freedom from correctness.

Focus lessons   Specific skill instruction in English conventions; involves grouping children temporarily to teach a particular skill and then disbanding.

Foot   A rhythmic unit that considers word syllables and accents as measures; a foot consists of one stressed syllable and one or two unstressed syllables.

Forms   The structures and shapes of writing; also a way to distinguish one type of writing from another within a particular function (for example, story is a form of literary writing).

Formula poems   Poems that are developed through specific word arrangements or set rules such as the syllable and count poems, imitation poems, or repetitive poems ("I remember").

Frame   A way of shaping an utterance for interpretation; allows for different understandings of reality.

Free verse   Lines of poetry that follow no specific rules of rhythm or rhyme, and often consist of an irregular beat or metrical pattern.

Function   The social purpose that writing serves for a particular audience; the intended use or effect of the writing. Interrelates with form.

Genres   Categories into which literary works are grouped according to purpose, form, content, or strategies; useful for descriptive purposes but, in reality, are rather arbitrary.

Genre-specific   Features of a particular written form that signal readers that they are reading a particular genre (for example, exaggeration, humor, clichés in tall tales).

Grand conversation   Discussion focused on content, ideas, and meanings in writing rather than talk about the craft.

Heuristics   Problem-solving strategies that writers use to engage in inquiry.

Hybrid   A combination of different forms of writing in a single text (such as journal entries in a story).

Idioms   Expressions in which meaning is not necessarily derived from the component words; a mismatch between literal and figurative meanings.

Indicators   Descriptions that denote and point out characteristics of a genre to be included in a rubric; the actual statements on a checklist that signal what to look for during observations.

Inner speech   Speech for oneself; absence of vocalization; speech turned into thought.

Inquiry   A multifaceted approach to solving problems.

Interaction   Exchange or flow of communication between teachers and students or among peers.

Introspection   Looking inward to take intellectual and emotional inventory; discovery tool for examining one's thoughts, habits, motives, and characteristic ways of behaving.

Invented poems   A category of free verse that requires no set meter or rhyme scheme and is particularly accessible to children.

Invention   The art of discovering a subject; term that can be used for prewriting.

Literacy   The ability to read, write, and use language.

Literacy habits   Routines associated with the writing process, handling of materials, class participation, and use of time.

Mechanics   Aspects of written communication that people can agree on, such as capitalization, punctuation, and spelling; also referred to as conventions.

Metalanguage   Term used in linguistics to make statements about language; talk about language as an object; also metalinguistics.

Meter   A recurring rhythmic pattern; rhythm is formalized into meter which consists of regular beats and stresses.

Mnemonic   A memory strategy that uses acronyms, rhymes, or associations; a mnemonic for distinguishing between the spelling of princi*pal* and princi*ple* might be associating the school administrator with being a *pal* and remembering the meaning of princi*ple* as a ru*le* of conduct.

Motifs   Repetitive events that unify the theme; an element that serves as a basis for expanded narrative.

Multiple forms of literacy   The complex amalgam of communicative channels, symbols, forms, and meanings inherent in oral and written language as well as the arts—visual arts, music, dance, theater, and film (including television, video, and technology).

Narrative   The recounting of real or fictitious events or situations.

Nonfiction   A genre of literature that is characterized by accurate information and documented facts; the writing often represents features of exposition.

Novice writers   Inexperienced writers of any age; beginners.

Onset   The consonants before the first vowel in a word; usually paired with rime.

Ownership   Writers' personal investments in their work and writing processes.

Pictionary   A book of words and corresponding pictures arranged alphabetically; word meanings amplified with picture cues.

Point of view   Writer's perspective, stance, and voice about a topic.

Products   Written works of students; writing samples.

Prompts   Idea starters to elicit writing during instruction or assessment.

Purposes   Writers' personal reasons for writing.

Referential words   Words that are associated or connected to a topic or genre; words that conceptually fit together; for example, the topic of rain forest might include words such as *climate, plant, flora, animal life.*

Response   A spoken or written answer to a question in text or conversation; a way to receive and take in meaning; stance adopted for talking about a text; in the broadest sense includes such activities as discussions, retellings, or creative drama.

Rhetoric   The study of effective communication that considers purpose, audience, and message.

Rime   The endings of words spelled the same (bla*ck*, cla*ck*, Ma*ck*).

Scaffolds   Instructional supports for guiding students in acquiring new information and gradually withdrawing the assistance to adjust to the learners' increasing writing development.

Scanning   Rapid, superficial reading to look over a text; previewing a text quickly for specific information during note taking or revising.

Schemas   Knowledge or semantic framework stored in memory as sets of organized and interconnected ideas; abstract representations of events, objects, or relationships.

Skills   Acquired abilities that require practice and repetition to achieve a high degree of competence and efficiency without full attention.

Standards   General expectations that serve as a framework for curriculum and classroom practice.

Stanza   A set of lines grouped together; similar to a paragraph in prose; divides sections of a poem according to idea, mood, rhythm, formula, visual effect, or other factors.

Storyboard   Panels with sketches to show the action and events of a narrative.

Strategies   Operations that reflect critical thinking; differentially portrayed depending on the type of text; results of strategic moves usually identified as naming, identifying, defining, describing, explaining, illustrating, analyzing, comparing, interpreting, arguing, generalizing, or evaluating.

Structure   The network of relations between the parts of the text that make the whole.

Style   Characteristic way of expressing self through language.

Stylistic devices   Strategies that create style such as producing alliteration and rhyme in poetry or dialogue and description in a story; differ according to genre.

Tacit knowledge   Something that one knows intuitively; implied or unspoken.

Task   A description of what participants are doing; an assignment that outlines the rhetorical context of purpose, audience, and message, resources to use, and strategies to explore.

Task talk   Student's discussion of written products and the writing craft; emphasizes the terminology or jargon of written discourse (paragraphs, dialogue, rhythm).

Teaching methods   A set of strategic procedures that are part of a teaching approach.

Terse verse   Short, pithy poems that range from a single line to a stanza and cross many genres (couplets, jokes, haiku, name poems).

Text   Written discourse, the whole of written communication; connected sentences.

Text analysis   Using words, sentences, paragraphs, and discourse structure as tools for examining an author's content and strategies; a subdiscipline of linguistics.

Text elements   Recognizable aspects of a particular text, such as plot or character in a story, or repetition or rhyme in poetry; chunks of discourse that can be labeled and studied.

Think aloud   The verbalizing of internal mental strategies; also talk aloud.

Think sheet   An open-ended, written exercise that scaffolds the planning or organizing of writing during the writing process (a graphic organizer, for instance); it is not a skill and drill worksheet or fill-in-the blank assessment.

Tone   The writer's attitude toward the subject, situation, or event presented; often characterized as friendly, sarcastic, angry, and so on.

Trade books   Informational books intended for sale to the public and often found in local libraries and bookstores; differ from textbooks which are typically designed for classroom use.

Traits   Identifiable qualities or attributes in a written product.

Word banks   Collections of words placed on cards and saved in file boxes or other containers; useful for word building activities; a personal dictionary.

Word sorts   Activity in which words and their features are organized and classified to reveal relationships and patterns.

Writing event   A happening in which a related set of instructional learning activities are organized around writing; an occasion in which writing is a part; social interactions, tasks, classroom practices and procedures, and everything involved with writing.

Index